THE AMERICAN PEOPLE

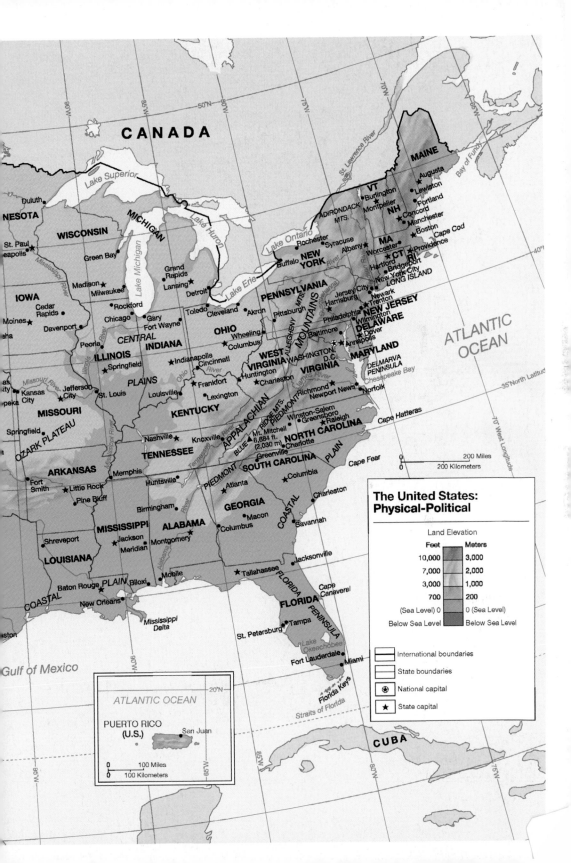

THE AMERICAN PEOPLE

Creating a Nation and a Society

Concise Sixth Edition

Volume I   To 1877

Gary B. Nash
University of California,
Los Angeles
General Editor

Julie Roy Jeffrey
Goucher College
General Editor

John R. Howe
University of Minnesota

Allan M. Winkler
Miami University

Allen F. Davis
Temple University

Charlene Mires
Villanova University

Peter J. Frederick
Wabash College

Carla Gardina Pestana
Miami University

PEARSON
Longman

New York   San Francisco   Boston
London   Toronto   Sydney   Tokyo   Singapore   Madrid
Mexico City   Munich   Paris   Cape Town   Hong Kong   Montréal

Executive Editor: Michael Boezi
Editorial Assistant: Vanessa Gennarelli
Executive Marketing Manager: Sue Westmoreland
Assistant Development Manager: David B. Kear
Supplements Editor: Brian Belardi
Media Supplements Editor: Melissa Edwards
Production Manager: Eric Jorgensen
Project Coordination, Text Design, and Electronic Page Makeup: Elm Street Publishing
    Services, Inc.
Senior Cover Design Manager/Cover Designer: Nancy Danahy
Cover Illustration/Photo: StockFood Creative/Photonica/Getty Images, Inc.
Photo Researcher: Julie Tesser
Manufacturing Buyer: Roy Pickering
Printer and Binder: Courier Corporation
Cover Printer: Phoenix Color Corp.

For permission to use copyrighted material, grateful acknowledgment is made to the following
copyright holder. Page 404, Jose Maria Sanchez, "A Trip to Texas in 1828," Southwestern Historical
Quarterly, v. 29 (1926), p. 251.

Library of Congress Cataloging-in-Publication Data
The American people: creating a nation and a society/general editors, Gary B. Nash,
  Julie Roy Jeffrey; with John R. Howe ... [et al.].—Concise 6th ed.
      p. cm.
    Includes bibliographical references and index.
    ISBN 978-0-205-56843-7
    1. United States History—History.   I. Nash, Gary B.   II. Jeffrey, Julie Roy.   III. Howe,
    John R.
    E178.1.A49355 2008
    973—dc22
                                                                      2007023088

Please visit us at www.ablongman.com

ISBN 10: 0-205-56843-2; ISBN 13: 978-0-205-56843-7 (Combined Volume)
ISBN 10: 0-205-57246-4; ISBN 13: 978-0-205-57246-5 (Volume One)
ISBN 10: 0-205-57247-2; ISBN 13: 978-0-205-57247-2 (Volume Two)
ISBN 10: 0-205-65665-X; ISBN 13: 978-0-205-65665-3 (Ala Carte)

4 5 6 7 8 9 10—CRK—10 09

Brief Contents

Detailed Contents

Features

RECOVERING THE PAST

HOW OTHERS SEE US

Maps

Preface

The Yoruba people of West Africa have an old saying: "However far the stream flows, it never forgets its source." Why, we wonder, do such ancient societies as the Yoruba find history so important, while modern American students question its relevance? This book aims to end such skepticism about the usefulness of history.

As we begin the twenty-first century in an ethnically and culturally diverse society caught up in an interdependent global system, history is of central importance in preparing us to exercise our rights and responsibilities as a free people. Studying history cannot make good citizens, but without a knowledge of history, we cannot understand the choices before us and think wisely about them. Lacking a collective memory of the past, we lapse into a kind of amnesia, unaware of the human condition and the long struggles of men and women everywhere to deal with the problems of their day and to create a better society. Unfurnished with historical knowledge, we deprive ourselves of knowing about the huge range of approaches people have taken to political, economic, and social life; to solving problems; and to surmounting the obstacles in their way.

History has a deeper, even more fundamental importance: the cultivation of the private person whose self-knowledge and self-respect provide the foundation for a life of dignity and fulfillment. Historical memory is the key to self-identity: to seeing one's place in the long stream of time, in the story of humankind.

When we study our own history, we see a rich and extraordinarily complex human story. This country, whose written history began with a convergence of Native Americans, Europeans, and Africans, has always been a nation of diverse peoples—a magnificent mosaic of cultures, religions, and skin shades. This book explores how American society assumed its present shape and developed its present forms of government; how as a nation we have conducted our foreign affairs and managed our economy; how science and technology and religion and reform have changed our lives; how as individuals and in groups we have lived, worked, loved, married, raised families, voted, argued, protested, and struggled to fulfill our dreams and the noble ideals of the American experiment.

Several ways of making the past understandable distinguish this book from traditional textbooks. The coverage of public events such as presidential elections, diplomatic treaties, and economic legislation is integrated with the private human stories that pervade them. Within a chronological framework, we have woven together our history as a nation, as a people, and as a society. When, for example, national political events are discussed, we analyze their impact on social and economic life at the state and local levels. Wars are described not only as they unfolded on the battlefield and in the salons of diplomats but also on the home front, where they have been history's greatest motor of social change. The interaction of ordinary and extraordinary Americans runs as a theme throughout this book.

Above all, we have tried to show the "humanness" of our history as it is revealed in people's everyday lives. Throughout these pages, we have often used the words of unnoticed Americans to capture the authentic human voices of those who participated in and responded to epic events such as war, slavery, industrialization, and reform movements.

GOALS AND THEMES OF THE BOOK

Our primary goal is to provide students with a rich, balanced, and thought-provoking treatment of the American past. By this we mean a history that treats the lives and experiences of Americans of all national origins and cultural backgrounds, at all levels of society, and in all regions of the country. It also means a history that seeks connections between the many factors—political, economic, technological, social, religious, intellectual, and biological—that have molded and remolded American society over four centuries. Finally, it means a history that encourages students to think about how we have all inherited a complex past filled with both notable achievements and thorny problems. The only history befitting a democratic nation is one that inspires students to initiate a frank and searching dialogue with their past.

To speak of a dialogue about the past presumes that history is interpretive rather than an agreed-upon account of what happened in the past and why history unfolded as it did. Students should understand that historians are continually reinterpreting the past. New interpretations may result from the discovery of new evidence, but more often they emerge because historians reevaluate old evidence in the light of new ideas that spring from the times in which they write and from their personal views of the world.

Through this book, we also hope to promote class discussions, which can be organized around six recurring themes basic to the American historical experience:

1. **The peopling of America**   How has this nation been peopled, from the first inhabitants to the many groups that arrived in slavery or servitude during the colonial period to the voluntary immigrants of today? How have these waves of newcomers contributed to and reshaped the American cultural mosaic? To what extent have different immigrant groups both assimilated into American culture and also preserved elements of their ethnic, racial, and religious heritages? How have the tensions between cultural assimilation and cultural preservation been played out, in the past and today?

2. **The development of American democracy**   To what extent have Americans developed a stable, democratic political system flexible enough to address the wholesale changes occurring in the last two centuries? To what degree has this political system been consistent with the principles of our nation's founding?

3. **Environmental, economic, and technological change**   How have environmental, economic, scientific, and technological changes affected the American landscape, attitudes toward nature, work, family life, leisure, sexual behavior, the division of wealth, and community relations in the United States?

4. **Religion and reform in American life**   What role has American religion played in the development of the nation? How have religion and religious values affected social change in our history? Whatever their varied sources, how have the recurring reform movements in our history dealt with economic, political, and social problems in attempting to square the ideals and realities of American life?

5. **America and the world**   In what ways have global events and trends had an impact on the shape and character of American life? How has the United

States affected the rest of the world? To what extent has the United States served as a model for other peoples, as an interventionist savior of other nations around the globe, and as an interfering expansionist in the affairs of other nations?

6. **Diversity, values, and American dreams** In the pursuit of American dreams, how have American beliefs and values changed over time? How have they varied between different groups: women and men; Americans of many colors and cultures; people of different regions, religions, sexual orientations, ages, and classes?

In writing a history that revolves around these themes, we have tried to convey two dynamics that operate in all societies. First, we observe people continuously adjusting to new developments, such as industrialization and urbanization, over which they seemingly have little control; we realize that people are not paralyzed by history but are the fundamental creators of it. They retain the ability, individually and collectively, to shape the world in which they live and thus in considerable degree to control their own lives. Second, we emphasize the connections that always exist among social, political, economic, and cultural events.

STRUCTURE OF THE BOOK

The chapters of this book are grouped into six parts that relate to major periods in American history. The titles for each part suggest a major theme that helps to characterize the period.

Each chapter has a clear structure, beginning with a chapter outline and then a personal story, called *American Stories,* recalling the experience of an ordinary or lesser-known American. Chapter 3, for example, is introduced with an account of the life of Anthony Johnson, who came to Virginia as a slave but who along with his wife, Mary, managed to gain his freedom. This brief anecdote introduces the overarching themes and major concepts of the chapter, in this case the tri-racial character of American society, the gradual tightening of racial slavery, and the instability of late seventeenth century colonial life. In addition, *American Stories* launches the chapter by engaging the student with a human account, suggesting that history was shaped by ordinary as well as extraordinary people. Following the personal story and easily identifiable by its visual separation from the anecdote and the body of the chapter, a *brief chapter overview* links the story and its themes to the text.

We aim to facilitate an exciting engagement with history for students in other ways as well. Every chapter ends with pedagogical features to reinforce and expand the presentation. A *timeline* reviews the major events and developments covered in the chapter. The *conclusion* briefly summarizes the chapter's main concepts and developments, revisits the individual described in *American Stories,* and serves as a bridge to the following chapter. *Questions for Review and Reflection* provide an opportunity to think about the chapter's major themes and their relation to the larger questions the text raises. An annotated section of suggested Web sites, *Discovering U.S. History Online,* offers students electronic resources relating to chapter content and themes and suggestions for further reading. *Fiction and Film* provides an annotated selection of historical novels and films. In addition, each map, figure, and table has been chosen to relate clearly to the narrative. *Captions* are specially written to help students understand and interpret these visual materials.

THE CONCISE SIXTH EDITION

This Concise Sixth Edition is condensed from the very successful comprehensive Seventh Edition of *The American People,* with its balance of political, social, and economic history. While we have eliminated detail and extra examples and have compressed the text, we have retained the interpretive connections and the "humanness" of history—the presentation of history as revealed through the lives of ordinary as well as extraordinary Americans and the interplay of social and political factors.

Continued Features

The Concise Sixth Edition continues the format and more compact size of the previous brief editions. The four-color design enhances the value of the maps and graphs and gives the book a vibrant appearance. This makes the book accessible, easy to read, and convenient for students to carry to and from class.

This edition contains one of the most popular features of *The American People:* the two-page sections entitled *Recovering the Past.* The RTPs, as the authors affectionately call them, introduce students to the fascinating variety of evidence—ranging from novels, political cartoons, and diaries to houses and popular music—that historians have learned to employ in reconstructing the past. Each RTP gives basic information about the source and its use by historians and then raises questions—called *Reflecting on the Past*—for students to consider as they study the example reproduced for their inspection.

In this edition, we have provided an international framework so students will think across international boundaries and understand the ways in which our history intersects with the world. Rather than developing a separate discussion of global events, we have woven an international narrative into our analysis of the American past. Chapter 13, for example, discusses the international context for American expansionism. Many maps underscore the international dimension of the text.

New Features

New to this edition and included in each section of the textbook are brief passages or, on occasion, illustrations such as posters or cartoons from non-Americans, commenting on **How Others See Us**. This feature is in keeping with our aim of putting American history into a global context and illustrating that those outside the United States (and often the "outsiders" within) sometimes know us better than we know ourselves.

Also new in the text are **review questions** at the end of each chapter. These questions not only help students identify, recall, and think about the major themes of the chapter but also encourage them to connect chapter themes to the book's large themes and questions.

Chapter Changes

Chapter-by-chapter changes include the following:

- *Chapter 3* contains the new feature, *How Others See Us*. In this case, the commentator is a traveler who describes New England, including its social structure and the presence of witches.
- *Chapter 4* also includes *How Others See Us*. Here a visitor analyzes Pennsylvania and includes his belief that exposure to British officers has improved its tone.
- *Chapter 7* reveals the attitudes of several English commentators after the Revolution in *How Others See Us*.
- *Chapter 9* has a new RTP focusing on federal census returns and what they can reveal. The chapter also contains insightful comments from an Englishwoman visiting the United States early in the nineteenth century for the feature *How Others See Us*.
- *Chapter 10* contains selections from Alexis de Tocqueville's visit to the United States in 1830, with his impression of American agriculture for *How Others See Us*.
- *Chapter 13* features the comments of a Mexican military officer as he observed American settlers in Texas in the feature *How Others See Us*.
- *Chapter 17* shows the Indian as outside observer in *How Others See Us*. Here Red Cloud's comments to the U.S. Secretary of the Interior in 1870 have been included.
- *Chapter 18* provides a different angle to understanding American industrial development with the comments of an English intellectual who argued that American businessmen worked too hard. His comments appear in *How Others See Us*.
- *Chapter 23* contains *How Others See Us* that provides the perspective of an Italian student who studied at Columbia University in the 1920s.
- *Chapter 24* has a new introductory vignette that focuses on how young people viewed the Great Depression and the Civilian Conservation Corps.
- *Chapter 25's How Others See Us* feature shows the experience of a young Japanese high school student who experienced the atom bomb explosion at Hiroshima.
- *Chapter 27* uses a West German poster on the Marshall Plan for *How Others See Us*.
- *Chapter 29* also uses posters, in this case French and German posters during the Vietnam War, for *How Others See Us*.
- *Chapter 31* takes the text up through the midterm elections of 2006 and provides coverage of the Iraq War. In addition, it also contains *How Others See Us* with the views of a European opponent to that war.

Our aim has been to write a balanced and vivid history of the development of the American nation and its society. We have also tried to provide the support materials necessary to make teaching and learning enjoyable and rewarding. The reader will be the judge of our success. We welcome your comments.

ACKNOWLEDGMENTS

Over the years, as new editions of this text were being developed, many of our colleagues read and critiqued the various drafts of the manuscript. For their thoughtful evaluations and constructive suggestions, the authors wish to express their gratitude to the following reviewers:

Richard H. Abbott, Eastern Michigan University; John Alexander, University of Cincinnati; Kenneth G. Alfers, Mountain View College; Terry Alford, Northern Virginia Community College; Donna Alvah, St. Lawrence University; Gregg Andrews, Southwest Texas State University; Robert Asher, University of Connecticut at Storrs; Patrick Ashwood, Hawkeye Community College; Arthur H. Auten, University of Hartford; Harry Baker, University of Arkansas at Little Rock; L. Diane Barnes, Youngstown State University; Michael Batinski, Southern Illinois University; Gary Bell, Sam Houston State University; Virginia Bellows, Tulsa Junior College; Spencer Bennett, Siena Heights College; Jackie R. Booker, Western Connecticut State University; Linda J. Borish, Western Michigan University; James Bradford, Texas A&M University; Thomas A. Britten, Briar Cliff College; Neal Brooks, Essex Community College; Jeffrey P. Brown, New Mexico State University; Dickson D. Bruce, Jr., University of California, Irvine; David Brundage, University of California, Santa Cruz; Steven J. Bucklin, University of South Dakota; Colin Calloway, Dartmouth University; D'Ann Campbell, Indiana University; Jane Censer, George Mason University; Vincent A. Clark, Johnson County Community College; Neil Clough, North Seattle Community College; Stacy A. Cordery, Monmouth College; Matthew Ware Coulter, Collin County Community College; A. Glenn Crothers, Indiana University Southeast; David Culbert, Louisiana State University; Jolane Culhane, Western New Mexico University; Mark T. Dalhouse, Northeast Missouri State University; Bruce Dierenfield, Canisius College; John Dittmer, DePauw University; Gordon Dodds, Portland State University; Richard Donley, Eastern Washington University; Dennis B. Downey, Millersville University; Robert Downtain, Tarrant County Community College; Robert C. Duncan, Western Oklahoma State College; Keith Edgerton, Montana State University at Billings; Trace Etienne-Gray, Southwest Texas State University; Robert Farrar, Spokane Falls Community College; Bernard Friedman, Indiana University–Purdue University at Indianapolis; Kathryn H. Fuller, Virginia Commonwealth University; Bruce Glasrud, California State University, Hayward; Brian Gordon, St. Louis Community College; Barbara Green, Wright State University; Richard Griswold del Castillo, San Diego State University; Carol Gruber, William Paterson College; Gretchen Grufman, Dominican University; Stephen A. Harmon, Pittsburgh State University; Thomas D. Hamm, Earlham College; Colonel William L. Harris, The Citadel Military College; Robert Haws, University of Mississippi; Jerrold Hirsch, Northeast Missouri State University; Frederick Hoxie, University of Illinois; John S. Hughes, University of Texas; Link Hullar, Kingwood College; Carol Sue Humphrey, Oklahoma Baptist University; Donald M. Jacobs, Northeastern University; Delores Janiewski, University of Idaho; David Johnson, Portland State University; Richard Kern, University of Findlay; Robert J. Kolesar, John Carroll University; Monte Lewis, Cisco Junior College; Xaio-bing Li, University of Central Oklahoma; William Link, University of North Carolina at Greensboro; Patricia M. Lisella, Iona College; Jeff Livingston, California State University, Chico; Ronald Lora, University of Toledo; Paul K. Longmore, San Francisco State University; Rita Loos, Framingham State College; George M. Lubick, Northern Arizona University; Suzanne Marshall, Jacksonville State University; John C. Massman, St. Cloud State University; Vernon Mattson, University of Nevada at Las Vegas; Joanne Maypole, Front Range Community College; Delove Nason McBroome, Humboldt State University; Arthur McCoole, Cuyamaca College; John McCormick, Delaware County Community College; George W. McDaniel, St. Ambrose University; David H. McGee, Central Virginia Community College; Sylvia McGrath, Stephen F. Austin University; James E. McMillan, Denison University; Otis L. Miller, Belleville Area College; Walter Miszczenko, Boise State University; Norma Mitchell, Troy State University; Gerald F. Moran, University of Michigan at Dearborn; William G. Morris, Midland College; Marian Morton, John Carroll University; Ting Ni, St. Mary's University; Roger Nichols, University of Arizona; Elizabeth Neumeyer, Kellogg Community College; Paul Palmer, Texas A&M University; Albert Parker, Riverside City College; Judith Parsons, Sul Ross State University; Carla Pestana, Ohio State University; Neva Peters, Tarrant County Community College; James Prickett, Santa Monica Community College; Noel Pugash, University of New Mexico; Juan Gomez-Quiñones, University of California, Los Angeles; George Rable, Anderson College; Joseph P. Reidy, Howard University; Leonard Riforgiato, Pennsylvania State University; Randy Roberts, Purdue University; Mary Robertson, Armstrong State University; David Robson, John Carroll University; Robert G. Rockwell, Mt. San Jacinto College; David E. Ruth, Pennsylvania State University; Judd Sage, Northern Virginia Community College; A. J. Scopino, Jr., Central Connecticut State University; Sylvia Sebesta, San Antonio College; Phil Schaeffer, Olympic College; Herbert Shapiro, University of Cincinnati; David R. Shibley, Santa Monica Community College; Ellen Shockro, Pasadena City College; Nancy Shoemaker, University of Connecticut; Bradley Skelcher, Delaware State University; Kathryn Kish Sklar, State University of New York at Binghamton; James Smith, Virginia State University; John Snetsinger, California Polytechnic State University at San Luis Obispo; Jo Snider, Southwest Texas State University; Randi Storch, State University of New York at Cortland; Stephen Strausberg, University of Arkansas; Katherine Scott Sturdevant, Pikes Peak Community College; Nan M. Sumner-Mack, Hawaii Community College; Cynthia Taylor, Santa Rosa Junior College; Thomas Tefft, Citrus College;

John A. Trickel, Richland College; Donna Van Raaphorst, Cuyahoga Community College; Morris Vogel, Temple University; Michael Wade, Appalachian State University; Jackie Walker, James Madison University; E. Sue Wamsley, University of Akron; Paul B. Weinstein, University of Akron-Wayne College; Joan Welker, Prince George's Community College; Michael Welsh, University of Northern Colorado; Seth Wigderson, University of Maine at Augusta; Kenneth H. Williams, Alcorn State University; Nelson E. Woodard, California State University, Fullerton; Mitch Yamasaki, Chaminade University; and Charles Zappia, San Diego Mesa College.

GARY B. NASH

JULIE ROY JEFFREY

SUPPLEMENTS FOR INSTRUCTORS AND STUDENTS

For Qualified College Adopters

Name of Supplement	Available in Print	Available Online	Instructor or Student Supplement	Description
Instructor's Resource Center (IRC)		✓	Instructor Supplement	Web site for downloading relevant supplements. Password protected. Please contact your local Pearson representative for an access code. *www.ablongman.com/irc*
MyHistoryLab		✓	Both	With the best of Longman's multimedia solutions for history in one easy-to-use place, MyHistory-Lab offers students and instructors a state-of-the-art interactive instructional solution for your U.S. History survey course. Built around a complete e-book version of this text, MyHistoryLab provides numerous study aids, review materials, and activities to make the study of history an enjoyable learning experience. Icons in the e-book link directly to relevant materials in context, many of which are assignable. MyHistoryLab includes several hundred primary source documents, videos, images and maps, all with accompanying analysis questions. It also includes a History Bookshelf with 50 of the most commonly assigned books in U.S. history courses and a History Toolkit with guided tutorials and helpful links. MyHistoryLab is flexible and easy-to-use as a supplement to a traditional lecture course or to administer a completely online course. *www.myhistorylab.com*
MyHistoryKit for American History		✓	Both	Online package of study materials, gradable quizzes and over 1,000 primary sources organized generically by typical American History themes to support your U.S. history survey text. Access code required. *www.myhistorykit.com*
American History Study Site		✓	Both	Online package of practice tests, Web links and flashcards organized generically by major history topics to support your U.S. history survey text. Open access. *www.longmanamericanhistory.com*
Instructor's Manual	✓	✓	Instructor Supplement	Each chapter includes a chapter overview, lecture supplements, and questions for class discussion. Text specific.
Test Bank	✓	✓	Instructor Supplement	Contains thousands of conceptual, objective, and essay questions. Text specific.
Computerized Test Bank	✓	✓	Instructor Supplement	Includes all items in the printed test bank. Questions can be edited, and tests can be printed in several different formats. Text specific.

(continued)

For Qualified College Adopters

Name of Supplement	Available in Print	Available Online	Instructor or Student Supplement	Description
PowerPoint Presentation		✓	Instructor Supplement	Designed to accompany the comprehensive version of *The American People*, these slides contain an outline of each chapter of the text and full-color images of maps and figures. *www.ablongman.com/irc*
Digital Transparency Masters		✓	Instructor Supplement	Designed to accompany the comprehensive version of *The American People*, these digital transparency masters are available exclusively on the Instructor's Resource Center. Text specific. *www.ablongman.com/irc*
Comprehensive American History Digital Transparency Masters		✓	Instructor Supplement	Vast collection of American history transparency masters. Available exclusively on the Instructor's Resource Center. *www.ablongman.com/irc*
Discovering American History Through Maps and Views Digital Transparency Masters		✓	Instructor Supplement	Set of 140 full-color digital transparency masters includes cartographic and pictorial maps, views, and photos, urban plans, building diagrams, and works of art. Available exclusively on the Instructor's Resource Center. *www.ablogman.com/irc*
History Digital Media Archive	CD		Instructor Supplement	Contains electronic images, interactive and static maps, and video. Available on CD only.
Visual Archives of American History, Updated Edition	CD		Instructor Supplement	Contains dozens of narrated vignettes and videos as well as hundreds of photos and illustrations. Available on CD only.
Study Guide	✓		Student Supplement	Contains chapter overviews, learning objectives, identifications, mapping exercises, multiple-choice and essay questions, and critical thinking exercises. Available in two volumes. Text specific.
VangoNotes		✓	Student Supplement	Downloadable MP3 audio topic reviews. Includes major themes, key terms, practice tests, and rapid reviews. *www.vangonotes.com*
Study Card for American History	✓		Student Supplement	Distills course information down to the basics, helping students quickly master the fundamentals and prepare for exams.
Research Navigator Guide	✓	✓	Student Supplement	A book that contains an access code to EBSCO ContentSelect, *New York Times,* and "Best of the Web."
Longman American History Atlas	✓		Both	100 full color maps.
Mapping America: A Guide to Historical Geography	✓		Student Supplement	18 exercises explore the role of geography in history.
Voices of *The American People*	✓		Student Supplement	Two volume collection of primary sources, organized to correspond to the table of contents of *The American People.*

For Qualified College Adopters

Name of Supplement	Available in Print	Available Online	Instructor or Student Supplement	Description
America Through the Eyes of Its People	✓		Student Supplement	Two-volume comprehensive anthology of primary sources expertly balances social and political history and includes up-to-date narrative material.
American History Timeline	✓		Student Supplement	Gives students a chronological context to help them understand important political, social, economic, cultural, and technology events.
Sources of the African-American Past	✓		Student Supplement	This collection of primary sources covers key themes in the African-American experience.
Women and the National Experience	✓		Student Supplement	Primary source reader contains both classic and unusual documents describing the history of women in the United States.
Reading the American West	✓		Student Supplement	Primary sources in the history of the American West.
A Short Guide to Writing About History	✓		Student Supplement	Teaches students to write cogent history papers.
American History Firsthand: Working with Primary Sources	✓		Student Supplement	Two-volume collection of looseleaf reproduced primary sources exposes students to archival research.
Longman–Penguin Putnam Inc. Value Packs	✓		Student Supplement	Variety of Penguin Putnam texts are available at discounted prices when bundled with *The American People*. Complete list of available titles at *www.ablongman.com/penguin*.
Library of American Biography Series	✓		Student Supplement	Renowned series of biographies that focus on figures who had a significant impact on American history. Complete list of available titles at *www.ablongman.com/html/lab*.

About the Authors

Gary B. Nash received his Ph.D. from Princeton University. He is currently Director of the National Center for History in the Schools at the University of California, Los Angeles, where he teaches colonial and revolutionary American history. Among the books Nash has authored are *Quakers and Politics: Pennsylvania, 1681–1726* (1968); *Red, White, and Black: The Peoples of Early America* (1974, 1982, 1992, 2000); *The Urban Crucible: Social Change, Political Consciousness, and the Origins of the American Revolution* (1979); *Forging Freedom: The Formation of Philadelphia's Black Community, 1720–1840* (1988); *First City: Philadelphia and the Forging of Historical Memory* (2002); and *The Unknown American Revolution: The Unruly Birth of Democracy and the Struggle to Create America* (2005). A former president of the Organization of American Historians, his scholarship is especially concerned with the role of common people in the making of history. He wrote Part One and served as a general editor of this book.

Julie Roy Jeffrey earned her Ph.D. in history from Rice University. Since then she has taught at Goucher College. Honored as an outstanding teacher, Jeffrey has been involved in faculty development activities and curriculum evaluation. She was Fulbright Chair in American Studies at the University of Southern Denmark, 1999–2000 and John Adams Chair of American History at the University of Utrecht, The Netherlands, 2006. Jeffrey's major publications include *Education for Children of the Poor* (1978); *Frontier Women: The Trans-Mississippi West, 1840–1880* (1979, 1997); *Converting the West: A Biography of Narcissa Whitman* (1991); *The Great Silent Army of Abolitionism: Ordinary Women in the Antislavery Movement* (1998) and *Abolitionists Remember* (forthcoming 2008). She collaborated with Peter Frederick on *American History Firsthand,* two volumes (2002, 2007). She is the author of many articles on the lives and perceptions of nineteenth-century women. Her research continues to focus on abolitionism as well as on history and film. She wrote Parts Three and Four in collaboration with Peter Frederick and acted as a general editor of this book.

John R. Howe received his Ph.D. from Yale University. At the University of Minnesota, he has taught the U.S. history survey and courses on the American revolutionary era and the early republic. His major publications include *The Changing Political Thought of John Adams* (1966), *From the Revolution Through the Age of Jackson* (1973), *The Role of Ideology in the American Revolution* (1977), and *Language and Political Meaning in Revolutionary America* (2003). His present research deals with the social politics of verbal discourse in late eighteenth- and early nineteenth-century Boston. He has received a Woodrow Wilson Graduate Fellowship, a John Simon Guggenheim Fellowship, and a Research Fellowship from the Charles Warren Center for Studies in American History. Howe wrote Part Two of this book.

Peter J. Frederick received his Ph.D. in history from the University of California, Berkeley. His career of innovative teaching began at California State University, Hayward, in the 1960s and continued at Wabash College (1970–2004) and Carleton College (1992–1994). He also served as distinguished Professor of American History and Culture at Heritage University on the Yakama Nation reservation in Washington between 2004 and 2006. Recognized nationally as a distinguished teacher and for his many articles and workshops on teaching and learning, Frederick was awarded the Eugene Asher Award for Excellence in Teaching by the AHA in 2000. He has also written several articles on life-writing and a book, *Knights of the Golden Rule: The Intellectual as Christian Social Reformer in the 1890s*. With Julie Jeffrey, he recently published *American History Firsthand*. He coordinated and edited all the "Recovering the Past" sections and coauthored Parts Three and Four.

Allen F. Davis earned his Ph.D. from the University of Wisconsin. A former president of the American Studies Association, he is a professor emeritus at Temple University and editor of *Conflict and Consensus in American History* (9th ed., 1997). He is the author of *Spearheads for Reform: The Social Settlements and the Progressive Movement* (1967); *American Heroine: The Life and Legend of Jane Addams* (1973); and *Postcards from Vermont: A Social History* (2002). He is coauthor of *Still Philadelphia* (1983); *Philadelphia Stories* (1987); and *One Hundred Years at Hull-House* (1990). Davis wrote Part Five of this book.

Allan M. Winkler received his Ph.D. from Yale University. He has taught at Yale and the University of Oregon, and he is now Distinguished Professor of History at Miami University of Ohio. An award-winning teacher, he has also published extensively about the recent past. His books include *The Politics of Propaganda: The Office of War Information, 1942–1945* (1978); *Home Front U.S.A.: America During World War II* (1986, 2000); *Life Under a Cloud: American Anxiety About the Atom* (1993, 1999); *The Cold War: A History in Documents* (2000), and *Franklin D. Roosevelt and the Making of Modern America* (2006). His research centers on the connections between public policy and popular mood in modern American history. Winkler wrote Part Six of this book.

Charlene Mires earned her Ph.D. in history at Temple University. At Villanova University, she teaches courses in nineteenth- and twentieth-century U.S. history, public history, and material culture. She is the author of *Independence Hall in American Memory* (2002) and serves as editor of the Pennsylvania History Studies Series for the Pennsylvania Historical Association. A former journalist, she was a co-recipient of the Pulitzer Prize for general local news reporting with other staff members of the Fort Wayne (Indiana) *News-Sentinel*. She has contributed to Part Five of *The American People*.

Carla Gardina Pestana received her Ph.D. from the University of California at Los Angeles. She taught at Ohio State University, where she served as a Lilly Teaching Fellow and launched an innovative on-demand publishing project. Currently she holds the W. E. Smith Professorship in History at Miami University.

Her publications include *Liberty of Conscience and the Growth of Religious Diversity in Early America* (1986), *Quakers and Baptists in Colonial Massachusetts* (1991), and *The English Atlantic in an Age of Revolution, 1640–1661* (2004). She is also the co-editor, with Sharon V. Salinger, of *Inequality in Early America* (1999). At present, she is completing a book on religion in the British Atlantic world to 1830 for classroom use. She has contributed to Part One of *The American People*.

Ancient America and Africa

American Stories

Four Women's Lives Highlight the Convergence of Three Continents

In what historians call the "early modern period" of world history—roughly the fifteenth to seventeenth century, when peoples from different regions of the earth came into close contact with each other—four women played key roles in the convergence and clash of societies from Europe, Africa, and the Americas. Their lives highlight some of this chapter's major themes, which developed in an era when the people of three continents began to encounter each other and the shape of the modern world began to take form.

Born in 1451, Isabella of Castile was a banner-bearer for *reconquista*—the centuries-long Christian crusade to expel the Muslim rulers who had controlled Spain for centuries. Pious and charitable, the queen of Castile married Ferdinand, the king of Aragon, in 1469. The union of their kingdoms forged a stronger Christian Spain now prepared to realize a new religious and military vision. Eleven years later, after ending hostilities with Portugal, Isabella and Ferdinand began consolidating their power. By expelling Muslims and Jews, the royal couple pressed to enforce Catholic religious conformity. Their religious zeal also led them to sponsor four voyages of Christopher Columbus as a means of extending Spanish power across the Atlantic. The first was commissioned in 1492, only a few months after what the Spanish considered a "just and holy war" against infidels culminated in the surrender of Moorish Granada, the last stronghold of Islam in Christian Europe. Sympathizing with Isabella's fervent piety and desire to convert the people of distant lands to Christianity, after 1493 Columbus signed his letters "Christopher Columbus, Christ Bearer."

On the other side of the Atlantic resided an Aztec woman of influence, also called Isabella by the Spanish, who soon symbolized the mixing of her people with the Spanish. Her real name was Tecuichpotzin, which meant "little royal maiden" in Nahuatl, the Aztec language. The first-born child of the Aztec ruler Moctezuma II and Teotlalco, his wife, she entered the world in 1509—before the Aztecs had seen a single Spaniard. But when she was 11, Tecuichpotzin witnessed the arrival of the conquistadors under Cortés. When her father was near death, he asked the conqueror to take custody of his daughter, hoping for an accommodation between the conquering Spanish and the conquered Aztecs. But Tecuichpotzin was reclaimed by her people and soon was married to her father's brother, who became the Aztec ruler in 1520. After he died of smallpox within two months, the last Aztec emperor claimed the young girl as his wife.

But then in 1521, the Spanish siege of Tenochtitlán, the Aztec island capital in Lake Texcoco, overturned the mighty Aztec Empire and soon brought Tecuichpotzin into the life of the victorious Spanish. In 1526, she learned that her husband had been tortured and hanged for plotting an insurrection against Cortés. Still only 19, she soon succumbed to the overtures of Cortés, agreeing to join his household and live among his Indian mistresses. Pregnant with Cortés's child, she was married off to a Spanish officer. Another marriage followed, and in all she bore seven children, all descendants of Moctezuma II. All became large landowners and figures of importance. Tecuichpotzin was in this way a pioneer of *mestizaje*—the mixing of races—and thus one of the leading Aztec women who launched the creation of a new society in Mexico.

Elizabeth I, daughter of Henry VIII, who had established the Church of England and rejected the authority of the Catholic pope in Rome, became the key figure in encouraging English expansion overseas. Through her long rule of nearly a half-century, she inspired Protestant England to challenge Catholic Spain and France. Even Pope Sixtus V acknowledged that she was "a great woman, and were she only Catholic she would be without her match." He also remarked, "She is only a woman, yet she makes herself feared by Spain, by France, by the Emperor, by all." Commissioning buccaneers such as John Hawkins and Francis Drake, and sponsoring promoters of colonization such as Walter Raleigh and the Richard Hakluyts (the two were cousins), Elizabeth assured the planting of English colonies in North America. They would grow mightily after her death in 1603 and eventually challenge the Dutch, French, and Spanish, who also saw the Americas as a source of great wealth and power.

Elizabeth I's vitality, ambition, and wit suited her perfectly to lead England forward, even though her nation, when she assumed the throne in 1558, was weak in comparison to France, Spain, and even Portugal. Investing her own money in voyages of exploration and settlement, she encouraged others from the middle and upper classes to do the same. In backing a 20-year conflict with the Spanish—a religious conflict and also a struggle for maritime power—she opened a gateway to the Americas for the English.

On the west coast of Africa was another powerful woman. Born around 1595 and named because she entered the world with the umbilical cord wrapped around her neck (which was believed to foretell a haughty character), Queen Njinga led fierce resistance to the Portuguese slave trade and the Portuguese attempts to control Angola. She knew the Portuguese had been trading for slaves in Angola and had even converted King Affonso I to Catholicism in the 1530s. She also knew that by the time Queen Elizabeth came to power in 1558 in England, the Portuguese had trapped her people into incessant wars in order to supply slaves to their Portuguese trading partners. Only when she assumed the throne of Ndongo (present-day Angola) in 1624 did Queen Njinga's people begin to resist Portuguese rule. Leading her troops in a series of wars, she gave a fierce battle cry that legend says was heard for miles, making her a heroic figure in Angolan history.

In opening this book, the stories of Queen Isabella of Castile, Aztec princess Tecuichpotzin, Queen Elizabeth I of England, and Angola's Queen Njinga set the scene for the intermingling of Europeans, Africans, and Native Americans in the New World—what Europeans called North and South America—by revealing the backgrounds of the peoples of three continents and the changes occurring in each of their societies as the time for a historic convergence neared. This allows us to better understand the advent of colliding cultures among societies rimming the Atlantic Ocean.

In narrating this historic meeting of societies previously distanced from each other, historians have too often portrayed Europeans reaching the Americas as the carriers of a superior culture that inevitably vanquished people living in a primitive, if not "savage," state. Such a view renders Native Americans and Africans passive and static people—so much dough to be kneaded by advanced Europeans. Modern historical scholarship, however, tells us that Africans and Native Americans played critically important roles in a complex, intercultural birthing of a "new world." Thus we examine the complexities of West African societies, delve into the societies of some of the peoples of North and South America, and study Western Europeans of the late fifteenth century. In drawing comparisons and contrasts, we equip ourselves to see three worlds meet as a new global age began.

THE PEOPLES OF AMERICA BEFORE COLUMBUS

Thousands of years before the European exploratory voyages in the 1490s, the history of humankind in North America began. American history can begin with some basic questions: Who were the first inhabitants of the Americas? Where did they come from? What were they like? How had the societies they formed changed over the millennia that preceded European arrival? Can their history be reconstructed from the mists of prehistoric time?

Migration to the Americas

Almost all the evidence suggesting answers to these questions comes from ancient sites of early life in North America. Archaeologists have unearthed skeletal remains, pots, tools, ornaments, and other objects to set a tentative date for the arrival of humans in America of about 35,000 B.C.E.—about the same time that humans began to settle Japan and Scandinavia.

DOCUMENT

Iroquois Creation Story

Nearly every Native American society has its own story about its origins in the Americas. However, paleoanthropologists, scientists who study ancient peoples, generally agree that the first inhabitants of the Americas were nomadic bands from Siberia hunting big-game animals. These sojourners began to migrate across a land bridge connecting northeastern Asia with Alaska. Geologists believe that this land bridge, perhaps 600 miles wide, existed most recently between 25,000 and 14,000 years ago. Ice-free passage through Canada was possible only briefly at the beginning and end of this period, however. Scholars are divided on the exact timing, but the main migration apparently occurred between 11,000 and 14,000 years ago. Some new archaeological finds suggest multiple migrations, both by sea and land, from several regions of Asia and even from Europe.

DOCUMENT

Pima Creation Story

Hunters, Farmers, and Environmental Factors

Once on the North American continent, these early wanderers began trekking southward and then eastward, following vegetation and game. Over centuries, they reached the tip of South America. American history has traditionally emphasized the "westward movement" of people, but for thousands of years before Columbus's arrival, the frontier moved southward and eastward. Thus did people from the "Old World" discover the "New World" thousands of years before Columbus.

Archaeologists have excavated ancient sites of early life in the Americas, tentatively reconstructing the dispersion of these first Americans over an immense land mass. Although much remains unknown, archaeological evidence suggests that as centuries passed and population increased, the earliest inhabitants evolved separate cultures, adjusting to various environments in distinct ways. Europeans who rediscovered the New World thousands of years later would lump together the myriad societies they found. By the late 1400s, the "Indians" of the Americas were enormously diverse in the size and complexity of their societies, the languages they spoke, and their forms of social organization.

MAP

Pre-Columbian Societies of the Americas

Native American history passed through several phases. The Beringian period of initial migration ended about 14,000 years ago. During the Paleo-Indian era, 14,000 to 10,000 years ago, big-game hunters flaked hard stones into spear points and chose "kill sites" where they slew herds of Pleistocene mammals. This more reliable food source allowed population growth, and nomadism began to give way to settled habitations or local migration within limited territories.

IMAGE

Clovis Points

During the Archaic era, from about 10,000 to 2,500 years ago, great geological changes brought further adaptations to the land. As the massive Ice Age glaciers slowly retreated, a warming trend turned vast grassland areas from Utah to the highlands of Central America into desert. The Pleistocene mammals were weakened by more arid conditions, but human populations ably adapted as they learned to exploit new sources of food, especially plants.

About 9,000 to 7,000 years ago, a technological breakthrough arose, probably independently in widely separated parts of the world. As humans learned how to plant, cultivate, and harvest—what historians call the agricultural revolution—they gained control over once-ungovernable natural forces. Agriculture slowly brought dramatic changes in human societies everywhere.

Recent archaeological evidence points to examples of environmental devastation that severely damaged the biodiversity of the Americas. The first wave of intruders found a wilderness teeming with so-called megafauna: saber-toothed tigers and woolly mammoths. But by about 10,000 years ago, overhunting and a massive shift of climate deprived these huge beasts of their grazing environment, bringing them to the brink of extinction. People were forced to kill new sources of food such as turkeys, ducks, and guinea pigs, and this may have gradually reduced human numbers.

Over many centuries, salinization and deforestation put the environment under additional stress. In what is today central Arizona, the Hohokam civilization collapsed hundreds of years ago when the irrigation system became too salty to support agriculture. At New Mexico's Chaco Canyon, the fast-growing Anasazi denuded a magnificently forested region for firewood and building materials. The resulting soil erosion impoverished the region.

As Native Americans learned to domesticate plant life, they began the long process of transforming their relationship to the physical world. Dating the advent of agriculture in the Americas is difficult, but archaeologists estimate it at about 5000 B.C.E. Agriculture had already been developed in southwestern Asia and in Africa and spread to Europe at about the time people in the Tehuacán valley of central Mexico first planted maize and squash. Over the millennia, humans progressed to systematic clearing and planting of fields, and settled village life began to replace nomadic existence. Increases in food supply triggered other major changes. As more ample food fueled population growth, large groups split off to form separate societies. Greater social and political complexity developed. Men cleared the land and hunted; women tended crops. Many societies empowered religious figures, trusting them to ward off hostile forces.

Everywhere in the Americas, regional trading networks formed. Along routes carrying commodities such as salt for food preservation, obsidian rock for projectile points, and copper for jewelry also traveled technology, religious ideas, and agricultural practices. By the end of the Archaic period, about 500 B.C.E., hundreds of independent kin-based groups had learned to exploit the resources of their particular area and to trade with other groups.

Mesoamerican Empires

Of all the large-scale societies developing in the Americas during Europe's medieval period, the most impressive were in Mesoamerica—the middle region bridging the great land masses of South and North America. The Valley of Mexico, now dominated by Mexico City, became the center of the largest societies that emerged in the centuries before the Spanish arrived early in the sixteenth century. In less than two centuries, the Aztecs, successor to the earlier Olmec and Toltec civilizations, built a mighty empire rivaling any known over the centuries in Europe, Asia, or Africa by subjugating smaller tribes. By the time of Columbus's first voyage in 1492, the Aztecs controlled most of central Mexico and had an estimated population of 10 to 20 million. Extracting tribute from conquered peoples, the Aztecs built a great capital in Tenochtitlán ("Place of the Prickly Pear Cactus"), a canal-ribbed city island in the great lake of Texcoco. Boasting a population of perhaps 150,000, it was certainly one of the world's greatest cities on the eve of the Columbian voyages. Aztec society was as stratified as any in Europe, and the supreme ruler's authority was as extensive as that of any European or African king. Every Aztec was born into one of four classes: nobility, free commoners, serfs, and slaves.

When they arrived in 1519, Spaniards could hardly believe the grandeur they saw in the immense Aztec capital that covered about 10 square miles and boasted some 40 towers. They had found their way to the most advanced civilization in the Americas, where through skilled hydraulic engineering the Aztecs cultivated

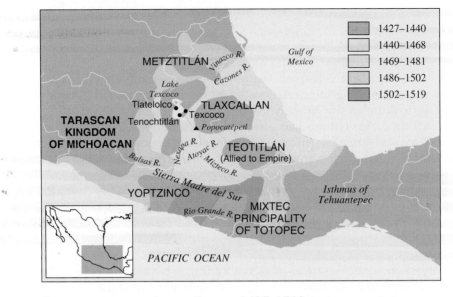

EXPANSION OF THE AZTEC EMPIRE, 1427–1519 In the century before Europeans breached the Atlantic to find the Americas, the Aztecs' rise to power brought 10 to 20 million people under their sway—more than the entire population of Spain and Portugal at this time.

chinampas, or "floating gardens," around their capital city in which a wide variety of flowers and vegetables grew. The Spaniards were unprepared for encountering such an advanced civilization built by what they considered savage people.

Regional North American Cultures

The regions north of Mesoamerica were never populated by societies of the size and complexity of the Aztecs, though some felt their influence. Throughout North America in the last epoch of the pre-Columbian (or post-Archaic) era, many distinct societies thrived. In the southwestern region of North America, for example, Hohokam and Anasazi societies (the ancestors of the present-day Hopi and Zuñi) had developed a sedentary village life thousands of years before the Spanish arrived in the 1540s.

By about 1200 C.E., "Pueblo" people, as the Spanish later called them, constructed planned villages composed of large, terraced, multistoried buildings, each with many rooms and often located on defensive sites that would afford the Anasazi protection from their northern enemies. By the time the Spanish arrived, the indigenous Pueblo people were using irrigation canals, dams, and hillside terracing to water their arid maize fields. In its agricultural techniques, skill in ceramics, use of woven textiles for clothing, and village life, Pueblo society resembled peasant communities in many parts of Europe and Asia.

IMAGE

Cliff Palace in Colorado

An Anasazi Village The ruins of Pueblo Bonita in Chaco Canyon, New Mexico, mark the center of Anasazi culture in the twelfth century C.E. This San Juan River basin town may have contained 1,000 people living in apartment-like structures larger than any built in North America until the late nineteenth century. (© *David Muench*)

Far to the north, on the Pacific coast of the Northwest, native Tlingit, Kwaki-utl, Salish, and Haida people lived in villages of several hundred, drawing their sustenance from salmon and other spawning fish and living in plank houses displaying elaborately carved red cedar pillars, guarded by gigantic carved totem poles. Reaching this region much later than most other parts of the hemisphere, European explorers were amazed at the architectural and artistic skills of the Northwest indigenous people. Northwest native people defined their place in the cosmos with ceremonial face masks, which often represented animals, birds, and fish—reminders of magical ancestral spirits that inhabited what they understood as the four interconnected zones of the cosmos: the Sky World, the Undersea World, the Mortal World, and the Spirit World.

Ceremonial masks played a pivotal place in the Potlatch, a great winter gathering with song, dance, and ritual. In Potlatch ceremonial dances, native leaders honored their family lineage and signified their chiefly authority in the tribe. By giving away many of their possessions, chiefs satisfied tribe members and in this way maintained their legitimacy, a largesse which mystified and often disturbed material-minded Europeans.

Far to the east, Native American societies have been traced as far back as about 9000 B.C.E. From the Great Plains of the midcontinent to the Atlantic tidewater region, four main language groups emerged: Algonquian, Iroquoian, Muskhogean, and Siouan. As in other tribal societies, agricultural revolution gradually trans- formed life, as people adopted semifixed settlements and developed trading net- works that linked together societies occupying a vast region.

Among the most impressive of these societies were the mound-building soci- eties of the Mississippi and Ohio valleys. When European settlers first crossed the Appalachian Mountains a century and a half after arriving on the continent, they were astounded to find hundreds of ceremonial mounds and gigantic sculp- tured earthworks. Believing "Indians" to be forest primitives, they reasoned that these must be the remains of some ancient civilization that had found its way to North America.

Archaeologists now conclude that the Mound Builders were the ancestors of the Creek, Choctaw, and Natchez. Their societies, evolving slowly over the cen- turies, had developed considerable complexity by the advent of Christianity in Europe. In southern Ohio alone about 10,000 mounds, used as burial sites, have been pinpointed, and archaeologists have excavated another 1,000 earth-walled enclosures, including one enormous fortification with a circumference of about $3\frac{1}{2}$ miles, enclosing 100 acres, or the equivalent of 50 modern city blocks. From the mounded tombs, archaeologists have recovered a great variety of items that have been traced to widely separated parts of the continent, showing that the Mound Builders participated in a vast trading network linking together hundreds of Indian villages.

The mound-building societies of the Ohio valley declined many centuries be- fore Europeans arrived, perhaps attacked by other tribes or damaged by severe climatic changes that undermined agriculture. By about 600 C.E., another mound- building agricultural society arose in the Mississippi valley. Its center, the city of Cahokia, with at least 20,000 (and possibly as many as 40,000) inhabitants, stood near present-day St. Louis. Great ceremonial plazas, flanked by a temple that rose in four terraces to a height of 100 feet, marked this first metropolis in America, an urban center of a far-flung Mississippi culture that encompassed hundreds of villages from Wisconsin to Louisiana and from Oklahoma to Tennessee.

IMAGE

Reconstructed
View of Cahokia

Before the mound-building cultures mysteriously declined, their influence was already transforming the woodland societies along the Atlantic. These nu- merous small tribes were far from the "savages" that the first European explorers described. They had added limited agriculture to their skill in using natural plants and had developed food procurement strategies that exploited all the re- sources around them.

In the far north people lived by the sea and supplemented their diet with maple sugar and a few foodstuffs. Farther south, in what was to become New England, were small tribes occupying fairly local areas and joined together only by occasional trade. In the mid-Atlantic area were various tribes who added lim- ited agriculture to their skill in using natural plants for food, medicine, dyes, and flavoring. Most eastern woodland residents lived in waterside villages. They of- ten migrated seasonally between inland and coastal village sites or situated them- selves astride two ecological zones. In the Northeast, their birchbark canoes, light enough to be carried by a single man, helped them trade and communicate over immense territories.

Mississippian Culture Shrine Figures Carved from marble seven to eight hundred years ago, these shrine figures, male and female, were found in a tomb in northwestern Georgia. The Indian carvings, known to us only as part of a South Appalachian Mississippi culture, are thought to be representations of ancestor gods. Are similar shrine figures found in African and European societies? *(Lynn Johnson/Aurora & Quanta Productions)*

In the Southeast were densely populated, rich and complex cultures that traced their ancestry back at least 8,000 years. Belonging to several language groups, some of them joined in loose confederacies. Called "Mississippian" societies by archaeologists, the tribes of the Southeast created elaborate pottery and baskets and conducted long-distance trade. These cultures also were influenced by burial mound techniques, some of which involved earthmoving on a vast scale. A global warming trend helped agriculture flourish in this region, leading in some cases, as with the Natchez, to the development of highly stratified societies. However, after the "Little Ice Age," which occurred for several centuries after about 1300, they abandoned their mounded urban centers and devolved into less populous, less stratified, and less centralized societies.

The Iroquois

Far to the north of the declining southeastern mound-building societies, between what would become French and English zones of settlement, five tribes comprised what Europeans later called the League of the Iroquois: the Mohawk, Oneida, Onondaga, Cayuga, and Senecas. The Iroquois Confederation began as a vast extension of the kinship group that characterized the northeastern woodland pattern of family settlement and embraced perhaps 10,000 people by the sixteenth century.

DOCUMENT

Dekanawida Myth and the Achievement of Iroquois Unity

Not long before Europeans began coming ashore in eastern North America, the loosely organized and strife-ridden Iroquois created a more cohesive political confederacy. As a result, villages gained stability, population increased, and the Iroquois developed political mechanisms for solving internal problems and presenting a more unified front to outsiders. This facilitated the development of a coordinated Iroquois policy for dealing with the European newcomers.

In the palisaded villages of Iroquoia, work, land use, hunting, and even living arrangements in longhouses were communal. While there might be individual farming or hunting efforts, it was understood that the bounty was to be divided among all. One historian has called this "upside-down capitalism," where the goal was not to pile up material possessions but to reach the happy situation where individuals could give what they had to others. This Iroquois societal structure would stand in contrast to that of the arriving Europeans, as would Iroquois gender roles, political structure, and familial customs.

Pre-Contact Population

For many decades, anthropologists and historians estimated that the population of the Americas, and especially North America, was small, only about 10 percent of Europe's population at the time of Columbus's first voyage in 1492. Recently scholars have conceded that most estimates made in the past were grossly understated due to the conventional view that Indian societies peopled by nomadic hunters and gatherers could not be very large.

Archaeological research in recent decades has indicated that sophisticated Native American agricultural techniques were capable of sustaining large societies. Therefore, population estimates have soared, with today's scholars estimating the pre-contact population north of the Rio Grande River to be at least 4 million people. Though estimates vary widely, the most reliable indicate that about 50 to 70 million people lived in the entire hemisphere when Europeans first arrived, contrasting with some 70 to 90 million in Europe (including Russia) around 1500, about 50 to 70 million in Africa, and 225 to 350 million in Asia. The colonizers were not coming to a "virgin wilderness," as they often described it, but to a land inhabited for thousands of years by people whose village existence in some ways resembled their own.

Contrasting Worldviews

IMAGE

Conquistadores Torturing Native Amerindians

Having evolved in complete isolation from each other, European and Indian cultures exhibited a wide difference in values. Colonizing Europeans called themselves "civilized" and typically described the people they met in the Americas as "savage," "heathen," or "barbarian." Lurking behind the confrontation that took place when Europeans and Native Americans met were latent conflicts over humans' relationship to the environment, the meaning of property, and personal identity.

Europeans and Native Americans conceptualized their relationship to nature in starkly different ways. Regarding the earth as filled with resources for humans to exploit for their own benefit, Europeans separated the secular and sacred parts of life, and they placed their own relationship to the natural environment mostly in the secular sphere. Native Americans, however, did not distinguish between the secular and sacred. For them, every aspect of the natural world was sacred and all were linked together to form a sacred whole.

Europeans believed that land, as a privately held commodity, was a resource to be exploited. They took for granted property lines, inheritance of land, and courts to settle the resulting land disputes. Property was the basis not only of sustenance but also of independence, wealth, status, social structure, political rights, and identity. Native Americans also had concepts of property and boundaries. But they believed that land had sacred qualities and should be held in common. Communal ownership sharply limited social stratification and increased a sense of sharing in most Native American communities.

There were exceptions. The Aztec and Inca empires in present-day Mexico and Peru were highly developed, populous, and stratified. So, in North America, were a few tribes such as the Natchez. But on the eastern and western coasts of the continent and in the Southwest—the regions of contact in the sixteenth and seventeenth centuries—lived people whose values differed strikingly.

European colonizers found the matrilineal organization of many tribal societies contrary to the European male-dominated hierarchy. Family membership among the Iroquois, for example, was determined through the female line. When a son or grandson married, he moved from his female-headed household to one headed by the matriarch of his wife's family.

Native American women were subordinate, but not nearly to the extent found among European women. For example, women were almost entirely excluded from European politics. But in Native American villages, again to take the Iroquois example, designated men sat in a circle to deliberate and make decisions, and the senior women of the village stood behind them, lobbying and instructing. Village chiefs, who were male, were chosen by the elder women of their clans. If they moved too far from the will of the women who appointed them, these chiefs were removed.

The role of women in the tribal economy reinforced male-female power-sharing. Men hunted, fished, and cleared land, but women controlled the raising and distribution of crops, supplying probably three-quarters of their family's nutritional needs. When the men were away hunting, women directed village life. Europeans perceived such sexual equality as another mark of "savagery."

In economic relations, Europeans and Indians differed in ways that sometimes led to misunderstanding and conflict. Over vast stretches of the continent, Indians had built trading networks for centuries before Europeans arrived, making it easy for them to incorporate new European goods into their cultures. However, Indian peoples saw trade as a way to preserve reciprocity between individuals and communities, while Europeans saw trade mostly as an economic transaction.

The English saw a final damning defect in Native American religious beliefs. While Europeans built their religious life around a single divinity, written scriptures, a trained clergy, and churches with structured ceremonies, Native American religion differed on all these counts. The Indians were polytheistic, and their religious leaders used medicinal plants and magical chants to

MAP

The First
Americans:
Location of Major
Indian Groups
and Culture Areas
in the 1600s

communicate with the spiritual world. For Europeans, the Indians' polytheism was pagan and devilish. Their fear and hatred of infidels intensified by the Protestant Reformation, Europeans saw a holy necessity to convert—or destroy—these enemies of God.

AFRICA ON THE EVE OF CONTACT

Half a century before Columbus reached the Americas, a Portuguese sea captain made the first European landing on the west coast of sub-Saharan Africa. If he had been able to travel the length and breadth of the immense continent, he would have encountered a rich variety of African states, peoples, and cultures. African "backwardness" was a myth perpetuated after the slave trade had begun transporting millions of Africans to the New World. During the period of early contact, Africa, like pre-Columbian America, hosted diverse cultures with complex histories.

The Spread of Islam

Spreading rapidly in Arabia after its founder Muhammad began preaching in 610 C.E., Islam rose to global eminence after several centuries. By the tenth century, Egypt was predominantly Muslim, and Islam was spreading southward from Mediterranean North Africa across the Sahara Desert into northern Sudan, where it took hold especially in the trading centers. In time, Islam encompassed much of the Eastern Hemisphere and became the main intermediary for exchanging goods, ideas, and technologies across a huge part of the world. When Portuguese traders initiated the slave traffic in West Africa in the 1400s, many of the Africans they forced onto slave ships were devout Muslims.

The Kingdoms of Central and West Africa

The region of West Africa, to which Islam was spreading by the tenth century, embraced widely varied ecological zones—including vast desert, grasslands, and tropical forests. Africa experienced an agricultural revolution similar to that which had occurred elsewhere. Most people tilled the soil, using sophisticated agricultural techniques and livestock management by the time of first contact with Europeans. About 450 B.C.E. the Nok in present-day Nigeria developed a method of iron production long before it reached Europe. Over many centuries, more efficient iron implements for cultivating and harvesting increased agricultural productivity, in turn spurring population growth, greater specialization of tasks, and thus greater efficiency and additional technical improvements.

Cultural and political development in West Africa proceeded at varying rates, depending on ecological conditions. Regions blessed by good soil, adequate rainfall, and abundance of minerals, as in coastal West Africa, engaged in interregional trade. Trade, in turn, brought population growth and cultural development. Where deserts were inhospitable or forests impenetrable, social systems remained small and changed slowly. The Sahara Desert had been depopulated by

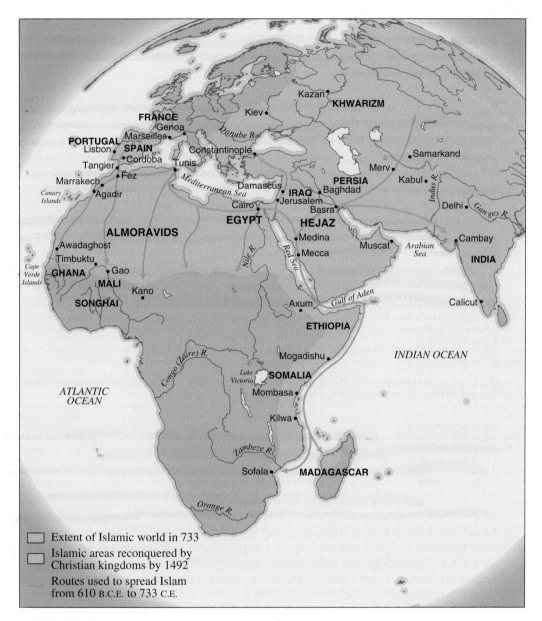

SPREAD OF ISLAM IN AFRICA, C. 1500 This map shows the extensive reach of Islam in Africa by 1500. On most of the North African Mediterranean coast and in the powerful Mali and Songhai kingdoms, the Muslim faith predominated.   ■ **Reflecting on the Past** Do you think enslaved Africans who had converted to Islam practiced their faith after arriving in the American colonies? How would they do so on slave plantations?

climate changes that brought higher temperatures and lower rainfall. Sahara people moved southward in search of more fertile land, eventually settling farther south to the fertile rain forests of the Niger River basin, where they built some of Africa's greatest empires.

The Ghana Empire   The first of these empires was Ghana. Developing between the fifth and eleventh centuries, it occupied an immense territory between the Sahara and the Gulf of Guinea and stretched from the Atlantic Ocean to the Niger River. Though mostly a land of small villages, Ghana became a major empire noted for its extensive urban settlement, sculpture and metalwork, long-distance commerce, and complex political and military structure. A wealthy empire built primarily on trade rather than military conquest, by the late 900s, Ghana controlled more than 100,000 square miles of land and hundreds of thousands of people. Gold was so plentiful that a pound of gold was traded for a pound of salt.

A thriving caravan trade with Arab peoples, fueled by gold, brought extensive Muslim influence by the eleventh century. Gold made Kumbi-Saleh, Ghana's capital, the busiest and wealthiest marketplace in West Africa. By Europe's Middle Ages, two-thirds of the gold circulating in the Christian Mediterranean region was coming from Ghana. Arab merchants came to live in the empire, often serving in government positions. They brought their number and writing systems as well as their Islamic religion. Ghanaian rulers adapted Arabic script but clung to their traditional religion. Many Ghanaians, especially in the cities, converted to Islam. By 1050, Kumbi-Saleh boasted 12 Muslim mosques.

The Mali Empire   An invasion of North African Muslim warriors beginning in the eleventh century eventually destroyed the kingdom of Ghana. The Islamic kingdom of Mali, dominated by Malinke, or Mandingo, people, rose to replace it. Through effective agricultural production and control of the gold trade, Mali flourished. Under Mansa Musa, a devout Muslim who assumed the throne in 1307, Mali came to control territory three times as great as the kingdom of Ghana. Famed for his 3,500-mile pilgrimage across the Sahara and through Cairo all the way to Mecca in 1324, Mansa Musa's image on maps of the world for centuries thereafter testified to his importance in advertising the treasures of western Africa. Muslim scholars and artisans who returned to Mali with Mansa Musa were instrumental in establishing Timbuktu, at the center of the Mali Empire, as a city of great importance. Noted for its extensive wealth, its Islamic university developed a distinguished faculty.

The Songhai Empire   After Mansa Musa died in 1332, power in West Africa began to shift to the Songhai, centered on the middle Niger River. A mixture of farmers, traders, fishermen, and warriors, the Songhai declared independence from Mali in 1435 and began a slow ascendancy. By the time Portuguese traders in the late 1400s were establishing firm commercial links with the Kongo, far to the south, the Songhai Empire was at its peak under the rule of Sonni Ali (1464–1492) and Muhammad Ture (1493–1528).

Yet Songhai, too, collapsed, as some tribes that were resentful of Muslim kings began to break away. The most dangerous threat came from Morocco, in North Africa, whose rulers coveted Songhai's sources of salt and gold—two critical commodities in the African trade. Equipped with guns procured in the Middle East, Morocco's ruler conquered Timbuktu and Gao in 1591. The North Africans remained in loose control of western Sudan for more than a century, as the last great trading empire of West Africa faded. These empires slowly devolved into smaller states. Local conflicts made it easier for European slave traders to convince tribal leaders to send out warrior parties to capture tradeable slaves.

The Kingdoms of Kongo and Benin   Farther south along the Atlantic coast and in Central Africa lay the vast kingdom of Kongo. In 1482 the Portuguese ship captain Diego Cao anchored in the mouth of the mighty Kongo River, the first European to encounter these people. Kongo's royal capital, Mbanza, was a trade center for a kingdom of several million people; Mbanza also became a center of trade with the Portuguese, who by the 1490s were sending Catholic missionaries to the court of King Mani-Kongo. Mani-Kongo's son was baptized Affonso I, and under Affonso's rule, in the early 1500s, a flourishing trade in slaves with the Portuguese began.

The kingdom of Benin, which would become important in the English slave trade, formed in about 1000 C.E. west of the Niger Delta. When Europeans reached

The African City of Loango   The city of Loango, at the mouth of the Kongo River on the west coast of Africa, was larger at the time of this drawing in the mid-eighteenth century than all but a few seaports in the British colonies in North America. *(The Granger Collection, New York)*

Benin City hundreds of years later, they found a walled city with broad streets and hundreds of buildings. Thousands of slaves procured in the interior passed through Benin City on their way for exchange with the Portuguese, and later the English, at coastal Calabar, where one of the main slave forts stood. One of Benin's most important chroniclers, Olaudah Equiano, endured just such a trip. Equiano's story has a timelessness that allows it to stand for the experiences over several centuries of millions of Africans who were born in western Africa, the ancestral homelands of most of today's African Americans.

African Slavery

The idea that slavery was a legitimate social condition in past societies offends modern values, and it is difficult for many Americans to understand why Africans would sell fellow Africans to European traders. But no people identified themselves as Africans four centuries ago; rather, they thought of themselves as Ibos or Mandingos, or Kongolese, or residents of Mali or Songhai. Moreover, slavery was not new for Africans or any other people in the fourteenth century. It had flourished in ancient Rome and Greece, in large parts of eastern Europe, in southwestern Asia, and in the Mediterranean world generally.

Slavery had existed in Africa for centuries. Unlike New World slavery, it had nothing to do with skin color. Like other peoples, Africans understood slavery as a condition of servitude or as a punishment for crimes and slaveholding as a mark of wealth. African societies for centuries conducted an overland slave trade that carried captured people from West Africa across the vast Sahara Desert to Christian Roman Europe and the Islamic Middle East. The peoples of West Africa held to a conception of slavery very different from that which would develop in colonies in the Americas. Slaves in Africa had restricted rights and blocked opportunities for upward movement. Yet they were entitled to certain rights including education, marriage, and parenthood. The enslaved served as soldiers, administrators, sometimes as royal advisors, and even occasionally as royal consorts. The status of slave was not necessarily lifelong and did not automatically pass on to the female slave's children.

The African Ethos

Those who eventually became African Americans made up at least two-thirds of all the immigrants who crossed the ocean to the Western Hemisphere in the three centuries after Europeans began colonizing there. They came from a rich diversity of African peoples and cultures, but most of them shared certain ways of life that differentiated them from Europeans.

As in Europe, the family was the basic unit of social organization. By maintaining intimate family connections, enslaved Africans developed an important defense against the cruelties of slavery. Europeans were patriarchal, putting the father and husband at the center of family life. For Africans, property rights and inheritance were matrilineal, descending through the mother, a tradition that carried over into slavery. In Africa identity was defined by family relationships, and individualism was an alien and distasteful, if not meaningless concept.

Africans brought a complex religious heritage to the Americas, which no amount of desolation or physical abuse could wipe out. Widespread across Africa was a belief in a supreme Creator of the cosmos and in a pantheon of lesser deities associated with natural forces that could intervene in human affairs and were therefore elaborately honored. West Africans, like most North American Indians, held that spirits dwelt in natural objects, and hence they exercised care in their treatment. They also believed in an invisible "other world" inhabited by the souls of the dead that could be known through revelations that spiritually gifted persons could interpret.

Africans venerated ancestors, who they believed mediated between the Creator and the living. Relatives held elaborate funeral rites to ensure the proper entrance into the spiritual world. The more ancient an ancestor, the greater that person's power to affect the living. Deep family loyalty and regard for family lineage flowed naturally from ancestor worship. West Africans also believed in spirit possession, in which gods spoke to men and women through priests and other religious figures. While their beliefs differed from the religious beliefs of Europeans, Africans shared some common ground that made it possible for a hybrid African Christianity to develop. Extensive contact with the Portuguese had allowed Christianity to graft itself onto African religious beliefs in the kingdom of Kongo and several small kingdoms by the seventeenth century.

Social organization in much of West Africa by the time Europeans arrived was as elaborate as in fifteenth-century Europe. At the top of society stood the king, supported by nobles and priests, usually elderly men. Beneath them were the great mass of people, mostly cultivators of the soil. In urban centers, craftsmen, traders, teachers, and artists lived beneath the ruling families. At the bottom of society toiled the slaves.

EUROPE ON THE EVE OF INVADING THE AMERICAS

In the ninth century, about the time that the Mound Builders of the Mississippi valley were constructing their urban center at Cahokia and the kingdom of Ghana was rising in West Africa, western Europe was an economic and cultural backwater. The center of political power and economic vitality in the Old World had shifted eastward to Christian Byzantium, which controlled Asia Minor, the Balkans, and parts of Italy. The other dynamic culture of this age, Islam, had spread through the Middle East, spilled across North Africa, and penetrated Spain and West Africa south of the Sahara.

Within a few centuries, an epic revitalization of western Europe occurred, creating the conditions that enabled its leading maritime nations vastly to extend their oceanic frontiers. By the late fifteenth century, a 400-year epoch of militant overseas European expansion was under way. Not until the second half of the twentieth century was this process of Europeanization reversed.

The Rebirth of Europe

The rebirth of western Europe, which began around 1000 C.E., owed much to a revival of long-distance trade from Italian ports on the Mediterranean and to the rediscovery of ancient knowledge that these contacts permitted. The once mighty cities of the Roman Empire had stagnated for centuries, but now Venice, Genoa, and other Italian ports began trading with peoples facing the Adriatic, the Baltic, and the North seas. These new contacts brought wealth and power to the Italian commercial cities, which gradually evolved into merchant-dominated city–states that freed themselves from the rule of feudal lords in control of the surrounding countryside. In the thirteenth and fourteenth centuries, however, kings began to reassert their political authority, unify their realms, and curb the power of the great feudal lords.

The Black Death (bubonic plague) first devastated China, wiping out nearly one-third of the population, and then moved eastward following trade routes to

A Procession in Venice   Venice's throbbing life along the Grand Canal is apparent in this painting of a procession making its way across the Rialto Bridge toward a balcony. Warehouses and handsome mansions flank the canal. Does this painting reflect the class structure of Venice? *(Scala/Art Resource, NY)*

India and the Middle East. By the time it reached western Europe and North Africa in 1348, famine and malnutrition had reduced the resistance of millions. Over the next quarter century, some 30 million Europeans died, producing economic disruption. Plague defied class distinction, promoting the unification of old realms into early modern states. Ironically, feudal lords treated their peasants better for a time because their labor, tremendously reduced by the plague, became more valuable.

England acquired a distinctive political system. In 1215, the English aristocracy curbed the powers of the king when they forced him to accept the Magna Carta. A parliament composed of elective and hereditary members eventually gained the right to meet regularly to pass money bills and therefore act as a check on the Crown. During the sixteenth century, the Crown and Parliament worked together toward a more unified state.

DOCUMENT

The Magna Carta

Economic changes of great significance also occurred in England during the sixteenth century. To practice more profitable agriculture, great landowners began to "enclose" (consolidate) their estates, throwing peasant farmers off their plots and turning many of them into wage laborers. The formation of this working class was the crucial first step toward industrial development.

Continental Europe lagged behind England in two respects. First, it was far less affected by the move to "enclose" agricultural land since continental aristocrats regarded the maximization of profit as unworthy of gentlemen. Second, continental rulers were less successful in engaging the interests of their nobles, who never shared governance with their king, as did English aristocrats. In France, a noble faction assassinated Henry III in 1589, and the nobles remained disruptive for nearly another century. In Spain, the final conquest of the Muslims and expulsion of the Jews, both in 1492, strengthened the monarchy's hold, but regional cultures and leaders remained strong. The continental monarchs would thus warmly embrace doctrines of royal absolutism developed in the sixteenth century.

The New Monarchies and the Expansionist Impulse

In the second half of the fifteenth century, ambitious monarchs coming to power in France, England, and Spain sought social and political stability in their kingdoms. They created armies and bureaucracies to quell internal conflict and to raise taxes. In these countries and in Portugal as well, economic revival and the reversal of more than a century of population decline and civil disorder nourished the impulse to expand. This impulse was also fed by Renaissance culture. The Renaissance (Rebirth) encouraged innovation, freedom of thought, and an emphasis on human abilities. Beginning in Italy and spreading northward through Europe, the Renaissance peaked in the late fifteenth century.

The exploratory urge had two initial objectives: first, to circumvent overland Muslim traders by finding an eastward oceanic route to Asia; second, to tap the African gold trade at its source, avoiding Muslim intermediaries in North Africa. Since 1291, when Marco Polo returned to Venice with tales of Eastern treasures, Europeans had bartered with the Orient via a long eastward overland route through the Muslim world. Eventually, Europe's mariners found they could voyage to Cathay (China) by both eastward and westward water routes.

Religious Wars Portuguese troops storm Tangiers in Morocco in 1471 as part of the ongoing struggle between Christianity and Islam in the mid-fifteenth century Mediterranean world. *(Pastrana Church/Dagli Orti/Art Archive)*

Prince Henry the Navigator, for whom trade was secondary to the conquest of the Muslim world, led a poor country of only 1 million inhabitants into the unknown. In the 1420s, Henry began dispatching Portuguese mariners to probe the Atlantic "sea of darkness." Important improvements in navigational instruments, mapmaking, and ship design aided his intrepid sailors.

Portuguese captains operated at sea on three ancient Ptolemaic principles: that the earth was round, that distances on its surface could be measured by degrees, and that navigators could "fix" their position at sea on a map by measuring the position of the stars. The invention in the 1450s of the quadrant, which allowed

TIMELINE

35,000 B.C.E.	First humans cross Bering Land Bridge to reach the Americas
500 B.C.E.–1000 C.E.	Post-Archaic era in North America
600 C.E.–1100	Rise of mound-building center at Cahokia
632–750	Islamic conquest of North Africa spreads Muslim faith
1000	Kingdom of Benin develops
1000–1500	Kingdoms of Ghana, Mali, Songhai, Kongo in Africa

1200s	Pueblo societies develop village life in southwestern North America
1300s	Rise of Aztec society in Valley of Mexico
1300–1450	Italian Renaissance
1324	Mansa Musa's pilgrimage to Mecca expands Muslim influence in West Africa
1420s	Portuguese sailors explore west coast of Africa
1469	Marriage of Castile's Isabella and Aragon's Ferdinand creates Spain

a precise measurement of star altitude necessary for determining latitude, represented a leap forward in navigation. A lateen-rigged caravel, adapted from a Moorish ship design, was equally important. Its triangular sails permitted ships to sail into the wind, allowing them to travel southward along the African coast and return northward against prevailing winds. By the 1430s, Prince Henry's captains had traveled to Madeira, the Canary Islands, and the more distant Azores. These islands soon developed as the first European-controlled agricultural plantations.

From islands off the West African coast, Portuguese sea captains pushed farther south, navigating down the west coast of Africa by 1460. While carrying their Christian faith to new lands, they began a profitable trade in ivory, slaves, and especially gold and were poised to capitalize on the connection between Europe and Africa. They did not yet know that a stupendous land mass, to become known as America, lay far across the Atlantic Ocean.

Conclusion

The Approach of a New Global Age

All the forces that have made the world of the past 500 years "modern" began to come into play by the late fifteenth century. As the stories about four important women of this era demonstrate, deep transformations were under way in West Africa, in southern and western Europe, and in the Americas. West African empires had reached new heights, some had been deeply influenced by the Islamic faith, and many had become experienced in transregional trade. Muslim scholars, merchants, and long-distance travelers were becoming the principal mediators in the interregional exchange of goods, ideas, and technical innovations. Meanwhile, the Renaissance, initiated in Italy, worked its way northward, bringing new energy and ambition to a weakened, disease-ridden, and tired Europe. Advances in maritime technology also allowed Europeans to make contact with the peoples of West Africa and develop the first slave-based plantation societies in tropical islands off the West African coast. In the Americas, large empires in Mexico and Peru were growing more populous and consolidating their power, while in North America the opposite was occurring—a decay of powerful mound-building societies and a long-range move toward decentralized tribal societies. The scene was set for the great leap of Europeans across the Atlantic, where the convergence between the peoples of Africa, the Americas, and Europe would occur.

Questions for Review and Reflection

1. To what do you attribute the remarkable diversity of cultures in the Americas in the centuries prior to contact with Europeans? What are the most marked examples of that diversity?

2. What were the major features of western African society and culture prior to contact with European traders?

3. What were the causes and major consequences of the revitalization of western Europe in the period after 1000 C.E.?

4. Africa, Europe, and the Americas at the start of the "early modern period" are often treated as dramatically different in every way, yet commonalities existed. What were the most striking of these common features?

5. Why did western Europeans expand out of their geographical confines to explore, conquer, and colonize the Americas? What factors were not present in Africa or the Americas to foster expansion into the Atlantic basin from those areas?

Discovering U.S. History Online

Cahokia Mounds http://www.cahokiamounds.com/cahokia.html
This online presentation of the historical Cahokia Mounds offers background information, an interactive map of the site, a satellite map, and other photos.

Civilizations in Africa www.wsu.edu:8080/~dee/CIVAFRCA/CIVAFRCA.HTM
This site offers a region-by-region broad overview of the pre-conquest civilizations in Africa.

The Slave Kingdoms www.pbs.org/wonders
Part of the PBS online exhibition "Wonders of the African World," this section describes the West African cultures during the slave trade as well as both African and European participation in the slave trade.

Life in Elizabethan England http://elizabethan.org/compendium/index.html
A compendium of information about everyday life, politics, and religion in England prior to "the westward fever."

Renaissance www.learner.org/exhibits/renaissance
An exploration of the European Renaissance, this interactive site seeks to discover and describe "the forces that drove this rebirth in Europe, and in Italy in particular."

Fiction and Film

Peter Forbath's *Lord of the Kongo* (1996) tells the dramatic story of a young Portuguese sailor counted among those interacting with the Kongo people of West Africa in the early 1500s. Chinua Achebe's *Things Fall Apart* (1958) is already a classic—an unsentimental depiction of tribal life in Nigeria before and after the arrival of Europeans. Barbara Tuckman's *A Distant Mirror* (1978) is the most engaging novel ever written about the European Middle Ages—and particularly about the calamitous fourteenth century, when England and France waged the Hundred Years War (1337–1429). In *The Man on a Donkey* (1952), H. F. M. Prescott brings alive the tumultuous English era of Henry VIII.

Search of the First Americans (1992), part of the Nova series produced by the Public Broadcasting System (PBS), provides a fascinating introduction to the peopling of the Americas before the Columbian voyages. *Secrets of the Lost Red Paint People,* also in this series, shows how archaeologists have reconstructed—always tentatively—the ancient world of the Americas. Films for the Humanities and Sciences in Princeton, New Jersey, has produced a five-part series of short films to recreate the history and culture of some of the great West African societies, particularly those from which today's African Americans in North America and the West Indies have derived. In *The Agony and the Ecstacy* (1965), derived from Irving Stone's biography of Michaelangelo, Charlton Heston and Rex Harrison bring alive the Italian Renaissance. A rendering of the life of *Luther,* based on an adaptation of John Osborne's play that captivated London theatergoers, appeared in 2003 with Ralph Fiennes playing the lead role. *The Return of Martin Guerre* (1982), called by some the best historical movie ever made, depicts French peasant life in the era when Europeans were awakening to overseas exploration and settlement.

Recommended Reading

www.ablongman.com/nash

The Companion Website has a list of recommended readings about American, African, and European societies in the 1500s and 1600s.

CHAPTER 2

Europeans and Africans Reach the Americas

American Stories

Old World Sojourners Mingle with New World Inhabitants

Just 15 years after conquistadors led by Hernán Cortés toppled the Aztec Empire in Mexico, Spanish horsemen, searching for Indians to capture as slaves, happened upon some 600 of them in northwestern Mexico. Traveling with the natives were an African and three Spaniards, all dressed in native garb. The horsemen were "thunderstruck to see me so strangely dressed and in the company of Indians," noted Alvar Núñez Cabeza de Vaca, one of the three Spaniards accompanying the Indians. "They went on staring at me for a long space of time, so astonished that they could neither speak to me nor manage to ask me anything."

De Vaca, his two Spanish companions, and the African had been lost for eight years and were presumed dead. They had been part of the 1528 expedition that had tried to plant a permanent Spanish settlement in what the Spanish called La Florida. Establishing themselves near the swamplands of Tampa Bay, the Spanish adventurers encountered starvation, disease, a leadership crisis, and hostile Native Americans. Captured by the Apalachee, who enslaved them, de Vaca and his companions soon adopted Native American ways, adapted to a new environment, and used their cleverness to convince the Indians that they possessed magical healing power. The African, already a slave of one of the captured Spaniards and known as Estevan (sometimes called Estanvanico or Esteban), became an accomplished linguist, healer, guide, and negotiator. When they fled their captors, the four fugitives plunged into the wilderness and headed west. Paddling crude boats across the Gulf of Mexico, they shipwrecked on the Texas coast and took refuge among merciful Indians.

Such forays into a rugged and uncharted territory cast the Spanish and African adventurers into unaccustomed roles and sorely tested their ability to survive among the indigenous people, who generally opposed their intrusion into their homelands. De Vaca, a conquistador experienced in enslaving Native Americans, had become a slave himself before the flight to Texas. Estevan's status as the slave of a Spanish conquistador all but dissolved in the process of becoming a Native American slave and then a refugee from enslavement. In his journal, de Vaca described Estevan as "a black," "a Moor," and "an Arabian." But these were only words describing his skin color (dark), his religion (Islam), and his geographical homeland (Morocco). What mattered in this strange and often hostile land was not Estevan's blackness or even his slave status. What counted, in this time before the idea of racial categories, were his linguistic abilities, his fortitude, and his cleverness as a go-between. Estevan, an Atlantic creole—a man who originated on one land bordering the Atlantic—became a new man in the process of the cultural, linguistic, and social braiding that was occurring throughout the sixteenth-century Atlantic world.

For five years, Estevan, his master Andrés Dorantes, de Vaca, and another Spaniard traveled west for about 2,500 miles. Often following friendly Native American guides, the four travelers came to be regarded as holy men, possessing the power to heal. Reaching present-day New Mexico, they found Native Americans who, according to de Vaca, described them as "four great doctors, one of them black, the other three white, who gave blessings [and] healed the sick." On one occasion, the natives gave Estevan a sacred gourd rattle. Then, in 1536, the foursome stumbled upon the Spanish expedition in northern Mexico. Three years later, after joining a new Spanish expedition, Estevan blazed a trail for Francisco Vásquez de Coronado's *entrada* of 1540. In what would later be called Arizona, Estevan was selected to forge ahead into Zuñi country with Native American guides, in search of the fabled seven gold-filled cities of Cibola. His gift for acquiring native languages and his long experience with peoples of the vast territory north of New Spain made him the logical choice. But on this trip, Estevan met his death at the hands of Zuñi warriors, perhaps angry at his consorting with Zuñi women.

The voyages of Christopher Columbus from 1492 to 1504 brought together people like Estevan and de Vaca from three previously unconnected continents. Together, they made a new world, their lives intersecting, their cultural attributes interacting. In this chapter, we follow the epoch-making voyages of Columbus, the arrival of Spanish conquistadors, their remarkable conquest of vast territories in Mesoamerica and the southern regions of North America, and the momentous effect on plants, animals, and germs as they traveled westward and eastward across the Atlantic. We will also see how the phenomenal exploits of Hernán Cortés and Francisco Pizarro, and the discovery of immense quantities of silver, attracted the attention of other Europeans—first the French, then the Dutch and English. Latecomers in the race to exploit the treasures of the Americas while providing a place for the downtrodden and opportunity-blocked settlers of Europe, the English, as we will see, finally appeared on the scene in the Americas a century after the Columbian voyages.

BREACHING THE ATLANTIC

When Ferdinand and Isabella married in 1469 to unite the independent states of Aragon and Castile, they launched Spain into its golden age, beginning with the four voyages of Christopher Columbus to the Americas between 1492 and 1504. Meanwhile, the Portuguese extended their influence along the west coast of Africa and all the way to East Asia. In a short period, contact between peoples in different parts of the world increased markedly, shrinking the globe. Then came the great leap across the Atlantic Ocean, triggering global changes of unimaginable significance. Western Europeans were becoming the most dynamic force in the world and were on the verge of exerting a greater global influence than the people of any single region had ever done before.

The Columbian Voyages

Christopher Columbus, an Italian sailor, led the way for Spain. Celebrated for hundreds of years as a heroic discoverer and now often attacked as the ruthless exploiter of Indian peoples and lands, Columbus is best understood in the context of his own times—an age of great brutality and violence. Columbus's urge to explore was nourished by ideas and questions about the geographic limits of his world, and he was inspired by notions of contributing to the reconquest of Moorish Spain.

Like many sailors, Columbus had listened to sea tales about lands to the west. He may have heard Icelandic sagas about the Norse voyages to Newfoundland five centuries before. Other ideas circulated that the Atlantic Ocean stretched to India and eastern Asia. Could one reach the Indies by sailing west rather than by sailing east around Africa, as the Portuguese were attempting? Columbus hungered to know.

DOCUMENT

From The Journal of Christopher Columbus (1492)

For nearly 10 years, Columbus tried unsuccessfully to secure financial backing and royal sanction in Portugal for exploratory voyages. Many mocked his modest estimates of the distance westward from Europe to Japan. Finally, in 1492, Queen Isabella commissioned him, and he sailed west with three tiny ships and a crew of about 90 men. In the fifth week at sea—longer than any European sailors had been out of the sight of land—mutinous rumblings swept through the crews. But on the seventieth day, long after Columbus had calculated he would reach Japan, a lookout sighted land. On October 12, 1492, the sailors clambered ashore on a tiny island in the Bahamas, which Columbus named San Salvador (Holy Savior).

IMAGE

Columbus Landing at Hispaniola— Woodcut

Believing he had reached Asia, Columbus explored the island-speckled Caribbean for 10 weeks. After landing on a heavily populated island that he named Hispaniola (today, Haiti and the Dominican Republic) and on Cuba, he set sail for Spain with cinnamon, coconuts, a bit of gold, and several kidnapped natives. Homeward bound, he penned a report of what he believed were his Asian discoveries: hospitable people, fertile soils, magnificent harbors, and gold-filled rivers. When he landed, his report was quickly distributed throughout Europe.

Columbus's report brought him financing between 1494 and 1504 for three much larger expeditions to explore the newfound lands. The second voyage, carrying over 1,200 Spanish in 17 ships, initiated the first extended contact between Europeans and Native Americans. In an ominous display of what was to come, Columbus's men captured some 1,600 Taínos on Hispaniola and carried 550 of them back to Spain as slaves in 1495. Although his discoveries seemed less significant than the Portuguese exploits, Columbus had led Spain to the threshold of a mighty empire. He died in 1506, to the end believing that he had found the water route to Asia.

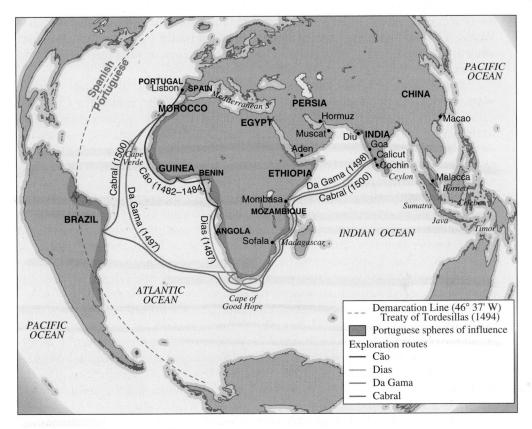

PORTUGUESE VOYAGES OF EXPLORATION The four voyages by Portuguese sea captains between 1482 and 1500 show how those who sailed southward and eastward opened up distant parts of the world to Europeans in the same era when Columbus was sailing westward to the Americas. ■ **Reflecting on the Past** Did Columbus share his Atlantic Ocean experiences with the Portuguese sea captains who reached the Indian Ocean? If so, how? What did Columbus learn from the Indian Ocean voyagers that helped him in his Atlantic Ocean voyages?

While Spain began to project its power westward across the Atlantic, the Portuguese extended their influence in different directions—southward toward West Africa and then eastward to East Asia. In 1497, Vasco da Gama became the first European to sail around the cape of Africa, allowing the Portuguese to colonize the Indian Ocean and to reach modern Indonesia and south China by 1513. By forcing trade concessions in the islands and coastal states of the East Indies, the Portuguese unlocked the fabulous Asian treasure houses that, since Marco Polo's time, had whetted European appetites. By 1500, they had captured control of the African gold trade monopolized for centuries by North African Muslims.

Religious Conflict During the Era of Reconnaissance

The expansion of Spain and Portugal into new areas of the world profoundly affected patterns of economic activity in Europe. Its commercial center now shifted away from the ports of the Mediterranean to the Atlantic ports facing the New World. This fast-growing commercial power also had a deeply religious aspect since it occurred in the midst of, and magnified, an era of religious conflict and reformation.

Shortly after Columbus's Atlantic voyages, the people of western Europe were torn by religious schisms. A continental movement to return the Christian Church to the purity of early Christianity was at the heart of Europe's religious strife. Criticism of the worldliness of the Church mounted during the Renaissance. Then a German monk, Martin Luther, broke successfully with Rome, initiating the Protestant Reformation. As Protestant sects multiplied, Catholics began to reform their own church.

Luther had lost faith in the power of the age-old rituals of the Church—the Mass, confession, and pilgrimages to holy places. He believed that salvation came through an inward faith, or "grace," that God conferred on those he chose. Good works, Luther believed, did not earn grace, but were the external evidence of faith. Insisting on "justification by faith," Luther had taken the revolutionary step of rejecting the Church's elaborate hierarchy of officials, who presided over the rituals that guided individuals toward salvation.

Luther's doctrine of "justification by faith" did not threaten the Church until 1517, when he openly attacked the sale of "indulgences" for sins, by which the pope raised money for the building of St. Peter's in Rome. By purchasing indulgences, individuals had been told, they could reduce their time (or that of a deceased relative) in purgatory. Printing, invented less than 70 years before, allowed the rapid circulation of Luther's protest. The printed word and the ability to read it were to become revolutionary weapons.

Luther's cry for reform soon inspired Germans of all classes. He denounced five of the seven sacraments of the Church, calling for a return to baptism and communion alone. He attacked the upper clergy for luxurious living and urged priests—who were nominally celibate but often involved in irregular sexual relationships—to marry respectably. He railed against the "detestable tyranny of the clergy over the laity" and called for a priesthood of all believers. He urged people to seek faith individually by reading the Bible, which he translated into German and made widely available for the first time. Most provocatively, he called on the German princes to assume control over religion in their states, directly challenging the authority of Rome.

The basic issue dividing Catholics and Protestants thus centered on the source of religious authority. To Catholics, religious authority resided in the organized Church, headed by the pope. To Protestants, the Bible was the sole authority, and access to God's word or God's grace did not require the mediation of the Church.

Building on Luther's redefinition of Christianity, John Calvin, a Frenchman, brought new intensity and meaning to the Protestant Reformation. By Calvin's doctrine, God had saved a few souls before Creation and damned the rest. Humans could not alter this predestination, but those who were good Christians must struggle to understand and accept God's saving grace if he chose to impart it. Without mediation of ritual or priest but by "straight-walking," one was to behave as one of God's elect, the "saints."

Calvin proposed reformed Christian communities structured around the elect few. To remake the corrupt world and follow God's will, communities of "saints" must control the state. Elected bodies of ministers and dedicated laymen, called presbyteries, were to govern the church, directing the affairs of society so that all, whether saved or damned, would work for God's ends.

Calvinism, a fine-tuned system of self-discipline and social control, was first put into practice in the 1550s in the city–state of Geneva, between France and Switzerland. Here Calvin established his intended model Christian community. A council of 12 elders drove nonbelievers from the city, disciplined daily life, and stripped the churches of every appeal to the senses. Religious reformers from all over Europe flocked to the new godly community, and Geneva soon became the continental center of Reformed Christianity. Calvin's radical program converted large numbers of people to Protestantism throughout Europe. Like Lutheranism, it recruited most successfully among merchants, landowners, lawyers, nobles, master artisans, and shopkeepers.

The most important monarch to break with Catholicism was Henry VIII of England. When the pope refused him permission to divorce and remarry, Henry declared himself head of the Church of England. Although it retained many Catholic features, the Church of England moved further in a Protestant direction under Henry's son Edward. But when Mary, Henry's older Catholic daughter, became queen, she vowed to reinstate her mother's religion by suppressing Protestants. Her policy created Protestant martyrs, and many were relieved when she died in 1558, bringing Henry's younger Protestant daughter, Elizabeth, to the throne. During her long rule, the flinty Elizabeth steered England's church along a middle course between the radicalism of Geneva and the Catholicism of Rome.

Some of the countries most affected by the Reformation—England, Holland, and France—were slow to colonize the New World, so Protestantism did not gain as early a foothold in the Americas as Catholicism, which remained the official church of both Spain and Portugal. Thus, Catholicism swept across the Atlantic almost unchallenged during the century after 1492.

THE SPANISH CONQUEST OF AMERICA

From 1492 to 1518, Spanish and Portuguese explorers made Europe aware of the Americas. Only modest attempts at settlement were made, mostly by the Spanish on the Caribbean islands. The three decades after 1518, however, were an age of conquest. In some of the bloodiest chapters in recorded history, the Spanish nearly exterminated the native Caribbean people, toppled and plundered the great Aztec and Inca empires in Mexico and Peru, discovered fabulous silver mines, and built an important oceanic trade. These conquests had immense consequences for global history.

Portugal, meanwhile, concentrated mostly on building an eastward oceanic trade to Asia. In 1493, the pope had demarcated Spanish and Portuguese spheres of exploration in the Atlantic. Drawing a north–south line 100 leagues (about 300 miles) west of the Azores, the pope confined Portugal to the eastern side. One year later, in the Treaty of Tordesillas, Portugal obtained Spanish agreement to move the line 270 leagues farther west. A large part of South America, as yet undiscovered by Europeans, bulged east of the new demarcation line and therefore fell within the Portuguese sphere. In time, Portugal would develop this region, Brazil, into one of the most profitable areas of the Americas. These lines were some of the most significant ever drawn on a map.

Caribbean Experiments

Columbus's second Atlantic expedition in 1493 established the first Spanish colony in the New World on the island of Hispaniola (or Santo Domingo). The inhabitants, the Taíno, were the first New World indigenous people to encounter Europeans, and the encounter provided a preview of what would soon occur elsewhere in the Americas: subjugation, biological disease, and eventually immense ecological alterations to the island.

Columbus arrived with 17 ships and about 1,200 men. He was seeking gold, and when he found none, he visited Cuba and then returned to Spain with six Taíno captives. What he left behind—seeds and cuttings for propagating European crops, livestock, and weeds—would prove to be the agents of great ecological change. Meantime, once the Spanish saw that the island was teeming with as many as 3 million Taíno, they used military force to subdue them and turn them into a captive labor force. Similar conquests brought the people of Puerto Rico under Spanish control in 1508 and the people of Cuba in 1511. Spanish diseases soon touched off a biological holocaust that killed most of the island's population within a single generation. Some Taíno women married Spanish men and produced the first mestizo society in the Americas, but by 1550, the Taíno no longer existed as a distinct people.

Spanish immigration to the Caribbean islands was under way by 1510, closely followed by the importation of enslaved Africans who were put to work on the first sugar plantations created in the Americas. Over the course of the sixteenth century, about a quarter million Spaniards—most of them young, single men—emigrated to the Americas. But the islands dotting the Caribbean did not reach their potential as cash-crop economies until much later. For now, they served as laboratories for larger experiments in Mexico and South America. The Spaniards launched invasions of the Mesoamerican mainland from these islands, while they fortified ports such as San Juan, Puerto Rico, and Havana, Cuba.

The Conquistadors' Onslaught at Tenochtitlán

Within a single generation of Columbus's death in 1506, Spanish conquistadors explored, claimed, and conquered most of South America except Brazil, as well as the southern parts of North America from present-day Florida to California. Led by audacious explorers and soldiers, and usually accompanied by enslaved Africans, they established Spanish authority and Catholicism over an area that dwarfed their homeland in size and population. "We came here," explained one Spanish foot soldier, "to serve God and the king, and also to get rich."

In two bold and bloody strokes, the Spanish overwhelmed the ancient civilizations of the Aztec and Inca. In 1519, Hernando Cortés, along with 550 soldiers, marched over rugged mountains to attack Tenochtitlán (now Mexico City), the capital of Moctezuma II's empire. Following two years of sparring between the Spaniards and the Aztecs, Cortés's assault succeeded and Tenochtitlán fell. The Spanish use of horses and firearms provided an important advantage, as did a murderous smallpox epidemic in 1520 that felled thousands of Aztecs. Cortés also benefited from the support of local peoples oppressed by Aztec tyranny. From the Valley of Mexico, the Spanish extended their dominion over the Maya of the Yucatán, Honduras, and Guatemala in the next few decades.

In the second conquest, Francisco Pizarro, marching from Panama through the jungles of Ecuador and into the towering mountains of Peru with a mere 168 men, most of them not even soldiers, toppled the Inca Empire. Like the Aztec, the populous Inca lived in a highly organized social system. They had also been weakened by internal violence and smallpox. This ensured Pizarro's success in capturing their capital at Cuzco in 1533, and soon other gold- and silver-rich cities. Further expeditions into Chile, New Granada (Colombia), Argentina, and Bolivia in the 1530s and 1540s brought under Spanish control an empire larger than any in the Western world since the fall of Rome.

By 1550, Spain had overwhelmed the major centers of native population in the Americas. Spanish ships carried gold, silver, dyewoods, and sugar east across the Atlantic and transported African slaves, colonizers, and finished goods west. In a brief half century, Spain had exploited the advances in geographic knowledge and maritime technology of its Portuguese rivals and brought into harsh but profitable contact with each other the people of three continents. The triracial character of the Americas was firmly established by 1600.

For nearly a century after Columbus's voyages, Spain enjoyed almost unchallenged dominion over the fabulous hemisphere newly revealed to Europeans. Greedy buccaneers snapped at the heels of homeward-bound Spanish treasure fleets, but this was only a nuisance. France tried to contest Spanish or Portuguese control by planting small settlements in Brazil and Florida in the mid-sixteenth century, but these were quickly wiped out. England remained island-bound until the 1580s. Until the seventeenth century, only Portugal, which staked out important claims in Brazil in the 1520s, challenged Spanish rule in the Americas.

The Great Dying

Spanish conquest of major areas of the Americas triggered a biological epidemic, setting in motion one of the most dramatic and disastrous population declines in history. The population of the Americas on the eve of European arrival had grown to an estimated 50 to 70 million. In central Mexico, the highlands of Peru, and certain Caribbean islands, population density exceeded that of most of Europe. Though far fewer than the peoples of the Americas, the European colonizers had one extraordinary advantage: Over the centuries, Europeans had built up immunities to nearly every lethal microbe that infects humans on an epidemic scale. Such biological defenses did not eliminate disease altogether, but they limited their deadly power. Geographic isolation had kept these diseases from the peoples of the Americas. So, too, did their lack of large domesticated animals, which were major disease carriers. The inhabitants of the Americas were utterly defenseless against the "domesticated" infections the Europeans and their animals carried.

Native American
Population Loss,
1500–1700

The results were catastrophic. Hispaniola, with a population of about 1 million when Columbus arrived, had only a few thousand survivors by 1530. Of some 15 million inhabitants in central Mexico before Cortés's arrival, nearly half perished within 15 years. Demographic disaster also struck the populous Inca peoples of the Peruvian Andes, speeding ahead of Pizarro's conquistadors. Smallpox "spread over the people as great destruction," an old man told a Spanish priest in the 1520s. "There was great havoc. Very many died of it. They could not stir, they could not change position, nor lie on one side, nor face down, nor on their backs. And if they stirred, much did they cry out. ... And very many starved; there was death from hunger, [for] none could take care of [the sick]." Such terrifying sickness convinced many natives that their gods had failed and left them ready to acknowledge the greater power of the Spaniards' God.

In most areas where Europeans intruded in the hemisphere for the next three centuries, the catastrophe repeated itself. Every European and African contributed to the spread of disease that typically eliminated, within a few generations, at least two-thirds of the native population. Moving in the other direction, syphilis and yaws, apparently not known in Europe until about 1500, were afflictions of the Americas that created misery in the Old World as they traveled eastward. The devastation they caused was never remotely on the scale of the smallpox epidemics.

The enslavement and brutal treatment of the native people intensified the lethal effects of European diseases. Having conquered the Inca and Aztec, the Spanish enslaved thousands of native people and assigned them work regimens that weakened them further. Some priests waged lifelong campaigns to reduce the exploitation of the Indians, but they had only limited power to control their colonizing compatriots.

The Columbian Exchange

Much more than lethal microbes crossed the Atlantic with the Spaniards as they conquered the Caribbean islands and then large parts of Central and South America. With them came animal and plant life that altered ecosystems and transformed the landscape. Most significant were the herd animals of the Europeans. Cattle, sheep, goats, and pigs caused the greatest transformation, flourishing as they grazed in the vast grasslands of the Americas safe from the large carnivores that attacked them in the Old World. Cattle reproduced so rapidly that feral livestock swarmed across the countryside, often increasing tenfold in three or four years. In time they ate themselves out of their new environment, stripping away plant life, which soon led to topsoil erosion and eventually to desertification.

Cattle Arrive in the New World

Pigs were even harder on the environment. Reproducing at staggering rates, they tore into the manioc tubers and sweet potatoes in the Greater Antilles where Columbus first introduced eight of them in 1493. They devoured guavas and pineapples, ravaged lizards and baby birds, and stripped the land clean. Similar swine explosions occurred on the mainland of Mexico and Central America, where along with cattle they devastated the grasslands.

Spaniards brought the flora and fauna that they prized most to the Americas, but also traveling with them were unwelcome passengers. Among the most de-

Aztec Corn Myth In this pictograph of an ancient Aztec myth, maize plays a central role; the first female spreads kernels of maize, or corn, while her husband tries to divine the future. Can you decipher some of the border figures? *(Bibliothèque de l'Assemblée Nationale, Paris)*

structive were weeds, their seeds hidden in sacks of fruit and vegetable seed. Once they took root, weeds spread rapidly. Rats and rabbits, which reproduced as fast as pigs, were also pesky stowaways on ships bound across the Atlantic. Rats especially decimated native small animals, spread diseases, and added a new dimension to the human struggle for life.

The "Columbian Exchange" had its eastbound dimension as well, one that mainly advantaged European, African, and eventually Asian recipients. Table foods from the Americas such as pumpkins, pineapples, squash, peanuts, beans, tomatoes, guinea pigs, and turkeys enriched the European diet. Llamas and alpacas produced wool for warmth. Over time, the most important food transfers to Europe proved to be maize and potatoes. The potato, with its fundamental advantage over Old World grains, slowly spread from its point of introduction in northern Spain northward and eastward through Europe. Farmers on the northern European plain learned slowly that by substituting potatoes for rye—the only grain that would thrive in the short and often rainy summers—they could quadruple their yield in calories per acre. The transition to the New World potato allowed for population growth and strengthened

New World Plants

Europe's diet. Likewise, maize (to be renamed corn) could be cultivated in mountain valleys such as in Spain, Greece, and the Balkans, where it became the staple grain. Maize also reached Africa and China as early as the 1550s; the New World sweet potato made its entry into China.

Silver, Sugar, and Their Consequences

The small amount of gold that Columbus brought home raised hopes that this metal, which along with silver formed the standard of wealth in Europe, might be found in the transatlantic paradise. Though some gold was gleaned from the Caribbean islands and later from Colombia, Brazil, and Peru, it would take three centuries before anyone would discover gold in windfall quantities in North America. Silver proved abundant—so plenteous, in fact, that when bonanza strikes were made in Bolivia in 1545 and in Mexico in the 1550s, much of Spain's New World enterprise focused on its extraction.

Native people, along with some African slaves, provided the first labor supply for the mines. The Spaniards permitted the highly organized Native American societies to maintain control of their own communities but exacted from them huge labor drafts for mining. At Potosí, in Bolivia, 58,000 workers labored at elevations of up to 13,000 feet to dig the precious metal from a fabulous "mountain of silver." The town's population reached 120,000 by 1570, making it larger than any in Spain at the time. Thousands of other workers toiled in Mexican mines. By 1660, they had extracted more than 7 million pounds of silver from the Americas, tripling the European supply.

The flood of American bullion into Europe triggered profound changes, including financing further conquests and settlement in Spain's American empire, spurring long-distance trading in East Asian silks and spices, and capitalizing agricultural development in the New World of sugar, coffee, cacao, and indigo. The bland diet of Europeans gradually changed as sugar and spices, previously luxury articles, became accessible to ordinary people.

The enormous increase of silver circulating in Europe after the mid-sixteenth century caused a "price revolution." The supply of silver increased faster than the demand for goods and services that Europeans could produce, so the value of silver coins declined. Put differently, prices rose, doubling in many parts of Europe between 1550 and 1600 and rising another 50 percent in the next half century. Farmers got more for their produce, and merchants thrived on the increased circulation of goods. The vast majority of the people, however, suffered when wages did not keep up with rising prices.

Overall, the price revolution brought a major redistribution of wealth and increased the number of people in western Europe living at the margins of society. It thus built up the pressure to immigrate to the Americas. At the same time, rising prices stimulated commercial development. Expansion overseas fed expansion at home and intensified changes toward capitalist modes of production already under way in the sixteenth century.

While the Spaniards organized their overseas empire around the extraction of silver from the highlands of Mexico, Bolivia, and Peru, the Portuguese staked their future on sugar production in Brazil. Spanish colonial agriculture supplied the huge mining centers, but the Portuguese, using cultivation techniques developed earlier on their Atlantic islands, produced sugar for export markets.

Whereas Spanish mining operations rested primarily on the backs of the native labor force, Portuguese sugar planters scattered the indigenous people and replaced them with platoons of African slaves. By 1570, this regimented workforce produced nearly 6 million pounds of sugar annually; by the 1630s, output reached 32 million pounds per year. The sweet "drug food" revolutionized the tastes of millions of Europeans and stimulated the transport of millions of African slaves across the Atlantic.

From Brazil, sugar production jumped to the Caribbean. Here, in the early seventeenth century, England, Holland, and France challenged Spain and Portugal. Once into the West Indies, Spain's enemies stood at the gates of the Hispanic New World empire. Through contraband trading with Spanish settlements, piratical attacks on Spanish treasure fleets, and outright seizure of Spanish-controlled islands, the Dutch, French, and English in the seventeenth century gradually sapped imperial Spain's strength.

Spain's Northern Frontier

Silver-rich Mexico and Peru were the crown jewels of Spain's New World empire, with the islands and coastal fringes of the Caribbean representing lesser, yet valuable, gemstones. Distinctly third in importance to Spain were the northern borderlands of New Spain—the present-day Sun Belt of the United States. Yet the early Spanish influence in Florida, the Gulf region, Texas, New Mexico, Arizona, and California indelibly marked the history of the United States. Spanish control of the southern fringes of North America began in the early 1500s and did not end for three centuries. Far outlasting the Spaniards' rule were the plants and animals they introduced to North America, ranging from sheep, cattle, and horses to weeds that crowded out native plants.

Spanish explorers began charting southeastern North America in the early sixteenth century. First came Juan Ponce de León's expeditions to Florida in 1515 and 1521 and a short-lived settlement in South Carolina in 1526. For the next half century, Spaniards planted small settlements as far north as Chesapeake Bay. The Spanish traded some with the natives, but the North American coast, especially Florida, was chiefly important to the Franciscan friars, who attempted to gather the local tribes into mission villages and convert them to Catholicism.

The Spanish made several attempts to bring the entire Gulf of Mexico region under their control. From 1539 to 1542, Hernán de Soto, a veteran of Pizarro's army, led a military expedition deep into the homelands of the Creek and Choctaw and explored from Tampa Bay to Arkansas. De Soto's expedition could not provide what the Spanish most wanted—gold. Pillaging Indian villages and seizing food supplies, de Soto's men cut a brutal swath, and disease followed in their wake. The Spanish unknowingly paved the way for later English-speaking conquerors by spreading lethal microbes that devastated Indian societies and broke up the great chiefdoms of the Southeast.

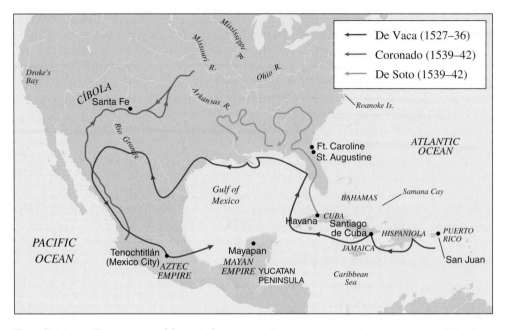

THE SPANISH *ENTRADAS* IN NORTH AMERICA The *entradas* of the Spanish conquistadors were all motivated by gold fever as well as the mission to claim vast territories across the lower tier of North America for the Spanish. Most of the early explorers became governors of Spanish colonies in South America.

In 1559, Spaniards again marched northward from Mexico in an attempt to establish their authority in the lower Gulf region. Everywhere they went, they enslaved Native Americans to carry provisions. In 1565, they sought to secure Florida. Building a fort at St. Augustine, they evicted their French rivals 40 miles to the north. St. Augustine became the center of Spain's northeastern frontier, and Florida remained Spanish for more than two centuries.

The Southwest became a more important region of early Spanish activity in North America. Francisco Vásquez de Coronado explored the region from 1540 to 1542. He never found the fabulous Seven Cities of Cíbola, reported by earlier Spanish explorers, but he opened much of Arizona, New Mexico, and Colorado to eventual Spanish control, happened upon the Grand Canyon, and probed as far north as the Great Plains.

Like Florida and the Gulf region, the Southwest had no golden cities. In New Mexico, however, Franciscans tried to harvest souls. A half century after Coronado's exploratory intrusions, Juan de Oñate led 400 Spanish soldiers and 10 Franciscan friars up the Rio Grande in 1598 to find some 60,000 Pueblo gathered in scores of settled towns where for centuries they had been practicing agriculture. For the next 80 years, the Franciscans tried to graft Catholicism onto Pueblo culture by building churches on the edges of ancient native villages. As long as the priests were content to overlay Indian culture with a Catholic veneer, they encountered little resistance. The Pueblo gained Spanish military protection from their Apache enemies and valued access to mission livestock and grain during years of drought. So, outwardly, they professed the Christian faith, while secretly adhering to their traditional religion.

ENGLAND LOOKS WEST

By the time England awoke to the promise of the New World, Spain and Portugal were firmly entrenched there. But by the late sixteenth century, the conditions necessary to propel England overseas had ripened. During the early seventeenth century, the English, as well as the Dutch and French, began overtaking their southern European rivals. For the English, the first challenge came in the Caribbean, where between 1604 and 1640 the English planted several small colonies producing tobacco and later sugar.

England Challenges Spain

England was the slowest of the Atlantic powers to begin exploring and colonizing the New World. Although far more numerous than the Portuguese, the English before the mid-sixteenth century had little experience with long-distance trade. Only the voyages of John Cabot (the Genoa-born Giovanni Caboto) gave England any claim in the New World sweepstakes. But England never followed up on Cabot's voyages to Newfoundland and Nova Scotia—the first northern crossing of the Atlantic since the Vikings.

At first, England's interest in the far side of the Atlantic centered primarily on fish. This high-protein food, basic to the European diet, was the gold of the North Atlantic. Early explorers found the waters off Newfoundland and Nova Scotia teeming with fish—not only the ordinary cod but also the delectable salmon. In the 1520s, it was the fishermen of Portugal, Spain, and France, more than those of England, who made annual spring trips to the offshore fisheries. Not until the end of the century would the French and English drive Spanish and Portuguese fishermen from the Newfoundland banks.

Exploratory voyages along the eastern coast of North America hardly interested the English. Between 1524 and 1535, Jacques Cartier and Giovanni da Verrazano sailed for France across the Atlantic. They sought straits so that India-bound ships could sail around the northern land mass (still thought to be an island). The two navigators encountered many Indian peoples, charted the coastline from the St. Lawrence River to the Carolinas, and realized that the northern latitudes of North America were suitable for settlement. The French were not yet interested in settlements, so their discoveries had no immediate value.

DOCUMENT

Jacques Cartier, "First Contact with the Indians" (1534)

Changes in the late sixteenth century, however, propelled the English overseas. The rising production of woolen cloth, a mainstay of the English economy, had sent merchants scurrying for new markets after 1550. Their success in establishing trading companies in Russia, Scandinavia, the Middle East, and India vastly widened England's commercial orbit and raised hopes for developing still other spheres. Meanwhile, population growth and rising prices depressed the

RECOVERING THE PAST

Illustrated Travel Accounts

English travel accounts of New World settlements had a threefold purpose: first, to convince investors that purchasing stock issued by colonizing companies would reward them richly; second, to attract colonists through promotional descriptions of an exotic new world; and third, to serve as a Protestant weapon against colonizing Catholic countries, especially Spain. These pamphlets have furnished historians with rich ethnographic evidence of Indian lifeways in the Americas, a source of information on English attitudes toward Native Americans, and insights into how new technologies in book publishing fed the Protestant–Catholic conflict.

In 1588, Thomas Harriot (1560–1623), a minister, mathematician, and scientist trained at Oxford, published the first popular pamphlet describing and promoting English colonization. It came off the press as the English were repelling the Spanish Armada as it tried to destroy the English navy. In *A Briefe and True Report of the New Found Land of Virginia, directed to the Investors, Farmers and Well-wishers of the project of Colonizing and Planting There,* Harriot described what he had seen in eastern North America as a member of the second expedition to the Roanoke colony in 1585. Harriot enthusiastically described the pleasant climate and fertile land that would make farming easy, while boasting the commodities that English colonists could easily procure in Virginia—furs, pearls, iron, timber, precious metals, and more. Also on this voyage was a talented watercolorist, John White, whose many paintings depicted Native Americans living in villages, practicing agriculture, and engaging in dances, religious activities, and child-rearing—a people who seemed to be ones with whom the English could settle peacefully.

Harriot's *Briefe and True Report* became a model for English colonial promotional pamphlets. In 1589, he teamed up with Théodore de Bry, a Protestant engraver who in 1570 had fled Liège, his Belgian hometown, to escape the Spanish Inquisition, and taken refuge in Strasbourg, a Protestant stronghold and a center of engraving and the book trade. Once in London, de Bry created new copperplate engravings of White's watercolor paintings for a second edition of the *Briefe and True Report.* Taking artistic liberties, de Bry made the Indians seem more civilized to the English. In 1590, Harriot's reissued, illustrated *Briefe Report* attracted great attention, appearing as the first volume of a series of European travel accounts gathered by de Bry and advertised as *The Grand Voyages to America.* When John Smith published his *Generall Historie of Virginia, New England, and the Summer Isles* in 1624, the first lengthy eyewitness account of early English settlement in North America, it used many of de Bry's engravings, copied from John White's watercolors.

De Bry's engravings introduced large numbers of Europeans to images of Native American life and to impressions of the first encounters of Europeans with the indigenous people. A few Europeans had seen crude woodcuts of native life in the Americas in earlier sixteenth-century travel accounts. But not until de Bry's copperplate engravings, which offered clear, precise details, did book illustration advance to the point where a panoramic view of the European colonization of the Americas become available to many. The great Catholic–Protestant conflict in sixteenth- and seventeenth-century Europe, being played out in the Americas, could thus be presented to a wide audience through the de Bry–illustrated travel accounts.

Just before he died in 1598, de Bry published a Latin version of Bartolomé de Las Casas's *Short Account of the Destruction of the Indies,* first published in 1541 by the Spanish Dominican friar, who had lived for nearly 40 years in New Spain. Las Casas gave his life to converting the natives to Catholicism and was intent on stopping the cruel Spanish treatment of them. His book was filled with details on horrific torture and killing of women and children as well as adult males. Protestants had earlier republished Las Casas's exposé in French, English, and other languages, eager to offer proof of Catholic

English viewers of this water-color of an Indian town on the bank of the Pamlico River (in present-day Beaufort County, North Carolina) might see that though they called them "savages," the Eastern Woodlands natives tilled their maize fields (shown on the right), enjoyed dancing (lower right), and buried their chiefs (see tomb in lower left) in ways familiar to Europeans. At the upper right is a small, elevated watchman's hut. (© *British Museum*)

Spain's depravity in the Americas. But de Bry's illustrations for the 1598 edition published in Frankfurt showed Spanish ruthlessness with such graphic horror as to terrify the reader.

After their father's death, Jean-Théodore and Jean-Israël de Bry published another 22 illustrated volumes of voyages to the Americas, including eight volumes with illustrations emphasizing how the Spanish Catholics brutalized the native people. Published in English, German, French, and Latin editions, the illustrated books promoted the idea of English superiority while providing Europeans with graphic material on the exotic peoples on the other side of the Atlantic.

REFLECTING ON THE PAST   Look at the illustration and imagine that you saw it in England as you prepared to cross the Atlantic among a group of colonists. Having never lived outside the small village where you had been born, how do you see the Native Americans? How will you prepare yourself for encounters with them? How will you be able to avert the violence of the Spanish colonists?

economic conditions of ordinary people and made them look across the ocean for new opportunities.

The cautious policy of Queen Elizabeth I, who ruled from 1558 to 1603, did not initially include promoting overseas colonies. She favored Protestantism, partly as a vehicle of national independence. Ambitious and talented, she had to contend with Philip II, the fervently Catholic king of Spain. Regarding Elizabeth as a Protestant heretic, Philip plotted incessantly against her. The pope added to Catholic–Protestant tensions in England by excommunicating Elizabeth in 1571 and absolving her subjects from paying her allegiance—in effect, inciting them to overthrow her.

The smoldering conflict between Catholic Spain and Protestant England broke into open flames in 1587. Two decades before, Philip II had sent 20,000 Spanish soldiers into his Netherlands provinces to suppress Protestantism. Then, in 1572, he facilitated the massacre of thousands of French Protestants. By the 1580s, Elizabeth was providing covert aid to the Protestant Dutch revolt against Catholic rule. Philip vowed to crush the rebellion and decided as well to attack England to wipe out this growing center of Protestant power.

Elizabeth fed the flames of the international Catholic–Protestant conflict in 1585 by sending 6,000 English troops to aid the Dutch Protestants. A year later, Francis Drake, who had been raiding Spanish shipping on the coasts of Mexico and Peru, bombarded Spanish St. Augustine in Florida for two days, looted the city, and touched off an epidemic that the Florida Indians attributed to the "English God that made them die so fast." Two years later, infuriated by English piracy and support of Protestant rebels in the Netherlands, Philip dispatched a Spanish armada of 130 ships to conquer Elizabeth's England. For two weeks in the summer of 1588, a sea battle raged off the English coast. A motley collection of smaller English ships, with Francis Drake in the lead, defeated the armada, sinking many of the lumbering Spanish galleons and then retiring as the legendary "Protestant wind" blew the crippled armada into the North Sea.

The Spanish defeat prevented a crushing Catholic victory in Europe and brought a temporary stalemate to the religious wars. It also solidified Protestantism in England and brewed a fierce nationalistic spirit there. Shakespeare's love of "this other Eden, this demi-paradise" summed up popular sentiments; and with Spanish naval power checked, both the English and the Dutch found the seas more open to their maritime and commercial interests.

The Westward Fever

In the last decades of the sixteenth century, the idea of overseas expansion captured the imagination of important elements of English society. Urging them on were two men both named Richard Hakluyt, who were cousins. In the 1580s and 1590s, they advertised the advantages of colonizing across the Atlantic. For nobles at court, colonies offered new baronies, fiefdoms, and estates. For merchants, the New World promised exotic produce to sell at home and a new outlet for English cloth. For militant Protestant clergy, there awaited a continent of heathen to be saved from devilish savagery and Spanish Catholicism. For the commoner, opportunity meant bounteous land, almost for the taking. The Hakluyts' pamphlets trumpeted that the time was ripe for England to break the Iberian monopoly on New World riches.

England first attempted colonizing, however, in Ireland. In the 1560s and 1570s, the English gradually extended control over the island through brutal military conquest. Ireland became a turbulent frontier for thousands of career-hungry younger sons of gentry families as well as landless commoners. Many of the leaders of England's initial New World colonization got their training in subjugating Ireland.

The first English attempts at transatlantic settlement were small, feeble, and ill-fated. Whereas the Spanish encountered unheard-of wealth and scored epic victories over ancient and populous civilizations, the English at first met only failure in relatively thinly settled lands. With the French already to the north, and the Spanish settled in the south, English settlement efforts centered on the temperate middle zone of the central North American coast. England began—unsuccessfully—to mount small settlements, first in Newfoundland in 1583. Others, organized by Walter Raleigh, planted a settlement from 1585 to 1588 at Roanoke Island, off the North Carolina coast. Small and poorly financed, the colony apparently failed to maintain peaceful relations with the local natives. By the time a relief expedition arrived in 1591, the colonists had vanished. A tiny colony in Guiana, off the South American coast, failed in 1604 and 1609. Another group, set down in Maine in 1607, lasted only a year. Although they would flourish in time, even the colonies founded in Virginia in 1607 and in Bermuda in 1612 floundered badly for several decades.

IMAGE

English Trade with Indians, as Seen by Théodore de Bry (1634)

English merchants, sometimes supported by gentry investors, undertook these first tentative efforts, risking capital in the hope of realizing profits similar to those from their other overseas commercial ventures. The Spanish and Portuguese colonizing efforts were sanctioned, capitalized, and coordinated by the crown. By contrast, English colonies had their queen's blessing, but were private ventures without royal subsidies or naval protection.

English colonization could not succeed until these first merchant adventurers solicited the wealth and support of the prospering middle class. This support grew steadily in the first half of the seventeenth century. Even then investors were drawn far more to the quick profits promised in West Indian tobacco production than to the uncertainties of mixed farming, lumbering, and fishing on the North American mainland. In the 1620s and 1630s, most of the English capital invested overseas went into establishing tobacco colonies in tiny Caribbean islands.

DOCUMENT

Thomas Hariot, "On Tabacco" (1588)

Apart from the considerable financing required, the vital element in launching a colony was a suitable body of colonists. The changing agricultural system, combined with population growth and the unrelenting increase in prices caused by the influx of silver, produced a surplus of unskilled labor, squeezed many small producers, and spread poverty and crime. Pushed in response to these conditions, about 80,000 streamed out of England between 1600 and 1640, at the same time that dreams of opportunity and adventure pulled them westward. In the next 20 years, another 80,000 departed.

Beginning in 1618, the renewed European religious wars between Protestants and Catholics devastated the continental market for English woolen cloth, bringing more unemployment. Probably half the households in England lived on the edge of poverty. Religious persecution and political considerations intensified the pressure to emigrate from England in the early seventeenth century. For the first time in their history, large numbers of English people were abandoning their island homeland to carry their destinies to new frontiers. The largest number went to the West Indies, about one-third migrated to the North American mainland, and fewer went to the plantations in northern Ireland.

Anticipating North America

The early English settlers in North America were far from uninformed about the indigenous people of the New World. Beginning with Columbus's first description of the New World, published in several European cities in 1493 and 1494, reports and promotional accounts circulated among the participants in early voyages of discovery, trade, and settlement. This literature became the basis for anticipating the world that had been discovered beyond the setting sun.

Colonists who read or listened to these accounts got a dual image of the native people. Some accounts depicted Indians as a gentle people who eagerly received Europeans. Verrazano, the first European to touch the eastern edge of North America, wrote optimistically about the native people in 1524. The natives, he related, "came toward us joyfully uttering loud cries of wonderment, and showing us the safest place to beach the boat."

This positive image of the Native Americans reflected both the friendly reception that Europeans often actually received and the European vision of the New World as an earthly paradise where war-torn, impoverished, and persecuted people could build a new life. The strong desire to trade with the native people also encouraged a favorable view because only a friendly Indian could become a suitable partner in commercial exchange.

IMAGE

How the Savages
Roast Their
Enemies (1575)

Early North American travel literature also portrayed a counterimage of a savage, hostile Indian. As early as 1502, Sebastian Cabot had paraded in England three Eskimos he had kidnapped on an Arctic voyage, describing them as flesh-eating savages and "brute beasts." Many other accounts portrayed the New World natives as "half men," who lived, as Amerigo Vespucci put it, without "law, religion, rulers, immortality of the soul, and private property."

The English had another reason for believing that all would not be peace and friendship when they came ashore. For years they had read accounts of the Spanish experience in the Caribbean, Mexico, and Peru—and the story was not pretty. Many books described in gory detail the wholesale violence that occurred when Spaniard met Mayan, Aztec, or Inca. Accounts of Spanish cruelty, even genocide, were useful to Protestant pamphleteers, who labeled the Catholic Spaniards "hell-hounds and wolves." Immigrants embarking for North America wondered whether similar violent confrontations awaited them.

For Englishmen, rooted in a tradition of private property ownership, the fact that Indians possessed the land necessary for settlement presented moral, legal, and practical problems. As early as the 1580s, George Peckham, an early pro-

Pomeiock Noblewoman and Daughter John White, governor of the second expedition to Virginia in 1587, rendered the first pictorial records of native life in the Americas. This watercolor of a tattooed noblewoman of Pomeiock shows her right arm resting in a chain of pearls or copper beads. Her young daughter holds a prized English doll in an Elizabethan dress. Do you think English colonizers would have found tattooing attractive? (© *British Museum*)

moter of colonization, had admitted that the English doubted their right to take the land of others. This problem could be partially solved by arguing that English settlers did not intend to take the Indians' land but only wanted to share it. In return, they would offer the natives the advantages of a more advanced culture and, most important, the Christian religion—a claim that would be repeated for generations.

A more ominous argument also justified English rights to native soil. By denying the humanity of the Native Americans, the English, like other Europeans, claimed that the native possessors of the land disqualified themselves from rightful ownership of it. "Although the Lord hath given the earth to children of men," one Englishman reasoned, "the greater part of it [is] possessed and wrongfully usurped by wild beasts and unreasonable creatures, or by brutish savages, which by reason of their godless ignorance and blasphemous idolatry, are worse than those beasts which are of the most wild and savage nature."

Defining the Native Americans as "savage" and "brutish" did not give the English arriving in the Americas the power to dispossess the Indians of their soil, but it armed them with a moral justification for doing so when their numbers became sufficient. Few settlers arriving in North America doubted that their technological superiority would allow them to overwhelm the indigenous people. For their part, the natives probably perceived the arriving Europeans as impractical, irreligious, aggressive, and strangely intent on accumulating things.

AFRICAN BONDAGE Don't Read

For almost four centuries after Columbus's voyages, European colonizers, in the largest forced migration in history, transported Africans from their homelands and used their labor to produce wealth. Estimates vary widely, but at least 9.6 million Africans were brought to the Americas, and millions more perished on the long, terrible journey. Nearly as many were traded across the Sahara to Red Sea and Indian Ocean slave markets from 650 to 1900 C.E.

Once the transatlantic African slave trade began, locales for producing desired commodities such as sugar, coffee, rice, and tobacco moved from the Old World to the Americas. As the first transoceanic European colonial empires were established, Europe's orientation shifted from the Mediterranean Sea to the Atlantic Ocean. African forced labor was an essential part of the immense Atlantic-basin system of trade and the success of the overseas colonies of European nations.

While the economic importance of enslaved Africans can hardly be overstated, it is equally important to understand the cultural interchange that occurred. From 1519 to the early nineteenth century, African newcomers probably outnumbered Europeans two or three to one. As a result, African slavery became the context in which European life would evolve in many parts of the Americas. At the same time, the slave trade etched lines of communication for the movement of crops, agricultural techniques, diseases, and medical knowledge among Africa, Europe, and the Americas.

North America remained a fringe area for slave traders until the early eighteenth century. Yet those slaves who came to the American colonies, about 10,000 in the seventeenth century and 350,000 in the eighteenth century, profoundly affected North American society. In a prolonged period of labor scarcity, they were indispensable to colonial economic development. Meanwhile, their African customs mixed continuously those that of their European masters. Moreover, the racial relations that grew out of slavery so deeply marked society that race has continued to be one of this nation's most difficult problems.

The Slave Trade

The African slave trade began as an attempt to fill a labor shortage in the Mediterranean world. As early as the eighth century, Arab and Moorish traders had driven slaves across Saharan caravan trails to Mediterranean ports. Seven centuries later, Portuguese merchants became the first Europeans to trade these slaves. Portuguese ship captains exploring the west coast of Africa tapped into a slave-trading network that had operated for many generations.

More than anything else, sugar transformed the African slave trade. By the sixteenth century, the center of production was Portugal's Atlantic island of

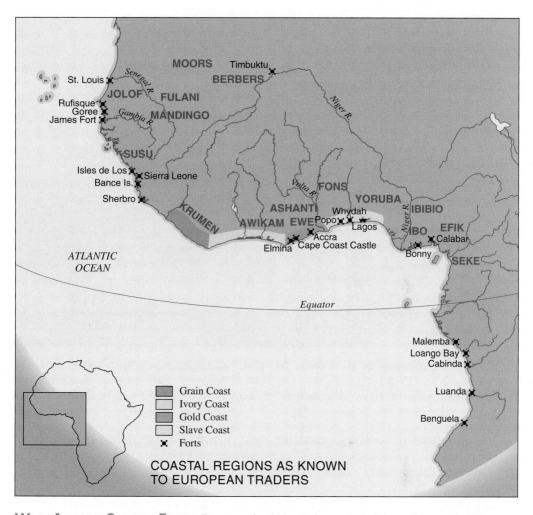

COASTAL REGIONS AS KNOWN
TO EUROPEAN TRADERS

WEST AFRICAN SLAVING FORTS Europeans fought lustily for control of slaving forts on the West African coast, and many forts changed hands several times during the long period of the Atlantic slave trade. ■ **Reflecting on the Past** How did West Africans participating in the slave trade adjust to the languages of different European slave traders? Or did the European slave traders learn a variety of African languages in order to trade at the coastal forts?

Madeira, the first European colony organized around slave labor. From it, sugar cultivation spread to Portuguese Brazil and Spanish Santo Domingo. By the seventeenth century, with Europeans developing a taste for sugar almost as insatiable as their craving for tobacco, they vied fiercely for Caribbean islands and West African coastal trading forts. African kingdoms, eager for European trade goods, fought each other to supply the "black gold" to white ship captains. Some Africans became slaves as punishment for crimes, but far more were war captives. This trend increased as the European demand for slaves led African kings highly desirous of a part in the trade to wage wars to acquire additional slaves to trade.

DOCUMENT

Alexander Falconbridge, The African Slave Trade (1788)

Crowded Conditions on Slave Ships *Slave Deck of the* Albanoz, *Prize to the* HMS Albatross, watercolor, by Lt. Francis Meynell (a young British naval officer) depicting a captured Spanish slave ship's deck, 1844–1845. *(National Maritime Museum, Greenwich, England)*

European nations competed for West African trading rights. In the seventeenth century, when about 1 million Africans were brought to the New World, the Dutch replaced the Portuguese as the major supplier. Not until the 1690s, when they began their century-long rise to maritime greatness, did the English challenge the Dutch. By 1790, the English were the foremost European slave traders.

In the eighteenth century, European traders carried at least 6 million Africans to the Americas. By then an Englishman called slavery the "strength and the sinews of this western world."

The slave trade's horrors were almost unimaginable. Olaudah Equiano, an eighteenth-century Ibo from what is now Nigeria, described how raiders from an-

DOCUMENT

Olaudah Equiano, The Middle Passage (1788)

other tribe kidnaped him and his younger sister when he was only 11 years old. He passed from one trader to another while being marched to the coast. Many on these forced marches attempted suicide or died from exhaustion or hunger. But Equiano survived. Reaching the coast, he encountered the next humiliation: confinement in barracoons, or fortified enclosures on the beach, where a surgeon from an English slave ship inspected him. Equiano was terrified by the light skins, strange language, and long hair of the English and was convinced that he "had got into a world of bad spirits and that they were going to kill me."

More cruelties followed. European traders often branded the African slaves. The next trauma came with the ferrying of slaves in large canoes to the ships an-

TIMELINE

1440s	Portuguese use enslaved Africans having kidnaped or traded them on Africa's western coast
1460s	Using African labor, sugar plantations in Portuguese Madeira become major exporters
1492	Christopher Columbus lands on Caribbean islands
	Spanish expel Moors (Muslims) and Jews
1493–1504	Columbus makes three additional voyages to the Americas
1493	Spain plants first colony in Americas on Hispaniola
1494	Treaty of Tordesillas
1497–1585	French and English explore northern part of the Americas
1498	Vasco da Gama reaches India after sailing around Africa
Early 1500s	First Africans reach the Americas with Spanish
1508–1511	Spanish conquistadors subjugate native people on Puerto Rico and Cuba
1517	Luther attacks Catholicism and begins Protestant Reformation
1521	Cortés conquers the Aztec
1528	Spain plants first settlement on Florida coast
1528–1536	Cabeza de Vaca *entrada* across southern region of North America
1530s	Calvin calls for religious reform
1533	Pizarro conquers the Inca
1540–1542	Coronado explores the Southwest
1558	Elizabeth I crowned queen of England
1585	English plant settlement on Roanoke Island
1588	English defeat the Spanish Armada
1590	Roanoke settlement fails

chored in the harbor. "The Negroes are so loath to leave their own country," wrote one Englishman, "that they have often leaped out of the canoes, boat and ship, into the sea, and kept under the water till they were drowned."

Conditions aboard the slave ships were miserable, even though the traders' goal was to deliver alive as many slaves as possible. Manacled slaves below decks were crowded together like corpses in coffins. "With the loathsomeness of the stench, and crying together," said Equiano, "I became so sick and low that I was not able to eat, nor had I the least desire to taste anything." Slavers brutally flogged the many people who tried to kill themselves by starvation and applied hot coals to their lips. If this did not suffice, they force-fed them with a mouth wrench.

The Atlantic passage usually took four to eight weeks, and one of every seven captives died en route. Many others arrived deranged or dying. In all, the relocation of any African may have averaged about six months from the time of capture to the time of arrival at the plantation of a colonial buyer. Ahead lay endless bondage.

Slavery in Early Spanish Colonies

Before a single enslaved African touched soil in the English colonies, thousands of slaves were already present in North America. They came first with fifteenth-century Spanish explorers such as Ponce de Leon, Vasquez de Ayllon, de Soto, and Coronado. The Morocco-born Estevan was indispensable to Coronado's expedition in North America's southwest, serving as guide, healer, linguist, and diplomat to Indian tribes. The importance of Africans on these arduous expeditions gave slavery a distinct character in the early Spanish colonies. Laboring in fields, in fort and church construction, and on supply trains, they were also valuable as soldiers, guides, and go-betweens with native people. In this setting, slavery had little of the caste-like character it developed in the English colonies. Also contributing to the greater flexibility of Spanish slavery was the frequent crossing of blood among Spaniards, Indians, and Africans.

Conclusion

Converging Worlds

The Iberian voyages of the late fifteenth and early sixteenth centuries, linking Europe and Africa with the Americas, brought together people such as the Spanish conquistador Alvar Núñez Cabeza de Vaca, the Moroccan captive Estevan, and chiefs of Creek villages in the southeastern sector of North America. Here were the beginnings of a communications network that ultimately joined every region of the globe and linked the destinies of widely disparate peoples living on many parts of the immense Atlantic basin. Other nations would follow Spain, but it was the Spanish who first erected colonial regimes that drew upon homeland traditions of law, religion, government, and culture. The Spanish also initiated maritime and commercial enterprises profoundly affecting patterns of production, with the Americas destined to become the great producer of foodstuffs to be exported to Europe. Part of this fledgling global economy was the trade in human beings—Africans carried to Spain and Portugal, then to the Atlantic islands off the west coast of Africa, and finally to the Americas in one of the most tragic chapters of human history. Accompanying this, and paving the way for European settlement, was the greatest weapon possessed by Europeans—the germs carried in their bodies that decimated the indigenous people of the Americas in the greatest biological holocaust in the annals of history.

The English immigrants who began arriving on the eastern edge of North America in the early seventeenth century came late to a New World that other Europeans had been colonizing for more than a century. The first English arrivals were but a small advance wave of the large, varied, and determined fragment of English society that would flock to the western Atlantic frontier during the next few generations. Like Spanish, Portuguese, and French colonizers before them, they would establish new societies in the newfound lands in contact with the people of two other cultures—one made up of ancient inhabitants of the lands they were settling and the other composed of those brought across the Atlantic against their will. We turn now to the richly diverse founding experience of the English latecomers in the seventeenth century and their contests with French, Dutch, and Spanish contenders for control of North America.

Questions for Review and Reflection

1. How did the religious changes in Europe affect European expansion into the Americas?

2. What was the Columbian Exchange, and what impact did it have on Europe and the Americas?

3. Why was England slow to become involved in exploration and colonization? How did the late arrival of the English affect their history in the New World?

4. What were the causes and consequences of the African slave trade with the European colonies in the Americas?

5. What was the impact of the collision of cultures that occurred in the Americas in the early colonial period?

Discovering U.S. History Online

1492: An Ongoing Voyage www.lcweb.loc.gov/exhibits/1492/intro.html
An exhibit of the Library of Congress in Washington, D.C., this site provides brief essays and images about early civilizations and contact in the Americas.

The European Voyages of Exploration www.ucalgary.ca/applied_history/tutor/eurvoya
This site has images and texts for nearly every facet of European exploration.

Spain, the United States, and the American Frontier http://international.loc.gov/intldl/eshtml/
A joint effort of American and Spanish national libraries, this bilingual site presents primary materials and several exhibits about the pre-conquest to contact period between the two countries.

Sir Francis Drake www.mcn.org/2/oseeler/drake.htm
This comprehensive site covers much of Drake's life and voyages.

John Cabot www.heritage.nf.ca/exploration/cabot.html
Giovanni Caboto, or John Cabot, sailed for England to the New World in the late fifteenth century. This site describes his voyages as well as England's goals.

African American Odyssey: Slavery—The Peculiar Institution http://lcweb2.loc.gov/ammem/aaohtml/exhibit/aopart1.html
A Web exhibit that includes paintings, original documents, engravings, and broadsides, along with background information on each.

Fiction and Film

In the feature film *Conquest of Paradise* (1992), Gerard Depardieu plays Christopher Columbus, but Boston's WGBH seven-part *Columbus and the Age of Discovery* (1991) is much more comprehensive and authentic. In the miniseries *Roanoke*, PBS explores the friction between Indians and colonizers in the first attempt of the English to plant a North American settlement. Louise Erdrich's poem titled "Captivity," which can be found in her *Jacklight* collection (1984), is a valuable Indian-centered reading of one of the most popular Indian captivity accounts ever published—Mary Rowlandson's *A Narrative of the Captivity, Sufferings and Removes of Mrs. Mary Rowlandson,* first published in 1682. Boston's WGBH has produced a superb four-part video series on *Africans in America* (1998). The first two parts cover slavery and slave culture in the seventeenth and eighteenth centuries. Much shorter is the BBC production *A Son of Africa: The Slave Narrative of Olaudah Equiano,* a half-hour video of the only eighteenth-century slave who wrote an autobiography.

Recommended Reading

www.ablongman.com/nash

The Companion Website has a list of recommended readings about the European conquest of the Americas and slavery in the New World.

Colonizing a Continent in the Seventeenth Century

American Stories

An African on the Virginia Frontier

Anthony Johnson, an African, arrived in Virginia in 1621 with only the name Antonio. Caught as a young man in the Portuguese slave-trading net, he had passed from one trader to another in the New World until he reached Virginia. There he was purchased by Richard Bennett and sent to work at Warrasquoke, Bennett's tobacco plantation on the James River. In the next year, Antonio was brought face-to-face with the world of triracial contact and conflict that would shape the remainder of his life. On March 22, 1622, the Powhatan tribes of tidewater Virginia fell on the colonizers in a determined attempt to drive them from the land. Of the 57 people on the Bennett plantation, only Antonio and four others survived.

Antonio—his name anglicized to Anthony—labored on the Bennett plantation for some 20 years, slave in fact if not in law, for legally defined bondage had not yet fully taken hold in the Virginia colony. During this time, he married Mary, another African trapped in the labyrinth of servitude, and fathered four children. In the 1640s, Anthony and Mary Johnson gained their freedom after half a lifetime of servitude. Probably at this point they chose a surname, Johnson, to signify their new status. Already past middle age, the Johnsons began carving out a niche for themselves on Virginia's eastern shore. By 1650, they owned 250 acres, a small herd of cattle, and two black servants. In a world in which racial boundaries were not yet firmly marked, the Johnsons had entered the scramble of small planters for economic security.

By schooling themselves in the workings of the English legal process, carefully cultivating white patronage, and working industriously on the land, the Johnsons gained their freedom, acquired property, established a family, warded off contentious neighbors, and hammered out a decent existence. But by the late 1650s, as the lines of racial slavery tightened, the customs of the country began closing in on Virginia's free blacks.

In 1664, convinced that ill winds were blowing away the chances for their children and grandchildren in Virginia, the Johnsons began selling their land to white neighbors. The following spring, most of the clan moved north to Maryland, where they rented land and again took up farming and cattle raising. Five years later, Anthony Johnson died, leaving his wife and four children.

The growing racial prejudice of Virginia followed Johnson beyond the grave. A jury of white men in Virginia declared that because Johnson "was a Negroe and by consequence an alien," the 50 acres he had deeded to his son Richard before moving to Maryland should be awarded to a local white planter.

Johnson's children and grandchildren, born in America, could not duplicate the modest success of the African-born patriarch. By the late seventeenth century, people of color faced much greater difficulties in extricating themselves from slavery. When they did, they found themselves forced to the margins of society. Anthony's sons never rose higher than the level of tenant farmer or small freeholder. John Johnson moved farther north into Delaware in the 1680s, following a period of great conflict with Native Americans in the Chesapeake region. Members of his family married local Native Americans and became part of a triracial community that has survived to the present day. Richard Johnson stayed behind in Virginia. When he died in 1689, just after a series of colonial insurrections connected with the overthrow of James II in England, he had little to leave his own four sons. They became tenant farmers and hired servants, laboring on plantations owned by whites. By now, slave ships were pouring Africans into Virginia and Maryland to replace white indentured servants, the backbone of the labor force for four generations. To be black had at first been a handicap. Now it became a fatal disability, an indelible mark of degradation and bondage.

Anthony and Mary Johnson's story is one of thousands detailing the experiences of seventeenth-century immigrants who arrived in North America. Their story is not about those European immigrants who sought both spiritual and economic renewal in the New World. But their lives became intertwined with those who were trying to escape European war, despotism, material want, and religious corruption. Like free immigrants and indentured servants from Europe, the Johnsons had to cope with new environments, new social situations, and new mixings of people who before had lived on different continents. Mastering the North American environment involved several processes that would echo down the corridors of American history. Prominent among them were the molding of an African labor force and the gradual subjection of Native American tribes that contested white expansion. Both developments occurred in the lifetimes of Anthony and Mary Johnson and their children. Both involved a level of violence that made this frontier of European expansion not a zone of pioneer equality and freedom but one of growing inequality and servitude.

This chapter reconstructs the manner of settlement and the character of immigrant life in six areas of early colonization: the Chesapeake Bay, southern New England, the French and Dutch area from the St. Lawrence River to the Hudson River, the Carolinas, Pennsylvania, and the Spanish toeholds on the northern boundaries of their empire. A comparison of these various colonies will show how the colonizers' backgrounds, ideologies, modes of settlement, and uses of labor—free, slave, and indentured—produced distinctly different societies in North America in the seventeenth century. The chapter also shows how these regional societies changed over the course of the seventeenth century and how they experienced internal strain, a series of Native American wars, a destructive and community-shattering witchcraft craze, and reactions to England's attempts to reorganize its overseas colonies.

THE CHESAPEAKE TOBACCO COAST

In 1607, a group of merchants established England's first permanent colony in North America at Jamestown, Virginia. But for the first generation, its permanence was anything but assured. Even into the second and third generation of settlement along the waters that flowed into the huge Chesapeake Bay, the English colonizers were plagued with internal discord and violent clashes with the native peoples.

Jamestown, Sot Weed, and Indentured Servants

Under a charter from James I, the Virginia Company of London sold shares of stock and used the pooled capital to finance overseas expeditions. They expected to find gold, a rewarding trade with Native Americans, and a water route to China. But investors and settlers got a rude shock. Dysentery, malaria, and malnutrition carried off most of the first colonists. More than 900 settlers arrived between 1607 and 1609; only 60 survived. There were no profits.

One-third of the first immigrants were gold-seeking adventurers, which meant the colony had six times the population of gentry back home in England. Many others were unskilled servants, some with criminal backgrounds, who (according to John Smith, the colony's first strong leader) "never did know what a day's work was." Both types adapted poorly, and Smith got few of the blacksmiths, carpenters, and farmers he wanted.

The colony was also hampered by the common assumption that Englishmen could exploit the Native Americans, as Cortés and Pizarro had done in Mexico and Peru. But the English found that the 24,000 local Powhatan Indians were not densely settled and so could not be easily subjugated. Unlike Spain, England had sent neither an army of conquistadors nor an army of priests to subdue the natives. Instead, relations with the small groups that the able Powhatan had united in a confederacy were bitter almost from the beginning. The Powhatan brought supplies of maize to the sick and starving Jamestown colony during the first autumn. However, John Smith, whose military experience in eastern Europe had schooled him in dealing with "barbarians," raided Native American food supplies and tried to cow the local tribes. In response, the Powhatan withdrew from trade with the English. Many settlers died in the "starving times" of the first years.

IMAGE

Mural of
Jamestown
Settlement

DOCUMENT

John Smith, "The
Starving Time"
(1624)

Still, the Virginia Company of London poured in more money and settlers, many enticed with promises of free land after seven years of labor. In 1618, the

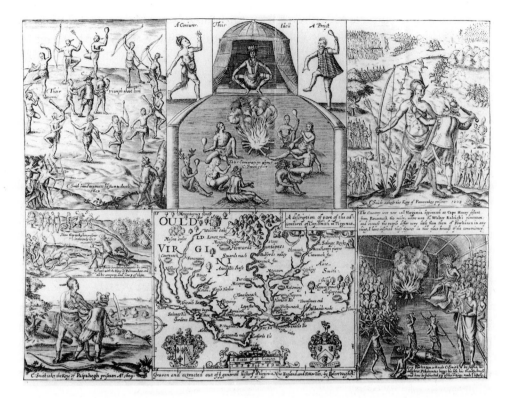

A History of Virginia   A small caption in the middle of this set of panels reads, "A description of part of the adventures of Cap: Smith in Virginia." The images were rendered by Robert Vaughan, an English engraver, and were published in *The Generall Historie of Virginia, 1624, by Captain John Smith*. In the lower right panel, an oversized Pocahontas (at the right) begs for the life of Smith, whose head is on a block, ready for dismemberment by an Indian executioner. What overall effect would this engraving have on readers of John Smith's history in England?

company even offered 50 acres of land outright to anyone journeying to Virginia. To people on the margins of English society, the promise of land in America seemed irresistible. More than 9,000 crossed the Atlantic between 1610 and 1622. Yet only 2,000 remained alive at the end of that period.

Beside the offer of free land, a crucial factor in the migration was the discovery that tobacco grew splendidly in Chesapeake soil. Francis Drake's boatload of the "jovial weed" (so named for its intoxicating effect), procured in the West Indies in 1586, popularized it among the upper class and launched an addiction that continues to this day.

Even James I's denunciation of smoking as "loathsome to the eye, hateful to the nose, harmful to the brain, and dangerous to the lungs" failed to halt the smoking craze. The "sot weed" became Virginia's salvation. Planters shipped the first crop in 1617, and cultivation spread rapidly. Tobacco yielded enough profit for settlers to plant it even in the streets and marketplace of Jamestown. By 1624, Virginia exported 200,000 pounds of the "stinking weed"; by 1638, though the price had plummeted, the crop exceeded 3 million pounds. Tobacco became to Virginia in the 1620s what sugar was to the West Indies and silver to Mexico and Peru.

Because tobacco required intensive care, Virginia's planters had to find a reliable supply of cheap labor. They found it by recruiting mostly English and Irish laborers to be indentured servants, who willingly sold years of their working lives in exchange for free passage to America. About four of every five seventeenth-century immigrants to Virginia and, later, Maryland, were indentured. About three-quarters of them were male, mostly between 15 and 24 years old, and nearly all came from the lower rungs of the social ladder at home.

Only about one in twenty indentured servants realized the dream of freedom and land. If malarial fever or dysentery did not quickly kill them, they often succumbed to brutal work routines. Even by the middle of the seventeenth century, about half died during the first few years of "seasoning." Masters bought and sold servants as property, gambled for them, and worked them to death, for there was little motive for keeping them alive beyond their term of service. When servants neared the end of their contract, masters found ways to add time and were backed by courts that they controlled.

Contrary to English custom, masters often put women servants to work at the hoe. Sexual abuse was common, and servant women paid dearly for illegitimate pregnancies. The courts fined them heavily and ordered them to serve an extra year or two to repay the time lost during pregnancy and childbirth. They also deprived mothers of their illegitimate children, indenturing them out at an early age. Many servant women accepted the purchase of their indenture by any man who suggested marriage as the best release from this hard life.

Expansion and Indian War

As tobacco production caused Virginia's population to increase, violence mounted between white colonizers and the Powhatan tribes. In 1614, the sporadic hostility of the early years ended temporarily with the arranged marriage of Powhatan's daughter, the fabled Pocahontas, to planter John Rolfe. However, the profitable cultivation of tobacco continued to create an intense demand for land.

In 1617, when Powhatan retired, leadership of the Chesapeake tribes fell to Opechancanough. This proud and talented leader began preparing an all-out attack on his English enemies. The English murder of a Powhatan war captain and religious prophet triggered a fierce assault in 1622 that wiped out more than one-quarter of the white population and much of the colony's physical infrastructure.

The devastating attack bankrupted the Virginia Company. The king annulled its charter in 1624 and established a royal government, allowing the elected legislative body established in 1619, the House of Burgesses, to continue lawmaking in concert with the royal governor and his council.

The Native American assault of 1622 fortified the determination of the surviving planters to pursue a ruthless new policy. John Smith, writing from England two years later, noted the grim satisfaction that had followed the attack. Many, he reported, believed that "now we have just cause to destroy them by all means possible." The Virginians conducted annual military expeditions against native villages. The population grew after 1630

IMAGE

John Smith
Threatening
Opechancanough

RECOVERING THE PAST

Homesteading is central to our national experience. For 300 years after the founding of the first colonies, most Americans were involved in taming and settling the land. On every frontier, families faced the tasks of clearing the fields, beginning farming operations, and building shelter for themselves and their livestock. The kinds of structures they built depended on available materials, their resources and aspirations, and their notions of a "fair dwelling." The plan of a house and the materials used in its construction reveal much about the needs, resources, priorities, and values of the people who built it.

By examining archaeological remains of early ordinary structures and by studying houses that are still standing, historians are reaching new understandings of the social life of pioneering societies. Since the 1960s, archaeologists and architectural historians have been studying seventeenth-century housing in the Chesapeake Bay and New England regions. They have discovered a familiar sequence of house types from temporary shanties and lean-tos to rough cabins and simple frame houses to larger and more substantial dwellings of brick and finished timber. This hovel-to-house-to-home pattern existed on every frontier as sodbusters, gold miners, planters, and cattle raisers secured their hold on the land and then struggled to move from subsistence to success.

What is unusual in the findings of the Chesapeake researchers is the discovery that the second phase in the sequence—the use of temporary, rough-built structures—lasted for more than a century. Whereas many New Englanders had rebuilt and extended their temporary clapboard houses into timber-framed, substantial dwellings by the 1680s, Chesapeake settlers continued to construct small, rickety buildings that had to be repaired continually or abandoned altogether every 10 to 15 years.

The house on the opposite page is a typical reconstructed tobacco planter's house. As opposed to New England structures, the chimney of the Chesapeake house is not built of brick but of mud and wood, and there is no window glass, only small shutters. The exterior is rough, unfinished planking. The placement of doors and windows and the overall dimensions indicate that this house has only one room downstairs and a loft above.

Historians have puzzled over this contrast between the architecture of the two regions. Part of the explanation may lie in the different climatic conditions and different immigration patterns of New England and the Chesapeake. In the southern region, disease killed thousands of settlers in the early decades. The imbalance of men and women produced a stunted and unstable family life, hardly conducive to an emphasis on constructing fine homes. In New England, good health prevailed almost from the beginning, and the family was at the heart of society. It made more sense, in this environment, to make a substantial investment in larger and more permanent houses. Some historians argue, moreover, that the Puritan work ethic impelled New Englanders to build solid homes—a compulsion unknown in the culturally backward, "lazy" South.

Archaeological evidence combined with data recovered from land, tax, and court records, however, suggests another reason for the impermanence of housing in the Chesapeake region. Living in a labor-intensive tobacco world, it is argued, planters large and small economized on everything possible in order to buy as many indentured servants and slaves as they could. Better to live in

Reconstructed Chesapeake planter's house, typical of such simply built and unpainted structures in the seventeenth century. *(Photograph by Julie Roy Jeffrey)*

a shanty and have 10 slaves than to have a handsome dwelling and nobody to cultivate the fields. As late as 1775, the author of *American Husbandry* calculated that in setting up a tobacco plantation, five times as much ought to be spent on purchasing 20 black fieldhands as on the "house, offices, and tobacco-house."

Only after the Chesapeake region had emerged from its prolonged era of mortality and gender imbalance and a mixed economy of tobacco, grain, and cattle had replaced the tobacco monoculture did the rebuilding of the region begin. Excavated house sites indicate that this occurred after 1720. New research reveals that the phases of home building and the social and economic history of a society were closely interwoven.

REFLECTING ON THE PAST   What do houses today reveal about the resources, economic livelihood, priorities, and values of contemporary Americans? Do class and regional differences in house design continue?

and tobacco quickly exhausted the soil and intensified the settlers' ambition for Indian land. The tough planters soon encroached on Indian territories, provoking war in 1644. The Chesapeake tribes, Virginians came to believe, were merely obstacles to be removed from the path of English settlement.

Proprietary Maryland

By the time Virginia had achieved commercial success in the 1630s, another colony on the Chesapeake took root. The founder's main aim was not profit but rather a refuge for Catholics and a New World version of England's manor-dotted countryside.

George Calvert, an English nobleman, designed and promoted the new colony. Closely connected to England's royal family, he had received a huge grant of land in Newfoundland in 1628, just three years after James I had made him Lord Baltimore. In 1632, Charles I, James's son, granted him a more hospitable domain of 10 million acres, which Calvert named Terra Maria, or Maryland, to honor the king's Catholic wife, Henrietta Maria.

Catholics were an oppressed minority in England, and Calvert planned his colony as a haven for them. But knowing that he needed more than a small band of Catholic settlers, the proprietor invited others, too. Protestants, who jumped at the offer of free land with only a modest yearly fee to the Calverts, quickly overwhelmed Catholics, never a majority in his colony.

Lord Baltimore died in 1632, leaving his 26-year-old son, Cecilius, to carry out his plans. The charter guaranteed the proprietor control over all branches of government, but young Calvert learned that his colonists would not be satisfied with fewer liberties than they enjoyed at home or could find in other colonies.

Arriving in 1634, immigrants ignored Calvert's plans for 6,000-acre manors for his relatives and 3,000-acre manors for lesser aristocrats, each to be worked by serflike tenants. The settlers took up their free land, imported as many indentured servants as they could afford, maintained generally peaceful relations with local Indian tribes, grew tobacco on scattered riverfront plantations like their Virginia neighbors, and governed themselves locally as much as possible. Although Maryland grew slowly at first—in 1650 it had a population of only 600—it developed rapidly in the second half of the seventeenth century. By 1700, its population of 33,000 was half that of Virginia.

Daily Life on the Chesapeake

Most immigrants found Chesapeake life dismal. Only a minority could marry and rear a family, because marriage had to be deferred until the indenture was completed. And there were three times more men than women. Marriages were fragile. Either husband or wife was likely to die of disease within about seven years. The vulnerability of pregnant women to malaria frequently terminated marriages, and death claimed half the children before they reached adulthood. Few children had two living parents while growing up. Grandparents were almost unknown. In a society so numerically dominated by men, widows were prized and often remarried quickly. Such conditions produced complex families full of stepchildren and stepparents, half-sisters and half-brothers.

Plagued by horrendous mortality, the Chesapeake remained, for most of the seventeenth century, a land of immigrants rather than a land of settled families. Churches and schools took root very slowly. The large number of indentured servants further destabilized community life. Strangers in a household, they served their time and moved on, or died, replaced by other strangers purchased fresh from England.

The region's architecture reflected the difficult conditions. Life was too uncertain, the tobacco economy too volatile, and the desire to invest every available shilling in field labor too great for men to build grandly. Even by the early eighteenth century, most Chesapeake families lived in a crude house without interior partitions. Eating, dressing, working, and loving all took place with hardly a semblance of privacy. For nearly two centuries, most ordinary Virginians and Marylanders were "pigg'd lovingly together," as one planter put it. Even prosperous planters did not begin constructing fully framed, substantial homesteads until a century after the colony was founded.

The crudity of life also showed in the household possessions of the Chesapeake colonists. Struggling farmers and tenants were likely to own only a straw mattress, a simple chest, and the tools for food preparation and eating. Most ordinary settlers owned no chairs, dressers, plates, or silverware. To be near the top of Chesapeake society meant having three or four rooms, sleeping more comfortably, sitting on chairs rather than squatting on the floor, and owning chamber pots, candlesticks, bed linen, a chest of drawers, and a desk. Only a few boasted such luxuries as clocks, books, punch bowls, wine glasses, and imported furniture. Four generations elapsed in the Chesapeake settlements before the frontier quality of life slowly gave way to more refined living.

Bacon's Rebellion Engulfs Virginia

In 1675 and 1676, the Chesapeake colonies became locked in a struggle involving both an external war between the native and white populations and a civil war among the colonizers. This deeply tangled conflict was called Bacon's Rebellion, after the headstrong Cambridge-educated planter Nathaniel Bacon, who had arrived in Virginia at age 28.

Bacon and many other ambitious young planters detested the Indian policy of Virginia's royal governor, Sir William Berkeley. In 1646, after the second native attack on the Virginians, the Powhatan tribes had been granted exclusive rights to territory beyond the limits of white settlement. Stable relations suited the established planters, some of whom traded profitably with the natives, but became obnoxious to new settlers. Nor did harmonious conditions please the white ex–indentured servants who hoped for cheap frontier land.

Land hunger and dissatisfaction with declining tobacco prices, rising taxes, and lack of opportunity erupted into violence in the summer of 1675. A group of frontiersmen used an incident with a local tribe as an excuse to attack the Susquehannock, whose rich land they coveted. Governor Berkeley denounced the attack, but few supported his position. The badly outnumbered Susquehannock prepared for war as rumors swept the colony that they were offering large sums to gain western native allies or that New England tribes would support them.

Thirsting for revenge, the Susquehannock attacked during the winter of 1675–1676 and killed 36 Virginians. That spring, hot-blooded Bacon became the frontiersmen's leader. Joined by hundreds of runaway servants and some slaves, he attacked friendly and hostile Native Americans alike. Governor Berkeley refused to sanction these attacks and declared Bacon a rebel, sending 300 militiamen to drag him to Jamestown for trial. Bacon recruited more followers, including many substantial planters. Frontier skirmishes thus turned into civil war. During the summer of 1676, Bacon's and Berkeley's troops maneuvered, while Bacon's men continued their forays against local tribes. Then Bacon boldly captured and razed Jamestown, obliging Berkeley to flee across Chesapeake Bay.

Virginians at all levels had chafed under Berkeley's rule. High taxes, an increase in the governor's powers at the expense of local officials, and the monopoly that Berkeley and his friends held on the Native American trade were especially unpopular. This opposition surfaced in the summer of 1676 as Berkeley's and Bacon's troops pursued each other through the wilderness. Berkeley tried to rally public support by holding new assembly elections and extending the vote to all freemen, but the new assembly turned on the governor, passing laws to make government more responsive to the common people and to end rapacious officeholding. It also legalized enslaving Native Americans.

Time was on the governor's side, however. Having crushed the Native Americans, Bacon's followers began drifting home to tend their crops. Meanwhile, 1,100 royal troops were dispatched from England. By the time they arrived in January 1677, Bacon had died of swamp fever and most of his followers had melted away. Berkeley hanged 23 rebel leaders without benefit of trial.

Royal investigators afterwards reported that Bacon's followers "seem[ed] to wish and aim at an utter extirpation of the Indians." This hatred of Native Americans, along with hopes of land ownership and independence, became a permanent feature of Virginia life. Even a royal governor could not restrain such men. A generation later, in 1711, the legislature spurned the governor's plea for quieting the frontier with educational missions and regulated trade, instead voting military appropriations of £20,000 "for extirpating all Indians without distinction of Friends or Enemys." The remnants of the once populous Powhatan Confederacy lost their last struggle for the world they had known. They moved west or submitted to a life on the margins of white society.

After Bacon's Rebellion, an emerging planter aristocracy annulled most of the reform laws of 1676. By making new land available, the war relieved much of the social tension among white Virginians. Equally important, Virginians with capital to invest were turning from the impoverished rural villages of England and Ireland to the villages of West Africa to supply their labor needs. This halted the influx of poor white servants who, once free, had formed a discontented mass at the bottom of Chesapeake society. A racial consensus, uniting whites of different ranks in the common pursuit of a prosperous slave-based economy, began to take shape.

Bacon's Rebellion caused rumblings outside Virginia. Many of his followers fled to North Carolina, joining disgruntled farmers there in briefly seizing power. In Maryland, Protestant settlers chafed under high taxes, quitrents, and venal or Catholic officeholders. Declining tobacco prices and a fear of Indian attacks increased their touchiness. A month after Bacon razed Jamestown, insurgent small planters tried to seize the Maryland government. Two leaders were hanged for the attempt.

In all three southern colonies, the volatility of late-seventeenth-century life owed much to the region's peculiar social development. Where family formation was retarded by imbalanced gender ratios and fearsome mortality, and where geographic mobility was high, little social cohesion or attachment to community could grow. Missing in the southern colonies were the stabilizing power of mature local institutions, a vision of a larger purpose, and the presence of experienced and responsive political leaders.

The Southern Transition to Slave Labor

English colonists on the mainland of North America at first regarded Native Americans as the obvious source of labor. But European diseases ravaged native societies, and native people, more at home in the environment than the white colonizers, were difficult to subjugate. Indentured white labor proved the best way to meet the demand for labor during most of the seventeenth century.

Though a few Africans entered the Chesapeake colonies as early as 1619 to labor in the tobacco fields alongside white servants, as late as 1671, when some 30,000 slaves toiled in English Barbados, fewer than 3,000 served in Virginia. They were still outnumbered there at least three to one by white indentured servants.

Only in the last quarter of the seventeenth century did southern field labor begin to shift to a black slave labor majority. This was due, first, to the rising commercial power of England, which swelled participation in the African slave trade and allowed southern planters to purchase slaves more readily and cheaply than before. Second, the supply of white servants from England began drying up. Third, Bacon's Rebellion, involving rebellious former servants seeking land, led white planters to seek a more pliable labor force. By the 1730s, the number of white indentured servants had dwindled to insignificance. Blacks tilled and harvested Chesapeake tobacco and Carolina rice, and slave labor became the priority in starting a plantation.

In enslaving Africans, English colonists in North America merely emulated their countrymen in Barbados, Jamaica, and the Leeward Islands, who had used brutal repression to mold Africans into a sugar- and tobacco-producing slave labor force. Human bondage would later become the subject of intense debate, but in the seventeenth century, all but a few whites accepted it without question.

The System of Bondage

The first Africans in the American colonies probably came as bound servants. They served their term, and if (like Anthony and Mary Johnson) they survived, they gained freedom. Then they could own land, hire out their labor, and move as they pleased. Their children, like those of white indentured servants, were born free.

Gradually, seventeenth-century Chesapeake planters began to draw tighter lines around the activities of black servants. By the 1640s, Virginia forbade blacks, free or bound, to carry firearms. In the 1660s, marriages between white women and black servants were banned as "shameful matches." By the end of the century, when incoming Africans increased from a trickle to a torrent, even the few free blacks found themselves pushed to the margins of society. Slavery, which had existed for centuries in many societies as the lowest social status, was becoming a caste reserved for those with black skin. White society was turning the black servant from a human being into chattel.

In this dehumanization of Africans, which the English largely copied from their colonial rivals, the key step was instituting hereditary lifetime service. Once servitude ended only with death, all other privileges quickly vanished. When a mother's slave condition legally passed to her newborn black infant (not the case in slavery in Africa), slavery became self-perpetuating.

Slavery became not only a system of forced labor but also a pattern of human relationships legitimated by law. By the early eighteenth century, most provincial legislatures limited black rights. Borrowed largely from England's Caribbean colonies, "Black Codes" forced Africans into an ever narrower world. Slaves could not testify in court, engage in commercial activity, hold property, participate in politics, congregate, travel without permission, or legally marry or be parents. Nearly stripped of human status, they became defined as property, and gradually all legal restraints on masters' treatment of them disappeared.

Eliminating slave rights did not eliminate resistance. With every African in chains a potential rebel, the rapid increase in the slave population brought demands for strict control and justifications for brutality. "The planters," wrote one Englishman in Jamaica, "do not want to be told that their Negroes are human creatures. If they believe them to be of human kind, they cannot regard them as no better than dogs or horses."

Dehumanizing slaves involved one of the great paradoxes of modern history. Many European immigrants saw the Americas as a liberating and regenerating arena. Yet the opportunity to exploit its resources led to a historic process by which masses of people were wrenched from their homelands and forced into a system of slavery that could be maintained only by increasing intimidation and brutality.

MASSACHUSETTS AND ITS OFFSPRING

While some English settlers in the reign of James I (1603–1625) scrambled for wealth on the Chesapeake, others in England looked to the wilds of North America as a place to build a tabernacle to God. The society they fashioned aimed at unity of purpose and utter dedication to reforming the corrupt world. American Puritanism would powerfully affect the nation's history by nurturing a belief in America's special mission in the world. It also attempted to banish diversity on a continent where the arrival of streams of immigrants from around the globe was destined to become the primary phenomenon.

Puritanism in England

England had been officially Protestant since 1558. Many English in the late sixteenth century, however, thought the Church of England was still riddled with Catholic vestiges. They wished to purify the Church of England, so were dubbed Puritans.

Religious reformers as well as men and women hoping to find in religion an antidote to the changes sweeping over English society were attracted to the Puritan movement. The growth of turbulent cities, the increase of wandering poor, rising prices, and accelerating commercial activity made them fear for the future and long for restraining institutions.

While the concept of the individual operating as freely as possible, maximizing both opportunities and personal potential, is at the core of our modern system of beliefs, many in Elizabethan England dreaded the crumbling of traditional restraints. They wanted to preserve the ideal of community and the belief that people were bound together by reciprocal rights and responsibilities. Symptoms of the "degeneracy of the times" included the defiling of the Sabbath by maypole dancing, card playing, fiddling, and bowling. Puritans vowed to reverse the march of disorder by imposing a new discipline.

Their plan included a social ethic stressing work as a primary way of serving God. This emphasis on work made the religious quest of every member of society equally worthy. The "work ethic" would banish idleness and impart discipline throughout the community. They also organized themselves into religious congregations in which each member hoped for personal salvation but also supported all others in their quest. Further, Puritans assumed responsibility for coercing and controlling "unconverted" people around them.

The relationship of Puritan reformers to the established church and the monarch had always been testy, but when Charles I succeeded to the throne in 1625, the situation worsened. Determined to strengthen the monarchy and stifle dissent, he harassed Puritans, removing dozens of Puritan ministers from their pulpits and threatening many others. In 1628, he summoned a new Parliament and, one year later, adjourned this venerable body (which was the Puritans' main instrument of reform) when it would not accede to royal demands.

By 1629, as the king began ruling without Parliament, many Puritans were turning their eyes to northern Ireland, Holland, the Caribbean, and, especially, North America. They were convinced that God intended them to carry their religious and social reforms beyond the reach of persecuting authorities. A declining economy added to their discouragement about England. Many Puritans decided that they should transport a fragment of English society to some distant shore and complete the Protestant Reformation.

Puritan Predecessors in New England

Puritans were not the first Europeans to reach northeastern North America. Fishermen of various European nations had dried their Newfoundland catches on the coast of Cape Cod and Maine since the early 1500s. They frequently encountered the Algonquian-speaking people. A short-lived attempt at settlement in Maine had also been made in 1607. Seven years later, the aging Chesapeake war dog John Smith coined the name "New England."

No permanent settlement took root, however, until "Pilgrims"—actually outnumbered by non-Pilgrims—arrived in Plymouth in 1620. Unlike the Puritans who followed, these humble Protestant farmers did not expect to convert a sinful world. Rather, they wanted to be left alone to realize

AUDIO

Plymouth Colony

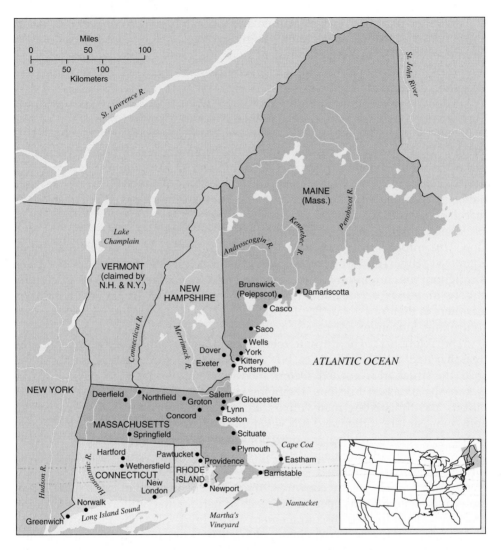

EARLY NEW ENGLAND Maine and New Hampshire became the frontier to which New England settlers migrated when their towns and farmlands became too crowded.

IMAGE

Mayflower
Replica at
Plymouth, MA

their radical vision of a pure and primitive life. Instead of reforming the Church of England, they were Separatists who left it. After James I threatened to "harry them out of the land," they fled first to Amsterdam in 1608, then to Leyden, Holland, and finally, in 1620, to North America.

Arriving at Cape Cod in November 1620, the Pilgrims were weakened by a stormy nine-week voyage and were ill-prepared for the harsh winter ahead. By the following spring, half the *Mayflower* passengers were dead, including 13 of the 18 married women.

The survivors, led by the staunch William Bradford, settled at Plymouth. Squabbles soon erupted with local Native Americans, whom Bradford considered "savage and brutish men." For two generations the Pilgrims tilled the soil, fished, and tried to keep intact their religious vision. But with the much larger Puritan migration that began in 1630, the Pilgrim villages around Cape Cod Bay became a backwater of the thriving, populous Massachusetts Bay Colony, which absorbed them in 1691.

Errand into the Wilderness

Their intention was to establish communities of pure Christians who collectively swore a covenant with God. Puritans believed that civil and religious transgressors should be harshly punished. They willingly gave up freedoms that other English settlers sought. An ideology of rebellion in England, Puritanism in North America became an ideology of control and of a powerful mission that is still part of American thinking. As Winthrop reminded the first settlers, "we shall be as a city upon a hill [and] the eyes of all people are upon us."

As in Plymouth and Virginia, the first winter tested the strongest souls. More than 200 of the first 700 settlers perished, and 100 others, disillusioned and sickened by the forbidding climate, soon returned to England. Still, Puritans kept coming, settling along the rivers that emptied into Massachusetts Bay. A few years later, they pushed south into what became Connecticut and Rhode Island, as well as northward along the rocky coast.

Motivated by their militant work ethic and sense of mission, and led by men experienced in local government, law, and exhortation, the Puritans thrived. The early leaders of Virginia were soldiers of fortune or roughneck adventurers with predatory instincts, men who had no families or had left them at home; ordinary Chesapeake settlers were mostly young men with little stake in English society who sold their labor to cross the Atlantic. But the early leaders in Massachusetts were university-trained ministers, experienced members of the lesser gentry, and men with a compulsion to fulfill God's prophecy for New England. Most ordinary settlers came as free men and women in families. Artisans and farmers from the middle ranks of English society, they established tight-knit communities in which, from the outset, the brutal exploitation of labor rampant in the Chesapeake had no place.

Relying mostly on free labor, the Puritans built an economy based on agriculture, fishing, timbering, and trading for beaver furs with local Native Americans. Even before leaving England, the directors of the Massachusetts Bay Company transformed their commercial charter into a rudimentary government. In North America, they laid the foundations of self-government. Free male church members annually elected a governor and deputies from each town. The latter formed one house of a colonial legislature, the General Court. The other house was composed of the governor's assistants, later to be called councillors. Consent of both houses was required to pass laws.The Puritans founded Harvard College, which opened its doors in 1636 to train clergymen, established the first printing press in the English colonies, and launched an innovative attempt in 1642 to create a tax-supported school system, open to all wanting an education.

DOCUMENT

The Cambridge Agreement (1629)

In spite of these accomplishments, the Puritan colony suffered many of the tensions besetting people bent on human perfection. Nor did Puritans prove any better at reaching an accommodation with the Native Americans than their less pious countrymen on the Chesapeake. Surrounded by seemingly boundless land, Puritans found it difficult to stifle acquisitive instincts and to keep families confined in compact communities. Those in Boston agitated for even broader political rights. After a few years, Governor Winthrop wondered if the Puritans had not gone "from the snare to the pit."

Winthrop's troubles multiplied in 1633 when Salem's minister, Roger Williams, began to voice disturbing opinions. He argued that the Massachusetts Puritans were not truly pure because they would not completely separate from the polluted Church of England (which most Puritans still hoped to reform). Williams denounced mandatory worship and contended that government officials should confine themselves to civil affairs and not interfere with religious matters. "Coerced religion," he warned, "on good days produces hypocrites, on bad days rivers of blood." Today honored as the earliest spokesman for the separation of church and state, in 1633 Williams seemed to strike at the heart of the Bible commonwealth, whose leaders regarded civil and religious affairs as inseparable. Williams also charged the Puritans with illegally intruding on Native American land.

For two years, Puritan leaders could not quiet the determined young Williams. Finally, warned by Winthrop that he was about to be deported to England, Williams fled southward through winter snow with a small band of followers to found Providence in what would become Rhode Island. Even as they were driving Williams out, the Puritan authorities confronted another threat: Anne Hutchinson, a devout and magnetic woman of extraordinary talent and intellect who arrived in 1634 with her husband and seven children. Quickly gaining respect among Boston's women as a midwife, healer, and spiritual counselor, she soon began to discuss religion and suggested that the "holy spirit" was absent in the preaching of some ministers. Before long Hutchinson was leading a movement labeled *antinomianism*, which stressed the mystical nature of God's free gift of grace while discounting the efforts the individual could make to gain salvation.

By 1636, Boston was dividing into two camps: those who followed the male clergy and those drawn to the theological views of a gifted though untrained woman without official standing. Her followers included most of the community's malcontents—merchants and artisans who chafed under price controls, young people resisting the rigid rule of their elders, and women disgruntled by male authority. Hutchinson doubly offended the male leaders of the colony because she boldly stepped outside the subordinate position expected of women.

Determined to remove this thorn from their sides, the clergy and magistrates put Hutchinson on trial in 1637, convicting her of sedition and contempt in a civil trial and banishing her from the colony "as a woman not fit for our society." Six months later, the Boston church excommunicated her for preaching 82 erroneous theological opinions. In the last month of her eighth pregnancy, Hutchinson, with a band of supporters, followed Roger Williams's route to Rhode Island. Ideas proved harder to banish. The magistrates could never enforce uniformity of belief nor curb the appetite for land. Growth, geographic expansion, and commerce with the outside world all eroded the ideal of integrated, self-contained communities vibrant with piety. Leaders faced the nearly impossible task of containing land-hungry immigrants in an expansive region. By 1636, groups of Puritans had swarmed not only to Rhode Island but also to Hartford and New Haven in what became Connecticut.

New Englanders and Indians

Though the charter of the Massachusetts Bay Company spoke of converting "the natives to the knowledge and obedience of the only true God and Saviour of mankind and the Christian faith," the instructions that Governor John Winthrop carried from England reveal other Puritan thoughts about the native inhabitants. According to Winthrop's orders, all men were to receive training in the use of firearms, a reversal of the sixteenth-century English policy of disarming the citizenry in order to quell public disorders. New England magistrates prohibited Native Americans from entering Puritan towns and threatened to deport any colonist selling arms to a native or instructing one in their use.

Only sporadic conflict with local tribes occurred at first since, in 1616, visiting English fishermen had triggered a ferocious outbreak of respiratory viruses and smallpox that wiped out three-quarters of some 125,000 Native Americans. Five years later, an Englishman exploring the area described walking through a forest where human skeletons covered the ground. The Puritans believed that God had intervened on their side, especially when smallpox returned in 1633, killing thousands more natives and allowing new settlers to find land. Many surviving natives welcomed the Puritans because they now had surplus land and through trade hoped to gain English protection against enemies to the north.

The settler pressure for new land, however, soon reached into areas untouched by disease. Land hunger mingled with the sense of mission made an explosive mix. Native Americans represented a mocking challenge to the building of a religious commonwealth that would "shine as a beacon" back to decadent England. Puritans believed that God would blame them for not civilizing and Christianizing the natives and would punish them with his wrath, so they tried to make the "savages" of New England strictly accountable to their ordinances. They succeeded with the smaller, disease-ravaged tribes of eastern Massachusetts, but control over the stronger Pequot required a bloody war in 1637. The Puritan victory ensured English domination over all the tribes of southern New England except the powerful Wampanoag and Narragansett of Rhode Island and removed the last obstacle to expansion into the Connecticut River valley. Missionary work, led by John Eliot, began among the remnant tribes in the 1640s. After a decade, about 1,000 Indians had been settled in four "praying villages," learning to live according to the white ways.

The Web of Village Life

Unlike the dispersed Chesapeake tobacco planters, the Puritans established small, tightly settled villages that were vital centers of life. Most were "open field" agricultural communities with narrow strip fields radiating out from the town. Farmers grazed their cattle on common meadowland and cut firewood on common woodland. Some towns employed the "closed field" system of self-contained

HOW OTHERS SEE US

John Josselyn, A Description of New Englanders

John Josselyn of Kent, England, on his second trip across the Atlantic, described New Englanders in the 1660s in this way.

The great masters [magistrates] as also some of their merchants, are damnable rich, generally all of [them] inexplicably covetous and proud. They receive your gifts but as an homage or tribute due to their transcendancy [high social position], which is a fault their clergy are also guilty of, whose living is upon the bounty of their hearers. ... But ... there are many sincere and religious people amongst them, descried by their charity and humility ... by their hearty submission to their sovereign, the king of England, by their diligent and honest labor in their callings. ... There are none that beg in the country, but there be witches too many—bottle-bellied witches amongst the Quakers and others that produce many strange apparitions (if you will believe reports of it): of a shallop [small ship] at sea manned with women; of a ship and a great red horse standing by the main mast; a ship being in a small cove to the eastward vanished of a sudden; of a witch that appeared aboard a ship twenty leagues to sea; of a mariner who took up the carpenter's broad axe and cleft her head with it; the witch dying of the wound at home.

- *Does Josselyn believe in witches?*
- *What do the many reports of apparitions tell you about the Salem witchcraft trials 30 years after this account was written?*

Source: John Josselyn, *Two Voyages to New England* (London, 1674), excerpted in James Axtell, *America Perceived: A View from Abroad in the 17th Century* (West Haven, Conn.: Pendulum Press, 1974), 102–103. Spelling and punctuation have been modernized.

farms. Both systems re-created common English patterns of agriculture with families living close together in towns built around a common, with a meetinghouse and tavern. These small, communal villages kept families in close touch so that each could be alert not only to its own transgressions, but also to those of its neighbors. To achieve godliness and communal unity, Puritans prohibited single men and women from living by themselves, beyond patriarchal authority and group observation. As Thomas Hooker put it, "every natural man and woman is born full of sin, as full as a toad of poison." Virginia planters counted the absence of restraint as a blessing. New Englanders feared it as the Devil.

Every community member gathered twice a week in the meetinghouse, a plain wooden structure at the center of each Puritan village. No man stood higher in the community than the minister, the spiritual leader in these small, family-based, community-oriented settlements. The unique Puritan mixture of strict authority and incipient democracy, of hierarchy and equality, can be seen in the way the Massachusetts town distributed land and devised local government. After receiving a grant, townsmen met to parcel out land. They awarded individual grants according to the size of a man's household, his wealth, and his usefulness to the church and town, perpetuating existing differences in wealth and status. Yet some towns wrote language into their covenants that to the modern ear has an almost socialistic ring. Puritans believed that the community's welfare transcended individual ambitions or accomplishments and that unity demanded limits on the accumulation of wealth. Every family should have enough land to sustain it, and prospering men were expected to use their wealth for such community projects as repairing the meetinghouse, building a school, or aiding a widowed neighbor.

Having felt the sting of centralized power in church and state, Puritans emphasized local exercise of authority. Until 1684, only male church members could vote. These voters elected selectmen who allocated land, passed local taxes, and settled disputes. Once a year, all townsmen gathered for the town meeting where they selected town officers for the next year and decided matters large and small. The appointment of many citizens to minor offices bred the tradition of local government.

The predominance of families lent cohesiveness to Puritan village life. Strengthening this family orientation was the remarkably healthy environment of the Puritans' "New Israel." Whereas the germs carried by English colonizers devastated neighboring Native American societies, the effect on the newcomers of entering a new environment was the opposite. The low density of settlement prevented infectious diseases from spreading, and the isolation of inland villages from Atlantic commerce, along which diseases as well as cargo flowed, minimized biological hazards.

The result was a spectacular natural increase in the population and a life span unknown in Europe. At a time when the population of western Europe was barely growing—deaths almost equaled births—the population of New England, discounting new immigrants, doubled every 27 years. The difference was not a higher birthrate. New England women typically bore about seven children during the course of a marriage, but this barely exceeded the European norm. The crucial factor was that chances for survival after birth were far greater than in England because of the healthier climate and better diet. In most of Europe, where life expectancy was less than 40 years, only half the babies born lived long enough to produce children themselves. In New England, nearly 90 percent of the infants born in the seventeenth century survived to marriageable age, and life expectancy exceeded 60 years—longer than for the American population as a whole at any time until the early twentieth century. About 25,000 people immigrated to New England in the seventeenth century, but by 1700 they had produced a population of 100,000. By contrast, some 75,000 immigrants to the Chesapeake colonies had yielded a population of only about 70,000 by the end of the century.

Women played a vital role in this family-centered society. The Puritan woman was not only a wife, mother, and housekeeper; she also kept a vegetable garden, salted and smoked meats, preserved vegetables and dairy products, spun yarn, wove cloth, and made clothes.

The presence of women and a stable family life strongly affected New England's regional architecture. As communities formed, the Puritans converted early economic gains into more substantial housing rather than investing in bound labor. Chesapeake colonists did the opposite, thereby retarding family formation and rendering the economy unstable. In New England, well-constructed one-room

The Mason Children Three of Arthur and Joanna Mason's five children were captured in this 1670 painting. The 9-year-old boy on the left holds a silver-headed walking
stick, signifying his status as male heir. His 6-year-old sister in the middle holds a yellow
fan and red and yellow ribbons. The 4-year-old sister to the right holds a rose, which
Puritans used as a symbol of innocence associated with childhood. Why do you think
the artists portrayed these children with faces typical of older boys and girls? (Fine Arts
Museum of San Francisco, Gift of Mr. and Mrs. John D. Rockefeller 3rd to The Fine Arts Museum of
San Francisco, 1979.7.3)

houses with sleeping lofts quickly replaced early "wigwams, huts, and hovels."
Families added parlors and lean-to kitchens as soon as they could. Within a half
century, New England immigrants accomplished a general rebuilding of their living structures. The Chesapeake lagged far behind.

A final binding element in Puritan communities was the stress on literacy and
education, which eventually became a hallmark of American society. Placing religion at the center of their lives, Puritans emphasized the ability to read cate-
chisms, psalmbooks, and especially the Bible. In literacy and education, Puritans
saw guarantees for preserving their central values.

Though eager to be left alone, Puritans could not escape events in England. In
1642, King Charles I pushed England into revolution by violating the country's
customary constitution and continuing earlier attacks against Puritans. By 1649,

the ensuing civil wars climaxed with the trial and beheading of the king. Thereafter, during the so-called Commonwealth period (1649–1660), Puritans in England could complete the reform of religion and society at home. Meanwhile, migration to New England abruptly ceased.

The 20,000 English immigrants who had come to New England by 1649 were scattered from Maine to Long Island. Governor Winthrop of Massachusetts and Roger Williams deplored the dispersal. Yet in this rock-strewn terrain, it was natural that farmers should seek better plow land.

In 1643, to combat the problems of dispersion, Puritan leaders established the Confederation of New England, intended to coordinate government among the various settlements (Rhode Island excluded) and to provide more effective defense against the French, Dutch, and Native Americans. This first American attempt at federalism functioned fitfully for a generation and then dissolved.

Although the Puritans fashioned stable communities, developed the economy, and constructed effective government, their leaders complained that the founding vision of Massachusetts Bay was faltering. If social diversity increased and the religious zeal of the founding generation waned, that was only to be expected. One second-generation Bay colonist put the matter bluntly. His minister had noticed his absence in church and found him later that day at the docks, unloading a boatload of cod. "Why were you not in church this morning?" asked the clergyman. Back came the reply: "My father came here for religion, but I came for fish."

King Philip's War in New England

For religious leaders concerned about declining piety, continued difficulties with Native Americans of southern New England signaled new signs of God's displeasure. Following the Pequot War of 1637, the Wampanoag and Narragansett tried to keep their distance from the New England colonists who coveted their territories. As colonists quarreled over provincial boundaries, they gradually reduced the natives' land base.

By the 1670s, when New England's population had grown to about 50,000, the Wampanoag leader was Metacomet (called King Philip by the English). The son of Massasoit, a chief who had allied with the first Plymouth settlers in 1620, Metacomet had watched his older brother preside over the deteriorating position of his people after their father's death in 1661. Becoming chief in his turn, Metacomet faced one humiliating challenge after another, including in 1671, when Plymouth forced him to surrender a large stock of guns and accept his people's subjection to English law.

Metacomet began organizing a resistance movement fed by the rising anger of the young Wampanoag males. Younger Native Americans refused to imitate their fathers, who had acquiesced to the colonizers' encroachments. For the young men, revitalization of their ancient culture through war became as important a goal as defeating the enemy. Rather than submit further, they attempted a pan-Indian offensive against an ever-stronger intruder.

In 1675 Puritans executed three Wampanoag for murdering John Sassamon, providing the spark for an insurrection. That summer, the Wampanoag unleashed daring hit-and-run attacks on villages in the Plymouth colony. By autumn, many

New England tribes, including the powerful Narragansett, had joined Meta-comet. Towns all along the frontier reeled under their attacks. By November, na-tive warriors had devastated the entire upper Connecticut River valley, and by March 1676, they were less than 20 miles from Boston and Providence. As as-sumptions about English military superiority faded, New England officials passed America's first draft laws. Widespread draft evasion and friction among the colonies hampered a counteroffensive.

Metacomet's offensive faltered in the spring of 1676, sapped by food short-ages, disease, and the refusal of the Mohawk to join the New England tribes. Metacomet fell in a battle. The head of this "hell-hound, fiend, serpent, caitiff and dog," as one colonial leader branded him, was displayed in Plymouth for 25 years.

Several thousand colonists and perhaps twice as many Native Americans lay dead. Of some 90 Puritan towns, 52 had been attacked and 13 completely de-stroyed; 1,200 homes lay in ruins and 8,000 cattle were dead. The estimated cost of the war exceeded the value of all personal property in New England. Not for 40 years would the frontier advance beyond the line it had reached in 1675. Native American towns were devastated even more completely, including several inhab-ited by "praying" Indians who had converted to Christianity and allied with the whites. An entire generation of young men had been nearly annihilated. Many of the survivors, including Metacomet's wife and son, were sold into slavery in the West Indies.

Slavery in New England

The Wampanoag captives sold as slaves in the West Indies continued New Eng-land's involvement in the dirty business of slavery. New England's crops were not labor-intensive, so coerced labor never became the foundation of its field workforce. Slavery did take root in the cities, though, where slaves worked as ar-tisans and domestic servants. Northern colonial economies also became en-meshed in the Atlantic commercial network, which depended on slavery and the slave trade. New England's merchants eagerly pursued profits in the slave trade as early as the 1640s. By 1750, half the merchant fleet of Newport, Rhode Island, reaped profits from carrying human cargo. In New York and Philadelphia, build-ing and outfitting slave vessels proved profitable.

New England's seaports became centers for distilling rum—the "hot, hellish and terrible liquor" made from West Indian sugar. Rum became one of the princi-pal commodities traded for slaves on the African coast. As the number of slaves in the Caribbean multiplied—from about 50,000 in 1650 to 500,000 in 1750—New England's large fishing fleet found important markets for its cod. Wheat from the middle colonies and barrel staves and hoops from North Carolina also serviced the slave-based West Indies economy. In short, every North American colony par-ticipated in the slave business.

FROM THE ST. LAWRENCE TO THE HUDSON

The New Englanders were not the only European settlers in the northern region, for both France and Holland created colonies there. While English settlers founded Jamestown, the French were settling Canada, where they had failed in the 1540s.

France's America

Henry IV, the first strong French king in half a century, sent Samuel de Champlain to explore deep into the territory even before the English had obtained a foothold on the Chesapeake. Champlain established a small settlement in Acadia (later Nova Scotia) in 1604 and another in Quebec in 1608. French trading with Indians for furs had already begun in Newfoundland, and his settlers hoped to keep making these easy profits. But the holders of the fur monopoly in France did not encourage immigration to the colony, fearing to reduce the forests from which the furs were harvested. New France remained lightly populated.

In 1609–1610, Champlain allied with the Algonquian Indians of the St. Lawrence region in attacking their Iroquois enemies to the south, earning their enmity. This drove the Iroquois to trade furs for European goods with the Dutch on the Hudson River; when the Iroquois exhausted the furs of their own territory, they turned north and west, determined to seize forest-rich resources from the Huron, French allies in the Great Lakes region.

When the Iroquois descended on them in the 1640s, the Huron were a people already decimated by epidemics that spread among them as Jesuit priests entered their villages. In the "beaver wars" of the 1640s and 1650s, the Iroquois used Dutch guns to attack Huron parties carrying beaver pelts to the French. By mid-century, Iroquois attacks had scattered the Huron, all but ending the French fur trade and reducing the Jesuit influence to a few villages of Christianized Huron.

The bitterness bred in these years colored future colonial warfare, driving the Iroquois to ally with the English against the French. By the mid-seventeenth century, the English remained unhindered by the beleaguered French colonists, who numbered only about 400.

England Challenges the Dutch

By 1650, the Chesapeake and New England regions each contained about 50,000 settlers. Between them lay the mid-Atlantic area controlled by the Dutch, who planted New Netherland at the mouth of the Hudson River in 1624. In the next four decades they extended their control to the Connecticut and Delaware river valleys. South of the Chesapeake lay a vast territory where only the Spanish, from their mission frontier in Florida, challenged the power of Native American tribes.

Although for generations they had been the Protestant bulwarks in a mostly Catholic Europe, England and Holland became bitter commercial rivals in the mid-seventeenth century. By the time the Puritans arrived in New England, the Dutch had become the mightiest carriers of seaborne commerce in western Europe. The Dutch had also muscled in on Spanish and Portuguese transatlantic commerce, trading illegally with Iberian colonists who gladly violated their government's commercial policies to obtain cloth and slaves more cheaply. By 1650, the Dutch had temporarily overwhelmed the Portuguese in Brazil, and soon their vast trading empire reached southeast and east Asia.

In North America, the Dutch West India Company's New Netherland colony was small, profitable, and multicultural. Agents fanned out from Fort Orange (Albany) and New Amsterdam (New York City) into the Hudson, Connecticut, and Delaware river valleys, establishing a lucrative fur trade with local tribes by hooking into the sophisticated trading network of the Iroquois Confederacy, which stretched to the Great Lakes. The Iroquois welcomed the Dutch, who were few in number, did not have voracious appetites for land, and willingly exchanged desirable goods for the pelts of animals plentiful in the vast Iroquois territory. At Albany, the center of the Dutch Iroquois trade, relations remained peaceful and profitable for several generations.

Although the Dutch never settled more than 10,000 people in their mid-Atlantic colonies, their commercial and naval powers were impressive. The Virginians learned this in 1667 when brazen Dutch raiders captured 20 tobacco ships on the James River and confiscated virtually the entire tobacco crop for that year. By 1650, England was ready to challenge Dutch maritime supremacy. War broke out three times between 1652 and 1675, as the two Protestant nations competed to control the emerging worldwide capitalist economy. In the second and third wars, New Netherland became an easy target for the English. They captured it in 1664 and then, after it fell to the Dutch in 1673, recaptured it almost immediately. By 1675, the Dutch had been permanently dislodged from the North American mainland. But they remained mighty commercial competitors of the English around the world.

New Netherland now became New York, so named because Charles II gave it (along with the former Dutch colonies on the Delaware River) to his brother the duke of York, later King James II. Under English rule, the Dutch colonists remained ethnically distinct for several generations, clinging to their language, their Dutch Reformed Calvinist churches, and their architecture. In time, however, English immigrants overwhelmed the Dutch, and gradual intermarriage among the Dutch, the French Huguenots, and the English diluted ethnic loyalties. New York retained its polyglot, religiously tolerant character, and its people never allowed religious concerns or utopian plans to interfere with the pragmatic conduct of business.

PROPRIETARY CAROLINA: A RESTORATION REWARD

In 1663, three years after he was restored to his father's throne, England's Charles II granted a vast territory named Carolina to a group who supported him during his exile. Its boundaries extended from Virginia to central Florida and westward to the Pacific. Within this potential empire, eight London-based proprietors, including several involved in Barbados sugar plantations, gained governmental powers and semifeudal land rights. The system of governance planned for Carolina had both feudal and modern features. To lure settlers, the proprietors promised religious freedom and free land. However, the generous land offer included a scheme for a semimedieval government in which they, their deputies, and a few noblemen would monopolize political power. Reacting to a generation of revolutionary turbulence in England, its founders designed Carolina as a model of social and political stability in which a hereditary aristocracy would check boisterous small landholders.

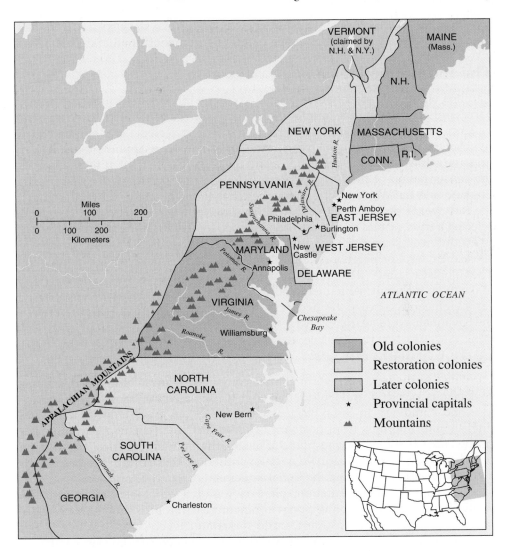

RESTORATION COLONIES: NEW YORK, THE JERSEYS, PENNSYLVANIA, AND THE CAROLINAS After founding the Restoration colonies from the 1660s to the 1680s, England's colonists claimed the entire seaboard between Spanish Florida and French Canada.

Carolina realities bore faint resemblance to their plan. Rugged sugar and to-bacco planters streamed in from economically depressed Barbados and Virginia and claimed their 150 acres of free land, as well as additional acreage for each family member or servant they brought. They ignored proprietary regulations about settling in compact rectangular patterns and reserving two-fifths of every county for appointed nobility. In government, they also did as they pleased. Meeting in assembly for the first time in 1670, they refused to accept the proprietors' Fundamental Constitutions of 1667 and disregarded orders from the proprietors' governor. Most of the settlers already knew how to run a slave society from having lived in Barbados, and they shaped local government from that experience.

The Indian Debacle

Carolina was the most elaborately planned colony in English history, yet the least successful in achieving the harmony the proprietors had intended. Mindful of the violence that had plagued other settlements, they projected a well-regulated Native American trade in deerskins, run exclusively by their appointed agents. Aggressive settlers from the West Indies and the Chesapeake flouted these plans. To the consternation of the London proprietors, capturing Indians for sale in New England and the West Indies became the cornerstone of commerce in Carolina in the early years, plunging the colony into a series of wars. Planters and merchants selected a tribe, armed it, and rewarded it handsomely for bringing in enemy captives. But even strong tribes found that after they had used English guns to enslave their weaker neighbors, they themselves were scheduled for elimination. The colonists claimed that "thinning the barbarous Indian natives" was needed to make room for white settlement, and the "thinning" was so thorough that by the early eighteenth century the two main tribes of the coastal plain, the Westo and the Savannah, were nearly extinct.

Early Carolina Society

Carolina's fertile land and warm climate convinced many that it was a "country so delicious, pleasant, and fruitful that were it cultivated doubtless it would prove a second Paradize." In came Barbadians, Swiss, Scots, Irish, French Huguenots, English, and migrants from northern colonies. Far from creating paradise, they clashed abrasively in an atmosphere of fierce competition, ecological exploitation, brutal race relations, and stunted social institutions. Decimating the coastal Indians made it easier to expand the initial settlements around Charleston.

After much experimentation, planters found a profitable staple crop that would flourish in this forbidding environment: rice. Its cultivation required backbreaking labor to drain swamps, build dams and levees, and hoe, weed, cut, thresh, and husk the crop. Many early settlers had owned African slaves in Barbados, so their early reliance on slave labor came naturally. On widely dispersed plantations, black labor came to predominate. In 1680, four-fifths of South Carolina's population was white. By 1720, when the colony had grown to 18,000, black slaves outnumbered whites two to one.

As in Virginia and Maryland, the low-lying areas of coastal Carolina were so disease-ridden that population grew slowly in the early years. "In the spring a paradise, in the summer a hell, and in the autumn a hospital," remarked one traveler. Malaria and yellow fever, especially dangerous to pregnant women, were the main killers that retarded population growth, and the scarcity of women further limited natural increase. Like the West Indies, the rice-growing region of Carolina was at first more a place to accumulate a fortune rather than to rear a family.

In healthier northern Carolina, a different kind of society emerged amid pine barrens along a sandy coast. Settled largely by small tobacco farmers from Virginia seeking free land, the Albemarle region developed a mixed economy of livestock grazing, tobacco and food production, and the extraction of naval stores of lumber, turpentine, resin, pitch, and tar. In 1701, North and South Carolina became separate colonies, but their distinctiveness had already emerged. Slavery took root only slowly in North Carolina. Still 85 percent white in 1720, North Carolina had the potential for sustained growth: a healthier climate and settlement by families rather than slave-owning single men. But in North as well as South Carolina, settlement patterns, ethnic and religious diversity, and a lack of shared assumptions about social and religious goals inhibited the growth of a strong colony-wide identity.

THE QUAKERS' PEACEABLE KINGDOM

Of all the utopian dreams imposed on the North American landscape in the seventeenth century, the most remarkable was the Quakers'. During the English civil wars, the Society of Friends, as the Quakers called themselves, had sprung up as one of the many radical sects searching for a more just society and a purer religion. Their visionary ideas and defiance of civil authority cost them dearly in fines, brutal punishment, and imprisonment. After Charles II and Parliament stifled radical dissent in the 1660s, the Quakers sent many converts across the Atlantic. More than any other colony, the society they founded in Pennsylvania foreshadowed the religious and ethnic pluralism of the future United States.

The Early Friends

Like Puritans, the Quakers regarded the Church of England as corrupt. But Quakers went much further, rejecting all Church officials and institutions and holding that every believer could find grace through the "inward light," a redemptive spark in every human soul. Rejecting original sin and eternal predestination, Quakers offered a radical alternative to Calvinism. Other Protestants regarded them as dangerous fanatics, for the Quakers' doctrine of the "light within" took precedence even over Scripture and elevated all laypeople to the position of the clergy.

Garbing themselves in plain black cloth and practicing civil disobedience, the Quakers also threatened social hierarchy and order. They refused to observe the customary marks of deference, believing that God made no social distinctions. They used the familiar "thee" and "thou" instead of the formal and deferential "you," resisted taxes supporting the Church of England, and refused to sign witnesses' oaths on the Bible, regarding this as profane. Most shocking, they renounced the use of force in human affairs and therefore refused to perform militia service.

Quakers also affronted traditional views when they insisted on the spiritual equality of the sexes and the right of women to participate in church matters on an equal, if usually separate, footing with men. Quaker women preached and established separate women's meetings. Among Quakers who fanned out from England to preach the doctrine of the inward light, 26 of the first 59 to cross the Atlantic were women. All but four of them were unmarried or without their husbands and therefore living, traveling, and ministering outside male authority.

Intensely committed to converting the world, Quakers ranged westward to North America and the Caribbean in the 1650s and 1660s. Nearly everywhere they faced jeers, prison, mutilation, deportation, and death. In 1659, Puritans in Massachusetts hanged two Quaker men on the Boston Common and threatened to do the same to Mary Dyer, an old woman who had followed Anne Hutchinson a quarter century before. Led from the colony, she returned the next year, undaunted, to meet her death at the end of a rope.

Early Quaker Designs

By the 1670s, the English Quakers were looking for a place in the New World to carry out their millennial dreams and escape severe repression. They found a leader in William Penn. His decision to identify with this radical and persecuted sect was surprising, for he was the son of Admiral Sir William Penn, who had captured Jamaica from Spain in 1654. In 1666, the 23-year-old Penn was converted to Quakerism and thereafter devoted himself to the Friends' cause.

In 1674, Penn joined other Friends in establishing a North American colony, West Jersey. They had bought the land from one of the proprietors of New Jersey, itself a new English colony recently carved out of the former New Netherland. For West Jersey, Penn helped fashion a constitution extraordinarily liberal for its time that allowed virtually all free males to vote for legislators and local officials. Settlers were guaranteed freedom of religion and trial by jury. As Penn and the other trustees of the colony explained, "We lay a foundation for [later] ages to understand their liberty as men and Christians, that they may not be brought in bondage, but by their own consent; for we put the power in the people."

The last phrase, summing up the document, shocked men of property and power in England or North America. Most regarded "the people" as ignorant, dangerous, and certain to bring society to a state of anarchy if allowed to rule themselves. Nowhere in the English world had ordinary citizens, especially those who did not own land, enjoyed such extensive privileges. Nowhere had a popularly elected legislature received such broad authority.

West Jersey sputtered at first. Only 1,500 immigrants arrived in the first five years, and for several decades the colony was caught up in legal tangles. The center of Quaker hopes lay across the Delaware River, where in 1681, Charles II granted William Penn a territory almost as large as England, paying off a large royal debt to Penn's father. Charles II also benefited by getting the pesky Quakers out of England. Thus Penn and the Quakers came into possession of the last unassigned segment of the eastern coast of North America, and one of the most fertile.

Pacifism in a Militant World: Quakers and Indians

On the day Penn received his royal charter for Pennsylvania, he wrote a friend,

DOCUMENT

William Penn, Description of Pennsylvania (1681)

"My God that has given it to me will, I believe, bless and make it the seed of a nation." The nation that Penn envisioned was unique among colonizing schemes. Penn intended to make his colony an asylum for the persecuted and a refuge from arbitrary state power. Puritans had strived for social homogeneity and religious uniformity. In the Chesapeake and Carolina colonies, aggressive, unidealistic men had sought to exploit their lands and bondspeople. Penn dreamed of inviting to his forested colony people of all

PENNS TREATY with the INDIANS, made 1681 with out an Oath.and never broken.The foundation of Religious and Civil LIBERTY, in the U.S. of AMERICA.

Concluding a Treaty with the Indians Edward Hicks painted *Penn's Treaty with the Indians* in the nineteenth century. It is a romanticized version of the Treaty of Shackamaxon by which the Lenape chiefs ceded the site of Philadelphia to Penn. The treaty was actually made in 1682, but Hicks was correct in implying that the Lenape held Penn in high regard for his fair treatment of them. What evidence of Quaker pacifism do you find in this painting? *(1980.62.11 [2796]/PA Gift of Edgar William and Bernice Chrysler Garbisch, © 2000 Board of Trustees, National Gallery of Art, Washington, D.C.)*

religions and national backgrounds, offering them peaceful coexistence. His government would neither claim authority over citizens' consciences nor demand military service of them.

Quakers began streaming into Pennsylvania in 1682, quickly absorbing earlier settlers. They participated in the government by electing representatives who initiated laws. Primarily farmers, they avidly acquired land, which Penn sold at reasonable rates. Unlike other colonizers, the Quakers practiced pacifism, holding the ethic of love and nonresistance embodied in the Sermon on the Mount as literally binding on them.

Even before arriving, Penn laid the foundation for peaceful relations with the Delaware tribe inhabiting his colony. "The king of the Country where I live, hath given me a great Province," he wrote to the Delaware chiefs, "but I desire to enjoy it with your Love and Consent, that we may always live together as Neighbors and friends." In this single statement Penn dissociated himself from the entire history of European colonization in the New World and from the widely held negative view of Native Americans. Recognizing them as the rightful owners of the land included in his grant, Penn pledged not to sell one acre until he had first purchased it from local chiefs. He also promised to regulate strictly the Indian trade and to ban alcohol sales.

The Quaker accomplishment is sometimes disparaged with the claim that there was little competition for land in eastern Pennsylvania between the natives and the newcomers. However, a comparison between Pennsylvania and South Carolina, both established after 1660, shows the power of pacifism. A quarter century after initial settlement, Pennsylvania had a population of about 20,000 whites. Penn's peaceful policy had so impressed Native American tribes that Indian refugees began migrating into Pennsylvania from all sides. During the same 25 years, South Carolina had grown to only about 4,000 whites, while becoming a cauldron of violence.

As long as the Quaker philosophy of pacifism and friendly relations with the local Native Americans held sway, interracial relations in the Delaware River valley contrasted sharply with those in other parts of North America. Ironically, the Quaker policies attracted thousands of land-hungry immigrants to the colony (especially in the eighteenth century) whose disdain for Native Americans undermined Quaker trust and friendship. Driven from their homelands by hunger and war, Germans and Scots–Irish flooded in, swelling the population to 31,000 by 1720. Neither shared Quaker idealism about racial harmony. They pressed inland and, sometimes encouraged by the land agents of Penn's heirs, encroached on the lands of the local tribes. By the mid-eighteenth century, white immigrants were spilling blood with the natives who had also sought sanctuary in Pennsylvania.

Building the Peaceable Kingdom

Although Pennsylvania came closer to matching its founder's goals than any other European colony, Penn's dreams never completely materialized. Unconvinced that they should settle in compact villages, which Penn believed necessary for his "holy experiment," settlers instead created open country networks without any particular centers or boundaries.

Still, because Quaker farmers prized family life and immigrated almost entirely in kinship groups, a sense of common endeavor persisted. This helped them maintain their distinctive identity. So did other practices such as allowing marriage only within their society, carefully providing land for their offspring, and guarding against too great a population increase (which would cause too rapid a division of farms) by limiting the size of their families.

Settled by religiously dedicated farming families, Pennsylvania boomed. Its countryside became a rich grainland. By 1700, the port capital of Philadelphia overtook New York City in population, and a half century later, it was the largest city in the colonies, bustling with artisans, mariners, merchants, and professionals.

The Limits of Perfectionism

Despite commercial success and peace with Native Americans, not all was harmonious in early Pennsylvania. Politics were often turbulent, in part because of Pennsylvania's weak leadership. Penn was a much-loved proprietor, but he returned to England in 1684, revisiting his colony again only briefly in 1700. This left a leadership vacuum.

A more important cause of disunity resided in the Quaker attitude toward authority. In England, balking at authority was almost a daily part of Quaker life. But in Pennsylvania, the absence of persecution eliminated a crucial binding element from Quaker society. The factionalism that developed among them demonstrated that people never unify so well as when under attack. Rather than looking inward and banding together, they looked outward to an environment filled with opportunity. Their squabbling filled Penn with dismay.

Meanwhile, Quaker industriousness and frugality helped produce great material success. After a generation, social radicalism and religious evangelicalism began to fade. As in other colonies, settlers discovered the door to prosperity wide open, and in they surged. Pennsylvania, it is said, was the first community since the Roman Empire to allow people of different national origins and religious persuasions to live together under the same government on terms of near equality. Their relations may not always have been friendly, but few attempts were made to discriminate against dissenting groups. Pennsylvanians thereby laid the foundations for the pluralism that was to become the hallmark of American society.

NEW SPAIN'S NORTHERN FRONTIER

Spain's outposts in Florida and New Mexico, preceding all English settlements on the eastern seaboard, fell into disarray between 1680 and the early eighteenth century just as the English colonies were sinking deep roots. Trying to secure a vast northern frontier with only small numbers of settlers, the Spanish relied on forced Native American labor. This reliance proved to be their undoing in Florida and New Mexico.

Popé's Revolt

During the 1670s, when the Franciscans developed a new zeal to root out traditional Native American religious ceremonies, the Pueblo people turned on the Spanish intruders. In years of harsh rule, the Spanish had extracted tribute labor from the Pueblo, who at the same time suffered the ravaging effects of European diseases. Both of these contributed to Pueblo alienation, but an assault on their religion pushed the Pueblo to the edge. Launching a campaign to restrict native religious ceremonies in the 1670s, the Spanish friars seized Pueblo kivas (underground ceremonial religious chambers), forbade native dances, and destroyed priestly Indian masks and prayer sticks. In August 1680, Popé, a medicine man, responded by leading about two dozen Pueblo villages scattered over several hundred miles to rise up in fury. They burned Spanish ranches and government

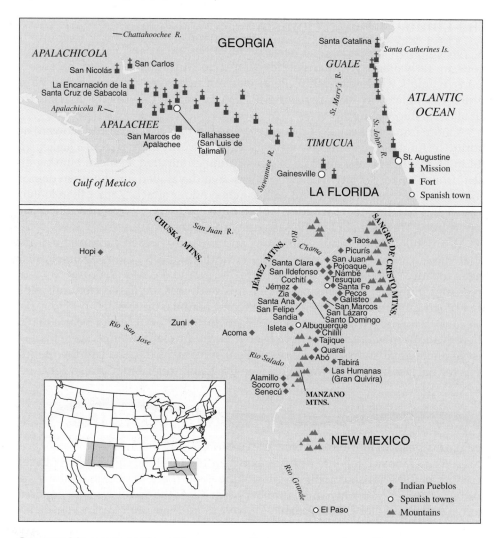

SPANISH MISSIONS IN NEW MEXICO AND FLORIDA IN THE LATE SEVENTEENTH CENTURY The extensive Spanish missionary activity in Florida and New Mexico had no English parallel.

buildings, systematically destroyed churches, lay waste to fields, and killed half of the friars.

Spanish settlers, soldiers, and friars streamed back to El Paso, abandoning their northern frontier in the Southwest for more than a decade. Only in 1694 did a new Spanish governor, the intrepid Diego de Vargas, regain Santa Fe and gradually subdue most of the Pueblo. Learning from Popé's rebellion, the Spanish declared a cultural truce, easing their demands for labor tribute and tolerating certain Pueblo rituals in return for nominal acceptance of Christianity. Periodic tension and animosity continued, but the Pueblo came to terms with the Spanish because of their need for defense against their old enemies, the Navajo, Ute, and Apache.

Decline of Florida's Missions

Franciscan missions had firmed up New Spain's grip of the southeast corner of North America. Yet few Spanish settlers could be persuaded to colonize Florida. In addition, the Florida Indians and their Franciscan spiritual shepherds were devastated by disease. English settlers in neighboring South Carolina were eager to use Native American allies to attack the Spanish Indian villages and sell the captives into slavery. The attacks of Carolinians in the early 1680s destroyed a number of Spanish missions. When England and Spain went to war in 1701—called Queen Anne's War in the colonies—the Carolinians attacked Florida. The Spanish mission frontier was devastated, and only St. Augustine remained as a Spanish stronghold. Unlike in New Mexico, no Spanish reconquest ensued. From this time onward, English and French traders, offering more attractive trade goods, would have the main influence over Florida Indians.

AN ERA OF INSTABILITY

A dozen years after King Philip's War in New England and Bacon's Rebellion in Virginia, a series of insurrections and a searing witchcraft incident convulsed colonial society. The Revolution of 1688 triggered rebellions and was known thereafter to English Protestants as the Glorious Revolution since it ended forever the notion that kings ruled by "divine right." Marking the last serious Catholic challenge to Protestant supremacy, it also signified a struggle for social and political dominance in the expanding colonies, as did the Salem witchcraft trials in Massachusetts.

Organizing the Empire

From the beginning of colonization, the English assumed that overseas settlements existed to promote the national interest at home. Mercantilist theory held that colonies served as outlets for English manufactured goods, provided foodstuffs and raw materials, stimulated trade (and hence promoted a larger merchant navy), and filled royal coffers by exporting commodities such as sugar and tobacco on which duties were paid. In return, colonists received English military protection and guaranteed markets.

Beginning with small steps in 1621, England slowly began to intervene in the colonies. Not until 1651, when the colonists traded freely with the commercially aggressive Dutch, did Parliament consider regulating colonial affairs. It passed a navigation act requiring that English or colonial ships carry all goods entering England, Ireland, and the colonies, no matter where those goods originated. These first steps toward a regulated empire were also the first moves to place England's power behind national economic development.

In 1660, after the monarchy was restored, Parliament passed a more comprehensive navigation act that listed colonial products (tobacco, sugar, indigo, dyewoods, and cotton) that could be shipped only to England or other English colonies. Like its predecessor, the act took dead aim at Holland's domination of Atlantic commerce, while increasing England's revenues by imposing duties on the articles. Later navigation acts added other enumerated articles. Regulation bore lightly on the colonists because the laws lacked enforcement.

After 1675, international competition and war led England to impose greater imperial control. That year marked the establishment of the Lords of Trade, a committee of the king's privy council empowered to make and enforce decisions regulating the colonies. Their chief aim was to create more uniform governments that would do the Crown's will. Although movement toward imperial centralization often sputtered, the trend was unmistakable, especially to colonists who felt the sting of royal customs agents sent to enforce the navigation acts. England was becoming the shipper of the world, and its state-regulated policy of economic nationalism was essential to achieving commercial greatness.

The Glorious Revolution in North America

When Charles II died in 1685, his brother, the duke of York, became King James II. This set in motion a chain of events that nearly led to civil war. Like Charles, James II professed the Catholic faith. Charles II, however, had disclosed this only on his deathbed, while the new king's faith was already well-known when he assumed the throne. Protestant England recoiled when James issued the Declaration of Indulgence, granting liberty of worship to all, appointed Catholics to high government posts, and demanded that Oxford and Cambridge open their doors to Catholic students. In 1687, the king dismissed a resistant Parliament. When his wife, supposedly too old for childbearing, bore a son in 1688, a Catholic succession loomed.

DOCUMENT

English Bill of Rights (1689)

Convinced that James aimed at absolute power, Protestant leaders in 1688 invited a Dutch prince, William of Orange, to seize the throne with his wife, Mary, who was James's Protestant daughter. James abdicated rather than fight. It was a bloodless victory for Protestantism, for parliamentary power and the limitation of kingly prerogatives, and for the merchants and gentry of England.

The response of New Englanders to these events stemmed from their previous experience with royal authority and their fear of "papists." In 1676, New England had become a prime target for efforts to reorganize the empire and crack down on smuggling. Charles II annulled the Massachusetts charter in 1684, and two years later James II appointed Sir Edmund Andros, a crusty professional soldier and former governor of New York, to rule over the newly created Dominion of New England. Soon the Dominion gathered under one government all the English colonies from Maine to New Jersey. Puritans now had to swallow the bitter fact that they were subjects of London bureaucrats who cared more about shaping a disciplined empire than about New England's special religious vision.

At first, New Englanders accepted Andros, though coolly. But he soon earned their hatred by imposing taxes without legislative consent, ending trial by jury, abolishing the General Court of Massachusetts (which had met annually since 1630), muzzling Boston's town meeting, and questioning land titles. He also converted a Boston Puritan meetinghouse into an Anglican chapel, held services there on Christmas Day—a gesture that to Puritans stank of popery—and insisted on religious toleration.

When news reached Boston in April 1689 that William of Orange had landed in England, Bostonians streamed into the streets. They imprisoned Andros and overwhelmed the fort in Boston harbor, which held most of the governor's small contingent of red-coated royal troops. Boston's ministers, along with merchants and former magistrates, led the rebellion. For three years, an interim government ruled Massachusetts while the Bay colonists awaited a new charter and a new royal governor.

Although Bostonians had dramatically rejected royal authority and the "bloody Devotees of Rome," no internal revolution occurred. However, growing social stratification and the emergence of a political elite caused some citizens to argue that men of modest means but common sense might better be trusted with power. "Anarchy" was the word chosen by Samuel Willard, a Boston minister, to tar the popular spirit unloosed in Boston in the aftermath of Andros's ouster.

In New York, the Glorious Revolution was similarly bloodless at first but far more disruptive. Royal government melted away on news of James's abdication. Displacing the governor's "popishly affected dogs and rogues," German-born militia captain Jacob Leisler established an interim government and ruled with an elected Committee of Safety for 13 months until a governor appointed by King William arrived.

Leisler's government enjoyed popularity among small landowners and urban laboring people who had resented the English seizing their colony in 1664 and crowding them out of the society they had built. Most of the upper echelon, however, had adjusted to English rule and many incoming English merchants had married into Dutch families. These New Yorkers detested Leisler as an upstart—a common foot soldier who had married a wealthy widow.

The Glorious Revolution ignited this smoldering social conflict. Leisler shared Dutch hostility toward New York's English elite, and his sympathy for the common people, mostly Dutch, earned him the hatred of the city's oligarchy. Leisler freed imprisoned debtors, planned a town-meeting system of government for New York City, and replaced merchants with artisans in important offices. By the autumn of 1689, Leislerian mobs were attacking the property of some of New York's wealthiest merchants. Two merchants, refusing to recognize Leisler's authority, were jailed.

Leisler's opponents were horrified at the power of the "rabble." They believed that ordinary people had no right to rebel against authority or to exercise political power. When a new English governor arrived in 1691, the anti-Leislerians embraced him and charged Leisler and seven of his assistants with treason for assuming the government without royal instructions.

In the ensuing trial, Leisler and Jacob Milbourne, his son-in-law and chief lieutenant, were convicted of treason by an all-English jury and hanged. Leisler's popularity among the artisans of the city was evident when his wealthy opponents could find no carpenter in the city who would make a ladder for the scaffold. After his execution, peace gradually returned to New York, but for years provincial and city politics reflected the deep rift between Leislerians and anti-Leislerians.

The Glorious Revolution also focused dissatisfactions in several southern colonies. Because a Catholic proprietor ruled Maryland, the Protestant majority seized power in July 1689 on word of the Glorious Revolution, using it for their own purposes. They vowed to cleanse Maryland of popery and to reform a corrupt customs service, cut taxes and fees, and extend the rights of the representative assembly. Militant Protestants held power until the arrival of Maryland's first royal governor in 1692.

In neighboring Virginia, the wounds of Bacon's Rebellion were still healing when word of the Glorious Revolution arrived. Virginia had a Catholic governor and a number of Catholic officials, fostering rumors of a Catholic plot. News of the revolution in England led a group of planters, suffering a prolonged drop in tobacco prices, to try to overthrow the governor, but the governor's council defended itself, partly by removing Catholics from positions of authority.

The Glorious Revolution brought lasting political changes to several colonies. The Dominion of New England collapsed. Connecticut and Rhode Island regained the right to elect their governors, but Massachusetts and New Hampshire became royal colonies with governors appointed by the king. In Massachusetts, a new royal charter in 1691 eliminated Church membership as a voting requirement. The Maryland proprietorship was abolished (to be restored in 1715 when the Calverts became Protestant), and Catholics were barred from office. Everywhere Protestant Englishmen celebrated their liberties.

The Social Basis of Politics

The colonial insurrections associated with the Glorious Revolution revealed social and political tensions that accompanied the transplanting of English society to the North American wilderness. Colonial societies were fluid, unruly, and competitive, lacking the stable political systems and leadership class thought necessary for social order.

The emerging colonial elite tried to foster stability by upholding a stratified Old World–style society where children were subordinate to parents, women to men, servants to masters, and the poor to the rich. Puritans did not file into church on Sundays and occupy the pews randomly; seats were assigned according to customary yardsticks of respectability: age, parentage, social position, wealth, and occupation. Even in fluid Virginia, lower-class people were hauled before courts for horse racing because this was a sport legally reserved for men of social distinction.

These social distinctions proved difficult to maintain. Regardless of previous rank, settlers rubbed elbows so frequently and faced such raw conditions together that those without pedigrees often saw little reason to defer to men of superior rank. "In Virginia," explained John Smith, "a plain soldier that can use a pickaxe and spade is better than five knights." Colonists everywhere gave respect not to those who claimed it by birth but to those who earned it by deed. A colonial elite gradually formed, but it had no basis, as in Europe, in legally defined and hereditary social rank. Planters and merchants, accumulating large estates, aped the

English gentry. Yet their place was rarely secure as new competitors nipped at their heels.

Amid such social flux, the elite never commanded general allegiance to the ideal of a fixed social structure. Ambitious men on the rise such as Nathaniel Bacon and Jacob Leisler, and their discontented followers, rose up against the constituted authorities, which they almost certainly would not have dared to do in their homelands. When they gained power during the Glorious Revolution, in every case only briefly, the leaders of these uprisings linked themselves with a tradition of English struggle against tyranny and oligarchical power. They vowed to make government more responsive to the ordinary people, who composed most of their societies.

Witchcraft in Salem

The ordinary people in the colonies, for whom Bacon and Leisler tried to speak, could sometimes be misled, as the tragic events of the Salem witch hunts demonstrated. In Massachusetts, deposing Governor Andros left the colony in political limbo for three years, and this allowed what might have been a brief outbreak of witchcraft in the little community of Salem to escalate into a bitter and bloody battle. The provincial government, caught in transition, reacted only belatedly.

On a winter's day in 1692, 9-year-old Betty Parris and her 11-year-old cousin Abigail Williams began to play at magic in the kitchen of a small house in Salem Village, Massachusetts. They enlisted the aid of Tituba, the slave of Betty's father, Samuel Parris, the minister of the small community. Tituba told voodoo tales from her Caribbean past and baked "witch cakes." The girls soon became seized with fits and began making wild gestures and speeches. Soon other young girls in the village were behaving strangely. Village elders extracted confessions that Tituba and two other women, both social outcasts, were tormenting them.

A Further Account of the Tryals of the New England Witches

What began as young girls' play turned into a ghastly rending of a farm community capped by the deaths of 20 villagers accused of witchcraft. In the seventeenth century, people still took literally the biblical injunction, "Thou shalt not suffer a witch to live." For centuries throughout western Europe, people had believed that witches followed Satan's bidding and did evil to anyone he designated. Communities accused and sentenced women to death for witchcraft far more often than men. In Massachusetts, more than 100 people, mostly older women, had been accused of witchcraft before 1692, and more than a dozen had been hanged.

In Salem, the initial accusations against three older women quickly multiplied. Within weeks, dozens had been charged, including several prominent figures. Formal prosecution of the accused witches could not proceed because neither the new royal charter of 1691 nor the royal governor to rule the colony had yet arrived. For three months, while charges spread, local authorities could only jail the accused without trial. When Governor William Phips arrived from England in May 1692, he ordered a special court to try the accused. By then, events had careened out of control.

All through the summer, the court listened to testimony. By September it had condemned about two dozen villagers. The authorities hanged 19 of them on

TIMELINE

1607	Jamestown settled
1616–1621	Native American population in New England decimated by European diseases
1619	First Africans arrive in Jamestown
1620	Pilgrims land at Plymouth
1622	Powhatan tribes attack Virginia settlements
1624	Dutch colonize mouth of Hudson River
1630	Puritan immigration to Massachusetts Bay
1632	Maryland grant to Lord Baltimore (George Calvert)
1636	Anne Hutchinson exiled to Rhode Island
1637	New England wages war against the Pequot people
1642–1649	English civil war ends great migration to New England
1650–1670	Judicial and legislative decisions in Chesapeake colonies solidify racial lines
1651	Parliament passes first navigation act
1660	Restoration of King Charles II in England
1663	Carolina charter granted to eight proprietors
1664	English capture New Netherland and rename it New York
	Royal grant of the Jersey lands to proprietors
1673–1685	French expand into Mississippi valley
1675–1677	King Philip's War in New England
1676	Bacon's Rebellion in Virginia
1680	Popé's revolt in New Mexico
1681	William Penn receives Pennsylvania grant
1688	Glorious Revolution in England, followed by accession of William and Mary
1689	Overthrow of Governor Andros in New England
	Leisler's Rebellion in New York
1690s	Transition from white indentured servitude to black slave labor begins in Chesapeake region
1692	Witchcraft hysteria in Salem

DOCUMENT

The Examination and Confession of Ann Foster at Salem (1692)

barren "Witches Hill" outside the town and crushed 80-year-old Giles Corey to death under heavy stones. The trials rolled on into 1693, but by then, colonial leaders, including many of the clergy, recognized that a feverish fear of one's neighbors, rather than witchcraft itself, had possessed Salem Village.

Many factors contributed to the hysteria. Among them were generational differences between older Puritan colonists and the sometimes less

religiously motivated younger generation, old family animosities, population growth and pressures on the available farmland, and tensions between
agricultural Salem Village and the nearby commercial center called Salem
Town. A new Indian war on the Massachusetts–Maine frontier caused
near-hysteria. Probably nobody will ever fully understand the exact mingling of causes, but the fact that most of the individuals charged with
witchcraft were women underscores the relatively weak position of women in Puritan society. The relentless spread of witchcraft accusations suggests the anxiety
of this tumultuous era of war, economic disruption, and political tension, and the
erosion of the early generation's utopian vision.

The Colonies to
1740

Conclusion

The Achievement of New Societies

Nearly 200,000 immigrants who had left their European homelands reached
North America in the seventeenth century. Coming from a variety of social backgrounds and spurred by different motives, they represented the rootstock of distinctive societies that matured in the colonies of England, France, Holland, and
Spain. For three generations, northern North America served as a social labora-
tory for religious and social visionaries, political theorists, fortune seekers, social
outcasts, and, most of all, ordinary men and women seeking a better life than they
had known in Europe.

By the end of the seventeenth century, 12 English colonies on the eastern edge
of North America (and several others in the West Indies) had secured footholds in
the hemisphere and erected the basic scaffolding of colonial life. So had Spanish
and French colonies lying north, south, and west of the English. The coastal Native American tribes were reeling from disease and a series of wars that secured
the English colonists' land base along 1,000 miles of coastal plain. Though never
controlling the powerful tribes of the interior, the colonists had established a profitable trade with them. English settlers had overcome a scarcity of labor by copy-
ing the other European colonists, who had linked the west coast of Africa to the
New World through the ghastly trade in human flesh. Finally, the English
colonists had engaged in insurrections against what they viewed as arbitrary and
tainted governments imposed by England.

The embryo of British America carried into the eighteenth century contained
peculiarly mixed features. Disease, stunted family life, and the harsh work regi-
men imposed by the planters who commanded the labor of the vast majority
ended the dreams of most who came to the southern colonies. Yet population
inched upward, and the bone and sinew of a workable economy formed. In the
northern colonies, to which the fewest immigrants came, life was more secure. Organized around family and community, favored by a healthier climate, and motivated by religion and social vision, the Puritan and Quaker societies thrived.

Still physically isolated from Europe, the colonists developed a large measure
of self-reliance. Slowly, they began to identify themselves as the permanent inhabitants of a new land rather than as transplanted English, Dutch, or Scots–Irish.

Viewing land and labor as the indispensable elements of a fruitful economy, they learned to exploit without apologies the land of one dark-skinned people and the labor of another. Yet even as they attained a precarious mastery in a triracial society, they were being culturally affected by the very people to whose land and labor they laid claim. Although utopian visions of life in North America still preoccupied some, most colonists had awakened to the reality that life in the New World was a mixture of unpredictable opportunity and sudden turbulence, unprecedented freedom and debilitating wars, racial intermingling and racial separation. It was a New World in much more than a geographic sense, for the people of three cultures who now inhabited it had remade it. And, while doing so, people like Anthony and Mary Johnson (whom we met at the beginning of the chapter) were remaking themselves.

Questions for Review and Reflection

1. What factors most shaped the development of the colonial Chesapeake region in the seventeenth century?

2. Early Massachusetts was organized around shared religious goals, yet it was riven by strife. How do you explain the tensions within this colony?

3. Seventeenth-century North America included a wide variety of colonial endeavors. What were the main regional divisions and distinguishing features of each area?

4. What were the causes and consequences of King Philip's War and Bacon's Rebellion? In what ways were the two conflicts similar or different?

5. What were the effects of the Glorious Revolution on the colonies and the empire?

6. Despite differences between colonial regions, it appears that prejudicial attitudes toward Africans and Native Americans were a common thread running through all colonial societies. Do you agree, and if so, do you see any exceptions to this rule?

Discovering U.S. History Online

Jamestown Rediscovery www.apva.org
This site has excellent material on the archaeological excavation of Jamestown.

Divining America: Religion and the National Culture www.nhc.rtp.nc.us/tserve/eighteen/ekeyinfo/puritan.htm
An illustrated essay on Puritan ideas and how they intersected with American history.

The People of Colonial Albany www.nysm.nysed.gov/albany/index.html
This site gives detailed information about the settlers of Albany using essays, biographical information, portraits, maps, architecture, and more. Some information is presented about the pre-European native settlers of the area.

William Penn xroads.virginia.edu/~CAP/PENN/pnhome.html
William Penn was an extraordinary colonial figure, and this site is a good introduction to the man and some of his achievements.

The Golden Crescent: Crossroads of Florida and Georgia www.cr.nps.gov/goldcres/
This site presents the cultural history and prehistory of the European, African, and native inhabitants of the region.

New Spain: The Frontiers of Faith www.humanities-interactive.org/newspain/
An illustrated exhibit of documents from the Thomas Gilcrease Institute pertaining to the Spanish colonies in the New World.

Salem Witchcraft Trials, 1692 www.law.umkc.edu/faculty/projects/ftrials/salem/salem.htm
Images and primary documents comprise this account of the events in Salem.

Fiction and Film

Nathaniel Hawthorne's *The Scarlet Letter* (1850) is an American classic on Puritan love, infidelity, and morality; Hollywood's version, by the same title, features Demi Moore and Gary Oldman (1995). John Barth's *The Sotweed Factor* (1960) is a rollicking and ribald novel about indentured servitude, tobacco planting, love, and brutishness in seventeenth-century Maryland. *Black Robe* (1991), a gripping film made in Canada, evokes all the cruelty of the contact between early French Jesuit missionaries and the Iroquois people. The film is based on Brian Manning's novel of the same name. Werner Herzog's *Aguirre: The Wrath of God* (1972) is a surreal film about the early Spanish conquest of much of the Americas in the sixteenth century. A much milder film on early Indian–European contact is *Squanto: A Warrior's Tale* (1994), featuring Adam Beach. *Three Sovereigns for Sarah* (1985), a PBS miniseries starring Vanessa Redgrave, stunningly dramatizes the Salem witchcraft trials. Arthur Miller's play *The Crucible* (1953), on the same topic, is as engaging today as it was decades ago when it played on stages around the country. A recent film version features Winona Ryder and Daniel Day Lewis (1996). Wayne Carlin, *The Wished For Country* (2002) is a compelling historical novel about the indentured servants, Africans, and Native Americans who met each other in early Maryland and how, from their intermingling, the triracial Wesort people emerged.

Recommended Reading

www.ablongman.com/nash
The Companion Website has a list of recommended readings about the European colonies in North America.

CHAPTER 4

The Maturing of Colonial Society

American Stories

A Struggling Farmer's Wife Finds True Religious Commitment

In 1758, 37-year-old Hannah Cook Heaton stood trial for her refusal to attend her local congregationalist church. A resident of North New Haven, Connecticut, Hannah was required by Connecticut law to attend Sunday worship services—a law derived from the belief that religious uniformity was a social good. Hannah did not object to churchgoing; in fact, she was a fervent Christian. She had been a member of Isaac Stiles's church—indeed, he had performed her marriage to Theophilus Heaton, Jr., in 1743. But later in that decade, after she had been caught up in the enthusiasm of the Great Awakening, a series of religious revivals that rocked New England in the 1740s, Hannah ceased to attend Sunday worship. Thereafter, finding that her minister's preaching and church admission policies left her cold and dissatisfied, Heaton quit the church, arguing that Stiles had never himself undergone conversion and was therefore a "blind guide" leading his flock astray.

Hannah's decision to leave the village church was prompted by the preaching of men she believed were imbued with the spirit. Hearing touring evangelists George Whitefield, James Davenport, and Gilbert Tennant sparked a profound conversion experience. As she later recorded in her diary, she "thought I see Jesus with the eyes of my soul." This religious transformation led her to join a small congregation headed by Benjamin Beach, a lay preacher. Uneducated and unlicensed, he was precisely the kind of man whom Harvard- and Yale-trained ministers regarded as a threat to well-ordered New England communities. Yet many like Hannah Heaton found him spiritually gifted, and so they separated themselves from the established church to meet regularly at Beach's home for worship and prayer.

Because she abandoned the established church for this community of believers, who called themselves Separatists, Hannah was pressured by both members of Stiles's church and local officials and then finally brought to trial. She remained defiant, telling the justice at her trial that "there was a day a-coming when justice would be done ... there is a dreadful day a-coming upon them that have no Christ." Declaring that Hannah "talked sass," the justice convicted her of breaking the law and fined her twelve shillings.

To Hannah's dismay and despite her efforts, her husband never shared her commitment to the dissenters. He remained a member of Stiles's church, urged Hannah to rejoin it, and, against Hannah's wishes, paid her fine in the trial of 1758. Resenting his wife's involvement with the

Separatists, he hid her spectacles so she could not read her Bible or write in her diary, threw her diary in the mud, and refused to provide her with a horse to ride to the Separatists' meetings. Hannah worried about his immortal soul, disheartened that even on his deathbed she could not persuade him to repent and seek after the Lord.

Hannah Cook Heaton was in many ways a typical colonial woman, married to a farmer and the mother of numerous children. Her life would be virtually unknown to us except that she kept a diary of her spiritual experiences, in which she revealed a life that was dramatically reshaped by the Great Awakening. Her identity as a Separatist was fundamental to her life, affecting her marriage and her intimate relationships. Her separatism also brought her briefly into public prominence, as one of the few members of her movement to be prosecuted in court in Connecticut in the 1750s. Her life suggests the significance of revivalism in the lives of many eighteenth-century colonists. Her religious convictions motivated her to defy various authorities in her life, including her husband, her minister, and the local magistrate.

The religious revivals that transformed Hannah Heaton's life were just one of the forces affecting colonial life during the eighteenth century. Between 1680 and 1750, a virtual population explosion occurred in the English colonies, swelling the number of settlers from 150,000 in 1680 to more than 1 million at midcentury. Such growth staggered English policymakers, who uneasily watched the population gap between England and its American colonies closing rapidly. A high marriage rate, large families, lower mortality than in Europe, and heavy immigration accounted for much of the population boom.

This chapter explains how population growth and economic development gradually transformed eighteenth-century British America. Three variations of colonial society emerged: the farming society of the North, the plantation society of the South, and the urban society of the seaboard commercial towns. Although they shared some important characteristics, each was distinct. Even within regions, diversity increased in the eighteenth century as incoming streams of immigrants, mostly from Germany, Ireland, France, and especially from Africa, added new pieces to the emerging American mosaic.

Until the late seventeenth century, the Spanish, French, and English settlements in North America were largely isolated from each other. But when a long period of war erupted in Europe between these colonizing nations, North America and the Caribbean became important theaters of international conflict that would reach a climax in the second half of the eighteenth century.

This chapter also explores the commercial orientation that spread from north to south, especially in the towns, as local economies matured and forged links with the Atlantic basin trade network. We will see how colonists such as Hannah Heaton experienced a deep-running religious awakening that established evangelical religion as a hallmark of American society. Connected to this democratization of religion was the changing exercise of political power. From increasingly powerful legislative assemblies and local instruments of governance emerged seasoned leaders, a tradition of local autonomy, and a widespread belief in a political ideology stressing the liberties that freeborn Englishmen should enjoy. In these ways, raw frontier settlements developed into mature provincial societies.

THE NORTH: A LAND OF FAMILY FARMS

Although New England strove to maintain its homogeneity by making non-English immigrants unwelcome, the mid-Atlantic colonies swarmed with waves of immigrants from the Rhineland and Ireland. About 90,000 Germans flocked in during the eighteenth century, many fleeing "God's three arrows": famine, war, and pestilence. They settled where promoters promised cheap and fertile land, low taxes, and freedom from military duty. Coming mostly in families, they turned much of the mid-Atlantic hinterland into a German-speaking region. Even more Protestant Scots–Irish arrived. Mostly poor farmers, they streamed into the same backcountry areas where Germans were settling, especially New York and Pennsylvania.

Northern Agricultural Society

In the mid-eighteenth-century northern colonies, especially New England, tight-knit farming families organized in communities of several thousand people dotted the landscape. New Englanders staked their future on a mixed economy. They cleared forests for timber used in barrels, ships, houses, and barns. They plumbed the offshore waters for fish that fed both local populations and the ballooning slave population of the West Indies. And they cultivated and grazed as much of the thin-soiled, rocky hills and bottomlands as they could recover from the forest.

The farmers of the middle colonies—Pennsylvania, Delaware, New Jersey, and New York—drove their wooden plows through much richer soils than New Englanders. They enjoyed the additional advantage of settling an area cleared by Native Americans who had relied more on agriculture than New England tribes. Thus favored, mid-Atlantic farm families produced modest surpluses of corn, wheat, beef, and pork. By the mid-eighteenth century, New York and Philadelphia ships were carrying these foodstuffs not only to the West Indies, always a primary market, but also to England, Spain, Portugal, and even New England, strengthening ties within the Atlantic basin.

In the North, the broad ownership of land distinguished farming society from every other agricultural region of the Western world. Although differences in circumstances and ability led gradually toward greater social stratification, in most communities, few were truly rich or abjectly poor. Except for indentured servants, most men lived to purchase or inherit a farm of at least 50 acres. With their family

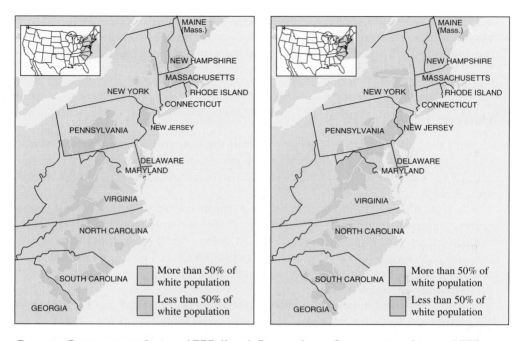

GERMAN SETTLEMENT AREAS, 1775 (*LEFT*) SCOTS–IRISH SETTLEMENT AREAS, 1775 (*RIGHT*) Most German and Scots–Irish immigrants in the 1700s were farmers, and they quickly moved into the interior, where land was cheapest and most available.

labor, they earned a decent existence and provided a small inheritance for each of their children. Settlers valued land highly, for freehold tenure ordinarily guaranteed both economic independence and political rights.

By the eighteenth century, with widespread property ownership, a rising population pressed against a limited land supply, especially in New England. Family farms could not be divided and subdivided indefinitely, for it took at least 50 acres to support a family. In Concord, Massachusetts, for example, the founders had worked farms averaging about 250 acres. A century later, in the 1730s, the average farm had shrunk by two-thirds, as farm owners struggled to provide an inheritance for the three or four sons that the average marriage produced.

Decreasing soil fertility compounded the problem. When land had been plentiful, farmers planted crops in the same field for three years and then let it lie fallow seven years or more until it regained its strength. On the smaller farms of the eighteenth century, farmers reduced fallowing to only a year or two, reducing crop yields and forcing farmers to plow marginal land or shift to livestock production.

The diminishing size and productivity of family farms drove many New Englanders to the frontier or out of the area. In Concord, one of every four adult males left town every decade from the 1740s on. In many towns, out-migration was even greater, with some drifting to New York and Pennsylvania, and others going to western Massachusetts, New Hampshire, Maine, and Nova Scotia. Still others sought opportunities as artisans in the coastal towns or took to the sea.

Northern farming was far less intense than in the South. The growing season was shorter, and cereal crops required incessant labor only during spring planting and autumn harvesting. This seasonal rhythm led many northern cultivators to fill out their calendars with work as clockmakers, shoemakers, carpenters, and weavers.

Unfree Labor

Though the shorter growing seasons curbed the demand for labor in the North, slaves and indentured servants still made up much of the incoming human tide after 1713. They became a regular part of the commerce linking Europe, Africa, and North America.

Despite official attempts to reduce the "tight packing" of indentured immigrants, shipboard conditions for both slaves and servants worsened in the eighteenth century. Crammed between decks in stifling air, they suffered from smallpox and fevers, rotten food, impure water, cold, and lice. The shipboard mortality rate of about 15 percent in the colonial era made this the most unhealthy of all times to seek American shores.

DOCUMENT

Virginia Law on
Indentured
Servitude (1705)

Most indentured servants, especially males, found the labor system harsh. Every servant's goal was to secure a foothold on the ladder of opportunity. However, many died before finishing their time; others won freedom only to toil for years as poor day laborers or tenant farmers. The chief beneficiaries of the system of bound white labor were the masters.

The number of enslaved Africans in the northern colonies grew in the eighteenth century, but not nearly as fast as the indentured servant population. Slaves made up less than 10 percent of the population in all northern colonies. Since in the North the typical slave labored alone or with only a few

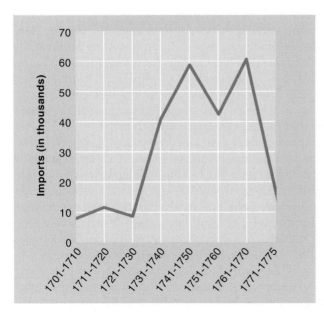

SLAVES IMPORTED TO NORTH AMERICA, 1701–1775 Overwhelmingly, Africans transported to the American colonies arrived from the 1730s to the 1770s. Rapid natural increase, as well as importation, swelled the African population to about 500,000 by the outbreak of the American Revolution. *(Source: R. C. Simmons, The American Colonies: From Settlement to Independence, 1976.)*

others while living in the same house as the master, slaves adapted to European ways much faster than in the South. Slavery was also less repressive in the North.

Northern slaves typically worked as artisans, farmhands, or personal servants. Slavery grew fastest in the northern ports. Artisans invested profitably in slaves; ship captains purchased them for maritime labor; and an emerging urban elite of merchants, lawyers, and landlords displayed its wealth with slave coachmen and personal servants. By the beginning of the eighteenth century, more than 40 percent of New York City households owned slaves. Even in Quaker Philadelphia, slaveholding increased sharply in the eighteenth century. Struggling white artisans resented slave workers for undercutting their wages, and the whites feared black arsonists and rebels. Yet high labor demand outweighed these reservations, and the advantage of purchasing lifelong servants for just two years' worth of a free white laborer's wages was obvious.

Phillis Wheatley

Changing Values

Boston weather on April 29, 1695, began warm and sunny, noted the devout merchant Samuel Sewall in his diary. But by afternoon, lightning and hailstones "as big as pistol and musket bullets" pummeled the town. Sewall dined that evening with Cotton Mather, New England's prominent clergyman. Mather wondered why "more ministers' houses than others proportionately had been smitten with lightning." The words were hardly out of his mouth before hailstones began to shatter the windows. Sewall and Mather fell to their knees in prayer "after this awful Providence." These two third-generation Massachusetts Puritans understood that God was angry with them as leaders of a people whose piety was giving way to worldliness. Massachusetts was becoming "sermon-proof," explained one dejected minister.

Throughout the North, the expansive environment and the Protestant emphasis on self-discipline and hard work were breeding qualities that would become hallmarks of American culture: ambitiousness, individualism, and materialism. One colonist remarked, "Every man expects one day or another to be upon a footing with his wealthiest neighbor." Commitment to religion, family, and community did not disappear, but fewer people saw daily existence just as a preparation for the afterlife. Land was not simply a source of livelihood, but a commodity to be bought and sold for profit.

A slender almanac, written by the twelfth child of a poor Boston candlemaker, captured the new outlook with wit and charm. Born in 1706, Benjamin Franklin climbed the ladder of success spectacularly. Running away from a harsh apprenticeship to an older brother when he was 16, he abandoned a declining Boston for a rising Philadelphia. By 23, he had learned the printer's trade and was publishing the *Pennsylvania Gazette*. Three years later, he began *Poor Richard's Almanack*, which, next to the Bible, was the most widely read book in the colonies. Franklin filled it with quips, adages, and homespun philosophy: "The sleeping fox gathers no poultry." "Lost time is never found again." Franklin caught the spirit of the rising secularism of the eighteenth century. He embodied the growing utilitarian doctrine that good is whatever is useful. For Franklin, the community was best served through individual self-improvement and accomplishment.

Women and the Family in the Northern Colonies

In 1662, Elnathan Chauncy, a Massachusetts schoolboy, copied into his writing book that the soul "consists of two portions, inferior and superior; the superior is masculine and eternal; the feminine inferior and mortal." Generations on both sides of the Atlantic had taught such ideas as part of a larger conception of God's design that assigned degrees of status and stations in life to all individuals. In that world, women were subordinate, taught from infancy to be modest, patient, and compliant. Regarded by men as weak of mind, they existed for and through men, subject first to their fathers and then to their husbands.

DOCUMENT

Church record of a marriage conflict, Brooklyn (1663)

European women usually accepted these narrowly circumscribed roles, and few openly complained that their work was generally limited to housewifery and midwifery. Women were excluded from the early public schools, laws transferred to their husbands any property or income they brought into a marriage, they had no legal voice in politics, and (except in Quaker meetinghouses) they could not speak or participate in their churches. In a society in which producing legal heirs was the means of transmitting property, parental guidance prevailed over love in choosing a husband. Once wed, women expected to remain so until death, for they could rarely obtain a divorce.

In the colonies, women's lives changed in modest ways. One in 10 European women did not marry. Colonial men outnumbered women for the first century, so a spinster was almost unheard of, and widows remarried with astounding speed. *Woman* and *wife* thus became nearly synonymous. Young colonial women slowly gained the right of consenting to a marriage partner—a right that came by default to the thousands of female indentured servants who completed their labor contracts and had no parents within 3,000 miles to dictate to them. Another change concerned property rights. As in England, single women and widows in the colonies could make contracts, hold and convey property, represent themselves in court, and conduct business. Colonial legislatures and courts, however, gave wives more control over property brought into marriage or left at their husband's death. They also enjoyed broader rights to act for and with their husbands in business transactions.

Although colonial society did not encourage or reward female individuality, women worked alongside their husbands in competent and complementary ways. Women had limited career choices and rights but broad responsibilities. The work spaces and daily routines of husband and wife overlapped and intersected far more than today. "Deputy husbands" and "yoke mates" were revealing terms used by New Englanders to describe eighteenth-century wives.

Despite conventional talk of inferiority, women within their families and neighborhoods nevertheless shaped the world around them. Older women molded the behavior of young women, aided the needy, and subtly affected menfolk, who held formal authority. Women outnumbered men in church life and, like Hannah Heaton, worked within their families to promote religion in outlying areas, to seat and unseat ministers, and to influence morals. Periodically, they appeared as visionaries and mystics.

Until the late eighteenth century, the "obstetrick art" was almost entirely in their hands. Midwives counseled pregnant women, delivered babies, supervised postpartum recovery, and participated in infant baptism and burial ceremonies. Because colonial women were pregnant or nursing infants for about half the years between the ages 20 and 40 and because childbirth was dangerous, the circle of female friends and relatives attending childbirth created strong networks of mutual assistance.

In her role as wife and mother, the eighteenth-century northern woman differed somewhat from her English counterpart. Whereas English women married in their mid-twenties, American women typically took husbands a few years earlier, increasing their childbearing years. Hence, the average colonial family included five children (two others typically died in infancy), whereas the English family had fewer than three.

Northern child-rearing patterns varied widely. In the seventeenth century, stern fathers dominated Puritan family life, and few were reluctant to punish unruly children, believing that breaking the young child's will created a pious and submissive personality. Quaker mothers, however, tended to use love to mold their children. Puritan parents usually arranged their children's marriages but allowed them the right to veto. Young Quaker men and women made their own matches, subject to parental veto. These differences aside, all children played roles in contributing to the family economy.

The father-dominated family of New England gradually declined in the eighteenth century, replaced by the mother-centered family, in which affectionate parents encouraged self-expression and independence in their children. This "modern" approach, on the rise in Europe as well, brought the colonists closer to the methods of parenthood found among the coastal Native Americans, who initially had been disparaged for their lax approach to rearing their young.

DOCUMENT

Benjamin Wadsworth, from *A Well-Ordered Family* (1712)

Ecological Transformation

Wherever Europeans settled in the Americas, they brought with them animals, plant life, diseases, and ways of viewing the natural resources—all with enormous consequences. In England's North American colonies, the rapid increase of settlers after 1715 affected the environment profoundly. First, the demand for wood—for building and heating houses, for producing the charcoal necessary for ironmaking, for shipbuilding and barrelmaking—swiftly depleted coastal forests. Rapid and often wasteful harvesting of the forests had many ill effects. Without the forest canopy, the winters became colder and the summers hotter. Early-melting snow caused watersheds to empty faster, and, in turn, triggered soil erosion and drought.

A second ecological transformation occurred when animals brought by Europeans began to replace animals already in North America. Multiplying rapidly in a favorable environment, pigs and cattle "swarm like vermin upon the earth," reported one Virginia account as early as 1700. In an environment generally free of animal predators, the grazing animals devoured the tall grasses and most palatable plant species. With depleted ground cover, new unwelcome plant species took hold—stinging nettles, dandelions, and nightshade. Native grasses and shrubs disappeared so quickly that the European livestock began to die for lack of grazing land.

Meanwhile, native fur-bearing animals—beaver, deer, bear, wolf, raccoon, and marten—rapidly became extinct in the areas of settlement. Prizing their skins or hating them as predators of domesticated animals, Native Americans and colonists hunted these species relentlessly. One broken link in the ecological chain affected others. For example, the dams and ponds of the beaver, which had been breeding grounds for many species of wild ducks, soon were drained and converted to meadows for cattle. Animals prized for dinner-table fare also quickly reached extinction along the East Coast. Wild turkeys were a rarity in Massachusetts by the 1670s. Deer disappeared by the early 1700s in settled areas.

All these environmental changes were linked not only to the numbers of Europeans arriving in North America but also to their ways of thinking about nature. Transplanted Europeans saw only the possibility of raising valuable crops as if the ecosystem were composed of unconnected elements, each ripe for exploitation. Land, lumber, fish, and fur-bearing animals could be converted into sources of cash that would buy imported commodities that improved one's material con-

Colonial Products

dition. Coming from homelands where land was scarce, the settlers viewed their ability to reap nature's abundance in North America as proof of their success. Yet the "rage for commerce" and for an improved life produced wasteful practices on farms and in forests and fisheries. "The grain fields, the meadows, the forests, the cattle, etc.," wrote a Swedish visitor in the 1750s, "are treated with equal carelessness." Once the native peoples had been driven from the land, and seeing no limits to the land that was available, the colonists embarked on ecologically destructive practices that over many generations profoundly altered the natural world of North America.

THE PLANTATION SOUTH

DOCUMENT

James Oglethorpe, "Establishing the Colony of Georgia" (1733)

Between 1680 and 1750, the southern white tidewater settlements changed from a frontier society with high immigration, a surplus of males, and an unstable social organization to a settled society composed mostly of native-born families. But while a mature southern culture took form from the ocean to the piedmont, after 1715 Scots–Irish and German immigrants flooded into the backcountry of Virginia, the Carolinas, and the new colony of Georgia. The fast-growing slave population accounted for much more of the population growth than in the North. Virginia, with a population of nearly 340,000 by 1760, remained by far the largest colony in North America.

The Tobacco Coast

Rapidly expanding tobacco production in seventeenth-century Virginia and Maryland sent exports to 25 million pounds annually during the 1680s. Two decades of war then drove up transportation costs, depressing the tobacco market until about 1715.

During this period the Upper South underwent a profound social transformation. First, African slaves replaced European indentured servants so rapidly that by 1730 the unfree labor force was overwhelmingly black. Second, planters responded to the depressed tobacco market by diversifying their crops. They shifted some tobacco fields to grain, hemp, and flax; increased their herds of cattle and swine; and became more self-sufficient by developing local industries to produce iron, leather, and textiles. By the 1720s, when a profitable tobacco trade with France created a new period of prosperity, the economy was much more diverse and resilient. Third, the population structure changed rapidly. African slaves grew from about 7 percent to more than 40 percent of the region's population between 1690 and 1750, and the drastic imbalance between white men and women disappeared. Families rather than single men now predominated. The earlier frontier society of white immigrants, mostly living short, unrewarding lives as indentured servants, grew into an eighteenth-century plantation society of native-born freeholder families.

Notwithstanding the influx of Africans, slave owning was far from universal. As late as 1750, a majority of families owned no slaves at all. Not more than one-tenth of slaveholders held more than 20 slaves. Nonetheless, the common goal was the large plantation where slaves made the earth yield up profits to support an aristocratic life for their masters.

The Chesapeake planters who acquired the best land and accumulated enough capital to invest heavily in slaves created a gentry lifestyle that set them apart from ordinary farmers. By the eighteenth century, the development of the northern colonies had produced prosperous farmers worth several thousand pounds. But such wealth paled alongside the estates of men who counted their slaves by the hundreds, their acres by the thousands, and their fortunes by the tens of thousands of pounds.

Ritual display of wealth marked southern gentry life. Racing thoroughbred horses and gambling on them recklessly became common sport for young gentlemen, who had often been educated in England. Planters built stately brick Georgian mansions, filled with imported furniture. The emerging Chesapeake planter elite controlled the county courts, officered the local militia, ruled the parish vestries of the Anglican Church, made law in their legislative assemblies, and passed to their sons the mantle of political and social leadership.

For all their airs, these southern squires were essentially agrarian businessmen. They spent their days haggling over credit, land, slaves, and tenant leases; scheduling planting and harvesting; conferring with overseers; and disciplining slaves. Tobacco cultivation (unlike that of wheat and corn) claimed the planter's year-round attention. A planter's reputation rested on the quality of his crop.

Planters' wives also shouldered many responsibilities. They superintended cloth production and the processing and preparation of food while ruling over households crowded with children, slaves, and visitors. An aristocratic veneer gave the luster of gentility to plantations from Maryland to North Carolina, but in fact these were large working farms, often completely isolated from one another.

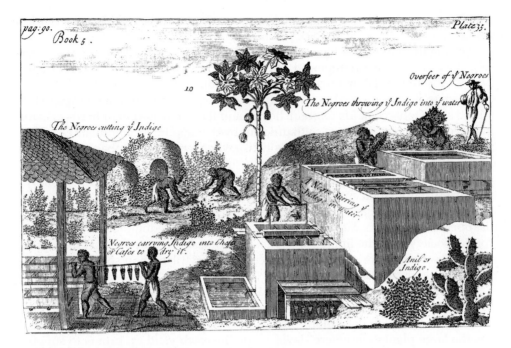

Slaves on an Indigo Plantation Indigo production, mostly the work of enslaved Africans in South Carolina, was dirty, smelly, and debilitating. This eighteenth-century engraving shows each step, from the plant at lower right to tending vats of boiling water. An overseer (top right) supervises the slaves. *(The Folger Shakespeare Library)*

The Rice Coast

The plantation economy of the Lower South in the eighteenth century rested on rice and indigo. Rice exports surpassed 1.5 million pounds per year by 1710 and reached 80 million pounds by the eve of the Revolution. Indigo, a smelly blue dye obtained from plants for use in textiles, became a staple crop in the 1740s after Eliza Lucas Pinckney, a wealthy South Carolina planter's wife, experimented successfully with its cultivation. Within a generation, indigo production had spread into Georgia, ranking among the leading colonial exports.

The expansion of rice production, exported to the West Indies and Europe, transformed the swampy coastal lowlands around Charleston, where planters imported thousands of slaves after 1720. By 1740, slaves comprised nearly 90 percent of the region's inhabitants. White population declined as wealthy planters entrusted their estates to resident overseers. At midcentury, a shocked New England visitor described it as a society "divided into opulent and lordly planters, poor and spiritless peasants, and vile slaves."

Throughout the plantation South, the courthouse became a central male gathering place. All classes came to settle debts, dispute over land, sue and be sued. When court was over, a multitude lingered on, drinking, gossiping, and staging horse races, cockfights, wrestling matches, footraces, and fiddling contests—all considered tests of male prowess.

The church, almost always Anglican in the South before 1750, also became a center of community gathering. A visiting northerner described the animated socializing before worship: men "giving and receiving letters of business, reading advertisements, consulting about the price of tobacco and grain, and settling either the lineage, age, or qualities of favourite horses." Then, people filed into church, with lesser planters entering first and standing attentively until the wealthy gentry, "in a body" took their pews at the front. After church, socializing continued with young people strolling together and older ones extending invitations to Sunday dinner. New England's pious Sabbath was little in evidence.

The Backcountry

As late as 1730, only hunters and Indian fur traders had known the upland backcountry, the vast expanse of hilly red clay and fertile limestone soils from Pennsylvania to Georgia. Over the next four decades, it attracted some 250,000 inhabitants, nearly half the southern white population.

Thousands of land-hungry Germans and Scots–Irish filled the valleys along the eastern side of the Appalachians. Living tensely with Indians, they created a subsistence society. Their enclaves remained isolated for several generations, which helped these pioneers cling fiercely to folkways they had brought across the Atlantic. Crude backcountry life appalled visitors from the more refined seaboard. "Through the licentiousness of the people," wrote one itinerant minister, "many hundreds live in concubinage—swopping their wives as cattle and living in a state of nature more irregularly and unchastely than the Indians."

This crudeness was actually a reflection of the poverty of frontier life and the lack of schools, churches, and towns. Most families plunged into the backcountry with only a few crude household possessions, tools, animals, and the clothes on their backs. They lived in log cabins and planted their crops between the tree stumps. Women toiled alongside men. For a generation, everyone endured a poor diet, endless work, and meager rewards.

By the 1760s, the southern backcountry had begun to emerge from the frontier stage. Small marketing towns became centers of craft activity, church life, and local government. Farms began producing surpluses for shipment east. Density of settlement increased, creating a social life known for harvest festivals, log-rolling contests, horse races, wedding celebrations, dances, and prodigious drinking bouts. Class distinctions remained narrow compared with the older seaboard settlements.

Family Life in the South

As the South emerged from the early era of withering mortality and stunted families, male and female roles gradually became separated. In most areas, the white gender ratio reached parity by the 1720s, depriving women of their leverage in the marriage market. The growth of slavery also changed white women's work role, with the wealthy planter wife becoming a domestic manager in "the great house."

The balanced gender ratio and the growth of slavery also brought changes for southern males. The planters' sons had always been trained in horsemanship, the use of a gun, and the rhythms of agricultural life. Learning how to manage and discipline slaves was as important as lessons with tutors. Bred to command, southern planters' sons developed a self-confidence and authority that propelled many of them into leadership roles during the American Revolution.

On the small farms of the tidewater region and throughout the back settlements, women's roles closely resembled those of northern women. Women labored in the fields alongside their menfolk. "She is a very civil woman," noted an observer of a southern frontierswoman, "and shows nothing of ruggedness or immodesty in her carriage; yet she will carry a gun in the woods and kill deer and turkeys, shoot down wild cattle, catch and tie hogs, knock down beeves with an ax, and perform the most manful exercises as well as most men in those parts."

Marriage and family life were more informal in the backcountry. With vast areas unattended by ministers and with courthouses out of reach, most couples married or "took up" with each other until an itinerant clergyman on horseback appeared to bless marriages and baptize children.

Enslaved Africans in the Southern Colonies

From the late seventeenth century, the slave population grew rapidly—from about 15,000 in 1690 to 80,000 in 1730 and 325,000 in 1760. In the entire period from 1700 to 1775, more than 350,000 African slaves entered the American colonies, with 90 percent of those going to the southern colonies.

The basic struggle for Africans toiling on plantations 5,000 miles from their homes was to create strategies for living as satisfactorily as possible despite horrifying treatment. The master hoped to convert the slave into a mindless drudge who obeyed every command and worked efficiently for his profit. He rarely enjoyed complete success. Masters could set the external boundaries of existence for their slaves, controlling physical location, work roles, diet, and shelter. They were less able to dictate how slaves established friendships, fell in love, formed kin groups, reared children, worshiped their gods, buried their dead, and organized their leisure time. At first, cultural differences divided slaves, who often came from many areas in Africa. In time, however, with the common experience of laboring in the South, a shared African American culture emerged.

Although slave codes severely restricted the lives of slaves, the possibility for family life increased as the southern colonies matured. Larger plantations employed dozens and even hundreds of slaves, and the growth of roads and market towns permitted them greater opportunities to forge relationships beyond their own plantation. By the 1740s, a growing proportion of Chesapeake slaves were American-born, established families, and lived in plantation outbuildings where after sundown they could fashion personal lives.

In South Carolina, slaves drew on agricultural skills they had practiced in Africa and made rice the keystone of the coastal economy by the early eighteenth century. Their numbers increased rapidly, from about 4,000 in 1708 to 90,000 by 1760. Working mostly on large plantations in swampy lowlands, they endured the worst conditions on the continent. But they also outnumbered whites three to one by 1760 and hence could maintain more of their African culture than slaves in the Chesapeake region. Many spoke Gullah, a "pidgin" mixing several African languages, gave African names to their children, and kept alive African religious customs.

Resistance and Rebellion

Slaves not only adapted to bondage but also resisted in ways that constantly reminded their masters that slavery's price was eternal vigilance. Slaveowners interpreted rebelliousness as evidence of the "barbarous, wild savage natures of Africans," as a South Carolina law of 1712 phrased it. But from the African point of view, resistance was essential to maintaining meaning and dignity in a life of degrading toil.

"Saltwater" Africans, fresh from their homelands, often fought slavery fiercely. "They often die before they can be conquered," said one white planter. Commonly, initial resistance took the form of fleeing—to renegade frontier settlements, to interior Native American tribes (which sometimes offered refuge), or to Spanish Florida. Rebellions, such as those in New York City in 1712 and at Stono, South Carolina, in 1739, mostly involved newly arrived slaves. There was no North American parallel, however, for the massive slave uprisings of the West Indies and Brazil, where Africans vastly outnumbered their European masters and therefore had a special incentive for rebelling.

The relatively small rebellions that did occur (or were feared) led to atrocious repression. Near Charleston in 1739, officials tortured and hanged 50 black rebels; their decapitated heads, impaled on posts, warned other potential insurrectionists. In New York City a year later, rumors of a planned insurrection caused the hanging of 18 slaves and 4 white allies and the burning of 13 other slaves.

Black Religion and Family

The balance of power was always massively stacked against the slaves. Only the most desperate challenged the system directly. As slaves struggled to find meaning and worth in their existence, religion and family became especially important.

Africans brought to the New World a complex religious heritage that no desolation or physical abuse could crush. Coming from cultures where the division between sacred and secular activities was less clear than in Europe, slaves made religion central to their existence. Most slaves died strangers to Christianity until the mid-eighteenth century. Then they began to blend African religious practices with the faith of the master class, using this hybrid religion both to light the spark of resistance and to find comfort from oppression.

The religious revival that began in the 1720s in the northern colonies and spread southward made important contributions to African American religion. Evangelicalism stressed personal rebirth, used music and body motion, and produced an intense emotional experience. The dancing, shouting, rhythmic clapping, and singing that came to characterize slaves' religious expression represented a creative mingling of West African and Christian religions.

Besides religion, the slaves' greatest refuge from their dreadful fate lay in their families. In West Africa, all social relations were centered in kinship, which included dead ancestors. Torn from their native societies, slaves placed great importance on rebuilding extended kin groups. Most English colonies prohibited slave marriages. But in practice, slaves and masters struck a bargain. Slaves desperately wanted families, and masters found that slaves with families would work harder and be less inclined to escape or rebel.

Slaves fashioned a family life only with difficulty, however. The general practice of importing three male slaves for every two females stunted family formation. Female slaves, much in demand, married in their late teens, but males usually had to wait until their mid- to late twenties. But as natural increase swelled the slave population in the eighteenth century, the gender ratio became more even.

Slave marriages were rarely secure. They were often severed by the sale of either husband or wife, especially when a deceased planter's estate was divided among his heirs or his slaves were sold to his creditors to satisfy debts. Children usually stayed with their mothers until about age eight; then they were frequently torn from their families through sale, often to small planters needing only a hand or two. Few slaves escaped separation from family members at some time during their lives.

White male exploitation of black women represented another assault on family life. How many black women were coerced or lured with favors into sexual relations with white masters and overseers cannot be known, but the sizable mulatto (mixed-race) population at the end of the eighteenth century indicates that the number was large.

In some interracial relationships, the coercion was subtle. In some cases, black women sought the liaison to gain advantages for themselves or their children. These unions nonetheless threatened both the slave community and the white plantation ideal. They bridged the supposedly unbridgeable gap between slave and free society and produced children who did not fit into the plantation ideal of separate racial categories.

Despite such obstacles, slaves fashioned intimate ties as husband and wife, parent and child. If monogamous relationships did not last as long as in white society, much of the explanation lies in slave life: the shorter life span of African Americans, the shattering of marriage through sale of one or both partners, and the call of freedom that impelled some slaves to run away.

Whereas slave men struggled to preserve their family role, many black women assumed a position in the family that differed from that of white women. Plantation mistresses usually worked hard in helping manage estates, but nonetheless the ideal grew that they should remain in the house guarding white virtue and setting standards for white culture. In contrast, the black woman remained indispensable to both the work of the plantation and the functioning of the slave quarters. She toiled in the fields and slave cabins alike. Paradoxically, black women's constant labor made them more equal to men than was the case of women in white society.

Above all, slavery was a set of power relationships designed to extract the maximum labor from its victims. Hence, it regularly involved cruelties that filled family life with tribulation. Still, slaves in North America toiled in less physically exhausting circumstances than slaves on sugar and coffee plantations and were better clothed, fed, and treated than Africans in the West Indies, Brazil, and other parts of the hemisphere. Therefore, they were unusually successful in establishing families. Slave family life in the American colonies brimmed with uncertainty and sorrow, but was nonetheless the greatest monument to slaves' will to endure captivity and eventually gain their freedom.

CONTENDING FOR A CONTINENT

By 1750, when English colonists numbered about 1.2 million, only a small fraction of them, along with their African slaves, lived farther than 100 miles from the Atlantic Ocean. Growing rapidly, the English colonies were beginning to press against the French and Spanish settlements in the rich river valleys of the Ohio and Mississippi and beyond. France posed the greatest threat to English colonists in the interior of North America, while the Spanish presented another challenge on their southern flank.

France's Inland Empire

In 1661, France's Louis XIV, determined to make his country the most powerful in Europe, looked with keen interest to North America and the Caribbean islands, with their precious sugar. New France's timber would build the royal navy, its fish would feed the growing mass of slaves in the French West Indies, and its fur trade, if greatly expanded, would fill the royal coffers.

New France grew in population, economic strength, and ambition in the late seventeenth century. In 1673, Louis Joliet and Father Jacques Marquette, a Jesuit priest, explored an immense territory watered by the Mississippi and Missouri rivers. A decade later, military engineers and priests began building forts and missions in the Great Lakes region and the Mississippi valley. In the first half of the eighteenth century, the French were able to develop a system of forts, trading posts, and agricultural villages throughout the heart of the continent, threatening to pin the English to the seaboard. Their success was partly due to their shrewd dealings with the Native Americans, who kept sovereignty over the land but gradually succumbed to French diseases and French-promoted intertribal wars.

Because France's interior empire was organized primarily as a military, trading, and missionizing operation, male French settlers arrived with few French women. For a long time, French men were in a state of need—not only for trading partners, allies, and converts, but also for wives. These needs produced a mingling of French and Native American economic, political, and social interests in the vast interior.

The French presence in the continent's vast heartland, thinly dotted with small farming communities, created a shield against the expansive British. The French population grew to about 70,000 by 1750, and almost all French settlements in the North American interior were mixed-race, or

DOCUMENT

Crèvecoeur,
Letters From an
American Farmer
(1782)

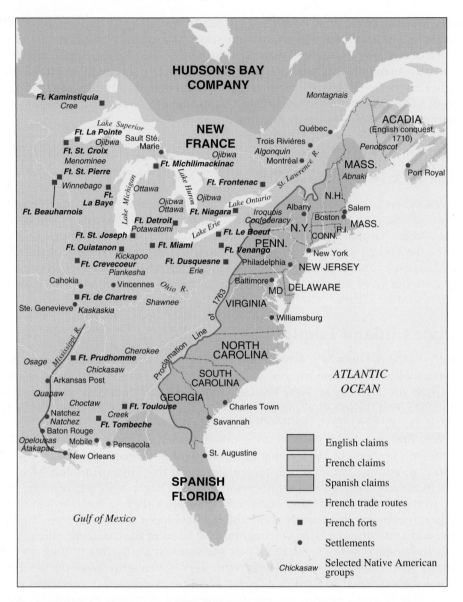

FRENCH NORTH AMERICA, 1608–1763 Though thinly settled by colonists, the vast region west of the Proclamation Line claimed by France was held by a combination of forts and trading posts.

meti, communities—a sharp contrast to the English colonies. They demonstrated how European settlers and Indian peoples could coexist.

In 1718, French pioneers of the interior and those along the Gulf of Mexico were inundated when France settled New Orleans at great cost by transporting almost 7,000 whites and 5,000 African slaves to the mouth of the Mississippi River.

Disease rapidly whittled down these numbers, and an uprising of the powerful Natchez in 1729 discouraged further French immigration. Most of the survivors settled around the little town of New Orleans and on long, narrow plantations stretching back from the Mississippi River. While its economy and society resembled early Charleston, South Carolina, New Orleans was run and financed by royal government and knew nothing of representative political institutions such as elections, assembly, newspapers, or taxes.

Slaves, with skills as rice growers, indigo processors, metal workers, river navigators, herbalists, and cattle keepers, became the backbone of the Louisiana economy. African slaves mingled with Native American women, producing mixed-race children known locally as *grifs*, while African women made interracial liaisons with French immigrants, often soldiers in search of partners. By 1765, blacks outnumbered whites. The chance of gaining freedom in fluid French Louisiana, especially for those of mixed-race descent, exceeded that of any other colony in North America's Southeast. When the Spanish took over the colony in 1769, they guaranteed slaves the right to buy freedom with money earned in their free time. A free black class emerged, but when Americans acquired the colony in 1803, they suppressed freedom purchase and discouraged manumission.

A Generation of War

The growth of French strength and ambitions brought British America and New France into deadly conflict beginning in the late seventeenth century. Protestant New Englanders regarded Catholic New France as a satanic challenge to their divinely sanctioned mission. When the European wars began in 1689, conflict between England and France quickly extended into every overseas theater where the two powers had colonies, including New York, New England, and eastern Canada.

In two wars, from 1689 to 1697 and 1702 to 1713, the English and French, while fighting in Europe, also sought to oust each other from the Americas. The zone of greatest importance was the Caribbean, where slaves produced huge sugar fortunes. Both home governments valued the North American settlements as a source of the timber and fish that sustained the important West Indian colonies.

The English struck three times at the centers of French power—at Port Royal, which commanded the access to the St. Lawrence River, and at Quebec, the capital of New France. In 1690, during King William's War (1689–1697), their small flotilla captured Port Royal, the hub of Acadia (which was returned to France at the end of the war). The English assault on Quebec, however, failed disastrously. In Queen Anne's War (1702–1713), New England attacked Port Royal three times before finally capturing it in 1710. A year later, when England sent a flotilla of 60 ships and 5,000 men to conquer Canada, the land and sea operations foundered before reaching their destination.

With European-style warfare miserably unsuccessful in America, both England and France attempted to subcontract military tasks to their Indian allies. This policy occasionally succeeded, especially for the French, who gladly sent their own troops into the fray alongside Indian partners. In both wars, French and Native American allies wiped out frontier posts in New York and Maine and battered other towns along New England's fringes. Retaliating, the English-supplied Iroquois left New France "bewildered and benumbed" after a massacre near Montreal in 1689. Assessing their own interests, and too powerful to be bullied by either France or England, the Iroquois sat out the second war in the early eighteenth century. Convinced that neutrality served their purposes better than acting as mercenaries for the English, they held to the principle that "we are a free people uniting ourselves to whatever sachem [chief] we wish."

Though England had rebuffed France after a generation of war, New England suffered grievous economic and human losses. Massachusetts bore the heaviest burden. Probably one-fifth of all able-bodied males in the colony participated in the Canadian campaigns, and of these, about one-quarter never lived to tell of the terrors of New England's first major experience with international warfare. The war debt was £50,000 sterling in Massachusetts alone, a greater per capita burden than the national debt today. At the end of the second conflict, in 1713, war widows were so numerous that the Bay Colony faced its first serious poverty problem.

War at sea between European rivals affected even those who escaped the land war. New York lost one of its best grain markets when Spain, allied with France, outlawed American foodstuffs in its Caribbean colonies. The French navy plucked off nearly one-quarter of the port's fleet and disrupted Philadelphia grain merchants' access to the Caribbean.

The burdens and rewards fell unevenly on the participants, as usually happens in wartime. Some lowborn men rose spectacularly. William Phips, the twenty-sixth child in his family, had been a poor sheep farmer and ship's carpenter in Maine who seemed destined to go nowhere. He then won a fortune by recovering a sunken Spanish treasure ship in the West Indies in 1687 and was given command of the expedition against Port Royal in 1690. Victory there catapulted him in 1691 to a secure status as governor of Massachusetts.

Other men, already rich, got richer. Andrew Belcher of Boston, who had grown wealthy on provisioning contracts during King Philip's War, supplied warships and outfitted the New England expeditions to Canada. He became a local titan, riding in London-built coaches, erecting a handsome mansion, and purchasing slaves.

Most men, especially those who did the fighting, gained little, and many lost all. The least securely placed New Englanders supplied most of the voluntary or involuntary recruits, dying in numbers that seem staggering today. Antipopery, dreams of glory, and promises of plunder in French Canada lured most of them into uniform. Having achieved no place on the paths leading upward, they grasped at straws and usually failed again.

In 1713, the Peace of Utrecht, which ended Queen Anne's War, capped a century-long rise for England and the decline of Spain in the rivalry for the sources of wealth outside Europe. England, the big winner, received Newfoundland and Acadia (renamed Nova Scotia), and France recognized English sovereignty over the fur-rich Hudson Bay territory. France retained Cape Breton Island, controlling the entrance to the St. Lawrence River. In the Caribbean, France returned St. Kitts and Nevis to England. Suffering various Old World losses, Spain awarded the English the lucrative privilege of supplying the Spanish empire in America with African slaves.

A Chart of Mixed-Race Families The mixing of races in Spain's New World colonies is vividly displayed in paintings of interracial families, widely produced in Mexico in the eighteenth century. In each painting shown here, the mother and father of different racial ancestries produces a child with a different racial term. In panel 5, for example, the mulatto mother and Spanish father produce a "Morisco" child. Paintings such as these spread the view that interracial mixing was the natural path of human affairs when people of different racial backgrounds converged.

Spain's Frail North American Grip

Spain's grip on its colonies in North America had always been tenuous. On the east coast, the growth of South Carolina slave-based plantation society in the late seventeenth century stemmed partly from the English use of Native American allies to attack Spanish Indian missions and outposts and sell the captives into slavery. From this time forward, English and French traders, with more attractive trade goods to offer, held sway over Florida Indians.

After 1713, Spain maintained a fragile hold on the southern tier of the continent. However, Spain learned how easily its thinly peopled missions and frontier outposts could be crippled or destroyed by chafing Native Americans and invading English. In the first half of the eighteenth century, the Spanish settlements stagnated, suffering from Spain's colonial policy that regarded them as marginal, money-losing affairs, useful only as defensive outposts.

Hispanics, mestizos, and detribalized Indians began to increase modestly in Texas, New Mexico, and California in the first half of the eighteenth century, but by 1745 in Florida they had only one-tenth the population of the English in South Carolina. New Mexico's Hispanic population of about 10,000 at midcentury could defend the vast region only because no European challenger appeared.

As in New France, there was more racial intermixture and social fluidity in New Spain than in the English colonies. Precisely how much is uncertain because the Spanish never defined racial groups as distinctly as the English. Social mobility was considerable: The crown would raise even a commoner to the status of *hidalgo* (minor nobleman) as an inducement to settle and ranch in New Mexico.

Native Americans had mixed success resisting Spanish domination. In New Mexico, an early nineteenth-century Spanish investigator saw the key to Pueblo cultural autonomy as the underground *kivas*, which were "like impenetrable temples, where they gather to discuss mysteriously their misfortunes or good fortunes, their happiness or grief." However, California tribes had a hard time maintaining cultural cohesion. In the 1770s, the Spanish completed their western land and sea routes from San Diego to Yerba Buena (San Francisco) to block Russian encroachment. California's Spanish pioneers were Franciscan missionaries, accompanied by royal soldiers. The priests would choose a good location and attract a few Indians to be baptized and resettle around the mission. Visiting relatives would then be induced to stay, and the Indians were eventually reduced to virtual slaves. The California mission, with its extensive and profitable herds and grain crops, theoretically belonged to the Indian converts, but they did not enjoy the profits. Ironically, the spiritual motives of the priests brought the same degradation of tribal Americans as elsewhere.

Cultural and Ecological Changes Among Interior Tribes

During the first half of the eighteenth century, the inland tribes proved their capacity to adapt to the contending European colonizers in their region while maintaining political independence. Yet extensive contact with Europeans slowly brought ominous changes. Trade goods, especially iron implements, textiles, firearms and ammunition, and alcohol, altered ways of life. Subsistence hunting turned into commercial hunting, restricted only by the quantity of trade goods desired. Native American males, gradually wiping out deer and beaver east of the Mississippi River, spent far more time away from the villages trapping and hunting. Women were also drawn into the new economy, skinning animals and fashioning pelts into robes. Among some tribes, all this became so time-consuming that they had to procure food from other tribes.

The fur trade altered much in traditional Native American life. Spiritual beliefs that the destinies of humans and animals were closely linked eroded when trappers and hunters declared all-out war on fur-bearing animals in order to exchange pelts for attractive trade goods. Competition for furs sharpened intertribal tensions, often to the point of war. The introduction of European weaponry, which Indians quickly mastered, intensified these conflicts. Tribal political organization in the interior changed too. Earlier, most tribes had been loose confederations of villages and clans, with primary loyalty directed to the village. But trade, diplomatic contact, and war with Europeans required coordinated policies, so villagers gradually adopted more centralized leadership.

While incorporating trade goods into their material culture and adapting their economies and political structures to new situations, the interior tribes held fast to many traditions. They saw little reason to replace what they valued in their own culture. What they saw of the colonists' law and justice, religion, education, family organization, and child rearing usually convinced Native Americans that their own ways were superior.

Their refusal to accept the superiority of white culture frustrated English missionaries, eager to win Native Americans from "savage" ways. A Carolinian admitted that "they are really better to us than we are to them. We look upon them with scorn and disdain, and think them little better than beasts in human shape, though if well examined, we shall find that, for all our religion and education, we possess more moral deformities and evils than these savages do."

Overall, interior tribes suffered from contact with the British colonizers. Decade by decade, the fur trade spread epidemic diseases, intensified warfare, depleted game animals, and drew Native Americans into a market economy where their trading partners gradually became trading masters.

THE URBAN WORLD OF COMMERCE AND IDEAS

Only about 5 percent of eighteenth-century colonists lived in towns as large as 2,500, and no city boasted a population above 16,000 in 1750 or 30,000 in 1775. Yet urban societies were at the leading edge of the transition to "modern" life. There, a barter economy first gave way to a commercial economy, a social order based on assigned status turned into one based on achievement, rank-conscious and deferential politics faded into participatory and contentious politics, and small-scale craftsmanship was gradually replaced by factory production. Into the cities flowed European ideas, which radiated outward to the hinterland.

Sinews of Trade

In the half century after 1690, Boston, New York, Philadelphia, and Charleston blossomed into thriving commercial centers. Their growth accompanied the development of the agricultural interior. As the colonial population rose and spread out, minor seaports such as Salem, Newport, Providence, Annapolis, Norfolk, and Savannah gathered 5,000 or more inhabitants.

Cities served as trade centers through which flowed colonial exports (tobacco, rice, furs, wheat, timber products, and fish) and the imported goods that colonists needed: manufactured and luxury goods from England (glass, paper, iron implements, and cloth); wine, spices, coffee, tea, and sugar; and laborers. The seaport merchant was a pivotal figure, frequently engaging in both retail and wholesale trade as well as serving as moneylender, shipbuilder, insurance agent, land developer, and often coordinator of artisan production.

The Connecticut Peddler

By the eighteenth century, the American economy was integrated into an Atlantic trading system that connected settlers to Great Britain, western Europe, Africa, the West Indies, and Newfoundland. Britain, like other major trading nations of western Europe, pursued mercantilist trade policies. Mercantilism's core idea was that a country gained wealth by increasing exports, taxing imports,

How Others See Us

Andrew Burnaby, On the Pennsylvanians

The English clergyman Andrew Burnaby toured the mid-Atlantic English colonies in 1759–1760, just a few years before relations between England and its North American colonies became severely strained. Here are some of his judgments on the Pennsylvanians he visited.

The Pennsylvanians, as to character, are a frugal and industrious people: not remarkably courteous and hospitable to strangers unless particularly recommended to them; but rather, like the denizens of most commercial cities, the reverse. They are great republicans, and have fallen into the same errors in their ideas of independency as most of the other colonies have. They are by far the most enterprizing people upon the continent. As they consist of several nations, and talk several languages, they are aliens in some respect to Great Britain; nor can it be expected that they should have the same filial attachment to her which her own immediate offspring have. However, they are quiet and concern themselves but little, except about getting money. The women are exceedingly handsome and polite; they are naturally sprightly and fond of pleasure; and, upon the whole, are much more agreeable and accomplished than the men. Since their intercourse with the English offices, they are greatly improved; and, without flattery, many of them would not make bad figures even in the first assemblies in Europe. Their amusements are chiefly dancing in the winter; and, in the summer, forming parties of pleasure upon the Schuylkill [River] and in the country.

- *What does Burnaby mean by calling the Pennsylvanians "great republicans"?*
- *Do you think he finds a connection between money-grubbing and his comments on the superiority of American women?*

Source: Andrew Burnaby, *Travels Through the Middle Settlements in North-America in the Years 1759 and 1760* (London, 1762; reprint, Ithaca, N.Y.: Cornell University Press, 1960), p. 61.

regulating production and trade, and exploiting colonies. These policies governed British treatment of North America.

Colonists could never produce enough exportable raw materials to pay for the imported goods they craved, so they had to earn credit in Britain by supplying the West Indies with foodstuffs and timber products. They also accumulated credit by providing shipping and distribution services, which Yankee merchant seamen and Yankee-built ships dominated.

The Artisan's World

Although merchants stood first in wealth and prestige in the colonial towns, artisans were far more numerous. About two-thirds of urban adult males (slaves excluded) labored at handicrafts. By the mid-eighteenth century, the colonial cities contained scores of specialized "leather apron men" besides the proverbial butcher, baker, and candlestick maker. Handicraft specialization increased as the cities matured, but every artisan worked with hand tools, usually in small shops.

Work patterns for artisans were irregular, dictated by weather, length of daylight, erratic delivery of raw materials, and shifting consumer demand. Ordinary laborers dreaded winter, for it was a season when cities had "little occasion for the labor of the poor," and firewood could cost several months' wages.

Urban artisans took fierce pride in their crafts. While deferring to those above them, they saw themselves as the backbone of the community, contributing essential products and services. "Our professions rendered us useful and necessary members of our community," the Philadelphia shoemakers asserted. "Proud of that rank, we aspired to no higher." This self-esteem and desire for community recognition sometimes jostled with the upper-class view of artisans as "mere mechanicks," part of the "vulgar herd."

Striving for respectability, artisans placed a premium on achieving economic independence. Every craftsman began as an apprentice, spending five or more teenage years in a master shop, then, after fulfilling his contract, becoming a "journeyman," selling his labor to a master and frequently living in his house, where he ate at his table and sometimes married his daughter. He hoped to complete within a few years the three-step climb from servitude to self-employment. In trades requiring greater organization and capital, such as distilling and shipbuilding, the rise from journeyman to master often proved impossible.

In good times, urban artisans did well. Success, however, was far from automatic, even for those following Poor Richard's advice. An advantageous marriage, luck in avoiding illness, and an ample inheritance were often critical. In Philadelphia, about half the artisans in the first half of the eighteenth century died leaving enough personal property to have ensured a comfortable standard of living. Their economy weaker, New England artisans did not fare as well.

Urban Social Structure

Population growth, economic development, and war altered the urban social structure between 1690 and 1765. Stately townhouses displayed fortunes built through trade, shipbuilding, war contracting, and—probably most profitable of all—urban land development. "It is almost a proverb," a Philadelphian observed in the 1760s, "that every great fortune made here within these 50 years has been by land." A merchant estate of £2,000 sterling was impressive in the early eighteenth century. Two generations later, North America's first millionaires were accumulating estates of £10,000 to £20,000 sterling.

Alongside urban wealth grew urban poverty. From the beginning, every city had its disabled, orphaned, and widowed who required aid. But after 1720, poverty marred the lives of many more city dwellers, including war widows without means of support, rural migrants, or recent immigrants. Boston was hit especially hard. Its economy stagnated in the 1740s, and taxpayers groaned under the burden of paying for heavy war expenditures. Though cities devised new ways of helping the needy, many of the indigent preferred "to starve in their homes" rather than endure the discipline and indignities of the poorhouse or leave their children alone to labor in America's first textile factory.

Urban eighteenth-century tax lists reveal the increasing gap between the wealthy and the poor. The top 5 percent of taxpayers increased their share of the cities' taxable assets from about 30 to 50 percent between 1690 and 1770. The bottom half of the taxable inhabitants saw their share of the wealth shrink from about 10 to 4 percent. Except in Boston, the urban middle classes continued to gain ground. Still, the growth of princely fortunes amid increasing poverty made some urban dwellers reflect that Old World ills were reappearing in the New.

The Entrepreneurial Ethos

As the cities grew, new values took hold. In the traditional view of society, economic life was supposed to operate according to what was fair, not what was profitable. Regulated prices and wages, quality controls, supervised public markets, and other such measures seemed natural because a community was defined as a single body of interrelated parts, where individual rights and responsibilities formed a seamless web.

In their commercialized cities, most urban dwellers grew to regard the subordinating of private interests to the commonweal as unrealistic. Prosperity required the encouragement of acquisitive appetites rather than self-denial. The new view held that, if people were allowed to pursue their material desires competitively, they would collectively form a natural, impersonal market of producers and consumers that would advantage everyone.

Hence, as the colonial port towns took their places in the Atlantic world of commerce, merchants became accustomed to making decisions according to the emerging commercial ethic that rejected traditional restraints on entrepreneurial activity. If wheat fetched eight shillings a bushel in the West Indies but only five in Boston, a grain merchant felt justified in sending all he could purchase from local farmers to the more distant buyer. The new transatlantic market responded only to the invisible laws of supply and demand.

Tension between the new economic freedom and the older concern for the public good erupted only with food shortages or galloping inflation. Because the American colonies experienced none of the famines that ravaged Europe in this period, such crises were rare, usually occurring during war, when demand for provisions rose sharply. Nonetheless, the two conceptions of community and economic life continued to rub against each other for decades, until by the mid-eighteenth century, the pursuit of a profit was winning out over the old community-oriented social compact.

The American Enlightenment

Ideas not only about economic life but also the nature of the universe and the improvement of the human condition filtered across the Atlantic. In the eighteenth century, an American version of the European intellectual movement called the Enlightenment emerged.

In what is called the Age of Reason, European thinkers rejected the pessimistic Calvinist concept of innate human depravity, replacing it with the optimistic notion that a benevolent God had blessed humankind with the supreme gift of reason. Thinkers like John Locke, in his influential *Essay Concerning Human*

The Quaker Benjamin Lay Benjamin Lay was regarded as eccentric and a troublemaker, even by his fellow Quakers. Known primarily as a fervent opponent of slavery and the slave trade as early as the 1730s, he was also in the vanguard of many reform movements such as temperance and vegetarianism. The portrait shows Lay's dwarflike stature. What does the basket at bottom left symbolize? *(National Portrait Gallery, Smithsonian Institution/Art Resource, NY)*

Understanding (1689), argued that God had not predetermined the content of the human mind but had instead given it the capacity to acquire knowledge. All Enlightenment thinkers prized this acquisition of knowledge, for it allowed humankind to improve its condition. As the great mathematician Isaac Newton demonstrated, systematic investigation could unlock the secrets of the physical universe. Moreover, scientific knowledge could be applied to improve society.

The scientific and intellectual advances of the seventeenth and eighteenth centuries encouraged a belief in "natural law" and fostered debate about the "natural" human rights. These ideas spread in Europe and the Americas, eventually finding expression in movements for reform, democracy, and liberation—all of deep interest to those beginning to oppose slavery and the slave trade as abominations. Even as the traffic in slaves peaked, religious and humanitarian opposition to slavery arose. The idea grew in the 1750s that slavery contradicted the Christian concept of brotherhood and the Enlightenment notion of the natural equality of all humans. Only a few hundred masters freed their slaves in the mid-eighteenth century, but the seeds of abolitionism had been planted.

Eighteenth-century Americans, including naturalist John Bartram of Philadelphia and Harvard Professor John Winthrop III, began to make significant contributions to the advancement of science. Foremost of all was Benjamin Franklin, whose spectacular (and dangerous) experiments with electricity, the properties of which were just becoming known, earned him an international reputation. Franklin's true genius as a figure of the Enlightenment came in his practical application of scientific knowledge. Among his inventions were the lightning rod; bifocal spectacles; and a stove that heated rooms more cost-effectively than the open fireplace. Franklin made his adopted city of Philadelphia a center of the American Enlightenment, helping found America's first circulating library in 1731, an artisans' debating club for "mutual improvement," and an intercolonial scientific association that in 1769 became the American Philosophical Society.

Most colonists were not educated enough to participate actively in the Enlightenment, and only a handful read French Enlightenment authors like Voltaire. But the efforts of men such as Franklin exposed thousands, especially in the cities, to new currents of thought. This kindled hopes that Americans, blessed by an abundant environment, might achieve the Enlightenment ideal of a perfect society.

THE GREAT AWAKENING

Many of the social, economic, and political changes occurring in eighteenth-century colonial society converged in the Great Awakening, the first of many religious revivals that would sweep America during the next two centuries. Though the timing and character of the Awakening varied from region to region, this quest for spiritual renewal challenged old sources of authority and produced patterns of thought and behavior that helped fuel a revolutionary movement in the next generation.

Fading Faith

Early eighteenth-century British America remained an overwhelmingly Protestant culture. Puritanism—institutionalized in Congregational churches—dominated all of New England except Rhode Island. Anglicanism held sway in much of New York and throughout the South except the backcountry. In the mid-Atlantic and in the back settlements, German Mennonites, Dunkers, Moravians, and Lutherans; Scots–Irish Presbyterians; and English Baptists and Quakers all mingled. Even so, two-thirds of the colonists went to no church at all, partly because in many areas, ministers and churches were simply unavailable. In the most populous colony, Virginia, only 60 parsons in 1761 served a population of 350,000—one for every 5,800 people.

Most colonial churches were voluntary ("congregated") groups, formed for reasons of conscience rather than government compulsion. Though Catholics, Jews, and nonbelievers could not vote or hold office, the persecution of Quakers and Catholics had largely passed, and by 1720 some dissenting groups had gained the right to use long-obligatory church taxes to support their own congregations.

Most efforts to tighten congregational organization and discipline failed. For example, Anglican ministers had to be ordained in England and regularly report to the bishop of London. But in his Chesapeake parish, an Anglican priest faced wealthy planters who controlled the vestry (the local church governing body), set his salary, and would drive him out if he challenged them too forcefully. In Connecticut, the Saybrook Platform of 1708 created a network of Congregational churches, but individual churches still preserved much of their autonomy.

As early as the 1660s, New England's Congregational clergy had adopted the Half-Way Covenant in order to combat religious indifference. It allowed children of church members, if they adhered to the "forms of godliness," to join the church even if they could not demonstrate that they had undergone a conversion experience. They could not, however, vote in church affairs or take communion. Such compromises and innovations could not halt the creeping religious apathy that many ministers observed. An educated clergy, its energies often drained by doctrinal disputes, appealed too much to the mind and not enough to the heart. As one Connecticut leader remembered it, "the spirit of God appeared to be awfully withdrawn."

The Awakeners' Message

The Great Awakening was not a unified movement; rather, it was a series of revivals that swept different regions between 1720 and 1760 with varying degrees of intensity. The first stirrings came in the 1720s in New Jersey, where a Dutch Reformed minister, Theodore Frelinghuysen, excited his congregation through emotional preaching about the need to be saved rather than offering the usual theological abstractions.

Jonathan Edwards

From New Jersey, the Awakening spread to Pennsylvania in the 1730s, especially among Presbyterians, and then broke out in the Connecticut River valley. There its greatest leader was Jonathan Edwards in Northampton, Massachusetts. Later a philosophical giant in the colonies, as a young man Edwards gained renown by frightening his parishioners with the fate of "sinners in the hands of an angry God." "How manifold have been the abominations of your life!" Edwards preached. Edwards paraded one sin after another before his trembling congregants and drew such graphic pictures of the hell awaiting the unrepentant that his Northampton neighbors were soon preparing frantically for the conversion by which they would be "born again." His *Faithful Narrative of the Surprizing Work of God* (1736), which described his town's awakening, was the first published revival narrative, a literary form that would be used many times in the future to fan the flames of evangelical religion.

Jonathan Edwards, "Sinners in the Hands of an Angry God" (1741)

In 1739, these regional brushfires of evangelicalism were drawn together by a 24-year-old Anglican priest from England, George Whitefield. Inspired by John Wesley, the founder of English Methodism, Whitefield used his magnificent speaking voice in dynamic open-air preaching before huge gatherings. Whitefield barnstormed seven times along the American seaboard, beginning in 1739. In Boston, he preached to 19,000 in three days and at a farewell sermon left 25,000 writhing in fear of damnation. In his wake came American preachers whom he had inspired, mostly young men.

The appeal of the Awakeners lay both in the medium and the message. They preached that the established, college-trained clergy was too intellectual and tradition-bound. Congregations were dead, Whitefield declared, "because dead men preach to them." The fires of Protestant belief could be reignited only if individuals assumed responsibility for their own conversion.

An important form of individual participation was "lay exhorting," which meant that anyone—young or old, female or male, black or white—could defy assigned roles and spontaneously recount a conversion experience and preach "the Lord's truth." This horrified trained clergy and shattered their monopoly. The oral culture of common people gained new importance, their impromptu outpourings contrasting sharply with the controlled literary culture of the gentry.

How religion, social change, and politics became interwoven in the Great Awakening can be seen by examining two regions swept by revivalism. Both Boston, the heartland of Puritanism, and interior Virginia, a land of struggling small planters and slave-rich aristocrats, experienced the Great Awakening, but in different ways and at different times.

Revivalism in the Urban North

In Boston, Whitefield-inspired revivalism blazed up amid political controversy about paper money and land banks, which pitted large merchants against local traders, artisans, and the laboring poor, who preferred the land bank. At first, Boston's elite applauded Whitefield's ability to call the masses to worship. It seemed that the master evangelist might restore social harmony by redirecting people from earthly matters such as the currency dispute toward concerns for their souls. But when he left Boston in 1740, others followed him. Men such as James Davenport were more critical of the "unconverted" clergy and the self-indulgent accumulation of wealth. Finding every meetinghouse closed to him, even those whose clergy had embraced the Awakening, the 25-year-old Davenport preached daily on the Boston Common, aroused religious ecstasy among thousands like Hannah Heaton, and stirred up feeling against the city's leading figures. Respectable people decided that revivalism had gotten out of hand when ordinary people began verbally attacking opponents of the land bank in the streets as "carnal wretches, hypocrites, fighters against God, children of the devil, cursed Pharisees." A revival that had begun as a return to religion among backsliding Christians had overlapped with political affairs, threatening polite culture, which stressed order and discipline from ordinary people.

Southern Revivalism

Although aftershocks continued for years, by 1744 the Great Awakening was ebbing in New England and the middle colonies. In Virginia, where the initial religious earthquake was barely felt, tremors of enthusiasm rippled through society from the mid-1740s onward.

Whitefield stirred some religious fervor during his early trips through Virginia. Traveling "New Light" preachers were soon gathering large crowds both in the backcountry and in the traditionally Anglican parishes of the older settled areas. By 1747, worried Anglican clergymen convinced the governor to issue a proclamation restraining "strolling preachers." As in other colonies, Virginia's leaders despised traveling evangelists, who, like lay exhorters, conjured up a world without properly constituted authority. When the Hanover County court gave the fiery James Davenport a license to preach in 1750, the governor ordered the suppression of all circuit riders.

Awakeners challenged the gentry-dominated Anglican church's spiritual monopoly. New Light Presbyterianism spread in the 1750s. Then, in the 1760s, came the Baptists. Renouncing finery and ostentatious display and addressing each other as "brother" and "sister," the Baptists reached out to thousands of unchurched people. Like northern revivalists, they focused on the conversion experience. Many of their preachers were uneducated farmers and artisans who called themselves "Christ's poor" and insisted that heaven was populated more by the humble poor than by the purse-proud rich. Among the poorest—Virginia's 140,000 slaves in 1760—the evangelical movement began to take hold. The insurgent Baptist movement offered a personal, emotionally satisfying religion among ordinary folk and a rejection of gentry values. Established Anglican pulpits denounced the Awakeners as furiously as had respectable New England divines. In both regions, social changes had weakened the cultural authority of the upper class and, in the context of religious revival, produced a vision of a society drawn along more equal lines.

Legacy of the Awakening

By the time George Whitefield returned to North America for his third tour in 1745, the revival had burned out in the North. Its effects, however, were long-lasting. Notably, it promoted religious pluralism and nourished the idea that all denominations were equally legitimate, giving the dissenting Protestant groups that had sprung up in seventeenth-century England a basis for living together in relative harmony. From this framework of denominationalism came a second change—the separation of church and state. Once a variety of churches gained legitimacy, it was hard to justify one denomination claiming special privileges. In the seventeenth century, Roger Williams had tried to sever church and state because he believed that ties with civil bodies would corrupt the Church. During the Awakening, groups such as the Baptists and Presbyterians in Virginia constituted their own religious bodies and broke the Anglican monopoly as *the* Church in the colony. This undermining of the church–state tie would be completed during the Revolutionary era.

A third effect of the revival was to legitimate community diversity, which had been valued in Rhode Island, the Carolinas, and the middle colonies almost from their beginnings. But uniformity had been prized elsewhere, especially in Massachusetts and Connecticut. There, the Awakening split Congregational churches into New Lights and Old Lights. Mid-Atlantic Presbyterian churches faced similar schisms. In hundreds of rural communities by the 1750s, two or three churches existed where only one had stood before. People learned that the fabric of community could be woven from threads of many hues.

New eighteenth-century colonial colleges reflected the religious pluralism. Before 1740, there existed only Puritan Harvard (1636) and Yale (1701) and Anglican William and Mary (1693). Between 1746 and 1769, six new colleges were added: Dartmouth, Brown, Princeton, and what are now Columbia, Rutgers, and the University of Pennsylvania. None was controlled by an established church, all had governing bodies composed of men of different faiths, and all admitted students regardless of religion. Eager for students and funds, they made nonsectarian appeals and combined the traditional Latin and Greek curricula with natural sciences and natural philosophy.

Last, the Awakening nurtured a subtle change in values that crossed over into politics and daily life. Especially for ordinary people, the revival experience created a new feeling of self-worth. People assumed new responsibilities in religious affairs and became skeptical of dogma and authority. Many, especially the Baptists, decried the growing materialism and deplored the new acceptance of self-interested behavior. By learning to oppose authority and create new churches, thousands of colonists unknowingly rehearsed for revolution.

POLITICAL LIFE

"Were it not for government, the world would soon run into all manner of disorders and confusions," wrote a Massachusetts clergyman early in the eighteenth century. Few colonists or Europeans would have disagreed. Government existed to protect life, liberty, and property.

How should political power be divided—in England, between the English government and the American colonies, and within each colony? Colonists naturally drew heavily on inherited political ideas and institutions—almost entirely English ones, for it was English charters that sanctioned settlement, English governors who ruled, and English common law that governed the courts. But meeting unexpected circumstances in a new environment, colonists modified familiar political forms.

Structuring Colonial Governments

All societies consider it essential to determine the final source of political authority. In England, the notion of the God-given, supreme monarchical authority was crumbling even before the planting of the colonies. In its place arose the belief that stable government depended on blending and balancing the three pure forms of government: monarchy, aristocracy, and democracy. Unalloyed, each would degenerate into oppression. Most colonists believed that the Revolution of 1688 in England had vindicated and strengthened a carefully balanced political system.

In the colonies, political balance was achieved somewhat differently. The governor, as the king's agent (or, in proprietary colonies, the agent of the proprietor to whom the king delegated authority), represented monarchy. Bicameral legislatures arose in most of the colonies in the seventeenth century, and in most provinces they had upper houses of wealthy men appointed by the governor; as a pale equivalent of Britain's House of Lords, it formed a nascent aristocracy. The assembly, elected by white male freeholders, replicated the House of Commons and was the democratic element. Every statute required the governor's assent (except in Rhode Island and Connecticut), and all colonial laws required final approval from the king's privy council. This royal check operated imperfectly, however. A law took months to reach England and months more before word of its final approval or rejection. In the meantime, the laws took force in the colony.

Behind the formal structure of politics stood rules governing who could participate as voters and officeholders. In England, male property owners with property producing at least an annual rental income of 40 shillings could vote or hold office. The colonists closely followed this principle, except in Massachusetts, where until 1691 Church membership was the basic requirement. As in England, the poor and propertyless were excluded, for they lacked the stake in society that supposedly produced responsible voters.

In England, the 40-shilling freehold requirement kept the electorate small; but in the colonies, where land was cheap, it conferred the vote on 50 to 75 percent of the adult free males. However, as the proportion of landless colonists increased in the eighteenth century, the franchise contracted.

Though voting rights were broadly based, most men assumed that the wealthy and socially prominent should hold the main political positions. Balancing this elitism, however, was the notion that the entire electorate should periodically judge the performance of those entrusted with political power and reject those who were found wanting. Following the precedent of England's Glorious Revolution, in British America the people were assumed to have the right to badger their leaders, to protest openly, and, in extreme cases of abuse of power, to assume control and put things right. Crowd action, frequently effective, gradually achieved a kind of legitimacy.

The Crowd in Action

Popular protests seldom faced effective police power. In the countryside, where most colonists lived, only the county sheriff insulated civil leaders from angry farmers. In the towns, the sheriff had only the night watch to keep order. In 1757, New York's night watch was described as a "parcell of idle, drinking vigilant snorers, who never quelled any nocturnal tumult in their lives." In theory, the militia stood ready to suppress public disturbances, but crowds usually included many militiamen.

The "Paxton Boys" in Philadelphia When frontier farmers marched on Philadelphia in 1763 to demand more protection on the frontier, a miniature civil war almost broke out. Philadelphians had little use for the "Paxton Boys," who had murdered 20 harmless Christian Indians in retaliation for frontier raids. Why are soldiers and mounted men commanding the public space? *(Henry Dawkins/Library Company of Philadelphia, Cartoon [1764])*

Boston's Impressment Riot of 1747 vividly illustrates the people's readiness to defend their inherited privileges and the weakness of law enforcement. It began when Commodore Charles Knowles brought his royal navy ships to Boston for provisioning and to replenish the ranks of mariners thinned by desertion. Knowles sent press gangs out to fill vacancies from Boston's waterfront population.

But before the press gangs could hustle away their victims, a crowd of angry Bostonians seized several British officers, surrounded the governor's house, and demanded the release of their townsmen. When the sheriff and his deputies attempted to intervene, the mob mauled them. The militia refused to respond. An enraged Knowles threatened to bombard the town, but negotiations amid further tumult averted a showdown. Finally, Knowles released the impressed Bostonians. After the riot, a young politician named Samuel Adams defended Boston's defiance of royal authority. The people, he argued, had a "natural right" to band together against press gangs that deprived them of their liberty. Local magnates who had supported the governor were "tools to arbitrary power."

The Growing Power of the Assemblies

While the Impressment Riot of 1747 was dramatic, a more gradual and restrained change was under way—the growing ambition and power of the legislative assemblies. For most of the seventeenth century, royal and proprietary governors had exercised greater power in relation to the elected legislatures than did England's king in relation to Parliament. Governors could dissolve the lower houses and delay their sitting, control the election of their speakers, and in most colonies initiate legislation with their appointed councils. They had authority to appoint and dismiss judges at all levels of the judiciary and to create chancery courts, which sat without juries. Governors also controlled the expenditure of public monies and had authority to grant land to individuals and groups, which they sometimes used to confer vast estates on their favorites. They lacked, however, the extensive patronage power that enabled ministers of government in England to manipulate elections and buy off opponents.

Since the seventeenth century, Virginia, Massachusetts, and New York had been royal colonies, with crown-appointed governors. In the eighteenth century, royal government came to New Jersey (1702), South Carolina (1719), and North Carolina (1729), replacing proprietary regimes.

Many royal governors were competent military officers or bureaucrats, but some were corrupt recipients of patronage posts. Some never even came over, preferring to pocket the salary and pay part of it to another man who went to serve as lieutenant governor. One committed suicide a week after arriving. Most, however, were merely mediocre.

Eighteenth-century legislatures challenged the swollen powers of the colonial governors. Bit by bit, they won new rights: to initiate legislation, to elect their own speakers, to settle contested elections, to discipline members, and to nominate provincial treasurers who disbursed public funds. Most important, they won the "power of the purse"—the authority to initiate money bills, specifying how much money should be raised by taxes and how it should be spent. Thus, the elected assemblies gradually transformed themselves into governing bodies reflecting the interests of the electorate.

Local Politics

Binding elected officeholders to their constituents became an important feature of the colonial political system. In England, the House of Commons claimed to represent the entire nation rather than narrow local interests, yet was filled with representatives from rotten boroughs (ancient places left virtually uninhabited by population shifts) and with men whose vote was controlled by the government because they had accepted offices, contracts, or gifts. American assemblies, by contrast, contained mostly representatives sent by voters who instructed them on particular issues and held them accountable.

Royal governors and colonial grandees who sat as councillors often deplored this localist, popular orientation. Sniffed one aristocratic New Yorker, the assemblies were crowded with "plain, illiterate husbandmen [small farmers], whose views seldom extended farther than the regulation of highways, the destruction of wolves, wildcats, and foxes, and the advancement of the other little interests of the particular counties which they were chosen to represent." In actuality, most lower-house members were merchants, lawyers, and substantial planters and farmers, who by the mid-eighteenth century constituted the political elite in most colonies. They took pride in upholding their constituents' interests, for they saw themselves as bulwarks against oppression and arbitrary rule, which history taught them were most frequently imposed by monarchs and their appointed agents.

Local government was usually more important to the colonists than provincial government. In the North, local political authority generally rested in the towns (which included surrounding rural areas). The New England town meeting decided a wide range of matters, arguing until it could express itself as a single unit.

In the South, the county was the primary unit of government, and by the mid-eighteenth century, a landed squirearchy of third- and fourth-generation families had achieved political dominance. They ruled the county courts and the legislature, and substantial farmers served in minor offices such as road surveyor and deputy sheriff. At court sessions, usually four times a year, deeds were read aloud and then recorded, juries impaneled and justice dispensed, elections held, licenses issued, and proclamations read aloud. On election days, gentlemen treated their neighbors (on whom they depended for votes) to alcoholic treats.

The Spread of Whig Ideology

Whether in local or provincial affairs, a political ideology called Whig, or "republican," had spread widely by the mid-eighteenth century. This body of thought, inherited from England, rested on the belief that concentrated power was historically the enemy of liberty and that too much power lodged in any person or group usually produced corruption and tyranny. The best defenses against concentrated power were balanced government, elected legislatures adept at checking executive authority, prohibition of standing armies (almost always controlled

TIMELINE

1682	La Salle canoes down Mississippi River and claims Louisiana for France
1689–1697	King William's War
1700	Spanish establish first mission in Arizona
1702–1713	Queen Anne's War
1704	*Boston News-Letter*, first regular colonial newspaper, published
1712	First northern slave revolt erupts in New York City
1713	Peace of Utrecht
1714	Beginning of Scots–Irish and German immigration
1715–1730	Volume of slave trade doubles
1718	French settle New Orleans
1720s	Natural increase of African population begins
1732	Benjamin Franklin publishes first *Poor Richard's Almanack*
1734–1736	Great Awakening begins in Northampton, Massachusetts

1735	Zenger acquitted of seditious libel in New York
1739	Slave revolt in Stono, South Carolina
1739–1740	Whitefield's first American tour spreads Great Awakening
1740s	Slaves compose 90 percent of population on Carolina rice coast
	Indigo becomes staple crop in Lower South
1747	Impressment riot in Boston
1750s	Quakers initiate campaign to halt slave trade and end slavery
1760	Africans compose 20 percent of colonial population
1760s–1770s	Spanish establish California mission system
1769	American Philosophical Society founded at Philadelphia

by tyrannical monarchs to oppress the people), and vigilance by the people in watching their leaders for telltale signs of corruption.

Much of this Whig ideology reached the people through the some 23 newspapers circulating in the colonies by 1763. Many papers reprinted pieces from English Whig writers railing against corruption and creeping despotism. Though limited to a few pages and published only once or twice a week, the papers passed from hand to hand and were read aloud in taverns and coffeehouses, so that their contents probably reached most urban households and a substantial minority of rural farms.

The new power of the press and its importance in guarding the people's liberties against would-be tyrants (such as haughty royal governors) were dramatically illustrated in the Zenger case in New York. Young John Peter Zenger, a printer's apprentice, had been hired in 1733 by the anti-government faction of Lewis Morris to start a newspaper, the *New-York Weekly Journal,* that would publicize the tyrannical actions of Governor William Cosby.

Arrested for seditious libel, Zenger was defended brilliantly by Andrew Hamilton, a Philadelphia lawyer hired by the Morris faction to convince the jury that Zenger had been simply trying to inform the people of attacks on their liberties. Although the jury acquitted Zenger, the libel laws remained very restrictive. The acquittal reinforced the notion that the government was the people's servant, and it brought home the point that public criticism could keep people with political authority responsible to the people they ruled. Such ideas about liberty and corruption, raised in the context of local politics, would shortly achieve a much broader significance.

Conclusion

America in 1750

The English colonies in North America, robust and expanding, matured rapidly between 1690 and 1750. Transatlantic commerce linked them closely to Europe, Africa, and other parts of the Americas. Churches, schools, and towns—the visible marks of the receding frontier—appeared everywhere. And everywhere people like Hannah Heaton had been energized by the Great Awakening and were introduced to the idea of ordinary people helping to shape the future. A balanced gender ratio and stable family life had been achieved throughout the colonies. Many men were able to move up in society despite frequent obstacles. Seasoned political leaders and familiar political institutions functioned from Maine to Georgia.

Yet the sinew, bone, and muscle of American society had not yet fully knit together. The polyglot population, one-fifth of it bound in chattel slavery and its Native American component still unassimilated and uneasily situated on the frontier, was a kaleidoscopic mixture of ethnic and religious groups. While developing rapidly, its economy showed weaknesses, particularly in New England, where land resources had been strained. The social structure reflected the colonizers' emergence from a frontier stage, but the consolidation of wealth by a landed and mercantile elite was matched by pockets of poverty appearing in the cities and some rural areas. Full of strength, yet marked by awkward incongruities, colonial America in 1750 approached an era of strife and momentous decisions. Much of that strife involved the growing power of France's inland empire in North America and the way that wars in Europe were becoming globe-encircling conflicts.

Questions for Review and Reflection

1. Regional variations within colonial society created different social and economic systems in areas of North America. What were the key regional divisions, and what differences characterized the societies and economies in each?

2. Why did slavery become a widespread institution in eighteenth-century colonial North America, and how did it shape society?

3. Was the Great Awakening compatible with other changes occurring in the society, or did it contradict most other trends? How do you see religious change relating to social, political, and intellectual changes?

4. Was colonial America more affected by transatlantic trends or local influences in the areas of politics, ideas, and social life?

5. What were the most important aspects of colonial society that enabled it to mature? Why do you think these particular factors most significant?

Discovering U.S. History Online

Bethlehem, Pennsylvania bdhp.moravian.edu/home/home.html
A cooperative effort of area libraries, this site examines the history of the Moravian community of Bethlehem, Pennsylvania.

Martha Ballard Diary www.dohistory.org
Focusing on the life of Martha Ballard, a late eighteenth-century New England woman, this site employs selections from her diary, excerpts from a book and film about her life, and other primary documents that enable students to conduct their own historical investigation.

Two Centuries of Louisiana History lsm.crt.state.la.us/cabildo/cabildo.htm
This state-run site focuses on the diverse ethnic heritage of Louisiana people. The early sections cover pre-contact and colonial Louisiana.

North American Womens' Letters and Diaries www.alexanderstreet2.com/NWLDlive/
At this site, students can find rich firsthand accounts of colonial life from women's perspectives.

White Oak Fur Post www.whiteoak.org
This site documents an eighteenth-century fur trading post among the Indians in the region that would become Minnesota.

Benjamin Franklin www.english.udel.edu/lemay/franklin
This richly illustrated site relates the story of Franklin's life and political involvement in seven parts.

Fiction and Film

Kenneth Roberts, king of historical novelists on eighteenth-century America, movingly describes the Seven Years War in *Northwest Passage* (1937); Spencer Tracy starred in the Hollywood version with the same title. James Fenimore Cooper's *The Last of the Mohicans* (1836) is another American classic, but much more to the taste of today's students is Hollywood's movie by the same title (1992), starring Daniel Day-Lewis and Madeleine Stowe.

Recommended Reading

www.ablongman.com/nash

The Companion Website has a list of recommended readings about agriculture in the northern and southern colonies, conflict with Indian tribes, colonial cities, the Great Awakening, and colonial political life.

The Strains of Empire

American Stories

A Shoemaker Leads a Boston Mob

In 1758, when he was 21 years old, Ebenezer MacIntosh of Boston laid down his shoemaker's awl and enlisted in the Massachusetts expedition against the French on Lake Champlain. The son of a poor Boston shoemaker who had fought against the French in a previous war, MacIntosh had known poverty all his life. Service against the French offered the hope of plunder or at least an enlistment bounty worth half a year's wages. One among thousands of colonists who fought against the "Gallic menace" in the Seven Years' War, MacIntosh did his bit in the climactic struggle that drove the French from North America.

But a greater role lay ahead for the Boston shoemaker. Two years after the Peace of Paris in 1763, England imposed a stamp tax on the American colonists. In the massive protests that followed, MacIntosh emerged as the street leader of Boston's ordinary people. In two nights of the most violent attacks on private property ever witnessed in North America, a Boston crowd nearly destroyed the houses of two of the colony's most important officials. On August 14, they tore through the house of Andrew Oliver, a wealthy merchant and the appointed distributor of stamps for Massachusetts. Twelve days later, MacIntosh led the crowd in attacking the mansion of Thomas Hutchinson, a wealthy merchant who served as lieutenant governor and chief justice of Massachusetts. "The mob was so general," wrote the governor, "and so supported that all civil power ceased in an instant."

For the next several months, the power of the poor Boston shoemaker grew. Called "General" MacIntosh and "Captain-General of the Liberty Tree," he soon sported a militia uniform of gold and blue and a hat laced with gold. Two thousand townsmen marched behind him in orderly ranks through the crooked streets of Boston on November 5 to demonstrate their solidarity in resisting the hated stamps.

Five weeks later, a crowd publicly humiliated stamp distributor Oliver. Demanding that he announce his resignation before the assembled citizenry, they marched him across town in a driving December rain. With MacIntosh at his elbow, he finally reached the "Liberty Tree," which had become a symbol of resistance to England's new colonial policies. There the aristocratic Oliver ate humble pie. He concluded his resignation remarks with bitter words, hissing sardonically that he would "always think myself very happy when it shall be in my power to serve the people."

"To serve the people" was an ancient idea embedded in English political culture, but it assumed new meaning in the American colonies during the epic third quarter of the eighteenth century. Few colonists in 1750 held even a faint desire to break the connection with England, and fewer still might have predicted the form of government that 13 independent states in an independent nation might fashion. Yet 2 million colonists moved haltingly toward a showdown with mighty England. Little-known men like Ebenezer MacIntosh as well as his well-known and historically celebrated townsmen Samuel Adams, John Hancock, and John Adams were part of the struggle. Collectively, ordinary people such as MacIntosh influenced—and, in fact, sometimes even dictated—the revolutionary movement in the colonies. Though we read and speak mostly of a small group of "founding fathers," the wellsprings of the American Revolution can be fully discovered only among a variety of people from different social groups, occupations, regions, and religions.

This chapter addresses the tensions in late colonial society, the imperial crisis that followed the Seven Years' War (in the colonies, often called the French and Indian War), and the tumultuous decade that led to the "shot heard round the world" fired at Concord Bridge in April 1775. It portrays the origins of a dual American Revolution. Ebenezer MacIntosh, in leading the Boston mob against Crown officers and colonial collaborators who tried to implement a new colonial policy after 1763, helped set in motion a revolutionary movement to restore ancient liberties thought by the Americans to be under deliberate attack in England. This movement eventually escalated into the war for American independence.

But MacIntosh's Boston followers were also venting years of resentment at the accumulation of wealth and power by Boston's aristocratic elite. Behind every swing of the ax, every shattered crystal goblet and splintered mahogany chair, lay the fury of a Bostonian who had seen the city's conservative elite try to dismantle the town meeting, had suffered economic hardship, and had lost faith that opportunity and just relations still prevailed in his town. This sentiment, flowing from resentment of what many believed was a corrupt, self-indulgent, and elite-dominated society, produced a commitment to reshape American society even while severing the colonial bond. As distinguished from the war for independence, this was the American Revolution.

THE CLIMACTIC SEVEN YEARS' WAR

After a brief period of peace following King George's War (1744–1748), France and England fought the fourth, largest, and by far most significant of the wars for empire that had begun in the late seventeenth century. Known variously as the Seven Years' War, the French and Indian War, and the Great War for Empire, this global conflict in part represented a showdown for control of North America between the Atlantic Ocean and the Mississippi River. In North America, the Anglo-American forces ultimately prevailed, and their victory dramatically affected the lives of all the diverse people living in the huge region east of the Mississippi.

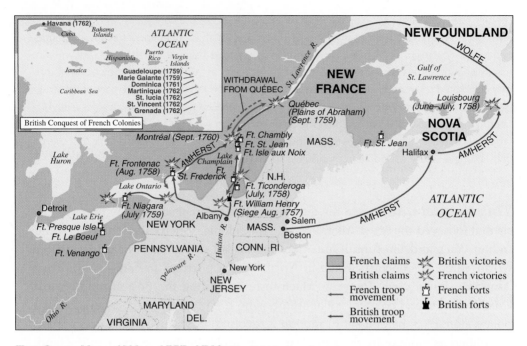

THE SEVEN YEARS' WAR, 1757–1760 The British-American victory over France and its Indian allies in the Seven Years' War did not bring peace on the western frontier. After the war, Pontiac led the warriors of several tribes in attacks on settlers and British forts.

War and the Management of Empire

England began constructing a more coherent imperial administration after the Glorious Revolution of 1688. In 1696, a professional Board of Trade replaced the old Lords of Trade; the Treasury strengthened the customs service; and Parliament created overseas vice-admiralty courts, which functioned without juries to prosecute smugglers who evaded the trade regulations set forth in the Navigation Acts. Parliament began playing a more active role after the reign of Queen Anne (1702–1714) and continued to do so when the weak, German-speaking King George I came to the throne. Royal governors received greater powers, got more detailed instructions, and came under more insistent demands from the Board of Trade to enforce British policies. England was quietly installing the machinery of imperial management tended by a corps of colonial bureaucrats.

The best test of an effectively organized state is its ability to wage war. Four times between 1689 and 1763, England matched its strength against France, its arch rival in Europe, North America, and the Caribbean. These wars of empire had tremendous consequences for the home governments, their colonial subjects, and the North American Indian tribes.

The Peace of Utrecht (see Chapter 4), which ended Queen Anne's War (1702–1713), brought victor's spoils of great importance to England. The generation of peace that followed was really only a time-out, during which both England and France strengthened their war-making capacity. Britain's productive and efficiently governed New World colonies made important contributions. Though known as a period of "salutary neglect," this was actually an era when king and Parliament increased their control over colonial affairs.

Concerned mainly with economic regulation, Parliament added new articles to the list of items produced in the colonies that had to be shipped to England before being exported to another country. Parliament also curtailed colonial production of articles important to England's economy: woolen cloth (1699), beaver hats (1732), and finished iron products (1750). Most important, Parliament passed the Molasses Act in 1733, an attempt to stop New England from trading with the French West Indies for molasses to convert into rum. Parliament imposed a prohibitive duty of six pence per gallon on French slave-produced molasses. This turned many of New England's largest merchants and distillers into smugglers, for a generation schooling them, their ship captains, crews, and allied waterfront artisans in defying royal authority.

The generation of peace ended abruptly in 1739 when England declared war on Spain. The immediate cause was the ear of an English sea captain, Robert Jenkins, which had been cut off eight years earlier when Spanish authorities caught him smuggling. Encouraged by his government, Jenkins publicly displayed his pickled ear in 1738 to whip up war fever against Spain. The real cause of the war, however, was England's determination to continue its drive toward commercial domination of the Atlantic basin.

From 1744 to 1748, the Anglo-Spanish war merged into a much larger Anglo-French conflict, called King George's War in North America and the War of Austrian Succession in Europe. Its scale far exceeded previous conflicts, highlighting the need for increased discipline within the empire. Unprecedented military expenditures led Britain to ask its West Indian and American colonies to share in the costs of defending—and extending—the empire and to tailor their behavior to home country needs. For the most part, war was costly for American colonists. Though proud of their part in capturing the French fortress of Louisbourg, the losses for the Massachusetts volunteers were staggering. Furthermore, they became bitter at war's end when England returned Louisbourg to France in exchange for other concessions.

Outbreak of Hostilities

The tension between British and French colonists in North America, which reached back to the early seventeenth century, was intensified by the spectacular population growth of the English colonies: from 250,000 in 1700 to 1.25 million in 1750, and to 1.75 million in the next decade. Three-quarters of the increase came in the colonies south of New York, propelling thousands of land-hungry settlers westward.

Fur traders and land speculators promoted this westward rush. In the 1740s and 1750s, speculators (including many future revolutionary leaders) formed land companies to capitalize on the seaboard population explosion. Colonial penetration of the Ohio valley in the 1740s established the first English outposts in the continental heartland, challenging French vital interests.

The French resisted. They attempted to block further English expansion west of the Alleghenies by constructing new forts in the Ohio valley and by prying some tribes loose from their new English connections. By 1753, the French were driving the English traders out of the Ohio River valley and establishing a line of forts between Lake Erie and the forks of the Ohio River, near present-day Pittsburgh. There, near Fort Duquesne on May 28, 1754, the French smartly rebuffed an ambitious 21-year-old Virginia militia colonel named George Washington, dispatched by his colony's government to expel them from the region.

Men in the capitals of Europe, not in the colonies, made the decision to force a showdown in the interior of North America. England's powerful merchants, supported by American clients, had been emboldened by English success in overwhelming the mighty French fortress at Louisbourg. Now, they argued, the time was ripe to destroy the French overseas trade. Convinced, the English ministry ordered several thousand troops to North America in 1754; in France, 3,000 regulars embarked to meet the English challenge.

With war looming, the colonial governments attempted to coordinate efforts. Representatives of seven colonies met at Albany, New York, in June 1754 to plan a colonial union and rewin the allegiance of the Iroquois. Both failed. The 150 Iroquois chiefs left with 30 wagonloads of gifts but made no firm commitment to fight the French. Benjamin Franklin designed a plan for an intercolonial government to manage Native American affairs, provide for defense, and have the power to pass laws and levy taxes. Even the clever woodcut displayed in the *Pennsylvania Gazette* that pictured a chopped-up snake with the insignia "Join or Die" failed to overcome long-standing jealousies, and the colonies rejected his plan.

With his newly arrived British regiments and hundreds of American recruits, General Edward Braddock slogged across Virginia in the summer of 1755, each day cutting a few miles of road through forests and across mountains. A headstrong professional soldier who regarded his European battlefield experience as sufficient for war in the American wilderness, Braddock had contempt for the woods-wise French regiments and their stealthy Native American allies.

As Braddock neared Fort Duquesne, the entire French force and the British suddenly surprised one another in the forest. The French had 218 soldiers and Canadian militiamen and 637 Native American allies; Braddock commanded 1,400 British regulars, supported by 450 Virginians and a few Indian scouts commanded by Washington. Pouring murderous fire into Braddock's tidy lines, the French and their native allies won. Braddock perished, and two-thirds of the British and Americans were killed or wounded. Washington, his uniform pierced by four bullets, had two horses shot from beneath him. Although they had 1,000 men in reserve down the road, the Anglo-American force beat a hasty retreat. This ignominious retreat brought almost every tribe north of the Ohio River to the French side. For the next two years, French-supplied Native American raiders torched the backcountry. Never was disunity within the English colonies so glaring.

Farther north, the Anglo-American forces had more success, overpowering French Fort Beauséjour, the French fort on the neck of land that connected Nova Scotia and the French Canadian mainland. This quickly led to the expulsion of the neutral French Acadians, Catholics who refused to swear oaths of unqualified allegiance to the English king, since that would revoke their religious freedom. The British rounded up about 6,000 Acadians, herded them aboard ships, and dispersed them among the English colonies, giving their confiscated land to New

Englanders. The English justified this ethnic cleansing—the first time a civilian population was relocated by force—as a wartime security measure.

In 1756, Britain officially declared war on France, and the French and Indian War in North America turned into a world war with France, Austria, and Russia pitting themselves against Britain and Prussia. The turning point in the war came after the energetic William Pitt became England's secretary of state in 1757. "I believe that I can save this nation and that no one else can," he boasted, abandoning Europe as the main theater of action against the French and throwing his nation's military might into the American campaign. The forces he dispatched to North America in 1757 and 1758 dwarfed all preceding commitments: about 23,000 British troops and a huge fleet with 14,000 mariners. But even forces of this magnitude, when asked to engage the enemy in the forests of North America, were not necessarily sufficient to the task without Native American support, or at least neutrality.

Tribal Strategies

The Iroquois knew that their interest lay in playing off one European power against the other. Anglo-American leaders knew that the support of the Iroquois and their tributary tribes was crucial and could be secured in only two ways: through purchase or by a demonstration of power that would convince the tribes that the English would prevail with or without their assistance.

The first stratagem failed. In 1754 colonial negotiators heaped gifts on the Iroquois chiefs, but received only tantalizing half-promises of support against the French. The second alternative fizzled because, for the first three years of the war, the English proved militarily inferior to the French. However, in 1758, the huge English military buildup began to produce victories. Troops under Sir Jeffrey Amherst captured Louisbourg on Cape Breton Island, and Fort Duquesne fell to another army of 6,000. These victories, and the fact that the English navy had cut the Iroquois off from French trade goods, finally moved the Iroquois away from neutrality. Added incentive to join the Anglo-American side came. By early 1759, foreseeing a French defeat in North America, the Iroquois pledged 800 warriors for an attack on Fort Niagara, the strategic French trading depot on Lake Ontario.

Dramatic Anglo-American victories did not always guarantee Indian support. Backcountry skirmishes with the Cherokee from Virginia to South Carolina turned into a costly war from 1759 to 1761. In 1760, the Cherokee mauled a British army of 1,300 under Amherst. The following summer, a much larger Anglo-American force invaded Cherokee country, burning towns and food supplies. English control of the sea interrupted the Native Americans' supply of French arms. Beset by food shortages, lack of ammunition, and a smallpox epidemic, the Cherokee finally sued for peace.

Other Anglo-American victories in 1759, the "year of miracles," decided the outcome of the bloodiest war yet known in the Americas. They captured Fort Niagara, the critical link in the system of forts that joined the French inland empire with the Atlantic, then conquered sugar-rich Martinique in the West Indies. The culminating stroke came at Québec. Led by 32-year-old General James Wolfe, 5,000 troops scaled a rocky cliff and overcame the French. The capture of Montréal late in 1760 completed the shattering of French power in North America. While fighting continued for three more years in the Caribbean and in Europe, in the American colonies, the old English dream of destroying the Gallic menace had finally come true.

Consequences of the Seven Years' War

The Seven Years' War

The Treaty of Paris, ending the Seven Years' War in 1763, brought astounding changes to European and native peoples in North America. Spain acquired New Orleans, the vast Louisiana territory west of the Mississippi, and Havana, and in turn surrendered Spanish Florida to the British. The interior tribes, which had adeptly forced Britain and France to compete for their support, suffered a severe setback when the French disappeared and the British became their sole source of trade goods.

After making peace, the British government launched a new policy designed to separate Native Americans and colonizers by creating a racial boundary roughly following the crestline of the Appalachian Mountains from Maine to Georgia. The Proclamation of 1763 reserved all land west of the line for Native American nations. White settlers who were already there were told to withdraw.

This well-meaning attempt to legislate interracial accord failed completely. Even before the proclamation was issued, the Ottawa chief Pontiac, concerned that the elimination of the French threatened the old treaty and gift-giving system, had gathered together many of the northern tribes that had aided the French assaults on the English forts during the Seven Years' War. Although Pontiac's pan-Indian movement to drive the British out of the Ohio valley collapsed in 1764, it served notice that the interior tribes would fight for their lands.

London could not enforce the proclamation. Staggering under an immense wartime debt, England decided to maintain only small army garrisons in America to regulate the interior. Nor could royal governors stop land speculators and settlers from privately purchasing land from trans-Appalachian tribes or simply encroaching on their land. The western frontier seethed after 1763.

Although the epic Anglo-American victory redrew the map of North America, the war also had important social and economic effects on colonial society. It convinced the colonists of their growing strength, yet left them debt-ridden and weakened in manpower. The war spurred economic development and poured British capital into the colonies, yet rendered them more vulnerable to cyclic fluctuations in the British economy.

When the war ended, so did the military contracts that had brought prosperity to most colonies during the war years. Huge orders for ships, arms, uniforms, and provisions enriched northern merchants and provided good prices for farmers as well. The war, however, required heavy taxes and took a huge human toll, especially in New England, which bore the brunt of the fighting. When peace came, Boston had a deficit of almost 700 men in a town of about 2,000 families. The high rate of war widowhood feminized poverty and required expanded poor relief to maintain husbandless women and fatherless children. Peace ended the casualties but also brought depression. When the bulk of the British forces left North America in 1760, the economy slumped badly, especially in the coastal towns.

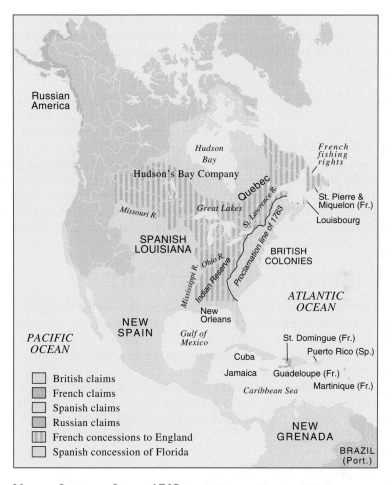

Russian America

Hudson Bay

French fishing rights

Hudson's Bay Company

Quebec

St. Pierre & Miquelon (Fr.)

Missouri R.   *Great Lakes*   *St. Lawrence R.*

Louisbourg

SPANISH LOUISIANA

Mississippi R.   *Ohio R.*   *Indian Reserve*   *Proclamation line of 1763*

BRITISH COLONIES

ATLANTIC OCEAN

New Orleans

PACIFIC OCEAN

NEW SPAIN   *Gulf of Mexico*

St. Domingue (Fr.)

Puerto Rico (Sp.)

Cuba

Jamaica   Guadeloupe (Fr.)

Caribbean Sea   Martinique (Fr.)

☐ British claims
☐ French claims
☐ Spanish claims
☐ Russian claims
▦ French concessions to England
☐ Spanish concession of Florida

NEW GRENADA

BRAZIL (Port.)

NORTH AMERICA AFTER 1763 At the Treaty of Paris in 1763, France surrendered huge claims west of the Mississippi River to Spain and east of the river to England. England also acquired Florida from Spain.

Although even some wealthy merchants went bankrupt, the greatest hardships after 1760 fell on laboring people. Established craftsmen and shopkeepers were caught between rising prices and reduced demand for their goods and services. A New York artisan expressed a common lament in 1762. Thankfully, he still had employment, he wrote in the *New-York Gazette*. But despite every effort at unceasing labor and frugal living, he had fallen into poverty and found it "beyond my ability to support my family ... [which] can scarcely appear with decency or have necessaries to subsist." His situation, he added, "is really the case with many of the inhabitants of this city."

The Seven Years' War paved the way for a far larger conflict in the next generation. The legislative assemblies, for example, which had been flexing their muscles at the expense of the governors in earlier decades, accelerated their bid for political power. The war also trained a new group of military and political leaders. In carrying out military operations on a scale unknown in the colonies and in shouldering heavier political responsibilities, men such as George Washington, Samuel Adams, Benjamin Franklin, Patrick Henry, and Christopher Gadsden acquired the experience that would serve them well in the future.

In spite of severe costs, the Seven Years' War left many colonists buoyant. New Englanders rejoiced at the final victory over the "Papist enemy of the North." Frontiersmen, fur traders, and land speculators also celebrated the French withdrawal, for the West now appeared open for exploitation. The colonists also felt a new sense of identity after the war. Surveying a world free of French and Spanish threats, they began reassessing subordination to England and the advantages of standing alone. The British, however, thought the colonists unreliable and poor fighters. He "could take a thousand grenadiers to America," boasted one officer, "and geld all the males, partly by force and partly by a little coaxing."

THE CRISIS WITH ENGLAND

At the end of the Seven Years' War, George Grenville became the chief minister of Britain's 25-year-old king, George III. By 1763, the national debt had billowed from £75 million to £145 million, straining a nation of wearied taxpayers. Grenville proposed new taxes in America, asking the colonists to bear their share of running the empire. His particular concern was financing the 10,000 British regulars left in North America after 1763 to police Canada and the Native Americans—and to remind unruly Americans that they were still subjects. In so doing, he opened a rift between England and its colonies that in a dozen years would become a revolution.

Sugar, Currency, and Stamps

DOCUMENT

Otis, the Rights of the British Colonies Asserted and Proved (1764)

In 1764, Grenville pushed through Parliament several bills that in combination pressed hard on colonial economies. First came the Revenue Act (or Sugar Act) of 1764. While reducing the tax on imported French molasses from six to three pence per gallon, it added various colonial products to the list of commodities that could be sent only to England. It also required American shippers to post bonds guaranteeing observance of the trade regulations before loading their cargoes, and it strengthened the vice-admiralty courts to prosecute violators of the trade acts.

Many colonial legislatures grumbled about the Sugar Act because a strictly enforced duty of three pence per gallon on molasses pinched more than the loosely enforced six-pence duty. But only New York objected that any tax by Parliament to raise revenue (rather than to control trade) violated the rights of overseas English subjects who were unrepresented in Parliament.

Next came the Currency Act. In 1751, Parliament had forbidden the New England colonies to issue paper money as legal tender, and now it extended that prohibition to all the colonies. In a colonial economy chronically short of cash, this constricted trade.

The move to tighten up the machinery of empire confused the colonists because many of the new regulations came from Parliament. For generations, colonists had viewed Parliament as a bastion of English liberty. Now Parliament began to seem like a violator of colonial rights. Colonial leaders were uncertain about where Parliament's authority began and ended.

Stamp Act Stamps

After Parliament passed the Sugar Act in 1764, Grenville announced his intention to extend to America the stamp duties—already imposed in England—on every newspaper, pamphlet, almanac, legal document, liquor license, college diploma, pack of playing cards, and pair of dice. He gave the colonies a year to suggest alternative ways of raising revenue. The colonies objected, but none provided another plan. Knowing that colonial property taxes were slight compared with those in England, Grenville drove the bill through Parliament. The Stamp Act became effective in November 1765.

Colonial reaction to the Stamp Act ranged from disgruntled submission to mass defiance. The breadth of the reaction shocked the British government—and many Americans as well. In many cases, resistance involved not only discontent over England's tightening of the screws on the American colonies but also internal resentments born out of local events. Especially in the cities, the defiance of authority and destruction of property by people from the middle and lower ranks redefined the dynamics of politics, setting the stage for a 10-year internal struggle for control among the various social elements alarmed by the new English policies.

Benjamin Franklin, Testimony Against the Stamp Act (1766)

Stamp Act Riots

In late 1764, Virginia's House of Burgesses strenuously objected to the proposed stamp tax, arguing that it was their "inherent" right to be taxed only by their own consent. It became the first legislature to react to the news of the Stamp Act. Virginians were already worried by a severe decline in tobacco prices and heavy war-related taxes, which mired most planters in debt. Led by newly elected 29-year-old Patrick Henry, in May 1765 the House of Burgesses debated seven strongly worded resolutions. Old-guard burgesses regarded some of them as treasonable, and they were revised. Many burgesses had left for home before Henry introduced his resolutions, so less than a quarter of Virginia's legislators voted for the four moderate resolves. But within a month, newspapers of other colonies published all seven resolutions, which included an assertion that Virginians did not have to pay externally imposed taxes and branded as an "enemy to this, his Majesty's colony" anyone who denied Virginia's exclusive right to tax itself.

Governor Francis Bernard of Massachusetts called the Virginia resolves an "alarm bell for the disaffected." August 1765 events in Boston amply confirmed his view. On August 14, Bostonians hung a rag-dressed effigy of stamp distributor Andrew Oliver. When the sheriff tried to remove it at the order of Lieutenant Governor Thomas Hutchinson, Oliver's brother-in-law, a hostile crowd intervened. In the evening, workingmen cut down Oliver's effigy, carried it boisterously through the streets, leveled his new brick office, and reduced his luxurious mansion to a shambles. The stamp distributor promptly asked to be relieved of his commission. Twelve days later, MacIntosh led the crowd as they destroyed the handsomely appointed homes of two British officials as well as that of the unpopular Hutchinson, a descendent of Anne Hutchinson.

In attacking the property of men associated with the stamp tax, the Boston crowd demonstrated not only its opposition to parliamentary policy but also its resentment of a local elite. For decades, ordinary Bostonians had aligned politically with the Boston "caucus," which led the colony's "popular party" against conservative aristocrats such as Hutchinson and Oliver. But the "rage-intoxicated rabble" had suddenly broken away from the leaders of the popular party and gone farther than they had intended. Hutchinson was one of their main targets. Characterized by young lawyer John Adams as "very ambitious and avaricious," Hutchinson was, in the popular view, chief among the "mean mercenary hirelings" of the British. Now, the more cautious political leaders knew that they would have to struggle to regain control of the protest movement.

"Bostonians Paying the Excise Man"—Cartoon

Protest took a more dignified form at the October 1765 Stamp Act Congress in New York. English authorities branded this first self-initiated intercolonial convention a "dangerous tendency." The delegates formulated 12 restrained resolutions that accepted Parliament's right to legislate for the colonies but denied its right to tax them directly.

Groups calling themselves the Sons of Liberty, composed mostly of artisans, shopkeepers, and ordinary citizens, led violent protests against the Stamp Act in New York and Newport, Rhode Island. By late 1765, effigy-burning crowds all over America were convincing stamp distributors to resign. Colonists defied English authority even more directly by forcing most customs officers and court officials to open the ports and courts for business after November 1 without using the hated stamps required after that date. This often took months of pressure and sometimes mob action, but the Sons of Liberty, frequently led by new faces in local politics, got their way by going outside the law.

In March 1766, Parliament debated the American reaction to the Stamp Act. Lobbied by many merchant friends of the Americans, Parliament voted to repeal it, bowing to expediency but also passing the Declaratory Act, which asserted Parliament's power to enact laws for the colonies in "all cases whatsoever."

The crisis had passed, yet nothing was solved. Americans had begun to recognize a grasping government trampling subjects' rights. The Stamp Act, one New England clergyman foresaw, "diffused a disgust through the colonies and laid the basis of an alienation which will never be healed." Stamp Act resisters had politicized their communities as never before. People lower down the social ladder often displaced generally cautious established leaders.

Gathering Storm Clouds

Ministerial instability in England hampered the quest for a coherent, workable American policy. Attempting to be a strong king, George III chose ministers who commanded little respect in Parliament. This led to strife between Parliament and the king's chief ministers, and a generally chaotic political situation just as the king was trying to overhaul the empire's administration. His goals included reor-

Patrick Henry, Forceful Patriot Orator From the time of his election to the Virginia House of Burgesses at the age of 29, Patrick Henry was an outspoken proponent of American rights. In this portrait, he pleads a case at a county courthouse crowded with local planters. *(Virginia Historical Society, Richmond, VA)*

ganizing the customs service, establishing a secretary of state for American affairs, and installing in the port cities three new vice-admiralty courts, which did not use juries to try accused smugglers. Still hard-pressed for revenue, the new ministry pushed through Parliament the relatively small Townshend duties on paper, lead, painters' colors, and tea. A final law suspended New York's assembly until that body ceased defying the Quartering Act of 1765, which required public funds for support of British troops garrisoned in the colony since the end of the Seven Years' War. New York knuckled under in order to save its legislature. Massachusetts led the colonial protests against the Townshend Acts. Its House of Representatives sent a circular letter written by Samuel Adams to each colony objecting to the new Townshend duties, attacking them as unconstitutional.

Showing more restraint than they had in resisting the Stamp Act, most colonists only grumbled and petitioned. But Bostonians protested stridently. In the summer of 1768, after customs officials seized a sloop owned by John Hancock for a violation of the trade regulations, an angry crowd mobbed them; for months, the officials took refuge on a British warship in Boston harbor. Newspapers warned of new measures designed to "suck the life blood" from the people and predicted that the English would send troops to "dragoon us into passive obedience." The belief grew that the English were plotting "designs for destroying our constitutional liberties."

RECOVERING THE PAST

Poetry is one of the most ancient and universal of the arts. Making its effect by the rhythmic sound and imagery of its language, poetry often expresses romantic love, grief, and responses to nature. But other kinds of poetry interest historians: reflections of human experience, often expressed with deep emotion; and political verses, often written to serve propagandistic goals. For generations, American historians have drawn on poetry to recapture feelings, ideas, and group experiences.

The revolutionary generation created such poetry. Many newspapers published weekly "Poet's Corner" satires, drinking songs, and versed commentary on issues of the day. Verse was widely used to provoke public discussion; in 1767 poets prompted the boycott of British goods to obtain Parliament's reversal of the Townshend duties.

A year later, Philadelphia's John Dickinson composed a "Liberty Song," the first set of verses learned in all the colonies. Boston's Sons of Liberty used this "Liberty Song" in annual ceremonies celebrating their resistance to the Stamp Act. Set to music and easily learned, the verses cultivated anti-British feeling and a sense of the need for intercolonial cooperation.

Of all the revolutionary era poets, none has fascinated historians more than Phillis Wheatley, a slave in Boston who wrote her first poem at age 14. In 1774 she became North America's first published black poet. Boston's "Ethiopian poetess" had been brought from Africa to Boston at age 7 and purchased by a prospering tailor named John Wheatley. Soon her master and his wife discovered that she was a prodigy. Learning English in 16 months so well that she could read the Bible, she showed an uncanny gift for writing. Much of her writing was inspired by deep religious feelings, but she was soon caught up in the dramatic events in Boston leading toward revolution. In "To the King's Most Excellent Majesty," she saluted King George III in poetry for repealing the Stamp Act; in "On the Death of Mr. Snider [Seider], Murder'd by Richardson," she lambasted the British customs officer who murdered a Boston teenager.

Wheatley was anything but radical. She had so thoroughly imbibed Christianity from her master and mistress that she wrote in one of her first poems that "Twas mercy brought me from my *Pagan* land." Many times she used poetry to implore slaves to "fly to Christ." But by 1772, she was inserting a muffled plea for an end of slavery in her odes to American rights and American resistance to British policies.

That Wheatley's poems were published in London in 1773 is remarkable. Women were not supposed to write publicly in the eighteenth century, especially not black women. Nonetheless, her master shipped a sheaf of poems to a bookseller in England, who obtained the support of the Countess of Huntingdon for publishing them. They appeared under the title *Poems on Various Subjects, Religious and Moral*. Even more remarkable was that Wheatley, only 20 years old, took ship to London to see her book come off the press. Her master and mistress financed the trip, hoping that sea air would clear her clogged lungs. There she was introduced to public dignitaries, received a copy of Milton's *Paradise Lost* from the lord mayor of London, and met with Benjamin Franklin.

Read the two poems that follow: "On the Death of Mr. Snider [Seider], Murder'd by Richardson" and her poem addressed to the King's minister for colonial affairs, penned in 1772.

On the Death of Mr. Snider, Murder'd by
  Richardson (1770)
In heaven's eternal court it was decreed
How the first martyr for the cause should bleed
To clear the country of the hated brood

We whet his courage for the common good.
Long hid before, a vile infernal here
Prevents Achilles in his mid career
Wherev'r this fury darts his Poisonous breath
All are endanger'd to the shafts of death

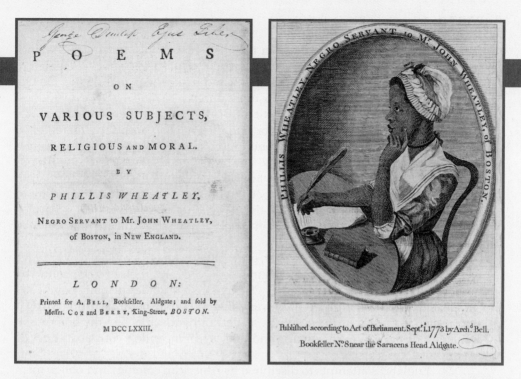

Wheatley worshiped at Old South Meeting House, where people frequently gathered for political rallies and deliberations. This partly explains Wheatley's growing interest in the political battles raging in Boston. Wheatley's patroness in England requested a drawing of Phillis for the frontispiece of this volume. *(Frontispiece and Scipio Moorehead, "Phillis Wheatley," ink drawing from the copy in the Rare Book Collection, The University of North Carolina at Chapel Hill)*

To the Right Honourable William, Earl of Dartmouth, His Majesty's Principal Secretary of State for North America (1772)

HAIL, happy day, when, smiling like the morn,
Fair Freedom rose New-England to adorn:
The northern clime beneath her genial ray,
Dartmouth, congratulates thy blissful sway:
Elate with hope her race no longer mourns,
Each soul expands, each grateful bosom burns,
While in thine hand with pleasure we behold
The silken reigns, and Freedom's charms unfold.
No more, America, in mournful strain
Of wrongs, and grievance unredress'd complain,
No longer shalt thou dread the iron chain,
Which wanton Tyranny with lawless hand
Had made, and with it meant t' enslave the land.
Should you, my lord, while you peruse my song,
Wonder from whence my love of Freedom sprung,
Whence flow these wishes for the common good,
By feeling hearts alone best understood,
I, young in life, by seeming cruel fate
Was snatch'd from Afric's fancy'd happy seat:
What pangs excruciating must molest,
What sorrows labour in my parent's breast?
Steel'd was that soul and by no misery mov'd
That from a father seiz'd his babe belov'd:
Such, such my case. And can I then but pray
Others may never feel tyrannic sway?

REFLECTING ON THE PAST   You may find the poetry stilted, but Wheatley's style was modeled on poetic conventions of the eighteenth century. What change can you discern in Wheatley's political consciousness between 1770 and 1772? Do you consider her poem on Seider's murder propagandistic? How does she relate the plight of enslaved Africans to the American colonists' struggle? More generally, how effective do you think poetry is in arousing sentiment and mobilizing political energy? Can you think of verse serving as lyrics in popular protest music today?

143

Troops indeed came. The attack on the customs officials convinced the English government that the Bostonians were insubordinate and selfish. It decided to bring them to a proper state of subordination and make them an example. On October 1, 1768, redcoats marched into Boston without resistance.

Thereafter, the colonists' main tactic of protest against the Townshend Acts became economic boycott. First in Boston and then in New York and Philadelphia, merchants and consumers adopted nonimportation and nonconsumption agreements, pledging neither to import nor to use British goods. These measures promised to bring the politically influential English merchants to their aid, for half of British shipping was engaged in commerce with the colonies, and one-quarter of all English exports were consumed there. When the southern colonies also adopted nonimportation agreements in 1768, a new step toward intercolonial union had been taken.

Many colonial merchants, however, especially those with official connections, saw nonimportation agreements as lacking legal force and refused to be bound by them. They had to be persuaded otherwise by street brigades, usually composed of artisans for whom nonimportation was a boon to home manufacturing. Crowd action welled up again in the seaports, as Patriot bands attacked the homes and warehouses of offending merchants and "rescued" incoming contraband goods seized by customs officials.

DOCUMENT

Boston Gazette, "Description of the Boston Massacre" (1770)

England's attempts to discipline its American colonies and oblige them to share the costs of governing their empire lay in shambles by the end of the 1760s. Using troops to restore order undermined the very respect needed for the colonial acceptance of parliamentary authority. The Townshend duties had failed miserably, yielding less than £21,000 by 1770 while costing British business £700,000 through the colonial nonimportation movement. On March 5, 1770, Parliament repealed all the Townshend duties except the one on tea.

On that same evening in Boston, British troops fired on an unruly crowd of heckling citizens. When the smoke cleared, five bloody bodies, including that of Ebenezer MacIntosh's brother-in-law, stained the snow-covered street. Bowing to furious popular reaction, Thomas Hutchinson, recently appointed governor, ordered the British troops out of town and arrested the commanding officer and the soldiers involved. They were later acquitted, with two young Patriot lawyers, John Adams and Josiah Quincy, Jr., providing a brilliant defense.

IMAGE

Paul Revere Etching of Boston Massacre

In spite of the potential of the "Boston Massacre" for galvanizing the colonies into further resistance, opposition to English policies, including boycotts, subsided in 1770. Popular leaders such as Samuel Adams in Boston and Alexander McDougall in New York, who had made names for themselves as the standard-bearers of American liberty, had few issues left, especially when the depression that had helped sow discontent ended. Yet the fires of revolution had not been extinguished but merely dampened.

The Growing Rift

In June 1772, the Crown created a new furor by announcing that it, rather than the provincial legislature, would henceforth pay the salaries of the royal governor and superior court judges in Massachusetts. Even though the measure saved the colony money, it looked like a scheme to impose despotic government. Judges paid from London presumably would obey London.

Boston's town meeting protested loudly and created a Committee of Correspondence to win other colonies' sympathy. By the end of 1772, another 80 towns in Massachusetts had created committees. In the next year, all but three colonies established Committees of Correspondence in their legislatures.

Samuel Adams was by now the leader of the Boston radicals, for the influence of laboring men like Ebenezer MacIntosh had been quietly reduced. Adams was an experienced caucus politicker, a skilled political journalist, and (despite his Harvard degree) had deep roots among the laboring people. He organized workers and secured the financial support of wealthy merchants such as John Hancock.

In 1772, Rhode Island gave Adams a new issue. The commander of the royal ship *Gaspee* was roundly hated by the fishermen and small traders of Narragansett Bay. When his ship ran aground while pursuing a suspected smuggler, Rhode Islanders burned it, and a local court convicted the captain of illegally seizing what he was convinced had been smuggled sugar and rum. London reacted with cries of high treason. Investigators found Rhode Islanders' lips sealed. The event was tailor-made for Samuel Adams, who used it to "awaken the American colonies, which have been too long dozing upon the brink of ruin."

The final plunge into revolution began when Parliament passed the Tea Act in early 1773, allowing the practically bankrupt East India Company to ship its tea directly to North America with the colonists paying only a small tax. Americans would get inexpensive tea, the Crown a modest revenue, and the East India Company a new lease on life. But colonists reacted furiously since their smuggled Dutch tea would be undersold. American merchants who competed with the East India Company denounced the monopoly, and colonists objected that the government's true object was to gain acceptance of Parliament's taxing power. As Americans drank the taxed tea, they would be swallowing the English right to tax them. Showing that their principles were not entirely in their pocketbooks, Americans staged mass meetings that soon forced the resignation of East India Company agents, and citizens vowed to stop the obnoxious tea at the water's edge.

Governor Hutchinson brought the tea crisis to a climax, convinced that to yield again to popular pressure would forever cripple English sovereignty in North America. Samuel Adams's Patriot party had been urging citizens to demonstrate that they were not yet prepared for the "yoke of slavery" by sending the tea back to England. When Hutchinson refused, a band of Bostonians, dressed as Native Americans, boarded the tea ships and flung £10,000 worth of the East India Company's property into Boston harbor.

Now the die was cast. Lord North, the king's chief minister, argued that the dispute was no longer about taxes but about whether England had any authority over the colonies. Parliament passed the Coercive Acts, stern laws that Bostonians promptly labeled the "Intolerable Acts." The acts closed the port of Boston to all shipping until the colony paid for the destroyed tea and barred local courts from trying British soldiers and officials for acts committed while suppressing civil disturbances. Parliament amended the Massachusetts charter, transforming the council into a body appointed by the governor and without veto power over the governor's decisions.

DOCUMENT

Hewes, "A Retrospect on the Boston Tea Party" (1834)

Portrait of Participant in the Boston Tea Party This portrait of George Robert Twelve Hewes was painted in 1835 when the last survivor of the Boston Tea Party was called "The Centenarian," though he was 93 years old. A biography of the poor shoemaker, written by Benjamin Busey Thatcher, came off the press in the same year. *(Courtesy of the Bostonian Society/Old State House)*

The act also struck at local government by authorizing the governor to prohibit all town meetings except one annual meeting to elect local officers of government. Finally, General Thomas Gage, commander in chief of British forces in America, replaced Thomas Hutchinson as governor.

Lord North's plan to strangle Massachusetts into submission and hope for acquiescence elsewhere in the colonies proved popular in England. The colonists found their maneuvering room severely narrowed. When the Intolerable Acts arrived in May 1774, Boston's town meeting urged all the colonies to ban trade with Britain. While this met with faint support, a second call, for a meeting in Philadelphia of delegates from all colonies, received a better response. Called the Continental Congress, it began to transform a 10-year debate conducted by separate colonies into a unified American cause.

In September 1774, 55 delegates from all the colonies except Georgia converged on Carpenters' Hall in Philadelphia. The discussions centered not on how to prepare for a war that many sensed was inevitable but on how to resolve sectional differences that most delegates feared were irreconcilable.

DOCUMENT

Petition of "A Grate Number of Blackes" (1774)

The Continental Congress was by no means a unified body. Some delegates, led by cousins Samuel and John Adams from Massachusetts and Richard Henry Lee and Patrick Henry of Virginia, argued for outright resistance to Parliament's Coercive Acts. Moderate delegates from the middle colonies urged restraint and further attempts at reconciliation. After weeks of debate, the delegates agreed to a restrained Declaration of Rights and Resolves, which attempted to define American grievances and justify the colonists' defiance of English policies and laws. Congress had a more concrete agreement on a plan of resistance. If England did not rescind the Intolerable Acts by December 1, 1774, all imports and exports between the colonies and Great Britain, Ireland, and the British West Indies would be banned. To keep reluctant southern colonies in the fold, some exceptions were made for the export of southern staple commodities.

By the time the Congress adjourned in late October, leaders from different colonies had transformed Boston's cause into a national movement. Patrick Henry argued dramatically, "Government is dissolved [and] we are in a state of nature. ... I am not a Virginian, but an American." Many other delegates were a long way from his conclusion; still, the Congress agreed to reconvene in May 1775.

By the time the Second Continental Congress met, the fabric of government was badly torn in most colonies. Illegal revolutionary committees, conventions, and congresses were replacing legal governing bodies. Assuming authority in defiance of royal governors, who suspended truculent legislatures in many colonies, they often operated on instructions from mass meetings where everyone, not just those entitled to vote, gave voice. These extralegal bodies created and armed militia units, bullied merchants and shopkeepers refusing to obey popularly authorized boycotts, levied taxes, operated the courts, and obstructed English customs officials. By the end of 1774, all but three colonies defied their own charters by appointing provincial assemblies without royal authority. In the next year, this independently created power became evident when trade with England practically ceased.

THE IDEOLOGY OF REVOLUTIONARY REPUBLICANISM

In the tumultuous years between 1763 and 1774, the colonists had many reactions to the crisis with Britain. Mostly these took the form of newspaper articles and pamphlets written by educated lawyers, clergymen, merchants, and planters. But the middling and lower ranks of society also expressed themselves in printed broadsides, appeals in the newspapers, and even ideologically laden popular rituals such as tarring and feathering and burning in effigy. Gradually, the colonists pieced together a political ideology, borrowed partly from English political thought, partly from the theories of the Enlightenment, and partly from their own experiences. While historians call this new ideology "revolutionary republicanism," no single coherent ideology united all the colonists' varied interests and experiences.

A Plot Against Liberty

Many American colonists agreed with earlier English Whig writers who charged that corrupt and power-hungry men were slowly extinguishing the lamp of liberty in England. The so-called "country" party represented by these Whig pamphleteers proclaimed itself the guardian of the true principles of the English constitution and opposed the "court" party—the king and his appointees.

American Liberty Abused   Liberty always had to struggle against power, as American colonists saw it; in this cartoon, England (power) forces Liberty (America in the form of a woman) to drink the "Bitter Draught" of tea. Uncompliant, America spits the tea into England's face while another corrupt Englishman peeks under her petticoat. *(Paul Revere, "The Able Doctor, or American Swallowing the Bitter Draught," engraving 1774. Courtesy of the Massachusetts Historical Society)*

From this perspective, every ministerial policy and parliamentary act in the decade after the Stamp Act appeared to be a subversion of English liberties. Most Americans regarded resistance to such blows against liberty as wholly justified.

Among many Americans, especially merchants, the attack on constitutional rights blended closely with the threats to their economic interests contained in the tough new trade policies. Merchants saw a coordinated attack on their "lives, liberties, and property." If a man was not secure in his property, he could not be secure in his citizenship, for it was property that gave a man the independence to shape his identity.

Revitalizing American Society

The continuing crisis over the imperial relationship by itself inspired many colonists to resist impending tyranny. But for others, the revolutionary mentality was also fed by a belief that an opportunity was at hand to revitalize American so-

ciety. They believed that the growing commercial connections with the decadent and corrupt mother country had injected poison into the American bloodstream. They worried about the luxury and vice around them and came to believe that resistance to England would return American so-

The Liberty Song   ciety to civic virtue, spartan living, and godly purpose.

The colonial protest movement got much of its high-toned moralism from its fervent supporters, the colonial clergy. This was especially true in New England, where even so secular a man as John Adams groaned at the "universal spirit of debauchery, dissipation, luxury, effeminacy and gaming." As in most revolutionary movements, talk of moral regeneration ennobled the cause, inspiring people in areas that had been stirred a generation before by the Great Awakening.

THE TURMOIL OF A REBELLIOUS PEOPLE

The long struggle with England over colonial rights between 1763 and 1774 did not occur in a unified society. Social and economic change, which accelerated in the late colonial period, brought deep unrest and calls for reform from many quarters.

As agitation against English policy intensified, previously passive people took a more active interest in politics. The constitutional struggle with England spread quickly into uncharted territory. Groups emerged—slaves, urban laboring people, backcountry farmers, evangelicals, women—whose enunciated goals were sometimes only loosely connected to the struggle with England. The stridency and potential power of these groups frightened many in the upper class. Losing control of protests they had initially led, many would abandon the resistance movement.

Urban People

Although the cities contained only about 5 percent of the colonial population, they were the core of revolutionary agitation. As centers of communications, government, and commerce, they led the way in protesting English policy, and they soon contained the most politicized citizens in America. Local politics could be rapidly transformed as the struggle against England meshed with calls for internal reform.

Philadelphia offers a good example of popular empowerment. Before the Seven Years' War, craftsmen had usually acquiesced to local leadership by merchant and lawyer politicos. But economic difficulties in the 1760s and 1770s led them to band together within their craft and community. Artisans played a central role in forging and enforcing a nonimportation agreement in 1768. Cautious merchants complained that mere artisans had "no right to give their sentiments respecting an importation" and called the craftsmen a "rabble." But artisans, casting off their customary deference, forged ahead. By 1772, they were filling elected municipal positions and insisting on their right to participate equally with their social superiors in nominating assemblymen and other important officeholders. They also began lobbying for reform laws, calling for elected representatives to be more accountable to their constituents. Genteel Philadelphians muttered, "It is time the tradesmen were checked—they ought not to intermeddle in state affairs—they will become too powerful."

By 1774, the Philadelphia working class's meddling in state affairs reached a bold new stage—de facto assumption of governmental powers by committees created by the people at large. Artisans had first assumed such extralegal author-ity in policing the nonimportation agreement in 1768. Now, responding to the Intolerable Acts, they proposed a radical slate of candidates for a committee to en-force a new economic boycott. Their ticket drubbed one nominated by conserva-tive merchants.

The political support of the new radical leaders centered in the 31 companies of the Philadelphia militia, composed mostly of laboring men, and in the extrale-gal committees now controlling the city's economic life. Their leadership helped overcome the conservatism of the regularly elected Pennsylvania legislature, which was resisting the movement of the Continental Congress toward independ-ence. The new radical leaders demanded internal reforms: curbing the accumula-tion of wealth by "our great merchants ... at the expense of the people"; abolish-ing the property requirement for voting; allowing militiamen to elect their officers; and imposing stiff fines, to be used for the support of the families of poor militiamen, on men who refused militia service.

Philadelphia's radicals never controlled the city. They always jostled for posi-tion with prosperous artisans and shopkeepers of more moderate views and with cautious lawyers and merchants. But mobilization among artisans, laborers, and mariners, in other cities as well as Philadelphia, became part of the chain of events that led toward independence. Whereas most of the Patriot elite fought only to change English colonial policy, the people of the cities also struggled for internal reforms and raised notions of how an independent American society might be reorganized.

Patriot Women

Colonial women also played a vital role in the movement toward revolution, and they drew upon revolutionary arguments to define their own goals. They signed nonimportation agreements, harassed noncomplying merchants, and helped or-ganize "fast days," on which communities prayed for deliverance from British oppression. But the women's most important role was to facilitate the boycott of English goods. The success of the nonconsumption pacts depended on substitut-ing homespun cloth for English textiles on which colonists of all classes had al-ways relied. From Georgia to Maine, women and children began spinning yarn and weaving cloth. Towns often vied patriotically in the manufacture of cotton, linen, and woollen cloth, the women staging spinning contests to publicize their commitment.

After the Tea Act in 1773, the interjection of politics into the household econ-omy increased as patriotic women boycotted their favorite drink. Newspapers carried recipes for tea substitutes and recommendations for herbal teas. In Wilm-ington, North Carolina, women paraded solemnly through the town and then made a ritual display of their patriotism by burning their imported tea.

Colonial protests and petitions against England's arbitrary uses of power changed women's perception of their role. The more male leaders talked about England's intentions to "enslave" the Americans and England's callous treatment of its colonial "subjects," the more American women began to rethink their own domestic situations. The language of protest against England reminded many

Satirizing Women's Activism As marketgoers and consumers, urban women played a crucial role in applying economic pressure on England during the prerevolutionary decade. This British cartoon, published in 1775, derisively depicts a group of North Carolina women signing an anti-tea agreement. *(Library of Congress)*

American women that they too were badly treated "subjects" of their husbands, who often dealt with them cruelly and exercised power over them arbitrarily.

Most American women, still bound by the social conventions of the day, were not ready to occupy such new territory. But the protests against England had stirred up new thoughts about what seemed "arbitrary" or "despotic" in their own society and a new feeling that what had been endured in the past was no longer acceptable.

Protesting Farmers

In most of the agricultural areas of the colonies, where the majority of settlers made their livelihoods, passions over English policies awakened only slowly. After about 1740, farmers had benefited from a sharp rise in the demand for foodstuffs in England, southern Europe, and the West Indies. Rising prices and brisk markets brought a higher standard of living to thousands of rural colonists, especially south of New England. Living far from harping English customs officers, impressment gangs, and occupying armies, the colonists of the interior had to be drawn gradually into the resistance movement by their urban cousins. Even in Concord, Massachusetts, only a dozen miles from the center of colonial agitation, townspeople found little to protest in English policies until England closed the port of Boston in 1774.

Still, other parts of rural America seethed with social tension in the prewar era. The dynamics of conflict, shaped by the social development of particular regions, eventually became part of the momentum for revolution. In three western

TIMELINE

1696	Parliament establishes Board of Trade
1701	Iroquois set policy of neutrality
1702–1713	Queen Anne's War
1713	Peace of Utrecht
1733	Molasses Act
1739–1742	War of Jenkins' Ear
1744–1748	King George's War
1754	Albany Conference
1755	Braddock defeated by French and Indian allies
	Acadians expelled from Nova Scotia
1756–1763	Seven Years' War
1759	Wolfe defeats the French at Québec
1759–1761	Cherokee War against the English
1760s	Economic slump
1763	Treaty of Paris ends Seven Years' War
	Proclamation Line limits westward expansion
1764	Sugar and Currency acts
	Pontiac's Rebellion in Ohio valley
1765	Colonists resist Stamp Act
	Virginia House of Burgesses issues Stamp Act resolutions
1766	Declaratory Act
	Tenant rent war in New York
	Slave insurrections in South Carolina
1767	Townshend duties imposed
1768	British troops occupy Boston
1770	"Boston Massacre"
	Townshend duties repealed (except on tea)
1771	North Carolina Regulators defeated
1772	*Gaspee* incident in Rhode Island
1773	Tea Act provokes Boston Tea Party
1774	"Intolerable Acts"
	First Continental Congress meets in Philadelphia

counties of North Carolina and in the Hudson River valley of New York, for example, widespread civil disorder marked the prerevolutionary decades.

For years, the small farmers of western North Carolina had suffered exploitation by corrupt county court officials appointed by the governor and a legislature dominated by eastern planter interests. Sheriffs and justices, allied with land speculators and lawyers, seized property when farmers could not pay their taxes and sold it, often at a fraction of its worth, to their cronies. The legislature rejected western petitions for lower taxes, paper currency, and lower court fees. In the mid-1760s, frustrated at getting no satisfaction from legal forms of protest, the farmers formed associations—the so-called Regulators—that forcibly closed the courts, attacked the property of their enemies, and whipped judges and lawyers. When their leaders were arrested, the Regulators stormed the jails and released them.

In 1768 and again in 1771, Governor William Tryon led troops against the Regulators. Bloodshed was averted on the first occasion. On the second, at the Battle of Alamance, two armies of more than 1,000 fired on each other. Nine men died on each side before the Regulators fled the field. Six leaders were executed in the ensuing trials. Though the Regulators lost the battle, their protests became part of the larger revolutionary struggle. They railed against the self-interested behavior of a wealthy elite and asserted the necessity for people of humble rank to throw off deference and assume political responsibilities.

Rural insurgency over land holdings in New York flared up in the 1750s, subsided, and then erupted again in 1766. A few wealthy families with enormous landholdings, acquired as virtually free gifts from royal governors, controlled the Hudson River valley. The Van Rensselaer manor, for example, totaled a million acres. Hundreds of tenants with their families paid substantial annual rents for the right to farm on these lands. When tenants resisted rent increases or purchased land from Indians who swore that manor lords had extended the boundaries of their manors by fraud, the landlords began evicting them.

As the wealthiest men of the region, the landlords had the power of government, including control of the courts, on their side. Organizing themselves and going outside the law became the tenants' main strategy, as with the Carolina Regulators. By 1766, while New York City was absorbed in the Stamp Act furor, tenants led by William Prendergast began resisting sheriffs who tried to evict them from lands they claimed. The militant tenants threatened landlords with death and broke open jails to rescue friends. British troops from New York were used to break the tenant rebellion. Prendergast was tried and sentenced to be hanged, beheaded, and quartered. Although he was pardoned, the bitterness of the Hudson River tenants endured through the Revolution. Most of them, unlike the Carolina Regulators, fought for the British because their landlords were Patriots.

Conclusion

On the Brink of Revolution

The colonial Americans who lived in the third quarter of the eighteenth century participated in an era of political tension and conflict that changed the lives of nearly everyone. The Seven Years' War removed French and Spanish challengers and nurtured the colonists' sense of separate identity. Yet it left them with difficult economic adjustments, heavy debts, and growing social divisions. The colonists heralded the Treaty of Paris in 1763 as the dawning of a new era, but it led to a reorganization of England's triumphant yet debt-torn empire that had profound repercussions in America.

In the prerevolutionary decade, as England and the colonies moved from crisis to crisis, a dual disillusionment penetrated ever deeper into the colonial consciousness. Pervasive doubt arose concerning both the colonies' role, as assigned by England, in the economic life of the empire and the sensitivity of the government in London to the colonists' needs. Meanwhile, the colonists began to perceive British policies—instituted by Parliament, the king, and his advisors—as a systematic attack on the fundamental liberties and natural rights of British citizens in North America.

The fluidity and diversity of colonial society and the differing experiences of Americans during and after the Seven Years' War evoked varying responses to the disruption that accompanied the English reorganization of the empire. In the course of resisting English policy, many previously inactive colonists, such as the humble shoemaker Ebenezer MacIntosh, entered public life to challenge gentry control of political affairs. Often occupying the most radical ground in the opposition to England, they simultaneously challenged the growing concentration of economic and political power in their own communities. What lay ahead was not only war with England but protracted arguments about how the American people, if they prevailed in their war for independence, should refashion their society.

Questions for Review and Reflection

1. What roles did Native Americans play in the imperial conflicts of the eighteenth century?

2. How did the Seven Years' War help pave the way for the colonies' break with Britain?

3. The British government pursued policies toward its colonies that it thought reasonable and just in the aftermath of the Treaty of Paris. Why did many colonists see these policies in an entirely different light?

4. What was the contribution of "republican ideology" to the revolutionary movement?

5. What does it mean to say that there were two American revolutions? How were the two related?

Discovering U.S. History Online

Exploring the West from Monticello: An Exhibition of Maps and Navigational Instruments
www.lib.virginia.edu/exhibits/lewis_clark/home.html
Maps and charts reveal knowledge and conceptions about the known and the unknown. This site includes a number of eighteenth-century maps.

Maps of the French and Indian War www.masshist.org/maps/MapsHome/Home.htm
In addition to contemporary maps, this site explains the political significance of the maps and gives a background of the wars.

1755: The French and Indian War web.syr.edu/~laroux/
This amateur site presents information about French soldiers who came to New France between 1755 and 1760 to fight in the French and Indian War as well as a list of key places.

Religion and the American Revolution www.lcweb.loc.gov/exhibits/religion/rel02.html
Providing an overview of eighteenth-century religion in the American colonies, this site draws on primary source material such as paintings of clergyman, title pages of published sermons, and other artifacts.

Journals of the Continental Congress www.memory.loc.gov/ammem/amlaw/lwjc.html
This site has a searchable version of "the daily proceedings of the Congress as kept by the office of its secretary, Charles Thomson."

The Freedom Trail www.thefreedomtrail.org/index.html
This site presents the story of colonial protest via Boston historical sites.

Fiction and Film

Americans have written novels about the American Revolution almost from the day the firing stopped. James Fenimore Cooper's *The Spy: A Tale of the Neutral Ground* (1822) is the best of the early ones. Historian Paul Leicester Ford's *Janice Meredith: A Story of the American Revolution* (1899) remains absorbing a century after its publication. In the modern period, Kenneth Roberts's four novels on the Revolution have entertained American readers for two generations: *Arundel* (1933); *Oliver Wiswell* (1940); *Rabble in Arms* (1953); and *The Battle of Cowpens: The Great Morale-Builder* (1958). *Oliver Wiswell* is especially notable for its recreation of a Loyalist's view of the Revolution. *Mary Silliman's War* (Heritage Film and Citadel Film, 1993) shows the Revolution through the eyes of a Connecticut family where husband and wife must reconcile their differing views on the Patriots and Loyalists. The English film on George III, *The Madness of King George* (1994), brings alive the era of the American Revolution and turns the king into the deeply psychotic ruler that some at the time believed he was. *Liberty* (Middlemarch Films, 1997) is a docudrama produced for television that has many high moments but neglects the internal struggles within the Patriot ranks for reforming American society.

Recommended Reading

www.ablongman.com/nash
The Companion Website has a list of recommended readings about the Seven Years' War, the crisis with England, revolutionary republicanism, and the turmoil of rebellious Americans.

A People in Revolution

American Stories

Struggling for Independence

Among the Americans wounded and captured at the Battle of Bunker Hill in the spring of 1775 was Lieutenant William Scott of Peterborough, New Hampshire. Asked by his captors how he had come to be a rebel, "Long Bill" Scott replied:

> The case was this Sir! I lived in a Country Town; I was a Shoemaker, & got [my] living by my labor. When this rebellion came on, I saw some of my neighbors get into commission, who were no better than myself. ... I was asked to enlist, as a private soldier. My ambition was too great for so low a rank. I offered to enlist upon having a lieutenant's commission, which was granted. I imagined my self now in a way of promotion. If I was killed in battle, there would be an end of me, but if my Captain was killed, I should rise in rank, & should still have a chance to rise higher. These Sir! were the only motives of my entering into the service. For as to the dispute between Great Britain & the colonies, I know nothing of it; neither am I capable of judging whether it is right or wrong.

Scott may have been trying to gain the sympathy of his captors, but people fought in America's Revolutionary War out of fear and ambition as well as on principle. We have no way of knowing whether Long Bill Scott's motives were typical. Certainly many Americans knew more than he about the colonies' struggle with England, but many did not.

In the spring of 1775, the Revolutionary War had just begun. So had Long Bill's adventures. When the British evacuated Boston a year later, Scott was transported to Halifax, Nova Scotia. After several months' captivity, he managed to escape and make his way home to fight once more. He was recaptured in November 1776 near New York City, when its garrison fell to a surprise British assault. Again Scott escaped, this time by swimming the Hudson River at night with his sword tied around his neck and his watch pinned to his hat.

During 1777, he returned to New Hampshire to recruit his own militia company. It included two of his eldest sons. In the fall, his unit helped defeat Burgoyne's army near Saratoga, New York, and later it took part in the fighting around Newport, Rhode Island. When his light infantry company was ordered to Virginia in early 1778, Scott's health broke, and he was permitted to resign from the army. After only a few months of recuperation, however, he was at it again. During the last years of the war, he served as a volunteer on a navy frigate.

For seven years, the war held Scott in its harsh grasp. His oldest son died of camp fever after six years of service. In 1777, Long Bill sold his New Hampshire farm to meet family expenses. He lost a second farm in Massachusetts shortly afterward. After his wife died, he helplessly turned their youngest children over to relatives and set off to beg a pension or job from the government.

Long Bill's saga was still not complete. In 1792, he rescued eight people when their boat capsized in New York harbor. Three years later, General Benjamin Lincoln took Scott with him to the Ohio country, where they surveyed land that was opening for white settlement. At last he had a respectable job and even a small government pension as compensation for his wounds. But trouble would still not let him go. While surveying on the Black River near Sandusky, Scott and his colleagues contracted "lake fever." Though ill, he guided part of the group back to Fort Stanwix in New York, then returned for the others. It was his last heroic act. A few days after his second trip, on September 16, 1796, Long Bill died.

American independence and the Revolutionary War that accompanied it were not as hard on everyone as they were on Long Bill Scott, yet together they transformed the lives of countless Americans. The war lasted longer than any other of America's wars until Vietnam nearly two centuries later. And unlike the nation's twentieth-century contests, it was fought on American soil. It called men by the thousands from shops and fields, disrupted families, destroyed communities, spread disease, and made a shambles of the economy. The war had far different consequences for men than women, black slaves than their white masters, Native Americans than frontier settlers, and overseas merchants than urban workers. This chapter examines each of these issues, as well as the war's military progress.

The chapter also explains how America's struggle for independence became internationalized as France and other nations, driven by their own imperial ambitions and the realities of European power politics, joined in the conflict against England. The Treaty of Paris (1783) that ended the war not only secured American independence, but also redrew the contours of imperial ambition in North America and recast relations between England and the nations of western Europe. More than that, America's fight for independence ushered in an extended Age of Revolution that over the following half century would see a king toppled and aristocratic privilege overthrown in France, political reforms erupt throughout much of Europe, and independence movements undercut European imperialism in Haiti and Latin America.

Amid the struggle for independence, the American people mounted a political revolution of profound importance, another topic of Chapter 6. Politics and government were transformed in keeping with republican principles and the clash of opposing interests. How much power should the new state governments have, and how democratic could they safely be? Could individual liberty be reconciled with the need for public order? Should women as well as men, and free blacks as well as whites be considered American citizens? And what should the new national government be like? Seldom has the nation's political agenda been more explosive, or more sharply contested, than during these critical years.

Our understanding of the experience out of which the American nation emerged must begin with the Revolutionary War, for as Long Bill Scott understood all too well, liberty came at a high cost.

BURSTING THE COLONIAL BONDS

By the spring of 1775, tension between the colonies and England was at the breaking point. In each of the colonies, extralegal committees and assemblies organized resistance to the Intolerable Acts, while in England, Parliament and the king's ministers prepared to crush the colonial challenge to British authority. The outbreak of fighting at Lexington and Concord transformed the imperial crisis. No longer was it limited to a struggle over competing theories of parliamentary authority and colonial rights, for now the firing had commenced and men on both sides lay dying. Within little more than a year of that fateful event, England's empire was severed.

The Final Rupture

DOCUMENT

Joseph Warren, "Account of the Battle of Lexington" (1775)

The final spark to the revolutionary powder keg was struck in April 1775. The government in London ordered General Gage, commander of the British troops occupying Boston, to arrest "the principal actors and abettors" of insurrection. Under cover of night, he sent 700 redcoats out of Boston to seize colonial arms in nearby Concord. But Americans learned of the plan, and when the troops reached Lexington at dawn, 70 armed Minutemen—townsmen available on a minute's notice—were waiting. In the ensuing skirmish, 18 Massachusetts farmers fell, 8 of them mortally wounded.

Marching farther west, to Concord, the British encountered another firefight. Withdrawing, the redcoats made their way back to Boston, harassed by militiamen firing from farmhouses and from behind stone walls. Before the bloody day ended, 273 British and 95 Americans lay dead or wounded. News of the bloodshed swept through the colonies. Within weeks, thousands of men besieged the British troops in Boston. According to one colonist, everywhere "you see the inhabitants training, making firelocks, casting mortars, shells, and shot."

IMAGE

Portrait of Benjamin Franklin, ca. 1794–1802

As fighting erupted around Boston, the Second Continental Congress assembled in May 1775 in Philadelphia. Many delegates knew one another from the earlier Congress. But fresh faces appeared, including Boston's wealthy merchant, John Hancock; a young planter-lawyer from Virginia, Thomas Jefferson; and Benjamin Franklin, who had recently arrived from London.

Meeting in the statehouse where the king's arms hung over the entrance and the inscription on the tower bell read "Proclaim liberty throughout the land unto all the inhabitants thereof," the Second Congress set to work. Though its powers were unclear and its legitimacy uncertain, the desperate situation required action. After a spirited debate, Congress authorized a continental army of 20,000 and, partly to cement Virginia to the cause, chose George Washington as commander in chief. Over succeeding weeks, it issued a "Declaration of Causes of Taking-up Arms," sent the king an "Olive Branch Petition" humbly begging him to remove the obstacles to reconciliation, made moves to secure the neutrality of the interior Indian tribes, issued paper money, and approved plans for a military hospital.

While debate continued over whether the colonies ought to declare themselves independent, military action grew more intense. The fiery Ethan Allen and his Green Mountain Boys from eastern New York captured Fort Ticonderoga, controlling the Champlain valley, in May 1775. On New Year's Day in 1776, the British shelled Norfolk, Virginia. Still, many members of Congress dreaded a final rupture and hoped for reconciliation. Such hopes finally crumbled at the end of 1775 when news arrived that the king, rejecting the Olive Branch Petition and proclaiming the colonies in "open and avowed rebellion," had dispatched 20,000 additional British troops to quell the insurrection. Those fatal words made Congress's actions treasonable and turned all who obeyed the Congress into traitors.

DOCUMENT

Royal Proclamation of Rebellion (1775)

Thomas Paine's *Common Sense*

As the crisis deepened, a pamphlet appeared that would speed the move toward independence. Published in Philadelphia on January 9, 1776, Thomas Paine's *Common Sense* soon appeared in bookstalls all over the colonies. In scathing language, Paine denied the very legitimacy of monarchy. "Of more worth is one honest man to society," he scoffed, "than all the crowned ruffians that ever lived." It was Paine's unsparing rejection of monarchy that made his pamphlet seem so radical. From that it was a logical step to call openly for Americans to act in defense of their liberties. "O ye that love mankind," he declared. "Ye that dare oppose not only the tyranny, but also the tyrant, stand forth!"

DOCUMENT

Thomas Paine, "Address to American Inhabitants" (Februay 14, 1776)

The pamphlet's astounding popularity—it went through 25 editions in 1776 and sold more copies than any printed piece in colonial history—stemmed not only from its argument but also from its style. Shunning the elaborate, legalistic language of most pamphlets written by lawyers and clergymen, Paine wrote for the common people who read little more than the Bible. Using biblical imagery and plain language, he appealed to their Calvinist heritage and millenial yearnings: "We have it in our power to begin the world over again," he exulted. "The birthday of a new world" is at hand. It was language that could be understood on the docks, in the taverns, on the streets, and in the farmyards.

Many Whig leaders found his pungent rhetoric and egalitarian call for ending hereditary privilege and leadership by the colonial elite too strong. Some denounced the disheveled immigrant as a "crack-brained zealot for democracy" who appealed to "every silly clown and illiterate mechanic." But thousands who read or listened to *Common Sense* were radicalized by it and came to believe not only that independence could be wrestled from England, but also that a new social and political order could be created in North America.

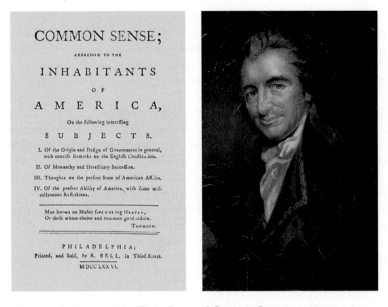

Thomas Paine and the Title Page of Comon Sense. In *Common Sense*, Thomas Paine took the radical step of attacking George III and the entire concept of monarchy in plain but muscular language that common folk could understand. Why do you suppose Paine did not put his name on the title page (though he was quickly identified as the author)? *(Left, Library of Congress; right, By courtesy of the National Portrait Gallery, London)*

Declaring Independence

DOCUMENT

Jefferson, "Rough Draft" of the Declaration of Independence (June 1776)

By the time Paine's hard-hitting pamphlet appeared, members of Congress were talking less gingerly about independence. When England embargoed all trade to the colonies and ordered the seizure of American ships, Congress declared American ports open to all countries. "Nothing is left now," Joseph Hewes of North Carolina admitted, "but to fight it out." It was almost anticlimactic when Richard Henry Lee introduced a congressional resolution on June 7 calling for independence. After two days of debate, Congress ordered a committee chaired by Jefferson to begin drafting such a document.

IMAGE

Independence Hall

Though it would become revered as the new nation's birth certificate, the Declaration of Independence was not a highly original statement. It drew heavily on Congress's earlier justifications of American resistance. The ringing phrases that "all men are created equal, that they are endowed by their Creator with certain unalienable Rights, that among these are Life, Liberty, and the pursuit of Happiness" were familiar in the writing of many American pamphleteers.

Congress began to debate the proposed declaration on Monday, July 1. The following day 12 delegations voted "yes," with New York abstaining, thus allowing Congress to say that the vote for independence was unanimous. Two more days were spent polishing the document. The major change was the elimination of a long argument blaming the king for slavery in America. On July 4, Congress sent the document to the printer.

IMAGE

The Signing of the Declaration of Independence, Copy of John Trumbull Painting (1817–1818)

Four days later, Philadelphians thronged to the state house to hear the Declaration of Independence read aloud. They "huzzahed" the reading, tore the king's arms from above the state house door, and later that night, amid cheers, toasts, and clanging church bells, hurled this symbol of more than a century and a half of colonial dependency on England into a roaring fire. Across the land, people raised toasts to the great event: "Liberty to those who have the spirit to preserve it," and "May Liberty expand sacred wings, and, in glorious effort, diffuse her influence o'er and o'er the globe." Independence had been declared; the war, however, was yet to be won.

THE WAR FOR AMERICAN INDEPENDENCE

The war began in Massachusetts in 1775, but within a year shifted to the middle states. After 1779, the South became the primary theater. Why did this geographic pattern develop, what was its significance, and why did the Americans win?

The War in the North

For a brief time following Lexington and Concord, British officials thought of launching forays out from Boston into the surrounding countryside. They soon reconsidered, however, for the growing size of the continental army and the absence of significant Loyalist strength in the New England region urged caution. More important, Boston became untenable after the Americans placed artillery on the strategic Dorchester Heights. On March 7, 1776, the British commander, General William Howe, decided to evacuate the city. Fearing retaliation against Loyalists and wishing not to destroy lingering hopes of reconciliation, Howe spared the city from the torch, but the departing British left it in shambles. "Almost everything here, appears gloomy and melancholy," lamented one returning resident.

For half a dozen years after Boston's evacuation, British ships prowled the New England coast, confiscating supplies and attacking coastal towns. Yet away from the coast, there was little fighting. Most New Englanders had reason to be thankful.

The British established their new military headquarters in New York City, which offered important strategic advantages: a fine harbor, control of the Hudson River route to the interior, and access to the abundant grain and livestock of the mid-Atlantic states. Loyalist sentiment ran deep there, too. When in the summer of 1776 Washington challenged the British for control of New York City, he was badly defeated. By late October, the city was firmly in British hands. It would remain so until the war's end.

MAP

The American Revolution

In the fall of 1776, King George III instructed his two chief commanders in North America, the brothers General William Howe and Admiral Richard Howe, to make a final effort at reconciliation with the colonists. In early September, the Howes met with three delegates from Congress on Staten Island in New York

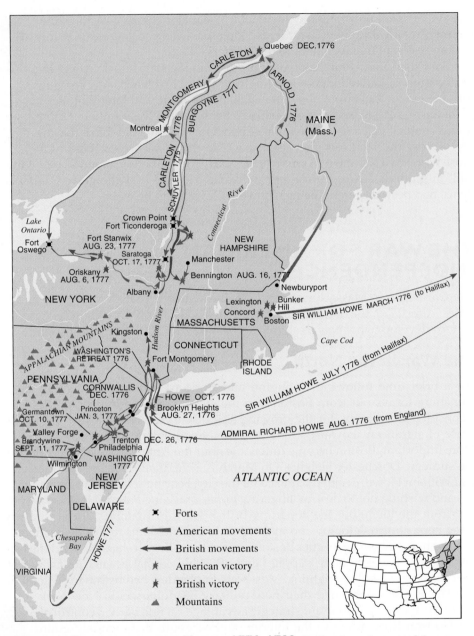

MILITARY OPERATIONS IN THE NORTH, 1776–1780 During the early years of the war, fighting was most intense in upper New York and the mid-Atlantic states. There, as in the South, the British and their Native American allies opened a second front far to the interior. Why did they do so, and how did this complicate American strategy?

harbor. But when the Howes demanded revocation of the Declaration of Independence before negotiations could begin, all hope of reconciliation vanished.

For the next two years, the war swept back and forth across New Jersey and Pennsylvania. Reinforced by German mercenaries hired in Europe, the British moved virtually at will. Neither the state militias nor the continental army—weakened by losses, low morale, and inadequate supplies—offered serious opposition. At Trenton, New Jersey, in December 1776 and at Princeton the following month, Washington surprised the British and scored victories that prevented the Americans' collapse. But survival remained the rebels' primary goal.

American efforts during the first year of the war to invade British Canada and bring it into the rebellion also fared badly. In November 1775, American forces had taken Montreal. But the subsequent assault against Québec ended with almost 100 Americans killed or wounded and more than 300 taken prisoner. The American cause could not survive many such losses.

Washington had learned the painful lesson at New York that his troops were no match for the British in frontal combat. He realized, moreover, that if the continental army was defeated, American independence would certainly be lost. Thus he decided to harass the British, make the war as costly for them as possible, and protect the civilian population as best he could while avoiding major battles. He followed that strategy for the rest of the war.

The war's middle years turned into a deadly chase that neither side could win. In September 1777, the British took Philadelphia, sending Congress fleeing into the countryside, but then hesitated to press their advantage. On numerous occasions British commanders failed to act decisively, either reluctant to move through the hostile countryside or uncertain of their instructions. In October 1777, the Americans won an important victory at Saratoga, New York, where General John Burgoyne surrendered with 5,700 British soldiers. That victory prompted France to join the struggle against England.

Congress and the Articles of Confederation

As war erupted, the Continental Congress turned to the task of creating a more permanent and effective national government. It was a daunting assignment, for prior to independence the colonies had quarreled over conflicting boundaries, control of the Indian trade, and commercial advantage within the empire. The crisis with England had forced them together, and Congress was the initial embodiment of that tenuous union.

As long as hope of reconciliation with England lingered, Congress's uncertain authority posed no serious problems. But as independence and the prospects of an extended war loomed, pressure to establish a more durable central government increased. On June 20, 1776, shortly before independence was declared, Congress appointed a committee, chaired by John Dickinson of Pennsylvania, to draw up a plan of perpetual union. So urgent was the crisis that the committee responded in a month's time and debate on the proposed Articles of Confederation soon began.

The delegates promptly clashed over whether to form a strong, consolidated government or a loose confederation of sovereign states. As discussions went on, those differences sharpened. Dickinson's draft, outlining a government of considerable power, generated strong opposition. American experience with a "tyrannous" king and Parliament had revealed the dangers of central governments unmindful of the people's liberties.

As finally approved, the Articles of Confederation represented a compromise. Article 9 gave Congress sole authority to regulate foreign affairs, declare war,

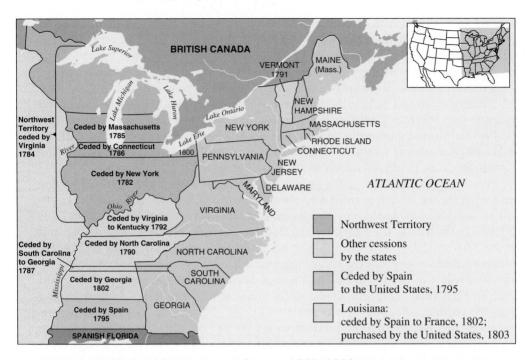

WESTERN LAND CLAIMS CEDED BY THE STATES, 1782–1802 Seven of the original states laid claim, based on their colonial charters, to lands west of the Appalachian Mountains. Eventually those states ceded those lands to Congress, thus making ratification of the Articles of Confederation and the creation of new states possible. Why were the western claims such a problem?

mediate interstate boundary disputes, manage the post office, and administer relations with Indians living outside state boundaries. The Articles also stipulated that the inhabitants of each state were to enjoy the "privileges and immunities" of the citizens of every other state. Embedded in that clause was the basis for national, as distinguished from state, citizenship.

But the Articles sharply limited what Congress could do and reserved broad governing powers to the states. For example, Congress could neither raise troops nor levy taxes, but only ask the states for support. Article 2 stipulated that each state was to "retain its sovereignty, freedom and independence," as well as "every power ... which is not by this confederation expressly delegated to the United States in Congress assembled." And the Articles could be amended only by the unanimous agreement of the 13 states.

Though Congress sent the Articles to the states for approval in November 1777, they were not ratified until March 1781. Ratification required approval by all 13 states, and that was hard to obtain. The biggest impediment was a bitter dispute over control of lands west of the Appalachian Mountains. Some states had western claims tracing back to their colonial charters, but other states, such as Maryland and New Jersey, did not. In December 1778, the Maryland assembly announced that it would not ratify until all the western lands had been ceded to

Congress. For several years, ratification hung in the balance while politicians and land speculators jockeyed for advantage. Finally, in 1780 New York and Virginia agreed to give up their western lands. Those decisions paved the way for Maryland's ratification in early 1781. Approval of the Articles was now assured.

Meanwhile, Congress managed the war effort as best it could, using the unratified Articles as a guide. Events quickly proved its inadequacy, because Congress could do little more than pass resolutions and implore the states for support. If they refused, as they frequently did, Congress could only protest and urge cooperation. Its ability to function was further limited by the stipulation that each state's delegation cast but one vote. Disagreements within state delegations sometimes prevented them from voting at all. That could paralyze Congress, because most important decisions required a nine-state majority.

As the war dragged on, Washington repeatedly criticized Congress for its failure to support the army. Acknowledging its own ineffectiveness, Congress in 1778 temporarily granted Washington extraordinary powers and asked him to manage the war on his own. In the end, Congress survived because enough of its members realized that disaster would follow its collapse.

The War Moves South

As the war in the North bogged down in a costly stalemate, Britain adopted an alternative strategy: invasion and pacification of the southern states. Royal officials in the South encouraged the idea with reports that thousands of Loyalists would rally to the British standard. Moreover, if the slaves could be lured to the British side, the balance might tip in Britain's favor. Even the threat of slave rebellion would weaken white southerners' will to resist. Persuaded by these arguments, the British shifted the war's focus southward for its last three years.

Georgia—small, isolated, and largely defenseless—was the initial target. In December 1778, Savannah, the state's major port, fell to a seaborne attack. For nearly two years, the Revolution in the state virtually ceased. Encouraged, the British turned to the Carolinas, with equally impressive results. On May 12, 1780, Charleston surrendered after a month's siege. At a cost of only 225 casualties, the British captured the entire 5,400-man American garrison. It was the costliest American defeat of the war.

After securing Charleston, the British quickly extended their control north and south along the coast. At Camden, South Carolina, the British killed nearly 1,000 Americans and captured 1,000 more, temporarily destroying the southern continental army. Scarcely pausing, the British pushed on into North Carolina. There, however, British officers quickly learned the difficulty of extending their lines into the interior: distances were too large, problems of supply too great, the reliability of Loyalist troops too uncertain, and popular support for the Revolutionary cause too strong.

In October 1780, Washington sent Nathanael Greene south to lead the continental forces. It was a fortunate choice, for Greene knew the region and the kind of war that had to be fought. Determined, like Washington, to avoid large-scale encounters, Greene divided his army into small, mobile bands. Employing what today would be called guerrilla tactics, he harassed the British and their Loyalist

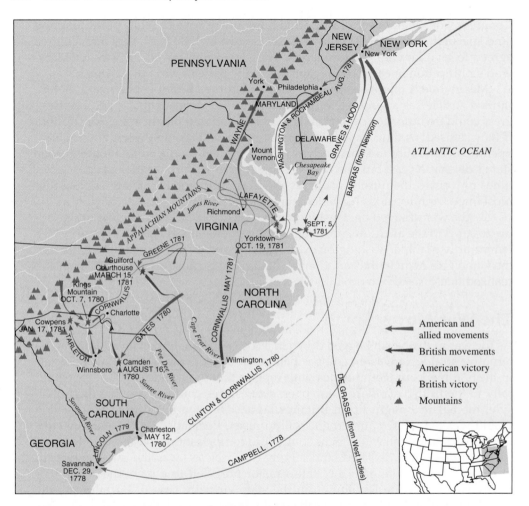

MILITARY OPERATIONS IN THE SOUTH, 1778–1781 The war in the South, as in the North, was fought along the coast and in the interior while British and French forces battled as well in the West Indies. Important water routes shaped the course of the war from beginning to end. Why was this so?

allies at every opportunity, striking by surprise and then disappearing into the interior. Nowhere was the war more fiercely contested than through the Georgia and Carolina countryside. Neither British nor American authorities could restrain the violence. Bands of private marauders, roving the land and seizing advantage from the war's confusion, compounded the chaos.

In time, the tide began to turn. At Cowpens, South Carolina, in January 1781, American troops under General Daniel Morgan won a decisive victory, suffering fewer than 75 casualties to 329 British deaths, and taking 600 prisoners. In March, at Guilford Court House in North Carolina, the British commander Cornwallis won, but at a cost that forced him to retreat to Wilmington, near the sea.

In April 1781, convinced that British authority could not be restored in the Carolinas while the rebels could still use Virginia as a supply and staging area, Cornwallis moved north. With a force of 7,500, he raided deep into Virginia, chasing Governor Jefferson and the state legislature from Charlottesville. But again Cornwallis found the costs of victory high, and turned back toward the coast for protection. On August 1, he reached Yorktown.

Cornwallis's position was secure as long as the British fleet controlled Chesapeake Bay, but that advantage did not last long. In 1778, the French government, still smarting from its defeat in the Seven Years' War and buoyed by the American victory at Saratoga, had signed an alliance with Congress, promising to send its naval forces into the war. Initially, the French concentrated their fleet in the West Indies, hoping to seize some of the British sugar islands. But on August 30, 1781, after repeated American urging, the French admiral Comte de Grasse arrived in the Chesapeake Bay and established naval supremacy. At the same time, Washington's continentals, supplemented by a French army, marched south from Pennsylvania.

As Washington had foreseen, French entry turned the tide of war. Cut off from the sea and pinned down on a peninsula between the York and James rivers by 17,000 French and American troops, Cornwallis's fate was sealed. On October 19, 1781, near the hamlet of Yorktown, he surrendered.

Surrender at Yorktown

Learning the news in London a month later, Lord North, the king's chief minister, exclaimed: "Oh, God! It is all over." On February 27, 1782, the House of Commons cut off further support of the war. North resigned the following month. In Philadelphia, citizens poured into the streets to celebrate while Congress held a solemn ceremony of thanksgiving. Though the preliminary articles of peace were not signed until November 1782, everyone knew after Yorktown that the Americans had won their independence.

Native Americans in the Revolution

The Revolutionary War drew in countless Native Americans as well as colonists and Englishmen. It could hardly have been otherwise, for the lives of all three peoples had been intertwined since the first English settlements.

By 1776, the major coastal tribes had been decimated by warfare and disease, their villages displaced by white settlement. Powerful tribes, however, still dominated the interior. The Iroquois Six Nations, a confederation numbering 15,000 people, controlled the area from the Hudson River to the Ohio Valley. Five tribes—the Choctaw, Chickasaw, Seminole, Creek, and Cherokee, 60,000 people in all—dominated the southern interior. As the imperial crisis between England and the colonies deepened, Native and European Americans eyed each other warily across this vast "middle ground."

When the Revolutionary War began, British and American officials urged neutrality on the Indians. The Native Americans, however, were too important militarily for either side to ignore. By the spring of 1776, both were seeking Indian alliances. Recognizing their stake in the white man's conflict, Native Americans up and down the interior debated their options.

Alarmed by encroaching white settlements, Cherokee bands led by the warrior Dragging Canoe launched a series of raids in 1776 in what is now eastern Tennessee. In retaliation, Virginia and Carolina militias laid waste a group of Cherokee towns. "I hope that the Cherokees will now be driven beyond the Mississippi," declared Jefferson. "Our contest with Britain is too ... great to permit any possibility of [threat] ... from the Indians." The Cherokee never again mounted a sustained military effort against the rebels. Seeing what had befallen their neighbors, the Creek stayed aloof. Their time for resistance would come in the early nineteenth century, when white settlers pushed onto their land.

In the Ohio country, the struggle lasted longer. For several decades before the Revolution, explorers such as Daniel Boone had contested the Shawnee and others for control of the region bordering the Ohio River. The Revolutionary War intensified these conflicts. In February 1778, George Rogers Clark led a ragtag band of Kentuckians across 180 miles of forbidding terrain to attack a British outpost at Vincennes, in present-day Indiana. Though heavily outnumbered, Clark fooled the British troops and their Indian allies into believing that his force was much larger, and the British surrendered without a shot. Clark's victory tipped the balance in the war's western theater.

The Devastation of the Iroquois

To the northeast, an even more deadly scenario unfolded. The initial Iroquois decision at a meeting of tribal leaders in Albany, New York, to regard the Revolution as a "family affair" between England and its colonies and stay aloof did not last long. In 1776, after American troops raided deep into Mohawk territory west of Albany, the British urged the Iroquois to join them against the rebels. Most did so in the summer of 1777 at the urging of Joseph Brant, a Mohawk warrior who had visited England several years earlier and proclaimed England's value as an ally against American expansion.

It was a fateful decision for Indians and whites alike. Over the next several years, the Iroquois and their British allies devastated large areas in central New York and Pennsylvania. The Americans' revenge came swiftly. During the summer of 1779, American troops launched a series of punishing raids into the Iroquois country, burning villages, killing men, women, and children, and destroying fields of corn. Their motto was blunt: "Civilization or death to all American savages." By war's end, the Iroquois had lost as many as one-third of their people as well as countless towns. Their domination of the northeastern interior was permanently shattered.

Not all the Eastern Woodland tribes sided with England in the Revolutionary War. The Oneida and Tuscarora, once members of the Iroquois confederation, fought with the Americans, their decision driven by intertribal politics and effective diplomacy by emissaries of the Continental Congress. Indians who fought for American independence, however, reaped little reward. Though the Americans spared the Oneida and Tuscarora villages, the British and their Iroquois allies destroyed them in turn. Tribes allied with the victorious Americans, moreover, gained no protection from the accelerating spread of white settlement.

Joseph Brant Mohawk chief Joseph Brant (Thayendanegea) played a major role in the Iroquois' decision to enter the war on the side of Britain. Can you identify the symbols of authority in his dress? *(George Romney, 1734–1802, Joseph Brant [Thayendanegea], 1776, oil on canvas, 127.6 × 101.6 cm. National Gallery of Canada, Ottawa, Ontario, Canada/Bridgeman Art Library International, Ltd.)*

Most Indians had sound reason for opposing American independence, because England provided them with trade goods, arms, and markets for their furs. England, moreover, had promised protection against colonial expansion, as the Proclamation Line of 1763 had demonstrated. Yet at the peace talks that ended the Revolutionary War, the British ignored their Indian allies. They received neither compensation for their losses nor guarantees of their land, for the boundary of the United States was set far to the west, at the Mississippi River.

Though the Indians' struggle against white expansion would continue, their anticolonial war of liberation had failed. The American Revolution, declared a gathering of Indian chiefs to the Spanish governor at Saint Louis in 1784, had been "the greatest blow that could have been dealt us."

Negotiating Peace

In September 1781, formal peace negotiations began in Paris between the British commissioner and the American emissaries, Benjamin Franklin, John Adams, and John Jay. The negotiations were complicated by involvement in the war of several European countries, seeking to weaken Great Britain. The Americans' main ally, France, had entered the war in February 1778. Eight months later, Spain declared war on England, though it declined to recognize American independence. Between 1780 and 1782, Russia, the Netherlands, and six other European countries joined in a League of Armed Neutrality aimed at protecting their maritime trade against British depredations. America's Revolutionary War had become internationalized.

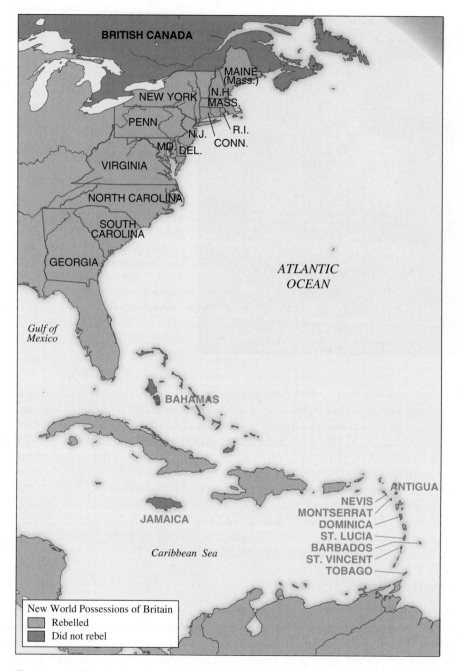

ENGLAND'S AMERICAN EMPIRE DIVIDES The majority of England's New World colonies did not rebel in 1776. ■ **Reflecting on the Past** What difference would it have made if Canada and England's Caribbean colonies had joined the 13 North American colonies in throwing off English rule?

It could hardly have been otherwise, given England's centrality to the European balance of power and the long-standing competition among European powers for colonial dominance in North America.

Dependent on French support, Congress instructed the American commissioners to follow the advice of French foreign minister Vergennes. But as the American commissioners soon learned, he was prepared to let the exhausting war continue in order to weaken England further and tighten America's dependence on France. Even more alarming, Vergennes suggested that the new nation's boundary should be set no farther west than the crest of the Appalachian Mountains and hinted that the British might retain areas they controlled at the war's end. That would have left New York City and other coastal enclaves in British hands.

In the end, the American commissioners ignored their instructions and, without a word to Vergennes, arranged a provisional peace agreement with the British emissaries. The British were prepared to be generous. In the Treaty of Paris, signed in September 1783, England recognized American independence and agreed to set the western boundary of the United States at the Mississippi River. England also promised U.S. fishermen the right to fish the waters off Newfoundland; also that British forces would evacuate American territory "with all convenient speed." In return, Congress would recommend that the states restore the rights and property of the Loyalists. Both sides agreed that prewar debts owed the citizens of one country by the citizens of the other would remain valid. Each of these issues would trouble Anglo-American relations in the years ahead, but for the moment it seemed a splendid outcome to a long and difficult war.

The Ingredients of Victory

In spite of English fears and congressional hopes, only half of Britain's New World colonies (13 out of 26) joined the rebellion against British authority. Congressional efforts to enlist Canadian support foundered because Canada's location at the western end of the North Atlantic sea routes made it a center of British military force. The colony's French Catholic majority, moreover, harbored bitter memories of conflicts during the Seven Years' War with England's Protestant colonists to the south.

Congress made overtures as well to white planters on Jamaica and other British sugar islands in the Caribbean. But the islands' sugar economies were heavily dependent on British markets. Planters depended as well on British military force for protection against Spanish and Dutch raiders, to say nothing of the slave majorities in their midst. Also, reports that slavery was being questioned in some of the rebellious colonies struck fear into planters' hearts.

Even without the support of Canada and the Caribbean islands, the 13 weak and disunited North American states were able to defeat Great Britain, the most powerful nation in the Atlantic world. How was that so? Certainly Dutch loans and French military resources were crucially important. At the height of the war, France fielded a force of more than 10,000 men in North America.

More decisive, though, was the American people's determination not to submit. Often the Americans were disorganized and uncooperative. Repeatedly, the war effort seemed about to collapse as continental troops drifted away, state militias refused to march, and supplies failed to materialize. Yet as the war progressed, the people's estrangement from England deepened and their commitment to the "glorious cause" grew stronger. To subdue the colonies, England would have had to occupy the entire eastern third of the continent, and that it could not do.

Though state militias engaged in relatively few battles after the first months of the war, they provided a reservoir of manpower capable of intimidating Loyalists, gathering intelligence, and harassing British forces. And though Washington frequently disparaged the militias' fighting qualities, he gradually learned to utilize them in the war effort.

The American victory owed much, as well, to Washington's organizational talents. Against massive odds, often by the sheer force of his will, he held the continental army together and created a military force capable of winning selected encounters and surviving over time. Had he failed, the Americans could not possibly have won.

In the end, however, it is as accurate to say that Britain lost the war as that the United States won it. With vast economic and military resources, Britain enjoyed clear military superiority over the Americans. Its troops were more numerous, better armed and supplied, and more professionally trained. Until the closing months of the contest, Britain enjoyed naval superiority as well, enabling its forces to move up and down the coast virtually at will.

Britain, however, could not capitalize on its advantages. It had difficulty extending its command structures and supply routes across several thousand miles of ocean. As a result, decisions made in London were often based on outdated intelligence. Given the difficulties of supply, British troops frequently lived off the land, thus reducing their mobility and increasing the resentment of Americans whose crops and animals were commandeered.

Faced with these circumstances, British leaders were often overly cautious. Burgoyne's attempt in 1777 to isolate New England by invading from Canada failed because Sir William Howe decided to attack Philadelphia rather than move northward up the Hudson River to join him. Similarly, neither Howe nor Cornwallis pressed his advantage in the central states during the middle years of the war, when more aggressive action might have crushed the continentals.

Just as important, British commanders generally failed to adapt European battlefield tactics to the realities of the American war. They were willing to fight only during specified times of the year and used formal battlefield maneuvers, even though the wooded American terrain was better suited to the use of smaller units and irregular tactics.

Washington and Greene were more flexible, often employing a patient strategy of raiding, harassment, and strategic retreat. Guiding this strategy was a willingness, grounded in necessity, to allow England control of territory along the coast. But it was based, as well, on the conviction that popular support for the revolutionary cause would grow and that the costs of subduing the colonial rebellion would become greater than the British government could bear. As a much later American war in Vietnam would also reveal, a guerrilla force can win if it does not lose, while a regular army loses if it does not consistently win.

The American strategy proved sound. As the war dragged on and its costs escalated, Britain's will wavered. After France and Spain entered the conflict, Britain had to worry about the European, Caribbean, and Mediterranean theatres, as well as North America. Unrest in Ireland and food riots in London tied down additional English troops. As the cost in money and lives increased and prospects of victory dimmed, political support for the war eroded. With the defeat at Yorktown, it finally collapsed.

THE EXPERIENCE OF WAR

In terms of the loss of life and destruction of property, the Revolutionary War pales by comparison with America's more recent wars. Yet modern comparisons are misleading, for the War of American Independence proved terrifying to the people caught up in it.

Recruiting an Army

Estimates vary, but on the American side as many as 250,000 men may at one time or another have borne arms. That amounted to one out of every two or three adult, white males. Though a majority of recruits were native born, many who fought for American freedom came from the thousands of British and European immigrants who streamed into North America during the middle decades of the eighteenth century. Of the 27 men enrolled in Captain John Wendell's New York company, for example, more than half had been born abroad, the majority in Ireland but others in Germany and the Netherlands. While the motives of these men varied, many had come to America seeking to better their lives and eagerly embraced the Revolution's democratic promise. They were the vanguard of transatlantic migrations that, over the late eighteenth and early nineteenth centuries, would tie American revolutionaries to English reformers and French radicals during what historians have called the age of democratic revolutions.

As the war began, most state militias were not effective fighting forces. This was especially true in the South, where Nathanael Greene complained that the men came "from home with all the tender feelings of domestic life" and were not "sufficiently fortified ... to stand the shocking scenes of war, to march over dead men, [or] to hear without concern the groans of the wounded." The militia served, however, as an efficient recruiting system, for men were already enrolled and could be called into the field on short notice. This was of special importance early in the war, before the continental army took shape. Given its grounding in local community life, the militia also legitimated the war among the people and secured their commitment to the revolutionary cause. What better way to separate Patriots from Loyalists, moreover, than by mustering the local company and seeing who turned out?

During the early years of the war, when enthusiasm ran high, men of all ranks—from the rich and middle classes as well as the poor—volunteered to fight the British. But as the war went on, casualties increased, enlistment terms grew longer, military discipline became more harsh, and the army filled with conscripts. Eventually, the war was transformed, as wars so often are, into a poor

RECOVERING THE PAST

In all of America's wars, patriotism and bombastic rhetoric have inspired citizens to arms. The American Revolutionary War was no exception, but people often fought for more than patriotic reasons, as the account of "Long Bill" Scott makes clear. It is always difficult to assess human motivations in something as complex as war. If we knew which Americans bore arms, however, it would help us understand why people fought and what the war meant to them.

As we see in this chapter, the social composition of the revolutionary army changed as the war went along. At the beginning, men from all walks of life and every class fought in defense of American liberty. As the war lengthened and its costs increased, however, men who could afford to hired substitutes or arranged to go home, while men of less wealth and influence increasingly carried the burden of fighting. Many of them did so out of choice, for the army promised adventure, an escape from the tedium of daily life, and even, as for Long Bill Scott, the chance to rise in the world. Such a decision was attractive to them because other opportunities were limited.

Enlistment lists of the continental army and state militias offer an important source for studying the social history of the Revolutionary War. Although eighteenth-century records are imperfect by modern standards, recruiting officers did keep track of the men they signed on so that bounties and wages could be paid accurately. These lists usually give the recruit's name, age, occupation, place of birth, residence, and length of service.

Such lists exist for some of America's earlier wars. The muster rolls for New York City and Philadelphia during the Seven Years' War, for example, show that most of the enlistees from these two cities in that conflict were immigrants—about 90 percent of New York's recruits and about 75 percent of Philadelphia's. Their occupations—mariner, laborer, shoemaker, weaver, tailor—indicate that they came primarily from the lowest ranks of the working class. Many were former indentured servants, while others were servants who ran away from their masters to answer the recruiting sergeant's drum. In these mid-Atlantic port towns, successful, American-born artisans left the bloody work of bearing arms against the French to those beneath them on the social ladder. Enlistment lists for Boston, however, reveal that soldiers from that city were drawn from higher social classes.

A comparison of Revolutionary War muster rolls from different towns and regions provides a view of the social composition of the revolutionary army and how it changed over time. It also offers clues to how social conditions in different regions might have affected military recruitment.

The muster rolls shown here of Captain Wendell's and Captain White's companies from New York and Virginia give "social facts" on several dozen men. (Because of space limitations only portions of each roster are included here.) What kind of group portrait can you draw from the data? Some occupations, such as tanner, cordwainer, and chandler, may be unfamiliar to modern readers, but they are defined in standard dictionaries. How many of the recruits come from middling occupations (bookkeeper, tobacconist, shopkeeper, and the like)? How many are skilled artisans? How many are unskilled laborers? What proportions are foreign and native born? Analyze the ages of the recruits. What does that tell you about the kind of fighting force that was assembled? How do the New York and Virginia companies differ in terms of these social categories and occupations? Can you explain these differences?

To extract the full meaning of the soldiers' profile, you would have to learn more about the economic and social conditions prevailing in the communities from which these men were drawn. But already you have glimpsed how social historians go beyond the history of military strategy, tactics, and battles to understand the "internal" social history of the Revolutionary War.

REFLECTING ON THE PAST   How would social historians describe and analyze more recent American wars? What would a social profile of soldiers who fought in Vietnam or Iraq—including their age, region, race, class, and extent of education—suggest to a social historian of these wars?

New York Line—1st Regiment

Captain John H. Wendell's Company, 1776–1777

Men's Names	Age	Occupation	Place of Birth	Place of Abode
Abraham Defreest	22	Yeoman	N. York	Claverack
Benjamin Goodales	20	do [ditto]	Nobletown	do
Hendrick Carman	24	do	Rynbeck	East Camp
Nathaniel Reed	32	Carpenter	Norwalk	Westchester
Jacob Crolrin	29	do	Germany	Bever Dam
James White	25	Weaver	Ireland	Rynbveck
Joseph Battina	39	Coppersmith	Ireland	Florida
John Wyatt	38	Carpenter	Maryland	
Jacob Reyning	25	Yeoman	Amsterdam	Albany
Patrick Kannely	36	Barber	Ireland	N. York
John Russell	29	Penman	Ireland	N. York
Patrick McCue	19	Tanner	Ireland	Scholary
James J. Atkson	21	Weaver	do	Stillwater
William Burke	23	Chandler	Ireland	N. York
Wm Miller	42	Yeoman	Scotland	Claverack
Ephraim H. Blancherd	18	Yeoman	Ireland	White Creek
Francis Acklin	40	Cordwainer	Ireland	Claverack
William Orr	29	Cordwainer	Ireland	Albany
Thomas Welch	31	Labourer	N. York	Norman's Kill
Peter Gasper	24	Labourer	N. Jersey	Greenbush
Martins Rees	19	Labourer	Fishkill	Flatts
Henck Able	24	do	Albany	Flatts

Virginia Line—6th Regiment

Captain Tarpley White's Company, December 13th, 1780

Name	Age	Trade	Where Born State or Country	Where Born Town or County	Place of Residence State or Country	Place of Residence Town or County
Win Bails, Serjt	25	Baker	England	Burningham	Virg.	Leesburg
Arthur Harrup"	24	Carpenter	Virg.	Southampton	Virg.	Brunswick
Charles Caffatey"	19	Planter	"	Caroline	"	Caroline
Elisha Osborn"	24	Planter	New Jersey	Trenton	"	Loudon
Benj Allday	19	"	Virg.	Henrico	"	Pawhatan
Wm Edwards Senr	25	"	"	Northumberland	"	Northumberland
James Hutcherson	17	Hatter	Jersey	Middlesex	"	P.Williams
Robert Low	31	Planter	"	Powhatan	"	Powhatan
Cannon Row	18	Planter	Virg.	Hanover	Virg.	Louisa
Wardon Pulley	18	"	"	Southampton	"	Hallifax
Richd Bond	29	Stone Mason	England	Cornwell	"	Orange
Tho Homont	17	Planter	Virg.	Loudon	"	Loudon
Tho Pope	19	Planter	"	Southampton	"	Southampton
Tho Morris	22	Planter	"	Orange	"	Orange
Littlebury Overby	24	Hatter	"	Dinwiddie	"	Brunswick
James [Pierce]	27	Planter	"	Nansemond	"	Nansemond
Joel Counsil	19	Planter	"	Southampton	"	Southampton
Elisha Walden	18	Planter	"	P.William	"	P.William
Wm Bush	19	S Carpenter	Virg.	Gloucester	Virg.	Glocester
Daniel Horton	22	Carpenter	"	Nansemond	"	Nansemond
John Soons	25	Weaver	England	Norfolk	"	Loudon
Mara Lumkin	18	Planter	Virg.	Amelia	"	Amelia
Wm Wetherford	27	Planter	"	Goochland	"	Lunenburg
John Bird	16	Planter	"	Southampton	"	Southampton
Tho Parsmore	22	Planter	England	London	"	Fairfax
Josiah Banks	27	Planter	Virg.	Gloucester	"	Gloucester
Richd Roach	28	Planter	England	London	"	Culpeper

American Uniforms This watercolor painting offers a humorous, even mocking, depiction of the variety of uniforms worn by American troops. *(De Verger, "American Soldiers." Anne S. K. Brown Military Collection, Brown University Library)*

man's fight as wealthier men hired substitutes and communities filled their quotas with strangers lured by enlistment bonuses. Convicts, out-of-work laborers, free and unfree blacks, even occasional British deserters filled the continental army with an array of "Tag, Rag, and Bobtail" soldiers.

For the poor and the jobless, whose ranks the war rapidly swelled, military bonuses and the promise of board and keep proved attractive. But often the bonuses failed to materialize, pay was long overdue, and soldiers frequently learned of their families' distress. As the war dragged on and desertion rose as high as 25 percent, Washington imposed harsher discipline in an effort to hold his troops in line.

DOCUMENT

Letter from a Revolutionary War Soldier (1778)

Throughout the war, soldiers suffered from shortages of supplies. At Valley Forge during the terrible winter of 1777–1778, men went without shoes or coats. Declared one despairing soul in the midst of that winter's gloom, "I am sick, discontented, and out of humour. Poor food, hard lodging, cold weather, fatigue, nasty cloathes, nasty cookery, vomit half my time, smoked out of my senses. The Devil's in't, I can't Endure it. Why are we sent here to starve and freeze?"

Neither state governments nor Congress could effectively administer a war effort of such magnitude. Though many individuals served honorably as supply officers, others exploited the army's distress. Washington commented bitterly on the "speculators, various tribes of money makers, and stock-jobbers" whose "avarice and thirst for gain" threatened the country's ruin.

Swarms of camp followers further complicated army life. Wives and prostitutes, personal servants and slaves, con men and provisioners swarmed around the continental army camps. While often providing essential services, they slowed its movement and threatened its discipline.

The Casualties of Combat

The death that soldiers dispensed to each other on the battlefield was intensely personal. Because the effective range of muskets was little more than 100 yards, soldiers came virtually face-to-face with the men they killed. According to eighteenth-century practice, armies formed in ranks on the battlefield and fired in unison. After massed volleys, the lines often closed for hand-to-hand combat with knives and bayonets. Partisan warfare in the South, with its emphasis on ambush and cyclical patterns of revenge, personalized combat even more.

British officers were shocked at the "implacable arder" with which the Americans fought. The Americans' ferocity is attributable in part to the fact that this was a civil war. Not only did Englishmen fight Anglo-Americans, but American Loyalists and Patriots fought each other as well. As many as 50,000 Americans fought for the king in some of the war's most bitter encounters. Conflicts between whites and Indians added to the brutality. The passion with which American Patriots fought derived as well from Americans' belief that the very future of human liberty depended on their success. In such a historic crusade, nothing was to be spared that might bring victory.

Medical treatment, whether for wounds or the diseases that raged through military camps, frequently did more harm than good. Casualties poured into hospitals, overcrowding them beyond capacity. Surgeons, operating without anesthetics and with the crudest of instruments, threatened life as often as they preserved it. Few understood the causes or proper treatment of infection. Doctoring consisted mostly of bleeding, blistering, and vomiting. One doctor reported that "we lost no less than from 10 to 20 of camp diseases, for one by weapons of the enemy."

No one kept accurate records of how many soldiers died. But the most conservative estimate runs to 25,000, a higher percentage of the total population than for any other American conflict except the Civil War. For Revolutionary War soldiers, death was an imminent reality.

Civilians and the War

While the experience of war varied from place to place, it touched the lives of virtually every American. Noncombatants felt the burden of war most heavily in densely settled areas along the coast. The British concentrated their military efforts there, taking advantage of their naval power and striking at the political and economic centers of American life. At one time or another, British troops occupied every major port city.

Urban dwellers suffered profound dislocations. About half of New York City's inhabitants fled when the British occupation began. An American officer somberly reported the scene as his troops entered the city at the war's end: "Close on the eve

New York City Burning In 1776, as the British took control of New York, nearly a quarter of the city was destroyed by a fire apparently set by a defiant Patriot woman. Among the gutted buildings was the elegant Trinity Church, the tallest structure in the city. Not until the British evacuated in 1783 did reconstruction of the city begin. *(Library of Congress)*

of an approaching winter, with an heterogeneous set of inhabitants, composed of almost ruined exiles, disbanded soldiery, mixed foreigners, disaffected Tories, and the refuse of the British army, we took possession of a ruined city."

In Philadelphia, the occupation was shorter and disruptions less severe, but the shock of invasion was no less real. Elizabeth Drinker, living alone after local Patriots had exiled her Quaker husband, found herself the unwilling landlady of a British officer and his friends. Though the officer's presence may have protected her from the plundering that went on all around, she was constantly anxious, confiding to her journal that "I often feel afraid to go to Bed." British soldiers frequently tore down fences for their campfires and confiscated food. Even Loyalists complained about the "dreadful consequences" of British occupation.

Along the entire coastal plain, British landing parties descended without warning, seizing supplies and terrorizing inhabitants. In 1780 and 1781, the British mounted punishing attacks along the Connecticut coast. The southern coast, with its broad, navigable rivers, was even more vulnerable. In December 1780, Benedict Arnold, the American traitor who by then was fighting for the British, ravaged Virginia's James River valley, uprooting tobacco, confiscating slaves, and creating panic among whites.

Such onslaughts sent civilians fleeing into the interior. During the first years of the war, the port cities lost nearly half their population. Not all the refugee traffic, however, was away from the coast. In western New York, Pennsylvania, Virginia, and the Carolinas, frontier settlements collapsed under British and Indian assaults, sending their residents fleeing to the east. Wherever the armies went, they generated a swirl of refugees who spread vivid tales of the war's devastation. This refugee traffic, together with the constant movement of soldiers between army and civilian life, brought the war home to countless people who did not experience it firsthand.

Disease, spread by the movement of people across the landscape, ravaged populations as well. During the 1770s and 1780s, a smallpox epidemic surged across North America, wreaking its devastating effects from the Atlantic coast to the Pacific, and from the Southwest to Hudson's Bay in Canada. The human toll is impossible to measure exactly, but the virus may have killed more than 130,000 people—Indians and Englishmen, African and European Americans among them. Because a crash program of inoculation launched by Washington in 1777 (the first large-scale immunization program in American history) protected much of the continental army and because many British troops carried immunity from earlier exposure to the disease, the plague did not significantly affect the war's outcome. Still, it took a terrible toll. In New England and the mid-Atlantic states, it was spread by returning soldiers and Britain's disease-infested prison ships. In the Chesapeake region, thousands of black Loyalists succumbed, while in the backcountry the virus raced through Indian populations, reducing their ability to resist the rebels. Beyond the Mississippi, agricultural tribes such as the Mandan, Hidatsa, and Arikara were virtually wiped out. The pox, declared one observer gloomily, "spread its destructive and desolating power, as the fire consumes the dry grass of the field."

The Loyalists

Among the Americans suffering the most grievous losses were those who remained loyal to the Crown. Though many Loyalist émigrés established successful lives in England, the Maritime Provinces of Canada, and the British West Indies, others found the uprooting an ordeal from which they never recovered. Several thousand Loyalists, appearing after the war before a royal commission in London appointed to hear their claims, gained partial reimbursement for their losses. But it proved meager compensation for the confiscation of house and property, expulsion from a familiar community, and relocation to a distant land. The vast majority of Loyalists never appeared before the commission and thus secured nothing.

Although we do not know how many colonists remained loyal to England, tens of thousands evacuated with British troops at the end of the war. At least as many slipped away while fighting was still going on. Additional thousands who wished the Revolution had never occurred stayed on in the new nation, struggling to rebuild their lives. The incidence of Loyalism differed from region to region. Loyalists were fewest in New England and most numerous around New York City, where British authority was most stable.

In each state, revolutionary assemblies exacted revenge against those who had rejected the revolutionary cause by depriving Loyalists of the vote, confiscating their property, and banishing them from their homes. In 1778, the Georgia assembly expelled 117 persons on pain of death. Probably not more than a few dozen Loyalists died at the hands of the revolutionary regimes, but thousands found their livelihoods destroyed, their families ostracized, and themselves subject to physical attack.

Punishing Loyalists—or people accused of loyalism, a distinction that was often unclear in the confusion of the times—was politically popular. Most Patriots argued that such "traitors" had put themselves outside the protection of American law. No other wartime issue raised so starkly the nettlesome question of balancing individual liberty against the requirements of public security. That issue would return to trouble the nation in the years ahead.

Why did so many Americans remain loyal to the Crown, often at the cost of personal danger and loss? Royal appointees such as customs officers, members of the governors' councils, and Anglican clergy often remained with the king. Loyalism was common, as well, among groups dependent on the British presence—for example, settlers on the Carolina frontier holding long-standing grievances against the planter elite along the coast and ethnic minorities, such as Germans, who feared domination by the Anglo-American majority. Others were Loyalist because they feared British military power, or doubted that independence could be won.

Still others based their Loyalism on principle. "Every person owes obedience to the laws of the government," insisted Samuel Seabury, "and is obliged in honour and duty to support them. Because if one has a right to disregard the laws of the society to which he belongs, all have the same right; and then government is at an end." Another Loyalist worried about the kind of society independence would bring when revolutionary crowds showed no respect for the rights of dissenters such as he. "If I differ in opinion from the multitude," he asked, "must I therefore be deprived of my character, and the confidence of my fellow-citizens; when in every station of life I discharge my duty with fidelity and honour?" Such individuals claimed to be upholding reason and the rule of law against revolutionary disorder. Their defeat weakened conservatism in American society and promoted revolutionary change.

African Americans and the War

DOCUMENT

Slave Petition to the Massachusetts House of Representatives (1774)

The Revolution caught up thousands of American blacks in its toils. In the northern states, free and enslaved blacks were enlisted in support of the revolutionary cause. The South's nearly 400,000 slaves were viewed by the British as a resource to be exploited and by southern whites as a source of vulnerability and danger. Sizing up the opportunities provided by the war's confusion, southern blacks struck out for their own freedom by seeking liberty behind British lines, journeying to the north, or fleeing to mixed-race settlements in the interior. Before the war was over, the conflict generated the largest slave rebellion in American history prior to the Civil War.

Hearing their masters talk about liberty, growing numbers of black Americans questioned their own oppression. In the North, slaves petitioned state legislatures for their freedom, while in the South pockets of insurrection appeared. In 1765, more than 100 South Carolina slaves, most of them young men in their twenties and thirties, fled their plantations. The next year, slaves paraded through the streets of Charleston chanting, "Liberty, liberty!"

In November 1775, Lord Dunmore, Virginia's royal governor, issued a proclamation offering freedom to all slaves and servants "able and willing to bear arms," who would leave their masters and join the British at Norfolk. Within weeks, 500 to 600 slaves responded. Among them was Thomas Peters, an African who had been brought to Spanish Louisiana about 1760. He resisted enslavement so fiercely that his master sold him into the English colonies. By the 1770s, he was toiling on William Campbell's plantation on the Cape Fear River, near Wilmington, North Carolina.

Peters's plans for his own declaration of independence may have ripened as a result of the rhetoric of liberty he heard around his master's house, for William Campbell was a leading member of Wilmington's Sons of Liberty and talked enthusiastically about inalienable rights. By mid-1775, the Cape Fear region, like many areas of the coastal South, buzzed with rumors of slave uprisings. In July, the state's revolutionary government imposed martial law when the British commander of Fort Johnston, near Wilmington, encouraged blacks to "elope from their masters." When 20 British ships entered the Cape Fear River in March 1776 and disembarked royal troops, Peters seized the moment to redefine himself as a man, instead of William Campbell's property, and escaped. Before long, he would fight with the British-officered Black Pioneers.

How many African Americans sought liberty behind British lines is unknown, but as many as 20 percent may have done so. Unlike their white masters, blacks saw in England the promise of freedom, not tyranny. As the war dragged on, English commanders pressed blacks into service. A regiment of black soldiers formed from Virginia slaves who responded to Dunmore's proclamation marched into battle, their chests covered by sashes emblazoned "Liberty to Slaves."

Some of the blacks who joined England achieved their freedom. At the war's end, several thousand were evacuated with the British to Nova Scotia. But their reception by the white inhabitants was generally hostile. By 1800, most had left Canada to help establish the free black colony of Sierra Leone in West Africa. Thomas Peters was a leader among them.

Many of the slaves who fled behind British lines never won their freedom. Under the terms of the peace treaty, hundreds were returned to their American owners. Several thousand others, their value as field hands too great to be ignored, were transported to harsher slavery on West Indian sugar plantations.

Other blacks took advantage of the war's confusion to flee. Some went north, following rumors that slavery had been abolished there. Others sought refuge among Indians in the southern interior. The Seminoles of Georgia and Florida generally welcomed black runaways and through intermarriage absorbed them into tribal society. Blacks met a more uncertain reception from the Cherokee and Creek. While some were taken in, others were returned to their white owners for bounties, and still others were held in slavelike conditions by new Indian masters.

Fewer blacks fought on the American side than on England's, in part because neither Congress nor the states were eager to see them armed. Faced with the increasing need for troops, however, Congress and all the states except Georgia and South Carolina eventually relented, pressing blacks into service. Of those who served the Patriot cause, many received the freedom they were promised. The patriotism of countless others, however, went unrewarded.

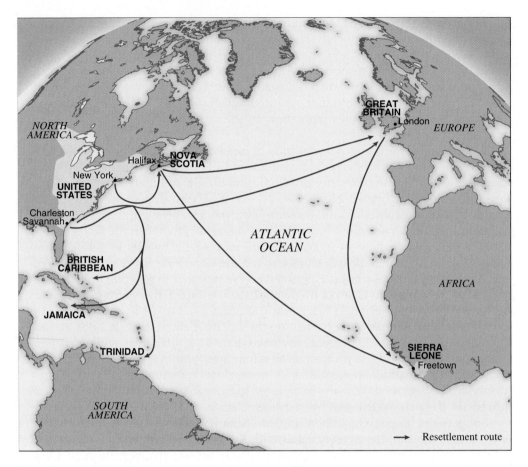

RESETTLEMENT OF BLACK LOYALISTS AFTER THE REVOLUTION Thousands of American blacks departed the new nation with British troops at the end of the Revolutionary War. As the map indicates, their destinations differed. ▪ **Reflecting on the Past** How did resettlement outside the United States reshape the lives of black Loyalists?

THE FERMENT OF REVOLUTIONARY POLITICS

The Revolution altered people's lives in countless ways that reached beyond the sights and sounds of battle. No areas of American life were more powerfully changed than politics and government. Who would have a voice in revolutionary politics, and who would be excluded? How vigorously would political equality be pursued, or how tenaciously would people cling to the traditional belief that citizens should defer to their political leaders? And how would the new state governments balance the need for order and the security of property against demands for democratic openness and accountability? Seldom has American politics struggled with more daunting problems than at the nation's founding.

Mobilizing the People

Under the pressure of revolutionary events, politics absorbed people's energies as never before. The politicization of American society was evident in the flood of printed material issuing from American presses. Newspapers multiplied and pamphlets by the thousands fanned political debate.

Pulpits rocked with political exhortations as well. While religion and politics had never been sharply separated in colonial America, the Revolution drew them more tightly together. In countless sermons, Congregational, Presbyterian, and Baptist clergy exhorted the American people to repent the sins that had brought English tyranny upon them and urged them to rededicate themselves to God's purposes by fighting for American freedom. It was language that people nurtured in Puritan piety and the Great Awakening instinctively understood.

The belief that God sanctioned their revolution strengthened Americans' resolve. It also encouraged them to equate their own interests with divine intent, and thus offered convenient justification for whatever they believed necessary to do. This was not the last time Americans would make that dangerous equation.

By contrast, Loyalist clergy, such as Maryland's Jonathan Boucher, urged their parishioners to support the king as head of the Anglican Church. During the months preceding independence, as the local Committee of Safety interrupted worship to harass him, Boucher carried a loaded pistol into the pulpit while he preached submission to royal authority.

Tearing Down the Statue of George III In celebration of American independence, Patriots and their slaves toppled the statue of King George III that stood at Bowling Green in New York City. *(Library of Congress)*

Belief in the momentous importance of what they were doing increased the intensity of revolutionary politics. As independence was declared, people throughout the land raised toasts to the great event: "Liberty to those who have the spirit to preserve it," and "May Liberty expand sacred wings, and, in glorious effort, diffuse her influence o'er and o'er the globe." Inspired by the searing experience of rebellion, war, and nation-building, Americans believed they held the future of human liberty in their hands. Small wonder they took their politics so seriously.

The expanding array of crowds and committees of safety and correspondence that formed during the 1770s and 1780s provided the most dramatic evidence of the people's political commitment. Prior to independence, crowds had taken to the streets to protest measures such as the Stamp Act. After 1776, direct political action increased as people gathered to administer roughhewn justice to Loyalists, and, as one individual protested, even direct "what we shall eat, drink, wear, speak, and think."

Patriots of more radical temperament defended these activities as legitimate expressions of the popular will. More cautious souls, however, worried that such behavior threatened political stability. Direct action by the people had been necessary in the struggle against England, but why such restlessness now, after the yoke of English tyranny had been thrown off? Even Thomas Paine expressed concern. "It is time to have done with tarring and feathering," he wrote in 1777. "I never did and never would encourage what may properly be called a mob, when any legal mode of redress can be had."

The expansion of popular politics resulted from an explosive combination of circumstances: the momentous events of revolution and war; the efforts of Patriot leaders to mobilize popular support for the struggle against England; and the determination of artisans, workingmen, farmers, and other common folk to apply the principles of liberty to the conditions of their own lives.

A Republican Ideology

As the American people moved from colonial subordination to independence, they struggled to establish their identity as a separate nation. What did it mean to be no longer English, but American? "Our style and manner of thinking," observed Thomas Paine, "have undergone a revolution. ... We see with other eyes, we hear with other ears, and think with other thoughts than those we formerly used." The ideology of revolutionary republicanism, pieced together from English political ideas, Enlightenment theories, and religious beliefs, constituted that revolution in thought. Many of its central tenets were broadly shared among the American people, but its larger meanings were sharply contested throughout the revolutionary era.

In addition to the rejection of monarchy that Paine had so eloquently expressed in *Common Sense,* the American people also rejected the system of hierarchical authority on which monarchy was based, a system that promised protection by the Crown in return for obedience by the people. Under a republican system, by contrast, the people, contracting together, created public authority for their mutual good. In that fundamental change lay much of the American Revolution's radical promise.

Basic to republican belief was the notion that governmental power, when removed from the people's close oversight, threatened to expand at the expense of liberty. Recent experience with England had made that lesson unmistakably clear. Although excessive liberty could degenerate into political chaos, history seemed to demonstrate that trouble most often arose from too much, not too little government.

Given the need to limit governmental power, how could political order be maintained? The revolutionary generation offered an extraordinary answer to that question. Order was not to be imposed from above through traditional agencies of control such as monarchies, standing armies, and state churches. In a republic, political discipline had to emerge from the willingness of citizens to put the public good ahead of their own private interests. In a republic, explained one pamphleteer, "each individual gives up all private interest that is not consistent with the general good." This radical principle of "public virtue" was an essential ingredient of republican belief.

By contrast, political "faction," or organized self-interest, constituted the "mortal disease" to which popular governments throughout history had succumbed. Given the absence in republics of a strong central authority capable of imposing political order, factional conflict could easily spin out of control. This fear added to the intensity of political conflict in revolutionary America, for it encouraged people to attribute the worst motives to their political opponents.

The idea of placing responsibility for political order with the people and counting on them to act selflessly for the good of the whole alarmed countless Americans. What if the people proved unworthy? If the attempt was made, warned one individual darkly, "the bands of society would be dissolved, the harmony of the world confused, and the order of nature subverted." A strong incentive toward Loyalism lurked in such concerns.

Few Patriots were so naive as to believe that the American people were altogether virtuous. During the first years of independence, when revolutionary enthusiasm ran high, however, many believed that public virtue was sufficiently widespread to support republican government. Others argued that the American people would learn public virtue by its practice. The revolutionary struggle would serve as a "furnace of affliction," refining the American character as it strengthened people's capacity for virtuous behavior. It was an extraordinarily hopeful but risk-filled undertaking.

The principle of political equality was another controversial touchstone of republicanism. It was broadly assumed that republican governments must be grounded in popular consent, that elections must be frequent, and that citizens must be vigilant in defense of their liberties. But there agreement often ended.

Some Americans took the principle of political equality literally, arguing that every citizen should have an equal voice and that public office should be open to all. This position was most forcefully articulated by tenants and small farmers in the interior, as well as workers and artisans in the coastal cities who had long struggled to claim a political voice. More cautious citizens emphasized that individual liberty must be balanced by political order, arguing that stable republics required leadership by men of ability and experience, an "aristocracy of talent" that could give the people direction. Merchants, planters, and large commercial farmers who were used to providing such leadership saw no need for radical changes in the existing distribution of political power.

Forming New Governments

Differences of ideology and self-interest burst through the surface of American politics during debates over new state constitutions. Fashioning new governments would not be easy, for the American people had no experience with government-making on such a scale and had to undertake it in the midst of a disruptive war. In addition, there were sharp divisions over the kinds of governmets they wanted to create. One person thought it the "most difficult and dangerous business" that was to be done.

Rather than create new written constitutions, Connecticut and Rhode Island continued under their colonial charters, simply deleting all reference to the British Crown. The other 11 states, however, set their charters aside and started anew. By 1778, all but Massachusetts had completed the task. Two years later, it had done so as well.

Constitution makers began with two overriding concerns: to limit the powers of government and to make public officials closely accountable. The only certain

Old Massachusetts Statehouse Massachusetts was the first state to elect a special convention to draw up a new constitution and then return that constitution to the people for approval. The new government—along with Boston's officials, courts, and the Merchants' Exchange—met in the old colonial statehouse. (I. N. Phelps Stokes Collection, Miriam and Ira D. Wallach Division of Art, Prints, and Photographs, The New York Public Library, Astor, Lenox and Tilden Foundations/Art Resource, NY)

way of accomplishing these goals was by establishing a fundamental law, in the form of a written constitution, that could serve as a standard for controlling governmental behavior.

In most states, the provincial congresses, extralegal successors to the defunct colonial assemblies, wrote the first constitutions. But this made people uneasy. If governmental bodies wrote the documents, they could change them as well, and what would then protect liberty against the abuse of governmental power? Some way had to be found of grounding the fundamental law not in the actions of government, but directly in the people's sovereign will. Massachusetts first perfected the new procedures. In 1779, its citizens elected a special convention for the sole purpose of preparing a new constitution, which was then returned to the people for ratification.

Through trial and argumentation, the revolutionary generation gradually worked out a clear understanding of what a constitution was and how it should be created. In the process it established some of the most basic doctrines of American constitutionalism: that sovereignty resides in the people, rather than government; that written constitutions embody the people's sovereign will; and that governments must function within clear constitutional limits. No principles have been more important to the preservation of American liberty.

Different Paths to the Republican Goal

Constitution-making generated heated controversy, especially over how democratic the new governments should be. In Pennsylvania, a coalition of western farmers, Philadelphia artisans, and radical leaders pushed through the most democratic state constitution of all. Drafted less than three months after independence, during the most intense period of political reform, it rejected the familiar English model of two legislative houses and an independent executive. Republican governments, the radicals insisted, should be simple and easily understood. The constitution thus provided for a single, all-powerful legislative house, its members annually elected, its debates open to the public. A truly radical assumption underlay this unitary design: that only the "common interest of society" and not "separate and jarring private interests" should be represented in public affairs.

There was to be no governor—legislative committees would handle executive duties. Property-holding requirements for public office were abolished, and the franchise was opened to every white, taxpaying male over 21. A bill of rights guaranteed every citizen religious freedom, trial by jury, and freedom of speech. The most radical proposal of all called for the partial redistribution of property. Alarmed conservatives just managed to fend off that dangerous proposal.

Debate over the proposed constitution polarized the state. Men of wealth condemned the document's supporters as "coffee-house demagogues" seeking to introduce a "tyranny of the people." The constitution's proponents—tradesmen, farmers, and other small producers—shot back that their critics were "the rich and great men" who had "no common interest with the body of the people."

In 1776, the radicals had their way, and the document was approved. For the moment, the lines of political power had been decisively redrawn. The

Pennsylvania constitution, together with its counterparts in Vermont and Georgia, represented the most radical thrust of revolutionary republicanism.

In Massachusetts, constitution-making followed a more cautious course. There the disruptions of war were less severe and the continuity of political leadership was greater. The constitution's main architect, John Adams, readily admitted that the new government must be firmly grounded in the people, yet he warned against "reckless experimentation" and regarded the Pennsylvania constitution as far too democratic. Believing that society was inescapably divided between "democratic" and "aristocratic" forces, Adams sought to isolate each in separate legislative houses where they could guard against each other. The constitution also provided for a governor empowered to veto legislation, make appointments, command the militia, and oversee state expenditures.

When the convention sent the document to the town meetings for approval on March 2, 1780, farmers and Boston artisans attacked it as "aristocratic." But when the convention reconvened in June, it declared the constitution approved, and the document went into effect four months later.

Women and the Limits of Republican Citizenship

While men of the revolutionary generation battled over sharing political power, they were virtually unanimous in the belief that women should be excluded from public politics. Though women participated in revolutionary crowds and other political activities, they continued to be denied the franchise. Except on scattered occasions, women had neither voted nor held public office during the colonial period. Nor, with rare exceptions, did they do so in revolutionary America. In New Jersey, the constitution of 1776 opened the franchise to "all free inhabitants" meeting property and residence requirements, and in the 1780s numerous women took advantage of that opening to vote, leading one disgruntled male to protest that "women, generally, are neither by nature, nor habit, nor education ... fitted to perform this duty with credit to themselves, or advantage to the public." Reflecting that widely held, male belief, the New Jersey assembly in 1807 again disfranchised women. Not until the twentieth century would women secure the vote, the most fundamental attribute of citizenship.

Prior to independence, most women had accepted the principle that political involvement fell outside the female sphere. Women, however, felt the urgency of the revolutionary crisis as intensely as men, writing and speaking to each other about public events, especially as their own lives were affected. As the war progressed, growing numbers of women spoke out publicly. A few, such as Mercy Otis Warren and Esther DeBerdt Reed, published essays explaining women's urgent desire to contribute to the Patriot cause. In her 1780 broadside, "The Sentiments of an American Woman," Reed declared that women wanted to serve like "those heroins of antiquity, who have rendered their sex illustrious," and called on women to renounce "vain ornament" as they had earlier renounced English tea. The money not spent on clothing and hairstyles would be the "offering of the Ladies" to Washington's army. In Philadelphia, women responded by collecting $300,000 in continental currency from more than 1,600 individuals. Refusing Washington's proposal that the money be mixed with general funds in

Mercy Otis Warren Though women were discouraged from public writing, Mercy Otis Warren, related by birth and marriage to leading Massachusetts Patriots, published pamphlets and plays dealing with revolutionary politics. *(Courtesy, Museum of Fine Arts, Boston. Reproduced with permission. © 1999 The Museum of Fine Arts, Boston. All Rights Reserved)*

the national treasury, they insisted on using it to purchase materials for shirts so that each soldier might know he had received a contribution directly from the women.

Even women's traditional roles took on new political meaning. With English imports cut off and the army badly in need of clothing, spinning and weaving assumed patriotic significance. Coming together as Daughters of Liberty, women made shirts and other items. Charity Clarke, a New York teenager, acknowledged that she "felt Nationaly" as she knitted "stockens" for the soldiers.

The most traditional female role, the care and nurture of children, assumed special political resonance during the revolutionary era. How would the republic be sustained once independence had been won? By a rising generation of republican citizens schooled in the principles of public virtue. How would they be prepared for the task? By their "Republican Mothers," the women of the Revolution.

Most women did not press for full political equality, since the idea flew in the face of long-standing social convention and its advocacy exposed a person to public ridicule. Women did, however, speak out in defense of their rights. Choosing words that had resonated so powerfully during the protests against England, Abigail Adams urged her husband John not to put "unlimited power" in the hands of husbands. Remember, she warned, that "all men would be tyrants if they could." John consulted Abigail on many things but turned this admonition quickly aside.

TIMELINE

1776	Declaration of Independence		Pennsylvania begins gradual abolition of slavery
1777	Washington's army winters at Valley Forge	**1781**	Cornwallis surrenders at Yorktown
1778	French treaty of alliance and commerce		Articles of Confederation ratified by states
1779	Sullivan destroys Iroquois villages in New York	**1783**	Peace treaty with England signed in Paris
1780	Massachusetts constitution ratified		

While women developed new ties to the public realm during the revolutionary years, the assumption that politics was an exclusively male domain did not easily die. Indeed, republican ideology, so effectively invoked in support of American liberty against the English king and Parliament, actually sharpened political distinctions between women and men. The independent judgment required of republican citizens assumed their economic self-sufficiency, and that was denied to married women by the long-established principle of *coverture*, a legal doctrine that transferred women's property to their husbands, in effect designating them economic as well as political dependents.

Republican virtue, moreover, was understood to encompass such "manly" qualities as rationality, self-discipline, and public sacrifice—qualities believed inconsistent with "feminine" attributes of emotion and self-indulgence. Finally, the desperate struggle against England strengthened patriarchal values by celebrating military heroism.

In the years ahead, new challenges to male political hegemony would emerge. When they did, women would find guidance in the universal principles enshrined in the Declaration of Independence that the women of the Revolution had helped to defend.

Conclusion

The Crucible of Revolution

When Congress launched its struggle for national liberation in July 1776, it steered the American people into uncharted seas. The break with England and accompanying war redrew the contours of American life and changed the destinies of countless Americans like Long Bill Scott. Though the war ended in victory, liberty had its costs, as lives were lost, property destroyed, and local economies deranged. The conflict altered relationships between Indians and whites, for it left the Iroquois and Cherokee severely weakened and opened the floodgates of western expansion. Though women participated in revolutionary activities and achieved enhanced status as "Republican Mothers," they were still denied the vote.

By 1783, a new nation had come into being, one based not on age-encrusted principles of monarchy and aristocratic privilege but on the doctrines of republican liberty. That was the greatest change of all. However, the political transformations that were set in motion generated angry disputes whose outcome could be but dimly foreseen. How might individual liberty be reconciled with the need for public order? Who should be accorded full republican citizenship, and to whom should it be denied? How should constitutions be written and republican governments be organized? Thomas Paine put the matter succinctly: "The answer to the question, can America be happy under a government of her own, is short and simple—as happy as she pleases; she hath a blank sheet to write upon." The years immediately ahead would determine whether America's republican experiment, launched with such hopefulness in 1776, would succeed.

Success would depend as well on the new nation's position in a hostile Atlantic world. Though American independence had been acknowledged, the long-established web of connections tying the United States to England and Europe remained strong. Wartime alliances had revealed that North America remained an object of imperial ambition and European power politics, while the cutoff of Atlantic trade had made clear how dependent the nation still was on overseas commerce. The new American republic, moreover, served as a model and, on occasion, an asylum for political radicals intent on reforming the corrupt systems of England and France. At the same time, many Americans regarded their republic as a beacon for the struggles of oppressed people elsewhere. In these ways as well, the full meaning of American independence was still to be worked out in the years immediately ahead.

Questions for Review and Reflection

1. Why were England and its North American colonies unable to resolve their differences peacefully?

2. Wars often produce unintended consequences. How was that the case for the American people during the Revolutionary War?

3. Loyalists and Patriots both argued that they sought to uphold the rule of law. How could that be true?

4. Many African Americans supported the struggle for American independence, but countless others did not. Explain the difference.

5. The conflict between the United States and England quickly became internationalized. Why was this so, and what difference did it make for the war's outcome?

Discovering U.S. History Online

The American Revolution and Its Era: Maps and Charts of North America and the West Indies, 1750–1789 www.memory.loc.gov/ammem/gmdhtml/armhtml/armhome.html
This site gives geographical context to the American Revolution.

Oneida Indian Nation, 1777 www.one-web.org/1777.html
This site presents a several-part essay that explains the Oneida tribe's role in the American Revolution. The discussion features quotes from Oneida oral history as well as contemporary publications.

Spy Letters of the American Revolution www.si.umich.edu/spies/
The story of the American Revolution is told through letters of its spies. This site gives context to the letters with a timeline, overall stories, maps of routes, and descriptions of their methods.

Black Loyalists www.collections.ic.gc.ca/blackloyalists
Using primary sources from the collections, this site explores the history of the African American Loyalists who earned their freedom by serving with the British and then fled to Canada to settle.

The American Revolution: National Discussions of Our Revolutionary Origins www.revolution. h-net.msu.edu
This site accompanies the PBS series *Liberty!* with essays and resource links to a rich array of sites containing information on the American Revolution. Included are the Bill of Rights, slave documents, and maps of the era.

Women in the American Revolution www.rims.k12.ca.us/women_american_revolution/
Brief biographies of 25 women who played a role in the Revolutionary War. This site also includes a comprehensive bibliography of online sources.

Fiction and Film

The Broken Chain, a made-for-television historical drama produced and aired in 1994, tells the story of the Mohawk war chief Joseph Brant, who fought with England during the Revolutionary War and then led many of his people to Canada following the peace of 1783. *The Way of Duty*, a PBS documentary-drama based on a book by historians Richard and Joy Buel, traces the challenging experiences of a Connecticut woman and her family during the American Revolution. James Fenimore Cooper's dramatic novel *The Pilot* (1824) offers an imaginative account of naval warfare and seafaring life during the Revolution. In the more recently published novel *Oliver Wiswell* (1940), Kenneth Roberts depicts the Revolution as seen through the eyes of an American Loyalist.

Recommended Reading

www.ablongman.com/nash
The Companion Website has a list of recommended readings about the military, social, and political aspects of the War for American Independence.

Consolidating the Revolution

American Stories

Extending the Revolution

Timothy Bloodworth of New Hanover County, North Carolina, experienced the American Revolution firsthand. A man of humble origins, Bloodworth had known poverty as a child. Lacking formal education, he worked as an innkeeper and ferry pilot, self-styled preacher and physician, blacksmith and farmer. Through hard work, he came to own nine slaves and 4,200 acres of land, considerably more than most of his neighbors.

His unpretentious manner and commitment to political equality earned Bloodworth the confidence of his community. In 1758, at the age of 22, he was elected to the North Carolina assembly. Over the following decades, he remained deeply involved in the political life of his home colony.

When the colonies' troubles with England drew toward a crisis, Bloodworth spoke ardently of American rights and mobilized support for independence. In 1775, he helped form the Wilmington Committee of Safety. Filled with revolutionary fervor, he endorsed republican political reform and, as commissioner of confiscated property for the district of Wilmington, pressed the attack on local Loyalists.

Shortly after the war ended, the North Carolina assembly named Bloodworth one of the state's delegates to the Confederation Congress. There he learned about the problems of governing a new nation. As Congress struggled through the middle years of the 1780s with problems of foreign trade, war debt, and control of the trans-Appalachian interior, Bloodworth shared the growing conviction that the Articles of Confederation were too weak. He supported Congress's call for a special convention to meet in Philadelphia in May 1787 for the purpose of taking action necessary "to render the constitution of the federal government adequate to the exigencies of the Union."

Like thousands of Americans, Bloodworth eagerly awaited the convention's work. And like them, he was stunned by the result, for the proposed constitution described a government that seemed designed not to preserve republican liberty but to threaten it.

Once again sniffing political tyranny on the breeze, Bloodworth resigned his congressional seat and in August 1787 hurried back to North Carolina to help organize opposition to the proposed constitution. For several years, he worked tirelessly for its defeat, protesting that "we cannot consent to the adoption of a Constitution whose revenues lead to aristocratic tyranny, or monarchical despotism, and open a door wide as fancy can point, for the introduction of dissipation, bribery and corruption to the exclusion of public virtue." Had Americans so quickly forgotten the dangers of consolidated power? Were they already prepared to turn aside their brief experiment in republicanism?

At the very least, Bloodworth demanded the addition of a federal bill of rights to protect individual liberties. Echoing the language of revolutionary republicanism, he warned the North Carolina ratifying convention that "without the most express restrictions, Congress may trample on your rights. Every possible precaution should be taken when we grant powers," he continued, for "Rulers are always disposed to abuse them."

Bloodworth feared the sweeping authority Congress would have to make "all laws which shall be necessary and proper" for carrying into execution "all other powers vested ... in the government of the United States." That language, he insisted, "would result in the abolition of the state governments."

In North Carolina, the arguments of Bloodworth and his Anti-Federalist colleagues carried the day. By a vote of 184 to 84, the ratifying convention declared that a bill of rights "asserting and securing from encroachment the great Principles of civil and religious Liberty, and the unalienable rights of the People" must be approved before North Carolina would concur. The convention was true to its word. Not until November 1789, well after the new government had gotten under way and Congress had forwarded a national bill of rights to the states for approval, did North Carolina, with Timothy Bloodworth's cautious endorsement, finally enter the new union.

Just as Timothy Bloodworth knew the difficulties of achieving American independence, so he learned the problems of preserving American liberty once independence had been won. This chapter examines the threats posed to the new nation by the continuing imperial ambitions of England and France in North America; Congress's inability to pay off the foreign-held war debt; the states' failure to join together in prying open foreign ports to American commerce; and continuing restrictions on free navigation of the Mississippi River, deemed essential to development of the nation's interior.

Chapter 7 also discusses an array of domestic issues that troubled the nation's affairs. Disputes over taxation and paper money, slavery and the separation of church and state, and democratic political reform generated turmoil in the states, in some cases leading discontented citizens to openly challenge public authority.

By 1786, Timothy Bloodworth, like countless other Americans, was caught up in an escalating debate between Federalists, who believed that the Articles of Confederation were failing and must be replaced by a stronger national government, and Anti-Federalists, who were alarmed by what they perceived to be the dangers to individual liberty posed by governmental power.

That debate over the future of America's republican experiment came to a head in the momentous Philadelphia convention of 1787, with its proposal for dramatic changes in the national government. With ratification of the new Constitution, the American people opened a portentous new era in their history and launched a dialogue over the very nature of American politics and government that continues to our own time.

STRUGGLING WITH THE PEACETIME AGENDA

As the war ended, daunting problems of demobilization and adjustment to the conditions of independence troubled the new nation. Whether the Confederation Congress could effectively deal with the problems of the postwar era remained unclear.

Demobilizing the Army

Demobilizing the army presented the Confederation government with immediate challenges, for when the fighting stopped, many of the troops refused to go home until Congress redressed their grievances. Trouble first arose in early 1783 when officers at the continental army camp in Newburgh, New York, sent a delegation to complain about arrears in pay and other benefits that Congress had promised them during the dark days of the war. When Congress called on the army to disband, an anonymous address circulated among the officers, attacking the "coldness and severity" of the Congress and hinting darkly at more direct action if grievances were not addressed.

Women Petition for War Compensation

Several Congressmen encouraged the officers' muttering, hoping the crisis would lend urgency to their own calls for a stronger central government. Most, however, found the challenge to Congress's authority alarming. Washington moved quickly to calm the situation. Promising that Congress would treat the officers justly, he counseled patience and urged his comrades not to tarnish the victory they had so recently won. His efforts succeeded, for the officers reaffirmed their confidence in Congress and agreed to disband.

Officers were not the only ones to take action. In June, several hundred disgruntled continental soldiers and Pennsylvania militiamen gathered in front of Philadelphia's Independence Hall, where Congress and Pennsylvania's Executive Council were meeting. When state authorities would not guarantee Congress's safety, it fled to Princeton, New Jersey. Once there, tension eased when it issued the soldiers three months' pay and furloughed them until they could be formally discharged. By early November, the crisis was over, but congressional authority had been seriously damaged.

Over the next several years, Congress shuffled between Princeton and Annapolis, Trenton and New York City, its transience visible evidence of its steadily eroding authority. A hot air balloon, scoffed the *Boston Evening Herald,* would "exactly accommodate the itinerant genius of Congress," because it could "float along from one end of the continent to the other ... and when occasion requires ... suddenly pop down into any of the states they please." Never had Congress been so openly mocked.

Opening the West

The Confederation Congress was not without significant accomplishments during the postwar years. Most notable were the two great land ordinances of 1785 and 1787. The first provided for the systematic survey and sale of the region west of Pennsylvania and north of the Ohio River. The area was to be laid out in townships six miles square, which were in turn to be subdivided into lots of 640 acres each. Thus began the rectangular grid pattern of land survey and settlement that to this day characterizes the Midwest, and distinguishes it so markedly from the irregular settlement patterns of the older, colonial areas to the east.

Western Land Claims Ceded by the States

Two years later, Congress passed the Northwest Ordinance. It provided for the political organization of the same interior region, first under congressionally appointed officials, then under popularly elected territorial assemblies, and ultimately as new states incorporated into the Union "on an equal footing with the original states in all respects whatsoever."

These laws represented a dramatic change from England's colonial administration. Rather than seeking to restrain white settlement as Parliament had attempted to do in the Proclamation Line of 1763, the central government in America's "Empire of Liberty" sought ways to promote settlement's expansion via land laws and Indian policies. In addition, settlements in the American West would not remain colonies subordinate to an imperial power, but would be fully incorporated into the expanding American nation.

Both ordinances enjoyed broad political support, for they opened land to settlers and profits to speculators. Income from land sales, moreover, promised to help reduce the national debt. While permitting slave owners already living north of the Ohio River to retain their chattels, the Ordinance of 1787 prohibited the importation of new slaves into the region. This made the area more attractive to white farmers who worried about competing with slave labor and living among blacks. Southern delegates in Congress accepted the restriction because they could look forward to slavery's expansion south of the Ohio River. During the 1780s, the country's interior seemed large enough to accommodate everyone's needs.

Columbia as Indian Maiden

Despite these accomplishments, various events fueled doubts that the Confederation government was capable of promoting westward expansion. During the postwar years, Congress operated as if the Native Americans of the interior were "conquered" peoples—allies of England who had lost the war and thus come under U.S. control.

For a few years, the conquest strategy seemed to work. During the mid-1780s, Congress imposed land treaties on the interior tribes, among them the Iroquois. Their numbers sharply reduced and their once-proud confederation shattered, many Iroquois had fled into Canada. At the Treaty of Fort Stanwix in 1784, those who remained ceded most of their lands to the United States and retreated to small reservations. By the 1790s, little remained of the once-imposing Iroquois domain but a few islands in a spreading sea of white settlement. On these "slums in the wilderness," the Iroquois struggled against disease and poverty, their traditional lifeways gone, their self-confidence broken. In January 1785, representa-

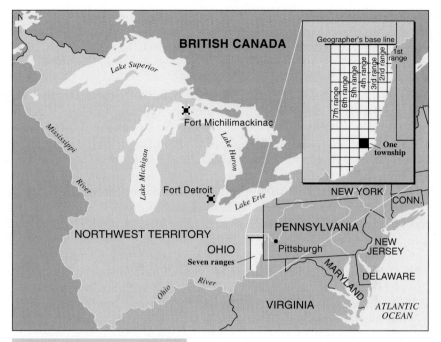

One township (6 miles square)

OLD NORTHWEST SURVEY PATTERNS The Land Ordinance passed by Congress in 1785 provided for the systematic, rectangular survey of lands west of Pennsylvania and north of the Ohio River. Townships were to be divided into lots of 640 acres. The purpose of the ordinance was to promote the rapid, orderly occupation of the Old Northwest. What differences might this new survey system have made in patterns of community settlement, land use, and social life compared to the older, irregular settlement patterns along the Atlantic coast?

tives of the Wyandotte, Chippewa, Delaware, and Ottawa tribes relinquished claim to most of present-day Ohio.

The treaties, often exacted under the threat of force, generated widespread resentment. Two years after the Fort Stanwix negotiations, the Iroquois repudiated the treaty. Within a few years, tribal groups above and below the Ohio River were resisting white expansion into the interior. While the Creek resumed hostilities in

Georgia, Indians north of the Ohio River strengthened their Western Confederacy and prepared to defend their homeland. As devastating Indian raids greeted settlers moving west, the entire region from the Great Lakes to the Gulf of Mexico was aflame with war. With the continental army disbanded, there was little that Congress could do.

Congress's inability to open the interior to white settlement alarmed speculators facing the loss of their investment; farmers wanting to leave the crowded lands of the East; revolutionary soldiers eager to start afresh on the rich soil of Kentucky and Ohio that they had been promised as payment for military service; and leaders such as Thomas Jefferson who believed that America's "empire of liberty" depended on an expanding nation of yeoman farmers.

Congress also failed to resolve problems with European nations that continued to claim areas of the trans-Appalachian west. In June 1784, Spain—still in possession of Florida, the Gulf Coast, and vast areas west of the Mississippi—closed the mouth of the river to American shipping. The act outraged western settlers dependent on getting their produce to market by floating it downstream to New Orleans. Rumors spread that Spanish agents were urging American frontiersmen to break away from the new nation and seek affiliation with Spain. Sensing the danger, Washington commented uneasily that settlers throughout the West were "on a pivot." "The touch of a feather," he warned, "would turn them away."

When Spain refused to reopen the Mississippi, Congress's secretary for foreign affairs, John Jay, offered to relinquish American claims to free transit of the river in return for a commercial treaty opening Spanish ports to American shipping. Though the bargain pleased merchants in the northeastern states, southern delegates in Congress were incensed at Jay's betrayal of their interests and opposed it. Stalemated, Congress could take no action at all.

Wrestling with the National Debt

Further evidence of the Confederation's weakness was Congress's inability to deal effectively with the nation's war debt. Estimated at $35 million, much was held by French and Dutch bankers. Unable to make regular payments against the loan's principal, Congress had to borrow additional money just to pay the accumulating interest. Things were no better at home. In response to the incessant demands of its creditors, the government could only delay and try to borrow more.

In 1781, Congress appointed Robert Morris, a wealthy Philadelphia merchant, as superintendent of finance and gave him broad authority to deal with the nation's troubled affairs. Morris urged the states to stop issuing paper money and persuaded Congress to demand that the states pay their requisitions in specie (gold and silver coin). In addition, he encouraged Congress to charter the Bank of North America and took steps to make federal bonds more attractive to investors.

Though Morris made considerable progress, the government's finances remained shaky. Lacking authority to tax, Congress depended on the states' willingness to meet their financial obligations. This arrangement, however, proved unworkable. In October 1781, a desperate Congress requested $8 million from the states. Two and a half years later, less than $1.5 million had come in. In January

HOW OTHERS SEE US

A View of Postwar America

The European Magazine *and* London Review, *in which this extract appeared in December 1784, reflected important segments of English opinion.*

North America ... appears to be in a very distracted and broken condition.... Their Indian neighbors threaten them with hostilities.... The different States are at a variance among themselves, disputing territories, removing boundaries, and contesting other questions of property! They are not less divided about ... the proportion each State shall contribute to the support of their Government-general, the Congress; what degree of power this ... body shall be invested with any authority at all.... These, and many other important questions, agitate them exceedingly. To crown all, their boasted friends the French and they hate one another most cordially....

Such are the blessed fruits of American Independency ...! How fatal has that chimera, that false light ... that shining nothing, that IGNIS FATUUS, called INDEPENDENCY, been to you! How it has led you through all the paths of error and delusion, from your ... safe dwelling, under the ... protecting wing of British Government.... Generations yet unborn will lament your folly, and curse your false policy and base ingratitude to your parent country.

- *Is this an accurate description of postwar conditions in the United States?*
- *What sources of information might have been available to the writer?*
- *What effect did the attitudes expressed here probably have on an Anglo-American relations?*

1784, Morris resigned. By 1786, federal revenue totaled $370,000 a year, not enough, one official lamented, to provide "the bare maintenance of the federal government."

Not all Americans were alarmed. Some noted approvingly that several state governments, having brought their own financial affairs under control, were beginning to assume portions of the national debt. Others, however, saw this as additional evidence of Congress's weakening condition and wondered how long a government unable to maintain its credit could endure.

Surviving in a Hostile Atlantic World

Congress's difficulties dealing with its creditors and failure to counter Spain's closure of the Mississippi River pointed to a broader problem in American foreign relations. Even after the United States had formally won independence, Britain, France, and Spain continued to harbor imperial ambitions in North America. Before the century was over, France would regain vast areas west of the Mississippi. Meanwhile, Great Britain's Union Jack still flew over Canada and British troops continued to occupy military outposts on American soil, while Spain still conjured up memories of past New World conquests.

The Revolutionary War had dramatically transformed America's relations with the outside world. England, once the nurturing "mother country," had become the enemy, while France, long the mortal foe of England and the colonies

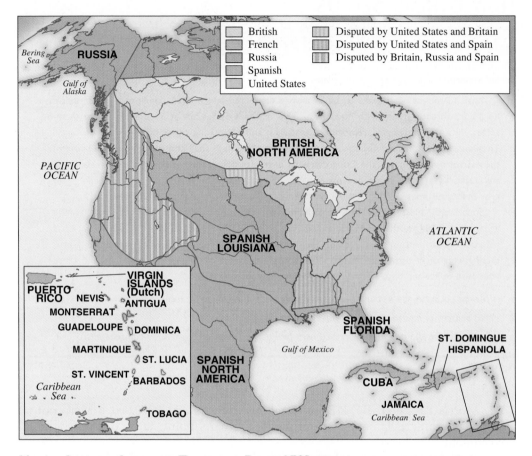

NORTH AMERICA AFTER THE TREATY OF PARIS, 1783 Though victorious in its struggle for independence, the United States was surrounded by British and Spanish possessions, while Russia and France continued to harbor imperial ambitions in the Americas as well. ■ **Reflecting on the Past** What problems and opportunities did European claims on areas of North America pose for the United States?

alike, had proven at best an uncertain friend. Given its imperial ambitions and entrenched monarchy, France feared colonial rebellions and regarded republicanism as deeply subversive. Moreover, French efforts to manipulate the peace process for its own advantage had taught the Americans a hard lesson in the dangers of power politics.

The reason for America's diplomatic troubles during the 1780s was clear: the country was new, weak, and republican in an Atlantic world dominated by strong, monarchical governments and divided into exclusive, warring empires. Nothing revealed the difficulties of national survival more starkly than Congress's futile efforts to rebuild America's overseas commerce. When the war ended, familiar English goods once again flooded American markets. Few American goods, however, flowed the other way. John Adams learned why. In 1785, he arrived in London as the first American minister to England, carrying instructions to negotiate a commercial treaty. After endless rebuffs, he reported in frustration that England had no intention of reopening the empire's ports to American shipping. British officials testily reminded him that Americans had desired independence and must now live with its consequences.

While England remained intractable, wartime allies such as France and Spain returned to a policy of maritime restrictions against American commerce. Congressional efforts to secure authorization from the states to regulate foreign trade were unavailing, because each state wanted to channel its trade for its own advantage. As a result, overseas trade continued to languish and economic hardship deepened.

By the late 1780s, the per capita value of American exports had fallen a startling 30 percent from the 1760s. No wonder that merchants and artisans, carpenters and shopkeepers, sailors and dockworkers—all dependent on shipbuilding and overseas commerce—suffered. In an Atlantic world divided into exclusive, imperial trading spheres, the United States lacked the political unity and economic muscle to protect its basic interests.

SOURCES OF POLITICAL CONFLICT

Revolutionary politics took different forms in different states, depending on the impact of the war, the extent of Loyalism, patterns of social conflict, and the disruptions of economic life. Everywhere, though, citizens struggled with an often intractable array of issues.

Separating Church and State

Among the most explosive issues was deciding the proper relationship between church and state. Prior to 1776, only Rhode Island, New Jersey, Pennsylvania, and Delaware had allowed full religious liberty. In the other colonies, established churches were endorsed by the government and supported by public taxes. There, civil authorities grudgingly tolerated "dissenters" such as Methodists and Baptists. Yet their numbers were growing rapidly and they noisily pressed their case for full religious liberty.

With independence, pressure built for severing all ties between church and state. Isaac Backus, the most outspoken of New England's Baptists, protested that "many, who are filling the nation with the cry of *liberty* and against *oppressors* are at the same time themselves violating that dearest of all rights, *liberty of conscience.*" Such arguments were strengthened by the belief that throughout history, alliances between government and church authorities had brought religious oppression, and that voluntary choice was the only safe basis for religious association.

In New England, Congregationalists fought to preserve their long-established privileges. To separate church and state, they argued, was to risk infidelity and disorder. Massachusetts's 1780 constitution guaranteed everyone the right to worship God "in the manner and season most agreeable to the dictates of his own conscience." But it also empowered the legislature to require towns to tax their residents to support local ministers. Backus argued that official support should be ended completely; "religious toleration," he insisted, fell far short of true religious

The Old Methodist Church, John Street, New York. This nineteenth-century print provides a view of the first Methodist Church erected in America (1786). Methodists and Baptists were among the "dissenting" groups pressing for full religious freedom during the Revolutionary era. *(The Metropolitan Museum of Art, Bequest of Edward W. C. Arnold, 1954. The Edward W. C. Arnold Collection of New York Prints, Maps and Pictures. 54.90.168/Art Resource, NY)*

freedom. Not until 1833 were laws linking church and state finally repealed in Massachusetts.

In Virginia, Baptists pressed their cause against the Protestant Episcopal Church, successor to the Church of England. The adoption in 1786 of Thomas Jefferson's Bill for Establishing Religious Freedom, rejecting all connections between church and state and removing all religious tests for public office, decisively settled the issue. Three years later, that statute served as a model for the First Amendment to the new federal Constitution.

But even the most ardent supporters of religious freedom were not prepared to extend it universally. The wartime alliance with Catholic France together with Congressional efforts to entice Catholic settlers in Québec to join the resistance against England had weakened long-established prejudices. Still, anti-Catholic biases remained strong, especially in New England. The people of Northbridge, Massachusetts, wanted to exclude "Roman Catholics, pagons, or Mahomitents" from public office. The legal separation of church and state did not end religious discrimination, but it implanted the principle of religious freedom firmly in American law.

Slavery Under Attack

The place of slavery in a republican society also vexed the revolutionary generation. How, wondered many, could slavery be reconciled with the inalienable right to life, liberty, and the pursuit of happiness?

DOCUMENT

Slave Petition to the General Assembly in Connecticut (1779)

During the several decades preceding 1776, the trade in human chattels had flourished. The 1760s witnessed the largest importation of slaves in colonial history. The Revolutionary War, however, halted the slave trade almost completely. Though southern planters talked of replacing their lost chattels once the war ended, a combination of revolutionary principles, a reduced need for field hands in the depressed Chesapeake tobacco economy, natural increase among the slave population, and anxiety over black rebelliousness argued for the slave trade's permanent extinction. By 1790, every state except South Carolina and Georgia had outlawed slave importations.

Ending the trade had powerful implications, for it reduced the infusion of new Africans into the black population. As a result, an ever higher proportion of blacks was American born, thus speeding the cultural transformation by which Africans became African Americans.

Slavery itself came under attack during the Revolutionary era, with immense consequences for blacks and the nation's future. As the crisis with England heated up, catchwords such as *liberty* and *tyranny*, mobilized by colonists against British policies, reminded citizens that one-fifth of the colonial population was in chains. Samuel Hopkins, a New England clergyman, accosted his compatriots for "making a vain parade of being advocates for the liberties of mankind, while ... continuing this lawless, cruel, inhuman, and abominable practice of enslaving your fellow creatures." Following independence, antislavery attacks intensified.

In Georgia and South Carolina, where blacks outnumbered whites more than two to one and where slave labor remained essential to the prosperous rice economy, slavery escaped significant challenge as whites tightened local slave codes, shuddering at the prospect of black freedom.

In Virginia and Maryland, by contrast, whites openly argued whether slavery was compatible with republicanism, and in these states significant change did occur. The weakened demand for slave labor in the depressed tobacco economy facilitated the debate. Though neither state abolished slavery, both passed laws making it easier for owners to free their slaves without continuing responsibility for their behavior. Moreover, increasing numbers of blacks purchased their own or their families' freedom, or simply ran away. By 1800, more than one of every ten blacks in the Chesapeake region was free, a dramatic increase from 30 years before. Even so, their freedom was limited, since many found themselves obligated to work for others as indentured servants.

The majority of free blacks lived and worked in towns such as Richmond and Baltimore, where they formed communities that served as centers of African American society, as well as havens for slaves escaping from the countryside. In the Chesapeake region, the conditions of life for black Americans slowly changed for the better.

The most dramatic breakthrough occurred in northern states, where slavery was either abolished or put on the road to gradual extinction. Such actions were

possible because blacks were a numerical minority—in most areas, they constituted less than 4 percent of the population—and slavery had neither the economic nor social importance that it did in the South. In 1780, the Pennsylvania assembly passed a law stipulating that all newborn blacks were to be free when
they reached age 21. It was a cautious but decisive step. Other northern states
adopted similar policies of gradual emancipation. Northern blacks joined in the
attacks on slavery. Following independence, they petitioned state assemblies for
their freedom.

In scattered instances, free blacks participated actively in revolutionary politics. "Would it not be ridiculous ... and unjust to exclude freemen from voting ...
though otherwise qualified, because their skins are black?" demanded William
Gordon, a white clergyman, during the debate over the Massachusetts constitution. "Why not ... for being long-nosed, short-faced, or ... lower than five feet
nine?" In the end, the new state constitution made no mention of race, and black
men occasionally cast their ballots.

If civic participation by blacks was scattered and temporary in the North, it
was almost totally absent in the South. With the brief exception of North Carolina,
free African Americans could neither vote nor enjoy protection of their persons
and property under the law. In the South, blacks remained almost entirely without political voice, other than the petitions against slavery and mistreatment that
they pressed on the state regimes.

Still, remarkable progress had been made. Prior to the Revolution, slavery
had been an accepted fact of northern life. After the Revolution, it no longer was.
That change made a vast difference in the lives of countless black Americans. The
abolition of slavery in the North, moreover, widened the sectional divergence between North and South, with enormous consequences for the years ahead. In addition, there now existed a coherent, publicly proclaimed antislavery argument,
closely linked in Americans' minds with the nation's founding. The first antislavery organizations had been created as well. Although another half century would
pass before antislavery became a powerful force in American politics, the ground-
work for slavery's final abolition had been laid.

Politics and the Economy

The devastating economic effects of independence and war plagued the American
economy throughout the 1780s. The cutoff of long-established overseas trade with
England sent American commerce into a 20-year tailspin. While English men-of-
war prowled the coast, American ships rocked idly at empty wharves, New England's once booming shipyards grew quiet, and communities whose livelihood
depended on the sea sank into depression. Virginia tobacco planters, their British
markets gone and their plantations open to seaborne attack, struggled to survive.
Farmers in the middle and New England states often prospered when hungry
armies were nearby, but their profits plummeted when the armies moved on.

Not everyone suffered equally. With the wearing of homespun deemed patriotic, American artisans often prospered. (The slogan "Buy American" has a long
tradition.) People with the right political connections, moreover, could make
handsome profits from government contracts. Henry Knox, sometime merchant

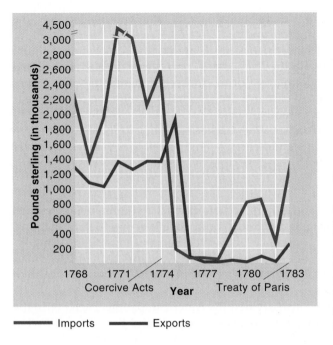

EXPORTS AND IMPORTS, 1768–1783 Nonimportation affected colonial commerce during the late 1760s and early 1770s, but both exports and imports plummeted in 1774 and 1775. Why? Can you explain why imports recovered somewhat beginning in 1778, while American exports remained flat? *(Source: U.S. Bureau of the Census.)*

and commander of the continental artillery, observed that he was "exceedingly anxious to effect something in these fluctuating times, which may make ... [me] easy for life." In the eighteenth century, as now, the boundary between private interest and public duty was often unclear.

But even as some prospered, countless others saw their affairs fall into disarray. Intractable issues such as price and wage inflation, skyrocketing taxation, and mushrooming debt set people sharply against each other. Heated debates arose over whether the states' war debts should be paid off at face value or at a reduced rate. Arguing for full value were state creditors—persons of wealth who had loaned the states money and had bought up large amounts of government securities at deep discounts. Such people spoke earnestly of upholding the public honor and giving fair return to those who had risked their resources in the revolutionary cause. Opposed were common folk angered by speculators' profits. No one, they argued, should reap personal advantage from public distress.

The issue of taxation, seared into Americans' consciousness by their troubles with England, generated similarly heated controversy. As the costs of the war mounted, so did taxes. Between 1774 and 1778, Massachusetts levied more than £400,000 in taxes, a stunning increase over colonial days. As taxes skyrocketed, farmers, artisans, and others of modest means argued that the taxes should be payable in depreciated paper money or government securities. Lacking the hard money that states required in payment, they faced foreclosure of their property. Officials responded that allowing payment in depreciated paper would deprive governments of critically needed revenue.

Controversy swirled as well around efforts to control soaring prices. The upward spiral of prices was staggering. In Massachusetts, a bushel of corn that sold for less than $1 in 1777 went for nearly $80 two years later, and in Maryland the price of wheat increased several thousandfold.

Every state experimented with price controls at one time or another. Seldom were such efforts effective; always they generated controversy. In Boston, a crowd of women angered by the escalating cost of food tossed a merchant suspected of monopolizing commodities into a cart and dragged him through the city's streets, while "a large concourse of men stood amazed."

Individuals not yet integrated into the market economy supported price controls. They believed that goods should carry a "just price" that was fair to buyer and seller alike. In keeping with that principle, a crowd in New Windsor, New York, seized a shipment of tea bound for Albany in 1777 and sold it for what they deemed a fair offering.

Merchants, shopkeepers, and others accustomed to a commercial economy, however, believed that supply and demand should govern economic transactions. "It is contrary to the nature of commerce," observed Benjamin Franklin, "for government to interfere in the prices of commodities." Attempts to regulate prices only created a disincentive to labor, which was "the principal part of the wealth of every country."

Disputes over paper money also divided the American people. Faced with the uncontrollable escalation of wartime expenses, Congress and the states did what colonial governments had done before and American governments have done ever since: they printed money. In the first year of the war alone, they issued more than $400 million in various kinds of paper money, and that was just the beginning. Citizens' willingness to accept such money at face value disappeared as the flood of paper increased. Congressional bills of credit that in 1776 were pegged against gold at the ratio of 1.5 to 1 had slipped five years later to 147 to 1. State currencies depreciated just as alarmingly.

The social consequences of such depreciation were at times alarming. James Lovell reported nervously that "sailors with clubs" were parading the streets of Boston "instead of working for paper." With property values in disarray, it seemed at times as if the very foundations of society were coming unhinged. "The war," wrote Thomas Paine, has "thrown property into channels where before it never was." While profiteers were "heaping up wealth," the rest of society was "jogging on in their old way, with few or no advantages." The poor suffered most severely, for they were most vulnerable to losses in the purchasing power of wages and military pay. But they were not alone. Farmers, merchants, planters, and artisans also faced growing debt and uncertainty.

Rarely has the American economy been in such disarray as at the nation's founding. Problems of debt, taxation, price control, and paper money seemed to exceed the capacity of politics for compromise and resolution.

POLITICAL TUMULT IN THE STATES

The many issues embroiling American politics came together with explosive force in the mid-1780s. The political crisis that resulted spurred demands for a new and more powerful national government.

The Limits of Republican Experimentation

In a pattern that would frequently recur in American history, the postwar era witnessed growing social and political conservatism. Exhausted by the war's ordeal, many Americans focused their energies on their personal lives. And with the patriotic crusade against England successfully concluded, the initial surge of republican reform subsided. As a consequence, political leadership fell increasingly to men convinced that republican experimentation had gone too far, that individual liberty threatened to overbalance political order, and that the "better sort" of men, not democratic newcomers, should occupy public office.

The most dramatic change occurred in Pennsylvania, where the democratic constitution of 1776 was replaced in 1790 by a far more conservative document. The new constitution provided for a strong governor who could veto legislation and control the militia, and a conservative senate designed to balance the more democratic assembly. Gaining control even of the assembly by the mid-1780s, the conservatives proceeded to dismantle much of the radicals' program, stopped issuing paper money, and rechartered the Bank of North America. Pennsylvania's experiment in radical republicanism was over.

Shays's Rebellion

The conservative resurgence generated little controversy in Pennsylvania. Elsewhere, however, popular opposition to hard money and high-tax policies generated vigorous protest. Nowhere was the situation more volatile than in Massachusetts. The controversy that erupted there in 1786 echoed strongly of equal rights and popular consent, staples of the rhetoric of 1776.

By the mid-1780s, increasing numbers of Massachusetts citizens found that they had to borrow money simply to pay their taxes and support their families. Those who were better off borrowed to speculate in western land and government securities. Because there were no commercial banks in the state, people borrowed from each other in a complicated, highly unstable pyramid of credit that reached from wealthy merchants along the coast to shopkeepers and farmers in the interior.

Trouble began when English goods glutted the American market, forcing down prices. In 1785, a number of English banks, heavily overcommitted in the American trade, called in their American loans. When American merchants tried in turn to collect debts due them by local shopkeepers, a credit crisis surged through the state's economy.

Hardest hit were farmers and laboring people in the countryside and small towns. Caught in a tightening financial bind, they turned to the state government for "stay laws" suspending the collection of private debts, thus easing the threat of foreclosure against their farms and shops. They also demanded new issues of paper money with which to pay debts and taxes. The largest creditors, most of whom lived in commercial towns along the coast, fought such relief proposals because they wanted repayment in hard money. They also feared that new paper money would quickly depreciate, further confounding economic affairs.

By 1786, Massachusetts farmers, desperate in the face of mounting debt and a lingering agricultural depression, were petitioning the Massachusetts assembly for relief in words that echoed the colonial protests of the 1760s. Their appeals, however, fell on deaf ears, for commercial and creditor interests now controlled the government. Turning aside appeals for tax relief, the government passed a law calling for full repayment of the state debt and levied a new round of taxes that would make repayment possible. No matter that, as one angry citizen charged, "there was not ... the money in possession or at command among the people" to pay what was due. Between 1784 and 1786, 29 towns defaulted on their tax obligations.

As frustrated Americans had done before and would do again when the law proved unresponsive to their needs, Massachusetts farmers took matters into their own hands. A Hampshire County convention of delegates from 50 towns condemned the state senate, court fees, and tax system. It advised against violence, but crowds began to form.

The county courts drew much of the farmers' wrath, because they issued the writs of foreclosure that private creditors and state officials demanded. In September 1786, armed men closed the court at Worcester. When farmers threatened similar actions elsewhere, the alarmed governor dispatched 600 militiamen to protect the state Supreme Court, then meeting in Springfield.

About 500 insurgents had gathered nearby under the leadership of Daniel Shays, a popular Revolutionary War captain recently fallen on hard times. A "brave and good soldier," Shays had returned home in 1780, tired and frustrated, to await payment for his military service. Like thousands of others, he had a long wait. Meanwhile, his farming went badly, debts accumulated, and, as he later recalled, "the spector of debtor's jail ... hovered close by." Most of the men who gathered around Shays were also veterans and debtors.

The Continental Congress, worried about a possible raid on the federal arsenal at Springfield and urged by the Massachusetts delegates to take action, authorized 1,300 troops, ostensibly for service against the Indians but actually to be ready for use against Shays and his supporters. For a few weeks, Massachusetts teetered on the brink of civil conflict.

The insurrection collapsed in eastern Massachusetts in late November, but to the west it was far from over. When several insurgent groups refused Governor James Bowdoin's order to disperse, he called out a force of 4,400 men, financed and led by worried eastern merchants. On January 26, 1787, Shays led 1,200 men toward the federal arsenal at Springfield. When they arrived, its frightened defenders opened fire, killing four of the attackers and sending the Shaysites into retreat. By the end of February, the rebellion was over. In March, the legislature pardoned all but Shays and three other leaders; in another year, they too were forgiven.

Similar challenges to public authority, fired by personal troubles and frustration over unresponsive governments, erupted in other states. In Charles County, Maryland, a "tumultuary assemblage" rushed into the courthouse and closed it down. The governor condemned the "riotous" proceedings and warned against further "violence and outrages." In South Carolina, an incensed Hezekiah Mayham, being served by the sheriff with a writ of foreclosure, forced him to eat it on the spot.

Across the states, politics was in turmoil. While many felt betrayed by the Revolution's promise of equal rights and were angered by the "arrogant unresponsiveness" of government, others were alarmed by the "democratic excesses" that the Revolution appeared to have unleashed. What the immediate future held in store seemed exceedingly uncertain.

TOWARD A NEW NATIONAL GOVERNMENT

By 1786, belief was spreading among members of Congress that the nation was in crisis and the republican experiment was in danger of foundering. Explanations for the crisis and prescriptions for its resolution varied, but attention focused on the inadequacies of the Articles of Confederation. Within two years, following a deeply divisive political struggle, a new constitution had replaced the Articles, altering forever the course of American history.

The Rise of Federalism

The supporters of a stronger national government called themselves Federalists (leading their opponents to adopt the name Anti-Federalists). Led by men such as Washington, Hamilton, Madison, and Jay, whose experiences in the continental army and Congress had strengthened their national vision, the Federalists believed that the nation's survival was at stake. Such men had never been comfortable with the more democratic impulses of the Revolution. While committed to moderate republicanism, they believed that democratic change had carried too far, property rights needed greater protection, and an "aristocracy of talent" should lead the country. The Revolution, lamented John Jay, "laid open a wide field for the operation of ambition," among men "raised from low degrees to high stations and rendered giddy by elevation." It was time, he insisted, to find ways of protecting "the worthy against the licentious."

Federalist leaders feared the loss of their own political power, but they were concerned as well about the collapse of the orderly world they believed essential to the preservation of republican liberty. In 1776, American liberty had required protection against overweening British power. Now, however, danger arose from excessive liberty that threatened to degenerate into license. "We have probably had too good an opinion of human nature," concluded Washington somberly. "Experience has taught us, that men will not adopt and carry into execution measures the best calculated for their own good, without the intervention of a coercive power." What America now needed was a "strong government, ably administered."

The Federalists regarded outbursts like Shays's uprising not as evidence of genuine social distress but as threats to social and political order. Although they were reassured by the speed with which the Shaysites had been dispatched, the episode persuaded them of the need for a stronger national government managed by the "better sort."

RECOVERING THE PAST

The work that historians do is limited only by their curiosity and the evidence left behind for them to study. In addition to written evidence such as household inventories and Indian treaties, and material artifacts such as the archaeological residue of burial mounds, historians also examine paintings and other forms of visual evidence for information about the past.

While revealing the development of artistic styles and techniques, paintings also provide important windows into past eras for social and cultural historians by revealing how people looked and did their work, as well as what the landscape and built environment were like. Paintings offer insights additionally into the values and attitudes of past times, for they are often intended to enlighten and instruct, as well as please the viewer's eye.

So it was with Charles Willson Peale, who, as a member of the Pennsylvania militia, carried paint kits and canvas along with his musket as he followed George Washington during the Revolutionary War. So it was, even more spectacularly, with the artist John Trumbull, who recorded on canvas some of the most dramatic events of the nation's founding. Slighted for promotion during the Rhode Island campaign early in the war, Trumbull resigned his commission to become a painter. After a frustrating start, he sailed for London, where he studied with the artist Benjamin West, another transplanted American. At the war's end, he was urged by West and Thomas Jefferson to paint an ambitious series of "national history" canvases. Over the next four decades, in addition to numerous portraits, religious subjects, and landscapes, Trumbull fashioned the most famous sequence of patriotic paintings ever undertaken by an American artist.

Included were four canvases, depicting crucial turning points in the struggle for American independence, commissioned by Congress in the early nineteenth century and now hanging in the capitol rotunda in Washington, D.C.—*The Surrender of General Burgoyne at Saratoga, The Surrender of Lord Cornwallis at Yorktown, The Declaration of Independence,* and *The Resignation of General Washington* as commander of the continental army. In addition to those monumental works, Trumbull fashioned a number of heroic battle scenes, including *The Death of General Warren at the Battle of Bunker Hill,* shown here.

Though Trumbull knew Warren and others who fought at Bunker Hill, had witnessed the battle from a distance, and was familiar with the techniques of military combat, he was not primarily concerned with literal accuracy as he composed his painting. Guided by the canons of classical aesthetics popular at the time, he was more interested in the power of artistic "invention" to impart "ideal" truths through the use of brush and pigment.

Examine the painting carefully. Note the positioning, posture, and facial expression of both British and American figures, as well as the banners, smoke, and uses of light. How do these various features contribute to the painting's overall effect? What messages about the Revolutionary War did Trumbull want viewers to carry away from the canvas?

In all his historical canvases, Trumbull was intent on constructing a usable public memory. How does this painting serve those purposes? Why was the creation of a shared public memory so important during the early years of the republic? Might Trumbull have had future generations of Americans as well as his own contemporaries in mind as he did his work?

John Trumbull, *The Death of General Warren at the Battle of Bunker Hill. (Francis G. Mayer/Corbis)*

REFLECTING ON THE PAST   Art and politics have been intimately related throughout our history, for painting, theater, music, and other forms of performance art have been employed to challenge as well as celebrate political leaders and their policies. Think for a moment about the connections between art and politics in our own time. Should the government provide financial assistance for the arts? If so, should such assistance be accompanied by restrictions on the political messages such art might convey? Is art ever nonpolitical?

Congress's inability to handle the national debt, establish public credit, and restore overseas trade also troubled the Federalists. Sensitive to America's economic and military weakness, smarting from French and English arrogance, and aware of continuing Anglo-European designs on North America, Federalists called for a new national government capable of extending American trade, spurring economic recovery, and protecting the national interest. Beyond that, Federalists shared a vision of an expanding commercial republic, its people spreading across the rich lands of the interior, its merchant ships connecting America with the markets of Europe and beyond. That vision, so rich in promise, seemed clearly at risk.

The Grand Convention

The first step toward governmental reform came in September 1786, when delegates from five states who were gathered in Annapolis, Maryland, to discuss interstate commerce issued a call for a convention to revise the Articles of Confederation. In February, the Confederation Congress cautiously endorsed the idea. Before long, it became clear that far more than a revision of the Articles was afoot.

During May 1787, delegates representing every state except Rhode Island began assembling in Philadelphia. The city bustled with excitement as they gathered, for the roster read like an honor roll of the Revolution. From Virginia came the distinguished lawyer George Mason, chief author of Virginia's trailblazing bill of rights, and the already legendary George Washington. Proponents of the convention had held their breath while Washington considered whether to attend. His presence vastly increased the prospects of success. James Madison was there as well. No one, with perhaps the single exception of Alexander Hamilton, was more committed to nationalist reform. Certainly, no one had worked harder to prepare for the convention. Poring over treatises on republican government and natural law that his friend Thomas Jefferson sent from France, Madison brought to Philadelphia a clear design for a new national government. That design, presented to the convention as the Virginia Plan, would serve as the basis for the new constitution. Nor did anyone rival the diminutive Madison's contributions to the convention's work. Tirelessly, he took the convention floor to argue the nationalist cause or buttonhole wavering delegates to strengthen their resolve. Somehow, he also found the energy to keep extensive notes of the debates in his personal shorthand. Those notes constitute the essential record of the convention's proceedings.

Two distinguished Virginians were conspicuously absent. Thomas Jefferson was in Paris as minister to France, and the old patriot Patrick Henry, an ardent champion of state supremacy, feared what the convention would do and wanted no part of it.

From Pennsylvania came the venerable Benjamin Franklin, too old to contribute significantly to the debates but still able to call quarreling members to account and reinspire them in their work. His colleagues from Pennsylvania included the erudite Scots lawyer James Wilson, whose nationalist sympathies had been inflamed when a democratic mob attacked his elegant Philadelphia town-

James Madison, Father of the Constitution James Madison of Virginia, only 36 years old when the Philadelphia convention met, worked tirelessly between 1786 and 1788 to replace the Articles of Confederation with a new and more effective national constitution. *(Mead Art Museum, Amherst Collection, Bequest of Herbert L. Pratt, 1895, [1945.82])*

house in 1779. Robert Morris, probably the richest man in America, was there as well. Massachusetts was ably represented by Elbridge Gerry and Rufus King, while South Carolina sent John Rutledge and Charles Pinckney. Roger Sherman led Connecticut's contingent.

The New York assembly sent a deeply divided delegation. Governor George Clinton, determined to protect New York's autonomy as well as his own political power, saw to it that several Anti-Federalist skeptics made the trip to Philadelphia. They were no match for Hamilton, however.

Born in the Leeward Islands, the "bastard brat of a Scots-peddlar" and a strong-willed woman with a troubled marriage, Hamilton used his intelligence and ingratiating charm to rise rapidly in the world. Sent to New York by wealthy sponsors, he quickly established himself as a favorite of the city's mercantile community. While still in his early twenties, he became Washington's wartime aide-de-camp. That relationship served Hamilton well for the next 20 years. Returning from the war, he married the wealthy Elizabeth Schuyler, thereby securing his personal fortune and strengthening his political connections. Together with Madison, Hamilton had promoted the abortive Annapolis convention. At Philadelphia, he was determined to drive his nationalist vision ahead.

Meeting in Independence Hall, where the Declaration of Independence had been proclaimed little more than a decade earlier, the convention elected Washington as its presiding officer, adopted rules of procedure, and, after spirited debate, voted to close the doors and conduct its business in secret.

Drafting the Constitution

DOCUMENT

James Madison, The Virginia (or Randolph) Plan (1787)

Debate focused first on the Virginia Plan, introduced on May 29 by Edmund Randolph. It outlined a potentially powerful national government and effectively set the convention's agenda. According to its provisions, there would be a bicameral Congress, with the lower house elected by the people and the upper house, or Senate, chosen by the lower house from nominees proposed by the state legislatures. The plan also called for a president who would be named by the Congress, a national judiciary, and a Council of Revision, whose task was to review the constitutionality of federal laws.

The smaller states quickly objected to the Virginia Plan's call for proportional rather than equal representation of the states. On June 15, William Paterson introduced a counterproposal, the New Jersey Plan. It urged retention of the Articles of Confederation as the basic structure of government while conferring on Congress the long-sought powers to tax and to regulate foreign and interstate commerce. After three days of heated debate, by a vote of seven states to three, the delegates adopted the Virginia Plan as the basis for further discussions. It was now clear that the convention would replace the Articles with a much stronger national government. The only question was how powerful the new government would be.

DOCUMENT

The New Jersey Plan (1787)

At times over the next four months, it seemed that the Grand Convention would collapse under the weight of its own disagreements and the oppressive summer heat. How were the conflicting interests of large and small states to be reconciled? How should the balance of power between national and state governments be struck? How could an executive be created that was strong enough to govern but not so strong as to endanger republican liberty? And what, if anything, would the convention say about slavery and the slave trade, issues on which northerners and southerners, antislavery and proslavery advocates so passionately disagreed?

Hamilton presented an audaciously conservative proposal, calling for a Congress and president elected for life and a national government so powerful that the states would become little more than administrative agencies. Finding his plan under attack and his influence eroding, Hamilton withdrew from the convention in late June. He would return a month later but make few additional contributions to the convention's work.

At the other extreme stood the ardent Anti-Federalist Luther Martin of Maryland. Rude and unkempt, Martin opposed anything that threatened state sovereignty or smacked of aristocracy. Increasingly isolated by the convention's nationalist inclinations, Martin also returned home, in his case to spread the alarm.

By early July, with tempers frayed and frustration growing over an apparent deadlock, the delegates agreed to recess, ostensibly for Independence Day but actually to let Franklin, Roger Sherman of Connecticut, and several others make a final effort at compromise. All agreed that only a bold stroke could prevent a collapse.

That stroke came on July 12, as part of what has become known as the Great Compromise. The reassembled delegates settled one major point of controversy by agreeing that representation in the lower house should be based on the total of each state's white population plus three-fifths of its blacks. Though African Americans were not accorded citizenship and could not vote, the southern delegates argued that they should be fully counted for this purpose. Delegates from the northern states, where relatively few blacks lived, did not want them counted at all, but the bargain was struck. As part of this compromise, the convention agreed that direct taxes would also be apportioned on the basis of population and that blacks would be counted similarly in that calculation. On July 16, the convention accepted the principle that the states should have equal votes in the Senate. Thus the interests of both large states and small were effectively accommodated.

The convention then submitted its work to a committee of detail for drafting in proper constitutional form. That group reported on August 6, and for the next month the delegates hammered out the language of the document's seven articles. On several occasions, differences seemed so great that it was uncertain whether the convention could proceed. In each instance, however, agreement was reached, and the discussion continued.

Determined to give the new government the stability that state governments lacked, the delegates created an electoral process designed to bring persons of wide experience and solid reputation into national office. An Electoral College of wise and experienced leaders, selected at the direction of state legislatures, would meet to choose the president. The process functioned exactly that way during the first several presidential elections.

Selection of the Senate would be similarly indirect, for its members were to be named by the state legislatures. (Not until 1913, with ratification of the Seventeenth Amendment, would the American people elect their senators directly.) Even the House of Representatives, the only popularly elected branch of the new government, was to be filled with people of standing and wealth, for the Federalists were confident that only such men would be able to attract the necessary votes.

The delegates' final set of compromises touched the fate of black Americans. At the insistence of southerners, the convention agreed that the slave trade would not formally end for another 20 years. As drafted, the Constitution did not contain the words *slavery* or *slave trade,* but spoke more vaguely about not prohibiting the "migration or importation of such persons as any of the states now existing shall think proper to admit." The meaning, however, was entirely clear.

Despite Gouverneur Morris's impassioned charge that slavery was a "nefarious institution" that would bring "the curse of Heaven on the states where it prevails," the delegates firmly rejected a proposal to abolish slavery, thereby tacitly acknowledging its legitimacy. More than that, they guaranteed slavery's protection, by writing in Section 2 of Article 4 that "No person held to service or labour in one state, ... [and] escaping into another, shall, in consequence of any law ... therein, be discharged from such service, but shall be delivered up on claim of the party to whom such service or labour may be due." Through such convoluted language, the delegates provided federal sanction for the capture and return of runaway slaves. This fugitive slave clause would return to haunt northern consciences in the years ahead. At the time, however, it seemed a small price to pay for sectional harmony and a new government.

Although the Constitution's unique federal system of government called for shared responsibilities between the nation and the states, it decisively strengthened the national government. Congress would now have the authority to levy and collect taxes, regulate commerce with foreign nations and between the states, devise uniform rules for naturalization, administer national patents and copyrights, and control the federal district in which it would eventually be located. Conspicuously missing was any statement reserving to the states all powers not explicitly conferred on the central government. Such language had proved crippling in the Articles of Confederation. On the contrary, the Constitution contained a number of clauses bestowing vaguely defined grants of power on the new government. Section 8 of Article 1, for example, granted Congress the authority to "provide for the ... general welfare of the United States" as well as to "make all laws ... necessary and proper for carrying into execution ... all ... powers vested by this Constitution in the government of the United States." Later generations would call these phrases "elastic clauses" and would use them to expand the federal government's activities.

In addition, Section 10 of Article 1 contained a litany of powers now denied the states, among them issuing paper money and entering into agreements with foreign powers without the consent of Congress. A final measure of the Federalists' determination to ensure the new government's supremacy over the states was the assertion in Article 6 that the Constitution and all laws and treaties passed under it were to be regarded as the "supreme Law of the Land."

When the convention had finished its business, 3 of the 42 remaining delegates refused to sign the document. The other 39, however, affixed their names and forwarded it to the Confederation Congress along with the request that it be sent on to the states for approval. On September 17, the Grand Convention adjourned.

Federalists Versus Anti-Federalists

Ratification presented the Federalists with a more difficult problem than they had faced at Philadelphia, for the debate now shifted to the states, where sentiment was sharply divided and the political situation was more difficult to control. Recognizing the unlikelihood of gaining quick agreement by all 13 states, the Federalists stipulated that the Constitution should go into effect when any nine agreed to it. Other states could then enter the Union as they were ready. Ratification was to be decided by specially elected conventions rather than by the state assemblies. Approval by such conventions would give the new Constitution greater legitimacy by grounding it in the consent of the people.

DOCUMENT

Patrick Henry, Against Ratification of the Constitution (1788)

In the Confederation Congress, opponents of the new Constitution charged that the Philadelphia Convention had grossly exceeded its authority. But after a few days' debate, Congress dutifully forwarded the document to the states for consideration. Word of the dramatic changes being proposed spread rapidly. In each state, Federalists and Anti-Federalists, the latter now actively opposing the Constitution, prepared to debate the new articles of government.

Opposition to the proposed Constitution was widespread and vocal. Some critics warned of the threat to state interests. Others, like Timothy Bloodworth, charged the Federalists with betraying revolutionary republicanism. Like all "energetic" governments, the one being proposed would be corrupted by its own power. Far from the watchful eyes of the citizenry, its officials would behave as power wielders always had, and American liberty, so recently preserved at such high cost, would again come under attack.

Anti-Federalists were aghast at their opponents' vision of an expanding "republican empire." "The idea of ... [a] republic, on an average of 1,000 miles in length, and 800 in breadth, and containing 6 millions of white inhabitants all reduced to the same standards of morals, ... habits ... [and] laws," exclaimed one incredulous critic, "is ... contrary to the whole experience of mankind." Such an extended republic would quickly fall prey to factional conflict and internal disorder. Anti-Federalists continued to believe that republican liberty could be preserved only in small, homogeneous societies, where the seeds of faction were few and public virtue guided citizens' behavior.

Nor did Anti-Federalists believe that the proposed separation of executive, legislative, and judicial branches or the intended balance between state and national governments would prevent power's abuse. Government, they insisted, must be kept simple, for complexity only confused the people and cloaked selfish ambition.

Not all Anti-Federalists were democratic in sympathy. In the South, many held slaves, and their appeals to local authority did not always mean support for political equality, even among whites. Yet along with their warnings against centralized power, many did speak fervently of democratic principles. Certainly they believed more firmly than their Federalist opponents that if government was to be safe, it must be tied closely to the people.

Federalist spokesmen moved quickly to counter the attacks, for many of the criticisms carried the sanction of the revolutionary past. Their most important effort was a series of essays penned by James Madison, Alexander Hamilton, and John Jay and published in New York under the pseudonym Publius. The *Federalist Papers*, as they came to be called, were written to promote ratification in New York but were quickly reprinted elsewhere.

DOCUMENT

James Madison Defends the Constitution (1788)

Madison, Hamilton, and Jay moved systematically through the Constitution, explaining its virtues and responding to the Anti-Federalists' charges. In the process, they described a political vision fundamentally different from that of their Anti-Federalist opponents. No difference was more dramatic than the Federalists' treatment of governmental power. Power, the Federalists now argued, was not the enemy of liberty but its guarantor. Where government was not sufficiently "energetic" and "efficient," demagogues and disorganizers would find opportunity to do their

IMAGE

Alexander Hamilton— Portrait

nefarious work. It is far better, Hamilton wrote in *Federalist No. 26*, "to hazard the abuse of ... confidence than to embarrass the government and endanger the public safety by impolitic restrictions of ... authority."

The authors of the *Federalist Papers* also countered Anti-Federalists' warning that a single, extended republic would lead inevitably to factional conflict and the end of republican liberty. Turning the Anti-Federalists' classic, republican argument on its head, they explained that political divisions were the inevitable accompaniment of human liberty. Wrote Madison in *Federalist No. 10*: "Liberty is to faction what air is to fire, an aliment without which it instantly expires." To suppress faction would bring the destruction of liberty itself.

Earlier emphasis on public virtue as the guarantor of political order, Federalists affirmed, had been naive, for few people would consistently put the public good

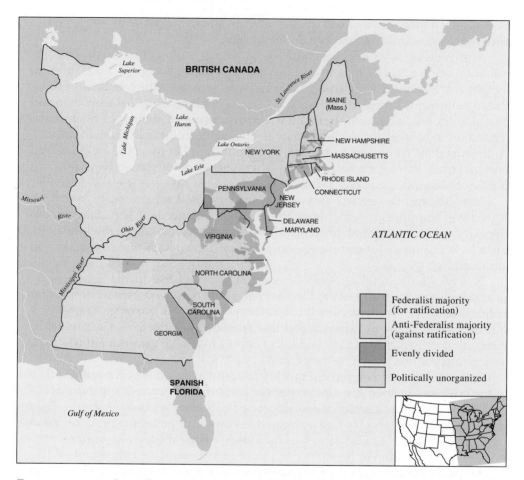

FEDERALIST AND ANTI-FEDERALIST AREAS, 1787–1788 Distinct geographic patterns of Federalist and Anti-Federalist strength appeared during the ratification debate. This map shows areas whose delegates to the state ratifying conventions voted for and against the Constitution. What do the patterns suggest concerning the economic and social bases of Federalist and Anti-Federalist support?

ahead of their own interests. Politics had to heed this harsh fact of human nature and provide for peaceful compromise among conflicting groups. That could best be accomplished by expanding the nation so that it included innumerable factions. Out of the clash and accommodation of multiple social and economic interests would emerge compromise and the best possible approximation of the public good.

In that argument is to be found the basic rationale for modern democratic politics, but it left Anti-Federalists sputtering in frustration. Where in the Federalists' scheme was there a place for that familiar abstraction, the public good? What would become of public virtue in a system built on the notion of competing, private interests? In such a free market of competition, Anti-Federalists warned, the wealthy and powerful would thrive, while ordinary folk would suffer.

As the ratification debate revealed, the two camps held sharply different visions of the new republic. Anti-Federalists remained much closer to the original republicanism of 1776, with its suspicion of power and wealth, its emphasis on the primacy of local government, and its fears of national development. They envisioned a decentralized republic filled with citizens who were self-reliant, guided by public virtue, and whose destiny was determined primarily by the states rather than the nation. Anxious about the future, they longed to preserve the political world of an idealized past.

Federalists, on the other hand, persuaded that America's situation had changed dramatically since 1776, embraced the idea of nationhood and looked forward eagerly to the development of a rising "republican empire," fueled by commercial development and led by men of wealth and talent. Both Federalists and Anti-Federalists claimed to be heirs of the Revolution, yet they differed fundamentally in what they understood that heritage to be.

The Struggle over Ratification

No one knows what most Americans thought of the proposed Constitution, for no national plebiscite on it was ever taken. Probably no more than several hundred thousand people participated in the elections for the state ratifying conventions, and many of the delegates carried no binding instructions from their constituents on how they should vote. It's likely that a majority of the people opposed the document, either out of indifference or alarm. Fortunately for the Federalists, they did not have to persuade most Americans but needed only to secure majorities in nine of the state ratifying conventions, a much less formidable task.

They set about it with determination. As soon as the Philadelphia Convention adjourned, its members hurried home to organize the ratification movement in their states. In Delaware and Georgia, New Jersey and Connecticut, where the Federalists were confident of their strength, they pressed quickly for a vote. Where the outcome was uncertain, as in New York, Massachusetts, and Virginia, they delayed, hoping that word of ratification elsewhere would work to their benefit.

It took less than a year to secure approval by the necessary nine states. Delaware, Pennsylvania, and New Jersey ratified first, in December 1787. Approval came a month later in Georgia and Connecticut. Massachusetts ratified in February 1788, but only after Federalist leaders agreed to forward a set of amendments outlining a federal bill of rights along with notice of ratification. The strategy worked, for it brought Samuel Adams and John Hancock into line, and with them the crucial convention votes that they controlled.

Maryland and South Carolina were the seventh and eighth states to approve. That left New Hampshire and Virginia vying for the honor of being ninth and putting the Constitution over the top. Sensing that they lacked the necessary votes, Federalists adjourned the New Hampshire convention and worked feverishly to build support. When the convention reconvened, it took but three days to secure a Federalist majority.

Two massive gaps in the new Union remained—Virginia and New York. Clearly, the nation could not endure without them. In Virginia, Madison gathered support by promising that the new Congress would immediately consider a federal bill of rights. Other Federalists spread the rumor that Patrick Henry, among the most influential Anti-Federalist leaders, had changed sides, a charge that Henry angrily denied. His oratory, however, proved no match for the careful politicking of Madison and others. On June 25, the Virginia convention voted to ratify by the narrow margin of 10 votes.

The New York convention gathered on June 17 at Poughkeepsie, with the Anti-Federalist followers of Governor Clinton firmly in command. Hamilton worked for delay, hoping that news of the results in New Hampshire and Virginia would turn the tide. For several weeks, approval hung in the balance. On July 27, approval squeaked through, 30 to 27. That left two states still uncommitted: North Carolina (with Timothy Bloodworth's cautious approval) finally ratified in November 1789; Rhode Island did not enter the Union until May 1790, more than a year after the new government had gotten under way.

The Social Geography of Ratification

Federalist strength in the ratifying conventions was concentrated in areas along the coast and navigable rivers and was strongest in cities and towns. Merchants and businessmen supported the Constitution most ardently. Enthusiasm also ran high among urban laborers, artisans, and shopkeepers—surprisingly so, given Anti-Federalist criticism of wealth and power and emphasis on democratic equality. City artisans and workers, after all, had been in the vanguard of democratic reform during the Revolution. But in the troubled circumstances of the late 1780s, they worried primarily about their livelihoods and believed that a stronger government could better promote overseas trade and protect American artisans from foreign competition.

DOCUMENT

The United States Constitution (1789)

On July 4, 1788, a grand procession celebrating the Constitution's ratification wound through the streets of Philadelphia. Seventeen thousand strong, it graphically demonstrated the breadth of support for the Constitution. At the head of the line marched lawyers, merchants, and others of the city's elite. Close behind came representatives of virtually every trade in the city, from ship's carpenters to shoemakers. For the moment, declared the democratic-minded physician Benjamin Rush in amazement, "rank ... forgot all its claims." Within a few years, political disputes would divide merchants and artisans once again. For the moment, however, people of all ranks joined in celebrating the new Constitution.

Outside coastal cities, political alignments were more sharply divided. The Constitution found support among commercial farmers and southern planters eager for profit and anxious about overseas markets. But in the interior, Federalist enthusiasm waned and Anti-Federalist sentiment increased. Among ordinary farmers living outside the market economy, local loyalties and the republicanism of 1776 still held sway. They found Federalist visions of an expanding "American empire" alarming.

Why did the Federalists prevail when their opponents had only to tap into people's deep-seated fears of central government and appeal to their local loyalties? The Federalists won, in part, because of the widespread perception that the

1784	Spain closes the Mississippi River to American navigation	**1786–1787**	Shays's Rebellion
1785	Land Ordinance for the Northwest Territory	**1787**	Northwest Ordinance
			Constitutional Convention
1786	Virginia adopts "Bill for Establishing Religious Freedom"		*Federalist Papers* published by Hamilton, Jay, and Madison
	Annapolis Convention calls for revision of the Articles of Confederation	**1788**	Constitution ratified

Articles of Confederation were inadequate and that America's experiment in republican independence was doomed unless decisive action was taken. More than anything, however, the Federalists succeeded because of their determination and political skill. Most of the Revolution's major leaders were Federalists. Time and again they spoke out for the Constitution, and time and again their support proved decisive. Their experience in the continental army and as members of the Continental and Confederation Congresses fired their vision of what the nation might become. They brought that vision to the ratification process and asked others to share it. Their success turned the American republic in a new and fateful direction.

Conclusion

Completing the Revolution

Only five years had passed between England's acknowledgment of American independence in 1783 and ratification of the new national Constitution, yet to many Americans it seemed far longer than that. At war's end, the difficulties of sustaining American liberty were abundantly evident. The experience of the 1780s added to these difficulties as the American people struggled to survive in a hostile Atlantic environment and cope with troublesome issues of church and state, slavery and the slave trade, and an economy shattered by the cutoff of overseas trade and rampant inflation. Amidst the resulting political turmoil, Americans continued to argue over how democratic their experiment in republicanism could safely be—even whether it could survive.

At the same time, the American people retained an immense reservoir of optimism about the future. Had they not defeated mighty England? Was not their Revolution destined to change the course of history and provide a model for all mankind? Did not America's wonderfully rich interior contain the promise of limitless economic and social opportunity? Though Timothy Bloodworth continued to worry, others, still filled with the enthusiasm of their new beginning, answered with a resounding "Yes." Much would depend on their new Constitution and the government soon to be created under it. As the ratification debate subsided and the Confederation Congress prepared to adjourn, the American people looked eagerly and anxiously ahead.

Questions for Review and Reflection

1. The peace treaty ending the Revolutionary War set the western boundary of the United States at the Mississippi River. What problems did the new territory west of the Appalachian Mountains pose for the new nation, and how effectively did Congress handle those problems during the 1780s?

2. With independence, the United States had to develop its own ways of dealing with other nations. What foreign policy problems did Congress face during the 1780s, and how effectively did it deal with them?

3. Throughout the nation's history, wars have disrupted the American economy. In what ways was this true of the Revolutionary War and what were the consequences?

4. The successful struggle for independence encouraged many Americans to apply the language of rights and equality, used against England, to the conditions of political, social, and religious life in the American states. Identify three examples of this during the 1780s and describe the outcomes.

5. The successful creation of the new American Constitution in 1787–1788 has often been interpreted as a conservative reaction to the more democratic pressures of the Revolution. Is this an accurate judgment? Explain.

Discovering U.S. History Online

Indian Affairs: Laws and Treaties www.digital.library.okstate.edu/kappler
This site offers a digitized and searchable version of U.S. treaties, laws, and executive orders pertaining to Native American tribes. Volume two contains treaties from 1770–1890.

Religion and the American Revolution www.lcweb.loc.gov/exhibits/religion/rel03.html
Providing an overview of eighteenth-century religion in the American colonies, this site draws on primary source material such as paintings of clergymen, title pages of published sermons, and other artifacts.

You Be the Historian www.americanhistory.si.edu/hohr/springer
Part of the Smithsonian's online museum, this exhibit enables students to examine artifacts from the home of New Castle, Delaware, residents Thomas and Elizabeth Springer and interpret the lives of a late eighteenth-century American family.

The Federalist www.law.emory.edu/FEDERAL/federalist www.law.emory.edu/FEDERAL/usconst.html
This searchable site, which presents a collection of the most important *Federalist Papers* as well as the complete text of the Constitution, is especially useful for its information about the Bill of Rights and other constitutional amendments.

Independence Hall National Historical Park www.nps.gov/inde/visit.html
This National Park Service site contains images and historical accounts of Independence Hall and other Philadelphia buildings closely associated with the founding of the United States.

Fiction and Film

The visually lush commercial film *Jefferson in Paris* (1995) combines a depiction of Jefferson's years as U.S. minister to France (1785–1789) with commentaries on themes of liberty and slavery involving events leading to the French Revolution and Jefferson's controversial liaison with his slave Sally Hemmings. The documentary film *Unearthing the Slave Trade* (1994) uses the recent discovery and excavation of an old black burying ground near Wall Street in New York City, where deceased slaves were interred from about 1712 to 1790, to depict the life of urban slaves in eighteenth-century America. Herman Melville's novel, *Israel Potter* (1855), tells the story of a fictitious Revolutionary War sailor who encounters Benjamin Franklin, Ethan Allen, and John Paul Jones during his adventures and ends up in England as a gardener to King George III. In *Those Who Love: A Biographical Novel of Abigail and John Adams* (1965), Irving Stone traces the life story of this remarkable couple, largely through Abigail's eyes, as they move from early courtship through the end of John's presidency in 1800.

Recommended Reading

www.ablongman.com/nash

The Companion Website has a list of recommended readings about the peacetime agenda, sources of political conflict, political tumult in the states, and the new national government.

CHAPTER 8

Creating a Nation

American Stories

Questioning Authority

In October 1789, David Brown arrived in Dedham, Massachusetts. After serving in the Revolutionary army, he had shipped out on an American merchantman to see the world. His travels took him to "nineteen different ... Kingdoms in Europe, and nearly all the United States." Before settling in Dedham, he visited scores of Massachusetts towns, supporting himself as a day laborer while discussing the troubled state of public affairs with local townspeople.

Initially, the people of Dedham took little notice of Brown, but he soon made his presence felt. Though he had little formal schooling, he was a man of powerful opinions and considerable natural ability. His reading and personal experience had persuaded him that government was a conspiracy of the rich to exploit farmers, artisans, and other common folk, and he was quick to make his opinions known.

The object of his wrath was the central government recently established under the new national Constitution. Though he could cite no evidence, he accused governmental leaders of engrossing the nation's western lands for themselves. "Five hundred [people] out of the union of five millions receive all the benefit of public property and live upon the ruins of the rest of the community," he declared. No government could survive, Brown warned, "after the confidence of the people was lost, for the people are the government."

In the highly charged political climate of the 1790s, Brown's explosive language brought a sharp response. In 1798, John Davis, the federal district attorney in Boston, issued a warrant for Brown's arrest on charges of sedition, while government-supported newspapers attacked him as a "rallying point of insurrection and disorder." Brown fled to Salem, where he was caught and charged with intent to defame the government and aid the country's enemies. Lacking $400 bail, he was clapped in prison.

In June 1799, Brown came before the U.S. Circuit Court, Justice Samuel Chase presiding. Convinced that critics of the administration were enemies of the republic, Chase was determined to make Brown an example. Confused and hoping for leniency, Brown pleaded guilty to seditious behavior. Ignoring Brown's plea, Chase directed the federal prosecutor to "examine the witness ... so that the degree of his guilt might be duly ascertained." Before passing sentence, Chase demanded that Brown provide a list of subscribers to his writings. When Brown refused, protesting that he would "lose all my friends," Chase sentenced him to a fine of $480 and 18 months in jail—no matter that Brown could not pay the fine and faced the prospect of indefinite imprisonment.

In rendering judgment, Chase castigated Brown for his "disorganizing doctrines and ... falsehoods, and the very alarming and dangerous excesses to which he attempted to incite the uninformed part of the community." Not all citizens, Chase thought, should be allowed to comment so brashly on public affairs. For nearly two years, Brown languished in prison. Not until the Federalist party was defeated in the election of 1800 and the Jeffersonian Republicans had taken office was he freed.

David Brown discovered how easy it was for critics of the government to get into trouble in the early republic, one of the most tumultuous eras in American political history. Though independence had been won, the struggle over political power and control of the revolutionary heritage continued. As Benjamin Rush, Philadelphia physician and revolutionary Patriot, explained: "The American War is over, but this is far from being the case with the American Revolution. On the contrary, nothing but the first act of the great drama is closed. It remains [for us] ... to establish and perfect our new forms of government." As Chapter 8 reveals, events would soon demonstrate how difficult, and how important to the nation's future, that task would be.

Controversy between Federalist supporters of the national government and the emerging Jeffersonian Republican opposition first erupted over domestic policies designed to stabilize the nation's finances and promote its economic development. Those policies revealed deep-seated conflicts between economic interests and raised urgent questions of how the new Constitution should be interpreted. What was the proper balance of power between state and national governments? How should governing authority be allocated between the executive branch and Congress? Much depended on the answers to those troubling questions.

The chapter then turns to international affairs, which further roiled American politics. The French Revolution and a successful revolt by black Haitians against French colonial power in the Caribbean—the two most dramatic events in a larger web of democratic insurgencies reaching from Europe to the Americas—inflamed congressional politics and roused the people at large. By the last years of the 1790s, the prospect of war with France and Federalist security measures such as the Alien and Sedition Acts brought the nation to the brink of political upheaval. That prospect was narrowly avoided by the Federalists' defeat and Thomas Jefferson's election as president in 1800.

Having captured the presidency and control of Congress, the Jeffersonian Republicans set about the task of refashioning the government, topics next addressed in Chapter 8. At home, the Jeffersonians dismantled the Federalists' war program, reduced the national debt, promoted westward expansion, and emphasized state rather than national authority. Abroad, they struggled less successfully to protect American commerce on the high seas and avoid embroilment in European war.

Adding to the political crisis was widespread anxiety over the nation's novel and still unproven "experiment" in creating a sprawling, diverse republic. The absence of fully developed political parties capable of forging compromise among leaders at the nation's capital and organizing the surging political energy among the people compounded the problem. As political controversy grew during these troubled years, it caught up countless people like David Brown in its toils. By the time Thomas Jefferson left the presidency in 1808, it was apparent how resilient and yet how fragile America's new government was proving to be.

LAUNCHING THE NATIONAL REPUBLIC

Once the Constitution had been ratified, its Anti-Federalist critics seemed ready to give the experiment a chance. They were determined, however, to watch closely for the first signs of danger. It was not many months before they sounded the alarm.

Beginning the New Government

On April 16, 1789, George Washington, unanimously elected president by the Electoral College, started north from Virginia to be inaugurated first president of the United States. His feelings were mixed as he set forth. "I bade adieu to Mount Vernon, to private life, and to domestic felicity," he confided to his diary, "and with a mind oppressed with more anxious and painful sensations than I have words to express, set out for New York ... with the best disposition to render service to my country in obedience to its call, but with less hope of answering its expectations." He had good reason for such foreboding.

The president-elect was the object of constant adulation as he journeyed north. In villages and towns, guns boomed their salutes, children danced in the streets, church bells pealed, and local dignitaries toasted his arrival. On April 23, he was rowed on a flower-festooned barge from the New Jersey shore to New York City, where throngs of citizens and newly elected members of Congress greeted him. That evening, bonfires illuminated the city.

Washington Taking the Oath of Office

Inaugural day was April 30. Shortly after noon, on a small balcony overlooking Wall Street, Washington took the oath of office. "It is done," exulted New York's chancellor, Robert Livingston. "Long live George Washington, President of the United States!" With the crowd roaring its approval and 13 guns booming in the harbor, the president bowed his way off the balcony. Celebrations lasted late into the night.

Though hopefulness attended the new government's beginning, the first weeks were tense. Everyone knew how important it was that the gov-

President-Elect Washington Travels to New York This imaginative scene of Washington's reception in Trenton, New Jersey, during his trip from Virginia to New York City for his first inauguration depicts the popular adulation that surrounded him. What other messages can you find in the picture's details? *(Library of Congress)*

ernment be set on a proper republican course. When Washington addressed the first Congress, republican purists complained that it smacked too much of the English monarch's speech from the throne at the opening of Parliament. Congress then had to decide whether it should accord Washington a title. Vice President Adams proposed "His Most Benign Highness," while others suggested the even gaudier "His Highness, the President of the United States, and Protector of the Rights of the Same." Howls of outrage arose from those who thought titles had no place in a republic. Good sense finally prevailing, Congress settled on the now-familiar "Mr. President." The belief that such decisions might determine the new government's direction for years to come gave politics a special intensity.

The Bill of Rights

Among Congress's first tasks was consideration of the constitutional amendments that several states had made conditions of their ratification. Although Madison and other Federalists had argued that a national bill of rights was unnecessary, they were ready to keep their promise that such amendments would be considered. That would reassure the fearful, fend off calls for a second constitutional convention, and build support for the new regime.

From the variety of proposals offered by the states, Madison culled a set of specific propositions. After extensive debate, Congress reached agreement in September 1789 on 12 amendments and sent them to the states for approval. By December 1791, 10 had been ratified and became the national Bill of Rights. Among other things, they guaranteed freedom of speech, press, and religion; pledged the right of trial by jury and due process of law; forbade "unreasonable searches and seizures"; and protected individuals against self-incrimination in criminal cases. The Bill of Rights was the most important achievement of these early years, for it has protected citizens' democratic rights ever since.

The People Divide

During its first months, Washington's administration enjoyed almost universal support. The honeymoon, however, did not last long. By the mid-1790s, opposition groups had formed a coalition known as the Jeffersonian Republicans, while the administration's supporters rallied under the name of Federalists.

Disagreement began in January 1790, when Secretary of the Treasury Alexander Hamilton submitted to Congress the first of several major policy statements on the country's economic future. Seldom in the nation's history has a single official so dominated public affairs as did Hamilton in these early years. A man of extraordinary intelligence and ambition, Hamilton preferred to act out of the public view, though his instincts for locating and seizing the levers of political power were unerring.

An ardent proponent of America's economic development, Hamilton, perhaps more than any of the nation's founders, foresaw the country's future

Alexander Hamilton Hamilton used the office of secretary of the treasury and his personal relationship with President Washington to shape national policy during the early 1790s. What personal qualities was the portraitist attempting to convey in this painting? *(White House Historical Association [White House Collection] [157])*

strength and was determined to promote its growth by encouraging domestic manufacturing and overseas trade. The United States, he was fond of saying, was a "Hercules in the cradle." Competitive self-interest, whether of nations or individuals, he thought the surest guide to behavior. He most admired ambitious entrepreneurs eager to tie their fortunes to America's rising empire, and believed that a close alliance between them and government officials was essential to achieving American greatness.

At the same time, Hamilton's politics were profoundly conservative. He was deeply impressed by the stability of the British monarchy and confident governing style of the British upper class. Hamilton distrusted the people's wisdom and feared their purposes. "The people," he asserted, "are turbulent and changing: they seldom judge or determine right." He thought the Constitution was not "high-toned" enough and was determined to give it proper direction. His opportunity came when Washington named him secretary of the treasury. Recognizing the potential importance of his office, he determined to build the kind of nation he envisioned.

In his first "Report on the Public Credit," Hamilton recommended funding the remaining Revolutionary War debt by enabling the government's creditors to exchange their badly depreciated securities at face value for new interest-bearing government bonds. Second, he proposed that the federal government assume responsibility for the $21.5 million in remaining state war debts. These actions, he hoped, would stabilize the government's finances, establish its credit, build confidence in the new nation at home and abroad, and tie business and commercial interests firmly to the new administration.

The proposal to fund the foreign debt aroused little controversy, but Hamilton's plans for handling the government's domestic obligations generated immediate opposition. In the House of Representatives, James Madison, Hamilton's recent ally in the ratification process, protested the unfairness of funding depreciated securities at their face value because speculators, some anticipating Hamilton's proposals, had acquired many of them at a fraction of their initial worth. Madison and his southern colleagues also knew that northern businessmen held most of the securities and that funding would bring little benefit to the South.

Hamilton was not impressed. The speculators, he observed, "paid what the commodity was worth in the market, and took the risks." They should therefore "reap the benefit." If his plan served the interests of the wealthy, that was exactly as he intended, for it would further strengthen ties between individual wealth and national power. After considerable grumbling, Congress endorsed the funding plan.

Federal assumption of the remaining state debts aroused sharper criticism. States with the largest unpaid obligations, such as Massachusetts, thought assumption a splendid idea. But others, such as Virginia and Pennsylvania, which had already retired much of their debt, were opposed. Critics also warned that assumption would strengthen the central government at the expense of the states, since wealthy individuals would now look to it rather than the states for a return on their investments. Moreover, with its increased need for revenue to pay off the accumulated debt, the federal government would have additional reason to exercise its newly acquired power of taxation. That was exactly as Hamilton intended.

Once again, Congress endorsed Hamilton's bill, in good measure because Madison and Jefferson supported it as part of a deal to move the seat of government from New York to Philadelphia, and eventually to a new federal district on the Potomac River. Southerners hoped that moving the government away from northern commercial centers would enable them to align it with their own agrarian interests.

Opposition to the funding and assumption scheme, however, did not die. In December 1790, the Virginia assembly passed a series of resolutions warning that southern agriculture was being subordinated to the interests of northern commerce, and that the national government's powers were expanding dangerously. In response, Hamilton confided privately that "This is the first symptom of a spirit which must either be killed, or will kill the Constitution."

As the controversy grew, Hamilton introduced the second phase of his financial program: a national bank capable of handling the government's financial affairs and pooling private investment capital for economic development. He had the Bank of England and its ties to the royal government in mind, though he did not say so publicly. Opposition to the bank came almost entirely from the South. It seemed obvious that the bank would serve the needs of northern merchants and manufacturers far better than those of southern agrarians. Still, in February 1792, Congress approved the bank bill.

When Washington asked his cabinet whether he should sign the bill, Hamilton said yes. Following the constitutional doctrine of "implied powers"—the principle that the government had the authority to make any laws "necessary and proper" for exercising the powers specifically granted it by the Constitution—he argued that Congress could charter such a bank under its power to collect taxes and regulate trade. Secretary of State Jefferson, however, urged a veto. He saw in Hamilton's argument a blueprint for the indefinite expansion of federal authority and insisted that the government possessed only those powers specifically listed in the Constitution. Because the Constitution said nothing about chartering banks, the bill was unconstitutional and should be rejected. To Jefferson's distress, Washington took Hamilton's advice and signed the bank bill into law.

In December 1790, in his second "Report on the Public Credit," Hamilton proposed a series of excise taxes, including one on the manufacture of distilled liquor. This so-called Whiskey Tax signaled the government's intention to use its taxing authority to increase federal revenue. The power to tax and spend, Hamilton knew, was the power to govern. The Whiskey Tax became law in March 1791.

DOCUMENT

Report on
Manufactures

Finally, in his "Report on Manufactures," issued in December 1791, Hamilton called for tariffs (i.e., taxes) on imported European goods as a way of protecting American industries; bounties to encourage the expansion of commercial agriculture; and a network of federally sponsored internal improvements such as roads and lighthouses. These were intended to stimulate commerce and bind the nation more securely together. Neither northern merchants nor Southern agrarians, however, wanted tariffs that might reduce overseas trade and raise the cost of living, so Congress never endorsed this report.

All the while, criticism of Hamilton's policies continued to grow. In October 1791, opposition leaders in Congress established a newspaper that attacked the

administration's program. Hamilton responded with a series of anonymous articles in the administration's paper, accusing Jefferson (inaccurately) of having opposed the Constitution and (also inaccurately) of fo-
menting opposition to the government. Alarmed, Washington pleaded for
restraint. The controversy showed how acrimonious politics had become at
the nation's capital.

VIDEO

The Hamiltonian
System

Political conflict was now spreading beyond the circle of governing officials in
Philadelphia. In northern towns and cities, artisans and other working people
supported Hamilton's efforts to improve credit and stimulate economic development. With their own economic circumstances improving, they seemed undis-
turbed by constitutional issues or the special benefits his policies brought to a few.
Within a few years, many of them would move into the Jeffersonian opposition,
but for the moment their support of the administration was secure.

The Whiskey Rebellion

The farmers of western Pennsylvania voiced their opposition to government policies in dramatic fashion. Their anger focused on the Whiskey Tax, for their livelihood depended on transporting surplus grain over the Appalachian Mountains to
eastern markets. Shipping it in bulk was prohibitively expensive, so they distilled
the grain and moved it more efficiently as whiskey. The Whiskey Tax threatened
to make this trade unprofitable. The farmers also protested that people charged
with tax evasion had to stand trial in federal court hundreds of miles away in
Philadelphia.

Westerners also sensed control of their local affairs slipping away as the backcountry became caught up in a market economy and political system dominated
by the more populous, commercialized areas to the east. In southern states such
as South Carolina, the integration of coastal and interior regions went more
smoothly because of similar agricultural interests and a shared antipathy to black
slaves. In the more economically diverse and racially homogenous states of the
north, however, conflicts between coastal and backcountry regions sharpened.

Hamilton cared little what western farmers thought about the Whiskey Tax.
The government needed revenue, and the farmers would have to bear the cost.
Angered by Federalist arrogance as much as the tax, farmers quickly made their
resentment known. In the summer of 1792, citizens began gathering in mass
meetings across western Pennsylvania. In August, a convention at Pittsburgh declared its intention to prevent the tax's collection. Like opponents of the Stamp
Act in 1765 and the Shays rebels in Massachusetts, they concluded that liberties
would be lost if resistance did not soon begin. Alarmed, Washington issued a
proclamation warning against such "unlawful" gatherings and insisting that the
tax would be enforced. As collections began, the farmers took matters into their
own hands.

In July 1794, when a federal marshal and a local excise inspector attempted to
serve papers on several recalcitrant farmers near Pittsburgh, an angry crowd cornered a dozen federal soldiers in the marshal's house. After an exchange of gun-
fire, the troops surrendered, and the house was torched. Similar episodes involving the erection of liberty poles reminiscent of the Revolution erupted across the

state, while a convention of 200 delegates debated armed resistance and talked about seceding from the United States.

DOCUMENT

Washington, Proclamation Regarding the Whiskey Rebellion (1794)

Fearing that the protests might spread through the entire backcountry from Maine to Georgia and alarmed by talk of secession, Washington called out federal troops to restore order. For more than a year, Hamilton had been urging the use of force against the protesters. To him, the insurrection was not evidence of an unjust policy needing change, but a test of the administration's ability to govern. He eagerly volunteered to accompany the troops west.

In late August, a federal force of nearly 13,000 men marched into western Pennsylvania. At its head rode the president and secretary of the treasury. Persuaded of the danger to his safety, Washington returned to Philadelphia, but Hamilton pressed ahead. The battle for which he had hoped never materialized, for as the army approached, the "Whiskey Rebels" dispersed. Of 20 prisoners taken, two were convicted of treason and sentenced to death. Later, in a calmer mood, Washington pardoned them both.

As people soon realized, the Whiskey Rebellion had never threatened the government. "An insurrection was ... proclaimed," Jefferson scoffed, "but could never be found." Even such an ardent Federalist as Fisher Ames was uneasy at the sight of federal troops marching against American citizens. "Elective rulers," he warned, "can scarcely ever employ the physical force of a democracy without turning the moral force or the power of public opinion against the government." The American people would have additional reason to ponder Ames's warning in the years immediately ahead.

THE REPUBLIC IN A THREATENING WORLD

Because the nation was new and the outside world so threatening, foreign policy generated extraordinary excitement during the 1790s. This was especially so after the tumultuous events of the French and Haitian Revolutions burst onto the international scene. The revolution in France and the European war that accompanied it threatened to draw America in, while across Europe, Ireland, and the Caribbean, political insurgents, invoking the Declaration of Independence and America's colonial rebellion as inspiration for their own cause, joined in what historians call the "Age of Democratic Revolution."

The Promise and Peril of the French Revolution

France's revolution began in 1789 as an effort to reform an arbitrary but weakened monarchy. Pent-up demands for social justice, however, quickly outran initial attempts at moderate reform and in January 1793, when the recently proclaimed republican regime beheaded Louis XVI, France plunged into a genuinely radical revolution. Soon Europe was locked in a deadly struggle between revolutionary France and a counterrevolutionary coalition led by Prussia and England. For more than a decade, the French Revolution dominated European affairs. It also cut like a plowshare through the surface of American politics, dividing Americans against each other.

The outbreak of European war posed thorny diplomatic problems for Washington's administration. By the 1790s, American merchants were earning handsome profits from "neutral trade" with both England and France. In 1800, American ships carried an astonishing 92 percent of all commerce between America and Europe. The economic benefits were most evident in the coastal cities, but radiated as well into the surrounding countryside, where cargoes of agricultural and forest goods and the provisions required by the ships' crews were produced.

America's expanding commerce, however, generated problems as well. While England and France sought access to American goods, each was determined to prevent those goods from reaching the other, if necessary by stopping American ships and confiscating their cargoes. America's relations with England were additionally complicated by the Royal Navy's practice of impressing American sailors into service aboard its warships to meet the growing demand for seamen. Washington faced the difficult problem of protecting the country's citizens without getting drawn into the European conflict.

The French treaty of 1778 compounded the government's dilemma. It appeared to require that the United States aid France much as France had assisted the American states against England a decade and a half earlier. Americans sympathetic to the French cause argued that the commitment still held. Others, fearing the consequences of American involvement and the political infection that closer ties with revolutionary France might bring, insisted that the treaty had lapsed when the French king was overthrown.

The American people's intense reaction to the revolution in France further complicated the situation. At first it seemed an extension of America's own struggle for liberty. Even the swing toward social revolution did not immediately dampen American enthusiasm. By the mid-1790s, however, especially after the revolutionary regime launched its attack on organized Christianity, many Americans pulled back in alarm. What connection could there be between the principles of 1776 and the chaos so evident in France? The differences were indeed profound.

To Federalists, revolutionary France now represented social anarchy and threatened the European order on which they believed America's commercial and diplomatic well-being depended. With increasing vehemence, they castigated the revolution, championed England as the defender of European civilization, and sought ways of linking England and the United States more closely together.

Many Americans, however, continued to support France. While decrying the revolution's excesses, they believed that liberty would ultimately emerge from the turmoil. Though Jefferson regretted the shedding of innocent blood, he thought it necessary if true liberty was to be achieved.

The turmoil in France challenged American assumptions about the gendered basis of politics as well. In France, women participated in revolutionary crowds and joined in arguments over issues of political equality. When word of radical feminist activity reached North American shores, it echoed loudly in the political consciousness of American women. In August 1794, Philadelphia citizens gathered to celebrate the progress of French liberty. Mimicking the public festivals popular in revolutionary France, a crowd of women and men paraded down Market Street to the French minister's residence. There, women dressed in gowns emblazoned with the French tricolor, gathered around an "altar of liberty" and recited patriotic odes before finally dispersing.

Upper-class women such as Anne Willing Bingham, wife of a Federalist senator and daughter of a socially prominent Philadelphia family, opened their dinner parties and social salons to political talk, a practice that became a common part of civic life at the nation's capital. In all of these ways, women explored the boundaries of American citizenship and claimed a wider presence in the public sphere.

Democratic Revolutions in Europe and the Atlantic World

The revolution in France was but the most dramatic among an array of political insurgencies that challenged aristocratic power and promoted democratic values throughout Europe and the Atlantic world during the 1790s. As with the French Revolution, they generated disputes among the American people.

Supported by invading armies of revolutionary France and inspired by the doctrine of natural rights voiced during the American and French revolutions, rebellions against long-entrenched privilege erupted from the Netherlands to the Italian peninsula. Democratic insurgencies broke out as well in Latin America and the Caribbean. The most important occurred on the island of Saint Domingue, soon to be known as Haiti. Beginning in 1791, a multiracial coalition rose in rebellion against French colonial rule. Conflict quickly developed between white landowners seeking to preserve their privileges while throwing off the colonial yoke, poor whites demanding access to land, mixed-race mulattoes chafing under years of discrimination, and black slaves angered by brutal repression. For more than a decade, black and white Haitians conducted a furious struggle against a French force of nearly 30,000. (England, fearing rebellion among the 300,000 slaves on Jamaica, its nearby possession, offered France military support, even though France was its mortal enemy in Europe.) The conflict devastated Haiti's sugar economy and caused more than 100,000 casualties among whites and blacks alike.

In 1798, the island's black majority, led by the charismatic Toussaint L'Ouverture, seized control of the rebellion, making the abolition of slavery its primary goal. Six years later, the victorious Haitian rebels established Haiti as the first black nation–state in the Americas.

While Haitian rebels celebrated the Declaration of Independence as a manifesto of universal freedom, North American whites followed events on that troubled island with a mixture of enthusiasm and dread. The Haitian revolt appeared to affirm the universal relevance of America's own struggle for liberty and struck another blow against European colonialism in the New World. During the height of the Haitian insurgency, American warships ferried black troops from one part of the island to another in preparation for battle.

U.S. citizens, however, contemplated with dread the effect on North American slaves of a successful black rebellion so close by. The Haitian achievement,

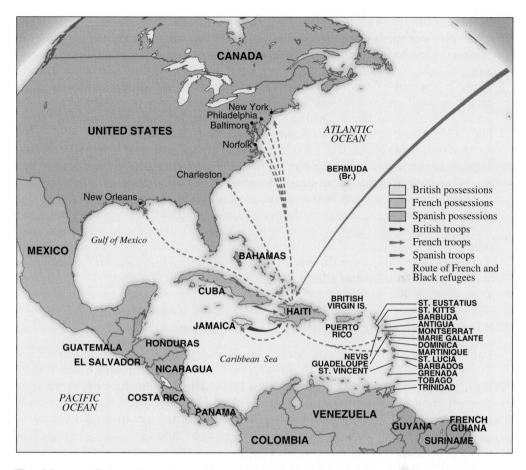

CANADA

UNITED STATES

New York
Philadelphia
Baltimore

Norfolk

Charleston

New Orleans

Gulf of Mexico

MEXICO

BAHAMAS

CUBA

JAMAICA

HAITI

GUATEMALA HONDURAS

EL SALVADOR

NICARAGUA

Caribbean Sea

COSTA RICA

*PACIFIC
OCEAN*

PANAMA

COLOMBIA

*ATLANTIC
OCEAN*

BERMUDA
(Br.)

BRITISH
VIRGIN IS.

PUERTO
RICO

NEVIS
GUADELOUPE
ST. VINCENT

ST. EUSTATIUS
ST. KITTS
BARBUDA
ANTIGUA
MONTSERRAT
MARIE GALANTE
DOMINICA
MARTINIQUE
ST. LUCIA
BARBADOS
GRENADA
TOBAGO
TRINIDAD

VENEZUELA

GUYANA
FRENCH
GUIANA
SURINAME

	British possessions
	French possessions
	Spanish possessions
→	British troops
→	French troops
→	Spanish troops
--→	Route of French and Black refugees

THE HAITIAN REVOLUTION Not only did the Haitian Revolution resonate with issues of racial ideology, it also proved a focal point of European imperial competition in the Americas and of French political battles at home. For white Americans, the Haitian Revolution conjured up frightening visions of black rebellion and cast doubt on the universal relevance of America's own revolution. ■ **Reflecting on the Past** In what ways was the United States sympathetic or unsympathetic to the Haitian Revolution?

moreover, cast doubt on the racial assumption that blacks were incapable of comprehending liberty's true meaning. White southerners were especially anxious. The governor of North Carolina issued a proclamation warning Haitians fleeing the island's chaos to stay away. When Haitian officials appealed "in the name of humanity" for "fraternal aid," Congress demurred. If Haiti became an independent state, warned a senator, it might become "a dangerous neighbor" offering asylum to runaway slaves. When the Haitian republic was proclaimed in 1804, the U.S. government withheld recognition. Not until after the American Civil War were diplomatic relations established.

Though each of the democratic insurgencies that erupted during the 1790s was inspired by local experiences of injustice, they shared a common dedication to human liberty. And though widely scattered across Europe and the Atlantic basin, news of them circulated in the United States via newspapers, networks of personal correspondence, and an expanding human traffic of soldiers, emigres, and political idealists who crisscrossed the Atlantic during these tumultuous years. In the mid-1790s, Joel Barlow and other Americans, motivated by curiosity and democratic principle, journeyed to France, eager to witness the further unfolding of universal liberty. At the same time, a stream of French émigrés, bringing vivid tales of political tumult, sought sanctuary in North America.

As the 1790s progressed, growing numbers of English and Irish radicals fleeing the deepening political conservatism in Britain took passage for North America. When they arrived, many joined the Jeffersonian opposition as newspaper editors and activists, adding to the party's democratic commitment and anti-British stance. The emerging transatlantic web of radical dissent was strengthened as well by a multiracial underclass of sailors, runaway slaves, and white common folk from the far corners of the Atlantic world circulating in and out of North American ports. Their rough appearance, vivid tales of injustice, and readiness to challenge local authorities added to the country's political clamor.

The Democratic–Republican Societies

Political clubs—providing safe havens where dissidents could gather to read political tracts and plot political change—served as weapons of democratic reform throughout the Atlantic world during the 1790s. The Jacobin clubs in France were the best known, but similar groups sprouted up in the United States.

As early as 1792, ordinary citizens began to form "constitutional societies" dedicated to "watching over the rights of the people" and giving the alarm in case of governmental encroachment on American liberties. Several dozen societies, modeled after the Sons of Liberty and Committees of Correspondence that had mobilized Patriots against England 20 years earlier, formed in opposition to Hamilton's financial program.

The French Revolution stoked the fires of democratic enthusiasm and spurred the societies' growth, as did the arrival in 1793 of Citizen Edmond Genêt, the French republic's new minister to the United States. Genêt landed at Charleston, South Carolina, to a tumultuous reception. His instructions were to court popular support and negotiate a commercial treaty with the United States. Shortly after his arrival, however, he began commissioning American privateers to attack British shipping in the Caribbean and enlisting American seamen for expeditions against Spanish Florida, clear violations of American neutrality.

As he traveled north toward Philadelphia, Genêt met more enthusiastic receptions. His popularity, however, soon led him into trouble. In open defiance of diplomatic protocol, he urged Congress to reject Washington's recently issued Neutrality Proclamation and side with revolutionary France. On August 2, the president demanded Genêt's recall.

Though Genêt failed as a diplomat, he succeeded in fanning popular enthusiasm for revolutionary France. With his open encouragement, the largest and most influential of the new societies, the Democratic Society of Pennsylvania, was founded in Philadelphia in June 1793. It called immediately for the formation of similar societies to join in supporting France and promoting "freedom and equality" at home. Washington and his colleagues might wonder whether that challenge was aimed at them.

About 40 popular societies scattered from Maine to Georgia sprang up during the next several years. Working people—artisans and laborers in the cities, small farmers and tenants in the countryside—provided the bulk of membership. Federalist critics derided them as "the lowest orders of ... draymen ... broken hucksters, and trans-Atlantic traitors." That canard referred to the growing tide of Irish immigrants, fleeing hard times and political repression at home, who combined demands for Irish independence from England with a commitment to political equality and a relish for rough-and-tumble politics.

The societies' leaders were often doctors, lawyers, and tradesmen—men of acknowledged respectability. All were united by a determination to preserve the "principles of '76" against the "royalizing" tendencies of Washington's administration. Committed to an awakened citizenry, the societies organized public celebrations, issued ringing addresses, and fired off petitions sharply critical of administration policies. Washington's proclamation of neutrality they labeled a "pusillanimous truckling to Britain, despotically conceived and unconstitutionally promulgated." Several of the societies openly urged the United States to enter the war on France's behalf.

West of the Appalachians, local democratic societies agitated against England's continuing occupation of the frontier posts south of the Great Lakes and berated Spain for closing the Mississippi River at New Orleans to American shipping. Everywhere, they protested the Excise Tax, opposed the administration's overtures to England, and called for a press free from control by Federalist "aristocrats."

President Washington and his supporters were incensed by the societies' support of Genêt and criticism of the government. Such "nurseries of sedition," thundered one Federalist, threatened to revolutionize America as the Jacobins had revolutionized France. Such polemics indicated how inflamed public discourse had become.

Jay's Controversial Treaty

The uproar over Jay's Treaty with England further heightened tensions at mid-decade. Alarmed by deteriorating relations with England, Washington sent Chief Justice John Jay to London in the spring of 1794 to negotiate a wide range of issues carried over from the Revolutionary War. The treaty that the chief justice brought home in early 1795 contained British promises on a number of sensitive matters but ignored a host of other problems. When its terms were made public, they triggered an explosion of protest.

The administration's pleas that the agreement headed off an open breach with England and was the best that could be obtained failed to pacify its critics. In New York City, Hamilton was stoned while defending the treaty at a mass meeting. Southern planters were angry because the agreement brought no compensation for their lost slaves. Westerners complained that the British were not evacuating the military posts, while merchants and sailors railed against Jay's failure to stop impressments and open the British West Indies to American trade. After a long and acrimonious debate, the Senate ratified the treaty by a narrow margin.

DOCUMENT

The Treaty of San Lorenzo (or Pinckney's Treaty) (1796)

The administration made better progress on the still volatile issue of free transit of the Mississippi. In the Treaty of San Lorenzo, negotiated by Thomas Pinckney in 1795, Spain for the first time recognized the Mississippi River to the west and 31st parallel to the south as U.S. boundaries and gave up all claim to U.S. territory. Spain also granted Americans free navigation of the Mississippi and the right to unload goods for transshipment at New Orleans—but only for three years.

By mid-decade, political harmony had disappeared as divisions deepened on virtually every important issue of foreign and domestic policy. Jefferson, increasingly estranged from the administration, resigned as secretary of state, joining Madison and others in open opposition to Washington's administration.

In September 1796, in what came to be called his Farewell Address, Washington deplored the deepening political divisions, warned against entangling alliances with foreign nations, and announced that he would not accept a third term. He had long been contemplating retirement, for he was now 64 and wearied by political attacks. "As to you, sir," fumed Thomas Paine in a letter published in an opposition newspaper, "treacherous in private friendship ... and a hypocrite in public life, the world will be puzzled to decide, whether you ... have abandoned good principles, or whether you ever had any." Few American presidents have been subjected to such public abuse.

THE POLITICAL CRISIS DEEPENS

By 1796, bitter controversy surrounded the national government. That controversy intensified during the last half of the 1790s until it seemed to threaten the very stability of the country.

The Election of 1796

With Washington out of the picture, the presidential election quickly narrowed to Adams versus Jefferson. Both had played distinguished roles during the Revolution, when they shared the task of drafting the Declaration of Independence. They had joined forces again during the 1780s, Adams serving as first U.S. minister to Great Britain and Jefferson as minister to France. They came together a third time during the early 1790s in Washington's administration, Adams as vice president and Jefferson as secretary of state.

By the mid-1790s, they differed sharply in their visions of the nation's future. While fearing Hamilton's ambition and distrusting his infatuation with England, Adams was a committed Federalist. He believed in a vigorous national government, was appalled by the French Revolution, and feared "excessive" democracy. Jefferson, while firmly supporting the Constitution, was alarmed by Hamilton's financial program, viewed France's revolution as a logical if chaotic extension of

John Adams John Adams, Washington's vice president, won a narrow victory over Jefferson for the presidency in 1796. His administration foundered on conflicts over foreign policy abroad and the suppression of political dissent at home. *(Adams National Historic Site/U.S. Department of the Interior, National Park Service)*

America's struggle for freedom, and hoped to expand democracy at home. By 1796, he had become the leader of an increasingly vocal opposition, the Jeffersonian Republican party.

The election of 1796 bound Jefferson and Adams together once again, this time in a deeply strained and ill-fated alliance. Adams received 71 electoral votes and became president. Jefferson came in second with 68 and, as then specified in the Constitution, assumed the vice presidency. The narrowness of Adams's majority foreshadowed the troubles that lay ahead.

The War Crisis with France

Adams had no sooner taken office than he confronted a deepening crisis with France generated by French naval vessels interfering with American merchant ships in the Caribbean. That crisis would push the nation to the brink of civil conflict.

Hoping to ease relations between the two countries, Adams sent three commissioners to Paris to negotiate an accord. When they arrived in Paris, agents of the French foreign minister Talleyrand (identified only as "X, Y, and Z") made it clear that the success of the American mission depended on a loan to the French government and a $240,000 "gratuity" (more accurately, a bribe) for themselves. The two staunchly Federalist commissioners, John Marshall and Charles Pinckney, indignantly sailed home. Elbridge Gerry, the third commissioner, alarmed by Talleyrand's intimation that France would declare war if all three Americans departed, stayed on.

AUDIO

Jefferson and Liberty

When Adams reported the so-called XYZ Affair to Congress, Federalists quickly exploited the French blunder. Secretary of State Pickering urged an immediate declaration of war, while Federalist congressmen thundered, "Millions for defense, but not one cent for tribute!" Caught up in the anti-French furor and emboldened by petitions of support that flooded in, Adams lashed out at "enemies" at home and abroad. Emotions were further inflamed by the so-called Quasi War, a series of naval encounters between American and French ships on the high seas.

For the moment, the Republicans were in disarray. Publicly, they deplored the French government's behavior and pledged to uphold the nation's honor. But they were alarmed about Federalist intentions—with good reason, because the Federalists soon mounted a crash program to repel invaders from abroad and root out "traitors" at home.

The Alien and Sedition Acts

In May 1798, Congress called for a naval force capable of defending the American coast against French attack. In July, it moved closer to an open breach by repealing the treaty of 1778 and calling for the formation of a 10,000-man army. The army's stated mission was to repel a French invasion, but this seemed an unlikely danger given France's desperate struggle in Europe. The Jeffersonians, remembering the speed with which the Federalists had deployed troops against the Whiskey Rebels, feared the army would be used against them.

As criticism of the army bill mounted, Adams had second thoughts. He was still enough of an old revolutionary to worry about the dangers of standing armies. "This damned army," he exclaimed, "will be the ruin of the country." He was further angered when members of his party sought to put Hamilton in command of the troops. To the dismay of hard-line Federalists, Adams issued only a few of the officers' commissions that Congress had authorized. Without officers, the army could not be mobilized.

DOCUMENT

The Alien and Sedition Acts (1798)

Fearful of foreign subversion and aware that French and Irish immigrants were active in the Jeffersonian opposition, the Federalist-dominated Congress acted to curb the flow of aliens into the country. In June 1798, the Naturalization Act raised the residence requirement for citizenship from 5 to 14 years, while the Alien Act authorized the president to expel aliens whom he judged "dangerous to the peace and safety of the United States." Another bill, the Alien Enemies Act, empowered the president in time of war to arrest, imprison, or banish the subjects of any hostile nation without specifying charges against them or providing opportunity for appeal. A Federalist congressman explained that there was no need "to invite ... the turbulent and disorderly of all parts of the world, to come here with a view to distract our tranquility."

The implications of these acts for political liberties were ominous enough, but the Federalists had not yet finished. In a move aimed directly at the Jeffersonians, Congress passed the Sedition Act, making it punishable by fine and imprisonment for anyone to conspire in opposition to "any measure or measures of the government," or to aid "any insurrection, riot, unlawful assembly, or combination." Fines and prison also awaited those who dared to "write, print, utter, or publish ... any false, scandalous and malicious writing" bringing the government, Congress, or the president into disrepute. The Federalist moves stunned the Jeffersonians, for they threatened to smother all political opposition.

Under the terms of the Alien Act, Secretary of State Pickering launched investigations intended to force foreigners to register with the government. He noted approvingly that large numbers of aliens were leaving the country. As Sedition Act prosecutions went forward, 25 people, among them David Brown of Dedham, were arrested. Fifteen were indicted, and 10 were ultimately convicted, the majority of them Jeffersonian printers and editors. In Congress, Representative Matthew Lyon, a cantankerous, Irish-born, acid-tongued Jeffersonian from Vermont, became embroiled in a heated debate over the Sedition Act and spat in the face of a Federalist opponent, Roger Griswold of Connecticut. Two weeks later, Griswold caned Lyon on the House floor. Later that year, Lyon was hauled into court, fined $1,000, and sentenced to four months in prison. His crime? Referring in a personal letter to President Adams's "unbounded thirst for ridiculous pomp, foolish adulation, and selfish avarice."

The Virginia and Kentucky Resolutions

The Alien and Sedition Acts generated a firestorm of protest across the country. On November 16, 1798, the Kentucky assembly passed a resolution declaring that the government had violated the Bill of Rights. Faced with such an arbitrary exercise of federal power, each state had "an equal right" to judge of infractions and "the mode and measure of redress." Nullification (declaring a federal law invalid within a state's borders) was the "rightful remedy" for unconstitutional laws. Similar resolutions, written by Madison and passed the following month by the Virginia Assembly, asserted that when the central government threatened the people's liberties, the states were "duty bound to interpose for arresting the progress of the evil." It would not be the last time in American history that state leaders would claim authority to set aside a federal law.

The Kentucky and Virginia resolutions received little support elsewhere, and as it turned out the Alien and Sedition Acts were not enforced in the South. Still, the resolutions indicated the depth of popular opposition to the Federalist program. As the Federalists pressed ahead, the Virginia assembly called for the formation of a state arsenal at Harpers Ferry and reorganization of the militia. In Philadelphia, Federalist patrols walked the streets to protect government officials from angry crowds. As a precaution, President Adams smuggled arms into his residence. As 1799 began, the country seemed on the brink of upheaval.

Within a year, however, the cycle turned once again, this time decisively against the Federalists. From Europe, the president's son, John Quincy Adams, sent assurances that Talleyrand was prepared to negotiate an honorable accord.

Fearful that war with France "would convulse the attachments of the country," Adams seized the opening and determined to appoint new peace commissioners. "The end of war is peace," he explained, "and peace was offered me." He also concluded that his only chance of reelection lay in fashioning a peace coalition out of both parties. Adams's cabinet was enraged, for the Federalist war program depended for its legitimacy on continuation of the French crisis. After Secretary of State Pickering ignored presidential orders to dispatch the new commissioners, Adams dismissed him and ordered them to depart. By year's end, the envoys had secured an agreement releasing the United States from the 1778 alliance and restoring peaceful relations.

The "Revolution of 1800"

As the election of 1800 approached, the Federalists were in disarray, having squandered the political advantage handed them by the XYZ Affair. With peace a reality, they stood before the nation charged with exercising federal power unconstitutionally, suppressing political dissent, and threatening to use a federal army against American citizens. Adams's opponents within the Federalist party were furious at his "betrayal." When he stood for reelection, they plotted his defeat.

Emotions ran high as the election approached. In Philadelphia, gangs of young Federalists and Jeffersonians clashed in the streets. "A fray ensued," one observer reported, "the light horse were called in, and the city was so filled with

Thomas Jefferson Principal author of the Declaration of Independence, U.S. minister to France, Washington's first secretary of state, vice president under John Adams, and leader of political opposition to the Federalists, Jefferson won the presidency (1800) in one of the most closely contested and significant elections in the nation's history. *(The Metropolitan Museum of Art, Bequest of Cornelia Cruger, 1923, 24.19.1/Art Resource, NY)*

confusion ... that it was dangerous going out." In Virginia, rumors of a slave insurrection briefly interrupted the political feuding, but the scare passed and Federalists and Jeffersonians were soon at each others' throats once again. This election, Jefferson warned, would determine whether republicanism or aristocracy would prevail.

Election day was tense throughout the country but passed without serious incident. As the results were tallied, it became clear that the Jeffersonians had won a decisive victory. The party's two candidates for president, Jefferson and Aaron Burr, each had 73 electoral votes. Adams trailed with 65.

Because of the tie vote, the election was thrown into the House of Representatives, as provided in the Constitution, where a deadlock quickly developed. After a bitter struggle, the House finally elected Jefferson, ten states to four, on the thirty-sixth ballot. (Seeking to prevent a recurrence of such a crisis, the next Congress passed and the states then ratified the Twelfth Amendment, providing for separate Electoral College ballots for president and vice president.) The magnitude of the Federalists' defeat was even more evident in congressional elections, where they lost their majorities in both the House and Senate.

The election's outcome revealed the strong sectional divisions now evident in the country's politics. The Federalists dominated New England because of regional loyalty to Adams, the area's commercial ties with England, and fears that the Jeffersonians intended to import social revolution from France. From Maryland south, political control by the Jeffersonians was almost as complete. In the middle states, the election was more closely contested.

The Federalist–Jeffersonian conflict was rooted as well in socioeconomic divisions among the American people. Federalist strength was strongest among merchants, manufacturers, and commercial farmers situated within easy reach of the coast. In New York City and Philadelphia, Federalists were most numerous in the wards where assessments were highest, houses largest, and addresses most fashionable. All had supported the Constitution in 1787–1788.

The Jeffersonian coalition included most of the old Anti-Federalists, but was much broader than that. It found support among urban workers and artisans, many of whom had once been staunch Federalists. The coalition, moreover, was led by individuals such as Madison and Jefferson who had helped create the Constitution and set the new government on its feet. Unlike the Anti-Federalists, the Jeffersonians were ardent supporters of the Constitution, but they insisted that it be implemented in ways consistent with political liberty and a strong dependence on the states.

Not all Jeffersonians were democratic in sympathy. Some continued to argue the importance of leadership by a "natural aristocracy of talent," most southern Jeffersonians found no inconsistency between black slavery and white liberty, and virtually all continued to believe that politics should remain an exclusively male domain. Still, the Jeffersonian coalition included countless individuals committed to the creation of a more democratic society. Motivated by electoral self-interest, political principle, and the determination of ordinary people to claim their rights as republican citizens, the Jeffersonian Republican party ushered in a growing tide of popular politics.

In the election of 1800, control of the federal government passed for the first time from one political party to another, not easily but peacefully. The "revolution of 1800," Jefferson claimed, was "as real a revolution in the principles of our government as that of 1776 was in its form." The years immediately ahead would reveal whether he was correct.

RESTORING AMERICAN LIBERTY

The Jeffersonians took office in 1801 determined to calm the political storms, consolidate their recent victory, rescue the government from Federalist mismanagement, and set it on a proper republican course.

The Jeffersonians Take Control

New Capitol—
Congress' First
Meeting—1800

In November 1800, the government had moved from Philadelphia to the new capital in the District of Columbia located on the Potomac River. To the consternation of arriving politicians, the new capital was nothing more than a swampy village of 5,000 inhabitants. Little had yet materialized of Pierre L'Enfant's grand design, commissioned by Congress, for a new capital intended to rise as the "Rome of the New World." One wing of the Capitol building containing the House of Representatives was finished, but the Senate chamber and president's house were uncompleted.

To rid the government of Federalist pomp, Jefferson planned a simple inauguration. Shortly before noon on March 4, he walked to the Capitol from his nearby boardinghouse. Dressed as a plain citizen, the president-elect read his short inaugural address; Chief Justice John Marshall, a fellow Virginian but staunch Federalist recently appointed to the Supreme Court by John Adams, administered the oath of office; and a militia company fired a 16-gun salute. Despite the modesty of the occasion, the moment was filled with significance. For the first time in American history, control of the government had shifted from one political party to another.

Thomas Jefferson,
First Inaugural
Address (1801)

In his inaugural speech, Jefferson enumerated the "essential principles" that would guide his administration: "equal and exact justice to all," support of the states as "the surest bulwarks against anti-republican tendencies," "absolute acquiescence" in the decisions of the majority, supremacy of civil over military authority, reduction of government spending, "honest payment" of the public debt, freedom of the press, and "freedom of the person under the protection of the habeas corpus." Though Jefferson never mentioned the Federalists, his litany of principles reverberated with the dark experience of the 1790s.

Jefferson spoke also of political reconciliation, asserting that "We are all republicans—we are all federalists." Not all his followers welcomed that final flourish. Acknowledging political reality, Jefferson agreed to a "general sweep" of Federalist officeholders. By 1808, virtually all government offices were in Jeffersonian hands.

Politics and the Federal Courts

Having lost Congress and the presidency, the Federalists turned to the federal judiciary for protection against the expected Jeffersonian onslaught. In the last months of the Adams administration, the Federalist-controlled Congress had passed a new Judiciary Act increasing the number of circuit courts, complete with judges, marshals, and clerks. Before leaving office, Adams filled many of those offices with staunch Federalists. When the new Jeffersonian-dominated Congress convened, it challenged the Federalist hold on the judiciary.

In early 1802, by a strict party vote, Congress repealed the Judiciary Act. As Federalists sputtered in anger, exultant Jeffersonians prepared to purge several highly partisan Federalist judges. In March 1803, the House of Representatives impeached District Judge John Pickering of New Hampshire. The grounds were not the "high crimes and misdemeanors" required by the Constitution but the Federalist diatribes with which Pickering regularly assaulted defendants and juries. Impeachment, claimed a Jeffersonian congressman, is nothing more than a declaration by Congress that an individual holds "dangerous opinions," which if allowed to go into effect "will work the destruction of the Union." Such phrases echoed the language of repression used by Federalists only a few years earlier. Still, the Jeffersonian-controlled Senate convicted Pickering by a straight party vote. Next, the Jeffersonians impeached Supreme Court Justice Samuel Chase, one of the most notorious Federalist partisans. When the trial revealed that Chase had committed no impeachable offense, he was acquitted and returned triumphantly to the bench.

Chase was a sorry hero, but constitutional principles are often established in defense of less than heroic people. Had Chase's impeachment succeeded, Chief Justice Marshall would almost certainly have been next, and that would have precipitated a constitutional crisis. Sensing the danger, the Jeffersonians pulled back, content to allow time and attrition to cleanse the courts of Federalist control. The vital principle of judicial independence had been narrowly preserved.

Dismantling the Federalist War Program

The Jeffersonians moved quickly to dismantle the Federalists' war program. They ended prosecutions under the Sedition Act, freed its victims, and in 1802 let it lapse. While several Federalist editors felt the government's displeasure, Jefferson never duplicated the Federalists' efforts to stifle dissent. As a consequence, freedom of the press, among the bedrock principles of American liberty, was solidly affirmed. Jefferson undercut the Alien Acts by dismantling the hated inspection system, and in 1802 Congress restored the requirement of 5 rather than 14 years of residence before a foreigner could become a citizen. The Federalists' provisional army was disbanded; no longer would federal troops intimidate American citizens.

Jefferson was determined as well to reduce the size of the federal government, even though it had fewer than 3,000 civilian employees, only 300 of them, including the cabinet and Congress, in Washington. The "principal care of our persons and property," he declared, should be left to the states because they were more closely attuned to the people's needs. The federal government should do little more than oversee foreign policy, deliver the mail, deal with Indians on federal lands, and administer the public domain. Though the Jeffersonians may not have "revolutionized" the government as they claimed, they pointed it in a new direction.

BUILDING AN AGRARIAN NATION

The Jeffersonians did more than reverse Federalist initiatives, for they were determined to implement their own vision of an expanding, agrarian nation. That vision was mixed and inconsistent, because the Jeffersonian party was made up of conflicting groups: southern planters, like Jefferson himself, determined to maintain a slavery-based agrarian order; lower- and middle-class southern whites committed to black servitude but ardent proponents of political equality among whites; northern artisans harboring an aversion to slavery (though rarely a commitment to racial equality) and a fierce dedication to honest toil and their own economic interests; western farmers devoted to self-sufficiency on the land; and northern intellectuals committed to political democracy. In time, this diversity would splinter the Jeffersonian coalition. For the moment, however, these groups found unity not only in opposition to their common Federalist enemies, but also in a set of broadly shared principles that guided government policies through Jefferson's two administrations (1801–1809).

The Jeffersonian Vision

Political liberty, the Jeffersonians believed, could survive only under conditions of broad economic and social equality. Their strategy centered on the independent, yeoman farmer—self-reliant, industrious, and concerned for the public good. Such qualities were deemed essential to democratic citizenship.

The Jeffersonian vision, however, was clouded because industriousness generated wealth, wealth bred social inequality, and inequality threatened to destroy the very foundation of a democratic society. The solution lay in rapid territorial expansion that would provide land for the nations' citizen farmers, draw restless people out of crowded eastern cities, preserve the social equality that democratic liberty required, and delay—perhaps even prevent—the cyclical process of growth, maturity, and decay that had been the fate of past nations.

There were other reasons for promoting expansion. Occupation of the West would secure U.S. borders against lingering British, French, and Spanish threats. Finally, Jeffersonians calculated that newly formed western states would strengthen their own political control and ensure the Federalists' demise.

Time would reveal that the United States' ability to avoid Europe's woes by continental expansion, a basic tenet of American exceptionalism, was more limited than Jefferson imagined. Yet from the perspective of the early nineteenth century, the Jeffersonians offered a compelling vision of the nation's future.

The Windfall Louisiana Purchase

The goal of securing agrarian democracy by territorial expansion explains Jefferson's most dramatic accomplishment, the Louisiana Purchase of 1803. It nearly doubled the nation's size.

The Louisiana Purchase

In 1800, Spain ceded the vast trans-Mississippi region called Louisiana to France. Jefferson was disturbed at this evidence that European nations still coveted North American territory. His fears were well grounded, for in October 1802 the Spanish commander at New Orleans, which Spain had retained, again closed the Mississippi to American commerce. Spain's action raised consternation both in Washington and the West.

In response, Jefferson instructed Robert Livingston, the American minister to France, to purchase a tract of land on the lower Mississippi that might serve as an American port, thus guaranteeing free transit for American shipping. By the time James Monroe arrived in April 1803 to assist in the negotiations, the French ruler, Napoleon Bonaparte, had decided to sell all of Louisiana. Faced with the threat of renewed war with England, as well as the successful black rebellion against French rule in Haiti, Napoleon feared American designs on Louisiana and knew he could not long keep American settlers out. Soon the deal was struck. For $15 million, the United States obtained nearly 830,000 square miles of new territory.

Federalists reacted with alarm, fearing correctly that the states to be carved from Louisiana would be staunchly Jeffersonian. They worried as well that a rapidly expanding frontier would "decivilize" the nation.

Territorial expansion did not stop with Louisiana. In 1810, American adventurers fomented a revolt in Spanish West Florida and proclaimed an independent republic. Two years later, over vigorous Spanish objections, Congress annexed the region. In the Adams-Onís (or Transcontinental) Treaty of 1819, Spain ceded East Florida. As part of that agreement, the United States also extended its territorial claims to include the Pacific Northwest.

Opening the Trans-Mississippi West

If America's expanding domain was to serve the needs of the agrarian nation, it would have to be explored and prepared for white settlement. In the summer of 1803, Jefferson dispatched an expedition led by Meriwether Lewis and William Clark to explore the far Northwest, make contact with the Native Americans there, open the fur trade, and bring back scientific information from the area. For nearly two and a half years, the intrepid explorers, assisted by the Shoshone woman Sacajawea, made their way across thousands of miles of hostile and unmapped terrain. Lewis and Clark's journey fanned American interest in the trans-Mississippi West, and demonstrated the feasibility of an overland route to the Pacific.

Meriwether Lewis—Portrait

In 1805 and 1806, Lieutenant Zebulon Pike explored the sources of the Mississippi River in northern Minnesota, then undertook an equally bold venture into the Rockies, where he traversed the peak that still bears his name. In the following decade, the government established a string of

William Clark—Portrait

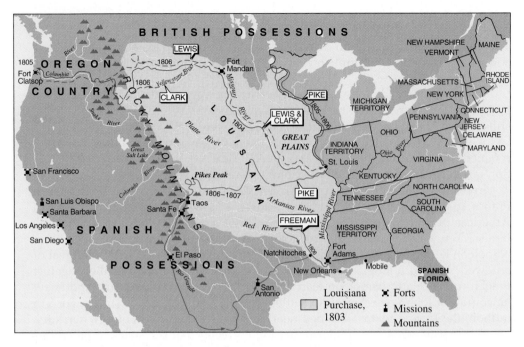

EXPLORING THE TRANS-MISSISSIPPI WEST, 1804–1807 During his two administrations, Jefferson sent several exploring expeditions into the vast Louisiana Territory and beyond. Why did he send them, and what did they accomplish?

military posts from Minnesota to Arkansas, all intended to secure the frontier, promote the fur trade, and support white settlement.

A FOREIGN POLICY FOR THE NEW NATION

While Jefferson was preoccupied with refashioning the government and extending American territory during his first term of office, his second term was dominated by foreign affairs. As Washington and John Adams had discovered, and as Jefferson soon learned, the Atlantic world was a dangerous place.

Jeffersonian Principles

During the early years of the nineteenth century, several goals guided the Jeffersonians' efforts to fashion a foreign policy appropriate for the expanding agrarian nation. Chief among them were protecting American interests on the high seas, clearing the Great Lakes region of British troops, and breaking free of the country's historic dependence on Europe.

Jeffersonian foreign policy was based on the principle of "no entangling alliances" with Europe that Washington had articulated in his Farewell Address of

TIMELINE

1789	George Washington inaugurated as first president	1798	Alien and Sedition Acts
			Virginia and Kentucky Resolutions
1790	Hamilton's "Reports on the Public Credit"	1801	Jefferson elected president
1794	Whiskey Rebellion in Pennsylvania	1803	Louisiana Purchase
1795	Controversy over Jay's Treaty with England	1803–1806	Lewis and Clark expedition
1796	John Adams elected president	1804	Jefferson reelected
1797	XYZ Affair	1807	Embargo Act

1796. England remained the principal enemy, but France, now that the revolution had ended in Bonaparte's dictatorial rule, was suspect as well.

Second, Jeffersonians emphasized the importance of overseas commerce for the nation's well-being. Foreign trade would provide markets for America's agricultural produce and bring manufactured goods in return. Unlike the Federalists, Jeffersonians hoped to keep large-scale manufacturing in Europe. They feared the concentrations of wealth and dependent working classes that domestic manufacturing would bring.

Peace was the Jeffersonians' third goal. War was objectionable not only because people were killed and property destroyed, but also because it endangered liberty by inflaming politics, stifling free speech, swelling public debt, and expanding government power. Jeffersonians understood the dangers lurking in the Atlantic world and knew that protecting the nation's interests might require force. Between 1801 and 1805, Jefferson dispatched naval vessels to defend American commerce against the Barbary States (Algiers, Morocco, Tripoli, and Tunis) in the Mediterranean Sea. War, however, was to be a policy of last resort.

Struggling for Neutral Rights

After a brief interlude of peace, European war resumed in 1803. Once again Britain and France seized American shipping. Britain's naval superiority made its attacks especially serious. Its continuing refusal to stop impressment, vacate its military posts south of the Great Lakes, and allow trade with its West Indian islands heightened the tension.

In response to British seizures of American shipping, Congress passed the Non-Importation Act in April 1806, banning British imports that could be produced domestically or acquired elsewhere. A month later, Britain blockaded the

European coast, thus shutting off American trade there. In retaliation, Napoleon forbade all commerce with the British Isles.

Tension between Britain and the United States reached the breaking point in June 1807, when the British warship *Leopard* stopped the American frigate *Chesapeake* off the Virginia coast and demanded that four crew members be handed over as British deserters. When the American commander refused, protesting that the sailors were U.S. citizens, the *Leopard* opened fire, killing 3 men and wounding 18. After the *Chesapeake* limped back into port with the story, cries of outrage rang across the land.

Knowing that the United States was not prepared to confront Britain, Jefferson proposed withdrawing American ships from the Atlantic. In December 1807, Congress passed the Embargo Act, forbidding American vessels from sailing for foreign ports. The embargo was one of Jefferson's most ill-fated decisions.

The embargo had relatively little effect on Britain, since British shipping profited from the withdrawal of American competition, and British merchants found new sources of agricultural produce in Latin America. The embargo's impact at home, however, was far-reaching. U.S. exports plummeted 80 percent in a year, while imports dropped by more than half. New England was hardest hit. In ports such as Boston and Providence, ships lay idle and thousands of jobs were lost as depression settled in.

Up and down the coast, communities openly violated the embargo. As attempts to police it failed, English goods were smuggled in across the Canadian border. Throughout the Federalist Northeast, bitterness threatened to escalate into rebellion. When federal officials declared martial law and sent in troops in an effort to control the situation near Lake Champlain in upstate New York, local citizens fired on U.S. revenue boats and recaptured confiscated goods. In language reminiscent of the Virginia and Kentucky Resolutions, Connecticut's Federalist governor declared that states were duty-bound "to interpose their protecting shield" between the liberties of the people and oppressive acts of the central government. Faced with the embargo's ineffectiveness abroad and disastrous political consequences at home, Congress repealed the measure in 1809.

As Jefferson's presidency ended, officials found themselves in a quandary. How could American rights on the high seas be protected and the country's honor upheld without being drawn into a European war and without further inflaming American politics? The nation would continue to struggle with that dilemma in the years immediately ahead.

Conclusion

A Period of Trial and Transition

The decade of the 1790s was a time of continuing political crisis. Scarcely had the new government been formed than divisions appeared, initially among political leaders at the capital, but increasingly among the people at large. Hamilton's domestic policies generated conflict first. It was the French Revolution, European war, Jay's Treaty, and Federalist war program, however, that galvanized political energies and set Federalists and Jeffersonian Republicans against each other, catching up countless citizens like David Brown in the confusion. The Haitian rebellion, together with other democratic insurgencies in Ireland, Europe, and the Americas, further inflamed the country's politics.

In control of the federal government following the election of 1800, the Jeffersonians labored to set it on a more democratic course. At home, they fashioned domestic policies designed to redirect authority to the states and promote the country's agrarian expansion. Abroad they attempted, with more ambiguous results and at considerable political cost, to protect American rights in a hostile Atlantic world, all the while avoiding European entanglements.

By the time Jefferson left the presidency and James Madison took office in 1809, politics at the seat of national government and in the states had drawn more closely together as leaders perfected such tools of democratic politics as a partisan press and political parties skilled in managing the expanding (white, male) electorate. These transitions, emerging in the midst of deep-seated controversy, would soon alter the very character of American political life.

Questions for Review and Reflection

1. Identify three foreign policy crises of the years 1790–1809, and explain why each was so controversial.

2. How did Federalists and Jeffersonians differ in political principles? In the kind of economy they envisioned for the nation?

3. Disputes over the proper balance between the national government and the states have been a recurring theme of American history from 1789 to the present. Why did the issue generate such controversy during the period covered in this chapter?

4. Tension between the demands of national security and the protection of citizens' rights has also been a recurrent theme of our history. Why did that tension become so severe during the 1790s?

Discovering U.S. History Online

The Bradford House—Whiskey Rebellion—Whiskey Insurrection www.bradfordhouse.org
David Bradford was a prominent figure in the "Whiskey Insurrection." His home has been restored as a museum; the online site includes a description of the rebellion, its causes, Bradford's role, and the end results.

The Haitian Revolution of 1791–1803 www.webster.edu/~corbetre/haiti/history/revolution/revolution1.htm
This site presents a four-part historical essay on the Haitian Revolution and its significance.

The Alien and Sedition Acts www.yale.edu/lawweb/avalon/alsedact.htm
The full text of these acts is available on this site.

Building the Capitol for a New Nation www.loc.gov/exhibits/us.capitol/s0.html
Compiled from holdings in the Library of Congress, this site contains detailed information on the design and early construction of the Capitol building in Washington, D.C.

Thomas Jefferson www.ipl.org/div/potus/tjefferson.html
This site contains basic factual data about Jefferson's election and presidency, speeches, and online biographies.

The Louisiana Purchase Exhibit www.sec.state.la.us/purchase/purchase-index.htm
A colorful, illustrated presentation of the details of the Louisiana Purchase, the negotiations, documents, and a series of historical maps.

Lewis and Clark: The Journey of the Corps of Discovery www.pbs.org/lewisandclark
This is a companion site to Ken Burns's film, containing a timeline of the expedition, a collection of related links, a bibliography, and 800 minutes of unedited, full-length Real Player interviews with seven experts featured in the film.

Fiction and Film

Adapted from Laurel Thatcher Ulrich's prize-winning book, the docudrama *A Midwife's Tale* (1997) depicts the daily life of nurse-midwife Martha Ballard, who delivered a thousand babies and served her New England community during the closing years of the eighteenth century. The initial installment of C-SPAN's *American Presidents: Life Portraits* series (1999) effectively portrays the challenges and accomplishments of the nation's first president, George Washington. In the novel *Fever* (1996), John Weidman offers a vivid account of the yellow fever plague that killed thousands of people and threatened social chaos in Philadelphia in 1793. Essayist and novelist Gore Vidal explores the tangled politics and personalities of the early republic via a largely sympathetic portrayal of Aaron Burr (who killed Alexander Hamilton in a duel in 1804) in *Burr: A Novel* (1973).

Recommended Reading

www.ablongman.com/nash
The Companion Website has a list of recommended readings about launching the national republic, global threats to the nation, and the political crisis of the new nation.

C H A P T E R   9

Society and Politics in the Early Republic

American Stories

Creating New Lives

In May 1809, Mary and James Harrod gathered their five children, loaded a few belongings onto a wagon, and headed west from Virginia toward a new life in Kentucky. They left behind 10 acres of marginal upland, 15 years of wearying effort at trying to wring a modest living from it, and a family cemetery holding two of their children and Mary's parents.

Beyond the Appalachian Mountains, 450 difficult miles ahead, lay more hard work and uncertainty. Though central Kentucky, where the Harrods would settle, contained few Native Americans, powerful tribes from north and south of the Ohio River hunted there and fought over its control. They also opposed the growing tide of white settlers. The first years would be especially hard for James and Mary as they "opened up" the land, planted crops, and built a cabin. They would be lonesome years as well, for Mary and James would be unlikely to see even the chimney smoke of their nearest neighbors.

They were hopeful, though, as they trudged west. The land agent who sold them their claim had promised rich, fertile soil that in time would support a good life. They were excited at the prospect of joining the swelling stream of migrants seeking new lives in the West, and were glad to leave behind Virginia's slave society with its arrogant planters and oppressed slaves. That was no place for poor whites to live. Once in Kentucky, Mary and James settled on their own plot of land and took responsibility for their lives.

In April 1795, Ben Thompson started north from Queen Anne's County, Maryland, for New York City. Ben knew little beyond farming, but he was ambitious, and when he arrived in New York he listened intently to the ships' captains as they talked about life at sea and recruited men for their crews. Ben was lucky, for he arrived just as American overseas commerce was entering a decade of unprecedented prosperity. Sailors were in demand, pay was good, and few questions were asked. For five years Ben sailed the seas. Having enough of travel, he returned to New York and hired out as an apprentice to a ship's carpenter.

About the same time, Phyllis Sherman left Norwalk, Connecticut. She also headed for New York, where she took a job as a maid in the household of one of the city's wealthy merchants. As fate would have it, Phyllis and Ben met, fell in love, and in the spring of 1802 were married.

There is little remarkable in their stories, except that Ben and Phyllis were former slaves and were married in the African Methodist Episcopal Zion Church. Ben had cast off his slave name, Cato, as a sign of liberation, while Phyllis kept the name her master had given her. Ben was doubly fortunate, for he had purchased his freedom just as cotton production began to expand through the southern interior, creating an accelerating demand for field hands shipped in from the Chesapeake region. In another decade, he would have faced greater difficulty securing his independence. Phyllis had been freed as a child when slavery ended in Connecticut. As she grew up, she tired of living as a servant with her former owner's family and longed for the companionship of other blacks. She had heard that there were people of color in New York, and she was correct. In 1800, it was home to 6,300 African Americans, more than half of them free.

Though life in New York was better than either Ben or Phyllis had known before, it was hardly easy. They shared marginally in the city's commercial prosperity. In 1804, they watched helplessly as yellow fever carried off their daughter and many of their friends. And while they found support in newly established African American churches and the expanding black community, they had to be constantly on guard because slave ships still moved in and out of the port and slave catchers pursued southern runaways in the city's streets.

In the early republic, thousands of Americans seized opportunities to improve their lives. Some, like Ben Thompson and Phyllis Sherman, moved from the countryside to the nation's burgeoning cities, while others, such as Mary and James Harrod, joined the swelling tide of westward expansion. By their actions, they strengthened American values of individual initiative, social equality, and personal autonomy.

They contributed as well to a process of social transformation that historians have called the "opening" of American society. That process was powered by an accelerating movement of people across the land that disrupted families, weakened long-established communities, and created countless new settlements. The transformation was fueled as well by an expanding market economy with its relentless discipline of supply and demand, pursuit of individual profit, and contract-based relationships. In addition, a wave of religious revivalism known as the Second Great Awakening swept through American society, strengthening belief in the equality of all believers before God and the individual's responsibility for his or her own soul. This chapter examines these processes of social, economic, and religious change that would continue to transform people's lives throughout the nineteenth century.

Chapter 9 deals as well with a variety of reform movements that sought to achieve social justice and bring the conditions of daily life into conformity with the nation's democratic ideals. Even so, not all Americans benefited equally during these early nineteenth-century years. Doctrines of equality and individual autonomy resonated more powerfully in the lives of men than of women. In the South, African Americans found their lives constrained by a revitalized system of slavery, while in the North free blacks faced an increasingly racist society. West of the Appalachians, Native Americans confronted a swelling tide of white settlement.

The chapter also explores the multiple ways in which America's diverse regions became more closely knit together, as well as the political tensions that resulted. The years of the early nineteenth century witnessed a diplomatic revolution of major importance. With the War of 1812, the American people broke free of their centuries-old dependence on Europe and turned their energies toward the settlement of the continental interior. Just as important, with the Monroe Doctrine of 1823 the United States asserted a bold, new framework for relations with other nations in the Americas as they also threw off the yoke of European colonialism.

Finally, Chapter 9 examines the collapse of the Federalist–Jeffersonian political system and the emergence of a new kind of American politics increasingly democratic in temper, organized by sophisticated political parties, and led by a new generation of political leaders eager to claim their place in shaping the nation's future.

A NATION OF REGIONS

In the early republic, the vast majority of Americans drew their living from the land. As the nineteenth century began, fully 83 percent of the labor force was engaged in agriculture, a figure that had hardly changed 25 years later. Yet across the nation, people occupied the land in very different ways.

The Northeast

In the Northeast, stretching from New Jersey and eastern Pennsylvania to New England, family farms dominated the landscape. On New England's rock-strewn land, farmers often abandoned field crops for the greater profits to be made from livestock. On the richer agricultural lands of New York and Pennsylvania, farmers cultivated the land intensively, planting crops year after year rather than following the time-honored practice of allowing worn-out fields to lie fallow and recover their productivity. In 1750, the mid-Atlantic landscape had looked unkempt, with wide areas still covered by timber and fallow lands lapsing into brush. Fifty years later, the countryside looked increasingly orderly, its carefully cultivated fields marked by hedges or stone walls.

	Wheat		Cotton	
	Worker-Hours per Acre	**Yield per Acre**	**Worker-Hours per Acre**	**Yield per Acre**
1800	56.0	15 bushels	185.0	147 pounds
2001	2.4	40 bushels	4.6	698 pounds

Agricultural Productivity in 1800 and 2001

Source: U.S. Bureau of the Census.

Farmers in southeastern Pennsylvania and New York's Hudson River valley produced an agricultural surplus, the produce left over after meeting their family's needs, and exchanged it in nearby towns for commodities such as tea, window glass, and tools. Across much of the rural Northeast, however, cash played only a small part in economic exchange. Noted an observant Frenchman, people "supply their needs in the countryside by direct reciprocal exchanges. The tailor and the bootmaker ... do the work of their calling at the home of the farmer ... who ... provides the raw material for it and pays for the work in goods. ... They write down what they give and receive on both sides, and at the end of the year they settle a large variety of exchanges with a very small quantity of coin."

Most farms were not large. By 1800, the average farm in longer-settled areas was no more than 100 to 150 acres, down substantially from half a century before. That was primarily a result of the continuing division of farm property from fathers to sons. Even in southeastern Pennsylvania, the most productive agricultural region in the Northeast, opportunity was declining. Continuous cropping had robbed the soil of fertility, forcing farmers to bring more marginal land under cultivation, thus bringing a steady decline in productivity. Nearly 20 percent of male taxpayers in southeastern Pennsylvania were single, clear evidence that young men were delaying marriage until they could establish themselves financially.

Whereas the majority of northeasterners made their living from the land, growing numbers of rural folk also worked for wages as artisans or day laborers in nearby towns, or toiled in the small-scale manufactories—grain and saw mills, potash works, and iron forges—that dotted the rural landscape. Farm women contributed to the family economy by helping with the livestock, preserving food, and making clothes for sale or exchange with neighbors. As the practice of men working for wages outside the family setting grew, women's unwaged domestic labor began to be regarded as less valuable.

By 1830, the demands of the Northeast's expanding population for new farmland and a wide variety of wood products had transformed much of the region's once heavily forested landscape. The numerous iron furnaces consumed firewood voraciously, while the production of potash, turpentine, planking for wooden houses, and fencing further depleted forest ranges. More than anything, though, it was the demand for heating fuel during the long winter months that made the woodcutter's axe ring. Rural households burned from 20 to 30 cords of firewood annually in highly inefficient open fireplaces. As the region's coastal cities grew and nearby woodlots were exhausted, fuel had to be fetched from as far away as 100 miles inland.

The South

Life was different in the South, a region stretching from Maryland to Georgia along the coast and west to the newly forming states of Alabama and Mississippi. In 1800, much of southern agriculture was in disarray. Low prices, worn-out land, war, and the loss of slaves had left the Chesapeake tobacco economy in shambles. In response, southern planters experimented with wheat and other grains in hopes of boosting their sagging fortunes. Regional recovery began in earnest, however, when they turned to a new staple crop—cotton.

In 1790, the South had produced 3,135 bales of cotton; by 1820, output had mushroomed to 334,378 bales. In 1805, cotton accounted for 30 percent of the nation's agricultural exports; by 1820, it exceeded half. Across the coastal South and the newly developing states of Alabama, Mississippi, and Tennessee, cotton was becoming king. A fortuitous combination of circumstances fueled the transformation: the growing demand of textile mills in England and the American Northeast; wonderfully productive virgin soil; a long, steamy growing season; ample slave labor; and southern planters' long experience in producing and marketing staple crops.

Eli Whitney's cotton gin speeded the process as well. The silky fibers of long-staple cotton could be easily separated from the cotton's seeds. The delicate, long-staple plant, however, grew only in the hot, humid climate along the southern coast. The hardier short-staple variety could be successfully cultivated in the southern interior, but its fibers clung tenaciously to the plant's sticky, green seeds. A slave could clean no more than a pound of short-staple cotton a day. Whitney's cotton gin was little more than a box containing a roller equipped with wire teeth designed to pull the fibers through a comblike barrier, thus stripping them from the seeds. A hand crank activated the mechanism. With this crude device, a laborer could clean as many as 50 pounds of short-staple cotton a day.

The swing to cotton marked a momentous turning point in the South's, and the nation's, history. It raised the value of southern land and opened economic opportunity for southern whites. It also increased the demand for black field hands and breathed new life into slavery. Some of the escalating demand for slave labor was met from overseas. In 1803, Georgia and South Carolina together imported 20,000 new slaves, as southern planters and northern suppliers rushed to fill the demand before the slave trade ended in 1808. Much of the demand for agricultural labor, however, was met by the internal slave trade that moved black labor from the worn-out lands of the Chesapeake to the lush cotton fields of the southern interior.

Trans-Appalachia

West of the Appalachian Mountains, a third region of white settlement was forming as the nineteenth century began. Trans-Appalachia, extending from the mountains to the Mississippi River and from the Great Lakes to the Gulf of Mexico, constituted a broad and shifting "middle ground," a zone of cultural, economic, and military interaction between Native and European Americans. In 1790, scarcely 100,000 white settlers had lived there. By 1810, their number, including Mary and James Harrod, had swollen to nearly a million. By 1820, over a million more had arrived. They came by wagon through mountain passes such as the Cumberland Gap and by flatboat down the Ohio River.

The human tide seemed to grow with each year. The woods were full of new settlers, wrote an amazed observer near Batavia in western New York in 1805. "Axes are resounding, and the trees literally falling around us as we passed." America, he exclaimed, is "breaking up and going west!"

Settlers were drawn by the promotions of speculators seeking their fortunes in the sale of western land. Between 1790 and 1820, land companies hawked vast

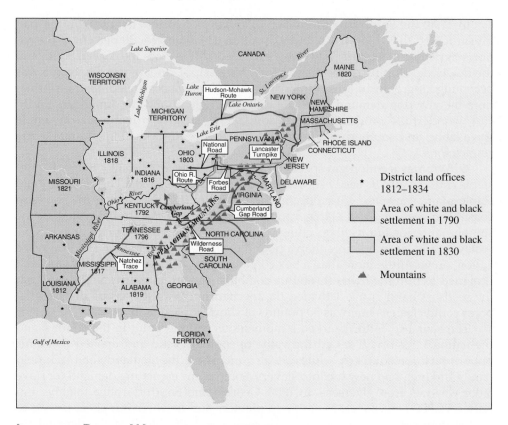

IMPORTANT ROUTES WESTWARD Through mountain passes and down the Ohio River, white settlers streamed into Trans-Appalachia in the early republic.

areas of New York, Ohio, and Kentucky to prospective settlers like the Harrods. Many ventures failed, but countless others proved profitable. Settlers joined in the speculative fever, often going deeply into debt to buy extra land for resale when population increased and land values rose.

North of the Ohio River, settlement followed the grid pattern prescribed in the Land Ordinance of 1785. There, free-labor agriculture took hold and towns such as Columbus and Cincinnati emerged as service and cultural centers for the surrounding population. South of the Ohio, white settlers and their black slaves distributed themselves more randomly across the land. In Kentucky and Tennessee, free-labor agriculture was soon challenged by the spread of slavery-based cotton.

In this constantly shifting borderland, people of different ethnicity, race, class, and regional origin mingled together. Their conflicting social and cultural values often generated tension. But as they built new communities, they fashioned new ways of life, in the process strengthening belief in America as a land of opportunity.

How Others See Us

Frances Trollope, born in England and wife of an English barrister, came to the United States in 1827. She settled for a few years in Cincinnati where she opened a lecture hall, had a shop for the sale of fancy goods, and made something of a name for herself. When her business venture failed, she returned to England where in 1832 she published Domestic Manners of Americans, *one of the most acerbic and yet insightful of the many travel accounts penned by foreign visitors to the early republic.*

The "simple" manner of living in Western America was more distasteful to me from its leveling effects on the manners of the people than necessary. ... The total and universal want of manners, both in males and females, is so remarkable that I was constantly endeavoring to account for it. It certainly does not proceed from want of intellect ... but there is no charm, no grace in their conversation. ... There is always something either in the expression or the accent that jars the feelings and shocks the taste. ... In America, that polish which removes the coarser and rougher parts of our nature is unknown and undreamed of. ... Nothing can exceed their activity and perseverance in all kinds of speculation, handicraft, and enterprise which promises a profitable pecuniary result. I heard an Englishman ... declare that he had never overheard Americans conversing without the word DOLLAR being pronounced between them. ... Yet the Americans declare that "they are the most moral people upon earth" ... My honest conviction is that the standard of moral character in the United States is greatly lower than Europe. ... It is amusing to observe how soothing the idea seems [to Americans] that they are more modern, more advanced than England. Our classic literature, our princely dignities, our noble institutions, are all [regarded as] bygone relics of the dark ages. ...

■ *What was it about the American people that sent Trollope's teeth on edge?*

Given its newness and diversity, Trans-Appalachia gained a reputation for rough and colorful ways. In towns such as Louisville along the Ohio River, boatmen, gamblers, con men, and speculators gave civic life a raucous quality. No characters were more famous in popular folklore than western adventurers such as Daniel Boone, and nothing revealed more graphically the West's rawness than the no-holds-barred, "rough and tumble" brawls that regularly erupted. Everywhere, the youthfulness and transience of the predominantly male population kept society unsettled.

As settlers arrived, they began the long process of transforming the region's heavily forested land. In mountainous areas, hillsides were denuded of trees to be dragged behind wagons, slowing their jolting rides downhill. Believing, erroneously, that open land was infertile, farmers cut girdles of bark off groves of trees, then set them on fire or left them to die while planting crops around the decaying hulks. By this method, a family could clear from three to five acres a year for cultivation. As expanding areas of Trans-Appalachia came under the farmer's plow, forests and wildlife gave way. The relentless demand for wood generated by the growing white population added to the assault on the region's forests.

The Nation's Cities

Though most Americans lived on the land or in small towns, increasing numbers dwelt in the nation's expanding cities. From 1790 to 1830, the nation's population increased by nearly 230 percent, but urban places of more than 2,500 residents grew almost twice as fast.

Patterns of urban development differed from region to region. The most dramatic growth occurred in the port cities of the Northeast. By 1830, the region contained four cities of more than 50,000. New York alone held over 100,000 people, while inland towns such as Springfield, Massachusetts, and Albany, New York, proliferated as service centers for their surrounding areas.

The cities of the Atlantic seaboard were socially diverse. In New York and Philadelphia, Irish, German, British, and African Americans, together with travelers from around the world, jostled for space on the cities' sidewalks. Sailors, often speaking strange tongues, added raucous behavior and at times an edge of danger to urban life.

Economic life still centered on the wharves, where sailing ships from around the world docked, and on the warehouses, where their cargoes were unloaded. At the same time, by the 1820s manufacturing was beginning to transform urban life. Philadelphia was becoming a textile manufacturing center, while New York produced shoes and iron goods. As these enterprises expanded, artisan production slowly gave way to factory-based wage labor.

Five Points, New York This rather humorous depiction of a bustling intersection in New York City in 1827 suggests the increasing crowdedness of the country's largest cities. How many different kinds of people and activities can you identify? *(Museum of the City of New York Gift of Lou Sepersky and Leida Snow, [97.227.3])*

Such changes widened the gap between richer and poorer inhabitants. Prosperous merchants rested securely at the top of the social pyramid, their households graced by fine table linens and store-bought furniture, the artifacts of an expanding consumer economy. Below them came an aspiring middle class of artisans, shopkeepers, and professional men whose families shared modestly in the general prosperity. At the bottom spread a growing underclass of common laborers, dockworkers, and the unemployed, their lives a continuous struggle for survival. Whereas rich and poor had often lived close together in colonial cities, rising land values now forced the lower classes into crowded alleys and tenements, while more prosperous urban dwellers began clustering in fashionable neighborhoods.

In the Southeast, urban development centered in long-established ports such as Charleston and Savannah. As during the colonial period, they continued to serve as commercial entrepots, exporting agricultural products and importing manufactured goods. Half their population was black, the majority of them slaves.

In Trans-Appalachia, fledgling cities such as Pittsburgh and Chicago dotted the region's rivers and lakes. Only small villages in 1790, these interior cities held 30 percent of the nation's urban population by 1830. Places such as New Orleans and St. Louis reflected their multinational origins.

Established as a French colony in 1718, New Orleans came under Spanish rule in 1763. When it became part of the United States in 1803, urban life was dominated by French and Spanish Creole families. For several decades, U.S. citizens remained a minority among the white population. Of the city's 27,000 people, nearly 13,000 were black. Upriver from New Orleans, the smaller town of St. Louis, at different times part of French and Spanish North America, had a similarly diverse population. Enslaved blacks constituted nearly one-third of the town's 1,000 souls, while people of French, Spanish, and U.S. origin made up the rest.

Though increasing rapidly in population, America's urban places remained small in area. In these "walking cities," residents could easily stroll from one side of town to the other. Rapid growth, however, brought increasing congestion, together with serious problems of public health and safety. Philadelphia led the way in street paving, but dust and mud constantly plagued urban life. More than mud clogged urban streets in the early nineteenth century, for residents dumped their garbage there, privies leached into open drains, and livestock roamed the streets, leaving their droppings behind. Though one urban dweller thought the scavenging hogs she encountered "disgusting," she acknowledged that without them the streets would soon be choked with filth. Under such conditions, typhoid and dysentery, spread by contaminated water, took a continuous toll.

INDIAN–WHITE RELATIONS IN THE EARLY REPUBLIC

Indian–white relations took a dramatic turn in the early years of the nineteenth century. In 1790, vast areas of Trans-Appalachia were still controlled by Native American tribes. North of the Ohio River, the Shawnee, Delaware, and Miami formed a western confederacy capable of mustering several thousand warriors.

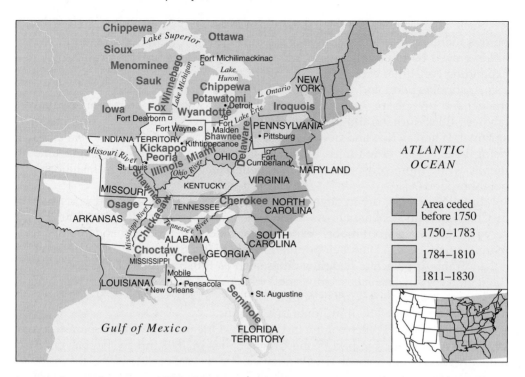

INDIAN LAND CESSIONS, 1750–1830 As white settlers streamed across the nation's interior, state and federal governments wrung land cessions from the Indians. By 1830, only the southeastern tribes still controlled significant areas of their ancestral land east of the Mississippi River. Labels in blue indicate the major Native American tribes.

MAP

Native American
Land Cessions to
1829

South of the river lived five major tribal groups: the Cherokee, Creek, Choctaw, Chickasaw, and Seminole. Together they totaled nearly 60,000 people. By 1830, however, the balance of power had shifted as white settlers, many of them bringing black slaves with them south of the Ohio, streamed into the region.

In response, tribal groups devised various strategies of resistance and survival. Among the Cherokee, many sought peaceful accommodation. Others, like the Shawnee and Creek, rose in armed resistance. Neither strategy was altogether successful, for by 1830 the Indians faced a future of continued acculturation, military defeat, or forced migration west of the Mississippi River.

Less dramatic but no less important, the social and cultural separation of Indians and white Americans sharpened during these years. As late as the 1780s, Indians still walked the streets of New York and Philadelphia, while countless Indians and white Americans interacted as friends or enemies, traders or marriage partners. By 1830, such contacts were much less common and racial separation had increased as Indians were confined on reservations or forced to move farther west.

The Goals of Indian Policy

During the years from 1790 to 1830, the federal government established policies that would govern Indian–white relations through much of the nineteenth century. Intended in part to promote the assimilation of Native Americans into white society, the policies speeded the transfer of Indian land to white settlers and set the stage for later, large-scale Indian removal.

With the government's initial "conquest" theory rendered obsolete by the Indians' refusal to regard themselves as a conquered people (see Chapter 7), U.S. officials shifted course by recognizing Indian rights to the land they inhabited and declaring that all future land transfers would come through treaty agreements.

Henry Knox, Washington's first secretary of war, laid out the government's new position in 1789. The Indians, he explained, "being the prior occupants of the soil, possess the right of the soil." It should not be taken from them "unless by their free consent, or by the right of conquest in case of just war." The Indian Intercourse Act of 1790 declared that public treaties, ratified by Congress, would henceforth be the only legal means of obtaining Indian land. Though it promised a more humane Indian policy, the acquisition of Indian land for white settlement remained the overarching goal.

The new, treaty-based strategy proved effective. Native American leaders frequently ceded land in return for trade goods, yearly annuity payments, and assurances that there would be no further demands. Reluctant tribal leaders could often be persuaded to cooperate by warnings about the inevitable spread of white settlement, or more tractable chieftains could be found. In these ways, vast areas of tribal land passed to white settlers.

Federal policy also attempted to regulate the fur trade, in which both Native Americans and white traders eagerly participated. The Indians, in return for their abundant furs, secured the blankets, guns, and rum that they valued highly, while white traders acquired valuable furs in exchange for inexpensive trade items.

The fur trade brought handsome profits to private trading companies such as John Jacob Astor's American Fur Company, but often worked to the Indians' disadvantage. Rum devastated Indian communities, while other trade goods frequently transmitted diseases such as measles and smallpox. Indians often became dependent on the trade because it provided the only reliable supplies of coveted goods. As demand for furs and pelts increased, Native Americans frequently overtrapped their hunting grounds, forcing them to compete with other tribes for new sources of furs farther west.

In an effort to reduce fraud and the resulting conflict, Congress created government trading posts, or "factories," where Indians could come for fair treatment. Native Americans, however, frequently found themselves deeply in debt to government traders. In 1822, the factory system was abolished.

A third objective of federal Indian policy was to "civilize" and Christianize the Native Americans, then assimilate them into white society. With the government's blessing, Moravians, Baptists, and other religious groups sent scores of missionaries to live among the Indians, preach the Gospel, and teach white ways. Among the most selfless were Quakers who labored with the Iroquois in New York. In

RECOVERING THE PAST

Throughout the nation's history, the American population has changed dramatically, not only in size and geographic distribution but also in birth and death rates, marriage age, and family size. In the early nineteenth century, for example, the average life expectancy of white Americans was about 45 years, and men tended to outlive women. In our own time, the average life expectancy has reached 74, and women on average live longer than men. Populations have differed as well across regions, in urban and rural settings, and among racial, ethnic, and class groups.

Changes in the demographic profile of the American population have powerful effects on the nation's economic, social, and political development. The changing size and makeup of the labor force shape economic activity, while changing proportions of older and younger Americans affect consumer habits and put different demands on health care and educational systems—as the aging of baby boomers in our own time is again making clear. When mortality rates were high, as was often the case in early American history, parents had more children in an effort to stabilize their families. As mortality declined during the nineteenth century, so too did birthrates and family size.

Demographic information can tell us a great deal about the life experiences of ordinary Americans. Indeed, demographic data is often the major source of information about otherwise anonymous individuals. For all these reasons, historians spend considerable time analyzing populations and the ways they change.

Two kinds of demographic data have proved most important. One consists of birth, death, and marriage records, often found in church or town registers. These records chronicle the basic demographic events in people's lives. If they are complete and continuous enough, they allow historians to trace the life course of individuals and to reconstruct patterns of family and community life.

Here we offer an example of the second kind of demographic data, a census. The material is from the federal census of 1820. Article 1, Section 2 of the Constitution called for an enumeration (or counting) of the nation's population every 10 years, "in such manner" as Congress required. The information was to be used in determining the periodic reapportionment of the House of Representatives and allocation of direct taxes to the states. The first decennial census was taken in 1790.

Compared with modern census inquiries, the first federal censuses collected limited information. The 1790s census, for example, gathered data under six headings: "Name of head of family," "Free white males, 16 years and upwards," "Free white males, under 16," "Free white females," "All other free persons," and "Slaves." As the nation grew, the demand for additional information increased. In 1820, Congress for the first time called for the collection of economic data. In the decades following, categories of social and economic data were gradually expanded.

The table provided here contains data from three cities—New York City; Charleston, South Carolina; and Cincinnati, Ohio—located in different sections of the country. What do the data tell you about the racial, gender, and age profiles of these cities? How do they differ? Do you find significant age and gender differences between white and black populations? Between free blacks and slaves? Can you explain the differences that you find? In making your calculations, be sure to take into account both absolute numbers and proportions of the total populations.

Why were there no slaves in Cincinnati, while there were still slaves in New York? What kinds of people might have been included under the heading. "Foreigners not naturalized?" The economic data included in the 1820 census was very general. What conclusions are you able to draw concerning economic activities in the three cities? Can you explain the differences?

Data from the Federal Census of 1820

	New York City	Charleston	Cincinnati
Free white males, 25 and under	36,122	3,780	3,419
Free white males, 26 and over	21,331	2,119	1,672
Free white males, total	57,453 (44)	5,899 (23)	5,091 (51)
Free white females, 25 and under	37,438	3,297	3,137
Free white females, 26 and over	20,070	2,033	1,152
Free white females, total	57,508 (44)	5,330 (21)	4,289 (43)
Total white population	114,961 (88)	11,229 (44)	9,380 (93)
Free colored males, 25 and under	2,201	394	120
Free colored males, 26 and over	1,993	229	99
Free colored males, total	4,191 (3)	623 (2)	219 (2)
Free colored females, 25 and under	3,342	467	132
Free colored females, 26 and over	2,832	385	82
Free colored females, total	6,174 (5)	852 (3)	214 (2)
Male slaves, 25 and under	144	3,656	0
Male slaves, 26 and over	33	2,039	0
Male slaves, total	177 (1)	5,695 (22)	0 (0)
Female slaves, 25 and under	233	4,347	0
Female slaves, 26 and over	108	2,610	0
Female slaves, total	341 (1)	6,957 (27)	0 (0)
Total black population	10,886 (8)	14,127 (55)	433 (0)
Foreigners not naturalized	5,390 (4)	425 (2)	241 (2)
Total city population	131,237	25,781	10,054
Persons engaged in agriculture	386	164	29
Persons engaged in commerce	3,142	1,138	63
Person engaged in manufacturing	9,523	887	211

Notes: New York City did not then include Kings, Queens, or Suffolk countries. Figures in parentheses represent percentages of each city's total population.

REFLECTING ON THE PAST   How would the federal census of 2000 differ from the census displayed here? Why do disputes often arise over the kinds of information that should be gathered?

spite of the missionaries' best efforts, however, most Native Americans remained aloof. The chasm between Christianity and their own religions was too wide.

Education was the other weapon of assimilation. In 1793, Congress appropriated $20,000 to promote literacy, agriculture, and vocational instruction among Indians. Federal officials encouraged missionaries to establish schools where Indian children could learn the three R's and vocational skills. But the vast majority of Indian children never attended, they and their parents distrusting the schools' alien environment.

Although white assimilationists cared deeply about the physical and spiritual fate of Native American people, they showed little sympathy for Indian culture, for they demanded that Native Americans give up their language, religion, and extended family arrangements and adopt the ways of white society. Assimilation or removal were the stark alternatives posed by even the most benevolent whites.

Strategies of Survival: The Iroquois and Cherokee

Faced with the loss of land and tribal autonomy, Native Americans devised various strategies of resistance and survival. Among the Iroquois, a prophet named Handsome Lake led his people through a religious renewal and cultural revitalization. In 1799, following a series of visions, he preached a combination of Indian and white ways: temperance, peace, land retention, and a new religion combining elements of Christianity and traditional Iroquois belief. His vision offered renewed pride in the midst of the Iroquois' radically changed lives.

Far to the south, the Cherokee followed a different path of accommodation. As the nineteenth century began, the Cherokee still controlled millions of acres in Tennessee, Georgia, and the western Carolinas. Their land base, however, was shrinking. Southern state governments, responding to white demands for Indian land, undercut tribal autonomy. In 1801, Tennessee unilaterally brought Cherokee lands under the authority of state courts. The Cherokee, who had their own system of justice and distrusted the state courts as biased, rejected Tennessee's demands. Soon a group of full-blood leaders called for armed resistance. Others, including mixed-bloods like John Ross, insisted that accommodation offered the best hope for survival.

After a bitter struggle, the accommodationists won out and brought the tribe's scattered villages under a common government, the better to protect their freedom and prevent the further loss of land. In 1808, the Cherokee National Council adopted a written legal code combining elements of U.S. and Indian law, and in 1827 it devised a written constitution patterned after those of nearby states. The Council also issued a bold declaration that the Cherokee were an independent nation with full sovereignty over their lands. In 1829, the Cherokee government made it an offense punishable by death for any member of the tribe to transfer land to white ownership without the consent of tribal authorities.

Meanwhile, the process of social and cultural accommodation, encouraged by Cherokee leaders such as Ross and promoted by white missionaries and government agents, went forward. As the Cherokee turned from their traditional hunting, gathering, and farming economy to settled agriculture, many moved from village settlements onto individual farmsteads. Others established sawmills, country stores, and blacksmith shops. In contrast to traditional practices of communal ownership, the concept of private property took hold. The majority of Cherokee kept their crude log cabins and continued to live a hand-to-mouth existence. But some mixed-bloods who learned English and understood how to deal with white authorities accumulated hundreds of acres of fertile land and scores of black slaves.

Since the mid-eighteenth century, the Cherokee had held a few runaway blacks in slavelike conditions. During the early nineteenth century, Cherokee slavery expanded and became harsher. By 1820, there were nearly 1,300 black slaves in the Cherokee nation. A tribal law of 1824 forbade intermarriage with blacks. The accelerating spread of cotton cultivation increased the demand for slave labor among the Cherokee, as among whites. As accommodation increased, slave ownership became a mark of social standing.

By 1820, the strategy of peaceful accommodation had brought clear rewards. Tribal government was stronger and the sense of Cherokee identity was reasonably secure. But success would prove the Cherokee people's undoing. As their self-confidence grew, so did the hostility of neighboring whites impatient to acquire their land. That hostility would soon erupt in a campaign to drive the Cherokee from their land forever (see Chapter 12).

Patterns of Armed Resistance: The Shawnee and Creek

Not all tribes proved so accommodating to white expansion. The Shawnee and Creek, faced with growing threats to their political and cultural survival, rose in armed resistance. Conflict, smoldering as the nineteenth century began, burst into open flame during the War of 1812.

DOCUMENT

Pennsylvania Gazette, "Indian Hostilities" (1812)

In the late 1780s, chieftains such as Little Turtle of the Miami and Blue Jacket of the Shawnee had led devastating raids across Indiana, Ohio, and western Pennsylvania, panicking white settlers and challenging U.S. control of the Old Northwest. In 1794, President Washington, determined to smash the Indians' resistance once and for all, sent a federal army led by the old Revolutionary War general Anthony Wayne into the area. It won a decisive victory over 2,000 Indian warriors in the Battle of Fallen Timbers. Shortly after, in the Treaty of Greenville, the assembled chiefs ceded the southern two-thirds of Ohio. That cession opened the heart of the Old Northwest to white control. Subsequent treaties further reduced the Indians' land base, driving the tribes more tightly in upon each other.

By 1809, two Shawnee leaders, the brothers Tecumseh and Elskwatawa, the latter known to whites as "the Prophet," were traveling among the region's tribes warning of their common dangers and forging an alliance against the invading whites. They established headquarters at an ancient Indian town named Kithtippecanoe in northern Indiana. Soon it became a gathering point for Native Americans from across the region responding to the messages of cultural pride, land retention, and pan-Indian resistance proclaimed by the Shawnee brothers.

Between 1809 and 1811, Tecumseh carried his message south to the Creek and the Cherokee. His speeches rang with bitterness. "The white race is a wicked race," he said. "Since the days when the white race first came in contact with the

Tecumseh Though Tecumseh's vision of a pan-Indian alliance reaching from the Great Lakes to the Gulf of Mexico never materialized, he led Indian tribes of the old Northwest in militant opposition to white territorial expansion. *(Woodfin Camp & Associates)*

red men, there has been a continual series of aggressions. The hunting grounds are fast disappearing, and they are driving the red men farther and farther to the west." The only hope was a "war of extermination against the paleface." Though the southern tribes refused to join, by 1811 more than 1,000 fighting men had gathered at Kithtippecanoe.

Alarmed, the governor of the Indiana Territory, William Henry Harrison, surrounded the Indian stronghold with a force of 1,000 soldiers. After an all-day battle, he burned Kithtippecanoe to the ground. The Indians, however, were not yet defeated. Tecumseh's followers, taking advantage of the recent outbreak of the War of 1812 with England and aided by British troops from Canada, mounted devastating raids across Indiana and southern Michigan. With the British, they crushed American forces at Detroit and followed up with an attack on Fort Wayne. The tide turned, however, at the Battle of the Thames near Detroit. There Harrison inflicted a grievous defeat on a combined British and Indian force. Among those slain was Tecumseh.

The American victory at the Thames signaled the collapse of Tecumseh's confederacy and an end to Indian resistance in the Old Northwest. Beginning in 1815, American settlers surged once more across Ohio and Indiana, then on into Illinois and Michigan. The balance of power in the Old Northwest had shifted decisively.

To the south, the Creek challenged white intruders with similar militancy. As the nineteenth century began, white settlers were pushing onto Creek lands in northwestern Georgia and central Alabama. Although some Creek leaders urged accommodation, others, called Red Sticks, prepared to fight. The embers of this conflict were fanned into flame by an aggressive Tennessee militia commander named Andrew Jackson. Citing Creek atrocities against "defenseless women and children," Jackson urged President Jefferson to endorse a campaign against the "ruthless foe." He got his chance in the summer of 1813, when the Red Sticks devastated the frontier and assaulted Fort Mims on the Alabama River, killing 500 men, women, and children. News of the tragedy elicited bitter cries for revenge. At the head of 5,000 Tennessee and Kentucky militia, augmented by warriors from other tribes eager to punish their traditional Creek enemies, Jackson attacked. As he moved south, the fighting grew more ferocious. Davey Crockett, one of Jackson's soldiers, later reported that the militia volunteers shot down the Red Sticks "like dogs." The Indians gave like measure in return.

The climactic battle of the Creek War came in March 1814 at Horseshoe Bend in central Alabama. Over 800 Native Americans died, more than in any other Indian-white battle in American history. Jackson followed up his victory with a scorched-earth sweep through the remaining Red Stick towns. He allowed the Creek survivors to return home, but exacted his final revenge by constructing Fort Jackson on the Creek nation's most sacred spot. During the following months, he seized 22 million acres, nearly two-thirds of the Creek domain. Before his Indian-fighting days were over, Jackson would acquire, through treaty or conquest, nearly three-fourths of Alabama and Florida, a third of Tennessee, and a fifth of Georgia and Mississippi.

Just as Tecumseh's death had signaled the end of Indian resistance in the North, so Jackson's defeat of the Creek at Horseshoe Bend broke the back of Indian defenses in the South. With all possibility of armed resistance gone, Native Americans gave way before the swelling tide of white settlement.

PERFECTING A DEMOCRATIC SOCIETY

Throughout our nation's history, the American people have launched a variety of reform movements aimed at achieving social justice and bringing the conditions of daily life into conformity with democratic ideals. The first of those reform eras occurred in the early nineteenth century.

The Impulse to Reform

Reform was inspired by democratic ideals fostered during the Revolution and still fresh in Americans' minds. Belief in American uniqueness as well as "youthfulness," compared to the "old" and "decadent" nations of Europe, together with the seemingly limitless land of the interior, offered the promise of creating a nation unlike any that had existed before, one in which ordinary citizens could create new lives if given the chance.

A surge of evangelical religion inspired the reform impulse as well. Throughout the nation's history, religion has been a major force in American public life. This was true in the early republic, when a wave of Protestant enthusiasm known as the Second Great Awakening swept across the nation. From its beginnings in the 1790s through the first half of the nineteenth century, in settings ranging from

A Camp Meeting During the Second Great Awakening, religious enthusiasts gathered at countless camp meetings to seek salvation and serve other needs as well. What does this depiction tell you about who attended and what took place? *(© Collection of the New York Historical Society)*

the Cane Ridge district of backwoods Kentucky to the cities of the Northeast, Americans by the tens of thousands sought personal salvation and social belonging in the shared experience of religious revivalism.

Displayed most spectacularly at Methodist and Baptist camp meetings, the revivals crossed boundaries of class and race. Rough-hewn itinerant preachers, black as well as white, many of them theologically untrained but afire with religious conviction, spread the Gospel message, in the process knitting networks of believers closely together.

Offering a simple message that ordinary folks could readily grasp, the Awakening emphasized the equality of all believers before God, held out the promise of universal salvation, and declared each individual responsible for his or her soul. The Awakening also called on believers to demonstrate their faith by going into the world to perfect American society and uplift the downtrodden. That mandate would provide much of the energy for later reforms such as temperance and abolition (see Chapter 12).

Alleviating Poverty and Distress

In the early republic, as at other times in the nation's history, social ideals jarred against social reality. One source of tension was the contrast between affirmations of democratic equality and deepening social divisions.

As the nineteenth century began, women continued to hold far less property than men. For black slaves, ownership of anything more than the most basic personal possessions was unattainable. Though the condition of free blacks such as Ben Thompson and Phyllis Sherman was better, they, too, held little of the country's wealth.

Among white males, property was broadly shared in rural areas of the North, where free-labor and family-farm agriculture predominated, and least so in the South, where planters' control of slave labor and the best land enabled them to monopolize the lion's share of the region's wealth. The most even distribution of property was to be found on the edges of white settlement in Trans-Appalachia, but it was an equality of want. As the frontier developed, differences in wealth appeared there as well.

Though America, unlike Europe, contained no permanent and destitute underclass (at least among white citizens), poverty was real and increasing. In the South, it was most evident among poor whites of the backcountry. In the North, port cities held growing numbers of the poor. Boston artisans and shopkeepers, who together had owned 20 percent of the city's wealth in 1700, held scarcely half as much a century later.

Recurring economic recessions hit the urban poor with particular force, while winter added to hard times as shipping slowed and jobs disappeared. During the winter of 1805, New York's mayor DeWitt Clinton, worried about the potentially disruptive behavior of 10,000 impoverished New Yorkers, asked the state legislature for help. During the winter of 1814–1815, relief agencies assisted nearly one-fifth of the city's population. Across New England and southeastern Pennsylvania, propertyless men and women, the "strolling poor," roamed the countryside searching for work.

Three other groups were conspicuous among the nation's poor. One consisted of old Revolutionary War veterans like Long Bill Scott, who had found poverty as well as adventure in the war. State and federal governments were peppered with petitions from grizzled veterans and widows describing their misery and seeking relief. Women and children also suffered disproportionately from poverty. Between 1816 and 1821, they outnumbered men in New York City's almshouses.

For every American who actually suffered poverty's effects, several others lived just beyond its reach. The thinness of their margin of safety became evident during the depression of 1819–1822. Triggered by a financial panic caused by the unsound practices of hundreds of newly chartered state banks, a deep depression settled over the land, generating bankruptcies and sending unemployment soaring. By the early 1820s, the depression was lifting, but it left behind broken fortunes and shattered dreams.

Alleviating poverty was one goal of the early reformers. In New York City, private and public authorities established more than 100 relief agencies to aid unfortunates, from orphans to poor seamen. Across the nation, a "charitable revolution" increased benevolent institutions from 50 in 1790 to nearly 2,000 by 1820. Most of these ventures drew a distinction between the "worthy poor" who merited help, and the "idle poor" who were deemed to lack character and thus deserved their fate. No matter that a New York commission in 1823 found only 46 able-bodied adults among the 851 inmates of the city's poorhouses.

Municipal authorities and private charities also established orphanages, insane asylums, and hospitals. Many efforts were short-lived, but they attested to the continuing strength of revolutionary and religious ideals and provided a foundation for the more ambitious reform efforts that would come later in the century.

Women's Lives

Women's lives did not change dramatically during the early nineteenth century, but developments occurred that helped set the stage for later, more significant breakthroughs.

DOCUMENT

Wilson Law
Lecture to
Women (1791)

Divorce was one area where women achieved greater equality. Securing a divorce was not easy. Most states allowed it only for adultery, and South Carolina did not permit it at all. Moreover, *coverture* laws required wives to transfer their property to their husbands, making divorce a risky economic proposition. New laws enabling women to file for divorce in court rather than having to secure legislative approval made the process

Young Women at School This painting captures a ceremony at the Raleigh Female Academy in Virginia about 1816. Examine the painting closely. Who is present, and perhaps not present? What does the painting tell you about the purposes and ideals of female education? *(Jacob Marling [American, 1774–1833] The May Queen [The Crowning of Flora], 1816, Oil on canvas, 30 × 39⅛ in., Chrysler Museum of Art, Norfolk, VA, Gift of Edgar William and Bernice Chrysler Garbisch [80.181.20])*

easier. Even so, women faced the uncomfortable task of persuading all-male juries of their husbands' transgressions.

Still, divorce was becoming more available to women. In Massachusetts during the decade after independence, 50 percent more women than men filed for divorce, with an almost equal rate of success. Part of the explanation lay in the war's disruptions that led large numbers of men to desert their families, thus encouraging their wives to take action. The trans-Appalachian West lured men away as well. It seems just as certain, however, that women took to heart prevailing values of individualism and equality, leading them to expect more of marriage.

Changes also occurred in women's education. Young women would have to be properly prepared for their role as "Republican Mothers," having prime responsibility for training future citizens in principles of republican virtue. Some women, such as Judith Sargeant Murray, demanded even more of women's education. In the 1790s, Murray criticized parents who pointed their daughters exclusively toward marriage and dependence. "They should be enabled to procure for themselves the necessaries of life; independence should be placed within their grasp," Murray wrote. "A woman should reverence herself."

Dolley Madison— Portrait

Between 1790 and 1830, numerous female academies were established, mostly in northeastern cities. Though some prescribed bookkeeping, reading, geography, and history as proper elements of girls' as well as boys' education, traditionalists were more conservative, warning that undue intellectual activity would "unsex" women. Even the most ardent supporters of female learning, like Murray, conceded that education was primarily important so that women might more effectively function within the domestic sphere. Still, by 1830 white female literacy was at an all-time high.

Women were affected as well by changes in American religious life. Though women had long outnumbered men in church membership, the Second Great Awakening drew them into the churches in even larger numbers, where ministers frequently relied on them to raise funds and promote charitable projects.

In important ways, however, the evangelical impulse reduced women's roles in the churches. Whereas women had previously served as religious exhorters and participated in Baptist and Methodist church governance, they found themselves increasingly marginalized as those rapidly growing denominations, striving for social acceptance, adopted older denominations' rigidly gendered rules. In matters of church discipline, women were more frequently charged with "disorderliness" than their male brethren, thus departing from an earlier tradition of piety in which men and women shared spiritual truth and ministered equally to each other's souls.

Race, Slavery, and the Limits of Reform

As we saw in Chapter 7, the Revolution initiated the end of slavery in the northern states and challenged it in the Upper South. As the new century began, however, private manumissions were declining in Virginia and Maryland, while antislavery sentiment was weakening and more rigid categories of racial exclusiveness were appearing in the North.

Slave Revolt, Saint Domingue (1791)

In the South, the spread of cotton cultivation sent the value of slave labor soaring just as revolutionary idealism was fading with the passage of time. Equally important were two slave rebellions that generated alarm among southern whites. Panic-stricken refugees fleeing the successful revolt of black Haitians on the island of Saint Domingue (see Chapter 8) spread terror through the South. In response, southern legislatures tightened their Black Codes, cut the importation of new slaves from the Caribbean, and weeded out malcontents among their chattels.

A second shock followed in the summer of 1800, when a rebellion just outside Richmond, Virginia, was nipped in the bud. A 24-year-old slave named Gabriel devised a plan to arm 1,000 slaves for an assault on the city. Gabriel and his accomplices were American-born blacks who spoke English and worked at skilled jobs that provided considerable personal autonomy. They fashioned their own ideology of liberation by appropriating the revolutionary tradition of Virginia's whites and applying it to the conditions of their own lives. A drenching downpour delayed the attack, giving time for several house servants (later granted their freedom by the Virginia Assembly) to sound the alarm. No whites died in the abortive rebellion, but scores of slaves and free blacks were arrested and 25 suspects, including Gabriel, were hanged at the order of Governor James Monroe.

In the early nineteenth century, antislavery appeals all but disappeared from the South. Even religious groups that had once denounced slavery grew quiet. "A majority of the [white] people of the southern states," declared a Georgia congressman in 1806, deprecate slavery as a "political evil" but do not consider slavery as a crime or believe it "immoral to hold human flesh in bondage." Confederate spokesmen would be saying much the same thing at the time of the Civil War. In the nation's capital, black servants attended the needs of southern congressmen, while slave markets thrived in the shadow of the Capitol building.

In the Northeast, the gradual abolition of slavery had soothed many consciences. With racial domination no longer enforced by slave laws, whites invoked the doctrine of black inferiority to justify racial exclusiveness and ensure their continued control. The belief in immutable racial differences also encouraged conciliatory attitudes toward slave owners in the South.

The hardening of racial attitudes was evident in growing sentiment for colonizing free blacks in west Africa, in areas that would become Liberia and Sierra Leone. The American Colonization Society, founded in 1816, typified these attitudes. While detesting slavery and proclaiming their benevolent intentions, northern members were uneasy over the growing number of free blacks in their midst. Southern slave owners saw in colonization a convenient way of reducing the region's free black population and ridding themselves of troublesome bondsmen. The Colonization Society never sent many American blacks abroad, but it did help allay white anxieties.

Although some blacks were sympathetic to colonization, believing it offered the best promise of true freedom, most black spokesmen vigorously opposed it. They condemned the ideology of black inferiority on which colonization was based and demanded their full rights as Americans. In joining together to oppose colonization, American blacks gained experience in forging a more effective polit-

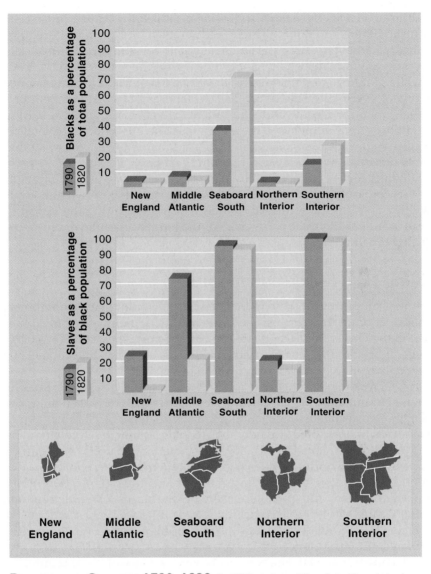

BLACKS AND SLAVERY, 1790–1820 In 1790, regions differed significantly in the proportion of blacks in their population and in the percentage of slaves among black residents. In the ensuing decades, those differences increased. Can you explain why? *(Source: U.S. Bureau of the Census)*

ical voice. That experience would prove valuable training for the abolitionist crusade that lay ahead.

Not all northern whites succumbed to the new racism. The states of Massachusetts, Rhode Island, and Pennsylvania would soon become hotbeds of a resurgent, multiracial abolitionist movement. Blacks, moreover, enjoyed greater liberty in the cities of the Northeast than elsewhere in the nation.

Racism reared its ugly head in the West as well. In 1823, a proslavery mob torched the Illinois capital and threatened the governor for his efforts to end *de facto* slavery in the state. Proposals for a new state constitution included calls, ultimately unsuccessful, for legalizing slavery within the state's borders. In Cincinnati, white citizens grew anxious as the city's black population expanded—by 1829, one of every 10 residents was black—and as black leaders petitioned the Ohio legislature for repeal of the city's "obnoxious" black laws. In late August, several hundred whites invaded the town's black neighborhoods. Several persons were killed in the ensuing melee. In the months that followed, over half the black population fled, many seeking sanctuary in Canada.

Though the slave trade officially ended in 1808, government efforts to suppress the continuing trade were sporadic. In addition, American diplomats pressed England for the return of chattels confiscated during the Revolutionary War and War of 1812. In the early years of the republic, the Revolution's promise of equality rang hollow for most black Americans.

Forming Free Black Communities

During the half century following independence, vibrant black communities, fed by emancipation in the Northeast and the increasing numbers of freed men and women in the Upper South, appeared in eastern port cities. In 1776, 4,000 slaves and several hundred free blacks had called the major port cities home; 50 years later, more than 40,000 African Americans did so.

Black men worked as laborers and dock hands, and black women as domestics. Family formation was eased by the fact that many of the urban migrants were women, thus correcting a long-standing imbalance in the black urban population. Former slaves often created extended households that included relatives, friends, and boarders. As circumstances allowed, single-family units were formed. By 1820, most blacks in northern cities lived in autonomous households.

As their numbers grew, African Americans created organizations independent of white control and capable of serving the needs of black communities. Schools educated black children excluded from white academies, mutual aid societies offered help to the down-and-out, and fraternal associations provided fellowship and mutual support.

Black churches quickly emerged as the cornerstones of black community life. Following the Revolution, growing numbers of free blacks joined integrated Methodist and Baptist congregations, drawn by their strongly biblical theology, enthusiastic forms of worship, and antislavery stand. As the number of black communicants grew, however, they found themselves segregated in church galleries, excluded from leadership roles, and even denied communion. In 1794, a small group of black Methodists led by Richard Allen, a slave-born itinerant preacher, organized the Bethel African American Methodist Church in Philadelphia. Originally established within American Methodism, Allen's congregation moved toward separatism by requiring that only "Africans and descendents of the African race" be admitted to membership. In 1815, it rejected all oversight by the white Methodist leadership, and a year later joined a similar congregation in Baltimore to form the African Methodist Episcopal Church—the first independent black denomination in the United States. Black Baptists also formed separate churches during the early nineteenth century.

Located in the heart of black communities, these churches nurtured distinctive African American forms of worship and provided education for black children and burial sites for families excluded from white cemeteries. Equally important, they offered secure places where the basic rituals of family and community life—marriages and births, funerals and anniversaries—could be celebrated, and where community norms could be enforced. By the 1830s, a rich cultural and institutional life had taken root in the black neighborhoods of northeastern cities.

Black life was far different in southern cities, where the vast majority remained enslaved. Of Charleston's 14,127 blacks (over half the city's population), 90 percent were slaves. That circumstance, together with the South's rigid Black Codes, frustrated black community building. In New Orleans, on the other hand, policies established during Spanish colonial rule had produced the largest free black (*libre*) and mixed race (*mulatto*) population in North America. While racial hierarchies existed, *libres*, their numbers augmented by manumitted slaves and refugees fleeing revolutionary Haiti, prospered. By 1820, *libres* numbered 46 percent of the black population. They constituted a uniquely prosperous and independent black community.

Yet several developments threatened their privileges. Among them were the thousands of new slaves imported to provide labor for the burgeoning sugar economy—what one historian has called the "re-Africanization" of Louisiana—alarm over the black rebellion in nearby Haiti, and the introduction of rigid racial ideologies by new white settlers.

THE END OF NEOCOLONIALISM

Following the election of 1808, James Madison, second in the "Virginia dynasty" of presidents, assumed office. As American ships once more ventured into the Atlantic following the embargo's collapse, and as the British Navy renewed its depredations, war fever continued to mount. Within a few years, conflict with England erupted in the War of 1812. The war brought an end to a period of neocolonialism when the United States, though formally independent, was still vulnerable to the actions of England and other European powers. During the two administrations of James Monroe (1817–1825), the Jeffersonian Republicans also fashioned a momentous new role for the United States within the Americas.

James Madison— Portrait

The War of 1812

As tensions grew, the loudest shouts for war came from the West and South. The election of 1810 brought to Congress a new group of leaders, firmly Jeffersonian in party loyalty but impatient with the administration's bumbling foreign policy and demanding tougher measures. These War Hawks included such future political giants as Henry Clay of Kentucky and John C. Calhoun of South Carolina.

For too long, the War Hawks cried, the United States had tolerated Britain's presence on American soil, encouragement of Indian raids, and attacks on American commerce. They talked freely of expanding the nation's boundaries north into Canada and south into Spanish Florida. Most of all, these young nationalists resented British arrogance and America's continuing humiliation. No government or political party, they warned, could long endure unless it protected the people's interests and upheld the nation's honor.

Responding to the pressure, President Madison finally asked Congress for a declaration of war on June 1, 1812. Opposition came entirely from the New England and mid-Atlantic states—ironically, the regions British poli-

The War of 1812

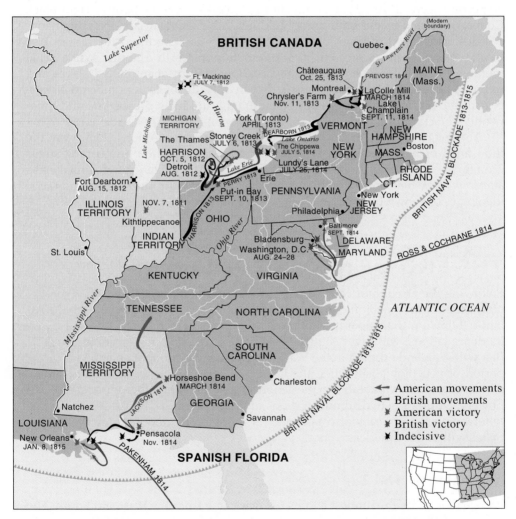

THE WAR OF 1812 The War of 1812 scarcely touched the lives of most Americans, but areas around the Great Lakes, Lake Champlain, Chesapeake Bay, and the Gulf Coast witnessed significant fighting. Why was the fighting concentrated in these areas?

cies affected most adversely—whereas the South and West voted solidly for war. Rarely had sectional alignments been more sharply drawn.

Rarely, either, had American foreign policy proven less effective. Madison decided to abandon economic for military coercion just as the British government, under domestic pressure to seek accommodation, suspended its European blockade. Three days later, unaware of Britain's action (it took three weeks for news to cross the Atlantic), Congress declared war.

The war proved a strange affair. Britain beat back several American forays into Canada and launched a series of attacks along the Gulf Coast. As it had done during the Revolutionary War, the British navy blockaded American coastal waters, while landing parties launched punishing attacks along the eastern seaboard. On August 14, a British force occupied Washington, torched the Capitol and president's mansion (soon to be called the White House after being repaired and whitewashed), and sent the president, Congress, and panic-stricken American troops fleeing into Virginia. Britain, however, did not press its advantage, for it was preoccupied with Napoleon's armies in Europe and wanted to end the American quarrel.

Burning of the White House in 1814

Emotions ran high among Federalist critics and Jeffersonian supporters of the war. In June 1812, during bloody riots in Baltimore, several people, including an old Federalist Revolutionary War general, were badly beaten in the streets. In Federalist New England, opposition to the war veered toward outright disloyalty. In December 1814, delegates from the five New England states met at Hartford, Connecticut, to debate proposals for secession. Cooler heads prevailed, but before adjourning, the Hartford Convention, echoing the Kentucky and Virginia Resolutions of 1798, asserted the right of a state "to interpose its authority" against "unconstitutional" acts of the government. Now it was New England's turn to play with the nullification fire. As the war dragged on, Federalist support soared in the Northeast, while elsewhere bitterness grew over New England's disloyalty.

Before the war ended, American forces won several impressive victories, among them Commander Oliver Hazard Perry's defeat of the British fleet on Lake Erie in 1813. The most dramatic American triumph was Andrew Jackson's victory in 1815 over an attacking British force at New Orleans, though it occurred after preliminary terms of peace had already been signed.

Increasingly concerned about Europe, the British government offered to begin peace negotiations. Madison eagerly accepted, and on Christmas Eve in 1814, at Ghent, Belgium, the two sides reached agreement. While Britain agreed to evacuate the western posts, the treaty ignored other long-standing issues, including impressment, neutral rights, and American access to Canadian fisheries. It simply declared the fighting over, called for the return of prisoners and captured territory, and provided for joint commissions to deal with lingering disputes.

Still, the war left its mark on the American nation. Four thousand African Americans, constituting nearly 20 percent of American seamen, fought in the war, demonstrating their patriotism and challenging white stereotypes. At least as many blacks served the British as spies, messengers, and guides, much as had occurred during the American Revolution. A hundred or so newly liberated slaves accompanied the British troops that burned the Capitol and president's house in 1814.

The war made Andrew Jackson a national hero and established him as a major political leader. The American people, moreover, regarded the contest as a "Second War of American Independence" that finally secured the nation from outside interference. In the years following 1815, the nation focused its energies on the task of internal development—occupying the continent, building the economy, and reforming American society. At the same time, Europe entered what would prove to be nearly a century free of general war. In the past, European wars had drawn America in; in the twentieth century, they would do so again. For the rest of the nineteenth century, however, that fateful link was broken. Finally, European colonialism was now shifting to Africa and Asia, and that diverted European attention from the Americas as well.

AUDIO

Star Spangled
Banner

The United States and the Americas

While disengaging from Europe, the president and Congress fashioned new policies for Latin America that would guide the nation's hemispheric relations for years to come. Many Americans cheered when Spain and Portugal's Latin American colonies, holding up the American Revolution as a model of liberation, began their struggle for independence in 1808. U.S. leaders were happy to see European colonialism weakened but were skeptical that the racially mixed populations of Latin America, with their history of brutal colonialism, could govern themselves effectively. After initial reluctance, primarily for fear of disrupting delicate efforts then under way to secure Florida from Spain, President Monroe sent Congress a message proposing formal recognition of the new Latin American republics. Congress quickly agreed.

Trouble, however, arose in November 1822, when several European powers talked of helping Spain regain its American empire. Such prospects alarmed Great Britain as well as the United States, and in August 1823 the British foreign secretary broached the idea of Anglo-American cooperation to thwart Spain's intentions.

DOCUMENT

Monroe Doctrine
(1823)

Secretary of State John Quincy Adams opposed the idea. Adams had joined the Jeffersonian camp some years earlier as part of the continuing exodus from the Federalist party. Filled with the new spirit of nationalism following the War of 1812 and suspicious of British intentions, Adams called for independent action based on two principles: a sharp separation between the Old World and the New, and U.S. dominance in the Western Hemisphere. Monroe agreed that the United States should issue its own declaration. In his annual message of December 1823, he outlined a new Latin American policy. Though known as the Monroe Doctrine, Adams had devised it.

The doctrine asserted four basic principles: (1) the American continents were closed to new European colonization, (2) the political systems of the Americas were separate from those of Europe, (3) the United States would consider as dangerous to its peace and safety any attempts to extend Europe's political influence into the Western Hemisphere, and (4) the United States would neither interfere with existing colonies in the New World nor meddle in Europe's affairs.

Monroe's bold declaration had little immediate effect, for the United States possessed neither the economic nor military power to enforce it. By the end of the nineteenth century when the nation's might had increased, however, it would become clear what a fateful moment in the history of the Western Hemisphere Monroe's declaration had been.

KNITTING THE NATION TOGETHER

At the Philadelphia convention in 1788, Federalists and Anti-Federalists had argued whether such a diverse and sprawling republic could long survive. After the vast area of Louisiana was added, those concerns increased. Given the country's primitive modes of travel, limited forms of communication, and small central government, problems of national unity continued to bedevil the American people. Although the nation would not be securely unified until after the Civil War, progress was clearly evident in the early republic.

Conquering Distance

It has been estimated that within half an hour of President Kennedy's assassination in Dallas, Texas, in 1963, 68 percent of the American people had learned the news. By contrast, when George Washington died in December 1799 in Alexandria, Virginia, it took five days for word to reach Philadelphia (scarcely 140 miles away), 11 days to get as far as Boston, and over three weeks to penetrate west to Lexington, Kentucky. In the absence of modern technologies such as telephones, television, and the Internet, human travel was the only way of communicating across space. By the 1820s, however, improvements in transportation and communication had begun to knit the nation more effectively together.

A flurry of turnpike construction in the northeastern states contributed to the improvements. Most consisted of little more than dirt roadways cut through the woods, with tree stumps sawed off low enough to clear wagon axles. Still, when a pike from Philadelphia to Lancaster, Pennsylvania, proved profitable, dozens of others quickly followed. By 1811, New York had chartered 137 turnpike companies and the New England states 200 more. By 1830, travel time along these roadways had been halved.

In the first federal road building project, Congress in 1806 authorized construction of a National Road from Cumberland, Maryland, to the West. By 1818, it had reached Wheeling on the Ohio River and had reduced travel time between its terminals from eight days to three.

Given the difficulties of overland routes, Americans traveled by water whenever possible. During the early years of the century, the first steamboats appeared along the Atlantic coast and began to ply the waters of the Ohio and Mississippi rivers. In 1807, Robert Fulton launched his 160-ton sidewheeler *Clermont*, demonstrating the feasibility of steam travel. Four years later, the *New Orleans* made the first successful run over the falls of the Ohio River at Cincinnati, then continued down the Mississippi to New Orleans. Within a few decades, steamboats would revolutionize transportation on the nation's interior river system.

Between 1790 and 1830, significant breakthroughs occurred in print communication as well. When Washington assumed the presidency, only 92 newspapers existed. Most were weeklies; virtually all were printed in cities along the Atlantic coast. The majority had no more than 600 subscribers. By 1830, the number of newspapers had increased to over 1,000, about one-third of them dailies. Some were published in places as far inland as Pittsburgh and St. Louis. By 1820, the ratio of newspapers to population was higher in the United States than in Great Britain.

The swelling demand for newspapers was spurred by rising literacy rates, the demand for information generated by the nation's expanding market economy, the democratic belief in the importance of an informed citizenry, and the growing importance of newspapers as instruments of party politics. The circulation of papers brought information about distant people and events into formerly isolated communities, expanding citizens' horizons and strengthening their sense of shared experience. Only a newspaper, noted one observer, "can drop the same thought into a thousand minds at the same moment."

During these years, the American postal system expanded similarly. When Washington was inaugurated, there were only 75 post offices in the entire country. As late as 1792, there were none in the trans-Appalachian West. By 1820, nearly 8,500 post offices lay scattered throughout the nation, while the number of letters carried by the postal system had increased ninefold. Though it cost 25 cents to send a letter 30 miles or more—a prohibitive sum for most folks when daily wages averaged only a dollar—the rate had declined by half.

Strengthening American Nationalism

If improvements in travel and communication, together with a sense of national pride fostered by the War of 1812, strengthened American nationalism, so, too, did the galvanizing experience of the Second Great Awakening. It reinforced belief in America as God's chosen nation and tied Americans together in networks of shared religious identity, woven by the hundreds of itinerant ministers who carried the Gospel message into communities in every part of the country. The flood of printed tracts circulated by religious organizations reinforced the sense of religious unity.

Rituals of patriotic celebration on occasions such as Washington's birthday and the Fourth of July also helped unify the country. Federalists and Jeffersonian Republicans, northerners and southerners, black and white Americans filled these occasions with their own, often conflicting meanings, yet all were eager to claim a voice in shaping the nation's heritage. Reports of these local celebrations, carried across the land via newspapers and correspondence, knitted communities together in a national conversation of patriotism.

DOCUMENT

Opinion of the Supreme Court for *Marbury* v. *Madison* (1803)

National unity was further strengthened by several key decisions of the Supreme Court. In a series of trailblazing cases, the Court, led by Chief Justice John Marshall, laid down some of the most basic doctrines of American constitutional law. In *Marbury* v. *Madison* (1803), the Court established the principle of judicial review, the assertion that the Court had the authority to judge the constitutionality of congressional laws and executive actions. In the case of *Martin* v. *Hunter's Lessee* (1816), the Court claimed appellate jurisdiction over the decisions of state courts.

Three years later, in another landmark decision, *McCulloch* v. *Maryland,* the Court set aside claims that Congress had exceeded its authority in chartering the Second Bank of the United States (1816). In a unanimous decision, Marshall issued

John Marshall Appointed chief justice of the United States by President Adams in 1801, Marshall served in that position for 34 years. Under his leadership, the Supreme Court established some of the most basic principles of American constitutional law. *(Boston Athenaeum)*

a ringing endorsement of the doctrine of loose, as opposed to strict, construction of the Constitution. "Let the end (of a Congressional law) be legitimate," he declared, "let it be within the scope of the constitution, and all means which are appropriate ... to that end, which are not prohibited, but consist with the letter and spirit of the constitution, are constitutional." The Bank's charter would thus stand.

No state, he further argued, possessed the right to tax a branch of the nationally chartered bank, as Maryland had attempted to do, because "the power to tax involves the power to destroy." The principle of national supremacy lay at the very center of Marshall's findings. The doctrines elaborated in these path-breaking decisions would continue to shape the nation's history in the years ahead.

The Specter of Sectionalism

Despite the surge of national spirit following the War of 1812, Federalist talk of disunion had revealed just how fragile national unity still was. That became starkly evident in the Missouri crisis of 1819–1820.

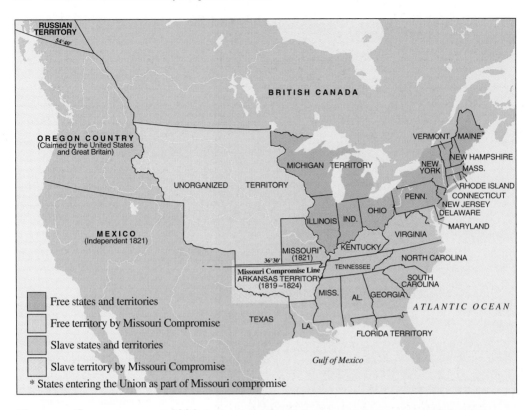

MISSOURI COMPROMISE OF 1820 In the early nineteenth century, politicians struggled to contain the explosive issue of slavery's expansion. How was this attempted in the Missouri Compromise?

Since 1789, politicians had labored to keep the explosive issue of slavery tucked safely beneath the surface of political life, for they understood how quickly it could jeopardize the nation. Their fears were borne out in 1819 when Missouri's application for admission to the Union raised anew the question of slavery's expansion. The Northwest Ordinance of 1787 had prohibited slavery north of the Ohio River while allowing its expansion to the south. But Congress had said nothing about slavery's place in the vast Louisiana territory west of the Mississippi.

Though there were several thousand slaves in the Missouri Territory, Senator Rufus King of New York demanded that Missouri prohibit slavery before entering the Union. The proposal triggered a fierce debate over Congress's authority to regulate slavery in the trans-Mississippi West. Southerners were adamant that the area must remain open to their slave property and were determined to preserve the equal balance of slave and free states in the Senate. Already by 1819, the more rapidly growing population of the free states had given them a 105-to-81 advantage in the House of Representatives. Equality in the Senate offered the only sure protection for southern interests. Northerners, however, vowed to keep the territories west of the Mississippi open to free labor, which meant closing them to slavery.

For nearly three months, Congress debated the issue. During much of the time, free blacks, listening intently to northern antislavery speeches, filled the House gallery. "This momentous question," worried the aged Jefferson, "like a fire-bell in the night, [has] awakened and filled me with terror." Northerners were similarly alarmed. The Missouri question, declared the editor of the New York *Daily Advertiser,* "involves not only the future character of our nation, but the future weight and influence of the free states. If now lost—it is lost forever."

In the end, compromise prevailed. Missouri gained admission as a slave state, while Maine (formerly part of Massachusetts) came in as a counterbalancing free state. A line was drawn west from Missouri at latitude 36°30' to the Rocky Mountains. Land south of that line would be open to slavery; areas to the north would not. For the moment, the issue of slavery's expansion had been put to rest. It would not be long, however, before the problem would set North and South even more violently against each other.

POLITICS IN TRANSITION

For two decades following the election of 1800, Jeffersonian Republicans monopolized the presidency and dominated Congress, while the Federalist party languished. By the late 1820s, however, the Jeffersonian ascendancy had ended, and the Federalist–Jeffersonian party system was in disarray. As that happened, new political alignments began to appear and America was poised on the threshold of a new political era.

The Collapse of the Federalist–Jeffersonian Party System

For a while following the election of 1800, Federalists had maintained a drumfire of attack on the Jeffersonians, including the charge published by a Federalist editor in 1803 that Jefferson had sired several children by his slave Sally Hemings. But Federalists were discredited by accusations of disloyalty during the War of 1812 and were tainted by their lingering aristocratic image. Some Federalists endorsed broadened suffrage as essential to social stability and governmental legitimacy, but others did not. "There is a tendency in the majority," declared one New York Federalist, "to tyrannize over the minority and trample down their rights." Saddled with this outlook, the Federalist party gradually collapsed.

The Jeffersonians' overwhelming political success after the War of 1812 proved their undoing. No single party could contain the nation's swelling diversity of economic and social interests, deepening sectional differences, and personal ambitions of new political leaders.

In response to growing pressures from the West and Northeast, as well as to nationalist sentiment stimulated by the War of 1812, Madison's administration launched a Federalist-like program of national development. In March 1816, he signed a bill creating a second Bank of the United States (the first bank's charter

DOCUMENT

Henry Clay, "Defense of the American System" (1832)

had expired in 1811), intended to stimulate economic expansion and regulate the loose currency-issuing practices of countless state-chartered banks. At Madison's urging, Congress passed America's first protective tariff, a set of duties on imported goods intended to protect America's "infant industries." Madison also launched a federally subsidized network of roads and canals. By the end of the 1820s, Henry Clay and others, now calling themselves National Republicans, were proposing an even more ambitious program of tariffs and internal improvements, under the name of the American System.

The administration's policies drew sharp criticism from so-called Old Republicans, southern politicians who regarded themselves as guardians of the Jeffersonian conscience and questioned whether the state governments were to be "swept away." They continued to sound the alarm, even as their numbers dwindled.

The final collapse of the Federalist–Jeffersonian party system was triggered by the presidential election of 1824. For the first time since 1800, when the "Virginia dynasty" of Jefferson, Madison, and Monroe began, there was competition for the presidency from every major wing of the Jeffersonian coalition. Of the five candidates, John Quincy Adams of Massachusetts and Henry Clay of Kentucky advocated bold programs of economic development. William Crawford of Georgia and Andrew Jackson of Tennessee clung to traditional Jeffersonian principles of limited government, agrarianism, and states' rights. In between stood John Calhoun of South Carolina, just beginning his fateful passage from nationalism to southern nullification.

When none of the presidential candidates received an electoral majority, the election, as in 1800, moved into the House of Representatives. There, an alliance of Adams and Clay supporters gave the New Englander the election, even though he trailed Jackson in electoral votes, 84 to 99. The Jacksonians' charges of a "corrupt bargain" gained credence when Adams appointed Clay secretary of state.

Adams's ill-fated administration revealed the disarray in American politics. His stirring calls for federal road and canal building, standardization of weights and measures, a national university, and government support for science and the arts quickly fell victim to sectional conflicts, political factionalism, and his own scorn for the increasingly democratic politics of the time. Within a year of his inauguration, Adams's administration had foundered. For the rest of his term, politicians jockeyed for position in the political realignment that was under way.

A New Style of Politics

While women, blacks, and Native Americans continued to be excluded from the franchise, white men now flocked to the polls in unprecedented numbers. In state elections, voter turnout at times reached as high as 80 percent of the qualifying electorate, far higher than previously.

The growing strength of democratic beliefs and decisions by state governments to abolish long-established property-owning requirements for the franchise help explain the dramatic increase. In addition, state programs of road and canal building, bank regulation, temperance enforcement, and poor relief activated people's self-interest, thus drawing them into the political arena. And it was in the states that a new generation of political leaders such as Martin Van Buren and Henry Clay, uninhibited by the revolutionary generation's fear of political "faction" and

Election Day, 1816 Election days were often raucous affairs in the increasingly democratic, male-dominated politics of the early republic, as this Philadelphia scene amply testifies. *(The Historical Society of Pennsylvania [HSP], India ink and watercolors on paper of "Election Day at the State House, 1816," by John Lewis Krimmel)*

skilled in party organization and the use of a partisan press, perfected the techniques of mass, democratic politics. By the 1820s, voter registration drives, party conventions, and popular campaigning had become commonplace in the states.

The election of Andrew Jackson to the presidency in 1828 represented the culmination of these democratic changes, for it brought the techniques of mass politics to presidential electioneering. When the presidential election became a genuine popular referendum, American politics had changed forever.

Conclusion

The Passing of an Era

As the nineteenth century began, the United States consisted of diverse, often conflicting, and loosely connected regions. Within those regions, ordinary citizens such as Mary and James Harrod, Ben Thompson, and Phyllis Sherman struggled to fashion new lives. Their efforts gave human expression to values of social equality, individual opportunity, and personal autonomy.

Those values, strengthened by the country's revolutionary heritage and the Great Awakening, inspired reforms intended to improve the conditions of American life. Though the lives of many white women were bettered, gendered restrictions continued to limit women's opportunities. The reinvigoration of chattel slavery in the South imperiled the lives of countless black slaves, while deepening racism in the North circumscribed the lives of free blacks. To the west, Native Americans, pursuing strategies of resistance and accommodation, gradually gave way in the face of expanding white settlement.

During these same years, American leaders fashioned important new relationships with the outside world. Following the War of 1812, the United States finally broke free from its neocolonial dependence on England and Europe. The Monroe Doctrine defined a portentous new relationship with the emerging nations of Latin America.

As the country grew, American nationalism was strengthened by improvements in travel and print communication, the widely shared experience of the Great Awakening, and a series of path-breaking decisions handed down by the Supreme Court. At the same time, sectional tensions continued to simmer, breaking ominously through the surface of political life in the Missouri Crisis.

These years brought important changes to American political life. While most women continued to find themselves politically marginalized, sophisticated political parties, skilled in new methods of organization and communication, enlisted white men by the tens of thousands in electoral politics.

By the 1820s, the American people had turned from an era of founding, when the nation was new and the outcome of its republican experiment uncertain, to an era of increased national security, accelerating development, and the emergence of a post-revolutionary generation of political leaders. That transition was dramatized on July 4, 1826, the fiftieth anniversary of American independence, when two of the remaining revolutionary patriarchs, John Adams and Thomas Jefferson, died within a few hours of each other. "The sterling virtues of the Revolution are silently passing away," mused George McDuffie of South Carolina during that jubilee year, "and the period is not distant when there will be no living monument to remind us of those glorious days of trial." As the anniversary celebrations ended and the revolutionary founders faded into memory, the American people had reason to ponder what the future would bring.

Questions for Review and Reflection

1. How did the nation's regions differ in the early republic? To what extent were these differences grounded in the colonial period, and to what extent did they reflect developments since the end of the Revolutionary War?

2. Why did some Indian tribes follow the path of accommodation to white expansion, while others rose in armed resistance? Which strategy was more successful?

3. What circumstances promoted and inhibited social reform in the early republic?

4. How and why did the United States refashion relations with the outside world in the early nineteenth century?

5. What circumstances served to unite and divide the nation during these years?

Discovering U.S. History Online

Birch's Views of Philadelphia in 1800 www.ushistory.org/birch
This site presents a facsimile of 29 engravings of Philadelphia at the beginning of the nineteenth century.

The Seminole Tribe of Florida www.seminoletribe.com/history/index.shtml
This site is dedicated to the rich history and culture of the Seminole, including the campaigns Andrew Jackson led against the tribe before and during his presidency.

Divining America: Religion and the National Culture, the 19th Century www.nhc.rtp.nc.us:8080/tserve/nineteen.htm
Using essays and contemporary photos and primary sources, this site offers several essays including "Evangelicalism, Revivalism, and Second Great Awakening" and "Evangelicalism as a Social Movement."

Colonization www.loc.gov/exhibits/african/afam002.html
This site explores the roots of the colonization movement, including the American Colonization Society.

Judith Sargent Murray Society www.hurdsmith.com/judith/
This site presents her biography, an illustrated tour of her world, and several of her published essays.

The Missouri Compromise www.darien.k12.ct.us/jburt/approject/civilwar/1820/per3/index.htm
Created for a class project, this site offers a topical presentation of the Missouri Compromise.

History of the Fourth of July www.pbs.org/capitolfourth/history.html
This site presents a colorful illustrated history of Fourth of July celebrations.

Fiction and Film

In the classic American novel *Rip Van Winkle* (1829), Washington Irving explores the transience of historical memory via the story of an eighteenth-century New Yorker who mysteriously falls asleep during the American Revolution and awakes decades later to find his community radically changed and himself the object of intense curiosity. *Scandalmonger* (2000), a novel by the *New York Times* columnist William Safire, describes personal intrigue within high political circles in the early republic. *Tecumseh: The Last Warrior* (1995), a made-for-television historical drama, offers an imaginative rendering of the Shawnee leader who sought to unite tribes north and south of the Ohio River against invading white settlers in the early nineteenth century. *Lewis and Clark: The Journey of the Corps of Discovery* (1997), a PBS documentary by Ken Burns, tells the story of this path-breaking expedition and reveals the dramatic landscape through which it passed.

Recommended Reading

www.ablongman.com/nash

The Companion Website has a list of recommended readings about the early republic, including the restoration of liberties, Indian–white relations, the development of a democratic society, foreign policy, and domestic politics.

CHAPTER 10

Currents of Change in the Northeast and the Old Northwest

American Stories

Discovering Success in the Midst of Financial Ruin

For her first 18 years, Susan Warner was little touched by the economic and social changes transforming the country and her own city of New York. Some New Yorkers toiled to make a living by taking in piecework; others responded to unsettling new means of producing goods by joining trade unions to agitate for wages that would enable them to "live as comfortable as others." But Susan was surrounded by luxuries. Much of the year was spent in the family's townhouse in St. Mark's Place. There Susan acquired the social graces and skills appropriate for a girl of her position: dancing, singing, Italian and French lessons, and the etiquette of receiving visitors and making calls. When hot weather made life in New York unpleasant, the Warners escaped to their summer house. Like any girl of her social class, Susan realized that marriage, which she confidently expected some time in the future, would bring significant new responsibilities, but not the end of her comfortable life.

It was not marriage and motherhood that disrupted the pattern of Susan's life, but financial disaster. Sheltered as she had been from the far-reaching and unsettling economic and social changes of the early nineteenth century, Susan found that she, too, was at the mercy of forces beyond her control. Her hitherto successful father lost most of his fortune in the Panic of 1837. Like others experiencing a sharp economic reversal, the Warners had to make radical adjustments. The fashionable home in St. Mark's Place and the pleasures of New York gave way to a modest existence on an island in the Hudson River. Susan turned "housekeeper" and learned tasks once relegated to others: sewing and making butter, pudding sauces, and johnny cake.

The change of residence and Susan's attempt to master domestic skills did not halt the family's financial decline. Prized possessions went up for auction. "When at last the men and the confusion were gone," Susan's younger sister, Anna, recalled, "then we woke up to life."

Waking up to life meant facing the necessity of making money. But what could Susan do? True, some women labored as factory operatives, domestics, seamstresses, or schoolteachers, but it was doubtful Susan could even imagine herself in any of these occupations. Her Aunt Fanny, however, had a more congenial suggestion. Knowing that the steam-powered printing press had revolutionized the publishing world and created a mass readership, much of it female, Aunt Fanny told her niece, "Sue, I believe if you would try, you could write a story." "Whether she added 'that ... would sell,' I am not sure," recalled Anna later, "but of course that was what she meant."

Taking Aunt Fanny's advice, Susan started to write a novel that would sell. She constructed her story around the trials of a young orphan girl, Ellen Montgomery. As Ellen suffered one reverse after another, she learned lessons that allowed her to survive and eventually triumph: piety, self-denial, discipline, and the power of a mother's love. Entitled *The Wide, Wide World,* the novel was accepted for publication only after the mother of the publisher, George Putnam, read it and told her son, "If you never publish another book, you must make *The Wide, Wide World* available for your fellow men." The cautious Putnam printed 750 copies. Much to his surprise, if not to his mother's, 13 editions appeared within two years. *The Wide, Wide World,* the first American novel to sell more than a million copies, became one of the best-sellers of the century.

Long before she realized the book's success, Susan, always aware of the need to make money, was working on a new story. Drawing on her own experience, Susan described the spiritual and intellectual life of a young girl thrust into poverty after an early life of luxury in New York. It was also a great success.

Though her fame as a writer made Susan Warner unusual, her books' popularity suggested how well they spoke to the concerns and interests of a broad readership. The background of social and financial uncertainty, with its sudden changes of fortune so prominent in several of the novels, captured the reality and fears of a fluid society in the process of transformation. While one French writer was amazed that "in America a three-volume novel is devoted to the history of the moral progress of a girl of thirteen," pious heroines like Ellen Montgomery, who struggled to master their passions and urges toward independence, were shining exemplars of the new norms for middle-class women. Their successful efforts to mold themselves heartened readers who believed that the future of the nation depended on virtuous mothers and those who strove to live up to new ideals. Susan's novels validated their efforts and the importance of the domestic sphere. "I feel strongly impelled to pour out to you my most heartful thanks," wrote one woman. None of the other leading writers of the day had been able to minister "to the highest and noblest feelings of my nature *so much as yourself*."

Susan Warner's life and her novels introduce the far-reaching changes that this chapter explores. Between 1820 and 1860, as Warner discovered, economic transformations in the Northeast and the Old Northwest reshaped economic, social, cultural, and political life. Though most Americans still lived in rural settings, not in factory towns or cities, economic growth and the new industrial mode of production affected them through the creation of new goods, opportunities, and markets. In urban communities and factory towns, the new economic order ushered in new forms of work, new class arrangements, and new forms of social strife.

After placing American economic change in an international context, another focus of this text, and discussing the factors that fueled antebellum growth, the chapter turns to the industrial world, where so many new patterns of work and life appeared. An investigation of urbanization reveals shifting class arrangements and values as well as rising social and racial tensions. Finally, an examination of rural communities in the East and on the frontier in the Old Northwest highlights the transformation of these two sections of the country. Between 1840 and 1860, industrialization and economic growth increasingly knit them together.

ECONOMIC GROWTH

Between 1820 and 1860, the American economy entered a new and more complex phase as it shifted from reliance on agriculture as the major source of growth toward an industrial and technological future. Amid general national expansion, real per capita output grew an average of 2 percent annually between 1820 and 1840 and slightly less between 1840 and 1860. This doubling of per capita income over a 40-year period suggests that many Americans were enjoying a rising standard of living.

Expanding America and Internal Improvements

But the economy was also unstable, as the Warners discovered. Periods of boom (1822–1834, mid-1840s–1850s) alternated with periods of bust (1816–1821, 1837–1843). As never before, Americans faced dramatic and recurrent shifts in the availability of jobs and goods and in prices and wages. Particularly at risk were working-class Americans, a third of whom lost their jobs in depression years. And because regional economies were increasingly linked, problems in one area tended to affect conditions in others.

The Trans-Atlantic Context for Growth

American economic growth was linked to and influenced by events elsewhere in the world, particularly in Great Britain. Britain was the home of the Industrial Revolution, the event that some historians believe to be among the most important of human history in terms of its impact on material life. For the first time, production of goods proceeded at a faster pace than the growth of population.

The Industrial Revolution beginning in Britain in the eighteenth century involved many technological innovations that spurred new developments and efficiencies. Among the most important developments was the discovery in the 1780s of a way to eliminate carbon and other substances from pig iron. This opened the way for cheap, durable iron machines that led to the increased production of goods. Another milestone, the improvement of the steam engine, originally used to pump water out of coal mines, eventually led to railroads and steamboats, thus revolutionizing transportation. Steam-powered machinery also transformed cloth production, moving it from cottages to factories. The British textile industry was the giant of the early Industrial Revolution. The use of machinery allowed the production of more and cheaper textiles. The industry became a prime market for American cotton as well as cotton from India and Brazil. British demand for raw cotton helped to cement the South's attachment to slavery.

By 1850, Great Britain was the most powerful country in the world, and its citizens were the richest. In the following decades, its factories and mines churned out most of the world's coal and over half of its iron and textiles. Not surprisingly, Americans would look to England and English know-how as they embarked on their own course of industrialization. While American industrial development

An Analysis of the Lure of Commerce and Manufacturing

In 1831 a French magistrate, Alexis de Tocqueville, came to the United States to examine the American prison system. While the exploration of the penal system was his official reason for spending nine months in the United States, he was actually more interested in understanding how American democracy operated. His book, Democracy in America, *published in 1835 and 1840, has become a classic study of this country in the 1830s.*

Agriculture is, perhaps, of all the useful arts, that which improves most slowly amongst democratic nations. Frequently, indeed, it would seem to be stationary, because other arts are making rapid strides toward perfection. On the other hand, almost all the tastes and habit which the equality of condition produces naturally lead men to commercial and industrial occupations.

Suppose an active, enlightened, and free man, enjoying a competency, but full of desires: he is too poor to live in idleness; he is rich enough to feel himself protected from the immediate fear of want, and he thinks how he can better his condition. ... life is slipping away time is urgent. ... The cultivation of the ground promises an almost certain result to his exertions, but a slow one; men are not enriched by it without patience and toil. Agriculture is therefore only suited to those who have already larger superfluous wealth, or to those who penury bids them only seek a bare subsistence. The choice of such a man as we have supposed is soon made; he sells his plot of ground, leaves his dwelling, and embarks in some hazardous but lucrative calling.

Democratic communities abound in men of this kind. ... Thus, democracy not only swells the number of working-men, but it leads men to prefer one kind of labor to another; and, whilst it diverts them from agriculture, it encourages their taste for commerce and manufactures.

- *What argument does de Tocqueville make to explain the American interest in commerce and manufacturing work?*
- *Does the discussion in this chapter support de Tocqueville's analysis about the supposed preference of Americans for industrial and commercial rather than agricultural pursuits?*

Source: Alexis de Tocqueville, Democracy in America *(Richard D. Heffner edition, 1956), p. 213.*

did not mimic the British, there were many similarities between the two countries' experiences.

Factors Fueling Economic Development

As the following table suggests, abundant natural resources and a growing population provided the raw materials, brawn, and brains for economic expansion. Because the size of American families was gradually shrinking, European immigrants played an essential role in supplying the workers, households, and consumers essential to economic development. They also contributed capital and technological ideas that helped shape American growth.

Improved transportation played a key role in promoting economic and geographical expansion. Early in the century, high freight rates discouraged produc-

Significant Factors Promoting Economic Growth, 1820–1860

Factor	Important Features	Contribution to Growth
Abundant natural resources	Acquisition of new territories (Louisiana Purchase, Florida, trans-Mississippi West); exploitation and discovery of eastern resources	Provided raw materials and energy vital to economic transformation
Substantial population growth	Increase from 9 million in 1820 to over 30 million in 1860—due to natural increase of population and, especially after 1840, to rising immigration; importance of immigration from Ireland, Germany	Provided workers and consumers necessary for economic growth; immigration increased diversity of workforce with complex results, among them supply of capital and technological know-how
Transportation revolution	Improvement of roads; extensive canal building, 1817–1837; increasing importance of railroad construction thereafter; by 1860, 30,000 miles of tracks; steamboats facilitate travel on water	Facilitated movement of people, goods, and information; drew people into national economic market; stimulated agricultural expansion, regional crop specialization; decreased costs of shipping goods; strengthened ties between Northeast and Midwest
Capital investment	Investments by European investors and U.S. interests; importance of mercantile capital and banks, insurance companies in funneling capital to economic enterprises	Provided capital to support variety of new economic enterprises, improvements in transportation
Government support	Local, state, and national legislation; loans favoring enterprise; judicial decisions	Provided capital, privileges, and supportive climate for economic enterprises

tion for distant markets and the exploitation of resources, while primitive transportation hindered western settlement. The construction of canals dramatically transformed this situation during the 1820s and 1830s. The most impressive was the 363-mile-long Erie Canal, the last link in a chain of waterways connecting New York City to the Northwest. The volume of goods and people it carried at low cost demonstrated the economic benefits of this mode of transportation and encouraged the construction of over 3,000 miles of canals by 1840.

But even at the height of the canal boom, politicians and promoters, impressed by Britain's success with railways, supported the construction

DOCUMENT

Erie Canal (1819)

AUDIO

The Erie Canal

of railroads. Unlike canals that froze in the winter, railroads could operate all year around and could be built almost anywhere. These advantages encouraged Baltimore merchants, envious of New York's water link to the Northwest, to begin the Baltimore & Ohio Railroad in 1828.

The first trains jumped their tracks and their sparks set fields ablaze, but such technical difficulties were quickly overcome. By 1840, there were 3,000 miles of track, mostly in the Northeast. Ten years later, total mileage soared to 30,000. Like canals, railroads strengthened links between the Old Northwest and the East and eventually fostered shared political outlooks.

DOCUMENT

"The Western Country," Letters in *Nile's Weekly Register* (1816)

Some historians use the term *Transportation Revolution* in recognition of the impact of improved transportation for economic development. Goods, people, and information flowed more predictably, rapidly, and cheaply. Canals and railroads gave farmers, merchants, and manufacturers inexpensive, reliable access to distant markets and goods and fostered technological innovations that, in turn, spurred production. Transportation links stimulated regional specialization and agricultural expansion as farmers began to plant larger, more specialized crops for the market—grain in the Old Northwest, dairy goods and produce in New England. By 1860, American farmers were producing four to five times as much wheat, corn, cattle, and hogs as in 1810. American workers had plentiful, cheap food, and farmers had more income to spend on new consumer goods.

Improved transportation encouraged Americans to settle the frontier. Railroads exerted enormous influence in shaping the pattern of western settlement. As the railroads followed—or led—settlers westward, their routes could determine whether a city, a town, or even a homestead survived and prospered. The railroad transformed Chicago from a small settlement into a bustling commercial and transportation center.

Capital and Government Support

Internal improvements, the exploitation of natural resources, and the cultivation of new lands demanded capital. Much came from abroad. Between 1790 and 1861, Europeans invested more than $500 million in the United States. These funds, along with savings brought by immigrant families, financed as much as a third of all canal construction and purchased almost a quarter of all railroad bonds.

American mercantile capital fueled growth as well. Those merchants prospering in the half century after the Revolution invested in schemes ranging from canals to textile factories. Many became manufacturers.

Local and state government enthusiastically supported economic growth. States often helped new ventures raise capital by passing laws of incorporation, by awarding entrepreneurs tax breaks or monopolies, by underwriting bonds for improvement projects (which increased their investment appeal), and by providing loans for internal improvements. New York, Pennsylvania, Ohio, Indiana, Illinois, and Virginia publicly financed almost 75 percent of the canal systems in their states between 1815 and 1860.

The national government also encouraged economic expansion by cooperating with states on some internal improvements, such as the national road from

Maryland to Illinois. Federal tariff policy shielded American products, and the second Bank of the United States provided the financial stability investors required. So widespread was the enthusiasm for growth that the line separating the public sector from the private often blurred.

The law also undergirded aggressive economic growth. Judicial decisions created a new understanding of property rights and increased predictability in the conduct of business. The case of *Palmer* v. *Mulligan,* decided by the New York State Supreme Court in 1805, determined that property ownership included the right to develop property for business purposes. Land was increasingly defined as a productive asset for exploitation, not merely subsistence. Contracts lay at the heart of commercial relationships, but contract law hardly existed in 1800. Between 1819 and 1824, major Supreme Court decisions established the basic principle that contracts were binding. In *Dartmouth College* v. *Woodward,* the Court held that a state charter could not be modified unless both parties agreed, and in *Sturges* v. *Crowninshield* it declared unconstitutional a New York law allowing debtors to repudiate debts.

A New Mentality

Economic expansion also depended on intangible factors. When a farmer decided to specialize in apples for the New York market rather than to concentrate on raising food for his family, he was thinking in a new way. So was a merchant who invested in banks that would, in turn, finance a variety of economic enterprises. The entrepreneurial outlook—the *"universal desire,"* as one newspaper editor put it, *"to get forward"*—was shared by millions of Americans. By encouraging investment, new business and agricultural ventures, and land speculation, it played a vital role in antebellum development.

Europeans often recognized other intangible factors. As one Frenchman observed in 1834, Americans were energetic and open to change. "All here is circulation, motion, and boiling agitation. Experiment follows experiment; enterprise succeeds to enterprise." Some saw an American mechanical "genius." "In Massachusetts and Connecticut," one Frenchman insisted, " there is not a labourer who had not invented a machine or tool." He exaggerated (many American innovations drew on British precedents and were introduced by immigrants familiar with the British originals), but every invention did attract scores of imitators.

Mechanically minded Americans prided themselves on developing efficient tools and machines. The McCormick harvester, the Colt revolver, Goodyear vulcanized rubber products, and the sewing machine—all were developed, refined, and developed further. Such improvements cut labor costs and increased efficiency. By 1840, the average American cotton textile mill was about 10 percent more efficient and 3 percent more profitable than its British counterpart.

Although the shortage of labor in the United States stimulated technological innovations that replaced humans with machines, the rapid spread of education after 1800 also spurred innovation and productivity. By 1840, most whites were literate, and public schools were educating 38.4 percent of white children between the ages of 5 and 19. The belief that education meant economic growth fostered enthusiasm for public education, particularly in the Northeast.

The development of the Massachusetts common school illustrates the connections many saw between education and progress. Although several states had decided to use tax monies for education by 1800, Massachusetts was the first to move toward mass education. In 1827, it mandated that taxes pay the whole cost of the state's public schools, and in 1836 it forbade factory managers to hire children who had not spent 3 of the previous 12 months in school. Still, the Massachusetts school system limped along with run-down school buildings, nonexistent curricula, and students with nothing to do.

Under the leadership of Horace Mann, the reform of state education for white children began in earnest in 1837. He and others pressed for graded schools, uniform curricula, and teacher training and fought the local control that often blocked progress. Mann's success inspired reformers everywhere. For the first time in American history, primary education became the rule for most children outside the South between ages 5 and 19. The expansion of education created a whole new career of schoolteaching, mostly attracting young women.

Mann believed that education promoted inventiveness. Businessmen often agreed. Prominent industrialists in the 1840s were convinced that education produced reliable workers who could handle complex machinery without undue supervision. Manufacturers valued education not merely because of its intellectual content, but also because it encouraged habits necessary for a disciplined and productive workforce.

Ambivalence Toward Change

While supporting education as a means to economic growth, many Americans also firmly believed in its social value. They expected public schools to mold student character and promote "virtuous habits." Rote learning taught discipline and concentration. The content of schoolbooks reinforced classroom goals.

This concern with education and character suggests that while Americans welcomed economic progress, they also feared its unsettling results. The improvements in transportation that encouraged trade and emigration also raised concerns that civilization might disintegrate as people moved far from familiar institutions. Others worried that rapid change undermined the American family and turned children into barbarians. Schools, which taught students to be deferential, obedient, and punctual, could counter the worst by-products of change.

Other signs of cultural uneasiness appeared. Popularizers in the 1830s reinforced Benjamin Franklin's message of hard work. As a publishing revolution lowered costs and speeded up printing, out poured tracts, stories, and self-help manuals touting diligence, punctuality, temperance, and thrift. All these habits probably assisted economic growth. But the success of early nineteenth-century economic ventures frequently depended on the ability to take risks. The emphasis these publicists gave to the safe but stolid virtues suggests their fear of social disintegration. Their books and tracts aimed to counter unsettling effects of change and reinforce middle-class values.

The Advance of Industrialization

As had been true for Great Britain in the eighteenth century, the advance of industrialization in the United States fueled economic growth in the decades before the

Civil War. As was also the case in Britain, economic changes spilled over to transform many other aspects of life. The types of work people did, the places where they labored, and the relationships they had with their bosses were all affected by new modes of production. The American class system was modified as a new working class dependent on wages emerged and as a new middle class took shape.

Factory production moved away from the decentralized system of artisan or family-based manufacturing using hand tools and reorganized work by breaking down the manufacture of an article into discrete steps. Manufacturers farmed out some steps to workers, both urban and rural, in shops and homes, paying them by the piece. This was the "putting-out" system. But other steps in the production process were consolidated in central shops, and eventually all the steps of production came under one roof, with hand labor gradually giving way to power-driven machinery such as "spinning jennies."

Sometimes, would-be American manufacturers sought the help of British immigrants with the experience and know-how that no American yet possessed. Thus in 1789 William Ashley and Moses Brown, Rhode Island merchants, hired 21-year-old Samuel Slater, a former apprentice in an English cotton textile mill, to devise a water-powered, yarn-spinning machine. Slater did that, but he also developed a machine capable of carding, or straightening, the cotton fibers. Within a year, Ashley and Brown's spinning mill had begun operations in Pawtucket, Rhode Island. Its initial workforce consisted of nine children, ranging in age from 7 to 12. Ten years later, their number had grown to more than 100. As factory workers replaced artisans and home manufacturers, the volume of goods rose, and prices dropped dramatically. The price of a yard of cotton cloth fell from 18 to 2 cents during the 45 years preceding the Civil War.

The transportation improvements that gave access to large markets after 1820 also encouraged the reorganization of production and the use of machinery. The simple tastes and rural character of the American people suggested the wisdom of manufacturing inexpensive everyday goods such as cloth and shoes rather than luxuries for the rich.

Between 1820 and 1860, textile manufacturing became the country's leading industry. Textile mills sprang up across the New England and middle Atlantic states. These regions had swift-flowing streams to power the mills, capitalists eager to finance ventures, children and women willing to tend machines, and numerous cities and towns with ready markets for cheap textiles. Early mills were small, containing only the machines for carding and spinning. The thread was then put out to home workers, who wove it into cloth. The early mechanization of cloth production supplemented, but did not replace, home manufacture.

Experiments were under way that would further transform the industry. In 1813, Boston merchant Francis Cabot Lowell and mechanic Paul Moody devised a power loom to weave cloth, based on Lowell's study of mechanical looms in England and Scotland. Eventually, they installed their loom in a mill at Waltham, Massachusetts, capitalized at $300,000 by Lowell and his Boston Associates.

The most important innovation of the Waltham operation was Lowell's decision to combine all the steps of cotton cloth production and all the workers under one roof. The Waltham mill thus differed from mills in Rhode Island and Great Britain, which separated spinning and weaving. Centralization allowed the profitable mass production of inexpensive cloth. In 1823, the Boston Associates

THE MANCHESTER PRINT WORKS, AT MANCHESTER, N. H.

A New Hampshire Printing Factory *Gleason's Pictorial,* one of the many modestly priced publications that the introduction of steam-powered printing presses put within reach of the reading public, pictures the Manchester Print Works in New Hampshire in 1854. How has the mill complex been depicted? What signs of pollution does the picture suggest? Men appear in the foreground, but over half the workers in this calico factory were female. *(Library of Congress)*

expanded their operations to Lowell, a renamed village on the Merrimack River. The Lowell system became the prototype for most New England mills. Although most of the South's cotton went to England, an increasing share flowed to northeastern mills.

The cumulative impact of the rise of the textile industry was to supplant the home production of cloth, though some women would continue to spin and weave for their families and hand-loom weavers would survive for another generation. More and more, Americans abandoned earth-colored homespun garments for clothes made of colorful manufactured cloth.

Textile mills and other manufacturing such as shoemaking gave the Northeast an increasingly industrial character. By 1860, fully 71 percent of all manufacturing workers lived there. Elsewhere, in communities of 200 families or more, power-driven machinery processed wheat, timber, and hides. Although a third of them were clustered in Philadelphia, paper mills were widespread. Ironworking and metalworking stretched from Albany, New York, to Maryland and Cincinnati.

Environmental Consequences

Although canals, railroads, steamboats, and the growth of industry stimulated economic growth, their impact on the environment was far-reaching and often harmful. Dams and canals supporting industrial activities contributed to erosion. The use of wood as fuel for steamboats, early railroads, and household stoves meant the destruction of eastern forests and their wildlife. Better transportation, which encouraged western migration, led to the disappearance of forest cover as settlers cleared land for crops and cut wood for housing. Sawmills and milldams interfered with the spawning of fish and changed the flow of rivers.

As late as 1840, wood provided for most of the country's energy needs. But its high price and the discovery of anthracite coal in Pennsylvania signaled the beginning of a shift to coal as the major power source. While the East gradually regained some of its forest cover, the heavy use of coal polluted the air. Acrid smells and black soot were part of urban life.

Anti-Railroad Poster in Philadelphia (1839)

Some Americans recognized the environmental consequences of rapid growth and change. "Industrial operations," declared the Vermont fish commissioner in 1857, are "destructive to fish that live or spawn in fresh water." Novelist James Fenimore Cooper had one of his characters in *The Pioneers* condemn those who destroyed nature "without remorse and without shame." Yet most Americans accepted a changing environment as the price of progress.

EARLY MANUFACTURING

Industrialization created a more efficient means of producing more goods at a much lower cost. A Philadelphian's diary described the new profusion and range of goods that he saw at an exhibition of American manufactures in 1833. "More than 700 articles have been sent," he noted. "Among this great variety, I distinguished the Philadelphia porcelains, beautiful Canton cotton, made at York in this state, soft and capacious blankets, silver plate, cabinet ware, marble mantels, splendid pianos and centre tables, chymical drugs, hardware, saddlery, and the most beautiful black broadcloth I ever saw."

Two examples illustrate how industrialization transformed American life in both simple and complex ways. Before the nineteenth century, local printing shops used manual labor to produce relatively expensive books and newspapers. Many literate families had little to read other than a Bible and an almanac. Between 1830 and 1850, however, the adoption and improvement of British inventions revolutionized the American printing and publishing industries. Like other changes in production, the transformation of publishing involved not only technological innovations, but also managerial and marketing changes. A $2.5 million market in 1830, the book business quintupled by 1850.

As books and magazines dropped in cost and grew in number, far more people could afford them. This new mass market of readers provided the basis for Susan Warner's literary success. Inexpensive reading material inspired and nourished literacy, and it encouraged a new sort of independence. Freed of depending on the "better sort" for information, people could form their own views from what they read. At the same time, however, readers everywhere were exposed repeatedly to the mainstream norms expressed in magazines and books. Even pioneer women could study inexpensive ladies' magazines or draw inspiration from *The Wide, Wide World*. Their husbands could follow political news, prices, and theories about scientific farming; their children learned to read from the moralistic McGuffey readers.

Meanwhile, the making of inexpensive timepieces affected the pace and rhythms of American life. Before the 1830s, owning a clock was a luxury, making exact planning and scheduling almost impossible. But by mid-century inexpensive mass-produced clocks could be found everywhere, encouraging a more disciplined use of time. Timepieces were essential for the successful operation of railroads and steamboats and imposed a new rhythm in many workplaces—for some Americans, representing a new form of oppression.

A NEW ENGLAND TEXTILE TOWN

The process of industrialization and its impact on work and the workforce are well illustrated by Lowell, the "model" Massachusetts textile town, and Cincinnati, a bustling midwestern industrial center. Though the communities shared certain traits, there were also significant differences. Lowell reveals the importance of women in the early stages of industrialization, while Cincinnati shows that industrialization was often an uneven and complex process.

Lowell was planned and built for industrial purposes in the 1820s. Planners focused on its shops, mills, and worker housing, but the bustling town had a charm that prompted visitors to see it as a model factory community. In 1836, Lowell, with 17,000 inhabitants, was the country's most important textile center.

DOCUMENT

Visit to the
Shakers, *Lowell
Offering* (1841)

Lowell's planners, understanding the difficulty of luring men away from farming, realized that they might recruit unmarried women relatively cheaply for a stint in the mills. Unlike factory owners farther south, they decided not to depend on child labor. By hiring women who would work only until marriage, they hoped to avoid the depraved and depressed workforce so evident in Great Britain. New England factory communities, they hoped, would become models for the world. By 1830, women composed nearly 70 percent of the Lowell textile workforce. As the first women to labor outside their homes in large numbers, they were also among the first Americans to experience the full impact of the factory system.

Working and Living in a Mill Town

IMAGE

Mill in West
Virginia

At the age of 15, Mary Paul wrote to her father asking him "to consent to let me go to Lowell if you can." This young woman from Vermont was typical of those drawn to work in Lowell. In 1830, more than 63 percent of Lowell's population was female, and most were between the ages of 15 and 29.

Women workers came from New England's middling rural families and took jobs in the mills for a variety of reasons, but desperate poverty was not one of them. The decline of home manufacture deprived many women, especially daughters in farming families, of their traditional productive role. Some had already earned money at home by taking in piecework. Millwork offered them a chance for economic independence, better wages than domestic service, and an interesting environment. Few made a permanent commitment by coming to Lowell. They came to work for a few years, felt free to go home or to school for a few months, and then return to millwork. Once married—and the majority of women did marry—they left the mill workforce forever.

Millwork was regimented and exhausting. Six days a week, the workers began their 12-hour day at dawn or earlier with only a half hour for breakfast and lunch. Within the factory, the organization of space facilitated production. In the basement was the waterwheel, the source of power. Above, successive floors were completely open, each containing the machines necessary for the different steps of cloth making. Elevators moved materials from one floor to another. Under the watchful eyes of male overseers, the women tended their machines. Work spaces were noisy, poorly lit, and badly ventilated, the windows often nailed shut.

Millwork required the women to adapt to both new work and new living situations. Hoping to attract respectable and productive female workers, mill owners built company boardinghouses for them. Headed by female housekeepers, the boardinghouse maintained strict rules, including a 10 P.M. curfew, and afforded little personal privacy. The cramped quarters encouraged close ties and a sense of community. Group norms dictated acceptable behavior, clothing, and speech. Shared leisure activities included lectures, night classes, sewing and literary circles, and church.

Female Responses to Work

Millwork offered better wages than other occupations open to women, but female workers had limited job mobility and received lower wages than men. Even those with the best female positions never earned as much as senior male employees. Economic and job discrimination characterized the American industrial system from the beginning.

DOCUMENT

"A Second Peep at Factory Life," *Lowell Offering* (1845)

Job discrimination generally went unquestioned; but the sense of sisterhood, so central to the Lowell work experience, encouraged protest against a system that workers feared was turning them into dependent wage earners. Lowell women's critique of the new industrial order drew on both the sense of female community and the revolutionary tradition.

Trouble began when hard times hit Lowell in February 1834. Falling prices, poor sales, and rising inventories prompted managers to announce a 15 percent wage cut. The millworkers sprang into action, threatening a strike. At one lunchtime gathering, the company agent, hoping to end the protests, fired an apparent ringleader. But, as the agent reported, "she declared that every girl in the room should leave with her," then "made a signal, and ... they all marched out and few returned the ensuing morning." Strikers roamed the streets appealing to other workers and visited other mills. In all, about a sixth of the workforce turned out.

Though this work stoppage was brief and failed to prevent the wage reduction, it demonstrated women workers' concern about the impact of industrialization on the labor force. Viewing wage reductions as an attack on their economic independence, strikers linked their protest to their fathers' and grandfathers' struggles against British oppression during the Revolution.

During the 1830s, wage cuts, long hours, increased workloads, and production speedups mandated by owners' desires to protect profits constantly reminded Lowell women and other textile workers of the possibility of "wage slavery." In Dover, New Hampshire, 800 women formed a union in 1834 to protest wage cuts. In the 1840s, women in several New

DOCUMENT

"A Week in the Mill," *Lowell Offering* (1845)

England states agitated for the 10-hour day, and petitions from Lowell prompted the Massachusetts legislature to hold the first official hearings on industrial working conditions.

The Changing Character of the Workforce

Most protest efforts had limited success. The short tenure of most women mill-workers prevented permanent labor organizations, and owners could easily replace strikers. Increasingly, owners found that they could do without the Yankee women altogether. The waves of immigration that deposited so many penniless foreigners in northeastern cities in the 1840s and 1850s created a new pool of labor, desperate for jobs and willing to work for less than New England farm girls. By 1860, Irish men composed nearly half the workers. A permanent workforce, once the owners' nightmare, became a reality by 1860. Lowell's reputation as a model factory town faded away.

The transformation of the Lowell workforce suggests the far-reaching impact of massive immigration on antebellum life. Immigration, of course, had been a constant part of the country's experience from the early seventeenth century. But what had been a trickle in the 1820s—some 128,502 foreigners came to U.S. shores during that decade—became a torrent in the 1850s, with more than 2.8 million migrants to the United States. The majority of the newcomers were young European men of working age.

This vast movement of people, which continued throughout the nineteenth century, resulted from dramatic changes in European life. Between 1750 and 1845, Europe experienced a population explosion. New farming and industrial practices undermined or destroyed traditional means of livelihood. Agricultural disaster uprooted the Irish from their homeland. In 1845, a terrible blight attacked and destroyed the potato crop, the staple of the Irish peasant diet. Years of famine followed. One million Irish starved to death between 1841 and 1851; another million and a half emigrated. The Irish were the most numerous of all newcomers to America in the two decades preceding the Civil War, usually arriving penniless and with only their unskilled labor to sell.

German immigrants, the second-largest group of immigrants during this period (1,361,506 arrived between 1840 and 1859), were not driven to the United States by the same kind of desperate circumstances as the Irish. Some even arrived with sufficient resources to go west and buy land. Others had the training to join the urban working class as shoemakers, cabinetmakers, and tailors.

The arrival of so many non-British newcomers made American society more diverse. Because more than half of the Irish and German immigrants were Roman Catholics, religious differences exacerbated economic and ethnic tensions.

FACTORIES ON THE FRONTIER

Cincinnati, a small Ohio River settlement of 2,540 in 1810, grew to be the country's third-largest industrial center by 1840. With a population of 40,382, it had a variety of industries at different stages of development. Manufacturers who turned out machines, machine parts, hardware, and furniture quickly mecha-

Cincinnati and the Ohio River In 1848, an unknown photographer took this picture of Cincinnati. What indications are there of the causes of the city's growth? While the countryside is visible in the background, what are the signs of Cincinnati's status as a bustling urban center? *(From the Collection of the Public Library of Cincinnati and Hamilton County. Photo by Charles Fontayne and William S. Porter)*

nized. Other trades, like carriage making and cigar making, moved far more slowly toward mechanization. Artisans still labored in small shops, using traditional hand tools. The new and the old coexisted in Cincinnati, as in most manufacturing towns.

No uniform work experience prevailed in Cincinnati. Some craftsmen continued to employ a wide array of skills to produce goods in time-honored ways. Others used their skills in new factories, focusing on more specialized tasks. Though in the long run machines threatened to replace them, skilled factory workers often had reason in the short run to praise the factory's opportunities. Less fortunate was the new class of unskilled factory laborers who performed limited operations at their jobs, with or without machinery. Having no skills, they were easily replaced, and during business slowdowns were casually dismissed.

Cincinnati's working women had a different work experience. A majority of black women labored as washerwomen, cooks, or maids. Many white women earned money as "outworkers" for the city's growing ready-to-wear clothing industry. Manufacturers purchased the cloth, cut it into basic patterns, and then contracted out the finishing work to women in small workshops or at home. Like many other urban women, Cincinnati women sought such employment because their husbands or fathers did not bring in enough to support the family and because outwork allowed them to earn money at home. Middle-class domestic ideology prescribed that home, not the workplace, was the proper sphere for women.

Many working men supported these views because they feared female labor would undercut their wages and destroy order in the family.

Paid by the piece, female outworkers were among the most exploited of Cincinnati's workers. Long days of sewing in darkened rooms not only often failed to bring an adequate financial reward, but also led to ruined eyes and curved spines. The introduction of sewing machines in the 1850s made stitching easier, increasing both the pool of potential workers and the volume of work expected.

Cincinnati employers claimed that the new industrial order offered great opportunities to most of the city's male citizens. Manufacturing work encouraged the "manly virtues" necessary for the "republican citizen." Not all Cincinnati workers agreed. The workingman's plight, as Cincinnati labor leaders analyzed it, stemmed from his loss of independence. The reorganization of work meant that few could expect to rise from apprentice to independent craftsman. The new worker, with only his raw labor to sell, toiled for others rather than for himself. His "wage slavery," or dependence on wages, promised to be lifelong.

Workers also resented attempts to control their lives. In the new factories, owners insisted on a steady pace of work and uninterrupted production. Artisans accustomed to working in spurts, stopping for a few moments of conversation or a drink, disliked the new routines. Those who took a dram or two at work got fired. Even outside the workplace, manufacturers attacked Cincinnati's working-class culture. Middle-class crusades to abolish "nonproductive" volunteer fire companies and saloons suggested how little equality the Cincinnati worker enjoyed in an industrializing society.

The fact that workers' wages in Cincinnati, as in other cities, lagged behind food and housing costs compounded discontent. The working class sensed it was losing ground just as the city's rich were visibly growing richer. In 1817, the top tenth of the city's taxpayers owned over half the wealth, whereas the bottom half possessed 10 percent. In 1860, the share of the top tenth had increased to two-thirds, and the bottom half's share had shrunk to 2.4 percent.

In the decades before the Civil War, Cincinnati workers, like workers in other communities, formed unions, struck for fair wages, and rallied for the 10-hour day. Using similar language as the Lowell mill girls, they cloaked their protest with the mantle of the Revolution. Because the republic depended on a free and independent citizenry, male workers warned that their bosses' policies undermined the republic itself.

Only in the early 1850s did Cincinnati workers begin to suspect that their employers formed a distinct class of parasitic "nonproducers." Although most strikes still revolved around familiar issues of better hours and wages, signs appeared of the more hostile labor relations that would emerge after the Civil War.

As elsewhere, skilled workers were in the forefront of Cincinnati's labor protest and union activities. But they won only temporary victories. Depression and bad times always hurt labor organizations and canceled employers' concessions. Furthermore, Cincinnati workers did not readily unite, for the uneven pace of industrialization meant that they, unlike the Lowell mill women, had no common working experience. Growing cultural, religious, and ethnic diversity compounded workplace differences. By 1850, almost half the people in the city were foreign-born (mostly German), whereas only 22 percent had been in 1825. Ethnic and religious tensions simmered. Immigrants faced limited job choices and cultural suspicions, which exploded in Cincinnati in the spring of 1855. Americans attacked barricades in German neighborhoods, shouting death threats. Their wrath visited the Irish as well. Ethnic, cultural, and social differences often drove workers apart, enabling businesses to maximize productivity and profits.

URBAN LIFE

Americans experienced the impact of economic growth most dramatically in the cities. In the four decades before the Civil War, the rate of urbanization in the United States rose faster than ever before or since. In 1820, about 9 percent of Americans lived in cities (defined as areas with a population of 2,500 or more). Forty years later, almost 20 percent of them did. Older cities such as Philadelphia and New York mushroomed, while new cities such as Cincinnati, Columbus, and Chicago sprang up "as if by enchantment." Urban growth was most dramatic in the East. By 1860, more than a third of the people living in the Northeast were urban residents, compared with only 14 percent of westerners and 7 percent of southerners.

Urbanization played an important role in sustaining economic expansion. The growing number of urban dwellers represented new markets for farmers and

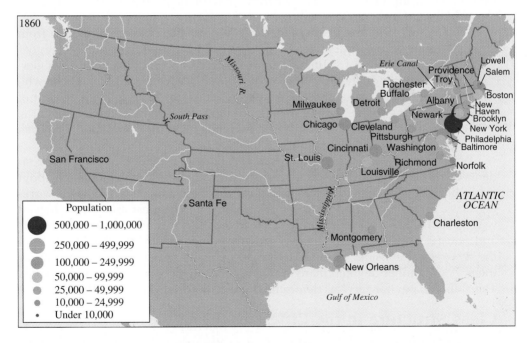

URBAN GROWTH IN 1820 AND 1850 In 1820, there were few very large cities in the United States, and most of them were located along the Atlantic coast. This map shows urban growth by 1850. What are the important features of the map and what forces lie behind them? *(Data Source: Statistical Abstract of the United States)*

for manufacturers of shoes and clothing, furniture and carriages, and cast-iron stoves. City governments purchased cast-iron pipes for sewers and water supply, and city merchants erected cast iron buildings.

The Process of Urbanization

Three distinct types of cities—commercial centers, mill towns, and transportation hubs—emerged during these years of rapid economic growth. Although a lack of waterpower limited industrial development, commercial seaports such as Boston, Philadelphia, and Baltimore expanded steadily and developed diversified manufacturing to supplement the older functions of importing, exporting, and providing services and credit. New York replaced Philadelphia as the country's largest and most important city. The completion of the Erie Canal allowed New York merchants to gain control of much of the trade with the West. By 1840, they had also seized the largest share of the country's import and export trade.

Access to waterpower spurred the development of a second kind of city, exemplified by Lowell, Massachusetts; Trenton, New Jersey; and Wilmington, Delaware. Situated inland along the waterfalls and rapids that provided the power to run their mills, these cities burgeoned.

A third type of city arose between 1820 and 1840, west of the Appalachian Mountains, where one-quarter of the nation's urban growth occurred. Louisville, Cleveland, and St. Louis typified cities that served as transportation and distribution centers from the earliest days of frontier settlement. In the 1850s, Chicago's most significant business was selling lumber to prairie farmers.

DOCUMENT

Samuel F. B. Morse, Foreign Immigration (1835)

Until 1840, the people eagerly crowding into cities came mostly from the American countryside. Then ships began to spill their human cargoes into eastern seaports. Immigrants who could afford it, many of them Germans or Scandinavians, left crowded port cities for the interior. Those who were penniless sought work in eastern cities. By 1860, fully 20 percent of those living in the Northeast were immigrants; in some of the largest cities, they and their children comprised more than half the population. The Irish were the largest foreign group in the Northeast.

While a few cities, such as New York and Boston, provided parks where residents could escape from the sounds, noises, and smells of urban life, much about urban life was grimy and difficult, especially for those who belonged to the working class. Speculators, finding the grid pattern the cheapest and most efficient way to divide land for development, created miles of monotonous new streets and houses. Overwhelmed by rapid growth, city governments provided few of the services we consider essential today, and usually only to those who paid for them. Poor families devoted many hours to securing necessities, including water. The ability to pay for services determined not only comfort, but health.

Class Structure in the Cities

The drastic differences in the quality of urban life reflected social fluidity and the growing economic inequality that characterized many American cities. In contrast to the colonial period, the first half of the nineteenth century witnessed a dramatic rise in the concentration of wealth in the United States. The pattern was most extreme in cities.

Because Americans believed that capitalists deserved most of their profits, the well-to-do profited handsomely from this period of growth, whereas workers lost ground. Philadelphia provides one example of these economic trends. The merchants, brokers, lawyers, bankers, and manufacturers of Philadelphia's upper class gained increasing control of the city's wealth. By the late 1840s, the wealthiest 4 percent of the population held about two-thirds of the wealth. Because more wealth was being generated, the widening gap between the upper class and the working class did not cause mass suffering. But growing inequality hardened class lines and contributed to labor protests.

Between 1820 and 1860, a new working and middle class took shape in Philadelphia and elsewhere. As preindustrial ways of producing goods yielded to factory production and as the pace of economic activity quickened, some former artisans and skilled workers seized newly created opportunities. Perhaps 10 to 15 percent of Philadelphians in each decade before the Civil War improved their occupations and places of residence. Increasingly, membership in this middle class meant having a nonmanual occupation and a special place of work suited to activities depending on brainpower rather than brawn. But downward occupational mobility increased. Former artisans or journeymen became part of a new class of permanent manual workers, dependent on wages. Fed by waves of immigrants, the lower class grew at an accelerating rate. The percentage of unskilled wage earners living in poverty or on its brink increased from 17 to 24 percent between 1820 and 1860, while the proportion of craftsmen, once the heart of the laboring class, shrank from 56 to 47 percent.

The Urban Working Class

As with so much else in urban life, housing patterns reflected social and economic divisions. Behind substantial houses on the main streets lay slums in back unpaved alleys and streets, where garbage accumulated and privies overflowed. The poorest rented quarters in crowded, flimsy shacks and two-room houses. Because they moved often, it was difficult for them to create close-knit neighborhoods and support networks.

Slums were not just abodes of poverty; they represented the transformation of working-class family life. Men could no longer be sure of supporting their wives and children; even when they were employed, they felt that they had lost much of their authority and power in the family. The shortage of money contributed to family tensions and misunderstandings. Some men thought their wives too independent or careless with money. One woman angered her husband by failing to explain clearly what she had done with the grocery money. This squabble over grocery money ended in murder. Although this was an extreme case, family violence that spilled out onto the streets was not uncommon in working-class quarters.

Middle-Class Life and Ideals

Members of the new middle class profited from the dramatic increase in wealth in antebellum America. They lived in pleasantly furnished houses, enjoying more peace, more privacy, and more comfort. Franklin stoves gave warmth in winter, and iron cookstoves made cooking easier. New lamps made it possible to read after dark. Bathing stands and bowls ensured higher standards of cleanliness.

African Americans in Philadelphia This cartoon was one of a series entitled "Life in Philadelphia." Philadelphia had a large, free African American community that often became the target for racial animosity. In what ways has the cartoonist presented a negative picture of the man and woman in the cartoon? Notice the exaggerated racial features of the two figures and the overelaborate clothing of the dandified man passing his card to the woman coming up from the basement. The verbal message reinforced the visual one. The man asks, "Is Miss Dinah at home?" The woman replies, "Yes sir but she bery potickly engaged in washing de dishes." He replies, "Ah! I'm sorry I cant have the honour to pay my devours to her. Give her my card." *(The Print & Picture Collection, The Free Library of Philadelphia)*

Genteel behavior, proper dress, and an elegantly furnished parlor all identified one as middle class.

New expectations about male and female roles, prompted partly by economic change, also shaped middle-class life. In the seventeenth and eighteenth centuries, the labor of men and women, adults and children, had all been necessary for the family's economic welfare. But in the nineteenth century, improved transportation, new products, and the rise of factory production and large businesses changed the family economy. Falling prices for processed and manufactured goods such as soap, candles, clothing, and even bread made it unnecessary for women (except those on the frontier) to continue making these items at home.

As men increasingly involved themselves in a money economy, whether through commerce or market farming, women's and children's economic contributions to the family welfare became relatively less significant. Even the rhythm of their lives, oriented to housework rather than the demands of the clock, separated them from their husbands' bustling commercial world. By 1820, these changing circumstances supported the conventional wisdom that the sexes had different innate characteristics and occupied separate spheres. Men were seen as naturally aggressive, intellectual, and active, at home in the public world of politics, business, and commerce. They were responsible for supporting their families in middle-class comfort—not always an easy duty, as Susan Warner's family experience suggested. Women, by contrast, were perceived as innately pious, virtuous, unselfish, and modest. This conception, based upon ideas first advanced in revolutionary days, suggested that women should operate in the private or domestic sphere, where they would train children in the virtues and habits necessary for the welfare of the republic and society. Just as important, they were expected to create peaceful retreats for husbands returning from the cares and harried rhythms of the public world.

No longer producers but housekeepers, women discovered both pleasures and frustrations in their new role. Susan Warner celebrated the coziness of domestic life in her novels. Yet it was sometimes impossible to create a harmonious home and meet the new standards of cleanliness, order, and beauty. Catharine Beecher's "Words of Comfort for a Discouraged Housekeeper" listed just some of the problems—inconvenient houses, sick children, poor domestics—that undermined efforts to meet the domestic ideal.

In actuality, the notion of separate spheres was far more flexible in real life than it appeared on paper. There was considerable overlap in the activities and roles of men and women. Many middle-class men were involved in child rearing and domestic life, for example, and some middle-class women, like Susan Warner, actually became breadwinners for their families. Furthermore, some aspects of reinterpretation of women's role and nature could encourage women to extend their interest in the public world.

Although the concept of domesticity emphasized women's domestic role, "Woman," as Sarah Hale, editor of the popular magazine *Godey's Lady's Book*, pointed out, was "God's appointed agent of *morality*." This insistence on women's moral nature encouraged women to join voluntary female associations that mushroomed in the early nineteenth century. Although initially most involved religious and charitable activities, women undertook activities in the public world, supporting orphanages, paying for and distributing religious tracts and Bibles, establishing Sunday schools, and ministering to the poor. By the 1830s, as we shall see in Chapter 12, women added specific moral concerns including the abolition of slavery to their missionary and benevolent efforts. As these women took on more active and controversial tasks, they often clashed with men and with social conventions about "woman's place."

While domesticity described norms rather than the actual conduct of white middle-class women, the ideas, expressed so movingly by novelists like Susan Warner, influenced how women thought of themselves. They also promoted "female" behavior by encouraging particular choices and helped many women make psychological sense of their lives. New standards for behavior also operated as a way of clarifying social boundaries between the middle class and those below them on the social scale.

Still, the new norms, effectively spread by the publishing industry, also influenced rural and urban working women. The insistence on marriage and service to family discouraged married women from entering the workforce. Those who had to work often bore a burden of guilt. Many accepted badly paid piecework so that they could stay home. Though the new feminine ideal may have suited middle-class women in cities and towns, it created difficult tensions in the lives of working-class women.

As family roles were reformulated, a new view of childhood emerged. Middle-class children were no longer expected to contribute economically to the family. Middle-class parents now came to see childhood as a special stage of life, a period of preparation for adulthood. In a child's early years, mothers were to impart important values, including the necessity of behaving in accordance with gender prescriptions. Harsh punishments lost favor. Children's fiction, which poured off the printing presses, reinforced maternal training, picturing modest youngsters happily making the correct choices of playmates and activities, obeying their parents, and being dutiful, religious, loving, and industrious. Schooling also prepared a child for the future, and urban middle-class parents supported the public school movement.

New notions of family life that emphasized a child's need for affection and careful preparation for adulthood suggested smaller families and the use of contraception. The declining birthrate evident first in the Northeast, particularly in cities and among the middle class, shows that families were limiting births. Abortion, which was legal in many states until 1860, terminated perhaps as many as a third of all pregnancies. Other birth control methods included coitus interruptus and abstinence. The success of these methods that relied on self-control suggests that many men and women may have internalized the view of the female sex as naturally affectionate but passionless and sexually restrained.

Mounting Urban Tensions

The social and economic changes transforming American cities and festering ethnic and racial tensions in the half century before the Civil War produced unprecedented urban violence. Mob actions sometimes lasted for days because there was no force strong enough to quell group disorder. American cities were slow to establish modern police forces. Traditional constables and night watches did not try to stop crimes, discover offenses, or "prevent a tumult."

An unsavory riot in Philadelphia in August 1834 revealed not only racial and social antagonisms but also the inability of the city's police force to control the mob. Starting off with the destruction of a merry-go-round patronized by both blacks and whites, the riot turned into an orgy of destruction, looting, and intimidation of black residents. In the several days of violence, at least one black was killed and numerous others injured. As one shocked eyewitness reported, "The mob exhibited more than fiendish brutality, beating and mutilating some of the old, confiding and unoffending blacks with a savageness surpassing anything we could have believed men capable of."

This racial explanation overlooked the range of causes underlying the rampage of fury and destruction. The rioters were young and generally of low social standing. Many were Irish; some had criminal records. A number of those arrested, however, were from a "class of mechanics of whom better things are expected," and middle-class onlookers egged the mob on. The rioters revealed that in the event of an "attack by the city police, they confidently counted" on the assistance of these bystanders.

The mob's composition hints at some of the reasons for participation. Many of the rioters were newly arrived Irish immigrants at the bottom of the economic ladder who competed with blacks for jobs. Subsequent violence against blacks suggested that economic rivalry was an important component of the riot. But if blacks threatened the dream of advancement of some whites, this was not the complaint of the skilled workers. These men were more likely to have believed themselves injured by a changing economic system that undermined the small-scale mode of production. Dreams of a better life seemed increasingly illusory as declining wages pushed them closer to unskilled workers than to the middle class. Like other rioters, they were living in one of the poorest and most crowded parts of the city. Their immediate scapegoats were blacks, but the intangible villain was the economic system itself.

Urban expansion also figured as a factor in the racial violence. Most of the rioters lived either in the riot area or nearby. Racial tensions generated by squalid surroundings and social proximity go far to explain the outbreak of violence. The same area would later become the scene of race riots and election trouble and became infamous for harboring criminals and juvenile gangs. The absence of middle- or upper-class participants did not mean that these groups were untroubled during times of growth and change, but their material circumstances cushioned them from some of the more unsettling forces.

Philadelphia, like other eastern cities, was beginning to create a police force, but only continued disorder would convince residents and city officials there (and in other large cities) to support an expanded, quasi-military, preventive, and uniformed police force. By 1855, most sizable eastern cities had such forces.

Finally, the character of the free black community itself was a factor in producing those gruesome August events. Not only was the community large and visible, but it also had created its own institutions and its own elite. The mob vented its rage against black affluence by targeting the solid brick houses of middle-class blacks and robbing them of silver and watches. Black wealth threatened the notion of the proper social order held by many white Philadelphians and seemed unspeakable when whites could not afford life's basic necessities or lacked jobs.

The Black Underclass

Despite the emergence of small African American elites, most blacks failed to benefit from economic expansion and industrial progress. Black men, often with little or no education, held transient and frequently dangerous jobs. Black women, many of whom headed their households because men were away working or had died, held jobs before and after marriage. In Philadelphia in 1849, almost half of the black women washed clothes for a living. Others took boarders into their homes, adding to their domestic chores.

Northern whites, like southerners, believed in black inferiority and depravity and feared black competition for jobs and resources. Although northern states had passed gradual abolition acts between 1780 and 1803 and the national government had banned slaves from the Northwest Territory, nowhere did any government extend equal rights and citizenship or economic opportunities to free blacks. In the 1830s, black men in most northern states began losing the right to vote, and by 1840 fully 93 percent of the northern free black population lived in states where law or custom kept them from the polls. In five northern states, blacks could not testify against whites or serve on juries. In most states, the two races were thoroughly segregated in railway cars, steamboats, hospitals, prisons, and other asylums. In some states, they could enter public buildings only as personal servants of white men. They sat in "Negro pews" in churches and took communion only after whites had left the church.

As the Philadelphia riot revealed, whites were driving blacks from their jobs. In 1839, *The Colored American* blamed the Irish. "These impoverished and destitute beings ... are crowding themselves into every place of business ... and driving the poor colored American citizen out." Increasingly after 1837, these "white niggers" became coachmen, stevedores, barbers, cooks, house servants—all occupations blacks had once held.

Educational opportunities for blacks were also severely limited. Only a few school systems admitted blacks, in separate facilities. In 1833, when Prudence Crandall, a Quaker schoolmistress in Canterbury, Connecticut, tried to admit "young colored ladies and Misses" to her private school, townspeople used intimidation and violence to block her. Eventually she was arrested, and after two trials—in which free blacks were declared to have no citizenship rights—she finally gave up and moved to Illinois.

Crandall likely did not find the Old Northwest much more hospitable. The fast-growing western states were intensely committed to white supremacy and black exclusion. In 1829 in Cincinnati, where evidence of freedom papers and $500 bond were demanded of blacks who wanted to live in the city, white rioters ran nearly 2,000 blacks out of town. An Indiana senator proclaimed in 1850 that a black could "never live together equally" with whites because "the same power that has given him a black skin, with less weight or volume of brain, has given us a white skin with greater volume of brain and intellect." Abraham Lincoln in neighboring Illinois, soon to be a nationally prominent politician, would not have disagreed.

RURAL COMMUNITIES

Although the percentage of families involved in farming fell from 72 to 60 percent between 1820 and 1860, agriculture represented the country's most significant economic activity and the source of most of its exports. The small family farm still characterized eastern and western agriculture.

Agriculture changed in the antebellum period, however. Vast new tracts of land came under cultivation in the West. Railroads, canals, and better roads drew rural Americans into a wider world. Some crops were shipped to regional markets; others, such as grain, hides, and pork, stimulated industrial processing. Manufactured goods, ranging from cloth to better tools, flowed in return to farm families. Like city dwellers, farmers and their families read books, magazines, and papers that exposed them to new ideas. Commercial farming encouraged different ways of thinking and acting and lessened the isolation that was so typical before 1820.

Farming in the East

Antebellum economic changes created new rural patterns in the Northeast. Marginal lands in New England, New York, and Pennsylvania, cultivated as more fertile lands ran out, yielded discouraging returns. Gradually, after 1830, farmers abandoned these farms, forest reclaimed farmland, and the New England hill country began a slow decline.

Those farmers who did not migrate west had to transform production. Unable to compete with western grain, they embraced new agricultural opportunities created by better transportation and growing urban markets. The extension of railroad lines into rural areas, for example, allowed farmers as far away as Vermont to

Preparing for Market This 1856 print shows the farm as a center of human and animal activity. What signs of the shifts in eastern agriculture can you find as farmers responded to competition from the Midwest? The rise of commercial farming also encouraged technological innovations like the McCormick reaper, patented in 1834. *(Art Resource, NY)*

ship cooled milk to the city. Other farmers used the new railroads to ship fruit and vegetables to the cities. By 1837, a Boston housewife could buy a wide variety of fresh vegetables and fruits, ranging from cauliflower to raspberries, at the central market. Cookbooks began to include recipes calling for fresh ingredients.

As northern farmers adopted new crops, they began to regard farming as a scientific endeavor. After 1800, northern farmers started using manure as fertilizer; by the 1820s, some farmers were rotating their crops and planting new grasses and clover to restore fertility to the soil. These techniques recovered worn-out wheat and tobacco lands in Maryland and Delaware for livestock farming. While farmers in the Delaware River valley were leaders in adopting new methods, interest in scientific farming was widespread. New journals informed readers of modern farming practices, and many states established agricultural agencies. Although wasteful farming practices did not disappear, they became less characteristic of the Northeast. Improved farming methods contributed to increased agricultural output and helped reverse a 200-year decline in farm productivity in some of the oldest areas of settlement. A "scientific" farmer in 1850 could often produce two to four times as much per acre as in 1820. Experimentation and the exchange of information also led to the development of thousands of special varieties of plants for local conditions by 1860.

Rural attitudes also changed. Cash transactions replaced the exchange of goods. Country stores became more reluctant to accept wood, rye, corn, oats, and butter as payment for goods instead of cash. As some farmers adopted the "get-ahead" ethic and entered the market economy, those who were content with just getting along fell behind. Wealth inequality increased throughout the rural Northeast.

Frontier Families

In 1820, less than one-fifth of the American population lived west of the Appalachians. By 1860, almost half did, and Ohio and Illinois had become two of the nation's most populous states.

American Stage Wagon

After the War of 1812, Americans flooded into the Old Northwest, settling first along the Ohio River and sending corn and pork down the Ohio and Mississippi to southern buyers. By 1830, Ohio, Indiana, and southern Illinois were heavily settled, but Michigan, northern Illinois, Wisconsin, and parts of Iowa and Missouri were still frontier.

The 1830s were boom times in the Old Northwest. Changes in federal land policy, which reduced both prices and the minimum acreage a settler had to buy, helped stimulate migration. Eastern capital contributed to the boom with loans, mortgages, and speculative buying. Internal improvement schemes after 1830 facilitated settlement and tied the Old Northwest firmly to the East. These links increasingly encouraged farmers to ship wheat east rather than concentrating on corn and hogs for the southern market. Between 1840 and 1860, Illinois, southern Wisconsin, and eastern Iowa became the country's fastest-growing grain regions.

Although the Old Northwest passed rapidly through the frontier stage between 1830 and 1860, its farming families faced severe challenges. Western farms were small, for there were limits to what a family with hand tools could manage. A family with two healthy men could care for about 50 acres. In wooded areas, it took several years to get even that much land under cultivation, for only a few acres could be cleared in a year.

It took capital to begin farming—a minimum initial investment of perhaps $100 for 80 acres of government land, $300 for basic farming equipment, and another $100 or $150 for livestock. To buy an already "improved" farm cost more, and free bidding at government auctions could drive the price of unimproved federal land far above the minimum price. Once farmers moved onto the prairies of Indiana and Illinois, they needed an initial investment of about $1,000, because they had to buy materials for fencing, housing, and expensive steel plows. If farmers invested in the new horse-drawn reapers, they could cultivate more land, but all their costs also increased.

Opportunities in the Old Northwest

It was possible to begin farming with less, however. Some farmers borrowed; others rented land from farmers who had bought more acres than they could manage. Tenants furnishing their own seeds and animals could expect to keep about a third of the yield, and within a few years some could buy their own farms. Those without capital could earn good wages as farmhands. Five to ten years of frugal living and steady work would bring the sum needed to get started. Probably about a quarter of the western farm population consisted of young men laboring as tenants or hired hands.

Widespread ownership of land characterized western rural communities. Unlike in the cities, there was no growing class of propertyless wage earners. But there were inequalities. In Butler County, Ohio, for example, 16 percent of people leaving wills in the 1830s held half the wealth; by 1860, the wealthiest 8 percent held half the wealth. Nevertheless, the Northwest offered many American families the chance to become independent producers and to enjoy a "pleasing competence." The rigors of frontier life faded with time.

Commercial farming brought new patterns of family life. As one Illinois farmer told his wife and daughter, "Store away ... all of your utensils for weaving cloth up in the loft. The boys and I can make enough by increasing our herds." Many farm families had money to spend on new goods. As early as 1836, the *Dubuque Visitor* was advertising the availability of ready-made clothing and "Calicoes, Ginghams, Muslins, Cambricks, Laces and Ribbands."

Agriculture and the Environment

Shifting agricultural patterns in the East and expanding settlement into the Old Northwest contributed to the changing character of the American landscape. John Audubon, the naturalist, mused in 1826 that "a century hence," the rivers, swamps, and mountains "will not be here as I see them." A French visitor remarked that Americans would never be satisfied until they had subdued nature.

More than the subjugation of nature was involved, however. When eastern farmers abandoned marginal lands, the process of reforestation was under way.

TIMELINE

1820	Lowell founded by Boston Associates
	Land Act of 1820
	The expression "woman's sphere" becomes current
1824–1850	Construction of canals in the Northeast
1825–1856	Construction of canals linking the Ohio, the Mississippi, and the Great Lakes

1828	Baltimore & Ohio Railroad begins operation
1830s	Boom in the Old Northwest
	Increasing discrimination against free blacks
	Public education movement spreads
1837–1844	Financial panic and depression
1840s–1850s	Rising tide of immigration

When they changed their agricultural practices as they became involved in the market economy, their decisions left an imprint on the land. Selling wood and potash stimulated clearing of forests. So did the desire for new tools, plow castings, threshing machines, or wagon boxes, which were produced in furnaces fueled by charcoal. As forests disappeared, so did their wildlife. Even using mineral manures such as gypsum or lime or organic fertilizers such as guano to revitalize worn-out soil and increase crop yields depleted land elsewhere.

When farmers moved into the Old Northwest, they used new steel plows, like the one developed in 1837 by Illinois blacksmith John Deere. Unlike older eastern plows, the new ones could cut through the dense, tough prairie cover. Deep plowing and the intensive cultivation of large cash crops had immediate benefits. But these practices could rob the soil of necessary minerals. When farmers built new timber houses as frontier conditions receded, they speeded the destruction of the country's forests.

Conclusion

The Character of Progress

Between 1820 and 1860, the United States experienced tremendous growth and economic development. Transportation improvements facilitated the movement of people, goods, and ideas. Larger markets stimulated both agricultural and industrial production. There were more goods and ample food for the American people. Cities and towns were established and thrived. Visitors constantly remarked on the amazing bustle and rapid pace of American life. The United States was, in the words of one Frenchman, "one gigantic workshop, over the entrance of which there is the blazing inscription 'no admission here, except on business.' "

Although the wonders of American development dazzled foreigners and Americans alike, economic growth had its costs, as the example of Susan Warner suggested at the chapter's beginning. Expansion was cyclic, and financial panics and depression punctuated the era. Even middle-class families like the Warners might face financial ruin. Workers discovered that industrial profits derived partly from low wages paid to them. Time-honored routes to economic independence disappeared, and a large class of unskilled, impoverished workers appeared in U.S. cities. Growing inequality characterized urban and rural life, prompting some labor activists to criticize new economic and social arrangements. But workers, still largely unorganized, did not speak with one voice. Ethnic, racial, and religious diversity divided Americans in new and troubling ways.

Yet a basic optimism and sense of pride also characterized the age. To observers, however, it frequently seemed as if the East and the Old Northwest were responsible for the country's achievements. During these decades, many noted that the paths between the East, Northwest, and South seemed to diverge. The rise of King Cotton in the South, where slave rather than free labor formed the foundation of the economy, created a new kind of tension in American life, as the next chapter will show.

Questions for Review and Reflection

1. List what you consider the most significant factors underlying American economic growth and explain why you think the factors you have chosen were so important.

2. Explain the ways in which Great Britain contributed to American economic development. How was American industry both similar to and different from British industry?

3. Compare and contrast industrialism in Lowell and Cincinnati.

4. How did economic changes transform the American class system and the relationship between classes?

Discovering U.S. History Online

Cloth: Discovering Science and Technology Through American History www.si.edu.lemelson/centerpieces/whole_cloth/
The Jerome and Dorothy Lemelson Center for the Study of Invention and Innovation/Society for the History of Technology put together this site, with excellent activities and sources concerning early American manufacturing and industry.

The Erie Canal www.syracuse.com/features/eriecanal/
This site features an overview of the history of the Erie Canal and the section "Life on the Erie Canal," built around the diary of a 14-year-old girl traveling from Amsterdam to Syracuse, New York, in the early nineteenth century. It explores the construction and importance of the Erie Canal.

The Gentleman's Page: A Practical Guide for the 19th Century American Man www.lahacal.org/
gentleman/
Drawing from contemporary photographs and nineteenth-century etiquette books, this site reveals the
attire and behavior expected of urban "gentlemen."

Common School Period www.nd.edu/~rbarger/www7/common.html
This site presents several topics relevant to the 1840–1880 period in American education, including a
brief illustrated biography of Horace Mann, information on the "Catholic Controversy," compulsory
attendance, and African American education.

Connor Prairie Living History Museum www.connerprairie.org/historyonline/
The online counterpart to a nineteenth-century living history museum that offers illustrated essays
such as "Clothing of the 1830s," "The American Woman of the Early Nineteenth Century," and "Jacksonian Medicine." The site includes a series of articles on "Life in the 1880s" and online versions of the
museum's exhibits.

Fiction and Film

Nathaniel Hawthorne's novel *The Scarlet Letter* (1850, but use any edition), although set in the Puritan
period, actually reveals much about the attitudes and controversies of the antebellum period. James
Fennimore Cooper's novels, such as *The Pioneers* (1823), depict the impact of social and economic
change on the frontier. Although not all her readers were female, Susan Warner's *The Wide, Wide World*
(any edition) and her other popular novels provide insights into female interests and concerns in this
period. *Little Women* (1994) is a feature film presenting a moving picture of domestic and family life so
idealized by the middle class. It also suggests the struggle of the middle class to maintain status in difficult times. Some critics have pointed out that this adaptation of Louisa May Alcott's novel has strong
overtones of contemporary feminism. *Out of Ireland: The Story of Irish Emigration to America* (1994) gives
a vivid picture of Irish emigration between 1840 and 1920. *Growing Up in New England* (1991) does an
excellent job of conveying the impact of industrialization on the family and small town.

Recommended Reading

www.ablongman.com/nash
The Companion Website has a list of recommended readings about economic growth, early manufacturing, urban life, and rural communities in the first half of the nineteenth century.

American Stories

A Young Slave Discovers the Path to Freedom

As a young slave, Frederick Douglass was sent by his master to live in Baltimore. When he first met his mistress, Sophia Auld, he was "astonished at her goodness" as she began to teach him to read. Her husband, however, ordered her to stop. Maryland law forbade teaching slaves to read. Master Auld's opposition, however, inspired Douglass "with a desire" to learn.

In the seven years he lived with the Aulds, young Frederick used "various stratagems" to teach himself to read and write. In the narrative of his early life, written after his escape to the North, Douglass acknowledged that his master's "bitter opposition" had helped him achieve his freedom as much as did Mrs. Auld's "kindly aid."

Most slaves did not, like Douglass, escape. But all were as tied to their masters as Douglass was to the Aulds. Nor could whites in antebellum America escape the influence of slavery. Otherwise decent people were often compelled by the "peculiar institution" to act inhumanely. After her husband's interference, Sophia Auld, Douglass observed, was transformed into a demon by the "fatal poison of irresponsible power." Her formerly tender heart turned to "stone" when she ceased teaching him. "Slavery proved as injurious to her," Douglass wrote, "as it did to me."

A slavebreaker, Mr. Covey, to whom Douglass was sent in 1833 to have his will broken, also paid the cost of slavery. Covey succeeded for a time, Douglass reported, in breaking his "body, soul, and spirit" by brutal work and discipline. But one hot August day in 1833, the two men fought a long, grueling battle. Douglass won. Victory, he said, "rekindled the few expiring embers of freedom, and revived within me a sense of my own manhood." Although it would be four more years before his escape north, the young man never again felt like a slave. The key to Douglass's resistance to Covey's power was not just his strong will, or even the magical root he carried in his pocket, but rather his knowledge of how to jeopardize Covey's livelihood as a slavebreaker. The oppressed survive by knowing their oppressors.

As Mrs. Auld and Covey discovered, as long as some people were not free, no one was free. Douglass observed, "You cannot outlaw one part of the people without endangering the rights and liberties of all people. You cannot put a chain on the ankle of the bondsman without finding the other end of it about your own necks." After quarreling with a house servant, one plantation mistress complained that she "exercises dominion over me—or tries to do it. One would have thought ... that I was the Servant, she the mistress." Many whites lived in constant fear of a slave revolt. A Louisiana planter recalled that he had "known times here when there was not a single planter who had a calm night's rest; they then never lay down to sleep without a brace of loaded pistols at their sides." In slave folktales, the clever Brer Rabbit usually outwitted the more powerful Brer Fox or Brer Wolf, thus reversing the roles of oppressed and oppressor.

Slavery in America was both an intricate web of human relationships and a labor system. After tracing the economic development of the Old South in a global context, in which slavery and cotton played vital roles, this chapter will emphasize the daily lives and relationships of masters and slaves who, like Douglass and the Aulds, lived, loved, learned, worked, and struggled with one another in the years before the Civil War.

Perhaps no issue in American history has generated as many interpretations or as much emotional controversy as slavery. Three interpretive schools developed over the years, each adding to our knowledge of the peculiar institution. The first saw slavery as a relatively humane and reasonable institution in which plantation owners took care of helpless, childlike slaves. The second depicted slavery as a harsh and cruel system of exploitation. The third, and most recent, interpretation has described slavery from the perspective of the slaves, who did indeed suffer brutal treatment yet nevertheless survived with integrity, self-esteem, and a sense of community and culture.

The first two interpretive schools emphasized sunup to sundown interactions among masters and mostly passive, victimized slaves; the third, however, focuses on the creative energies, agency, and vibrant life in the slave quarters from sundown to sunup. In a unique structure, this chapter follows these masters and slaves through their day, from morning in the Big House through hot afternoon in the fields to the slave cabins at night. Although slavery was the crucial institution in defining the Old South, diverse social groups and patterns contributed to the tremendous economic growth of the South from 1820 to 1860. We will look first at these aspects of antebellum southern life, and then follow whites and blacks through a southern day from morning to noon to night.

BUILDING A DIVERSE COTTON KINGDOM

Many myths obscure our understanding of the antebellum South. It was not a monolithic society filled only with large cotton plantations worked by hundreds of slaves. The realities were much more complex. Large-plantation agriculture was dominant, but most southern whites were not even slaveholders. Most southern farmers lived in two-room cabins. Cotton was the key cash crop in the South, but it was not the only crop grown. Some masters were kindly, but many were not; some slaves were contented, but most were not.

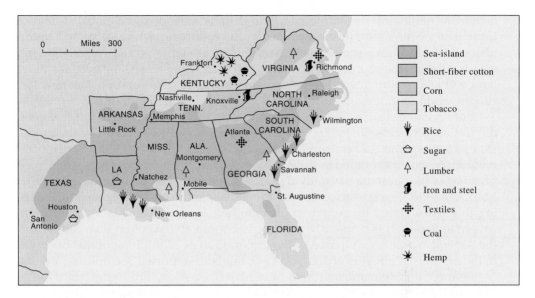

THE VARIED ECONOMIC LIFE IN THE SOUTH Can you identify the "Black Belt" and indicate which two states had more African slaves than whites? If short-fiber cotton was "king," what crop was "queen"—second most important? Why do you think so?

There were many Souths. The older Upper South of Virginia, Maryland, North Carolina, and Kentucky grew different staple crops from those grown in the newer, Lower or "Black Belt" South, from South Carolina to eastern Texas. Within each state, the economies of flat coastal areas and inland upcountry pine forests differed. A still further diversity existed between these areas and the Appalachian highlands. Cities such as New Orleans, Charleston, and Richmond differed dramatically from rural areas.

Although the South was diverse, agriculture dominated industry and commerce. In 1859, a Virginia planter complained about a neighbor who was considering abandoning his farm to become a merchant. "To me it seems to be a wild idea," the planter wrote in his diary. Southerners placed a high value on agricultural labor. Slavery was primarily a labor system intended to produce wealth for landowners. A paternalistic institution, with masters and slaves owing mutual obligations, slavery increasingly became a capitalistic enterprise intended to maximize profits.

The Expansion of Slavery in a Global Economy

In the 20 years preceding the Civil War, the South's economy grew slightly faster than the North's. If the South had become an independent nation in 1860, it would have ranked as one of the wealthiest countries in the world per capita, a wealth based mainly on cotton.

The world was deeply involved in the tremendous economic growth of the South in the early nineteenth century. The expansion of cotton depended on five factors: technological developments, land, labor, demand, and a global system of trade. The technological breakthrough was the cotton gin, which separated cotton fibers from the sticky seeds in the hardier "short staple" cotton plant. The gin wedded the southern economy to cotton production, increased the need for more land and labor, stimulated slavery's southwestward expansion into vast new territories, and brought the South deeper into a global economy of trade.

For several centuries, British, French, Dutch, and Spanish merchants had been developing a worldwide system of trade. In the late eighteenth century, the industrial factory system, in England especially, was made possible by an agricultural revolution, which provided surplus food and labor for urban workers, and by inventions of the spinning jenny, flying shuttle, and steam engine. At the same time, European working classes were demanding inexpensive, lightweight cotton clothing to replace heavy linen and woolen clothes. As British textile manufacturers sought to supply this demand, they eagerly bought all the cotton they could from the American South. Compared to the importation of 22 million pounds of cotton in the pre–cotton gin year of 1787, by 1840, England imported 366 million pounds!

To meet this demand, southern farmers rushed westward to the fresh, fertile lands of the Gulf states to plant cotton. Large-plantation owners, who alone could afford to purchase the gins, slaves, and vast lands needed to grow cotton, spread the plantation system southwestward. Despite the abolition of slavery in the North and occasional talk of emancipation in the South, slavery became more entrenched in southern life. Thoughts of ending slavery were dispelled by one word: cotton.

Although more acreage was planted in corn, cotton was the largest cash crop and for that reason was called "king." In 1820, the South became the world's largest producer of cotton, and from 1815 to 1860 cotton represented more than half of all American exports. Cotton spurred economic growth throughout the country. New England textile mills bought it, northern merchants profitably shipped, insured, and marketed it, and northern bankers acquired capital from cotton sales. The supply of American cotton to Old and New England grew at an astonishing rate. Cotton production soared from 461,000 bales in 1817 to 4.8 million bales in 1860, a more than tenfold jump.

Slavery in the South

Slavery in Latin America

Europeans depended on the slave-based economy in Latin America as well as the American South. Africans were enslaved not only in Virginia and the Carolinas but also in Jamaica, Barbados, Cuba, and other European-owned islands in the West Indies, in Spanish Mexico and Central America, and throughout South America, including Portuguese Brazil, which at 1 million in 1800 had the largest slave population in all the Americas.

Slavery emerged in Latin America out of economic necessity to provide labor where the indigenous population of Indians, decimated by both disease and intermarriage, could not be replaced. Sugar was to Latin America as cotton was to the southern United States, doubling in output at the beginning of the nineteenth century to meet growing European demands. In the Caribbean and Brazil, slaves were indispensable to the sugarcane industry, providing refined sugar for a growing global market that included rum and other liquor distilleries. By 1840, Cuba was the world's largest producer of cane sugar.

Enslaved Africans also worked in Peruvian and Chilean vineyards and in cacao, coca, cotton, and tobacco fields throughout Central and South America. They toiled in Mexican and South American gold, silver, and copper mines; as construction menials, cowboys, tradesmen, dockworkers, and muleteers for overland and maritime transportation; and as servants to royal and religious officials. Women were generally expected to perform the same physical labor as men.

The conditions of work in Bolivian mines or Brazilian sugar fields were as harsh as in American cotton fields. Slaves labored in gangs yet were held accountable as individuals. As market demands for sugar increased in the nineteenth century, sugar growers pressured slaves to increase their productivity, which rose from 1,500 to 2,500 pounds per year. Slaves were literally worked to debilitation and death, the average working life in the fields falling from 15 to 7 years. Whippings were used to enforce obedience, and strict supervision and control were maintained to prevent Africans from mixing with Indians or Europeans and from fleeing to communities of escaped slaves in nearby jungles, called maroons.

Perhaps the most distinctive aspect of Latin American slavery was the preponderance of enslaved African men and the absence of women and families compared to the United States. By the nineteenth century, the gender ratio was three men to every two women, with a 2:1 ratio on the sugar estates of Brazil and Cuba; as late as 1875, only one in six Brazilian slaves was recorded as married. The death rate in Latin America was appalling, the result of hard work, tropical epidemic diseases, malnutrition, and an extremely high infant mortality rate. With low birthrates and lower life expectancy (age 23 in Brazil, 35 in the United States), the slave population in Latin America actually dropped in the nineteenth century. While Brazil's slave population only climbed to 1,510,000, U.S. numbers reached over 4 million by 1860.

Unlike in the United States, where natural births increased the slave population, Latin Americans used the African slave trade to replenish lost labor. Between 1810 and 1870, after the 1807 abolition of the slave trade by Great Britain and the United States, nearly 2 million Africans were taken to the Americas, 60 percent to Brazil and 32 percent to Cuba and Puerto Rico, as compared to only 2.7 percent smuggled illegally to the American South. The last American countries to abolish slavery were Cuba (1880) and Brazil (1888). Although Latin America was slow to abolish slavery officially, intermarriages among Europeans, Indians, and Africans led to an increase in the population of free people of color, who by midcentury vastly outnumbered slaves (80 percent in Brazil). It was strikingly different in the United States, where free blacks constituted only 12 percent of all African Americans.

Latin American slaves obtained their freedom by various means: racial intermarriage, as payment for special favors, in wills upon a master's death, and by purchasing their own freedom by extra work and hiring out. Relative autonomy and incentives such as presents, privileges, extra rations, holidays, and their own gardens were given to many Latin American slaves. As one slaveholder manual said: "the slave who owns neither flees nor causes disorder." Thus, although slave conditions in Latin America were often harsher than in the American South, rights were more fluid, shifting with changing economic and demographic conditions.

White and Black Migrations

Conditions changed in the United States, too. Seeking profits from the British and worldwide demand for cotton, southerners migrated southwestward between 1830 and 1860, pushing the southeastern Indians and Mexicans in Texas out of the way. Like northern grain farmers, southern farmers followed parallel migration paths westward. From the coastal states they trekked westward into the lower Midwest and into the Lower South. By the 1830s, the center of cotton production had shifted from the Southeast to Alabama and Mississippi. This process continued in the 1850s as southerners forged into Arkansas, Louisiana, and eastern Texas.

Slave Dealers

Not only were these migrating southern families pulled by the prospect of fresh land and cheap slave labor, but they also were pushed westward by deteriorating economic conditions. A long depression in the Upper South beginning in the 1820s affected tobacco and cotton prices, as years of constant use had exhausted formerly fertile lands. In a society that valued land ownership, farmers had several choices. One was to move west; another was to stay and diversify. Farmers of the Upper South therefore shifted to grains, mainly corn and wheat, which required less slave labor, and to selling slaves.

Nat Turner
Rebellion (1831)

The internal slave trade from Virginia "down the river" to the Old Southwest thus became a multimillion-dollar "industry" in the 1830s. Between 1830 and 1860, an estimated 300,000 Virginia slaves were transported south for sale. One of the busiest routes was from Alexandria, Virginia, almost within view of the nation's capital, to a huge depot near Natchez, Mississippi. Although most southern states occasionally attempted to control the traffic in slaves, these efforts were poorly enforced. Besides, the reason for outlawing the slave trade was generally not humanitarian, but rather reflected fear of a rapid increase in the slave population. Alabama, Mississippi, and Louisiana all banned the importation of slaves after the Nat Turner revolt in Virginia in 1831 (described later in this chapter), resuming only in the profitable 1850s.

Congress formally ended external slave imports on January 1, 1808, the earliest date permitted by the Constitution. Enforcement by the United States was weak, and many thousands of Africans continued to be smuggled to North America until the end of the Civil War. The tremendous increase in the slave population was the result not of this illegal trade, however, but of natural reproduction, often encouraged by slave owners.

Southern Dependence on Slavery

Frances E. W.
Harper, "The Slave
Auction" (1854)

The rapid increase in the number of slaves, from 1.5 million in 1820 to 4 million in 1860, directly contributed to southern economic growth and its dependence on slavery. A Tennessee senator said that slavery was "sacred," the basis of civilization, and an English traveler noted that it would be easier to attack popery in Rome or Islam in Constantinople than slavery in the American South.

Although most slaves worked on plantations and medium-size farms, they were found in all segments of the southern economy. In 1850, some 75 percent of all slaves were engaged in agricultural labor: 55 percent growing cotton, 10 percent tobacco, and 10 percent rice, sugar, and hemp. Of the remaining one-fourth, about 15 percent were domestic servants, while others were involved in mining, lumbering, construction, dock and steamship labor, and iron and tobacco factories. A visitor to Natchez in 1835, noting that slaves were "trained to every kind of manual labour," saw them working as "mechanics, draymen, hostelers, labourers, hucksters, and washwomen."

The Tredegar Iron Company of Richmond decided in 1847 to shift from white labor "almost exclusively" to slave laborers, who were cheaper and not likely to organize. This strategy foreshadowed the many future companies that exploited black labor while putting an economic squeeze on organized white workers who, along with white artisans, were threatened by black slave competition. Some white workers even opposed slavery.

Whether in factories, mines, or cotton fields, slavery was profitable as a source of labor and as an investment. In 1859, the average plantation slave produced $78 in cotton earnings for his master annually while costing only about $32 to be fed, clothed, and housed. Enslaved women were likely to bear from two to six children, increasing their value. Slaves were a good investment. In 1844, a "prime field hand" sold for $600. A cotton boom beginning in 1849 raised this price to $1800 by 1860. A slave owner could prosper by buying slaves, working them for several years, and selling them for a profit.

The economic growth of the South was impressive, but the dependence on a cotton and slave economy was limiting. Generally, agricultural growth spurs the rise of cities and industry, but not in the Old South. In 1860, the South had 35 percent of the U.S. population but only 15 percent of its manufacturing. Just before the Civil War, one southerner in 14 was a city dweller, compared with one of every three northerners.

Some southerners were aware of the dangers of the single focus on cotton. De Bow's *Review,* an important journal published in New Orleans, called for more economic independence in the South through agricultural diversification, industrialization, and an improved transportation system. De Bow urged using slave labor in factories. But the planter class disagreed. As long as money could be made through an agricultural slave system that also valued honor and regulated race and gender relationships, plantation owners saw no reason to risk capital in new ventures.

Paternalism and Honor in the Planter Class

The aversion to industrialism in the South stemmed from the fact that most southerners, inheriting traditions of medieval chivalry from their Celtic Scots–Irish cultural heritage, espoused a lifestyle of refined paternalism based on a rigid sense of social-class hierarchy and obligations. Wealthy planters, emulating the aristocratic English landowning class, claimed a privileged status as social "betters" and insisted on being treated with deference by those below them. This was especially important for those living in elegant mansions in isolated areas surrounded by black slaves and envious poor whites, circumstances that led to a violent undercurrent throughout the South.

The head of the plantation had to care for his "inferiors," much like a kindly father. This meant providing the necessities of life to slaves (and white overseers), treating them as humanely as he could, and expecting faithful obedience, loyalty, and hard work in return. The plantation wife was an essential part of this culture. Placed on a pedestal and expected to uphold genteel values of sexual purity, spiritual piety, and submissive patience, she managed the household and extended gracious hospitality to social equals. She also had to put up with a double sexual standard and the hypermasculinity of plantation life, which made it all the more important that she reflect ladylike virtues and be fiercely protected.

This masculine code, which valued activities such as politics, war, hunting, and gambling, carried with it a rigid code of honor. Southern men enjoyed leisure activities of the hunt, cards, cockfighting, and horse racing. They were sensitive to lapses of appropriate, chivalrous behavior and to insults and challenges to their honor. Such slights led to duels, regulated by strict rules. One southern visitor said that the "smallest breach of courtesy" was "sufficient grounds for a challenge." Although duels were eventually outlawed in most states, the laws were routinely ignored.

Slavery, Class, and Yeoman Farmers

Slavery clearly served social as well as economic purposes. Although the proportion of southern white families that owned slaves slowly declined from 40 to 25 percent, the ideal of slave ownership permeated all classes and determined southern society's patriarchal and hierarchical character. At the top stood the planter aristocracy, much of it new wealth, elbowing its way among old established families. Some 10,000 rich families owned 50 or more slaves in 1860; about 3,000 of these owned over 100. A slightly larger group of small planters held from 10 to 50 slaves. But the largest group, 70 percent of all slaveholders in 1860, comprised 270,000 middle-level farm families with fewer than 10 slaves. The typical slaveholder worked a small family farm of about 100 acres with less than 10 slaves. The typical slave, however, was more likely to be one of 20 or more on a large farm or small plantation.

In 1841, a young white North Carolinian, John Flintoff, went to Mississippi dreaming of wealth and prestige. Beginning as an overseer managing an uncle's farm, he bought a "negro boy 7 years old" even before he owned any land. After several years of unrewarding struggle, Flintoff married and returned to North Carolina. There he finally bought 124 acres and a few cheap, young blacks, and by 1860 he had a modest farm with several slaves growing corn, wheat, and tobacco. Although he never realized his grandest dreams, his son went to college, and his wife, he reported proudly, "has lived a Lady." Economic, social, and political standing for middle-level farmers like Flintoff depended on owning slaves. Aspiring southern whites hoped to purchase one slave, preferably a female who would bear children, and then climb the socioeconomic ladder.

Middling white southerners defended slavery not only for economic reasons but also because it gave them feelings of superiority over blacks and of kinship, if not quite equality, with other whites. Although a few southern whites believed in emancipation, most did not. An Alabama farmer told a northern visitor in the

1850s that if the slaves got their freedom, "they'd all think themselves just as good as we.... How would you like to hev a nigger feelin' just as good as a white man?"

Yeoman farmers also stoutly defended their independence (from both the national government and local elites), their property and lands as "self-working farmers," and their "households of faith." They believed in an evangelical Christianity that endorsed the divine sanctity of both the male-headed family and slavery.

The Nonslaveholding South

Below Flintoff and other yeoman farmers lived the majority of white southerners, who owned no slaves at all. Some 30 to 50 percent were landless. This nonslaveholding class, 75 percent of all southerners, was scattered throughout the South. Newton Knight, for example, worked a harsh piece of land cut out of the pines of southern Mississippi. He and his wife lived in a crude log cabin, scratching out their livelihood by growing corn and sweet potatoes and raising chickens and hogs. A staunch Baptist given to fits of violence, Knight had once killed a black.

Living throughout the South but especially upcountry in the Appalachian highlands, whites like Knight worked poorer lands than yeomen and planters. Far from commercial centers, they were largely self-sufficient, raising almost all their food and trading hogs, eggs, small game, and homemade items for cash and necessary manufactured items like kettles and rifles. With the indispensable help of their wives and children, they maintained a subsistence household economy, making soap, shoes, candles, whiskey, coarse textiles, and ax handles. They lived in two-room log houses separated by a "dog run." Their drab, isolated life was brightened when neighbors and families gathered at corn huskings and quilting parties, logrolling and wrestling matches, and political stump and revivalist Baptist or Methodist camp meetings.

These nonslaveholding farmers were certainly in the majority. In 1860 in North Carolina and even in the large plantation states of Mississippi and Louisiana, 60–70 percent of farms were less than 100 acres. Despite numerical majorities, these farmers were politically marginalized. Resenting the tradition of political deference to "betters," they were unable to challenge planters for political power. Most fought with the Confederacy during the Civil War; a few silently harbored Unionist views.

Another group was herdsmen raising hogs and other livestock, fed on corn or allowed to roam in the woods. These whites supplied bacon and pork to local slaveholders (who often thought hog growing beneath their dignity) and drove herds to stockyards in Nashville, Louisville, and Savannah. The South raised two-thirds of the nation's hogs. In 1860, the value of southern livestock was $500 million, twice that of cotton. Although the hog business was large and valued, hog herdsmen were low on the southern social ladder.

Below them were the poorest whites of the South, about 10 percent of the population. Often sneeringly called "crackers," they eked out a living in isolated, inhospitable areas. Some made corn whiskey, and many hired out as farmhands for an average wage of $14 per month. Because of poor diet and bad living conditions, these poor whites often suffered from hookworm and malaria. This, along with the natural debilitation of heat and poverty, gave them a reputation as lazy, shiftless, and illiterate.

The Life of Yeoman Farm Families Study these two images and describe what you see. What do the pictures tell you about the daily lives of women and men in southern non-plantation rural cultures? How self-sufficient do they seem to be? How isolated are they? What many social purposes did the quilting party fulfill (other than revealing a uniquely female American work of useful art)? Note that men were also at the party, talking (politics, perhaps) by the stove, bouncing a baby, carrying food, and courting a young woman by the quilt. *(Above, Abby Aldrich Rockefeller Folk Art Museum, Colonial Williamsburg Foundation, Williamsburg, VA; left, North Wind Picture Archives)*

Poor whites stayed poor partly because the slave system allowed the planter class to accumulate a disproportionate amount of land and political power. High slave prices made entry into the planter class increasingly difficult, raising class tensions. Because large planters dominated southern life and owned the most slaves, slavery and the relations between slaves and masters are best understood by looking closely at this group.

MORNING: MASTER AND MISTRESS IN THE BIG HOUSE

It is early morning in the South. Imagine four scenes. In the first, William Waller of Virginia is preparing to leave with 20 choice slaves on a long trip to the slave market in Natchez, Mississippi. Waller is making this "intolerable" journey to sell some of his slaves in order to ease his heavy debts. Although he "loaths the vocation of slave trading," he must recover some money to see his family "freed" from the "bondage" of indebtedness. To ease his conscience, he intends to supervise the sale personally, thus securing the best possible deal not only for himself but also for his departing slaves.

On another plantation, owned by the wealthy James Hammond of South Carolina, the horn blows an hour before daylight to awaken slaves for field work. Hammond rises soon after, aware that to run an efficient plantation he must hold his slaves "in complete check." "In general 15 to 20 lashes will be sufficient flogging" for most offenses, but "in extreme cases" the punishment "must not exceed 100 lashes in one day."

On an Alabama plantation, Hugh Lawson is up early, writing a sorrowful letter about the death of a "devotedly attached and faithful" slave, Jim. A female slave, already awake, "walked across a frosty field in the early morning ... to the big house to build a fire" for her mistress. As the mistress wakes up, she says to the slave, a grown woman taking care of two families, "Well, how's my little nigger today?"

In a fourth household, a middling farm in upcountry Georgia, Charles Brock awakens at dawn to join two sons and four slaves digging up stumps and plowing fields of grains and sweet potatoes, while Brock's wife and a female slave tend cows.

As these diverse scenes suggest, slavery thoroughly permeated the lives of southern slaveholders. For slaves, morning was a time for getting up early for a long day of tedious, hard work. But for white slaveholders, morning involved contact with slaves in many ways: as burdens of figuring profit and loss, as objects to be kept obedient and orderly, as intimates and fellow workers, but also as ever-present reminders of fear, hate, and uncertainty.

The Burdens of Slaveholding and the Plantation Mistress

Robert Francis Withers Allston (1801–1864) was a major rice planter in the Georgetown district of South Carolina, a low, swampy, mosquito-infested tidal area. It was a perfect spot for growing rice, but so unhealthy that few whites wanted to live there. The death rate among slaves was appallingly high. Robert was the fifth generation of Allstons to live in this inhospitable land. By 1860, he owned seven plantations along the Peedee River, totaling some 4,000 acres, and another 9,500 acres of pasture and timberland. He held nearly 600 slaves. The total value of his land and slaves in the 1850s was approximately $300,000. Rich in land and labor, he had large mortgages and debts.

Allston was an enlightened, talented, public-spirited man. Educated at West Point but trained in the law, he both practiced agriculture and served South Carolina many years as state senator and governor. His political creed, he wrote in 1838, was based on "the principles of Thomas Jefferson." The core of his conviction was a "plain, honest, commonsense reading of the Constitution," which for Allston meant the constitutionality of slavery and the illegitimacy of abolitionism and the United States Bank. Allston also reflected Jefferson's humane side. Active in the Episcopal Church, he advocated the liberalization of South Carolina's poor laws;

an improved system of public education open to rich and poor; humanitarian care of the disabled; and the improvement of conditions for the Catawba Indians.

In 1832, Allston married the equally enlightened Adele Petigru. She participated fully in the management of the plantation and ran it while Robert was away doing politics. In a letter to her husband in 1850, Adele demonstrated her diverse interests by reporting on family affairs and the children's learning, sickness among the slaves, the status of spring plowing, the building of a canal, the bottling of wine, and current politics. After Robert's death during the Civil War, she would assume control of the Allston plantations, abandoned when Union troops arrived (see Chapter 16). Except during the worst periods of mosquitoes and heat, both Allstons were fully engaged in plantation operations. Managing thousands of acres of rice required not only an enormous investment in labor and equipment, but also careful supervision of slaves. Although working rice rather than cotton, Allston's concerns were typical of large planters.

His letters frequently expressed the burdens of owning slaves. Although Allston was careful to distribute enough cloth, blankets, and shoes to his slaves and to give them rest, the sickness and death of slaves, especially young fieldworkers, headed his list of concerns. "I lost in one year 28 negroes," he complained. He tried to keep slave families together, but sold slaves when necessary. In a letter to his son Benjamin, he expressed concern over the bad example set by a slave driver who was "abandon'd by his hands" because he had not worked with them the previous Sunday. In the same letter, Allston urged Benjamin to keep up the "patrol duty," less to guard against runaway slaves, he said, than to restrain "vagabond whites." Clearly, the planter class felt a duty to control lower-class whites as well as black slaves.

Other planters likewise saw slavery as both a duty and a burden. Many insisted that they worked harder than their slaves to feed and clothe them. R. L. Dabney of Virginia exclaimed, "there could be no greater curse inflicted on us than to be compelled to manage a parcel of Negroes." Curse or not, Dabney and other planters profited from their burdens, a point they seldom admitted.

Their wives experienced other kinds of burdens. "The mistress of a plantation," wrote one, "was the most complete slave on it." Another complained, "It is the slaves who own me. Morning, noon, and night, I'm obliged to look after them," burdens Adele Allston would have understood. In accord with the southern code of honor, plantation mistresses were expected to improve their husbands' morals and beautify their parlors. They also suffered under a double standard of morality. Expected themselves to act as chaste ladies, their husbands had nearly unrestricted sexual access to slave women. "God forgive us, but ours is a monstrous system," Mary Boykin Chesnut wrote in her diary. "Any lady is ready to tell you who is the father of all the mulatto children in everybody's household but her own. Those, she seems to think, drop from the clouds." But plantation wives had their own double standard: a former slave woman said of her mistress that, "though a warm-hearted woman, [she] was a violent advocate of slavery. I have ... puzzled how to reconcile this with her otherwise Christian character."

Chesnut called the sexual dynamics of slavery "the sorest spot." There were others. Together with female slaves, plantation mistresses had to tend to the food, clothing, health, and welfare of not just their husbands and children, but the slaves, too. The plantation mistress, then, served many roles: as a potential humanizing influence on men; as a resourceful, responsible manager of numerous plantation affairs; as a perpetuator of the system; and sometimes as a victim herself.

Justifying Slavery

The behavior of Douglass's mistress discussed at the beginning of this chapter suggests that slavery led otherwise good people to act inhumanely. Increasingly attacked as immoral, slaveholders felt compelled to justify the institution, not only to opponents of the "peculiar institution" but perhaps also to themselves. Until the 1830s, they explained away slavery as a "necessary evil." After abolitionist attacks in that decade, however, they shifted to justifying slavery in five arguments as a "positive good."

A biblical justification was based in part on the curse that had fallen upon the son of Ham, one of Noah's children, and in part on Old and New Testament admonitions to servants to obey their masters. In a historical justification, southerners claimed slavery had always existed and all the great ancient civilizations were built on it.

The legal justification rested on the U.S. Constitution's refusal to forbid slavery and on three passages clearly implying its legality: the "three-fifths" clause,

A Slave Coffle This engraving of a group of slaves in chains depicts the stark inhumanity of the institution of slavery. Note the white man (in the right corner) raising the whip to hurry the slaves along. In front of him are a woman and child, and another woman stares at him in moral disbelief. What is your response to this engraving? *(Library of Congress)*

the protection of the overseas slave trade for 20 years, and the mandate for return-ing fugitive slaves.

A fourth justification for slavery was pseudoscientific. Until the 1830s, most white southerners believed that blacks were degraded not by nature but by African climate and their slave condition. With the rise of the "positive good" de-fense in the 1830s, southerners began to argue that blacks had been created sepa-rately as an inherently inferior race, and therefore the destiny of the inferior Africans was to work for the superior Caucasians. At best, the patriarchal slave system would domesticate uncivilized blacks. As Allston put it, "The educated master is the negro's best friend upon earth."

A sociological defense of slavery was implicit in Allston's paternalistic state-ment. George Fitzhugh, a leading advocate of this view, argued, "the Negro is but

DOCUMENT

George Fitzhugh, Slavery Justified (1854)

a grown child and must be governed as a child," and so needed the pater-nal guidance and protection of a white master. Many southerners believed that chaos and miscegenation would ensue if slaves were freed. Fitzhugh compared the treatment of southern slaves favorably with that of free la-borers working in northern factories. These "wage slaves," he argued, worked as hard as slaves, yet with their paltry wages they had to feed, clothe, and shelter themselves. Since southern masters took care of these necessities, to free their slaves would be a heartless burden on both blacks and whites.

Southern apologists for slavery faced the difficult intellectual task of justify-ing a system that ran against the main ideological directions of nineteenth-cen-tury American society: the expansion of individual liberty, economic opportunity, and democratic political participation. The southern defense of slavery had also to take into account the 75 percent of white families who owned no slaves but en-vied those who did. To deflect potential for class antagonisms among whites, wealthy planters developed a justification of slavery that emphasized white supe-riority regardless of class.

The underlying but rarely admitted motive behind all these justifications was that slavery was profitable. As the southern defense of slavery intensified in the 1840s and 1850s, it aroused greater opposition from northerners and from slaves themselves. Perhaps slavery's worst cruelty was not physical but psychological: to be enslaved and barred from participation in a nation that espoused freedom and equality of opportunity.

NOON: SLAVES IN HOUSE AND FIELDS

It is two o'clock on a hot July afternoon on the plantation. The midday lunch break is over, and the slaves are returning to work in the fields. Lunch was the usual cornmeal and pork. The slaves now work listlessly, their low stamina result-ing from a deficient diet and suffocating heat and humidity. Douglass remem-bered that "we worked all weathers. ... It was never too hot, or too cold." Mary Reynolds, a Louisiana slave, recalled that she hated most having to pick cotton "when the frost was on the bolls," which made her hands "git sore and crack open and bleed."

Daily Toil

The daily work schedule for most slaves, whether in the fields or the Big House, was long and demanding. Awakened before daybreak, they worked on an average day 14 hours in the summer and 10 hours in the winter; during harvest, an 18-hour workday was not uncommon. Depending on the size of the workforce and the crop, the slaves were organized either in gangs or according to tasks. Gangs, usually of 20 to 25, worked the cotton rows under the watchful eye and quick whip of a driver. Ben Simpson, a Georgia slave, remembered vividly his master's "great, long whip platted out of rawhide" that struck any slave who would "fall behind or give out."

Under the task system, which slaves preferred and negotiated for cleverly, each slave had a specific task to complete daily. It gave slaves incentive to work hard enough to finish early, but their work was scrutinized constantly. An overseer's weekly report to Robert Allston in 1860 noted that he had "flogged for hoeing corn bad Fanny 12 lashes, Sylvia 12, Monday 12, Phoebee 12, Susanna 12, Salina 12, Celia 12, Iris 12." Black slave drivers were no less demanding.

An average slave was expected to pick 130 to 150 pounds of cotton per day; work on sugar and rice plantations was even harder. Sugar demanded constant cultivation, digging ditches in snake-infested fields. At harvest time, cutting, stripping, and carrying the cane to the sugar house for boiling was exhausting, as was cutting and hauling huge quantities of firewood. Working in the low-country rice fields was worse: slaves spent long hours standing in water up to their knees.

House slaves, mostly women, had relatively easier assignments, though they were usually called on to help with the harvest. Their usual work was in or near the Big House as maids, "mammies," cooks, seamstresses, laundresses, coachmen, drivers, and gardeners. Slaves did most of the skilled artisan work on the plantation. More intimacy between whites and blacks occurred near the house. House slaves ate and dressed better than those in the fields. But there were disadvantages: close supervision, duty day and night, and conflicts with whites that could range from being given unpleasant jobs to insults, spontaneous angry whippings, and sexual assault. The most feared punishment, however, other than sale to the Deep South, was to be sent to the fields.

Slave Health and Punishments

Although slave owners had an interest in keeping their workforce healthy, slaves led sickly lives. Home was a crude, one-room log cabin with a dirt floor and a fireplace. Mosquitoes found easy entry through cracks and holes. Typical furnishings included a table, some stools or boxes to sit on, an iron pot and wooden dishes, and perhaps a bed. Cabins were crowded, usually housing more than one family. Clothing was shabby and uncomfortable.

Studies on the adequacy of slave diet disagree. But compared with Latin American slaves, American slaves were fed well. Once a week, each slave got an average ration of a peck of cornmeal, three to four pounds of salt pork or bacon, some molasses, and perhaps some sweet potatoes. The mainstay was corn. While some slaves were able to grow vegetables and to fish or hunt, they rarely enjoyed fresh meat, dairy products, fruits, or vegetables. The limitations of their diet led to theft of food and the practice of eating dirt, which caused worms. The slave diet also resulted in skin disorders, cracked lips, sore eyes, vitamin deficiency diseases, and even mental illness.

Enslaved women especially suffered weaknesses caused by vitamin deficiency, hard work, and disease, as well as those associated with menstruation and childbirth. Women were expected to do the same tasks in the fields as the men, in addition to cooking, sewing, child care, and traditional female jobs in the quarters when the fieldwork was finished. "Pregnant women," the usual rule stated, "should not plough or lift" and had a three-week recovery period following birth. But these guidelines were often violated. Mortality of slave children under five years of age was twice as high as for white children.

Life expectancy for American slaves in 1850 was 21.4 years as compared to 25.5 years for whites. In part because of poor diet and the climate, slaves were highly susceptible to epidemics. Despite some resistance as a result of the sickle-cell trait, many slaves died from malaria, yellow fever, cholera, and other diseases spread by mosquitoes or bad water. Slaves everywhere suffered and died from intestinal ailments in the summer and respiratory diseases in the winter. An average of 20 percent (and sometimes more than 50 percent) of the slaves on a given plantation would be sick at one time, and no overseer's report was complete without recording sicknesses and days of lost labor.

The relatively frequent incidence of whippings and other physical punishments aggravated the poor physical condition of the slaves. Many slaveholders offered rewards—a garden plot, an extra holiday, hiring out, and passes—as inducements for faithful labor and withheld these privileges as punishment. But southern court records, newspapers, plantation diaries, and slave memoirs reveal that sadistic punishments were frequent. Slaveholders had many theories on the appropriate kind of lash to inflict sufficient pain and punishment without damaging a valuable laborer. Other punishments included confinement in stocks and jails during leisure hours, chains, muzzling, salting lash wounds, branding, burning, and castration.

Nothing testifies better to the physical brutality of slavery than the advertisements for runaways that slaveholders printed in antebellum newspapers. In searching for the best way to describe the physical characteristics or brands of a missing slave, slave owners unwittingly condemned their own behavior. A Mississippi runaway was described as having "large raised scars ... in the small of his back and on his abdomen nearly as large as a person's finger." A female fugitive, Betty, was described as recently "burnt ... with a hot iron on the left side of her face. I tried to make the letter M," her master admitted in his diary.

Slave Law and the Family

Complicating master–slave relationships was the status of slaves as both human and property, a legal and psychological ambiguity the South never resolved. On the one hand, the slaves had names, personalities, families, and wills of their own, making them fellow humans. On the other hand, they were items of property, purchased to perform specific profit-making tasks.

A Slave Market The breakup of families and friendships was an ever-present fear for slaves, who could be sold for economic reasons or for uncooperative behavior. Study this painting of a slave market by an unidentified artist, and describe what you see. Note the varied colors and conditions of the African Americans in the painting, and note the varied classes of whites—*and blacks*. What differences between the two women do you see? How many different men are gazing at them, and in what ways? What conclusions do you draw about slavery from this one complex image? *(American, Slave Market, c. 1850–1860. Oil on canvas. 29 × 39 in. Carnegie Museum of Art, Pittsburgh; Gift of Mrs. W. Fitch Ingersoll. Photograph © 2007 Carnegie Museum of Art, Pittsburgh)*

This ambiguity led to confusion in the laws governing treatment of slaves. Until the early 1830s, some southern abolitionist activity persisted, primarily in the Upper South, and slaves had slight hopes of being freed. But they also suffered careless, often brutal treatment. This confusion changed with the threatening convergence in 1831 of Nat Turner's revolt and William Lloyd Garrison's publication of the abolitionist newspaper the *Liberator*. After 1831, the South tightened up the slave system. Laws prohibited manumission, and slaves' hopes of freedom other than by revolt or escape vanished. At the same time, laws protecting them from overly severe treatment were strengthened.

Treatment varied with individual slaveholders and depended on their mood and other circumstances. Most planters, like Robert Allston, encouraged their slaves to marry and sought to keep families intact; they believed that families made enslaved males more docile and less inclined to run away. But some masters failed to respect slave marriages or broke them up because of financial problems, which southern law permitted them to do.

Adding to the pain of forced breakup of the slave family was the sexual abuse of black women. Although the frequency of such abuse is unknown, the presence of thousands of mulattoes in the antebellum era points to the practice. White men in the South took advantage of black enslaved women by offering gifts for sexual "favors," by threatening those who refused sex with physical punishment or the sale of a child or loved one, by purchasing concubines, and by outright rape.

To obtain cheap additional slaves for the workforce, slaveholders encouraged young enslaved women to bear children, whether married or not. If verbal prodding and inducements such as less work and more rations did not work, masters would force mates on slave women. Massa Hawkins, for example, selected Rufus to bed with an unwilling 16-year-old Rose Williams. At first, Rose repulsed him by shoving him on the floor with her feet, but when Rufus persisted, she took a poker and "lets him have it over de head." Hawkins then threatened Rose with a "whippin' at de stake" or sale away "from my folks." This was too much for her. "What am I's to do?"

Slaves, however, usually chose their own mates on the basis of mutual attraction during a courtship complicated by the threat of white interference. As among poor whites, premarital intercourse was frequent, but promiscuous behavior was rare. Most couples maintained affectionate, lasting relationships. This, too, led to numerous sorrows. Members of slave families, powerless to invervene, had to witness the flogging or physical abuse of loved ones. William Wells Brown remembered that "cold chills ran over me and I wept aloud" when he saw his mother whipped. For this reason, some slaves preferred to marry a spouse from another plantation.

Although motherhood was the key event in an enslaved woman's life, bearing children and the double burden of work and family responsibilities challenged her resourcefulness. Some masters provided time off for nursing mothers, but the more common practice was for them to work in the fields with their newborn infants lying nearby. Women developed support networks, looking after one another's children; meeting to sew, quilt, cook, or do laundry; and attending births, caring for the sick and dying, and praying together.

The worst trauma for slaves was the separation of families, a haunting fear rarely absent from slave consciousness. Although many slaveholders had both moral and economic reasons to maintain families, inevitably they found themselves destroying them. One study of 30 years of data from the Deep South shows that masters dissolved one-third of all slave marriages. Even then, the slaves tried to maintain contact with loved ones sold elsewhere. "My Dear Wife for you and my Children my pen cannot Express the Griffe I feel to be parted from you all," wrote Abream Scriven.

There was a sound basis, in fact, for the abolitionists' contention that slavery was a harsh, brutal system. However, two points need to be emphasized. First, although slavery led otherwise decent human beings to commit inhumane acts, many slaveholders throughout the South were not cruel; they did what they could for their slaves, out of both economic self-interest and Christian morality. Second, whether under kind or cruel masters, the slaves endured with dignity, communal strength, and occasional joy. If daytime in the fields describes slavery at its worst, nighttime in the quarters, as examined from the black perspective, reveals noble survival powers and the capacity to mold an African American community culture even under slavery.

NIGHT: SLAVES IN THEIR QUARTERS

It is near sundown, and the workday is almost over. Some slaves begin singing the gentle spiritual "Steal Away to Jesus," and others join in. To the unwary over-seer or master, the song suggests happy slaves, looking forward to heaven. To the slaves, however, the song is a signal that, as ex-slave Wash Wilson put it, they are to "steal away to Jesus" because "dere gwine be a 'ligious meetin' dat night."

In the slave quarters, away from whites and daily work, a black community helped the slaves make sense out of and cope with their lives. In family life, reli-gion, song, dance, the playing of musical instruments, and the telling of stories, the slaves both sought release from suffering and created a vibrant community and culture.

Black Christianity

As suggested by the scene Wash Wilson described, Christian worship was indis-pensable to life in the slave quarters. The revivals of the early nineteenth century led to an enormous growth of Christianity among black Americans. Independent black Baptist and Methodist churches, especially in border states and cities, served slaves, free blacks, and occasionally even whites. These black churches steered a careful path to maintain their autonomy and avoid white interference. The vast majority of southern blacks, however, were slaves, attending plantation churches set up by their masters.

Robert Allston built a prayer house for his slaves, reporting with pride that they were "attentive ... and greatly improved in intelligence and morals." For the slaveholders, religion represented a form of social control. Black religious gather-ings were usually forbidden unless white observers were present or white preach-ers led them. Whether in slave or white churches (where blacks sat in the back), sermons emphasized the importance of work, obedience, honesty, and respect for the master's property. "All that preacher talked about," one slave remembered, "was for us slaves to obey our master and not to lie and steal."

There were limits, however, to white control. Although some slaves accom-modated to the master's brand of Christianity and patiently waited for heavenly deliverance, others rebelled and sought earthly liberty. Not far from Allston's plantation, several slaves were discovered—and imprisoned—for singing "We'll soon be free / We'll fight for liberty / When de Lord will call us home." Douglass had an illegal Sabbath school on one plantation, "the sweetest engagement with which I was ever blessed," where he and others risked whippings while learning about Christianity and how to read. In religious meetings like these, the slaves created an "invisible" church. On Sunday morning, they dutifully sat through the master's service and waited for "real preachin'" later that night.

Long into the night, they would sing, dance, shout, and pray. "Ya' see," one enslaved woman explained, "niggers lack ta shout a whole lot an' wid de white fo'ks al'round 'em, dey couldn't shout jes' lack dey want to." But at night they could, taking care to deaden the sound to keep the whites away. Dance, forbidden by Methodists, was transformed into the "ecstatic shout," praising the Lord. The religious ceremony itself, with its camp meeting features, relieved the day's burdens and expressed communal religious values when blacks "really did have they freedom of spirit," one recalled.

Although many of the expressive forms were African, the message stressed the Judeo-Christian themes of suffering and deliverance from bondage. "We prayed a lot to be free," Anderson Edwards recalled, but the freedom the slaves sought was a complex blend of a peaceful soul and an earthly escape from slavery, as reflected in spirituals.

The Power of Song

Pharaoh's Host
Got Lost

A group of slaves gathers at night in the woods behind their quarters to sing and shout together. Two moods are expressed. First, they mourn being stolen from Africa, with families "sold apart." But second, they sing: "There's a better day a-coming. / Will you go along with me? / There's a better day a-coming. / Go sound the jubilee."

Music was a crucial form of expression in the slave quarters on both secular and religious occasions. The slaves were adept at creating a song, as one woman recalled, "on de spurn of de moment." Jeanette Robinson Murphy described a process of spontaneous creation that, whether in rural church music or urban jazz, describes black music to this day. "We'd all be at the 'prayer house' de Lord's day," she said, when all of a sudden in the midst of a white preacher's sermon, "de Lord would come a-shinin' thoo dem pages and revive dis ole nigger's heart." She continued, "I'd jump up dar and den and holler and shout and sing and pat, and dey would all cotch de words and I'd sing it to some ole shout song I'd heard 'em sing from Africa, and dey'd all take it up and keep at it, and keep a-addin' to it, and den it would be a spiritual."

Spirituals reiterated a basic Judeo-Christian theme: a chosen people, the children of God, were held in bondage but would be delivered. What they meant by deliverance often had a double meaning: freedom in heaven and freedom in the North. Where, exactly, was the desired destination of "Oh Canaan, sweet Canaan / I am bound for the land of Canaan"? Was it heaven? Was it the North? Was it a literal reference to the terminus of the Underground Railroad in Canada? Or was it freedom "anyplace else but here"? For different slaves, and at different times for the same person, it meant all of these.

Slave songs did not always contain hidden meanings. Sometimes slaves gathered simply for music, to play fiddles, drums, and other instruments fashioned in imitation of West African models. Some musicians were invited to perform at white ceremonies and parties, but most played for the slave community. Weddings, funerals, holiday celebrations, family reunions, and a successful harvest were all occasions for a communal gathering, usually with music.

So, too, was news of external events that affected their lives—a crisis in the master's situation, a change in the slave code, a Civil War battle, or emancipation. "The songs of the slave," Douglass wrote, "represent the sorrows of his heart." But they also expressed joy, triumph, and deliverance. Each expression of sorrow usually ended in an outburst of eventual liberation and justice: from "sometimes I feel like a motherless chile" to "a eagle in de air.... / Gonna spread my wings an' Fly, fly, fly."

The Enduring Family

The role of music in all milestones of family life suggests that the family was central to life in the slave quarters. Although sexual abuse and family separation were all too real, so was the hope for family continuity. Naming practices, for example, show that children were connected to large extended families.

The benefits of family cohesion were those of any group: love, protection, education, moral guidance, cultural transmission, role models, and basic support. All these existed in the slave quarters. In this way, blacks preserved cultural traditions, which enhanced the identity and self-esteem of parents and children alike. Parents taught their children how to cope with slavery and survive in the world. As young ones neared the age for full-time fieldwork, their parents instructed them in the best ways to pick cotton, how to avoid the overseer's whip, whom to trust and learn from, and ways of fooling their master.

Opportunities existed on many plantations for parents to perform extra work for money to buy sugar or clothing; to hunt and fish, thereby adding protein to their family's diet; or to tend a small garden to grow vegetables. In such small ways, they improved the welfare of their families.

Slaves were not always totally at the mercy of abusive masters and overseers. Mary Prince used to sass her Antigua mistress "not to use me so." Harriet Jacobs fended off her master's sexual advances partly by her cleverness and sass, and partly by a threat to use her free black grandmother's considerable influence in the community against him. That enraged but stopped him. When family intervention, appeals for mercy, or conjurers' magic did not work, some slaves resorted to force. In 1800, a slave called Ben shot dead a white man for living with Ben's wife, and another slave killed an overseer in 1859 for raping his wife. Enslaved women risked serious consequences to protect themselves or family members. When Cherry Loguen was attacked by a knife-wielding would-be rapist, she knocked him out with a large branch.

Despite numerous incidents of mutual support, the love and affection that slaves had for each other was sometimes a liability. Many slaves, women especially, were reluctant to run away because they did not want to leave their families. Those who fled were easily caught because, as an overseer near Natchez, Mississippi, told a northern visitor, they "almost always kept in the neighborhood, because they did not like to go where they could not sometimes get back and see their families."

As these episodes suggest, violence, sexual abuse, and separation constantly threatened slave families. Yet slave parents continued to serve as protectors, providers, comforters, transmitters of culture, and role models for their children.

Slave Families in Their Quarters In these two photographs of the slave quarters at "night," men, women, and children, despite separation, sale, and sexual abuse by white masters, created a vibrant black community and provided love, support, and pride to family members. How many generations do you see in the 1862 photograph of a Hilton Head, South Carolina, family at the top, and what activities are going on in the bottom picture? What do you observe about gender roles from these two photographs? *(Top: Library of Congress; bottom: Collection of the New York Historical Society)*

RESISTANCE AND FREEDOM

Songs, folktales, and other forms of cultural expression enabled slaves to articulate their resistance to slavery. For example, in the song "Ole Jim," on Jim's "journey" to the "kingdom," he invited others to "go 'long" with him, taunting his owner: "O blow, blow, Ole Massa, blow de cotton horn / Ole Jim'll neber wuck no mo' in de cotton an' de corn." From refusal to work, it was a short step to outright revolt. In another song, "Samson," the slaves stated their determination to abolish the house of bondage: "An' if I had-'n my way / I'd tear the buildin' down! / ... And now I got my way / And I'll tear this buildin' down." Every defiant song, story, or event, like Douglass's victory over Covey, was an act of resistance.

Forms of Black Protest

Slaves protested the burdensome demands of continuous forced labor in various "day-to-day" acts of resistance. These ranged from breaking tools to burning houses, from stealing food to defending fellow slaves from punishment, from self-mutilation to work slowdowns, and from poisoning masters to feigning illness.

Slave women, aware of their childbearing value, were adept at missing work on account of "disorders and irregularities." They established networks of support while winnowing and pounding rice or shucking corn, sharing miseries but also encouraging each other in private acts of subtle defiance such as ruining the master's meals and faking sickness or painful menstrual cramps.

Overseers also suffered from these acts of disobedience, for their job depended on productivity, which in turn depended on the goodwill of the slave workers. Slaves adeptly played on the frequent struggle between overseer and master.

Many slaveholders resorted to using black drivers rather than overseers, but this created other problems. Slave drivers were "men between," charged with the tricky job of getting the master's work done without alienating fellow slaves or compromising their own loyalties. Although some drivers were as brutal as white overseers, many became leaders and role models for other slaves. A common practice of the drivers was to appear to punish without really doing so. Solomon Northrup reported that he "learned to handle the whip with marvelous dexterity and precision, throwing the lash within a hair's breadth of the back, the ear, the nose, without, however, touching either of them."

Another form of resistance was to run away. The typical runaway was a young male who ran off alone and hid out in a nearby wood or swamp. He left to avoid a whipping or because he had just been whipped, to protest excessive work demands, or, as one master put it, for "no cause" at all. But there was a cause—the need to experience a period of freedom away from the restraints and discipline of the plantation. Many runaways would sneak back to the quarters for food, and after a few days, if not tracked down by hounds, they would return, perhaps to be whipped, but also perhaps with some concessions for better treatment.

Some slaves left again and again. Remus and his wife Patty ran away from their master in Alabama. Caught and jailed three times, each time they escaped again. Runaways hid out for months and years in communities of escaped slaves, especially in Florida, where Seminole Indians befriended them. In these maroons,

DOCUMENT

Runaway Slave
Advertisements
(1838–1839)

black Seminoles intermarried and shared a common hostility to whites, though sometimes other southeastern natives were hired to track down runaway slaves.

The means of escape were manifold: forging passes, posing as master and servant, disguising one's sex, sneaking aboard ships, and pretending loyalty until taken by the master on a trip to the North. One slave even had himself mailed to the North in a large box. The Underground Railroad, organized by abolitionists, was a series of safe houses and stations where runaway slaves could rest, eat, and spend the night before continuing. Harriet Tubman, who led some 300 slaves out of the South on 19 separate trips, was the railroad's most famous "conductor." It is difficult to know exactly how many slaves actually

DOCUMENT

Slave Narrative,
"The History of
Mary Prince, A
West Indian
Slave," Related by
Herself, London
(1831)

escaped to the North and Canada, but the numbers were not large. One estimate suggests that in 1850, about 1,000 slaves (out of over 3 million) attempted to run away, and most were returned. Nightly patrols by white militiamen reduced the chances for any slave to escape and probably deterred many from even trying.

Other ways in which slaves sought their freedom included petitioning Congress and state legislatures, bringing suit against their masters that they were being held in bondage illegally, and persuading masters to provide for emancipation in their wills. Many toiled to purchase their own freedom by hiring out to do extra work at night and on holidays.

Slave Revolts

The ultimate act of resistance was rebellion. Countless slaves committed individual acts of revolt. In addition, there were hundreds of conspiracies whereby slaves met to plan a group escape and often the massacre of whites. Most of these conspiracies never led to action, either because circumstances changed, or the slaves lost the will to follow through, or, more often, because some fellow slave—perhaps planted by the master—betrayed the plot. Such spies thwarted the elaborate

IMAGE

Slave
Dockworkers
(1860)—Brady
Photo

conspiracies of Gabriel in Virginia in 1800 and Denmark Vesey in South Carolina in 1822. Both men were skilled, knowledgeable leaders who planned their revolts in hopes that larger events would support them—a possible war with France in 1800 and the Missouri debates in 1820. Both conspiracies were thwarted before revolts could begin, and both resulted in severe reprisals by whites, including mass executions of leaders and the random killing of innocent blacks. The severity of these responses indicated southern whites' enormous fear of slave revolt.

Only a few organized revolts ever actually took place. The most famous slave revolt, led by Nat Turner, occurred in Southampton County, Virginia, in 1831. Turner was an intelligent, skilled, unmarried, religious slave who had experienced many visions of "white spirits and black spirits engaged in battle."

DOCUMENT

Nat Turner, *The
Confession of
Nat Turner*
(1831)

He believed himself "ordained for some great purpose in the hands of the Almighty." He and his followers intended, Turner said, "to carry terror and devastation" throughout the country. They crept into the home of Turner's master—a "kind master" with "the greatest confidence in me"—and killed the entire family. Before the insurrection was finally put down, 55 white men, women, and children had been murdered and twice as many blacks

Abolition of Slavery

1777–1802	U.S. Northern states (effective gradually)
1794	French West Indies (revoked in Haiti in 1802, finally in 1848)
1804	Haitian independence
1808–1825	Revolutionary movements throughout South and Central America for independence from Spain and Portugal (Brazil)
1823	Chile
1824	Central American republics
1829	Mexico (gradually)
1820s–1850s	Venezuela, Colombia, Ecuador (gradually)
1833	British West Indies (effective in 1834)
1848	Virgin Islands
1853	Argentina
1854	Peru
1861	Russian serfs
1865	United States
1873	Puerto Rico
1886	Cuba
1888	Brazil

SLAVE REVOLTS, MAROONS, AND THE ABOLITION OF SLAVERY IN THE AMERICAS, 1790–1888 Throughout the Americas, enslaved Africans found many ways to protest their enslavement, including revolt, escape, and petitioning the abolition of slavery altogether. Maroons were communities of successful runaway slaves who fled to dense forested and largely inaccessible areas where they often intermarried with Native Americans. Some carried on a kind of guerilla warfare with Europeans who tried to track them down. ■ **Reflecting on the Past** Do you see any patterns in the outbreaks of this partial mapping of slave revolts, either by place or time? What relationships do you see, if any, between slave revolts and abolition, or between national independence movements and abolition? What other observations would you make about the data on this map?

killed in the aftermath. Turner hid for two weeks before he was apprehended and executed, but not before dictating a chilling confession to a white lawyer. The Nat Turner revolt was a crucial moment for southern whites. A Virginia legislator said that he suspected there was "a Nat Turner ... in every family."

Frederick Douglass, "What to the Slave is the 4th of July?"

Although Frederick Douglass lived in the United States, as a slave—and even as a free person—he was not considered a citizen and had no rights. Therefore, his view of America was definitely that of an outsider. Douglass's remarks were made in 1852 at a meeting of the Rochester, New York, Ladies Anti-Slavery Society. His title: "What to the Slave is the 4th of July?"

What, to the American slave, is your Fourth of July? I answer: a day that reveals to him, more than all other days in the year, the gross injustice and cruelty to which he is the constant victim. To him, your celebration is a sham; your boasted liberty, an unholy license; your national greatness, swelling vanity; your sounds of rejoicing are empty and heartless; your denunciation of tyrants, brass-fronted impudence; your shouts of liberty and equality, hollow mockery; your prayers and hymns, your sermons and thanksgivings, with all your religious parade and solemnity, are to Him, mere bombast, fraud, deception, impiety, and hypocrisy—a thin veil to cover up crimes which would disgrace a nation of savages. There is not a nation on the earth guilty of practices more shocking and bloody than are the people of the United States at this very hour.

- How accurate and how fair do you think Douglass was with these charges?
- Could such a speech be given today? If so, what changes would you make?

The fact that Turner was an intelligent and trusted slave and yet led such a terrible revolt suggests again how difficult it is to generalize about slavery and slave behavior. Slaves, like masters, had diverse personalities and changeable moods, and their behavior could not be predicted easily. Sometimes humble and deferential, at other times obstinate and rebellious, the slaves made the best of a bad situation and did what they needed to do to survive with a measure of self-worth.

Free Blacks: Becoming One's Own Master

DOCUMENT

Passages from *The Autobiography of Frederick Douglass* (1883)

Frederick Douglass said of the slave, "Give him a bad master, and he aspires to a good master; give him a good master, and he wishes to become his own master." In 1838, Douglass forged a free black's papers as a seaman and sailed from Baltimore to become his own master in the North, where he found "great insecurity and loneliness." Apart from the immediate difficulties of finding food, shelter, and work, he realized that he was a fugitive in a land "whose inhabitants are legalized kidnappers" who could at any moment seize and return him to the South. Douglass thus joined the 11 to 12 percent of the African American population who were not slaves.

Between 1820 and 1860, the number of free blacks in the United States doubled, from 233,500 to 488,000. This rise resulted from natural increase, successful escapes, "passing" as whites, purchasing of freedom, and manumission.

More than half the free blacks lived in the South, most (85 percent in 1860) in the Upper South. They were found scattered on impoverished rural farmlands and in small towns, feared by whites as an inducement to slave unrest. One-third

Frederick Douglass The young Douglass, shown here in a photograph from about 1855, understood as well as any American the profound human, social, and political complexities and consequences of slavery. What qualities do you see in his face? Do they match the Douglass whose words and actions are described in this chapter? *(Schomburg Center for Research in Black Culture, Art and Artifacts Division, The New York Public Library; Astor, Lenox and Tilden Foundations/Art Resource, NY)*

of the southern free African American population lived in cities or towns. In part because it took a long time to buy freedom, free blacks tended to be older, more literate, and lighter-skinned than other African Americans. In 1860, more than 40 percent of free blacks were mulattoes (compared with 10 percent of the slaves). With strong leadership, Baltimore, Richmond, Charleston, New Orleans, and other southern cities developed black communities—their churches, schools, and benevolent societies vibrant in the midst of white hostility.

Most free African Americans in the antebellum South were poor farmhands, day laborers, or woodcutters. In the cities, they worked in factories and lived in appalling poverty. A few skilled jobs, such as barbering, shoemaking, and plastering, were reserved for black men, but they were barred from more than 50 other trades. Women worked as cooks, laundresses, and domestics. The 15 percent of free African Americans who lived in the Lower South were divided into two distinct castes. Most were poor. But in New Orleans, Charleston, and other southern cities, a small, mixed-blood free black elite emerged, closely connected to white society and distant from poor blacks. A handful even owned land and slaves.

Most free blacks had no such privileges. In most states, they could not vote, bear arms, buy liquor, assemble, speak in public, form societies, or testify against whites in court. Nevertheless, the African American persistence in supporting each other in prayer meetings, burial societies, and back alleys was stronger than white efforts to impede it.

Urban whites sought to restrain free blacks from mixing with whites in working-class grogshops, gambling halls, and brothels, as well as to confine them to certain sections of the city or (increasingly by the 1850s) to compel them to leave altogether. Those who stayed had trouble finding work, were required to carry papers, and had to have their actions supervised by a white guardian. Southern whites especially feared contact between free blacks and slaves.

The key institution in these developments was the African American church, "the Alpha and Omega of all things," Martin Delaney wrote to Douglass. Welcoming the freedom from white control, the independent African Methodist Episcopal (AME) church grew enormously in the two decades before the Civil War. By 1860, Baltimore had 15 African American churches representing five different denominations, and in Virginia 14 new black Baptist churches were founded between 1841 and 1860. These institutions gave spiritual solace, set community standards, and offered a host of educational, insurance, self-help, and recreational opportunities.

Nor were African American Catholics left out. Baltimore and New Orleans had strong black Catholic communities made up of Creoles, converts, former slaves, and refugees from Haiti. The Sisters of the Holy Family and other Catholic black women started schools and ministered to the infirm and aged in community religious work reaching Louisville and St. Louis.

African American churches were centers of vital urban black community activities and springboards for activist black preachers seeking larger changes in American society. The Reverend J. C. Pennington, an escaped slave, attended lectures at Yale Divinity School (though he was denied the right to enroll or borrow books). Licensed to preach in 1838, he headed prominent black churches in New Haven, Hartford, and New York City. Pennington started several schools, was an abolitionist leader of the National Negro Convention movement (described in Chapter 12), and founded a black missionary society focused on Africa. Such black religious leaders prepared the way not only for Civil War, but also for an unprecedented postwar growth of African American churches.

A young AME minister, Henry Turner, proclaimed in the 1850s, "We, as a race, have a chance to be Somebody, and if we are ever going to be a people, now is the time." As free blacks became more of a "people," they faced a crisis in the 1850s. The worsening conflict between the North and South over slavery in the territories caused many white southerners to be even more concerned than usual with the presence of free blacks. Pressures increased in the late 1850s either to deport or enslave them. Some black leaders, not surprisingly, began to look more favorably on migration to Africa. That quest was interrupted, however, by the outbreak of the Civil War, rekindling in Douglass the "expiring embers of freedom."

Conclusion

Douglass's Dream of Freedom

When Frederick Douglass forged a free black sailor's pass and escaped to the North, in a real sense he wrote himself into freedom. The *Narrative of the Life of Frederick Douglass,* "written by himself" in 1845, was a way for Douglass both to expose the many evils of slavery and to create his own identity, even choosing his own name. Ironically, Douglass had learned to value reading and writing from his Baltimore masters, the Aulds. This reminds us again of the intricate ways in which the lives of slaves and masters were tied together in the antebellum South.

TIMELINE

1787	Constitution adopted with proslavery provisions
1793	Eli Whitney invents cotton gin
1820	South becomes world's largest cotton producer
1830s	Southern justification of slavery changes from a necessary evil to a positive good

1831	Nat Turner's slave revolt in Virginia
1845	*Narrative of the Life of Frederick Douglass* published
1852	Harriet Beecher Stowe publishes best-selling *Uncle Tom's Cabin*
1860	Cotton production and prices peak

Our understanding of the complexities of this relationship is enhanced as we consider the variations of life in the Big House in the morning, in the fields during the afternoon, in the slave quarters at night, and in the degrees of freedom blacks achieved through resistance and revolt.

In a poignant moment in his *Narrative,* Douglass described his boyhood dreams of freedom as he looked out at the boats on the waters of Chesapeake Bay. Contrasting his own enslavement with the boats he saw as "freedom's swift-winged angels," Douglass vowed to escape: "This very bay shall yet bear me into freedom. ... There is a better day coming." Many other Americans also were concerned with various evil aspects in their society, slavery among them, and sought ways of shaping a better America. We turn to these other dreams in the next chapter.

Questions for Review and Reflection

1. How much variety—social and economic—existed in the Old South? In what ways—social and economic—was the South dependent on slavery and cotton, and what were the consequences of this dependency?

2. Compare and contrast North American with Latin American slavery.

3. Show your understanding of the morning, noon, and night structure of this chapter by explaining it to a friend not in the course. How does this structure reflect three different interpretations of slavery?

4. List five or six different ways in which slaves resisted their enslavement and achieved a measure of autonomy, agency, and self-esteem. Can you identify in any way with these methods of resistance?

5. What does the author of this chapter—and Frederick Douglass—think was the worst thing about slavery? What do you think? What does the institution of slavery suggest about American values and how they have changed over time?

Discovering U.S. History Online ─────────────────────

Slave Culture www.kingtisdell.org/exhibit.htm
An illustrated explanation of slavery culture in Savannah from antebellum Savannah to the end of the Reconstruction era.

Letters from the Slave States www.fordham.edu/halsall/mod/1857stirling.html
A reprint of an article with interviews of plantation owners and former slaves.

Africans in America, 1791–1831 www.pbs.org/wgbh/aia/part3/index.html
PBS images and documents (both primary source and modern commentaries) on the growth and entrenchment of slavery, the rise of abolitionism (especially in Philadelphia), and the black church.

Songs of the Underground Railroad www.appleseedrec.com/underground/sounds.html
Samples of popular slavery songs and interpretations of the meaning of the lyrics.

Virginia Runaways www.wise.virginia.edu/history/runaways
This Web site presents a "digital database" of the detailed "runaway and captured slave and servant advertisements from 18th-century Virginia newspapers."

North American Slave Narratives, Beginnings to 1920 http://www.metalab.unc.edu/docsouth
From the University of North Carolina, a rich collection of narratives about slavery, edited by William Andrews, who has written widely and well about slave narratives.

Fiction and Film ────────────────────────────────

The Bondswoman's Narrative (2002) by Hannah Crafts, recently discovered and edited by Henry Louis Gates, Jr., is perhaps the earliest known novel by an African American woman. Written in the 1850s, hers is a captivating story of a light-skinned North Carolina slave whose escape to New Jersey involved a series of horrifying experiences. Harriet Beecher Stowe's classic *Uncle Tom's Cabin* (1852) follows various black and white lives in antebellum Kentucky and the Deep South. Charles Johnson's *Middle Passage* (1990) is a novel about antebellum life in New Orleans and on slave trade ships between West Africa and the Caribbean. Toni Morrison's novel, *Beloved* (1988), made into a film in 1998, is a powerful and moving account of African American life both during and after slavery. Alice Randall's *The Wind Done Gone* (2001) is a parody of Margaret Mitchell's *Gone With the Wind* (1936). *Kindred* (1979), by Octavia Butler, a contemporary African American science fiction writer, is about a Los Angeles black woman who is transported back to 1815, where she endures the brutality of slavery even as she seeks to save the life of the son of her slave-owning white ancestors. A recent novel about slavery, Edward P. Jones's *The Known World* (2003), won the Pulitzer Prize for literature. His exquisitely written story of a black slaveholder examines all aspects of the morality of slavery and depicts the complex dimensions of black and white relations going far beyond conventions of evil white slaveholders and victimized slaves. *Amistad* is a 1997 Hollywood film based on a successful mutiny on a slave ship in 1839 near Cuba and subsequent capture and trial of the mutineers in Connecticut, where they were defended by former-president John Quincy Adams. The film, featuring the rebel leader Cinque, contains vivid scenes aboard slave ships. *Nat Turner: A Troublesome Property* (2002) is a magnificent recent documentary film.

Recommended Reading ──────────────────────────────

www.ablongman.com/nash
The Companion Website has a list of recommended readings about slavery in the Old South.

CHAPTER 12
Shaping America in the Antebellum Age

CHAPTER OUTLINE

- Religious Revival and Reform Philosophy
- The Political Response to Change
- Perfectionist Reform and Utopianism
- Reforming Society
- Abolitionism and Women's Rights
- Conclusion: Perfecting America

American Stories

Experiencing the Costs of a Commitment

In November 1836, as the second term of Andrew Jackson neared its end, 30-year-old Marius Robinson and Emily Rakestraw were married near Cincinnati, Ohio. Two months later, Marius went on the road to speak against slavery and organize abolitionist societies in Ohio. Emily stayed in Cincinnati to teach in a school for free blacks. During their 10-month separation, their affectionate letters told of their love and work.

Writing to Emily after midnight from Concord, Ohio, Marius complained of the "desolation of loneliness" he felt without her. Emily responded that she felt "about our separation just as you do" and confessed that her "womanish nature" did not enjoy self-denial. In their letters, each imagined the "form and features" of the other and chided the other for not writing more often. Each thought of the burdens of the other's work. Each expressed comfort, doubted his or her own abilities ("a miserable comforter I am"), and agreed that in their separation "we must look alone to God."

With such love for each other, what prompted this painful early separation? Emily wrote of their duty "to labor long in this cause so near and dear to us both," together if possible, but apart if so decreed by God. Marius, who had been converted by revivalist Charles G. Finney and his abolitionist disciple Theodore Weld, described the reason for their separation: "God and humanity bleeding and suffering demand our services apart." Driven by a strong religious commitment to serve others, these two young reformers dedicated themselves to several social causes: the abolition of slavery, equal rights and education for free blacks, temperance, and women's rights.

Their commitments cost more than separation. When Emily went to Cincinnati to work with other young reformers, her parents disapproved. When she married Marius, who already had a reputation as a "rebel," her parents disowned her. Emily wrote with sadness that her sisters and friends also "love me less ... than they did in by-gone days." Marius responded that he wished he could "dry your tears" and sought to heal the rift. Although Emily's family eventually accepted their marriage, there were other griefs. Teaching at the school in Cincinnati was demanding, and Emily could not get rid of a persistent cough. Furthermore, the white citizens of the city treated the school and the young abolitionists in their midst with contempt. Earlier in the year, Marius had escaped an angry mob by disguising himself and mingling with the crowd that came to sack the

351

offices of a reformist journal edited by James G. Birney. Emily, meanwhile, tirelessly persisted in the work of "our school" while worrying about the health and safety of her husband.

She had good reason for concern, for Marius's letters were full of reports of mob attacks, disrupted meetings, stonings, and narrow escapes. At two lectures, he was "mobbed thrice, once most rousingly," by crowds of "the veriest savages I ever saw," armed with clubs and intense hatred for those speaking against slavery. In June, he was dragged from his Quaker host's home, beaten, and tarred and feathered. Never quite recovering his health, Marius spent six months in bed, weak and dispirited. For nearly 10 years after that, the Robinsons lived on an Ohio farm, only slightly involved in abolitionist activity. Despite the joyous birth of two daughters, they felt lonely, restless, and guilt-ridden, "tired of days blank of benevolent effort and almost of benevolent desires."

The work of Emily and Marius Robinson represents one response by the American people to the rapid social and economic changes of the antebellum era described in Chapters 10 and 11. In September 1835, a year before the Robinsons' marriage, the *Niles Register* commented on some 500 recent incidents of mob violence and social upheaval. "Society seems everywhere unhinged, and the demon of 'blood and slaughter' has been let loose upon us. ... [The] character of our countrymen seems suddenly changed." How did Americans adapt to these changes? In a world that seemed everywhere "unhinged," in which old rules and patterns no longer provided guidance, how did people maintain some sense of control over their lives? How did they seek to shape their altered world? How could they both adopt the benefits of change and reduce the accompanying disruptions?

One way was to embrace the changes fully. Thus, some Americans became entrepreneurs in new industries; invested in banks, canals, and railroads; bought more land and slaves; and invented new machines. Others went west or to the new textile mills, enrolled in common schools, joined trade unions, specialized their labor in the workplace and the home, and celebrated modernization's practical benefits. Marius Robinson eventually went into life insurance, though he and Emily never fully gave up their reformist efforts and idealism.

But many Americans were uncomfortable with the character of the new era. Some worried about the unrestrained power and materialism symbolized by the slavemaster's control over his slaves. Others feared that institutions like the U.S. Bank represented a "monied aristocracy" capable of undermining the country's honest producers. Seeking positions of leadership and authority, these critics of the new order tried to shape a nation that retained the benefits of economic change without sacrificing humane principles of liberty, equality of opportunity, and community virtue. This chapter examines four ways in which the American people responded to change by attempting to influence their country's development: religious revivalism, party politics, utopian communitarianism, and social reform.

RELIGIOUS REVIVAL AND REFORM PHILOSOPHY

When the Frenchman Alexis de Tocqueville visited the United States in 1831 and 1832, he observed that he could find "no country in the whole world in which the Christian religion retains a greater influence over the souls of men than in America." Tocqueville was describing a new and powerful religious enthusiasm among American Protestants. Religious rebirth gave some Americans a mooring in a fast-changing world, while others were inspired to refashion their society, working through new political parties to shape an agenda for the nation or through reform associations targeting a particular social evil. Although not all evangelicals agreed about politics or even about what needed reform, religion was the lens through which they viewed events and sought change.

Finney and the Second Great Awakening

From the late 1790s until the late 1830s, a wave of religious revivals matching the intensity of the Great Awakening in the 1730s and 1740s swept through the United States. While there were many links between Protestant denominations in the United States and in Great Britain, the popular character of American revivalism gave it a distinctive stamp. British religion was becoming more conservative, while American Protestantism was becoming more democratic.

The turn-of-the-century frontier camp meeting revivals and the New England revivals sparked by Lyman Beecher took on a new emphasis and location after 1830. Led by the spellbinding Charles G. Finney, revivalism shifted to upstate New York and the Old Northwest. Both areas had been gripped by profound economic and social changes.

Rochester, New York, was typical. Located on the Erie Canal, it was changed by the canal from a sleepy village of 300 in 1815 to a bustling city of nearly 20,000 by 1830. As in other cities, booming economic growth created a gulf between masters and workers. As that gulf widened, masters' control over laborers weakened. Saloons and unions sprang up, and workers became more transient, following opportunities westward.

In 1830, prompted partly by their concerns about poverty and absenteeism, both caused presumably by alcohol, prominent Rochester citizens invited Charles Finney to the city. He led what became one of the most successful revivals of the Second Great Awakening. Finney preached nearly every night and three times on Sundays, first converting the city's business elite, often through their wives, and then many workers. For six months, Rochester experienced a citywide prayer meeting in which one conversion led to another.

Jonathan Edwards had believed that revivals were God's miracles. Revivalist preachers like Finney emphasized the role of human effort and faith in bringing about individual salvation and highlighted emotion over doctrine. Understanding that the human "agency" of the minister was crucial in causing a revival, Finney even published a do-it-yourself manual for revivalists. But few could match his powerful preaching style that relied upon both logic and emotion to trigger conversions. When he threw an imaginary brick at the Devil, people ducked.

The Rochester revival was part of a wave of religious enthusiasm in America that contributed to the tremendous growth of Methodists, Baptists, and other evangelical denominations in the first half of the nineteenth century. By 1844, Methodism became the country's largest denomination with over a million members.

American Catholics also caught the revival fervor in the 1830s. Scattered in small but growing numbers, urban Catholic leaders recognized that survival as a small, often despised religion depended on constant reinvigoration and evangelism. Focusing on the parish mission, energetic retreats and revivals gathered Catholics from miles around to preserve a religious heritage seriously threatened by life in Protestant America.

Finney believed that humans were not passive objects of God's predestined plan, but moral free agents who could choose good over evil and thereby eradicate sin. Unlike Catholic and southern revivalism, which sought personal conversion and personal salvation, Finney revivals insisted that conversion and salvation were not the end of religious experience but the beginning. Finney encouraged not only individual reformation but also the commitment on the part of converted Christians to embrace the sacred duty of reforming society.

The Transcendentalists

No one knew this better than Ralph Waldo Emerson, a Concord, Massachusetts, essayist and the era's foremost intellectual figure. Emerson's essays of the 1830s influenced the midcentury generation of reformist American intellectuals, artists, and writers. The small but influential group of New England intellectuals who lived near Emerson were called Transcendentalists because of their belief that truth was found beyond (transcended) experience. Casting off the European intellectual tradition, Emerson urged Americans to look inward and to nature for self-knowledge, self-reliance, and the spark of divinity within them. Such examinations would lead to social reform. "What is man born for," Emerson asked, "but to be a Reformer?"

Inspired by self-reflection, Transcendentalists asked troublesome questions. They challenged not only slavery, an obvious evil, but also the obsessive, competitive pace of economic life, the overriding materialism, and the restrictive conformity of social life. Although not Transcendentalists, Nathaniel Hawthorne and Herman Melville, two literary giants of midcentury, expressed similar concerns. Like Emerson, they celebrated emotion over reason. Hawthorne's great subject was the "truth of the human heart." In his greatest novel, *The Scarlet Letter* (1850), Hawthorne sympathetically told the story of a courageous Puritan woman's adultery and her eventual loving triumph over the narrowness of both cold intellect and intolerant conformity. Herman Melville's epic novel *Moby Dick* (1851) was both a rousing adventure story and an allegory of good and evil, bravery and weakness, innocence and experience. Like Emerson, Hawthorne and Melville mirrored the tensions of the age as they explored issues of freedom and control.

When Emerson wrote, "Whoso would be a man, must be a nonconformist," he described his friend Henry David Thoreau. No one thought more deeply about the virtuous natural life than Thoreau. On July 4, 1845, he went to live in a small hut by Walden Pond, near Concord, to confront the "essential facts of life"—to discover who he was and how to live well. When Thoreau left Walden two years later, he protested against slavery and the Mexican War by refusing to pay his taxes. He went to jail briefly and wrote an essay, "On Civil Disobedience" (1849), and a book, *Walden* (1854), both classic statements of what one person can do to protest unjust laws and wars and live a life of principle.

THE POLITICAL RESPONSE TO CHANGE

Although transcendentalism touched only a few elite New Englanders, evangelical Protestantism affected perhaps 40 percent of Americans. Evangelical values and religious loyalties colored many people's understanding of the appropriate role of government and influenced their politics. As politics became more a popular than an elite vocation, it was not surprising that religious commitments spilled over into it.

At the heart of American politics was the concern for the continued health of the republican experiment. As American society changed, so did the understanding of what was needed to maintain that health. In the late 1850s, a Maine newspaper warned that the preservation of the nation's freedom depended on the willingness of its citizens to go to the polls. This insistence on voting as crucial to the well-being of the country was a new emphasis in the United States and unique in the world at that time.

Before the 1820s, politics in both the United States and Europe primarily engaged the social and economic elite. In the United States, however, the power of the Revolution's ideas and the relative weakness of the country's upper classes led to a gradual extension of the franchise to all white men. During the early nineteenth century, many states were voluntarily removing voting restrictions even though the majority of white men did not trouble themselves with political matters. But the Panic of 1819 and the spirited presidential campaigns for Andrew Jackson helped create widespread interest in politics and a distinctive American style of politics. For many Americans, political participation became an important way of asserting and supporting important values and promoting their vision of the republic.

Changing Political Culture

Jackson's presidency was crucial in bringing politics to the center of many Americans' lives. Styling himself the people's candidate in 1828, Jackson derided the Adams administration as corrupt and aristocratic and promised a more democratic political system. He told voters he would "purify" and "reform the Government," purging all "who have been appointed from political considerations or against the will of the people." Most Americans believed campaign rhetoric. Four times more men turned out to vote in the election of 1828 than four years earlier. They gave Jackson a resounding 56 percent of their ballots. No other president in the century would equal that percentage of popular support.

Despite campaign rhetoric and his image as a democratic hero, Jackson was not personally very democratic, nor did the era he symbolized involve any significant redistribution of wealth. Jackson owned slaves, defended slavery, and condoned mob attacks on abolitionists like Marius Robinson. He disliked Indians and ordered the forcible removal of southeastern Native Americans to west of the Mississippi River in blatant disregard of treaty rights and a Supreme Court decision. Belying promises of widening opportunity, the rich got richer during the Jacksonian era, and most farming and urban laboring families did not prosper.

But the nation's political life had changed in important ways. The old system of politics, based on elite coalitions and dependent on voters deferring to their "betters," largely disappeared. In its place emerged a competitive party system, begun early in the republic but now oriented toward heavy voter participation. The major parties grew adept at raising money, selecting and promoting candidates, and bringing voters to the polls. A new "democratic" style of political life emerged as parties sponsored conventions, rallies (much like evangelical revivals), and parades to encourage political identification and participation. Party politics became a central preoccupation for many adult white males. In both the North and South, even women who were formally excluded from voting might become caught up in party politics and turn up at rallies and speeches.

Political parties appealed to popular emotions, religious views, and ethnic prejudices. Party-subsidized newspapers regularly indulged in scurrilous attacks on political candidates. The language of politics became contentious and militaristic. Jackson's rhetoric exemplified the new trends. He described an opponent as an "enemy." Politicians talked of elections as battles and of their disciplined "rank and file." Strong party identification became part of the new political culture.

Jackson's Path to the White House

The early career of Andrew Jackson gave few hints of his future political importance. Orphaned at age 14, young Jackson was often in trouble. As a law student, he was "a most roaring ... horse-racing, card-playing, mischievous fellow." Still, he passed the bar and set out to seek his fortune in frontier Nashville. There he built a successful law practice and became state attorney general, a substantial landowner, and a prominent citizen of Nashville.

Jackson's national reputation stemmed mainly from his military exploits, primarily against Indians. As major general of the Tennessee militia, he proved able and popular, winning the nickname of "Old Hickory." His savage victory over the Creek in 1813 and 1814 brought notoriety and an appointment as major general in the U.S. Army. Victory at New Orleans in 1815 made him a national hero. Within two years, he was talked of as a presidential candidate. While aggressive military forays into Spanish Florida in 1818 bothered rival politicians and added to Jackson's reputation for scandal, they increased both his popularity and interest in the presidency. Jackson recognized that his greatest appeal lay with ordinary people,

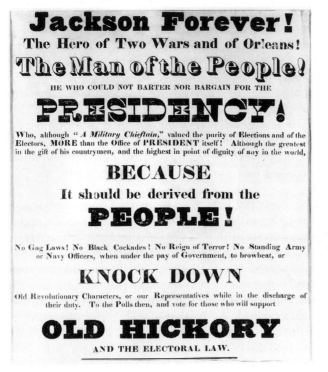

Jackson Forever!

The Hero of Two Wars and of Orleans!

The Man of the People!

HE WHO COULD NOT BARTER NOR BARGAIN FOR THE

PRESIDENCY!

Who, although "*A Military Chieftain,*" valued the purity of Elections and of the Electors, **MORE** than the Office of **PRESIDENT** itself! Although the greatest in the gift of his countrymen, and the highest in point of dignity of any in the world,

BECAUSE

It should be derived from the

PEOPLE!

No Gag Laws! No Black Cockades! No Reign of Terror! No Standing Army or Navy Officers, when under the pay of Government, to browbeat, or

KNOCK DOWN

Old Revolutionary Characters, or our Representatives while in the discharge of their duty. To the Polls then, and vote for those who will support

OLD HICKORY

AND THE ELECTORAL LAW.

The Man of the People Unlike rivals J. Q. Adams and Henry Clay, who deprived Jackson of the presidency in 1824, Jackson (nicknamed "Old Hickory" after America's toughest hardwood) claimed to honor the constitutional electoral system and the will of the people. To what historical events does this poster refer? Was Jackson a man of the people? (© Collection of the New-York Historical Society)

whom he cultivated. But he also secured effective political backing. Careful political maneuvering in Tennessee in the early 1820s brought him election as U.S. senator and nomination for the presidency in 1824.

Jackson won both the popular and the electoral votes in 1824, but lost in the House of Representatives to John Quincy Adams. This failure highlighted the importance of political organization. Confident of his strength in the West and helped by Adams's vice president, Calhoun, in the South, Jackson organized his campaign by setting up committees and newspapers in many states and by encouraging efforts to undermine Adams and Clay.

A loose coalition promoting Jackson's candidacy began to call itself the Democratic party. Politicians of diverse views from all sections of the country were drawn to it, including Martin Van Buren of New York. Jackson masterfully waffled on controversial issues. He concealed his dislike of banks and paper money and vaguely advocated a "middle and just course" on the tariff. He also promised to cleanse government of corruption and privilege.

The Jackson–Adams campaign in 1828 degenerated into a nasty but entertaining contest. The Democrats whipped up enthusiasm with barbecues, mass rallies, and parades and distributed buttons and hats with hickory leaves attached. Few people discussed issues. Both sides indulged in slanderous personal attacks. Supporters of Adams and Clay, who called themselves National Republicans, branded Jackson "an adulterer, a gambler, a cockfighter, a brawler, a drunkard, and a murderer" and maligned his wife Rachel as immoral.

The Jacksonians charged Adams with buying Clay's support in 1824 and described him as a "stingy, undemocratic" aristocrat determined to destroy the people's liberties. Worse yet, they said, Adams was an intellectual. Campaign slogans contrasted the hero of New Orleans, "a man who can fight," with a wimpy Adams, "a man who can write."

Jackson's supporters in Washington worked to ensure his election by devising a tariff bill to win necessary support in key states. Under the leadership of Van Buren, who hoped to replace Calhoun as Jackson's heir apparent, the Democrats in Congress managed to pass what opponents called the "Tariff of Abominations." It arbitrarily raised rates to protect New England textiles, Pennsylvania iron, and some agricultural goods, securing voters in those states where the Democrats needed more support.

The efforts of Jackson and his party paid off as he won an astonishing 647,286 votes, about 56 percent of the total. Organization, money, effective publicity, and a popular style of campaigning had brought the 60-year-old Jackson to the presidency. His inauguration, however, horrified many. Washington was packed for the ceremonies. When Jackson appeared to take the oath of office, wild cheering broke out. Few heard him, but many hoped to shake the new president's hand, and Jackson was all but mobbed. At the White House reception, the crowd got completely out of hand. As Justice Joseph Story observed, a throng of people, "from the highest and most polished, down to the most vulgar and gross," poured into the White House, overturning furniture in a rush for food and punch. Jackson had to leave by a side door. When wine and ice cream were carried out to the lawn, many guests followed by diving through the windows. The inauguration, to Story, meant the "reign of King Mob." But another observer called it a "proud day for the people." Their contrasting views on the inauguration captured the essence of the Jackson era.

Andrew Jackson's Inauguration— Lithograph

Old Hickory's Vigorous Presidency

Although Jackson adopted vague positions on important issues during the campaign, as president he needed to confront many of them. His decisions, often controversial, helped sharpen what it meant to be a Democrat.

A few key convictions, drawn from Jeffersonian principles—the principle of majority rule, the limited power of the national government, the obligation of the national government to defend the interests of the nation's average people against the "monied aristocracy"—guided Jackson's actions as president. As he drew upon Jeffersonian ideals, Jackson helped to transform them and to create a new political environment. Seeing himself as the people's most authentic representative (only the president was elected by all the people), Jackson intended to be a vigorous executive. More than any predecessor, Jackson used presidential power in the name of the people and justified his actions by appeals to the voters. Jackson asserted his power most dramatically through the veto. His six predecessors had cast only nine vetoes, mostly against measures that they had believed unconstitutional. Jackson vetoed 12 bills during his two terms, often because they conflicted with his political agenda.

Jackson had promised to correct what he called an undemocratic and corrupt system of government officeholding. Too often, "unfaithful or incompetent" men clung to government jobs for years. Jackson proposed to throw these "scoundrels" out and establish rotation of office. The duties of public office were so "plain and simple," he said, that ordinary men could fulfill them.

Jackson's rhetoric was more extreme than his actions. He did not replace officeholders wholesale. In the first year and a half of his presidency, he removed 919 officeholders of a total of 10,093, mostly for corruption or incompetence. Nor were the new Democratic appointees especially plain, untutored, or honest; they were much like their predecessors. Still, Jackson's rhetoric helped create a new democratic political culture for most of the nineteenth century.

His policy on internal improvements—roads, canals, and other forms of transportation—was less far-seeing. Like most Americans, Jackson recognized their economic importance. But Jackson opposed infringement on states' rights. When proposals for federal support for internal improvements seemed to rob local and state authorities of their proper function, he opposed them. In 1830, he vetoed the Maysville Road bill, which proposed federal funding for a road in Henry Clay's Kentucky. But projects of national significance, like river improvements or lighthouses, were different. During his presidency, Jackson supported an annual average of $1.3 million in internal improvements.

In a period of rapid economic change, tariffs stirred heated debate. New England and the mid-Atlantic states, the center of manufacturing, favored tariffs. The South had long opposed them because they made it more expensive to buy manufactured goods from the North or abroad and threatened to provoke retaliation against southern cotton and tobacco exports. Feelings ran particularly high in South Carolina. Some of that state's leaders mistakenly believed the tariff was the prime reason for the depression that hung over their state. In addition, some worried that the federal government might eventually interfere with slavery, a frightening prospect in a state where slaves outnumbered whites.

Vice President Calhoun, a brilliant political thinker and opponent of the tariff, provided the appropriate theory to check federal power and protect minority rights. "We are not a nation," he once remarked, "but a Union, a confederacy of equal and sovereign states." In 1828, the same year as the hateful tariff, Calhoun anonymously published *Exposition and Protest,* presenting nullification as a means by which southern states could protect themselves from harmful national action by declaring legislation null and void.

Two years later, Calhoun's doctrine was aired in a Senate debate over public land policy. South Carolina's Robert Hayne defined nullification and urged western states to adopt it. New England's Daniel Webster responded. The federal government, he said, was no mere agent of the state legislatures. It was "made for the people, made by the people, and answerable to the people." Aware that nullification could mean a "once glorious Union ... drenched ... in fraternal blood," Webster cried in his powerful closing words that the appropriate motto for the nation was not "Liberty first and Union afterwards, but Liberty and Union, now and forever, one and inseparable!"

The drama was repeated a month later in a dinner toast, when President Jackson declared his position. Despite his support of states' rights, Jackson did not believe that any state had the right to reject the will of the majority or to destroy the Union. Jackson rose for a toast, held high his glass, and said, "Our Union—it must be preserved." Challenged, Calhoun followed: "The Union—next to our liberty most dear." The split between them widened over personal as well as ideological issues, and in 1832 Calhoun resigned as vice president. Final rupture came in a collision over the tariff and nullification.

DOCUMENT

South Carolina's Ordinance of Nullification (1832)

In 1832, hewing to Jackson's "middle course," Congress modified the tariff of 1828 by retaining high duties on some goods but lowering other rates to an earlier level. A South Carolina convention later that year adopted an Ordinance of Nullification, voiding the tariffs of 1828 and 1832 in the state. The legislature funded a volunteer army and threatened secession if the federal government tried to force the state to comply.

South Carolina had attacked the principles of union and majority rule, and Jackson responded forcefully. To the "ambitious malcontents" in South Carolina, he proclaimed emphatically that "the laws of the United States must be executed. ... Disunion by armed force is treason. ... The Union will be preserved and treason and rebellion promptly put down."

Jackson's proclamation stimulated an outburst of patriotism all over the country. South Carolina stood alone, abandoned even by other southern states. Jackson asked Congress for legislation to enforce tariff duties (the Force Bill of 1833), and new tariff revisions, engineered by Clay and supported by Calhoun, called for reductions over a 10-year period. Having secured its objective, South Carolina quickly repealed its nullification of the tariff laws. But the state saved face by nullifying the Force Bill, which Jackson ignored. The crisis was over, but left unresolved were the constitutional issues it raised. Was the Union permanent? Was secession a valid way to protect minority rights? Such questions would trouble Americans for three decades.

Jackson's Native American Policy

Jackson threatened force on South Carolina; he used it on southeastern Indians. His policy of forcible relocation defined governmental and private practice toward Native Americans for the rest of the century.

DOCUMENT

Memorial of the Cherokee Nation (1830)

In the early nineteenth century, the vast lands of the five "civilized nations" of the Southeast (the Cherokee, Choctaw, Chickasaw, Seminole, and Creek) had been seriously eroded by land-hungry whites supported by military campaigns led by professional Indian fighters like Jackson. The Creek lost 22 million acres in Georgia and Alabama after Jackson defeated them in 1814. Cessions to the government and private sales accounted for even bigger losses: Cherokee holdings of more than 50 million acres in 1802 dwindled to only 9 million 20 years later.

A Supreme Court decision in 1823 declaring that Indians could occupy but not hold title to land in the United States bolstered the trend. Seeing that their survival was threatened, Indian nations acted to protect tribal lands. By 1825, the Creek, Cherokee, and Chickasaw restricted land sales to government agents. The Cherokee, having already assimilated such elements of white culture as agricultural practices, slaveholding (see Chapter 9), Christianity, and constitutionalism established a police force to prevent local leaders from selling off tribal lands.

Jackson's election in 1828 boosted white efforts to relocate the Indians west of the Mississippi, however. In 1829, Jackson recommended to Congress removal of

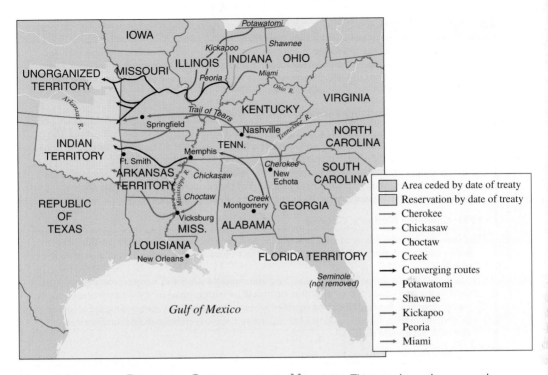

NATIVE AMERICAN REMOVALS: SOUTHEAST AND MIDWEST This map shows the westward routes of Indians removed from the Southeast to the new Indian territory in Oklahoma and from the Midwest (Old Northwest Territory) to present-day Kansas. Why Kansas and Oklahoma? Who already lived there?

the southeastern tribes. Appealing at first to sympathy, Jackson argued that because the Indians were "surrounded by the whites," they were inevitably doomed to "weakness and decay." Removal was justified by "humanity and national honor." He also insisted that state laws should prevail over the claims of either Indians or the federal government (thus contradicting his tariff policy).

The crisis came to a head that same year, when the Georgia legislature declared the Cherokee tribal council illegal and claimed jurisdiction over both the tribe and its lands. In 1830, the Cherokee were forbidden to bring suits or testify against whites in the Georgia courts. The Cherokee protested to the Supreme Court. In 1832, Chief Justice Marshall supported them in *Worcester v. Georgia*, saying that state laws could "have no force" over the Cherokee.

Legal victory did not suppress white land hunger. With Jackson's blessing, Georgia defied the Court ruling. By 1835, harassment, intimidation, and bribery had persuaded a minority of chiefs to sign a removal treaty. That year, Jackson informed the Cherokee, "You cannot remain where you are. Circumstances ... render it impossible that you can flourish in the midst of a civilized community." But most Cherokee refused to leave. Chief John Ross protested to Congress that the treaty was illegitimate. "We are stripped of every attribute of freedom. ... Our property may be plundered ... our lives may be taken away." His words did no good. So in

---

Key Court Cases on Indian Rights

These Supreme Court cases decided in the nineteenth century have provided the legal basis for Native American activism in the twentieth century. Although Indian victories in court during the Jacksonian period did not halt the determination of whites to take over tribal lands, in the twentieth century, these court decisions allowed Indian tribes to win numerous court victories.

1823: Johnson & Graham's Lessee v. William Mcintosh

This case focused on the status of a land grant from an Indian tribe to an individual person. The decision recognized tribal sovereignty and the tribe's rights to land. The court stated that only the federal government was competent to negotiate with tribes for their lands.

"It has been contested that the Indian claims amounted to nothing. Their right of possession has never been questioned ... the Court is decidedly of the opinion, that the plaintiffs do not exhibit a title which can be sustained in the Courts of the United States."

1831: Cherokee Nation v. Georgia

This case involved the status of state law within the Cherokee nation. The court classified the Indian tribes as domestic dependent nations whose relationship was like that of a ward to a guardian.

"Though the Indians are acknowledged to have an unquestionable, and, heretofore, unquestioned right to the lands they occupy until that right shall be extinguished by a voluntary cession to our government, yet it may well be doubted whether those tribes ... can, with strict accuracy, be denominated as foreign nations. They may more correctly, perhaps, be denominated as domestic dependent nations."

1832: Worcester v. Georgia

This case was prompted by the state of Georgia's attempt to extend state law over the Cherokee nation. The decision reaffirmed Indian political rights, stating that Georgia laws had no force in Native American territories and that only the federal government had jurisdiction in Indian territories.

"The Indian nations had always been considered as distinct, independent, political communities ... the settled doctrine of the law of nations is, that a weaker power does not surrender its independence—its rights to self-government—by associating with a stronger."

1835: Mitchell v. The United States

This decision affirmed the rights Native Americans have as occupants (not owners) of the land.

"It is enough to consider as a settled principle, that the right of occupancy is considered as sacred as the fee simple of the white."

1837 and 1838, the U.S. Army gathered the terrified Indians in stockades before herding them west to the "Indian Territory" in present-day Oklahoma.

The removal, whose $6 million cost was deducted from the $9 million awarded the Cherokee for its eastern lands, killed perhaps a quarter of the 15,000 who set out. The Cherokee, following the earlier experiences of the Creek, Choctaw, and Chickasaw remember this as the "Trail of Tears." Between 1821 and 1840, tribes in the Old Northwest, as well as the southeast, were also forced westward to Kansas and Oklahoma. Despite resistance from some tribes, most nations were removed. Although both Jackson and the Removal Act of 1830 had promised to protect and forever guarantee the Indian lands in the West, within a generation those promises, like others

Cherokee Trail of Tears—Painting

before and since, would be broken. Indian removal left the eastern United States open for the enormous economic expansion described in Chapter 10.

Jackson's Bank War and "Van Ruin's" Depression

As the (white) people's advocate, Jackson could not ignore the Second Bank of the United States, which in 1816 had received a charter for 20 years. The bank generated intense feelings. Jackson called it a "monster" that threatened the people's liberties. But it was not so irresponsible as Jacksonians imagined.

Guided since 1823 by the aristocratic Nicholas Biddle, the Philadelphia bank and its 29 branches generally played a responsible economic role in an expansionary period. As the nation's largest commercial bank, "the B.U.S." could shift funds around the country as needed and could influence state banking activity. It restrained state banks from making unwise loans by insisting that they back their notes with specie (gold or silver coin) and by calling in its loans to them. The bank accepted federal deposits, made commercial loans, and bought and sold government bonds. Businessmen, state bankers needing credit, and nationalist politicians such as Webster and Clay, who were on the bank's payroll, all favored it.

Other Americans, led by the president, distrusted the bank. Businessmen and speculators in western lands resented its careful control over state banking and wanted cheap, inflated money to finance new projects and expansion. Some state bankers resented its power over their actions. Southern and western farmers regarded it as immoral because it dealt with paper rather than landed property. Others simply thought it was unconstitutional.

Jackson had long opposed the B.U.S. He hated banks in general because of a near financial disaster in his own past, and also because he and his advisers considered the B.U.S. the chief example of a special privilege monopoly that hurt the common man—farmers, craftsmen, and debtors. Jackson called the bank a threat to the Republic. Its power and financial resources, he thought, made it a "vast electioneering engine."

DOCUMENT

Andrew Jackson, Veto of the Bank Bill (1832)

Aware of Jackson's hostility, Clay and Webster persuaded Biddle to ask Congress for a new charter in 1832, four years ahead of schedule. They reasoned that in an election year, Jackson would not risk a veto. The bill to recharter the bank swept through Congress. Jackson took up the challenge. "The bank ... is trying to kill me," he told Van Buren, "but I will kill it."

Jackson determined not only to veto the bill, but also to carry his case to the public. His veto message, condemning the bank as undemocratic, un-American, and unconstitutional, was meant to stir up voters. He presented the bank as a dangerous monopoly that gave the rich special privileges and harmed "the humble members of society." He also pointed to the high percentage of foreign investors in the bank. Jackson's veto message turned the rechartering issue into a struggle between the people and the aristocracy. His oversimplified analysis made the bank into a symbol of everything that worried many Americans in a time of change.

The bank furor helped to clarify party differences. In 1832, the National Republicans, now calling themselves Whigs, nominated Henry Clay, and they and Biddle spent thousands of dollars trying to defeat "King Andrew." Democratic campaign rhetoric pitted Jackson, the people, and democracy against Clay, the bank, and aristocracy. The Anti-Masons, the first third party in American political life and the first to hold a nominating convention, expressed popular resentments against the elitist Masonic order (Jackson was a member) and other secret societies.

Jackson won handsomely, with 124,000 more popular votes than the combined total for Clay and the Anti-Mason candidate, William Wirt. "He may be President for life if he chooses," said Wirt of Jackson.

Jackson, seeing the election as a victory for his bank policy, closed in on Biddle, even though the bank's charter had four years to run. He decided to weaken the bank by transferring $10 million in government funds to state banks. Although two secretaries of the treasury balked at the request as financially unsound, Jackson persisted until he found one, Roger Taney, willing to do it.

Jackson's war with Biddle and the bank had serious economic consequences. A wave of speculation in western lands and ambitious new state internal-improvement schemes in the mid-1830s produced inflated land prices and a flood of paper money. Even Jackson was concerned, and he tried to curtail irresponsible economic activity. In July 1836, he issued the Specie Circular, announcing that the government would accept only gold and silver in payment for public lands. Panicky investors rushed to change paper notes into specie, and banks started calling in loans. The result was the Panic of 1837. Jackson was blamed for this rapid monetary expansion followed by sudden deflation, but international trade problems probably contributed more to the panic and to the ensuing seven years of depression.

Whatever the primary cause, Jackson left his successor, Martin Van Buren, who was elected in 1836 over a trio of Whig opponents, with an economic crisis.

Van Buren

Van Buren had barely taken the oath of office in 1837 when banks and businesses began to collapse. "Martin Van Ruin's" presidency was dominated by a severe depression. As New York banks suspended credit and began calling in loans, some $6 million was lost on defaulted debts. By the fall of 1837, one-third of America's workers were unemployed, and thousands of others had only part-time work. Those who kept their jobs saw wages fall by 30 to 50 percent within two years. The price of necessities nearly doubled. As winter neared in 1837, a journalist estimated that 200,000 New Yorkers were "in utter hopeless distress with no means of surviving the winter but those provided by charity." They took to the streets, but as one worker said, most laborers called "not for the bread and fuel of charity, but for Work!"

The pride of workers was dampened as soup kitchens and bread lines grew faster than jobs. Laboring families found themselves defenseless, for the depression destroyed the trade union movement begun a decade earlier—a demise hastened by employers who imposed longer hours, cut wages and piece rates, and divided workers. Job competition, poverty, and ethnic animosities led to violent clashes in other eastern cities, as we saw in Chapter 10.

The Second American Party System

By the mid-1830s, a new two-party system and a lively national political culture had emerged in the United States. The parties had taken shape amid the conflicts of Jackson's presidency and the religious fervor and commitments stimulated by the Second Great Awakening. Although both parties included wealthy and influential leaders and mirrored the nation's growing diversity, Democrats had the better claim to be "the party of the common man," with strength in all sections of the country.

Whigs represented greater wealth than Democrats and were strongest in New England and in areas settled by New Englanders across the Upper Midwest. Appealing to businessmen and manufacturers, Whigs generally endorsed Clay's American System: a national bank, federally supported internal improvements, and tariff protection for industry. Many large southern cotton planters joined the Whig party because of its position on bank credit and internal improvements. Whigs ran almost evenly with Democrats in the South for a decade, and artisans and laborers belonged equally to each party. The difficulty in drawing clear regional or class distinctions between Whigs and Democrats suggests that ethnic, religious, and cultural background also influenced party choice.

In the Jeffersonian tradition, the Democrats espoused liberty and local rule. They wanted freedom from those who legislated morality, from religious tyranny, from special privilege, and from too much government. For them, the best society was one in which all Americans were free to follow individual interests. The Democrats appealed to members of denominations that had suffered discrimination in colonies and states where there had been an established church. Scots–Irish, German, French, and Irish Catholic immigrants, as well as free thinkers and labor organizers, tended to be Jacksonians. Democrats were less moralistic than Whigs on matters like drinking and slavery. Their religious background generally taught the inevitability of sin and evil, and Democrats sought to separate politics from moral issues.

By contrast, for many Whigs religious and moral commitments shaped political goals and the ways they understood issues. Calling themselves the party of law and order, most Whigs did not think Americans needed more freedom; rather, they had to learn to use the freedom they already had. If all men were to vote, they should learn how to use their political privileges. Old-stock Yankee Congregationalists and Presbyterians were usually Whigs. So were Quakers and evangelical Protestants, who believed in government action to change moral behavior and eradicate sin. Whigs supported a wide variety of reforms, such as temperance, public education, and strict observance of the Sabbath, as well as government action to promote economic development.

Party identification played an increasingly large part in the lives of American men. Gaudy new electioneering styles were designed to recruit new voters into the political process and ensure loyalty. Politics offered excitement, entertainment, camaraderie, and a way to shape the changing world.

The election of 1840 illustrated the new political culture. Passing over Henry Clay, the Whigs nominated William Henry Harrison, the aging hero of the Battle of Tippecanoe of 1811. Virginian John Tyler was nominated as vice president to underline the regional diversity of the party. The Democrats had no choice but to renominate Van Buren, who conducted a quiet campaign. The Whig campaign, however, used every form of popularized appeal: songs, cartoons, barbecues, and torchlight parades.

The Whigs reversed conventional images by labeling Van Buren an aristocratic dandy and their man as a simple candidate. Harrison reminded voters of General Jackson, and they swept him into office, with 234 electoral votes to Van Buren's 60. In one of the largest turnouts in American history, over 80 percent of eligible voters

The Second American Party System		
	Democrats	**Whigs**
Leaders	Andrew Jackson	Henry Clay
	John C. Calhoun	Daniel Webster
	Martin Van Buren	John Quincy Adams
	Thomas Hart Benton	William Henry Harrison
Political tradition	Republican party (Jefferson, Madison)	Federalist party (Hamilton, John Adams)

Major Political Beliefs

State and local autonomy	National power
Opposition to monopoly and privilege	Support for U.S. Bank, high tariff
Low land prices and tariffs	Internal improvements
Freedom from government interference	Broad government role in reforming America

Primary Sources of Support

Region	South and West	New England, Middle Atlantic, Upper Midwest
Class	Middle-class and small farmers, northeastern urban laborers and artisans	Big southern planters and wealthy businessmen, pockets of middling farmers in Midwest and South, artisans
Ethnicity	Scots–Irish, Irish, French, German, and Canadian immigrants	English, New England old stock
Religion	Catholics, frontier Baptists and Methodists, free thinkers	Presbyterians, Congregationalists, Quakers, moralists, reformers

marched to the polls. A Democratic party journal acknowledged that the Whigs had out-Jacksoned the Jacksonians: "We taught them how to conquer us."

During the campaign, one man had complained that he was tired of all the hoopla over "the Old Hero. Nothing but politics ... mass-meetings are held in every groggery." The implied criticism of the role that alcohol played in party politics highlights the moral and religious perspective many Americans, especially Whigs, brought to politics. Others, however, rejected the political route and sought other means to impose order and morality on American society.

PERFECTIONIST REFORM AND UTOPIANISM

"Be ye therefore perfect even as your Father in heaven is perfect," commanded the Bible. Mid-nineteenth-century reformers, inspired by the Finney revivals, took the challenge seriously. Eventually, a perfected millennial era—1,000 years of peace, harmony, and Christian brotherhood—would bring the Second Coming of Christ.

This perfectionist thrust in religion fit America's sense of itself as chosen by God to reform the world. The impulse to reform in the 1830s had deep-rooted causes: the Puritan idea of American mission; the secular examples of founding fathers like Benjamin Franklin to do good, reinforced by Republican ideology and romantic beliefs in the natural goodness of human nature; the social activist ten-

Motivations and Causes of Reform in America, 1830–1850
• Changing relationships between men and women, masters and workers as a result of the market economy, growth of cities, and increasing immigration
• Finney and other religious revivalists in the Second Great Awakening
• Social activist and ethical impulses of the Whig party
• Psychological anxieties over shifting class and ethnic relationships
• Family traditions and youthful idealism
• Puritan and Revolutionary traditions of the American mission to remake the world
• Republican ideology and Enlightenment emphasis on virtue and good citizenship
• Romantic literary influences such as Transcendentalism

dencies in Whig political ideology; anxiety over shifting class relationships and socioeconomic change; family influence and the desire of young people to choose careers of principled service; and the direct influence of the revivals.

The International Character of Reform

Yet not all the forces leading to reformism came from within. During the early decades of the nineteenth century, the Atlantic Ocean was a highway for reform ideas and reformers. Many of the conditions that troubled Americans, often spawned by industrialization, also troubled Europeans. Women organized in Britain and the United States to reform prostitutes. Societies to encourage temperance flourished in Germany, Ireland, and England as well as the United States. French and British liberals agitated to end the slave trade as did their American counterparts.

A steady stream of men and women traveled from one side of the Atlantic to the other, raising money, publicizing their ideas, studying what had been done outside of their own country, and setting up social experiments. Abolitionists Frederick Douglass and William Lloyd Garrison visited England to gain support for their struggle against slavery, while English abolitionist George Thompson toured in the northern states to assist abolitionists there. Scottish cotton mill owner Robert Owen came to the United States in the 1820s to set up a socialist community after having created a model factory town in Scotland.

There was cross-fertilization across national boundaries of ideas and reform strategies. Owen's book, *The Book of the Moral World* (1820), inspired cooperative efforts of many kinds, while the work of female antislavery societies in Britain and Scotland served as models for American women. Letters between reformers in different countries also helped to firm the reform commitment and inspire action. Hearing of a success elsewhere gave faith that change might come at home, while hearing about failures prompted discussions of appropriate strategies.

The Dilemmas of Reform

Throughout the Atlantic world reformers faced timeless dilemmas about how best to effect change. Is it more effective to appeal to people's minds in order to change bad institutions, or to change institutions first, assuming that altered behavior will then change attitudes? Taking the first path, the reformer relies on education, sermons, tracts, literature, argument, and personal testimony. Following the second, the reformer acts politically and institutionally, seeking to pass laws, win elections, encourage unions, boycott goods, and create or abolish institutions. Reformers must also decide whether to attempt to bring about limited, piecemeal, practical change on a single issue or whether to go for perfection. Should they use or recommend force or enter into coalitions with less principled potential allies?

As Marius and Emily Robinson understood, promoting change has its costs. Reformers invariably disagree on appropriate ideology and tactics, and so they end up quarreling with one another. Although reformers suffer pressure to conform and cease questioning things, their duty to themselves, their society, and their God sustains their commitment.

Utopian Communities: Oneida and the Shakers

Utopian
Communities
Before the Civil
War

Thoreau tried to lead an ideal solitary life. Others tried to redeem a flawed society that was losing the cohesion and traditional values of small community life by creating miniature utopian societies—alternatives to a world of factories, foreigners, immorality, and entrepreneurs. Many also rejected the new middle-class ideals of marriage and family.

In 1831, as Jackson and the nullifiers squared off, as Nat Turner planned his revolt, and as the citizens of Rochester sought ways of controlling their workers' drinking habits, a young man in Putney, Vermont, heard Charles Finney preach. John Humphrey Noyes was an instant, if unorthodox, convert.

Noyes believed that spiritual conversion led to perfection and complete release from sin. But his earthly happiness was soon sorely tested when a woman he loved rejected both his doctrine and his marriage offer. Among those who were perfect, he argued, all men and women belonged equally to each other. Others called his doctrines "free love" and socialism. Noyes recovered from his unhappy love affair and married a loyal follower. When she bore four stillborn babies within six years, Noyes again revised his unconventional ideas about sex.

In 1848, Noyes and 51 followers founded a "perfectionist" community at Oneida, New York. Under his strong leadership, it prospered, although many

John H. Noyes on
Free Love at
Oneida (1865)

Americans found the community's rejection of middle-class marriage norms immoral. Sexual life at the commune was subject to many regulations, including male continence except under carefully prescribed conditions. Only certain spiritually advanced males (usually Noyes) could father children. Other controversial practices included communal child rearing, sexual equality in work, the removal of the competitive spirit from both work and play, and an elaborate program of "mutual criticism" at community meetings presided over by "Father" Noyes. Wise economic decisions bound community members in mutual prosperity. Noyes opted for modern manufacturing, first producing steel animal traps and later silverware.

Noyes greatly admired the Shakers, who also believed in perfectionism, communal property, and bringing on the millennial kingdom of heaven. Unlike the Oneidans, Shakers condemned sexuality and demanded absolute chastity, so that only conversions could bring in new members. Founded by an Englishwoman, Mother Ann Lee, Shaker conversions grew in the Second Great Awakening and peaked around 6,000 souls by the 1850s, with communities from Maine to Kentucky. Shakers believed that God had a dual personality, male and female, and that Mother Ann was the female counterpart to the masculine Christ. Shaker communities, some of which survived long into the twentieth century, were known for their communal ownership of property, equality of women and men, simplicity, and beautifully crafted furniture.

Other Utopias

Over 100 utopian communities were founded. Some were religiously motivated; others were secular. Most were small and lasted only a few months or years. All eventually collapsed, but not before giving birth to significant social ideas.

While pietist German-speaking immigrants founded the earliest utopian communities in America to preserve their language, spirituality, and ascetic lifestyle, other antebellum utopian communities focused on the regeneration of this world or responded more directly to the social misery and wretched working conditions accompanying industrialization. Evil, these communities assumed, came from bad environments, not from individual sin.

Robert Owen was the best-known of the secular communalists. A Scottish industrialist who saw the miserable lives of cotton mill workers, he envisioned a society of small towns with good schools and healthy work. In 1824, he established his first town in America at New Harmony, Indiana. But little harmony prevailed, and it failed within three years.

Brook Farm, founded by two Concord friends of Emerson, tried to integrate "intellectual and manual labor." Residents would hoe for a few hours each day and then recite poetry. Although the colony lasted less than three years, it produced some notable literature in a journal, *The Dial,* edited by Margaret Fuller. Hawthorne briefly lived at Brook Farm and wrote a novel, *The Blithedale Romance* (1852), criticizing the utopians' naive optimism.

The utopian communities all failed for similar reasons. Americans seemed unwilling to share either their property or their spouses. Nor did celibacy arouse much enthusiasm. Other recurring problems included unstable leadership, financial bickering, local hostility toward sexual experimentation and other unorthodox practices, the indiscriminate admission of members, and waning enthusiasm. As Emerson said of Brook Farm, "It met every test but life itself."

Millerites and Mormons

If utopian communities failed to bring about the peaceful millennium, an alternative hope was to leap directly to the Second Coming of Christ. William Miller, a shy farmer from upstate New York, figured out its exact time: 1843, probably in March. A sect gathered around him to prepare for Christ's return and the Day of Judgment. Excitement and fear grew as the day came closer. Some people gave away all their belongings, put on robes, and flocked to high hills and rooftops. When 1843 passed without the end of the world, Miller recalculated. Each new disappointment diminished his followers, and he died discredited in 1848. But a small Millerite sect, the Seventh-Day Adventists, abandoned predicting the date of the Second Coming, living rather with the expectation that it will be "right soon." It continues to this day.

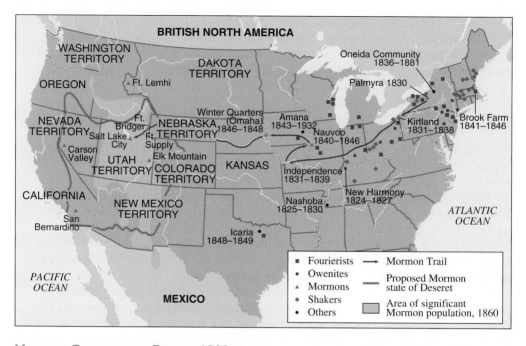

UTOPIAN COMMUNITIES BEFORE 1860 The Mormons migrated to the trans-Mississippi West to realize their vision of a better society, but most communitarians did not go so far away from "civilization" to establish their experiments. Where were the communities located? Why did members not flee more settled and ordinary communities? Why did they avoid the South?

Other groups that emerged from the same religiously active area of upstate New York were more successful. As Palmyra, New York, was being swept by Finney revivalism, young Joseph Smith, a recent convert, claimed to be visited by the angel Moroni, who led him to golden tablets buried near his home. On these were inscribed *The Book of Mormon,* which described the one true church and a "lost tribe of Israel" missing for centuries. The book also predicted the appearance of an American prophet who would establish a new and pure kingdom of Christ in America. Smith published his book in 1830 and soon founded the Church of Jesus Christ of Latter-Day Saints (the Mormons). His visionary leadership attracted thousands of ordinary people trying to escape what they viewed as social disorder, religious impurity, and commercial degradation in the 1830s.

Smith and a steadily growing band of converts migrated first to Ohio, next to Missouri, and then back to Illinois. The frequent migrations were partly a consequence of the ridicule, persecution, and violence that they encountered. Hostility stemmed in part from their active missionary work, in part from their beliefs and support for local Indian tribes, and in part from rumors of unorthodox sexual practices.

Despite persecution and dissension over Smith's strong leadership style, the Mormons prospered. Converts from England and northern Europe added substantially to their numbers. By the mid-1840s, Nauvoo, Illinois, with a thriving population of nearly 15,000, was the showplace of Mormonism. Smith petitioned

Congress for territorial status and ran for president of the United States in 1844. Smith's behavior was too much for local citizens. Violence culminated in Smith's trial for treason and his lynching. Under the brilliant leadership of his successor, Brigham Young, the Mormons headed west in 1846.

Mormon Emigrants (1879)

REFORMING SOCIETY

The Mormons and the utopian communitarians had as their common goal, in Young's words, "the spread of righteousness upon the earth." Most people, however, preferred to focus on a specific social evil.

"We are all a little wild here," Emerson wrote in 1840, "with numberless projects of social reform." Mobilized in part by their increased participation in the political parties of Jacksonian America, the reformers created and joined all kinds of social-uplift societies. The reform ranks were swelled by thousands of women, stirred to action by the religious revivals and freed from domestic burdens by delayed marriage and smaller families. In hundreds of voluntary societies, people like Emily Rakestraw and Marius Robinson tackled such issues as alcohol, diet and health, sexuality, the institutional treatment of social outcasts, education, the rights of labor, slavery, and women's rights.

Temperance

On New Year's Eve in 1831, a Finney disciple, Theodore Dwight Weld, delivered a four-hour temperance lecture in Rochester. Graphically he described the awful fate of those who refused to stop drinking and urged his audience not only to cease their tippling, but also to stop others. Several were converted on the spot. The next day, the largest providers of whiskey in Rochester smashed their barrels as cheering Christians applauded.

Nineteenth-century Americans drank heavily. It was said that "a house could not be raised, a field of wheat cut down, nor could there be a log rolling, a husking, a quilting, a wedding, or a funeral without the aid of alcohol." With drinking came poverty, crime, illness, insanity, battered and broken families, and corrupt politics.

Early efforts at curbing alcohol emphasized moderation. Local societies agreed to limit what they drank. Some met in taverns to toast moderation. But, influenced by the revivals, the movement achieved better organization and clearer goals. The American Temperance Society, founded in 1826, aimed at the "teetotal" pledge. Within a few years, thousands of local and state societies had formed.

Temperance advocates copied revival techniques. Fiery lecturers expounded on the evil consequences of drink and urged group pressure on the weak-willed. A deluge of graphic and sometimes gory temperance tracts poured out. One "intemperate man," it was claimed, died when his "breath caught fire by coming in contact with a lighted candle."

By 1840, disagreements split the temperance movement into many separate organizations. In depression times, when jobs and stable families were harder to

RECOVERING THE PAST

Although paintings are often admired and studied for artistic reasons alone, their value as historical documents should not be overlooked. In an age before the camera, paintings, sketches, and even pictures done in needlework captured Americans at different moments of life and memorialized their significant rituals. Paintings of American families in their homes, for example, reveal both an idealized conception of family life and the details of its reality. In addition, the paintings provide us with a sense of what the houses of the middle and upper classes (who could afford to commission art) were like.

Artists trained in the European tradition of realism painted family scenes and portraits, but so did many painters who lacked formal academic training, the so-called primitive artists. Their art was abstract in the sense that the artists tended to emphasize what they knew or felt rather than what they actually saw.

Some primitive artists were women who had received some drawing instruction at school. They often worked primarily for their own pleasure. Other artists were craftsmen, perhaps house or sign painters, who painted pictures in their leisure time. Some traveling house decorators made a living by making paintings and wall decorations. Many primitive paintings are unsigned, and even when we know the painter's identity, we rarely know more than a name and perhaps a date. Primitive artists flourished in the first three-quarters of the nineteenth century, eventually supplanted by the camera and inexpensive prints.

We see here a painting of the Sargent family by an unknown artist around 1800. Though not an exact representation of reality, it does convey what the artist and the buyer considered important and how the family wished to be viewed. Like any piece of historical evidence, this painting must be approached critically and carefully. First, study the family itself. How many family members are there, and what is each one doing? What objects are associated with each person? What seems to be the relationship between husband and wife? Why do you think Mr. Sargent is painted with his hat on? Who seems to dominate the painting, and how is this dominance conveyed?

Why do you think the artist included a ball and a dog in this scene of family life? What do these choices suggest about attitudes toward children and their upbringing? What seems to be the role of the children in the family?

Finally, observe the objects and decoration of the room. How would you compare it to present-day interiors? Why do you think the chairs are placed near the window and door? What kind of scene does the window frame? What can we learn about daily life from the painting?

The *Family at Home,* painted by H. Knight in 1836, is a more detailed painting showing a larger family gathering almost 40 years later. Similar questions can be asked about this painting, particularly in relationship to the different treatment of boys and girls and the positioning and objects associated with each sex. The family's living room can be contrasted with that of the Sargent family to reveal some of the changes brought about by industrialization.

Note the depiction of husband and wife. How is it different from the portrayal of the Sargents? Why does the woman in this painting have her hat on?

REFLECTING ON THE PAST   As you compare these two paintings, can you find hints that the position of middle-class women was changing as the nineteenth century progressed? Are there any ways to connect the images here with the emergence of women's reform work?

The Sargent Family, 1800. (© Board of Trustees, National Gallery of Art, Washington, D.C.)

H. Knight, *The Family at Home*, 1836. *(Private collection)*

Temperance Propaganda This piece of temperance propaganda comes from a journal entitled *Cold Water Magazine*. Why that title? What does the picture suggest are the effects of drinking? *(Library Company of Philadelphia)*

find than whiskey and beer, laboring men and women moved more by practical concerns than religious fervor joined the crusade. The Washington Temperance Society, founded in a Baltimore tavern in 1840, was enormously popular with unemployed young workers and grew to an estimated 600,000 members in three years. The Washingtonians, arguing that alcoholism was a disease rather than moral failure, changed the shape of the temperance movement. They replaced revivalist techniques with those of the new party politics by organizing parades, picnics, melodramas, and festivals to encourage people to take the pledge.

Tactics in the 1840s also shifted away from moral suasion to political action. Temperance societies lobbied for local option laws, which allowed communities to prohibit the sale, manufacture, and consumption of alcohol. The first such law in the nation was passed in Maine in 1851. Fifteen other states followed with similar laws before the Civil War. Despite weak enforcement, per capita drinking fell dramatically in the 1850s. Interrupted by the Civil War, the movement reached its ultimate objective with passage of the Eighteenth Amendment in 1919.

The temperance crusade reveals the many practical motivations for Americans to join reform societies. For some, as in Rochester, temperance provided an opportunity for the Protestant middle class to exert some control over laborers, immigrants, and Catholics. Perfectionists saw abstinence as a way of practicing self-control. For many women, the temperance effort represented a way to control drunken abusers. For many young men, especially after the onset of the depression of 1837, a temperance society provided entertainment, fellowship, and contacts to help their careers. In temperance societies as in political parties, Americans found jobs, purpose, support, spouses, and relief from loneliness and uncertainty.

Health and Sexuality

It was a short step from the physical and psychological ravages of drink to other potentially harmful effects on the body. Reformers were quick to attack too much eating, too many stimulants, and, above all, too much sex. Many endorsed a variety of special diets and exercise programs for maintaining good health. Some promoted panaceas, including hydropathy (bathing and water purges), hypnotism, phrenology (the study of bumps on the head), and "spiritualist" seances.

Sylvester Graham, inventor of the graham cracker, combined all these enthusiasms. In 1834, he delivered a series of lectures on chastity, later published as an advice book. To those "troubled" by sexual desire, he recommended cold baths and open-air exercise. Women were advised to "have intercourse only for procreation." Although females learned to control sexuality for their own purposes, male "sexual purity" advocates urged restraint to protect various male interests. One doctor argued that women ought not to be educated because blood needed for the womb would be diverted to the head, thus breeding "puny men."

The authors of antebellum "health" manuals advocated abstinence from sex as vehemently as from alcohol. Semen must be saved for reproductive purposes and should not be wasted, either in masturbation or intercourse. Such waste would cause enervation, disease, insanity, and death. Some argued that the "expenditure" of sperm meant a loss of energy from the economy.

Humanizing the Asylum

Struggling to restore order to American society, some reformers preferred to work not to influence individuals but to change institutions like asylums, almshouses, prisons, schools, and even factories. Dealing with social outcasts presented special challenges. Colonial families or communities had looked after orphans, paupers, the insane, and even criminals. Beginning early in the nineteenth century, states built various institutions to uplift and house social victims. In some, like prisons and almshouses, the sane and the insane, children and hardened adult criminals, were thrown together in terrible conditions. In 1843, Dorothea Dix reported to a horrified Massachusetts legislature that the state's imprisoned insane people lived in the "extremest state of degradation and misery," confined in "cages, closets, stalls, pens! Chained, naked, beaten with rods, and lashed into obedience!" Dix recommended special asylums where the insane could be "humanly and properly controlled" by trained attendants.

Many perfectionist reformers like Dix believed that asylums could reform outcasts. Convinced that bad institutions corrupted basically good human beings, they reasoned that reformed institutions could rehabilitate them. In 1853, Charles Loring Brace started a Children's Aid Society in New York City that was a model of change through effective education and self-help. Reformers like Dix and Brace, as well as Samuel Gridley Howe and Thomas Gallaudet, who founded institutions for the care and education of the blind and deaf, achieved remarkable results.

But all too often, results were disappointing. Reformers believed that a proper penitentiary could bring a criminal "back to virtue." Some preferred the prison at Auburn, New York, with its tiny cells and common workrooms; others praised Pennsylvania's penitentiaries, each inmate in solitary confinement. All prison reformers assumed that "penitents" in isolated cells, studying the Bible and reflecting on their wrongdoing, would eventually decide to become good citizens. In fact, many inmates went mad or committed suicide. Institutions built by well-intentioned reformers became dumping places for society's outcasts. By midcentury, American prisons and mental asylums had become what they remain today: sadly impersonal, understaffed, and overcrowded.

Working-Class Reform

Efforts to improve the institutional conditions of American life were not all top-down movements initiated and led by middle-class reformers. For working-class Americans, as in England, the institution most in need of transformation was the factory. Workers, many of them involved in other issues such as temperance, peace, and abolitionism, tried to improve their own lives.

Between 1828 and 1832, dozens of workingmen's parties arose. They advocated free, tax-supported schools, free public lands in the West, equal rights for the poor, and elimination of monopolistic privilege. Trade union activity began in Philadelphia in 1827 as skilled workers organized journeymen carpenters, plasterers, printers, weavers, tailors, and other tradesmen. That same year, 15 unions combined into a citywide federation, a process followed in other cities. The National Trades Union, founded in 1834, was the first attempt at a national labor organization.

Trade unions fared better than labor parties as Jacksonian Democrats siphoned off workers' votes. Union programs set more practical goals, including shorter hours, wages that would keep pace with rising prices, and ways (such as the closed shop) of warding off the competitive threat of cheap labor. In addition, both workers and their middle-class supporters sought free public education, improved living conditions for workers, and the right to organize as well as the elimination of imprisonment for debt and compulsory militia duty (both often cost workers their jobs). Discouraged by anti-union decisions of New York State courts, workers compared themselves to the rebels of the Boston Tea Party.

Fired by revolutionary tradition, rising political influence, and a union membership of near 300,000, workers struck some 168 times between 1834 and 1836. Over two-thirds of the strikes were over wages (see Chapter 10); the others were for shorter hours. The Panic of 1837 ushered in a depression that dashed the hopes and efforts of American workers. But the organizational work of the 1830s promised that the labor movement would reemerge, strengthened, later in the century.

ABOLITIONISM AND WOMEN'S RIGHTS

As American workers struggled for better wages and hours in 1834, Emily and Marius Robinson arrived in Cincinnati to fight for their causes. Along with many other young idealists, they had been attracted by the newly founded Lane Seminary, a center of reformist activity. When nervous citizens persuaded the school's president, Lyman Beecher, to crack down, 75 "Lane rebels" fled to Oberlin in northern Ohio. The rebels turned Oberlin College into the first institution in the United States open to women and men, blacks and whites. The movements to abolish slavery and for equal rights for women and free blacks coalesced.

The goals of the struggle against slavery and subtle forms of racism and sexism often seemed as distant as the millennium itself. Yet antislavery and feminist advocates persisted in their efforts to abolish what they believed were visible, ingrained social wrongs. Whether seeking to eliminate coercion in the cotton fields or in the kitchen, they faced the dual challenge of pursuing elusive goals while achieving practical changes.

Tensions Within the Antislavery Movement

Although the antislavery movement was smaller than the temperance movement, it revealed more clearly the difficulties of pursuing significant social change. William Lloyd Garrison passionately desired to improve, if not to perfect, a flawed world. On January 1, 1831, eight months before Nat Turner's revolt, Garrison published the first issue of *The Liberator,* soon to become the leading antislavery journal in the United States. "I am in earnest," he wrote. "I will not equivocate—*and I will be heard.*" After organizing the New England Anti-Slavery Society with a group of blacks and whites, in 1833 Garrison and 62 others established the American Anti-Slavery Society, which called for an immediate end to slavery.

Until then, most antislavery whites had advocated gradual emancipation by individual slave owners. Many joined the American Colonization Society, founded in 1816, which sent a few ex-slaves to Liberia. But these efforts proved inadequate and racist, the main goal being to rid the country of free blacks. Rejected by African Americans and violently attacked by Garrisonians, colonization lost much of its support.

Garrison and others in the American Anti-Slavery Society viewed slavery as a sin that had to be eliminated and called for immediate emancipation in uncompromising language. As Garrison declared, "I do not wish to think, or speak, or write, with moderation." There could be "no Union with slaveholders," he argued, condemning the Constitution that perpetuated slavery as "an agreement with Hell." Inspired by the *Liberator* and antislavery lecturers like Garrison and Marius Robinson, dozens of local male and female abolitionist societies dedicated to the immediate emancipation of the slaves arose, mostly in the Northeast and Northwest. Yet others who opposed slavery found the Garrisonian abolitionists far too radical for their tastes.

Abolitionists also differed over tactics. Their primary method was to convince slaveholders and their supporters that slavery was a sin. Slaveholding whites, black abolitionist David Walker declared, were morally inferior. But as Marius

An Abolitionist Gathering This woodcut illustration of an abolitionist convention from *Harper's Weekly* magazine in 1859 shows the mixture of both black and women delegates in the hall. The black man on the stage could be Frederick Douglass. How many other black (and female) abolitionists do you see, and where are they sitting? *(Boston Public Library/Rare Books Department. Courtesy of The Trustees.)*

wrote to Emily Robinson, "The spirit of slavery is not confined to the South." His Ohio trip suggests that northerners were equally guilty in providing the ships and support necessary to maintain the slave system.

Illustrations from the *American Anti-Slavery Almanac for 1840*

The abolitionists by 1837 flooded the nation with over a million pieces of antislavery literature. Their writing described slave owners as "manstealers" who gave up all claim to humanity. In 1839, Weld published *American Slavery as It Is,* which described in the goriest possible detail the inhumane treatment of slaves.

Other abolitionists preferred more direct methods. Some brought antislavery petitions before Congress and formed third parties. Boycotting goods made by slave labor was another tactic. Still another approach, although rare, was to call for slave rebellion, as did two northern blacks, David Walker in an 1829 pamphlet and Henry Highland Garnet in a speech at a convention of black Americans in 1843. As Garnet recognized, Walker's work represented "among the first, and ... the boldest and most direct appeals in behalf of freedom" of the early abolitionist movement.

Abolitionists' tactical disagreements helped splinter the movement. Garrison's unyielding style and commitment to even less popular causes such as women's rights offended many abolitionists. In 1840, at its annual meeting in New York, the American Anti-Slavery Society split. Several delegates walked out when a woman, Abby Kelley, was elected to a previously all-male committee. One group, which supported multiple issues and moral suasion, stayed with Garrison; the other left to pursue political action and the Liberty party.

Class differences and race further divided abolitionists. Northern workers, though fearful of the potential job competition with blacks implicit in emancipation, nevertheless saw their "wage slavery" as similar to chattel slavery. Strains between northern labor leaders and middle-class abolitionists (who minimized workingmen's concerns) were similar to those between white and black antislavery forces. Whites like Wendell Phillips decried slavery as a moral blot on American society; blacks like Douglass were more concerned with the effects of slavery and discrimination on African Americans. Moreover, white abolitionists tended to see slavery and freedom as absolute opposites: a person was either slave or free. Blacks knew that there were degrees of freedom and that northern blacks had less of it.

Furthermore, black abolitionists experienced prejudice, not just from ordinary northern citizens, but also from white abolitionists. Many antislavery businessmen refused to hire blacks. The antislavery societies usually provided less than full membership rights for blacks, and, sometimes unknowingly, perpetuated black stereotypes in their literature. Conflict between Garrison and Douglass reflected these tensions. The famous runaway was one of the most effective orators in the movement. But after a while, rather than simply describing his life as a slave, Douglass began skillfully to analyze abolitionist policies. Garrison warned him that if he sounded too sophisticated, audiences would doubt he had been a slave; other whites told him to stick to the facts and let them take care of the philosophy.

Douglass gradually moved away from Garrison's views, endorsing political action and sometimes even slave rebellion. Garrison's response, particularly when Douglass came out for the Liberty party, was to denounce his independence as "ungrateful ... and malevolent in spirit." In 1847, Douglass started his own journal, the *North Star,* later called *Frederick Douglass's Paper.* In it, he expressed his appreciation for the help of that "noble band of white laborers," but declared that it was time for those who "suffered the wrong" to lead the way in advocating liberty.

Moving beyond Garrison, a few black nationalists, like fiery Martin Delaney, totally rejected white society and advocated emigration to Africa. Most blacks, however, were practical and agreed with Douglass to work to end slavery and discrimination in the United States. David Ruggles in New York and William Still in Philadelphia led black vigilance groups that helped fugitive slaves escape to Canada or to safe northern black settlements. Ministers, writers, and orators such as Douglass, Garnet, William Wells Brown, Samuel Cornish, Lewis Hayden, and Sojourner Truth lectured and wrote journals and slave narratives on the evils of slavery. They also organized a National Negro Convention Movement, which began annual meetings in 1830. These blacks met not only to condemn slavery but also to discuss issues of discrimination facing free blacks in the North.

Flood Tide of Abolitionism

Black and white abolitionists, however, usually worked together well. Weld and Garrison often stayed in the homes of black abolitionists when they traveled. In addition, black and white "stations" cooperated on the Underground Railroad, passing fugitives from one hiding place to the next.

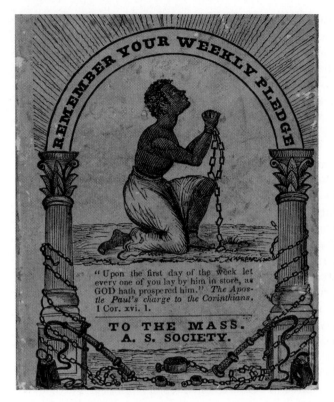

An Abolitionist Message This image of an imploring slave was one of the favorite abolitionist devices. Sometimes the caption asked, "Am I not a Man and a Brother?" In this case, the caption has been changed to encourage antislavery supporters to make weekly donations to the Massachusetts Anti-Slavery Society. What does the biblical text suggest? How do the objects portrayed reinforce the message? *(Courtesy of The Newberry Library, Chicago)*

The two races worked together to fight discrimination as well as slavery. When David Ruggles was dragged from the "white car" of a New Bedford, Massachusetts, railway in 1841, Garrison, Douglass, and 40 other protesters organized what may have been the first successful integrated "sit-in" in American history. Blacks and whites also worked harmoniously in protesting segregated public schools; after several years of boycotts and legal challenges, they forced Massachusetts in 1855 to became the first state to outlaw them. Not for 99 years would the U.S. Supreme Court begin desegregating schools throughout the country.

White and black abolitionists were united perhaps most closely by defending themselves against attacks by people who regarded them as dangerous fanatics bent on disrupting society. As abolitionists organized to rid the nation of slavery, they aroused many people—northerners as well as southerners—who were eager to rid the nation of abolitionists. Mob attacks, like the one on Marius Robinson in Ohio, occurred frequently in the mid-1830s. Abolitionists were stoned, dragged through streets, and reviled by northern mobs. Weld could hardly finish a speech without disruption. Douglass endured similar attacks. Garrison was saved from a Boston mob only by being put in jail. In 1837 Elijah Lovejoy, an antislavery editor from Illinois, was murdered.

Antiabolitionsts were as fervid as the abolitionists. "I warn the abolitionists, ignorant and infatuated barbarians as they are," growled one South Carolinian, "that if chance shall throw any of them into our hands, they may expect a felon's death." One widely circulated book in 1836 described opponents of slavery, led by "gloomy, wild, and malignant" Garrison, as "crack-brained enthusiasts" and "female fanatics." Jackson denounced abolitionists in his annual message in 1835 as "incendiaries" who deserved to have their "unconstitutional and wicked" activities broken up by mobs, and he urged Congress to ban antislavery literature from the U.S. mails. A year later, southern Democratic congressmen, with crucial support from Van Buren, passed a "gag rule" to stop the flood of abolitionist petitions in Congress.

By the 1840s the antislavery movement had gained significant strength. Many northerners, including workers otherwise unsympathetic to ending slavery, decried mob violence, supported free speech, and denounced the South and its northern defenders as undemocratic. The gag rule, interference with the mails, and Lovejoy's killing seemed proof of the growing influence of an evil slave power. Former president John Quincy Adams, now a Massachusetts congressman, devoted himself for several years to the repeal of the gag rule, which he finally achieved in 1844, keeping the matter alive until the question of slavery in the territories became the dominant political issue of the 1850s (see Chapter 14). Meanwhile, black and white abolitionists struggled on with many different tactics.

Women Reformers and Women's Rights

As a young Quaker teacher in Massachusetts in 1836, Abby Kelley circulated petitions for the local antislavery society. She came to reform through religious conviction. In 1838, she braved a crowd in Philadelphia by delivering an abolitionist speech to a convention of antislavery women so eloquently that Weld told her that if she did not join the movement full time, "God will smite you." Before the convention was over, a mob, incensed by both abolitionists and women speaking in public, burned the hall to the ground.

After a soul-searching year, Kelley left teaching to focus on antislavery and women's rights. When she married, she retained her own name and went on lecture tours of the West while her husband stayed home to care for their daughter. Other young women were also defining unconventional new relationships while illustrating the profound difficulty of both fulfilling traditional roles and speaking out for change. Angelina and Sarah Grimké, outspoken Quaker sisters from Philadelphia who had grown up in South Carolina, went to New England in 1837 to lecture on abolitionism. Criticized for speaking to audiences containing both men and women, Angelina defended women's rights to speak in public. After the tour, Angelina married Theodore Weld and stopped her public lectures to show that she could also be a good wife and mother. But she and Sarah, who moved in with her, undertook most of the research and writing for Weld's book attacking American slavery.

Young couples like these, while pursuing reform, also experimented with equal relationships in an age that assigned distinctly unequal roles to husbands and wives. On the one hand, women were told that their sphere was the home,

Marriage Expectations Examine the respective marital requirements of husband and wife detailed in this certificate (you may need a magnifying glass). What are male responsibilities and what are female duties? How might the views expressed here relate to the meeting the same year at Seneca Falls, New York? *(Library of Congress)*

upholding piety and virtue. On the other hand, they were assured that their ethical influence would be "felt around the globe." Not surprisingly, many women joined the perfectionist movement to cleanse America of its sins. Active in every reform movement, women discovered the need to improve their own condition.

To achieve greater personal autonomy, antebellum American women, like their English counterparts, pursued several paths depending on their class, cultural background, and situation. In 1834, Lowell textile workers went on strike against wage reductions while looking to marriage as an escape from millwork. Catharine Beecher argued that it was by accepting marriage and the home as a woman's sphere and by mastering domestic duties there that women could best achieve power and autonomy. In another form of "domestic feminism," American wives exerted considerable control over their bodies by convincing their husbands to practice abstinence, coitus interruptus, and other forms of birth control.

Other women found an outlet for their role as moral guardians by attacking the sexual double standard. In 1834, a group of Presbyterian women formed the New York Female Moral Reform Society. Inspired by revivalism, they visited brothels, opened a refuge to convert prostitutes, and even publicly identified brothel patrons. Within five years, there were 445 auxiliaries of the society.

Lowell millworkers and New York moral reformers generally accepted the duties—and attractions—of female domesticity. Other women, usually from upper-middle-class families, did not. They sought to devote their lives to working directly for more legally protected rights. Campaigns to secure married women's control of their property and custody of their children involved many of them. Others gained from abolitionism a growing awareness of similarities between the oppression of women and of slaves. Collecting antislavery signatures and speaking out publicly, they continually faced denials of their right to speak or act politically. American women "have good cause to be grateful to the slave," Kelley wrote, for in "striving to strike his iron off, we found most surely, that we were manacled *ourselves.*"

The more active women became in antislavery activities, the more hostility they encountered, especially from conservative clergymen. Sarah Grimké was criticized once too often. She struck back in 1837 with *Letters on the Condition of Women and the Equality of the Sexes,* concluding that she sought "no favors for my sex. I surrender not our claim to equality. All I ask of our brethren is, that they will take their feet from off our necks and permit us to stand upright on that ground which God designed us to occupy."

Grimké's strong message was soon translated into an active movement for women's rights, and illustrative of its international character, the American movement was born in London. At the World Anti-Slavery Convention in London in 1840, attended by many American abolitionists, male delegates refused to let women participate. Two of the women, Elizabeth Cady Stanton and Lucretia Mott, had to sit behind curtains and were forbidden to speak. When they returned home, they resolved to "form a society to advocate the rights of women." In 1848, in Seneca Falls, New York, their intentions, though delayed, were fulfilled in one of the most significant antebellum protest gatherings.

In preparing for the meeting, Mott and Stanton drew up a list of women's grievances. For example, even though some states had awarded married women control over their property, they still had no control over their earnings. Modeling their "Declaration of Sentiments" on the Declaration of Independence, the women at Seneca Falls proclaimed it a self-evident truth that "all men and women are created equal" and that men had usurped women's freedom and dignity. The remedy was expressed in 11 resolutions calling for equal opportunities in education and work, equality before the law, and the right to appear on public platforms. The most controversial resolution called for women's "sacred right to the elective franchise." The convention approved Mott and Stanton's list of resolutions.

Throughout the 1850s, led by Stanton and Susan B. Anthony, women continued to meet in annual conventions, working by resolution, persuasion, and petition campaign to achieve equal political, legal, and property rights with men. The right to vote, however, was considered the cornerstone of the movement. It remained so for 72 years of struggle until 1920. The Seneca Falls convention was crucial in beginning the campaign for equal public rights. The seeds of psychological autonomy and self-respect, still continuing, were sown in the struggles of countless women like Abby Kelley, Sarah Grimké, and Emily Robinson.

TIMELINE

1828	Jackson defeats Adams for the presidency		**1832–1836**	Removal of funds from U.S. Bank to state banks
	Tariff of Abominations		**1833**	American Anti-Slavery Society founded
1830–1831	Charles Finney's religious revivals			
1832	Jackson vetoes U.S. Bank charter		**1834**	Whig party established
	Jackson reelected		**1836**	Van Buren elected president
	Worcester v. Georgia		**1837**	Financial panic and depression
1832–1833	Nullification crisis			
			1837–1838	Cherokee "Trail of Tears"

Conclusion

Perfecting America

Inspired by religious revivalism, advocates for women's rights and temperance, abolitionists like Marius and Emily Robinson, and other reformers carried on very different crusades from those waged by Andrew Jackson against Indians, nullificationists, and the U.S. Bank. In fact, Jacksonian politics and antebellum reform were often at odds. Most abolitionists and temperance reformers were anti-Jackson Whigs. Jackson and most Democrats repudiated the passionate moralism of reformers.

Yet both sides shared more than either side would admit. Reformers and political parties were both organized rationally. Both mirrored new tensions in a changing, growing society. Both had an abiding faith in change and the idea of progress yet feared that sinister forces jeopardized that progress. Whether ridding the nation of alcohol or the national bank, slavery or nullification, mob violence or political opponents, both forces saw these responsibilities in terms of patriotic duty. Whether inspired by religious revivalism or political party loyalty, both believed that by stamping out evil forces, they could shape a better America. In this effort, they turned to politics, religion, reform, and new lifestyles. Whether politicians like Jackson and Clay, religious community leaders like Noyes and Ann Lee, or reformers like Garrison and the Grimkés, these antebellum Americans sought to remake their country politically and morally as it underwent social and economic change.

As the United States neared midcentury, slavery emerged as the most divisive issue. Against much opposition, the reformers had made slavery a matter of national political debate by the 1840s. Although both major political parties tried to evade the question, westward expansion and the addition of new territories to the nation would soon make avoidance impossible. Would new states be slave or free? The question increasingly aroused the deepest passions of the American people. For the pioneer family, who formed the driving force behind the westward movement, however, questions involving their fears and dreams seemed more important. We turn to this family and that movement in the next chapter.

Questions for Review and Reflection

1. How does the story of Marius Robinson and Emily Rakestraw introduce the major themes and structure of the chapter?

2. What social, economic, and political forces motivated Americans to seek ways of controlling their lives? How did they try to shape both their own lives and also America?

3. What were the major issues of Jackson's administration? Was he primarily a unifier or divider? Did he advance or set back the development of American democracy? Explain your responses.

4. Explain the key differences between Democrats and Whigs and their basis of support. Which party would you have supported and why?

5. Describe the role of religion in antebellum American life and the ways in which revivalism sought to affect social change. Do you agree that this was the proper function for religion?

6. Characterize three or four major antebellum reform movements, pointing out what motivations, values, challenges, and resources were common to each of them. Would you have been a reformer? Why or why not?

Discovering U.S. History Online

Godey's Lady's Book Online Home Page www.history.rochester.edu/godeys/
Here is online text of this interesting nineteenth-century journal.

Influence of Prominent Abolitionists www.loc.gov/exhibits/african/influ.html
This Library of Congress exhibit site, with pictures and text, discusses some key African American abolitionists.

Religion and the National Culture in the Nineteenth Century www.nhc.rtp.nc.us:8080/tserve/nineteen.htm
Using essays and contemporary photos and primary sources, this site was "designed to help teachers of American history bring their students to a greater understanding of the role religion has played in the development of the United States."

The Trail of Tears www.ourgeorgiahistory.com/indians/cherokee/trail_of_tears.html
A thorough interactive essay explains the history of the Trail of Tears and provides information on Cherokee forts and a map of the various routes traveled during this period of Indian removal.

Reform Movements www.womhist.binghamton.edu/datelist.htm
This site includes many essays and primary sources relevant to the antebellum reform movements including "The Appeal of Female Moral Reform," "The Nineteenth-Century Dress Reform Movement, 1838–1881," and "Lucretia Mott's Reform Networks, 1840–1860."

Fiction and Film

Nathaniel Hawthorne's *The Blithedale Romance* (1852), a novel set in a utopian community much like Brook Farm, reveals the challenges of perfecting America. Hawthorne's *Celestial Railroad and Other Stories* (1963 edition)— in particular, "The Birthmark," "Rappaccini's Daughter," and the title story—and *The Scarlet Letter* (1850) show the author's struggles to balance the head and the heart, scientific and romantic perfectionism. Charles Frazier's compelling historical novel, *Thirteen Moons* (2006), is an excellent social history of the rugged, blurred lives of frontier southern whites and Cherokees in mid-century, as well as a captivating love and coming of age story. *Not for Ourselves Alone: The Story of Elizabeth Cady Stanton and Susan B. Anthony* is Ken Burns's superb 1999 documentary. Other film possibilities include *Frederick Douglass: When the Lion Wrote History* (1994), a dramatization of *Uncle Tom's Cabin* (1987), and *The Journey of August King*, a 1996 film based on a 1971 novel. The film deals with the decision of a North Carolina frontiersman to help a female fugitive slave.

Recommended Reading

www.ablongman.com/nash

The Companion Website has a list of recommended readings about religious revival, reform, utopianism, abolitionism, and the women's rights movement.

American Stories

The Surprises of a Missionary Life

It was July 4, 1836, but nothing in her 28 years had prepared Narcissa Whitman for the sights and sounds marking this particular holiday. Earlier in the day, Narcissa and the party with which she was traveling had crossed over the South Pass of the Rocky Mountains, a memorable milestone for the nation's birthday. Now, evening had come, and the caravan set up camp for the night. Suddenly, wild cries and the sound of gunshots and galloping horses broke the silence. Fourteen or fifteen men, most dressed as Indians, advanced toward the camp. Frightened by the threatening appearance of the horsemen, the noise, and the bullets whizzing over her head, Narcissa may well have wondered if her journey and even her life were to end. But as the horsemen approached, the anxious travelers could make out a white flag tied to one of the rider's rifles. These were not foes but friends who had ridden out from the annual fur traders' rendezvous to greet the caravan.

Two days later, Narcissa reached the rendezvous site where hundreds of Indians as well as 200 whites, mostly traders and trappers, were gathered to exchange furs, tell stories, drink, and enjoy themselves. Some of the mounted Indians, "carrying their war weapons, wearing their war emblems and implements of music," put on a special display. The exhibition was a novelty for Narcissa, as was her presence for the Indians. Narcissa found herself the center of attention "in the midst of [a] gazing throng" of curious Indians. The experience was not unpleasant, and Narcissa's impression of the Indians was favorable. "They all like us and that we have come to live with them."

Narcissa Whitman was one of the first white women to cross the Rocky Mountains and live in Oregon territory in the 1830s. While many more Americans would follow her, only a few would share her reasons for coming west. They would come to farm, dig for gold, speculate in land, open a store, or practice law. However, Narcissa and her husband, Dr. Marcus Whitman, did not go west to better their lives but to carry God's word to the Native Americans. Inspired by the revivals of the Second Great Awakening and convinced that all non-Christians were headed toward eternal damnation, Narcissa and her husband came to settle among the Indians in Oregon territory and to convert them to Christianity and the American way of life.

This dream of becoming a missionary was one Narcissa had nourished since her early teens. But once the Whitmans reached their mission station in the Walla Walla valley, Narcissa slowly discovered that missionary work was nothing like her youthful fantasies. Although the Cayuse Indians listened to the missionaries and adopted some Christian practices, they never lived up to the Whitmans' high standards. None experienced conversion. They continued to consult their medicine men and refused to settle permanently next to the mission station. Cayuse women seemed little interested in the middle-class domestic skills Narcissa wished to teach them. Narcissa's positive impression of Native Americans disappeared. The Cayuse, she wrote, were "insolent, proud, domineering, arrogant, and ferocious."

There were other disappointments and personal tragedies. Marcus was often away from the mission on medical business, leaving Narcissa lonely and sometimes frightened. Her only daughter fell into the river and drowned.

As time passed, however, Narcissa's dismay and depression faded as hopeful signs of new possibilities other than Indian missionary work appeared. As she wrote to her mother in 1840, "a tide of immigration appears to be moving this way rapidly." In the following years, many American families passed the mission station. One wagon train included a family of children orphaned during their journey. The Whitmans adopted all seven children. Narcissa threw herself into caring for them and found herself too busy to work actively with the Cayuse.

The Indians were troubled by the numbers of whites coming into the territory, but the Whitmans, convinced that the future of the West lay with the emigrants, welcomed them. The day of the Indians had passed. As a "hunted, despised and unprotected" people, the Whitmans believed that the Native Americans were headed toward "entire extinction." But in an unexpected turn of events, some of the Cayuse rejected this vision, turned against the Whitmans, and killed them both. Such violent actions did nothing to slow the swarm of Americans heading west.

Narcissa Whitman and her husband, Marcus, were among thousands of Americans participating in the nation's expansion into the trans-Mississippi West. While the religious faith that drove them west differentiated them from many crossing the western plains and prairies, the Whitmans' cultural beliefs about the inferiority of the Native Americans and the necessity of American settlement were widely shared. Shared too was the conviction that the American values and way of life were superior to those of the Native Americans and Mexicans who occupied the land.

This chapter explores the trans-Mississippi West between 1830 and 1865. First we will consider how and when Americans moved west, by what means the United States acquired the vast territories that in 1840 belonged to other nations, and the meaning of "Manifest Destiny," the slogan used to defend the conquest of the continent west of the Mississippi River. Then we explore the nature of life on the western farms, in western mining communities where Latin American, Chinese, and European adventurers mingled with American fortune seekers, and in western cities. Finally, the chapter examines responses of Native Americans and Mexican Americans to expansion and illuminates the ways different cultural traditions intersected in the West.

PROBING THE TRANS-MISSISSIPPI WEST

Until the 1840s, most Americans lived east of the Mississippi. By 1860, however, some 4.3 million Americans had moved beyond the great river into the trans-Mississippi West.

The International Context for American Expansionism

When the Whitmans arrived in Oregon territory, they stayed at a bustling British fur trading post with hundreds of workers: French Canadians, English, Scots, and many from mixed European-Indian backgrounds. The establishment symbolized the international setting within which American expansionism occurred. The shifting interests and fortunes of several European nations helped to shape the character and timing of westward emigration even though individual settlers might not recognize the large forces affecting their experiences.

In 1815, except for Louisiana territory, Spain held title to most of the trans-Mississippi West. For hundreds of years, Spaniards had marched north from Mexico to explore, settle, and spread Spanish culture to native peoples. Eventually, Spanish holdings included present-day Texas, Arizona, New Mexico, Nevada, Utah, western Colorado, California, and parts of Wyoming, Kansas, and Oklahoma. Spanish rulers tried to exclude foreigners from these frontier areas but increasingly found this policy difficult to enforce. The area was vast, and Spain itself was experiencing internal difficulties that weakened its hold on its New World colonies. In 1820, the conservative Spanish monarch faced liberal revolt at home. Its ideas sparked liberation movements in the New World.

In 1821, Mexico declared its independence and acquired Spain's territories in the trans-Mississippi West with a population that included 75,000 Spanish-speaking inhabitants and numerous Native American tribes. While maintaining control of this distant region and its peoples would have been difficult under any circumstances, Mexico was not successful in forming a strong or a stable government until the 1860s. It was in a weak position to resist the avid American appetite for expansion.

North of California lay Oregon country, a vaguely defined area extending to Alaska. Russia, Spain, and Great Britain all had claims to Oregon, but negotiations with Russia and Spain in 1819 and 1824 left just the United States and Britain contending for the territory. Joint British-American occupation, agreed upon in 1818 and 1827, delayed settling the boundary question. With only a handful of Americans in the territory, Oregon's future would depend partly on how Britain, the world's richest and most powerful country, defined its interests there as Americans began to stream into Oregon in the 1840s.

Early Interest in the West

Some Americans penetrated the trans-Mississippi West long before the great migrations of the 1840s and 1850s. The fur business attracted American trappers and traders to Oregon by 1811 and a decade later to the Rockies. Many married Indian

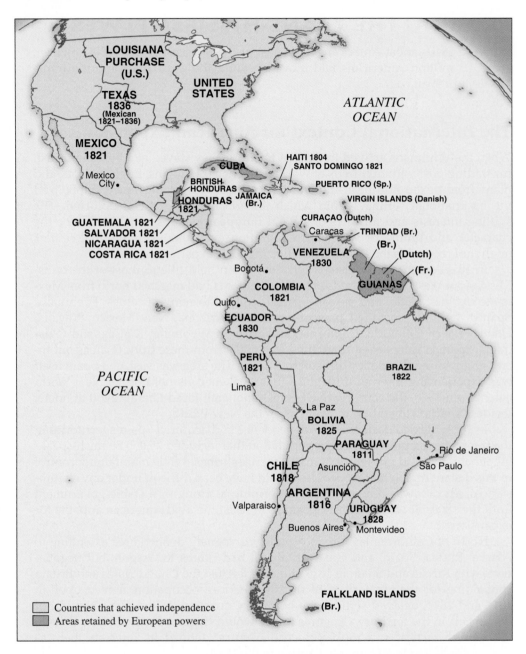

NORTH AND SOUTH AMERICA, 1800–1836 Events in Europe had a dramatic impact on the Americas. Napoleon's defeat of the Spanish king in 1808 and the popularization of the ideas of the French Revolution contributed to ending Spanish rule in the New World. Note how rapidly countries claimed their independence in the southern hemisphere and Latin America.   ■   **Reflecting on the Past** How did the changing political landscape of the Americas affect the power and influence of the United States in the region?

women and established valuable connections with Indian tribes involved in trapping. Along with their wives, they occupied a cultural middle ground characterized by elements from both American and native ways of life. Some ultimately became guides for Americans who emigrated later to the West.

Like the Whitmans, Methodist missionaries established early outposts in Oregon territory to teach native tribes Christian and American practices. Roman Catholic priests, sent from Europe, also worked among the native peoples. More tolerant of Indian culture than their Protestant counterparts, the Catholics had greater initial success in converting native peoples to Christianity.

The collapse of the Spanish Empire in 1821 provided Americans with a variety of opportunities. Each year American caravans followed the Santa Fe Trail, loaded with weapons, tools, and brightly colored calicoes for New Mexico's 40,000 inhabitants. Eventually, some "Anglos" settled there. In Texas, cheap land for cotton rather than commerce attracted settlers and squatters just as the small local Tejano population was adjusting to Mexico's independence. By 1835, almost 30,000 had migrated to Texas, the largest group of Americans living outside the nation's boundaries.

On the Pacific, a handful of New England traders carrying sea-otter skins to China anchored in the harbors of Spanish California in the early nineteenth century. By the 1830s, as the near extermination of the animals ruined this trade, a commerce exchanging California cowhides and tallow for clothes, boots, hardware, and furniture manufactured in the East developed.

Tribes driven from the South and the Old Northwest by the American government into present-day Oklahoma and Kansas were among the earliest easterners in the trans-Mississippi West. Ironically, some of these tribes acted as agents of white civilization by introducing cotton, the plantation system, black slavery, and schools. Other tribes triggered conflicts that weakened the western tribes with whom they came into contact. These disruptions foreshadowed white incursions later in the century.

The fact that much of the trans-Mississippi West lay outside U.S. boundaries and that the government had guaranteed Indian tribes permanent possession of some western territories did not deter American economic or missionary activities. By the 1840s, a growing volume of detailed published information about the interior made emigration feasible. Lansford Hastings's *Emigrants' Guide to Oregon and California* (1845) provided practical information and a rationale for emigration, arguing that Americans would bring "genuine Republicanism and unsophisticated Democracy" to the West, replacing "ignorance, superstition, and despotism."

Hastings's vision of the future materialized rapidly. During the 1840s the United States used war and diplomacy to acquire Mexico's possessions in the West as well as the title to the Oregon country up to the 49th parallel. The 1853 Gadsden Purchase secured yet another chunk of Mexican territory for the nation.

Manifest Destiny

Florid rhetoric accompanied territorial growth, and Americans used the slogan "Manifest Destiny" to justify it. The phrase, coined in 1845, suggested that the country's superior institutions and culture constituted a God-given right, even an obligation, to spread American civilization across the entire continent. This sense of uniqueness and mission had roots in Puritan utopianism and revolutionary republicanism but also owed much to the rapid growth and progress of the early nineteenth century. The idea that the nation could and should expand enjoyed wide popular support.

WINNING THE TRANS-MISSISSIPPI WEST

Manifest Destiny justified expansion, but events in Texas triggered the national government's determination to move west of the Mississippi. The Texas question dated back to the years of Spanish control. Primarily a buffer zone for Mexico, the sparsely populated area of the Southwest had scattered centers of Spanish settlement, distant from one another and thousands of miles from Mexico City. Vulnerable as this defensive perimeter of the Spanish Empire was, the United States had recognized its legal status with the Adams-Onis Treaty of 1819, which, in return for Florida, specifically conceded Texas to Spain.

Annexing Texas, 1845

By the time that treaty was ratified in 1821, Mexico was independent but unable to defend its borderlands or to develop powerful bonds of national identity. Mexicans soon had reason to wonder whether Americans would honor the 1819 treaty.

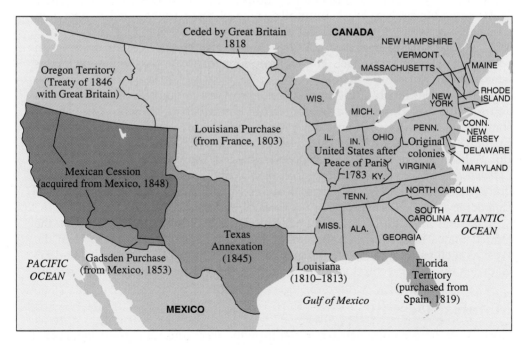

UNITED STATES TERRITORIAL EXPANSION BY 1860 This map makes the rapidity of the acquisition of the Far West clear.

As American politicians like Henry Clay called for "reannexation" of Texas, Mexican fears grew.

In 1823, the Mexican government resolved to strengthen Texas by increasing its population. In return for token payments and pledges to adopt Catholicism and Mexican citizenship, settlers were promised land. Stephen F. Austin was among the first Americans to take up the offer. Most settlers were southerners, and some brought slaves. By the end of the decade, some 15,000 white Americans, 1,000 slaves, but just 5,000 Tejanos lived in Texas.

Mexican officials began to question the wisdom of their policies. Although Austin converted to Roman Catholicism, few settlers honored their bargain. Some were malcontents who disliked Mexican laws and limitations on their opportunities. In late 1826, a small group declared the Republic of Fredonia. Although Stephen Austin helped crush the brief uprising, American newspapers praised the rebels as "apostles of democracy."

Mexican anxiety rose. Secretary of Foreign Relations Lucas Aláman branded American settlers advance agents of the United States. In 1829, the Mexican government determined to curb American influence by abolishing slavery in Texas. In 1830, it forbade further American emigration. But little changed. American residents evaded the mandate to abolish slavery while emigrants still crossed the border into Texas.

Tensions escalated, and in October 1835, a skirmish between the colonial militia and Mexican forces opened hostilities. Sam Houston, onetime governor of Tennessee and army officer, headed the Texas forces. Although Texans called the war a revolution, it was in fact, as one Vermont soldier observed, "a rebellion."

Mexican dictator and general Antonio López de Santa Anna hurried north with an army of 6,000 conscripts, many of them Mayan Indians who spoke no Spanish. All were exhausted by the long march. Supply lines were spread thin. Nevertheless, Santa Anna and his men won initial engagements. They took the Alamo in San Antonio, defended by 187 Americans—all of whom were killed—and then the fortress of Goliad, to the southeast, where more than 300 Americans lost their lives.

William Barret Travis, Letter from the Alamo (1836)

As he pursued Houston and the Texans toward the San Jacinto River, carelessness proved Santa Anna's undoing. Although anticipating an American attack, the Mexican general and his men settled down to their usual siesta on April 21, 1836, without posting an adequate guard. As the Mexicans dozed, the Americans attacked. With cries of "Remember the Alamo! Remember Goliad!" the Texans overcame the army, captured its commander in his slippers, and won the war within 20 minutes. American casualties were minimal, but 630 Mexicans lay dead.

The Alamo

Vanquished and threatened with lynching, Santa Anna signed treaties recognizing Texan independence. When news of the disaster reached Mexico City, however, the Mexican Congress repudiated an agreement carried out under "threat of death," insisting that Texas was still part of Mexico.

The new republic, financially unstable with a questionable diplomatic status, sought admission to the United States. Jackson, whose Texas agent declared that the republic's "future security must depend more upon the weakness and imbecility of her enemy than upon her own strength," was reluctant to act quickly.

With 13 free and 13 slave states, many northerners violently opposed taking in another slave state. Petitions poured into Congress in 1837 opposing annexation. Soon the explosive idea was dropped.

For the next few years, the Lone Star Republic limped along. Mexico refused to recognize it, but sent only an occasional raiding party across the border. Texans failed ignominiously in their ill-conceived attempt to capture Santa Fe in 1841. While diplomatic maneuvering in European capitals for financial aid and recognition was only moderately successful, financial ties with the United States increased.

Texas became headline news again in 1844. One Alabama expansionist rightly predicted that it would "agitate the country more than all the other public questions ever have." Hoping to ensure his reelection, President John Tyler reopened the annexation issue. Powerful sectional, national, and political tensions exploded, demonstrating the divisiveness of the slavery-expansion question. Southern Democrats insisted that their region's future hinged on annexing Texas.

Other wings of the Democratic party capitalized more successfully on the issue, however. Stephen Douglas of Illinois, among others, vigorously supported annexation not because it would expand slavery (a topic he avoided), but because it would spread American civilization. Such arguments, classic examples of Manifest Destiny, put the question into a national context of expanding American freedom. So powerfully did these Democrats link Texas to Manifest Destiny that their candidate, James Polk of Tennessee, secured the 1844 Democratic nomination. Polk called for both "the reannexation of Texas at the earliest practicable period" and the occupation of the Oregon Territory.

Fearing the addition of another slave state, most Whigs opposed annexation. They accused the Democrats of exploiting Manifest Destiny to gain office rather than to bring freedom to Texas. As the Whigs feared, Polk rode the issue to win a close election in 1844.

DOCUMENT

John O'Sullivan, "Annexation" (1845)

But by the time Polk assumed office in March 1845, Tyler had resolved the question of annexation by pushing through Congress a joint resolution admitting Texas to the Union. Unlike a treaty, requiring the approval of two-thirds of the Senate, a joint resolution needed only majority support. Nine years after its revolution, Texas finally joined the Union, with the right to split into five states if it chose.

War with Mexico, 1846–1848

When Mexico learned of Texas's annexation, it severed diplomatic ties with the United States. Mexicans could easily interpret events from the 1820s on as part of a gigantic American plot to steal Texas. During the war for Texas independence, American papers, especially those in the South, had hailed the rebels, while

IMAGE

The Storming of Chapultepec

southern money and volunteers assisted the Texans. Now, in his inaugural address in 1845, Polk was arguing "that our system may easily be extended to the utmost bounds of our territorial limits, and that as it shall be extended the bonds of our Union, so far from being weakened will become stronger." Did his remarks suggest further territorial designs, this time on Mexico?

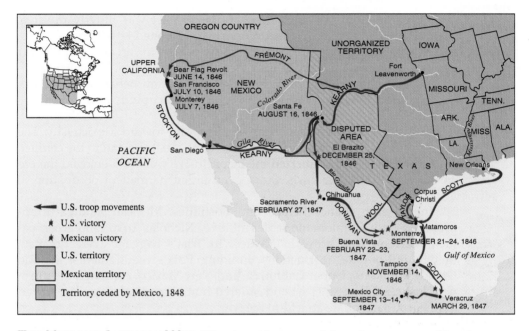

THE MEXICAN-AMERICAN WAR What does this map reveal about the movements of American troops during the Mexican-American war? Would you consider American actions equivalent to an invasion? How large an area was in dispute between the Americans and the Mexicans?

Like many Americans, Polk failed to appreciate how the annexation of Texas humiliated Mexico and encouraged its government to respond belligerently. The president anticipated that a weak Mexico would grant his grandiose demands: Texas bounded by the Rio Grande rather than the Nueces River 150 miles to its north, as well as California and New Mexico.

As a precaution, Polk ordered General Zachary Taylor to move "on or near the Rio Grande." By October 1845, Taylor and 3,500 American troops had reached the Nueces River. The positioning of an American army in Texas did not mean that Polk expected war. Rather, he hoped that a show of military force, coupled with secret diplomacy, would bring the desired concessions. In November, the president sent his secret agent, John L. Slidell, to Mexico City with instructions to secure the Rio Grande border and to buy Upper California and New Mexico. When the Mexican government refused to receive Slidell, Polk decided to make Mexico accept American terms. He ordered Taylor south to the Rio Grande, a move Mexicans saw as an act of war. Democratic newspapers and expansionists enthusiastically hailed Polk's provocative decision; Whigs opposed it.

In late April, the Mexican government declared a state of defensive war. Two days later, a skirmish between Mexican and American troops resulted in 16 American casualties. When Polk heard the news, he quickly drafted a war message for Congress. Despite the fact that the skirmish had occurred on both contested and Mexican territory, Polk claimed that Mexico had "invaded our territory and shed American blood upon American soil." "Notwithstanding all our efforts to avoid it," Polk asserted, war "exists by act of Mexico."

Although Congress declared war, the conflict was bitterly divisive. Many Whigs, including Abraham Lincoln, questioned Polk's truthfulness, and, with time, their opposition grew more vocal. Lincoln declared the war one "of conquest brought into existence to catch votes." The American Peace Society revealed sordid examples of army misbehavior in Mexico, and Frederick Douglass accused the country of "cupidity and love of dominion." Many workers also censured the war.

Debate continued as American troops swept toward Mexico City. The Mexican government refused to admit defeat or to negotiate an end to the conflict. Yet even as some Americans criticized the inconclusive war, Polk enjoyed the enthusiastic support of expansionists. Some even urged permanent occupation of Mexico.

In the end, chance helped end hostilities. Mexican moderates approached Polk's diplomatic representative, Nicholas Trist, who accompanied the American army in Mexico. In Trist's baggage were detailed, though out-of-date, instructions outlining Polk's requirements: the Rio Grande boundary, Upper California, and New Mexico. Although the president lost confidence in Trist and ordered him home in chains, Trist stayed in Mexico to negotiate an end to the war.

California and New Mexico

While Texas and Mexico dominated the headlines, Polk considered California and New Mexico part of any resolution of the Mexico crisis. Serious American interest in California dated from the late 1830s. Before then, few Americans were living in California. Many had married into California families and taken Mexican citizenship. But gradual recognition of California's fine harbors, its favorable position for the China trade, and suspicion that Great Britain had designs on it fed the conviction that California must become part of the United States. The arrival of 1,500 overland emigrants in the 1840s increased the likelihood that California would not long remain a Mexican outpost.

In 1845, Polk appointed Thomas Larkin, a successful American merchant in Monterey, as his confidential agent. "If the people [of California] should desire to unite their destiny with ours," wrote Polk's secretary of state, James Buchanan, to Larkin, "they would be received as brethren." Polk's efforts to buy California suggested that he was sensitive to the fragility of American claims to the region. But Santa Anna, carrying the burden of having lost Texas, was in no position to sell.

New Mexico was also on Polk's list. Profitable economic ties with the United States dating back to the 1820s stimulated American territorial ambitions. As part of the oldest and largest Mexican community in North America, however, most New Mexicans had little desire for annexation. The unsuccessful Texan assault on Santa Fe in 1841 and border clashes in the two following years did not enhance the attractiveness of Anglo neighbors. But standing awkwardly in the path of westward expansion and further isolated from Mexico by the annexation of Texas in 1846, New Mexico's future was uncertain.

In June 1846, shortly after the declaration of war with Mexico, American troops led by Colonel Stephen W. Kearney left Fort Leavenworth, Kansas, for

New Mexico. Kearney had orders to occupy Mexico's northern provinces and to protect the lucrative Santa Fe trade. Two months later, the army took Santa Fe without a shot. Having already made strategic alliances with Americans, New Mexico's upper class readily accepted the new rulers. However, ordinary Mexicans and Pueblo Indians did not take conquest so lightly. After Kearney departed for California, resistance erupted first in New Mexico and then in California. Kearney was wounded, and the first appointed American governor of New Mexico was killed. In the end, superior American military strength won the day. By January 1847, both California and New Mexico were firmly in American hands.

The Treaty of Guadalupe Hidalgo, 1848

Negotiated by Trist and signed on February 2, 1848, the Treaty of Guadalupe Hidalgo resolved the original issues by setting the Rio Grande as the boundary between Mexico and the United States and by transferring the Southwest and California into American hands. At a cost of 13,000 American lives, mostly due to disease, the United States gained 75,000 Spanish-speaking inhabitants, 150,000 Native Americans, and 529,017 square miles, almost a third of prewar Mexico. It paid Mexico $15 million (and another $10 million in 1853 for the Gadsden Purchase), agreed to honor American claims against Mexico, and guaranteed the civil, political, and property rights of former Mexican citizens. Although sporadic violence would continue for years in the Southwest as Mexicans protested the outcome, the war was over, and the Americans had won.

The Oregon Question, 1844–1846

In the Pacific Northwest, the presence of mighty Great Britain suggested reliance on diplomacy rather than war. Glossing over the disputed nature of American claims to the Oregon Territory, Polk assured the inauguration day crowd that "our title to the country of Oregon is 'clear and unquestionable.'" The British did not agree.

Though the British considered the president's speech belligerent, Polk correctly noted that Americans had begun to settle in the disputed territories. Between 1842 and 1845, the number of Americans in Oregon grew from 400 to more than 5,000, mostly south of the Columbia River in the Willamette valley. By 1843, these settlers had written a constitution and soon after elected a legislature. At the same time, declining British interest in the area set the stage for an eventual compromise. The near destruction of the beaver undermined the fur trade, while the riches created by Britain's Industrial Revolution reduced the appeal of colonies. Britain had already granted Canada self-rule. Attractive commercial opportunities were opening up in other parts of the world like India and China, while New Zealand, annexed in 1840, and Australia became magnets for British emigration.

Polk's flamboyant posture and the expansive American claims made mediation difficult, however. Polk's campaign slogan claimed a boundary of 54°40'. But Polk was not willing to go to war with Great Britain for Oregon. Privately, he considered reasonable a boundary at the 49th parallel, which would extend the existing Canadian-American border to the Pacific.

Soon after his inauguration, Polk offered his compromise to Great Britain, but his tone antagonized the British. In his year-end address to Congress in 1845, the president increased diplomatic tensions by again claiming Oregon and giving the required one-year's notice of American intention to cancel the joint occupation.

Despite slogans, most Americans did not want to fight for Oregon. As war with Mexico loomed, the task of resolving the disagreement became more urgent. The British, too, were eager to settle, and in June 1846 they agreed to the 49th parallel boundary if Vancouver Island remained British. Polk ended the crisis just weeks before the declaration of war with Mexico; he escaped some of the responsibility for retreating from slogans by sharing it with the Senate, who approved the compromise.

As these events show, Manifest Destiny was an idea that supported and justified expansionist policies. It corresponded to Americans' basic belief that expansion was necessary and right. As early as 1816, American geography books pictured the nation's western boundary at the Pacific and included Texas. Popular literature typically described Indians as a dying race and Mexicans as "injurious neighbor[s]." Only whites could make the wilderness flower. Thus, as lands east of the Mississippi filled up, Americans automatically called on familiar ideas to justify expansion.

GOING WEST AND EAST

IMAGE

American Progress, 1872

Americans lost little time in moving into the new territories. Between 1841 and 1867, thousands of Americans left their homes for the West. By 1860, California alone had 380,000 settlers. At the same time, thousands of Chinese headed south and east to destinations like Australia, Hawaii, and North and South America to escape the unrest caused by opium wars with Great Britain, internal unrest, and poor economic conditions. Sixty-three thousand had come to the United States by 1870, most settling in California.

One Chinese folk song depicted the "perilous journey" to the United States "sailing [in] a boat with bamboo poles across the sea." The Chinese, of course, had little choice on their travel route to the American West, but American migrants did. Some chose the expensive sea route from Atlantic or Gulf Coast ports around South America to the West Coast or across Panama and then by sea to the coast. Most American emigrants, however, chose land routes. In 1843, the first large party succeeded in crossing the plains and mountains to Oregon. More followed. Between 1841 and 1867, some 350,000 traveled the overland trails to California or Oregon, while others trekked part of the way to intermediate points like Colorado and Utah.

IMAGE

A Forty-Niner's Covered Wagon

Unlike earlier migrations west, the trip to the Far West involved considerable expense: $600 paid for one person on the relatively comfortable Cape Horn voyage or for four people overland. (If emigrants sold their wagons and oxen at the journey's end, the final expenses might be only $220.) Such outlays ruled out the very poor. Migration to the Far West (with the exception of group migration to Utah) was a movement of middle-class Americans.

The Emigrants

Most of the emigrants heading for the Far West, where slavery was prohibited, were white and American-born. They came from the Midwest and the Upper South. A few free blacks made the trip as well. Emigrants from the Deep South usually headed for Arkansas or Texas, many with their slaves. By 1840, over 11,000 slaves toiled in Texas and 20,000 in Arkansas.

Except for the Gold Rush, white migration was a family experience, usually involving men and women from their late twenties to early forties. A sizable number had recently married. For most, migration to the Far West was the latest in a series of moves, often as children or as newlyweds. But this time, vast distances seemed to mean a final separation from home.

Migrants' Motives

While emigrant expectations varied, many believed that the West would offer rich opportunities. Thousands sought gold. Others anticipated making their fortune as merchants, shopkeepers, and peddlers. Some intended to speculate in land, acquiring large blocks of public lands and reselling to later settlers at a handsome profit. Practicing law or medicine on the frontier attracted still others.

Most migrants dreamed of bettering their life by farming, and government policies made it easier to get land. During the 1830s and 1840s, preemption acts allowed "squatters" to settle public lands before the government offered them for sale and then purchase them at the minimum price once they came on the market. The amount of land a family had to buy shrank to only 40 acres. (In 1862, the Homestead Act would offer 160 acres of government land free to citizens or future citizens over 21 who lived on the property, improved it, and paid a small registration fee.) Oregon's land policy was even more generous. It awarded a single man 320 acres of free land and a married man 640 acres, provided he occupied his claim for four years and made improvements.

Some emigrants went west for their health. Others pursued religious or cultural missions in the West. Missionary couples like David and Catherine Blaine, who settled in frontier Seattle, were determined to bring Protestantism and education to white settlers. Stirred by stories of the "deplorable morals" on the frontier, they left the comforts of home to evangelize and educate westerners. Still others, like the Mormons, made the long trek to Utah to establish a society conforming to their religious beliefs.

Like Americans, Chinese migrants also dreamed of bettering their condition. Most were married men facing limited opportunities in their villages. Labor circulars insisted that Americans "want the Chinaman to come and make him very welcome. ... Money is in great plenty and to spare in America." Emigrants to Hawaii and the United States reinforced the message when they returned with money in their pockets. In the 1860s, Chinese laborers could earn $30 a month

Recovering the Past

Nineteenth-century journals kept by hundreds of ordinary men and women traveling west on the overland trails constitute a rich source for exploring the nature of the westward experience. They are also an example of how private sources can be used to deepen our understanding of the past. Diaries, journals, and letters all provide us with a personal perspective on major happenings. These sources tend to focus on the concrete, so they convey the texture of daily life in the nineteenth century, daily routines and amusements, clothing, habits, and interactions with family and friends. They also provide evidence of the varied concerns, attitudes, and prejudices of the writers, thus providing a test of commonly accepted generalizations about individual and group behavior.

Like any historical source, personal documents must be used carefully. It is important to note the writer's age, gender, class, and regional identification. Although this information may not be available, some of the writer's background can be deduced from what he or she has written. It is also important to consider for what purpose and for whom the document was composed. This information will help explain the tone or character of the source and what has been included or left out. It is, of course, important to avoid generalizing too much from one or even several similar sources. Only after reading many diaries, letters, and journals is it possible to make valid generalizations about life in the past.

Here we present excerpts from two travel journals of the 1850s. Few of the writers considered their journals to be strictly private. Often, they were intended as a family record or as information for friends back home. Therefore, material of a personal nature has often been excluded. Nineteenth-century Americans referred to certain topics, such as pregnancy, only indirectly or not at all.

One excerpt comes from Mary Bailey's 1852 journal. Mary was 22 years old when she crossed the plains to California with her 32-year-old doctor husband. Originally a New Englander, Mary had lived in Ohio for six years before moving west. The Baileys were reasonably prosperous and were able to restock necessary supplies on the road west. The other writer, Robert Robe, was 30 years old when he crossed along the same route a year earlier than the Baileys, headed for Oregon. Robert was a native of Ohio and a Presbyterian minister.

REFLECTING ON THE PAST   As you read these brief excerpts, notice what each journal reveals about the trip west. What kinds of challenges did the emigrants face on their journey? Can you see indications of the divisions of work based on gender? How is the focus of their interests different? What sorts of interactions seem to have occurred between men and women?

Even these short excerpts suggest that men and women, as they traveled west, had different concerns and different perspectives on the journey. How are the two accounts similar and different?

Journal of Robert Robe

[MAY] [1851]

29. Have arrived in the region abounding in Buffalo. At noon a considerable herd came in sight. The first any of us had ever seen. Thus now for the chase—the horsemen proved too swift in pursuit and frightened them into the Bluffs without capturing any—the footmen pursued however and killed three pretty good success for the first.

30. Nothing remarkable today.

31. Game being abundant we resolved to rest our stock and hunt today—Started in the morning on foot. Saw probably 1,000 Buffalo. Shot at several and killed one. Where ever we found them

---

wolves were prowling around as if to guard them. Their real object is however no doubt to seize the calves as their prey. Saw a town of Prairie dogs, they are nearly as large as a gray squirrel. They bark fiercely when at a little distance but on near approach flee to their holes. Wherever they are we see numerous owls. After a very extensive ramble and having seen a variety of game we returned at sunset with most voracious appetites.

[JUNE]

1. The Bluffs became beautifully undulating losing their precipitous aspect and the country further back is beautifully rolling prairie.

2. In the evening camped beside our old friends Miller and Dovey. They had met with a great loss this morning their 3 horses having taken fright at a drove of buffalo and ran entirely away. Some of our company killed more buffalo this evening & a company went in the night with teams to bring them in.

3. Spent the forenoon in an unsuccessful search for the above mentioned horses. In the afternoon pursued & caught our company after.

4. Crossed the south fork of the Platte at 2 p.m.

Source: Journal of Robert Robe [1851] from *Washington Historical Quarterly* (now *Pacific Northwest Quarterly*), January 1928. Reprinted with permission.

Journal of Mary Stuart Bailey

WEDNESDAY, APRIL 13, 1852
Left our hitherto happy home in Sylvania amid the tears of parting kisses of dear friends, many of whom were endeared to me by their kindness shown to me when I was a stranger in a strange land, when sickness and death visited our small family & removed our darling, our only child in a moment, as it were. Such kindness I can never forget. ...

FRIDAY, 21ST [MAY]
Rained last night. Slept in the tent for the first time. I was Yankee enough to protect myself by pinning up blankets over my head. I am quite at home in my tent.

12:00 Have traveled in the rain all day & we are stuck in the mud. I sit in the wagon writing while the men are at work doubling the teams to draw us out. ...

SUNDAY, 23RD.
Walked to the top of the hill where I could be quiet & commune with nature and nature's God. This afternoon I was annoyed by something very unpleasant & shed many tears and felt very unhappy. ...

SUNDAY, 4TH [JULY]
Started at 3 o'clock to find feed or know where it was. Had to go 4 or 5 miles off the road. Found water & good grass. Camped on the sand with sage roots for fuel. It is wintery, cold & somewhat inclined to rain, not pleasant. Rather a dreary Independence Day. We speak of our friends at home. We think they are thinking of us. ...

MONDAY, 12TH.
Stayed in camp another day to get our horse better. He is much improved. It is cold enough. Washed in the morning & had the sick headache in the afternoon. ...

SATURDAY, 18TH [SEPTEMBER]
Very pleasant, delightful weather. Feel much better today. We are not stirring this afternoon. We have heard to a great deal of suffering, people being thrown out on the desert to die & being picked up & brought to the hospital. ...

TUESDAY, NOVEMBER 8TH
Sacramento city has been nearly consumed. The Dr. has had all his instruments & a good deal of clothing burned, loss not exceeding $300. It really seems as though it was not right for us to come to California & lose so much. I do not think that we shall be as well off as at home.

Source: Sandra L. Myers, ed., *Ho for California! Women's Overland Diaries from the Huntington Library* (San Marino, CA: Henry E. Huntington Library, 1980). Reprinted with the permission of the Henry E. Huntington Library.

A Mormon Wagon Train What does this view of a Mormon wagon train in the 1850s suggest about the terrain that emigrant families encountered as they went west? The Mormon migrations were the most organized of the migrations into the trans-Mississippi West, although not all Mormons were lucky enough to travel by wagon. Some emigrants to Utah pushed handcarts across the plains to their destination. *(Used by permission, Utah State Historical Society, all rights reserved.)*

working for the railroad, far more than the $3 to $5 they could expect if they stayed home.

The Overland Trails

The trip for American emigrants began at starting points in Iowa and Missouri. When the grass was up for the stock in the late spring, the emigrant trains set out.

IMAGE

Oregon Trail Marker

Making only 15 miles a day, emigrants first followed the valley of the Platte River up to South Pass in the Rockies. This part of the trip seemed novel, even enjoyable. Until the 1850s, conflict with Indians was rare. The traditional division of labor persisted: Men did "outdoor" work like driving and repairing wagons, and women handled domestic chores. Young children stayed out of the way in wagons, while older brothers and sisters walked alongside and lent a hand. Wagon trains might stop to observe the Sabbath, allowing for rest and laundry.

Later, difficulties multiplied. Cholera often took a heavy toll. Deserts and mountains replaced rolling prairies. Emigrants had to cross the final mountain ranges—the Sierras and the Cascades—before the first snowfall, so they pushed on relentlessly. Animals weakened by constant travel, poor feed, and bad water sickened, collapsed, and often died. Families had to lighten wagons by throwing

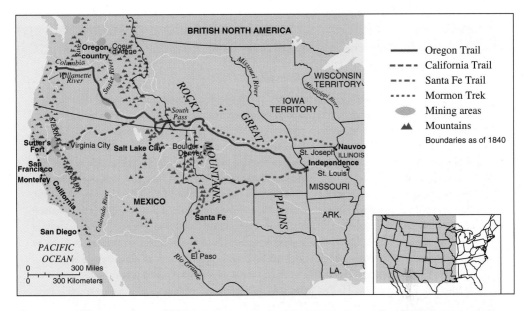

OVERLAND TRAILS TO THE WEST The various trails over which thousands of Americans traveled during the 1840s, 1850s, and 1860s are depicted on this map. What natural obstacles do the map's geographic features suggest the travelers faced and at what point during their trip did travelers encounter them?

out treasured possessions. Food supplies dwindled, and the familiar division of responsibilities often collapsed. Women found themselves loading and driving wagons, even helping to drag them over rocky mountain trails. Their husbands worked frantically with the animals and the wagons as the time of the first snowfall approached. Tempers frayed. Family harmony often collapsed. Mary Power, who with her husband and three children crossed in 1853, revealed exasperation and depression in her journal: "I felt my courage must fail me, for there we were in a strange land, almost without anything to eat, [with] a team that was not able to pull an empty wagon."

DOCUMENT

Elizabeth Dixon Smith Geer, *Oregon Trail Journal* (1847, 1848)

Finally, five or six months after setting out, emigrants arrived, exhausted and often penniless, in Oregon or California. As one wrote at the end of her journey in 1854, its "care, fatigue, tediousness, perplexities and dangers of various kinds, can not be excelled."

LIVING IN THE WEST

Whether elated or depressed after months of travel, emigrants had no choice but to start anew. As they did so, they naturally drew on their experiences back East. "Pioneers though we are, and proud of it, we are not content with the wilds ... with the idleness of the land, the rudely construct[ed] log cabin," one Oregon settler explained.

How Others See Us

Sent by the Mexican government in 1828 to assess American immigration to Texas, Lieutenant Jose Maria Sanchez gave his views on the settlement of San Felipe de Austin.

Village has been settled by Mr. Stephen Austin, a native of the United States of the North. It consists, at present, of forty or fifty wooden houses ... not arranged systematically so as to form streets; but on the contrary, lie in an irregular and desultory manner. Its population is nearly two hundred persons, of which only ten are Mexicans, for the balance are all Americans from the North with an occasional European. Two wretched little stores supply the inhabitants of the colony: one sells only whiskey, rum, sugar and coffee; the other, rice, flour, lard, and cheap cloth. ... To these the greater part of those who live in the village add strong liquor, for they are in general, in my opinion, lazy people of vicious character. Some of them cultivate their small farms by planting corn; but this task they usually entrust to their negro slaves, whom they treat with considerable harshness. Beyond the village in an immense stretch of land ... are scattered families brought by Stephen Austin ... The diplomatic policy of this empresario, evidence in all his actions, has ... lulled the authorities into a sense of security, while he works diligently for his own ends. In my judgment, the spark that will start the conflagration that will deprive us of Texas, will start from this colony.

- How does Sanchez characterize American immigrants to Texas?
- What do you think were American goals?
- How would you compare this account with the current view of many Americans toward Mexican immigrants to the United States?

Source: Jose Maria Sanchez, "A Trip to Texas in 1828," *Southwestern Historical Quarterly*, v. 29 (1926), p. 251.

Farming in the West

Pioneer farmers faced the urgent task of establishing homesteads and beginning farming. First, they had to locate a suitable claim, then clear land, and construct a shelter. Only then could they plant crops.

As farmers labored "to get the land subdued and the wilde nature out of it," they repeated a process occurring on earlier frontiers. Felling timber, pulling out native plants that seemed without value, and planting familiar crops began to transform the landscape, often with unanticipated results. When they planted seed brought from home, farmers unknowingly also introduced weeds that did all too well, like the Canadian thistle that gradually displaced native grass and rendered land useless for grazing.

Emigrants did not recognize the ecological transformation they set in motion. The goal of taming nature was so central and difficult that there was little time or inclination to wonder about long-range consequences.

The task of getting started presented many challenges. Since emigrant families had brought only a few possessions with them, they had to work without familiar tools and implements. The Oregon bride who set up housekeeping in the 1840s with only a stew kettle and three knives was not unusual. Men often found themselves assisting wives in unfamiliar domestic chores, while women helped men with their heavy outdoor work. After months of intense interaction with other travelers, families often felt lonely and thought longingly of friends and family back home. Although they might interact with nearby Indians, cultural biases made close friendships difficult.

One pioneer remembered that "in those days anyone residing within twenty miles was considered a neighbor." But the isolation usually ended within a few years as new emigrants arrived and old settlers sought better claims. As rural communities grew, settlers established schools, churches, and clubs. These organizations redefined acceptable forms of behavior and enforced conventional standards.

Determination to reestablish familiar institutions was most apparent in law and politics. In Oregon, pioneers set up a political system based on eastern models before territorial status was resolved. Before permanent schools or churches existed, men resumed familiar political rituals of electioneering, voting, and talking politics. They went to court to ensure law and order.

Establishing a common school system and churches was more difficult and less urgent than beginning political life. Few settlers initially thought education important enough to tax themselves for permanent public schools. Schools operated sporadically and only for students paying at least part of the fees. While confirmed believers attended early church services, they often discovered that there were too few members of individual denominations to support separate churches. Nor were converts plentiful, for many settlers had lost the habit of regular churchgoing. David Blaine learned the "unwelcome lesson" that "separation from gospel influences" had left many "quite indifferent to gospel truth."

The chronic shortage of cash on the frontier hampered the growth of both schools and churches. Until farmers could send their goods to market, they had little cash to spare. Geographic mobility also contributed to institutional instability. Up to three-quarters of the population of a frontier county might vanish within a 10-year period. Some farmed in as many as four locations before finding a satisfactory claim. Institutions relying on continuing personal and financial support suffered accordingly.

Yet newspapers, journals, and books, which circulated early on the frontier, reinforced familiar norms and determination. As more settlers arrived, support for educational, religious, and cultural institutions grew. In the end, as one pioneer pointed out, "We have a telegraph line from the East, a daily rail road train, daily mail and I am beginning to feel quite civilized. And here ended my pioneer experience." Only 16 years had passed since she had crossed the Plains.

Although the belief in frontier economic and social opportunities encouraged emigration, the dream was often illusory. Western society rapidly acquired a social and economic structure resembling that of the East. Frontier newspapers referred to leading settlers as the "better" sort, while workers for hire and tenant farmers appeared. Widespread geographic mobility also suggests that many failed to capitalize on the benefits of homesteading. Those who left communities were generally less successful than the core of stable residents, who became economic and social leaders. Those on the move believed that fortune would finally smile at their next stop. Said one wife when her husband announced another move: "I seemed to have heard all this before."

Mining Western Resources

In 1848, news of the discovery of gold in California swept the country and prompted thousands to abandon their ordinary lives in hopes of a fortune. Within a year, California's population ballooned from 14,000 to almost 100,000. By 1852, that figure more than doubled.

United States Territorial Expansion in the 1850s

Unlike farming pioneers, the "forty-niners" were mostly unmarried young men. (In 1850, over half the people in California were in their twenties.) Of those pouring into California in 1849, about 80 percent came from the United States and 13 percent from Mexico and South America; the rest were Europeans and Asians. California was thus one of the most diverse places in the country. Few, however, thought of settling in the West; instead, they dreamed of going home rich.

California was only the first and most dramatic of the western mining discoveries. In 1858, 25,000 to 30,000 emigrants, many from California, hurried to British Columbia; the next year gold strikes in Colorado precipitated another frantic rush. Precious metals lured prospectors to the Pacific Northwest, Montana, and Idaho in the 1860s and, in the next decade, to the Black Hills of South Dakota.

Unlike isolated farming settlements, the mining communities sprang up almost overnight after a strike. Mining camps, often hastily constructed, soon housed hundreds or even thousands of miners and the merchants, saloonkeepers, cooks, druggists, gamblers, and prostitutes serving them. Usually about half of a mining camp's residents were there to prospect the miners.

Given the motivation, character, and ethnic diversity of those flocking to boomtowns and the feeble attempts to set up local government in what were perceived as temporary communities, it was hardly surprising that mining life was disorderly. Racial antagonisms led to ugly riots and lynchings. Miners had few qualms about eliminating Indians and others who got in the way. Fistfights, drunkenness, and murder occurred often enough to become part of the lore of the gold rush. In less than a month, one woman wrote, "we have had murders, fearful accidents, bloody deaths, a mob, whippings, a hanging, an attempt at suicide, and a fatal duel."

Mining life was not usually this violent, but it did tolerate behavior that would have been unacceptable farther east. Miners were trying to get rich, not to recreate eastern communities. Married men, knowing the raucous and immoral character of mining communities, hesitated to bring wives and families west.

Although the lucky few struck it rich or at least made enough money to return home with pride intact, miners' journals and letters reveal that many made only enough to keep going. Easily mined silver and gold deposits soon ran out. Although Chinese miners proved adept at finding what early miners overlooked, the remaining rich deposits lay deeply embedded in rock or gravel. Extraction required capital, technological experience, and expensive machinery.

Eventually, mining became a corporate industrial concern and miners industrial wage workers.

Probably 5 percent of early gold rush emigrants to California were women and children. Many of the women also anticipated getting "rich in a hurry." Because there were so few of them, the cooking, nursing, laundry, and hotel services women provided had a high value. When Luzena Wilson arrived in Sacramento, a miner offered her $10 for a biscuit. Yet the work was tiring, and some wondered if the money compensated for the exhaustion. Mary Ballou thought it over and decided, "I would not advise any Lady to come out here and suffer to toil and fatigue I have suffered for the sake of a little gold." As men's profits shrank, so, too, did those of the women who served them.

Some of the first women to arrive on the mining frontier were prostitutes, hoping that the gender ratio would make their profession especially profitable. Prostitutes may have constituted as much as 20 percent of California's female population in 1850, and they probably vastly outnumbered other women in early mining camps. During boom days, they made good money and sometimes won a recognized place in society. But prostitution was a risky business in such a disorderly environment.

The Mexicans, South Americans, Chinese, and small numbers of blacks seeking their fortunes in California soon discovered that although they contributed substantially to California's growth, racial discrimination flourished vigorously. At first, American miners tried to force foreigners out of the gold fields altogether. An attempt to declare mining illegal for all foreigners failed, but a high tax on them was more successful. Thousands of Mexicans left the mines, and the Chinese found other jobs in San Francisco and Sacramento. As business stagnated in mining towns, however, white miners reduced the levy. By 1870, when the tax was declared unconstitutional, the Chinese, paying 85 percent of it, had "contributed" $5 million to California for the right to prospect. The hostility that led to this legislation also fed widespread violence against Chinese and Mexicans.

Black Americans found that their skin color placed them in a situation akin to that of foreigners. Deprived of the vote, forbidden to testify in civil or criminal cases involving whites, excluded from the bounties of the state's homestead law, blacks led a precarious existence in Golden California.

For the Native American tribes of the interior, the mining rushes were disasters. Accustomed to foraging for food, they found fish and game increasingly scarce as miners diverted streams, hunted game, or drove it from mining areas altogether. When Indians responded by raiding mining camps, miners erupted with fury. They stalked and killed native men and women, sometimes collecting bounties offered by some mining communities for their scalps. Indian women were raped; children were kidnaped and offered as apprentices. As one miner pointed out, "Indians seven or eight years old are worth $100 ... [and] it is a damn poor Indian that's not worth $50." Without legal recourse because of their skin color, Native Americans could not withstand the onslaught of white society. Subjected not only to violence but to white disease, Indians died by the thousands. In 1849, there had been about 150,000 Indians in California. In just over 20 years, numbers had tumbled to fewer than 30,000.

In fact, fantasies of riches rarely came true. Western ghost towns testified to the typical pattern: boom, bust, decay, death. The landscape bore the scars of careless exploitation. Forests were devastated to provide timber for the flumes miners constructed to divert rivers from their channels in the hopes of exposing gold in dry riverbeds. During heavy rains, mounds of debris oozed over fields and choked waterways.

Yet for all the negative consequences, gold had many positive effects on the country and the West. Between 1848 and 1883, California mines supplied two-thirds of the country's gold. Gold transformed sleepy San Francisco into a bustling metropolis. It fueled the agricultural and commercial development of California and Oregon, as miners provided a market for goods and services. Gold built harbors, railroads, and irrigation systems all over the West. Though few people made large fortunes, both the region and the nation profited from gold.

Establishing God's Kingdom

In the decades before 1860, many emigrants heading for the Far West stopped to rest and buy supplies in Salt Lake City, the heart of the Mormon state of Deseret. There they encountered a society both familiar and also shockingly foreign. Visitors admired the attractively laid-out town, but they also gossiped about polygamy and searched the faces of Mormon women for signs of rebellion—and were amazed that so few Mormon women seemed interested in escaping the bonds of plural marriage, which outsiders equated with slavery.

Violence drove the Mormons to the Great Basin area. Two years after Joseph Smith's murder in 1844, angry mobs had chased the last of the "Saints" out of Nauvoo, Illinois. Smith's successor, Brigham Young, realized that the Saints' best hope for survival lay in situating the Kingdom of God somewhere in the West, far removed from the United States. The Mexican-American War unexpectedly furthered his plans. By raising 500 Mormon young men for Kearney's Army of the West, Young acquired sorely needed capital. The battalion's advance pay bought wagonloads of supplies for starving and sick Mormons strung out along the trail between Missouri and Iowa and helped finance the impending great migration.

Young selected the Great Basin area, technically part of Mexico, for the future settlement. One thousand miles from its nearest "civilized" neighbors, it was remote and arid. But if irrigated, Mormon leaders concluded it might prove as fertile as ancient Israel. In April 1847, Young led an exploratory expedition west. After reaching Salt Lake in late July, he exclaimed, "This is the place," and announced his land policy. Settlers would receive virtually free land on the basis of a family's size and ability to cultivate it. While he returned to lead the main body, the expeditionary group dug irrigation ditches and began planting.

Young's organizational talents and his followers' cooperative abilities were fully tested. By September 1847, fully 566 wagons and 1,500 Saints made the arduous trek to Salt Lake City; more came the next year. Church leaders directed everything. By 1850, the Mormon frontier had over 11,000 settlers. Missionary efforts in the United States, Great Britain, and Scandinavia drew thousands of converts to the Great Basin, with a Church-administered loan fund facilitating the journey for many. By the end of the decade, over 30,000 Saints lived in Utah, not only in Salt Lake City but also in more than 90 village colonies. Despite hardship, the Mormons thrived.

Most Mormons were farmers; many came from New England and the Midwest and shared many customs, attitudes, and political structures with other Americans. But "Gentile" outsiders perceived profound differences, for the heart of Mormon society was not the individual farmer on his own homestead, but the cooperative village. Years of persecution had promoted a strong group identity and acceptance of Church guidance. With Church leaders making essential decisions, farming became a collective enterprise. All farmers received land and access to community water. During Sunday services, the local bishop might provide farming instructions along with his sermon.

Nothing separated Church and state in Utah. Church leaders occupied all of the important political posts. Young's Governing Quorum included the Church's high priests, who made both religious and political decisions. When it became clear that Utah would become a territory, however, Mormon leaders drew up a constitution separating religious and political power. But little changed. As one Gentile pointed out, "This intimate connection of church and state seems to pervade everything that is done. The supreme power in both being lodged in the hands of the same individuals, it is difficult to separate their two official characters, and to determine whether in any one instance they act as spiritual or merely temporal officers." The Treaty of Guadalupe Hidalgo officially incorporating Utah into the United States hardly affected political and religious arrangements. Young became territorial governor. Bishops continued as spiritual and civil leaders.

Although most Gentiles accepted some of the peculiarities of the Mormon settlement, few could tolerate polygamy. Smith and other Church leaders had secretly practiced it in the early 1840s, but Young only publicly revealed the doctrine in 1852, when the Saints were safely in Utah. Smith believed that the highest or "celestial" form of marriage brought special rewards in the afterlife. Because wives and children contributed to these rewards, plural marriage was a means of sanctification. From a practical standpoint, polygamy incorporated into Mormon society single female converts who had left their families to come to Utah.

Although most Mormons accepted the doctrine and its religious justification, perhaps only 10 to 20 percent of Mormon families were polygamous. Few men had more than two wives. Personal strains and the expense of maintaining several families ensured that usually only the most successful and visible Mormon leaders practiced plural marriage during the 40 years in which polygamy was practiced openly.

Polygamous family life hardly resembled outsiders' fantasies of sexual excess. Since jealousy among wives could destroy families, Mormon leaders minimized romantic love and sexual attraction in courtship and marriage. Instead, they encouraged marriages founded on mutual attachment, with sex primarily for procreation.

To the shock of outsiders, Mormon women considered themselves not slaves but highly regarded members of the community. Whether plural wives or not, they saw polygamy as the cutting edge of their society and defended it to outsiders. Polygamy was preferable to monogamy, which left the single woman outside family life and forced some into prostitution.

Although they faced obvious difficulties, many plural wives found rewards in polygamy. Without the constant presence of husbands, they had an unusual opportunity for independence. Many treated visiting husbands as revered friends, deriving day-to-day emotional satisfaction from their children. Occasionally, plural wives lived together and became close friends.

The Mormon frontier succeeded in terms of its numbers, its growing prosperity, and its unity. Long-term threats loomed, however, once the area became part of the United States. Attacks on Young's power as well as heated verbal denunciations of polygamy proliferated. Efforts began in Congress to outlaw polygamy. In the years before the Civil War, Mormons withstood these assaults. But as Utah became more connected to the rest of the country, the pressures on the institution of plural marriage would increase.

Cities in the West

Many emigrants went west not to farm or pan for gold but to live in cities like San Francisco, Denver, and Portland. There they pursued business and professional opportunities or perhaps speculated in real estate.

Cities were integral to frontier life. Some, like St. Joseph, Missouri, which catered to the emigrant trade, preceded agricultural settlement. Others, like Portland, were destinations for overland travelers or were market and supply centers for emigrant farmers. San Francisco and Denver were "instant cities," transformed as the discovery of precious metals sent thousands of miners to and through them. Once the strike ran out, many miners returned to these cities to make a new start. In San Francisco, a Chinese community took shape as Chinese laborers abandoned mining and railroad work. In 1860, almost 3,000 Chinese lived in Chinatown; 10 years later, that number grew to 12,022.

Bustling commercial life offered residents a wide range of occupations and services. As a Portland emigrant remarked in 1852, "In many ways life here ... was more primitive than it was in the early times in Illinois and Missouri. But in others it was far more advanced. ... We could get the world's commodities here which could not be had then, or scarcely at all, in the interior of Illinois or Missouri."

Young, single men seeking their fortunes made up a disproportionate share of urban populations. Frontier Portland had more than three men for every woman. Predictably, urban life was often noisy, rowdy, and occasionally violent. Some women tried to reform the atmosphere by attempting to close stores on Sunday or to prohibit drinking. Others, of course, enjoyed all the attention that came with the presence of so many young men. Eventually, the gender ratio became balanced, but as late as 1880, fully 18 of the 24 largest western cities had more men than women.

Western cities soon lost their distinctiveness. The history of Portland suggests the common pattern of development. In 1845, it was only a clearing in the forest, with lively speculation in town lots. By the early 1850s, Portland had become a small trading center with a few rough log structures and muddy tracks for streets. As farmers poured into Oregon, the city became a regional commercial center. More permanent structures were built, giving it an "eastern" appearance.

The belief that western cities offered special opportunities initially drew many young men to Portland and other urban areas. Success was greatest, however, for those arriving with assets. By the 1860s, when the city's population had reached 2,874, Portland's Social Club symbolized the emergence of an elite. Portland's businessmen, lawyers, and editors controlled an increasing share of the community's wealth and set its social standards, showing how rapidly and far Portland had traveled from its raw frontier beginnings.

CULTURES IN CONFLICT

Looking at westward expansion through the eyes of white emigrants provides only one view of the frontier experience. In such a diverse region, many other views existed.

Some of those heading to the American West came from south China. Mostly men, they planned to work for a few years and then return home. Initially, California welcomed them. One San Francisco merchant reported in 1855 that the Chinese were "received like guests" and treated "with politeness. From far and near we came and were pleased." However, such tolerance soon disappeared as more Chinese arrived on the West Coast and took jobs in mining camps, on the railroads, and elsewhere. A telegram from Chinese miners in the California mountains betrayed anxieties many must have felt: "Am afraid there will be big fight." Increasingly whites perceived the Chinese as racial threats, calling them "nagurs" only slightly removed "from the African race." Chinese workers faced many forms of harassment. In 1880, California legislators expressed white hostility by passing a law that made any marriage between a white person and a "negro, mulatto, or Mongolian" illegal.

A View of Chinese Miners This magazine illustration shows Chinese miners searching for gold deposits in areas probably abandoned by other miners. How does the illustration highlight the foreign character of these miners? What point of view towards the miners does this illustration seem to convey?

Confronting the Plains Tribes

Some likened the Chinese to the Native Americans, another group that would see the western experience differently from white emigrants. An entry from an Oregon Trail journal hints at what one such perspective might be. On May 7, 1864, Mary Warner, a bride of only a few months, described a frightening event. That day, a "fine-looking" Indian had visited the wagon train and tried to buy her. Mary's husband, probably uncertain how to handle the situation, played along, agreeing to trade his wife for two ponies. The Indian generously offered three. "Then," wrote Mary, "he took hold of my shawl to make me understand to get out [of the wagon]. About this time I got frightened and really was so hysterical [that] I began to cry." Everyone laughed at her, she reported, though surely the Indian found the whole incident no more amusing than she had.

This ordinary encounter on the overland trail begins to hint at the social and cultural differences separating white Americans moving west and the peoples they met. Confident of their values and rights, emigrants had little regard for those who had lived in the West for centuries and no compunction in seizing their lands. Many predicted that the Indians would soon disappear from the continent.

During the 1840s, white Americans for the first time came into extensive contact with the powerful Plains tribes, whose culture differed from that of the more familiar eastern Woodland peoples. Probably a quarter million Native Americans occupied the Plains. "Border" tribes along the Plains' eastern edge lived in villages and raised crops, supplemented with buffalo meat during summer months. On the Central Plains lived Brulé and Oglala Sioux, Cheyenne, Shoshone, and Arapaho, all aggressive tribes who followed the buffalo and often raided the border tribes. In the Southwest were Comanche, Ute, Navajo, and some Apache bands; northern and western Texas were hunting grounds for the Kiowa, Wichita, Apache, and southern Comanche. Many southwestern tribes had adopted aspects of Spanish culture and European domestic animals such as cattle, sheep, and horses.

The Plains tribes shared certain characteristics. Most became nomads after the introduction of Spanish horses in the sixteenth century increased their seasonal mobility from 50 to 500 miles. Horses allowed Indian men to hunt the buffalo so successfully that tribes (with the exclusion of the border groups) came to depend on the beasts for food, clothing, fuel, teepee dwellings, and trading purposes. Women were responsible for processing buffalo products, and some men had more than one wife to tan skins for trading.

Mobility also increased tribal contact and conflict. War was central to the lives of the Plains tribes. Unlike whites, Indians sought not to exterminate their enemies or to claim territory but to steal horses and prove individual prowess. They considered it braver to touch an enemy than to kill or scalp him. Under such conditions, political unity was difficult. No male became a fully accepted member of his tribe until proven in battle, and chiefs, who enjoyed only limited authority, often could not restrain young men intent on proving their courage.

With guns, fast ponies, and skills in warfare and raiding, the Plains tribes posed a fearsome obstacle to white expansion. They had signed no treaties with

An Indian Contrast This drawing, done by an unknown Indian artist sometime in the 1840s, contrasts the traditionally clad Indians and the wild animals they hunted with the formally dressed white men and their stock animals. Has the artist depicted whites in a sympathetic manner? *(Archives de Jesuites, St. Jerome, Québec)*

the United States and had few friendly feelings toward whites. While their contact with white society had brought gains through trade in skins, it had also brought alcohol and epidemics.

When the first emigrants drove their wagons across the plains and prairies in the early 1840s, Indian-white relations were peaceable. But the intrusion of whites set in motion an environmental cycle that eventually made for conflict. Indians depended on the buffalo but respected this source of life. The grasses that nourished the buffalo also sustained the Indians' ponies and the animals that supported horse traders like the Cheyenne.

Whites, however, fed their oxen and horses on the grass that the Indians' ponies and the buffalo needed. And they adopted that "most exciting sport," the buffalo hunt. As the great herds began to shrink, Native American tribes began to battle one another for hunting grounds and food. The powerful Sioux swooped down into the hunting grounds of their enemies and mounted destructive raids against the Pawnee and other smaller tribes.

In 1846, the Sioux petitioned President Polk for compensation for damages to their hunting grounds caused by emigrating whites. When the president denied their request, they tried to tax emigrants, who were outraged at what they considered Indian effrontery. However, little was done to relieve the suffering of the tribes bearing the brunt of Sioux aggression, the dismay of the Sioux at the white invasion, or the fears of the emigrants themselves.

The discovery of gold in California, luring over 20,000 across the Plains in 1849 alone, became the catalyst for federal action. The horde of gold seekers and their animals wrought such devastation in the Platte valley that it rapidly became a wasteland for the Indians. Cholera spread from whites to Indians, killing thousands.

Government officials devised a two-pronged plan. The government would construct a chain of forts to protect emigrants and, simultaneously, call the tribes to a general conference. Officials expected that in return for generous presents, Indians would end tribal warfare and limit their movements. They instructed tribes to select chiefs to speak for them at the conference.

The Fort Laramie Council, 1851

In 1851, the council convened at Fort Laramie. As many as 10,000 Indians gathered, hopeful of ending the destruction of their way of life and eager for the presents. Tribal animosities simmered, however. Skirmishes occurred on the way to the fort. Border tribes, fearful of the Sioux, refused to come; so did the Comanche, Kiowa, and Apache because their Sioux and Crow enemies would be there.

Whites informed the tribes that times had changed. In the past, "you had plenty of buffalo and game ... and your Great Father well knows that war has always been your favorite amusement and pursuit. He then left the question of peace and war to yourselves. Now, since the settling of the districts West ... by the white men, your condition has changed." In return for compensation for the destruction of grass, timber, and buffalo and annual payments of goods and services, tribes must give up their rights of free movement. The government drew tribal boundaries, and chiefs promised to stay within them. Some tribal lands were sold.

The Fort Laramie Treaty was the first agreement between the Plains tribes and the United States government. It expressed whites' conviction that Indians must stay apart in clearly defined areas. But even during the conference, ominous signs of trouble appeared. The Sioux refused to remain north of the Platte, for south of the river lay their recently conquered lands. "These lands once belonged to the Kiowas and the Crows," one Sioux explained, "but we whipped those nations out of them and in this we did what the white men do when they want the lands of the Indians." Elsewhere in the trans-Mississippi West, other tribes, like the fierce Navajo of New Mexico, also resisted white Americans' attempts to restrict them.

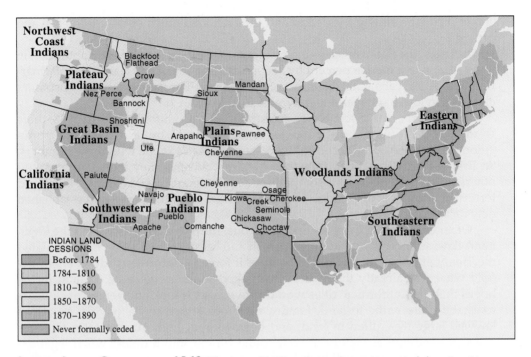

INDIAN LAND CESSIONS IN 1840 This map of Indian tribes and groupings reveals locations in 1840, but it presents too static a picture of tribal territories. Some of the Indian groups in the West had been forced across the Mississippi by events in the Midwest. What does the map show about the pace of Indian land cessions in the nineteenth century, especially in the trans-Mississippi West?

Overwhelming the Mexican Settlers

In the Southwest, in Texas, and in California, Americans encountered a Spanish-speaking population and Hispanic culture. Americans regarded Mexicans, whom they often outnumbered and usually disparaged, as the "dregs of society." Although Anglo-Mexican interaction differed from place to place, few Anglos heeded the Treaty of Guadalupe Hidalgo's assurances that Mexicans would have citizens' rights.

Most Spanish-speaking people lived in New Mexico, and, of all former Mexican citizens, they probably fared the best. Most were of mixed blood, living marginally as ranch hands for rich landowners or as farmers and herdsmen in small villages dominated by a *patron,* or headman. As the century wore on, Americans produced legal titles and took over lands long occupied by peasant farmers and stock raisers. But despite economic reversals, New Mexicans survived, carrying their rural culture well into the twentieth century.

Disinterested in the situation of their poor rural countrymen, upper-class landowners looked out for themselves. Even before the conquest, rich New Mexicans had protected their future by establishing contacts with American businessmen and sending their sons east to American schools. When the United States annexed New Mexico, they made strategic marriage and business alliances with the

Anglo men who slowly trickled in and thus retained much of their influence and prestige.

In Texas, the Spanish-speaking residents, only 10 percent of the population in 1840, shrank to a mere 6 percent by 1860. Although the upper class also intermarried with Americans, they lost most of their power. Poor, dark-skinned Hispanics clustered in low-paying and largely unskilled jobs.

In California, the discovery of gold transformed California life. In 1848, there were 7,000 Californios and about twice as many Anglos; by 1860, the Anglo population reached 360,000. Californios were hard pressed to cope with these numbers. At first, along with several thousand Mexican citizens, they joined Anglos and others in the gold fields. But competition fed antagonism and conflict. Taxes and terrorism ultimately drove most Spanish speakers from the mines and established new racial contours.

Other changes were even more disastrous. In 1851, Congress passed the Gwin Land Law, supposedly validating Spanish and Mexican land titles. But it violated the Treaty of Guadalupe Hidalgo because it forced California landowners to defend what was already theirs and encouraged squatters to settle on land in the hopes that the Californios' titles would prove false. It took an average of 17 years to establish clear title to land. Landowners found themselves paying American lawyers large fees, often in land, and borrowing at high interest rates to cover court proceedings. A victory at court often turned into a defeat when legal expenses forced owners to sell their lands to pay debts.

Working-class Hispanic Americans, laboring for Anglo farmers or for mining and later railroad companies, earned less money and did more unpleasant jobs than Anglo workers. By 1870, the average Hispanic American worker's property was worth only about a third of its value of 20 years earlier.

Various forms of resistance to American expansion emerged. Some, like Tiburcio Vásquez in southern California, became *bandidos*. As he explained, the American presence provoked a "spirit of hatred and revenge ... I believed we were unjustly and wrongfully deprived of the social rights that belonged to us." Others, like the members of Las Gorras Blancas in New Mexico, ripped up railroad ties and cut the barbed wire fences of Anglo ranchers and farmers, while the religiously oriented Penitentes tried to work through the ballot box. Ordinary men, women, and children resisted efforts to convert them to Protestantism and held on to familiar customs and beliefs while learning some of the skills they hoped would enable them to flourish in a changing culture.

Conclusion

Fruits of Manifest Destiny

Like Narcissa Whitman and her husband, many nineteenth-century Americans decided that they had a unique right to settle the West and make it flower. They were not much concerned with the fate of those who had lived for centuries on the land. The process of acquiring the western half of the continent was so swift that there seemed little point in worrying about the losers. The tale of western ex-

TIMELINE

1818	Treaty on joint U.S.–British occupation of Oregon		1846	Mexico declares defensive war
1821	Mexican independence			United States declares war and takes Santa Fe
	Opening of Santa Fe Trail			Resolution of Oregon question
	Stephen Austin leads American settlement of Texas		1848	Treaty of Guadalupe Hidalgo
1836	Texas declares independence		1849	California Gold Rush begins
1840s	Emigrant crossings of overland trail		1851	Fort Laramie Treaty

pansion loomed large in the imagination of the American people for many years. Some western settlers became folk heroes. The Whitmans were remembered by the founding of Whitman College in Walla Walla, Washington. All white Americans could be thankful for the special opportunities and the new chance that the West seemed to hold out. Certainly, the nation did gain vast natural wealth in the trans-Mississippi West. But only a small fraction of the hopeful emigrants heading for the frontier realized their dreams of success. And the move west and east had a dark side, as the acquisition of new territories fueled the controversy over the future of slavery.

Questions for Review and Reflection

1. Explain how and why the westward movement entangled the United States in the affairs of foreign powers.

2. Compare and contrast the acquisition of Texas and the Southwest with the annexation of Oregon.

3. What racial and ethnic tensions emerged in the West because of American expansionism?

4. What factors caused problems and tensions between Native Americans and whites?

5. What were the important American beliefs and values that were involved in the westward movement? How did they shape the westward experience?

Discovering U.S. History Online

The Mexican-American War www.sunsite.unam.mx/revistas/1847/

This well-illustrated site offers several sections (each available in English or Spanish) explaining the causes, courses, and outcomes of the Mexican-American War.

The Oregon Trail www.ukans.edu/carrie/kancoll/index.html www.isu.edu/~trinmich/Oregontrail.html
The Kansas Collection site contains good primary sources with images on the Oregon Trail and the early movement westward. The second site is a companion to the PBS film *The Oregon Trail*.

California in the Gold Rush Decade www.huntington.org/Education/GoldRush www.museumca.org/goldrush
The first site presents the Huntington Library's remarkable collection of Gold Rush manuscripts, drawings, and rare printed materials. The second is a well-illustrated interactive site on the Gold Rush exhibit formerly on display at the Oakland Museum of California.

The National Museum of the American Indian, Smithsonian Institution and The George Gustav Heye Center www.conexus.si.edu/main.htm
A cooperative effort of these two institutions, this site hosts several virtual exhibits about Native American culture and history.

Fiction and Film

Mark Twain's *Roughing It* (1872) is often humorous, but you can see Twain's insightful comments about westerners' values and standards. James C. Work's *Gunfight!* (1996) contains a selection of gunfight stories originally printed in popular magazines. Ann Sophia Winterbotham Stephens's *Malaeska: Indian Wife of the White Hunter* (1861) is an early example of a "dime novel." *The West* (1996) is a nine-part series by Ken Burns shown on television that provides a sympathetic and critical account of the settlement and its impact on Native Americans. *The Donner Party* (1992) is a PBS video on the disastrous experience of a party of emigrants caught in the Sierra Nevadas during the winter of 1846–1847.

Recommended Reading

www.ablongman.com/nash
The Companion Website has a list of recommended readings about the trans-Mississippi West, living on the frontier, and cultural conflicts in the West.

American Stories

Four Men Respond to the Union in Peril

The autumn of 1860 was a time of ominous rumors. The election was held on November 6 in an atmosphere of crisis. In Springfield, Illinois, Abraham Lincoln, taking coffee and sandwiches prepared by the "ladies of Springfield," waited as the telegraph brought in the returns. By 1 A.M., victory was certain. "I went home, but not to get much sleep, for I then felt, as I never had before, the responsibility that was upon me." He and the American people faced the most serious crisis since the founding of the Republic.

Lincoln won a four-party election with only 39 percent of the popular vote. He appealed almost exclusively to northern voters in a blatantly sectional campaign, defeating his three opponents by carrying every free state except New Jersey. Only Illinois Senator Stephen Douglas campaigned actively in every section of the country. For his efforts, he received the second-highest number of votes. Douglas's appeal, especially in the closing days of the campaign, was "on behalf of the Union," which he feared—correctly—was in imminent danger of splitting apart.

That fall, other Americans sensed the crisis and faced their own fears and responsibilities. A month before the election, South Carolina plantation owner Robert Allston wrote his oldest son, Benjamin, that "disastrous consequences" would follow from a Lincoln victory. Although his letter mentioned the possibility of secession, he dealt mostly with plantation concerns: a new horse, the mood of the slaves, ordering supplies from the city, instructions for making trousers on a sewing machine. After Lincoln's election, Allston corresponded with a southern colleague about the need for an "effective military organization" to resist "Northern and Federal aggression." In his shift from sewing machines to military ones, Allston prepared for what he called the "impending crisis."

Frederick Douglass greeted the election of 1860 with characteristic optimism. Not only was this an opportunity to "educate ... the people in their moral and political duties," he said, but "slaveholders know that the day of their power is over when a Republican President is elected." But no sooner had Lincoln's victory been determined than Douglass's hopes turned sour. He noted that Republican leaders, who were trying to keep border states from seceding, sounded more antiabolitionist than antislavery. They vowed not to touch slavery in areas where it already existed (including the District of Columbia), not to enforce the hated Fugitive Slave Act, and not to put down slave rebellions. In fact, Douglass bitterly concluded, slavery would "be as safe, and safer" with Lincoln than with a Democrat.

419

Iowa farmer Michael Luark was not so sure. Born in Virginia, he was a typically mobile nine-teenth-century American. Growing up in Indiana, he followed the mining booms of the 1850s to Colorado and California, then returned to the Midwest to farm. Luark sought a good living and re-sented the furor over slavery. He could not, however, avoid the issue. Writing in his diary on the last day of 1860, Luark looked ahead to 1861 with a deep sense of fear. "Startling" political changes would occur, he predicted, perhaps even the "Dissolution of the Union and Civil War with all its train of horrors." He blamed abolitionist agitators, perhaps reflecting his Virginia origins. On New Year's Day, he expressed his fears that Lincoln would let the "most ultra sectional and Abolition" men dis-turb the "vexed Slavery question" even further, as Frederick Douglass wanted. But if this happened, Luark warned, "then farewell to our beloved Union of States." Within four months, the guns of the Confederate States of America fired on a U.S. fort in South Carolina. The Civil War had begun.

The firing on Fort Sumter made real Luark's fears, Douglass's hopes, and Lincoln's and Allston's preparations for responsibility. America's shaky democratic political system faced its worst crisis. The explanation of the peril and dissolution of the Union forms the theme of this chapter.

Such a calamitous event as the Civil War had numerous causes, large and small. The reactions of Allston, Douglass, and Luark to Lincoln's election suggest some of them: moral duties, sectional politics, growing apprehensions over emotional agita-tors, and a concern for freedom and independence on the part of blacks, white south-erners, and western farmers. But as Douglass understood, by 1860 it was clear that "slavery is the real issue ... between all parties and sections. It is the one disturbing force, and explains the confused and irregular motion of our political machine."

This chapter analyzes how the momentous issue of slavery disrupted the po-litical system and eventually the Union itself. We will look at how four major de-velopments between 1848 and 1861 contributed to the Civil War: first, a sectional dispute over the extension of slavery into the western territories; second, the breakdown of the political party system; third, growing cultural differences in the views and lifestyles of southerners and northerners; and fourth, intensifying emo-tional and ideological polarization between the two regions over losing their way of life and sacred republican rights at the hands of the other. A preview of civil war, bringing all four causes together, occurred in Kansas in 1855 to 1856. Eventu-ally, emotional events, mistrust, and irreconcilable differences made conflict in-evitable. Lincoln's election was the spark that touched off the conflagration of civil war, with all its "train of horrors."

SLAVERY IN THE TERRITORIES

As Narcissa Whitman sadly discovered with the Cayuse Indians in eastern Wash-ington (see Chapter 13), white migration westward was discouraging and down-right dangerous. It was especially damaging to the lives, lands, and cultural integrity of Native Americans and Mexicans. Moreover, the westward movement imperiled freedom and eventually the Union by causing a collision between Yankees and southern slaveholders.

The North and the South had mostly contained and compromised their differences over slavery for 60 years after the Constitutional Convention. Compromise in 1787 had resolved questions of the slave trade and how to count slaves for congressional representation. Although slavery threatened the uneasy sectional harmony in 1820, the Missouri Compromise had established a workable balance of free and slave states and defined a geographic line (36°30′) across the Louisiana Purchase to determine future decisions. In 1833, compromise had defused South Carolina's attempt at nullification, and the gag rule in 1836 had kept the abolitionists' antislavery petitions off the floor of Congress.

Each apparent resolution, however, raised the level of emotional conflict between North and South and postponed ultimate settlement of the slavery question. One reason these compromises temporarily worked was the two-party system, with Whigs and Democrats in both North and South. The parties differed over cultural and economic issues, but slavery was largely kept out of political campaigns and congressional debates. This changed in the late 1840s.

Free Soil or Constitutional Protection?

When war with Mexico broke out in 1846, Pennsylvania congressman David Wilmot added an amendment to an appropriations bill, declaring that "neither slavery nor involuntary servitude shall ever exist" in any territories acquired from Mexico. Legislators debated the Wilmot Proviso not as Whigs and Democrats, but as northerners and southerners.

A Boston newspaper prophetically observed that Wilmot's resolution "brought to a head the great question which is about to divide the American people." When the war ended, several solutions were presented to deal with slavery in the territories. First was the "free-soil" idea of preventing any extensions of slavery. Two precedents suggested that Congress could do this. One was the Northwest Ordinance, which had barred slaves from the Upper Midwest; the other was the Missouri Compromise.

Free-Soilers had mixed motives. For some, slavery was an evil to be destroyed. But for many northern white farmers looking westward, the threat of economic competition with an expanding system of large-scale slave labor was even more serious. Nor did they wish to compete with free blacks. As Wilmot put it, his proviso was intended to preserve the area for the "sons of toil, of my own race and own color." Other northerners supported it as a means of restraining the growing political power and "insufferable arrogance" of the "spirit and demands of the Slave Power."

An opposing position to the Free-Soilers was the argument of South Carolina Senator John C. Calhoun. Congress not only lacked the constitutional right to exclude slavery from the territories, he argued, but also had a duty to protect it. Therefore, the Wilmot Proviso was unconstitutional. So were the Missouri Compromise and other federal acts that prevented slaveholders from taking their slave property into the territories.

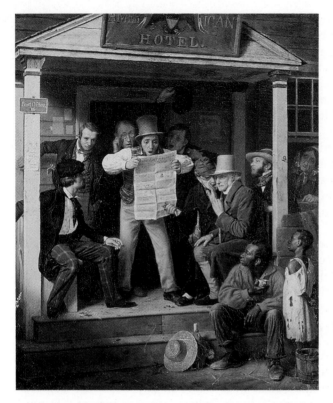

War News Describe what you see in this 1848 painting by Richard Caton Woodville, titled *War News from Mexico.* What do you suppose the men are hearing about the war in Mexico, and how are they reacting? Do you think this "American Hotel" is in the North or South? How would the war news be heard in each place? What are the black man and little girl doing there, and how do you think they are responding to the news? Why would the Mexican War and its outcomes interest them? *(© 2004 Board of Trustees, National Gallery of Art, Washington, D.C.)*

Economic, political, and moral considerations stood behind Calhoun's position. Many southerners hungered for new cotton lands in the West and Southwest, even in Central America and the Caribbean. Southerners feared that northerners wanted to trample their right to protect their institutions against abolitionism. Southern leaders saw the Wilmot Proviso as a moral issue touching basic Republican principles. One congressman called it "treason to the Constitution," and Senator Robert Toombs of Georgia warned that if Congress passed the proviso, he would favor disunion rather than "degradation."

Popular Sovereignty and the Election of 1848

With such divisive potential, it was natural that many Americans sought a compromise solution to exclude slavery from politics. Polk's secretary of state, James Buchanan, proposed extending the Missouri Compromise line to the Pacific Ocean, thereby avoiding thorny questions about the morality of slavery and the constitutionality of congressional authority. So would "popular sovereignty," the proposal of Michigan Senator Lewis Cass to leave decisions about permitting slavery to territorial legislatures. The idea appealed to the American democratic belief in local self-government, but it left many details unanswered. At what point in the progress toward statehood could a territorial legislature decide about slavery?

Democrats, liking popular sovereignty because it could mean all things to all people, nominated Cass for president in 1848. Cass denounced abolitionists and the

Wilmot Proviso, but otherwise avoided the slavery issue. The Democrats printed two campaign biographies of Cass, one for the South and one for the North.

The Whigs found an even better way to maintain party unity. Rejecting Henry Clay, they nominated the Mexican-American War hero General Zachary Taylor, who was a Louisiana slaveholder. Taylor compared himself to Washington as a "no party" man above politics. This was about all he stood for. Southern Whigs supported Taylor because they thought he might understand the burdens of slaveholding, and northern Whigs were pleased that he took no stand on the Wilmot Proviso.

The evasions of the two major parties disappointed Calhoun, who tried to create a new, unified southern party. His "Address to the People of the Southern States" threatened secession and called for a united stand against further attempts to interfere with the southern right to extend slavery. Although only 48 of 121 southern representatives signed the address, Calhoun's argument raised the specter of secession and disunion.

Warnings also came from the North. A New York Democratic faction bolted to support Van Buren for president. At first, the split had more to do with state politics than moral principles, but it soon involved the question of slavery in the territories. Disaffected "conscience" Whigs from Massachusetts also explored a third-party alternative. These groups met in Buffalo, New York, to form the Free-Soil party and nominated Van Buren. The platform of the new party, an uneasy mixture of ardent abolitionists and opponents of free blacks moving into western lands, pledged to fight for "free soil, free speech, free labor and free men."

Taylor won easily, largely because defections from Cass to the Free-Soilers cost the Democrats New York and Pennsylvania. Although weakened, the two-party system survived. Purely sectional parties had failed. The Free-Soilers took only about 10 percent of the popular vote.

The Compromise of 1850

Taylor won the election by avoiding slavery questions. But as president, he had to deal with them. When he was inaugurated in 1849, four issues faced the nation. First, the rush of some 80,000 gold miners to California qualified it for statehood. But California's entry as a free state would upset the slave–free state balance in the Senate. The unresolved status of the Mexican cession in the Southwest posed a second problem. The longer the area remained unorganized, local inhabitants called for an application of either the Wilmot Proviso or the Calhoun doctrine. The Texas–New Mexico boundary was also disputed, with Texas claiming everything east of Santa Fe. Northerners feared that Texas might split into five or six slave states. A third problem, especially for abolitionists, was the existence of slavery and a huge slave market in the nation's capital. Fourth, southerners resented the lax federal enforcement of the Fugitive Slave Act of 1793. They called for a stronger act that would end protection for runaways fleeing to Canada.

Taylor was a political novice (he had never voted in a presidential election before 1848) and tackled these problems somewhat evasively. Sidestepping the issue of slavery in the territories, he invited California and New Mexico to seek statehood immediately, presumably as free states. But soon he alienated both southern supporters such as Calhoun and mainstream Whig leaders such as Clay and Webster.

Early in 1850, the old compromiser Henry Clay sought to regain control of the Whig party by proposing solutions to the divisive issues before the nation. With Webster's support, Clay introduced a series of resolutions in an omnibus package intended to settle these issues once and for all. The stormy debates, great speeches, and political maneuvering that followed made up a crucial and dramatic moment in American history. Yet after 70 speeches on behalf of the compromise, the Senate defeated Clay's Omnibus Bill. Tired and disheartened, the 73-year-old Clay left Washington and died two years later. Into the gap stepped Senator Stephen Douglas of Illinois, who saw that Clay's resolutions had a better chance of passing if voted on individually. Under Douglas's leadership, in variously strange political alignments and with the support of Millard Fillmore, who succeeded to the presidency upon Taylor's sudden death, a series of bills finally passed.

MAP

The Compromise of 1850 and the Kansas–Nebraska Act

The "Compromise of 1850" put Clay's resolutions, slightly altered, into law. First, California entered the Union as a free state, ending the balance of free and slave states. Second, territorial governments were organized in New Mexico and Utah, letting local people decide whether to permit slavery. The Texas–New Mexico border was settled, denying Texas the disputed area. In return, the federal government gave Texas $10 million to pay debts owed to Mexico. Third, the slave trade, but not slavery, was abolished in the District of Columbia.

DOCUMENT

The Fugitive Slave Act (1850)

The fourth and most controversial part of the compromise was a new Fugitive Slave Act, containing many provisions that offended northerners. One denied alleged fugitives a jury trial, leaving special cases for decision by commissioners (who were paid $5 for setting a fugitive free, but $10 for returning a fugitive). An especially repugnant provision compelled northern citizens to help catch runaways.

Consequences of Compromise

The Compromise of 1850 was the last attempt to keep slavery out of politics. Voting on the different bills followed sectional lines on some issues and party lines on others. Douglas felt pleased with his "final settlement" of the slavery question.

But the Compromise only delayed more serious sectional conflict, and it added two new ingredients to American politics. First, political realignment along sectional lines moved closer. Second, although repudiated by most ordinary citizens, ideas like secessionism, disunion, and a "higher law" than the Constitution entered political discussions. People wondered whether the question of slavery in the territories could be "compromised away" next time.

Others were immediately upset. The new fugitive slave law angered many northerners. Owners of runaway slaves hired agents (labeled "kidnappers" in the North) to hunt down fugitives. In a few dramatic episodes, notably in Boston, literary and religious intellectuals led mass protests to resist slave hunters. When Webster supported the law, New England abolitionists denounced him. Emerson said that he would not obey the "filthy law."

Frederick Douglass would not obey it either. As a runaway slave, he faced arrest and return to the South until friends overcame his objections and purchased his freedom. Douglass still risked harm by his strong defiance of the Fugitive

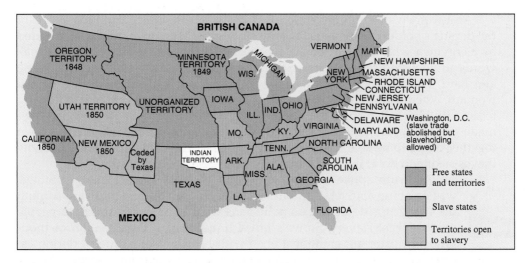

BRITISH CANADA

Free states and territories

Slave states

Territories open to slavery

THE COMPROMISE OF 1850 "I have seen many periods of great anxiety, of peril, and of danger in this country," Henry Clay told the Congress in February of 1850, "and I have never before risen to address any assemblage so oppressed, so appalled, and so anxious." What followed were the debates that led eventually to the passage of his great compromise. Can you find three of the four major parts of the bill on the map? What was the fourth, and how might you represent it on the map?

Slave Act. Arguing the "rightfulness of forcible resistance," he urged free blacks to arm themselves. "The only way to make the Fugitive Slave Law a dead letter," he said in Pittsburgh in 1853, "is to make a half dozen or more dead kidnappers." Douglass raised money for black fugitives, hid runaways in his home, helped hundreds escape to Canada, and supported black organizations such as the League of Freedom in Boston.

"Hypocrisy of Fugitive Slave Act"—Cartoon (1851)

Other northerners, both white and black, stepped up work for the Underground Railroad and helped runaway slaves evade capture. Several states passed "personal liberty laws" that prohibited using state officials and institutions in the recovery of fugitive slaves. But most northerners complied. Of some 200 blacks arrested in the first six years of the law, only 15 were rescued, and only 3 of these by force. Failed rescues, in fact, had more emotional impact than did successful ones. In two cases in the early 1850s, angry mobs of abolitionists in Boston failed to prevent the forcible return of blacks to the South. These celebrated cases aroused antislavery emotions in more northerners than abolitionists had been able to do by their tracts and speeches.

But the spoken and written word also fueled emotions over slavery in the aftermath of 1850. In an Independence Day speech in 1852, Douglass wondered aloud: "What, to the American slave, is your 4th of July?" It was, he said, the day that revealed to the slave the "gross injustice and cruelty to which he is the constant victim. To him, your celebration is a sham; your boasted liberty, an unholy license; your national greatness, swelling vanity; your sounds of rejoicing are empty and heartless; your denunciation of tyrants, brass-fronted impudence; your shouts of liberty and equality, hollow mockery." Douglass's speeches, like those of another ex-slave, Sojourner Truth, became increasingly strident.

Frederick Douglass, Independence Day Speech (1852)

At a women's rights convention in 1851 in Akron, Ohio, Truth made one of the decade's boldest statements for minority rights. The convention was attended by clergymen who heckled female speakers. Sojourner Truth stood up to speak words still debated by historians. She pointed to her many years of childbearing and hard, backbreaking work as a slave, crying out a refrain, "And ar'n't I a woman? Where had Jesus came from? From God and a woman: Man had nothing to do with Him." Referring to Eve, she concluded, "If the first woman God ever made was strong enough to turn the world upside down all alone, these women together ought to be able to turn it back, and get it right side up again! And now they is asking to do it, the men better let them." She silenced the hecklers.

DOCUMENT

Harriet Beecher
Stowe, *Uncle
Tom's Cabin*
(1852)

As Truth spoke, another American woman, Harriet Beecher Stowe, was finishing a novel, *Uncle Tom's Cabin,* that would go far toward turning the world upside down. As politicians were hoping the American people would forget slavery, Stowe's novel brought it to the attention of thousands. In gripping emotional style with heartbreaking cruelty, daring escapes, and reunited family members, she gave readers an absorbing indictment of the horrors of slavery and its impact on both northerners and southerners. Published initially as magazine serials, each month's chapter ended at a nail-biting moment.

Although it outraged the white South when published in full in 1852, *Uncle Tom's Cabin* became one of the all-time best-sellers in American history. In the first year, more than 300,000 copies were printed, and Stowe's novel was eventually published in 20 languages. When President Lincoln met Stowe in 1863, he is reported to have said to her, with a twinkle in his eye, "So you're the little woman who wrote the book that made this great war!"

POLITICAL DISINTEGRATION

The response to *Uncle Tom's Cabin* and the Fugitive Slave Act indicated that politicians had congratulated themselves too soon for saving the Republic in 1850. Political developments, not all dealing with slavery, were already weakening the ability of political parties—and ultimately the nation—to withstand the passions slavery aroused.

Weakened Party Politics in the Early 1850s

As we see in modern elections, political parties attempt to convince voters that they stand for moral values and economic policies crucially different from those of the opposition. Between 1850 and 1854, these differences blurred, undermining party loyalty.

Both parties scrambled to convince voters that they had favored the Compromise of 1850. In addition, several states rewrote their constitutions and remodeled their laws. These changes reduced the number of patronage jobs that politicians could dispense and regularized the process for securing banking, railroad, and other corporate charters, ending the role formerly played by the legislature and undermining the importance of parties in citizens' lives. The return of prosperity in

Celebrating a Political Victory In George Caleb Bingham's *Verdict of the People* (after 1855), the American flag flies proudly over a happy throng celebrating the outcome of democratic politics. How well did the political process work in the 1850s? In an earlier version of this same painting, the women on the hotel balcony in the upper right display a banner announcing (ironically?) "Freedom for Virtue." What do you think that means? *(Courtesy of the R.W. Norton Art Gallery, Shreveport, Louisiana)*

the early 1850s also weakened parties. For almost a quarter of a century, Whigs and Democrats had disagreed over the tariff, money and banking, and government-supported internal improvements. Now, in better times, party distinctions over economic policies seemed less important.

The election of 1852 illustrated the lessening significance of political parties. The Whigs nominated General Winfield Scott, another Mexican-American War hero, who they hoped would repeat Taylor's success four years earlier. With the passing prominence of Clay and Webster (who died in 1852), Senator William Seward of New York aspired to party leadership and desired a president he could influence more successfully than the moderate Fillmore. Still, it took 52 ballots to nominate Scott over Fillmore, alienating southern Whigs. Democrats had their own problems. After 49 ballots, the party turned to a lackluster compromise candidate, Franklin Pierce of New Hampshire.

The two parties offered little choice and downplayed issues so as not to widen intraparty divisions. Voter interest diminished. "Genl. Apathy is the strongest candidate out here," was a typical report from Ohio. Democratic leaders resorted to bribes and drinks to buy the support of thousands of new Catholic immigrants from Ireland and Germany, who could be naturalized and were eligible to vote after only three years. Pierce won easily, 254 to 42 electoral votes.

The Kansas–Nebraska Act

The Whig party's final disintegration came on a February day in 1854 when southern Whigs, choosing to be more southern than Whig, supported Stephen Douglas's Nebraska bill. The Illinois senator had many reasons for introducing a bill organizing the Nebraska Territory (which included Kansas). An ardent nationalist, he was interested in the continuing development of the West. He wanted the eastern terminus for a transcontinental railroad in Chicago rather than in rival St. Louis. This meant organizing the lands west of Iowa and Missouri.

Politics also played a role. Douglas hoped to recapture the party leadership he had held in passing the Compromise of 1850 and aspired to the presidency. Although he had replaced Cass as the great advocate of popular sovereignty, thus winning favor among northern Democrats, he needed southern Democratic support. Many southerners, especially neighboring Missouri slaveholders, opposed organizing the Nebraska Territory unless open to slavery. But the Nebraska Territory lay north of the Missouri Compromise line prohibiting slavery.

Douglas's bill, introduced early in 1854, in effect repealed the Missouri Compromise restriction and recommended using popular sovereignty in organizing two territories, Kansas and Nebraska. Inhabitants thus could vote slavery in. Douglas reasoned, however, that Kansas and Nebraska would never support slavery-based agriculture and that the people would choose to be a free state. Therefore, he could win the votes he needed for the railroad without also getting slavery. By stating that the states created out of the Nebraska Territory would enter the Union "with or without slavery, as their constitution may prescribe at the time of their admission," his bill ignored the Missouri Compromise.

Douglas miscalculated. Northerners from his own party immediately attacked him and his bill as a "criminal betrayal of precious rights" and as part of a plot promoting his own presidential ambitions by turning free Nebraska over to "slavery despotism." Whigs and abolitionists were even more outraged. Frederick Douglass branded the act the result of the "audacious villainy of the slave power."

But the more Stephen Douglas was attacked, the harder he fought. Eventually his bill passed, but it seriously damaged the party system. What began as a railroad measure ended in reopening the question of slavery in the territories, which Douglas had thought finally settled in 1850. What began as a way of avoiding conflict ended in violence over whether Kansas would enter the Union slave or free. What began as a way of strengthening party lines ended up destroying one party (Whigs), planting irreconcilable divisions in another (Democrats), and creating two new parties (Know-Nothings and Republicans).

Expansionist "Young America" in the Larger World

The Democratic party was weakened in the early 1850s not only by the Kansas–Nebraska Act, but also by an expansive energy that led Americans to adventures far beyond Kansas. Americans had hailed the European revolutions of

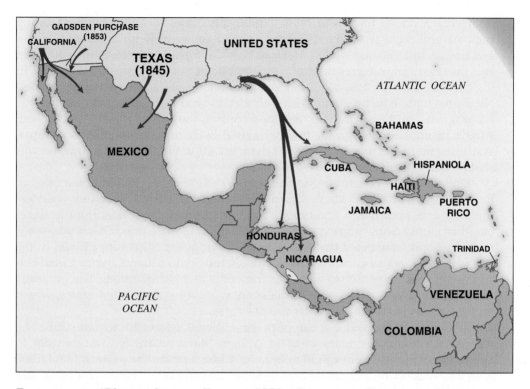

EXPANSIONIST "YOUNG AMERICA" IN THE 1850S: ATTEMPTED RAIDS INTO LATIN AMERICA Note the flurry of expansionist American raids and forays southward into Mexico and the Caribbean between the mid-1840s and the mid-1850s. ■ **Reflecting on the Past** What major events and motives caused the expansionist interest? Why was Cuba a key target?

1848 as evidence that republicanism was the wave of the future. "Young America" was the label assumed by patriots eager to spread Americanism abroad; however, these ardent republican nationalists ironically abetted the spread of the idea of slavery.

Pierce's platform in 1852 reflected this nationalism, declaring that the war with Mexico had been "just and necessary." Many Democrats took their overwhelming victory as a mandate to continue adding territory. A Philadelphia newspaper in 1853 described the United States as bound on the "East by sunrise, West by sunset, North by the Arctic Expedition, and South as far as we darn please."

Many of Pierce's diplomatic appointees were southerners interested in adding new cotton-growing lands to the Union. Pierce's ambassador to Mexico, for example, South Carolinian James Gadsden, had instructions to negotiate with Mexican president Santa Anna for the acquisition of large parts of northern Mexico. Gadsden did not get all he wanted, but he did manage to buy a strip of southwestern desert for a transcontinental railroad linking the Deep South with the Pacific Coast.

Failure to acquire more territory from Mexico legally did not discourage expansionist Americans from pursuing illegal means. During the 1850s, Texans and

Californians staged dozens of raids ("filibusters") into Mexico. The most daring such adventurer was William Walker, a tiny Tennessean with a zest for danger and power. In 1853, he invaded Mexican Baja California with fewer than 300 men and declared himself president of the Republic of Sonora. Arrested and tried in the United States, he was acquitted in eight minutes. Two years later, he invaded Nicaragua, where he proclaimed himself dictator and legalized slavery. When the Nicaraguans, with British help, regained control, the U.S. Navy rescued Walker. After a triumphant tour in the South, he tried twice more to conquer Nicaragua. Walker came to a fitting end in 1860 when, invading Honduras this time, he was shot by a firing squad.

Undaunted by failures in the Southwest, the Pierce administration looked to the acquisition of Cuba. Many Americans thought this Spanish colony was destined for U.S. annexation and would be an ideal place for expanding the slave-based economy. Some argued that Cuba belonged to the United States because it was physically connected by alluvial deposits from the Mississippi River. In the 1840s, the Polk administration had vainly offered Spain $10 million for Cuba. Unsuccessful efforts were then made to foment a revolution among Cuban sugar planters, who were expected to request annexation by the United States, which might then divide Cuba into several slave states.

Although Pierce did not support these illegal efforts to acquire Cuba, he wanted the island. Secretary of State William Marcy instructed the minister to Spain, Pierre Soulé, to offer $130 million for Cuba, upping the price. If that failed, Marcy suggested stronger measures. In 1854, the secretary arranged for Soulé and the American ministers to France and England to meet in Belgium, where they issued the Ostend Manifesto to pressure Spain to sell Cuba to the United States.

The manifesto argued that Cuba "belongs naturally" to the United States and that they were "one people with one destiny." Moreover, southern slaveholders feared that a slave rebellion would "Africanize" Cuba, like Haiti, and suggested all kinds of "horrors to the white race" in the nearby southern United States. American acquisition of Cuba was necessary, therefore, to "preserve our rectitude and self-respect." If Spain refused to sell, the ministers at Ostend threatened a Cuban revolution with American support. If that failed, "we should be justified in wresting it from Spain."

Even Marcy was shocked, and he quickly repudiated the manifesto. As with the Kansas–Nebraska Act, Democrats supported the Ostend Manifesto in order to further the expansion of slavery. The outraged reaction of northerners in both cases divided and further weakened the Democratic party.

Nativism, Know-Nothings, and Republicans

Increasing immigration also damaged an already enfeebled Whig party and alarmed many native-born Americans. To the average hardworking Protestant American, the foreigners pouring into the nation and following the railroads westward spoke unfamiliar languages rather than English, wore funny clothes, drank alcohol freely, and bred crime and pauperism. Moreover, they seemed content with a lower standard of living and thus threatened to take jobs away from native-born American workers, themselves descended from former immigrants.

Immigration and Politics Describe what you see in this cartoon from the mid-1850s (top). What stereotypes of Irish and Germans are shown? What does it mean that they are stealing the ballot box, and what is going on in the background by the "election polls"? The Know-Nothing flag (bottom) makes starkly clear that party's view on the origins of the danger. Who are the "Native Americans" referred to on the flag, and what do you think the original "Native" Americans would think of this flag and its warning? *(Photo courtesy of the Milwaukee County Historical Society)*

Worst of all from the Protestant perspective, Irish and German immigrants spearheaded an unprecedented growth of American Catholicism. By the 1850s, there were nearly 3 million Catholics in the United States, not only in eastern cities but expanding westward and—to the shocked surprise of many old-stock Americans—converting Protestants. A wave of Catholic revivals to gain converts and the opening of Catholic schools compounded their offensiveness to Protestants.

Many Protestants charged that Catholic immigrants corrupted American politics. Indeed, most Catholics did prefer the Democratic party, which was less inclined than the Whigs to interfere with religion, schooling, drinking, and other aspects of personal behavior and rights. It was mostly former Whigs, therefore, who in 1854 founded the American party to oppose the new immigrants. Members wanted a longer period of naturalization to guarantee the "vital principles of Republican Government" and pledged never to vote for Irish Catholics, whose highest loyalty was supposedly to the pope. They also agreed to keep information about their order secret. If asked, they would say, "I know nothing." Hence, they were dubbed the Know-Nothing party.

The Know-Nothings appealed to the middle and lower classes—to workers worried about their jobs and to farmers and small-town Americans nervous about change. A New Yorker said in 1854, "Roman Catholicism is feared more than American slavery." It was widely believed that Catholics slavishly obeyed their priests, who represented a Church associated with European despotism. In the 1854 and 1855 elections, the Know-Nothings gave anti-Catholicism as well as anti-immigration a national political focus for the first time.

To other northerners, however, the "slave power" seemed a more serious threat than alleged schemes of the pope. No sooner had debates over Nebraska ended than the nucleus of another new party appeared: the Republican party. Drawn almost entirely from "conscience" Whigs and disaffected Democrats (including ex–Free-Soilers), the Republicans combined four main elements.

Moral fervor led the first group, headed by senators William Seward, Charles Sumner (Massachusetts), and Salmon P. Chase (Ohio), to demand prohibiting slavery in the territories, freeing slaves in the District of Columbia, repealing the Fugitive Slave Act, and banning the internal slave trade. There were, however, limits to most Republicans' idealism. A more moderate and larger group, typified by Abraham Lincoln, opposed slavery in the western territories, but would not interfere with it where it already existed. This group also opposed equal rights for northern free blacks.

Many Republicans were anti-Catholic as well as antislavery. A third element of the party, true to traditional Whig reformist impulses, wanted to cleanse America of intemperance, impiety, parochial schooling, and other forms of immorality—including voting for Democrats, who catered to the "grog shops, foreign vote, and Catholic brethren" and combined the "forces of Jesuitism and Slavery."

The fourth element of the Republican party, a Whig legacy from Clay's American System, included those who wanted the federal government to promote economic development and the dignity of labor. This group, like the antislavery and anti-Catholic elements, idealized free labor. At the heart of both the new party and the future of America were hardworking, middle-class, mobile, free white laborers—farmers, small businessmen, and independent craftsmen, people who, in the words of the Springfield, Illinois *Republican*, valued "work with their hands" and "home and family."

The strengths of the Republican and Know-Nothing (American) parties were tested in 1856. The American party nominated Fillmore, who had strong support in the Upper South. The Republicans chose John C. Frémont, an ardent Free-Soiler from Missouri with virtually no political experience but with fame as an explorer of the West and a military record against the Mexicans in California. The Democrats nominated Pennsylvanian James Buchanan, a "northern man with southern principles." Frémont carried several free states, while Fillmore took only Maryland. Buchanan, benefiting from a divided opposition, won with only 45 percent of the popular vote.

After 1856, the Know-Nothings died out, largely because Republican leaders cleverly redirected nativist fears—and voters—to their broader program. Moreover, Know-Nothing secrecy, hatreds, and occasional violent attacks on Catholic voters damaged their image. Still, the Know-Nothings represented a powerful current in American politics that would return each time social and economic changes seemed to threaten. It became convenient to label certain people "un-American" or "illegal" immigrants, and try to root them out. The Know-Nothing party disappeared, but nativist hostility to new immigrants did not, as we clearly see in the current opposition to Mexican and Central American migrants.

KANSAS AND THE TWO CULTURES

The slavery issue also would not go away. As Democrats sought to expand slavery and other American institutions westward across the Plains and south into Cuba, Republicans wanted to halt the advance of slavery. In 1854, Lincoln worried that slavery "deprives our republican example of its just influence in the world." The specific cause of his concern was the likelihood that slavery might be extended into Kansas as a result of the passage that year of Stephen Douglas's Kansas–Nebraska Act.

Competing for Kansas

During the congressional debates over the Kansas–Nebraska bill, Seward accepted the challenge of slave-state senators to "engage in competition for the virgin soil of Kansas." No sooner had the Kansas–Nebraska Act passed Congress in 1854 than the Massachusetts Emigrant Aid Society was founded to recruit free-soil settlers for Kansas. By the summer of 1855, about 1,200 New England colonists had migrated to Kansas.

One migrant was Julia Louisa Lovejoy, a Vermont minister's wife. As a riverboat carried her into a slave state for the first time in her life, she wrote of the dilapidated plantation homes on the monotonous Missouri shore as the "blighting mildew of slavery." By the time she and her husband arrived in the Kansas Territory, Julia had concluded that the "morals" of the slaveholding Missourians moving into Kansas were of an "*undescribably repulsive* and undesirable character." To her, northerners came to bring the "energetic Yankee" virtues of morality and economic enterprise to drunken, unclean slaveholders.

Perhaps she had in mind David Atchison, Democratic senator from Missouri. Atchison believed that Congress must protect slavery in the territories, allowing Missouri slaveholders into Kansas. In 1853, he pledged "to extend the institutions of Missouri over the Territory at whatever sacrifice of blood or treasure." He recommended to fellow Missourians if need be "to kill every God-damned abolitionist in the district."

Under Atchison's inflammatory leadership, secret societies sprang up in the Missouri counties adjacent to Kansas dedicated to combatting the Free-Soilers. One editor exclaimed that northerners came to Kansas "for the express purpose of stealing, running off and hiding runaway negroes from Missouri [and] taking to their own bed ... a stinking negro wench." Not slaveholders, he said, but New Englanders were immoral, uncivilized, and hypocritical. Rumors of 20,000 such Massachusetts migrants spurred Missourians to action. Thousands poured across the border late in 1854 to vote on permitting slavery in the territory. Twice as many ballots were cast as the number of registered voters.

The proslavery forces overreacted. The permanent population of Kansas consisted primarily of migrants from Missouri and other border states, people more concerned with land titles than slavery. They opposed any blacks—slave or free—moving into their state.

In March 1855, a second election was held to select a territorial legislature. The pattern of border crossings, intimidation, and illegal voting was repeated. Atchison himself, drinking "considerable whiskey," led an armed band across the state line to vote and frighten away would-be Free-Soil voters. Not surprisingly, swollen numbers of illegal voters elected a proslavery territorial legislature. Free-Soilers, meanwhile, held their own convention in Lawrence and created a Free-Soil government at Topeka. It banned blacks from the state. The proslavery legislature settled eventually in Lecompton, giving Kansas two governments.

The struggle shifted to Washington. Although Pierce could have nullified the illegal election, he did nothing. Congress debated and sent an investigating committee to Kansas, which further inflamed passions. Throughout 1855, the call to arms grew more strident. In South Carolina, Robert Allston wrote his son Benjamin that he was "raising men and money ... to counteract the effect of the Northern hordes. ... We are disposed to fight the battle of our rights ... on the field of Kansas."

Both sides saw Kansas as a holy battleground. An Alabaman sold his slaves to raise money to hire an army of 300 men to fight for slavery in Kansas, promising free land to his recruits. A Baptist minister blessed their departure from Montgomery, promised them God's favor, and gave each man a Bible. Northern Christians responded in kind. At Yale University, the noted minister Henry Ward Beecher presented 25 Bibles and 25 Sharps rifles to young men who would go fight for the Lord in Kansas. "There are times," he said, "when self-defense is a religious duty." Beecher suggested that rifles would be of greater use than Bibles. Missourians dubbed them "Beecher's Bibles" and vowed, as one newspaper put it, "Blood for Blood!"

"Bleeding Kansas"

As civil war threatened in Kansas, a Brooklyn poet, Walt Whitman, heralded American democracy in his epic poem *Leaves of Grass* (1855). Whitman identified himself as the embodiment of average Americans "of every hue and caste ... of every rank and religion," and celebrated urban mechanics, southern woodcutters, runaway slaves, mining camp prostitutes, and long lists of average Americans. But Whitman's faith in the democratic American masses faltered in the mid-1850s.

He worried that a knife plunged into the "breast" of the Union would bring on the "red blood of civil war."

Blood indeed flowed in Kansas. In May 1856, supported by a pro-southern federal marshal, a mob entered Lawrence, smashed the offices and presses of a Free-Soil newspaper, fired several cannonballs into the Free State Hotel, and destroyed homes and shops. Three nights later, believing he was doing God's will, John Brown led a small New England band, including four of his sons, to a proslavery settlement near Pottawatomie Creek and hacked five men to death with swords.

That same week, abolitionist senator Charles Sumner delivered a tirade known as "The Crime Against Kansas." He lashed out at the "incredible atrocities of the Assassins and ... Thugs" from the South. He accused proslavery Senate leaders, especially Andrew Butler of South Carolina and Stephen Douglas, of cavorting with the "harlot, Slavery." Two days later, Butler's cousin, Congressman Preston Brooks, avenged his honor by viciously beating Sumner senseless with his cane as he sat at his Senate desk.

The sack of Lawrence, the Pottawatomie massacre, and the caning of Sumner set off a minor civil war in "Bleeding Kansas" that lasted throughout the summer. Crops were burned, homes were destroyed, fights broke out in saloons and streets, and night raiders murdered enemies. For Charles Lines, who just wanted to farm in peace, it was impossible to remain neutral. Lines hoped his neighbors near Lawrence would avoid "involving themselves in trouble." But when proslavery forces tortured a neighbor to death, Lines joined the battle. "Blood," he wrote, "must end in the triumph of the right."

Even before the bleeding of Kansas began, the New York *Tribune* warned, "We are two peoples. We are a people for Freedom and a people for Slavery. Between the two, conflict is inevitable." As the rhetoric and violence in Kansas demonstrated, competing visions of two separate cultures for the future destiny of the United States were at stake. Despite many similarities between the North and the South, the gap between the two sides widened with the hostilities of the 1850s.

Northern Views and Visions

As Julia Lovejoy suggested, the North saw itself as a prosperous land of bustling commerce and expanding, independent agriculture. Northern farmers and workers were self-made free men who believed in individualism and democracy. The "free labor system" of the North, as both Seward and Lincoln often said, offered equality of opportunity and upward mobility. Both generated more wealth. Although the North contained many growing cities, northerners revered the values of the small towns that spread from New England across the Upper Midwest. These values included a respect for the rights of the people, tempered by the rule of law; individual enterprise, balanced by a concern for one's neighbors; and a fierce morality, rooted in Protestantism. Northerners would regulate morality—by persuasion if possible, by legislation if necessary—to purge irreligion, illiteracy, and intemperance from American society.

Northerners valued the kind of republican government that guaranteed the rights of free men, enabling them to achieve economic progress. This belief

Scenes from North and South Describe the socioeconomic contrasts in these two pictures. How many differences can you identify? Any similarities? Chicago (top) was a rapidly growing, bustling northern city in the 1850s; situated on the Great Lakes and a developing railroad hub, Chicago became the distribution center for industrial and agricultural goods throughout the Midwest. The vital unit of southern commerce was, by contrast, the individual plantation (bottom), with steamboats and flatboats carrying cotton and sugar to port cities for trade with Europe. Are there examples today of cultural contrasts similar to this? *(top: Corbis; bottom: Library of Congress)*

supported government action to promote free labor, industrial growth, some immigration, foreign trade (protected by tariffs), and the extension of railroads and free farm homesteads westward across the continent. Energetic mobility, both westward and upward, would dissolve state, regional, and class loyalties and increase the sense of nationhood. A strong Union could achieve national and even international greatness. These were the conditions, befitting a chosen people, who would, as Seward put it, spread American institutions around the world and "renovate the condition of mankind." These were also the principles of the Republican party.

Only free men could achieve economic progress and moral society. In northerners' eyes, therefore, the worst sin was the loss of one's freedom. Slavery was the root of evil. It was, Seward said, "incompatible with all ... the elements of the security, welfare, and greatness of nations." The South was the antithesis of everything that such northerners saw as good. Southerners were unfree, backward, economically stagnant, uneducated, lawless, immoral, and in conflict with the values and ideals of the nineteenth century. Julia Lovejoy's denunciation of slaveholding Missourians was mild. Other Yankee migrants saw southerners as "wild beasts" who guzzled whiskey, ate dirt, swore, raped slave women, and fought or dueled at the slightest excuse. In the slang of the day, they were "Pukes."

The Southern Perspective

Southerners were a diverse people who, like northerners, shared certain broad values, generally those of the planter class. If in the North the values of economic enterprise were most important, southerners revered social values most. They admired the English gentry and saw themselves as courteous, refined, hospitable, and chivalrous—and saw "Yankees" as rude, aggressive, and materialistic. In a society where one person in three was a black slave, racial distinctions and paternalistic relationships were crucial in maintaining order and white supremacy. Fear of slave revolt was ever-present. The South had five times as many military schools as the North. Northerners educated the many for economic utility; southerners educated the few for character. In short, the white South saw itself as an ordered society guided by the planters' genteel code.

Southerners agreed with northerners that republican sovereignty rested in the people, who created a government of laws to protect life, liberty, and property. But unlike northerners, southerners believed that the democratic principle of self-government was best preserved in local political units such as the states. They were ready to fight to resist any tyrannical encroachment on their liberty, as they had in 1776. They saw themselves as true revolutionary patriots. Like northerners, southerners cherished the Union. But they preferred the loose confederacy of the Jeffersonian past, not Seward's centralized nationalism.

To southerners, Yankees were in too much of a hurry—to make money, to reform others' behavior, to put dreamy theories (like racial equality) into practice. Two images dominated the white South's view of northerners: either they were stingy, hypocritical, moralizing Puritans, or they were grubby, slum-dwelling, Catholic immigrants. These northerners, one paper said, "are devoid of society fitted for well-bred gentlemen."

Each side saw the other threatening its freedom and degrading proper republican society. Each saw the other imposing barriers to its vision for America's future, which included the economic systems described in Chapter 10 and Chapter 11. As hostilities rose, the views each section had of the other grew steadily more rigid and conspiratorial. Northerners saw the South as a "slave power," determined to foist the slave system on free labor throughout the land. Southerners saw the North as full of "black Republicanism," determined to destroy their way of life.

POLARIZATION AND THE ROAD TO WAR

The struggle over Kansas solidified the image of the Republicans as a northern party and seriously weakened the Democrats. Further events, mostly over the question of slavery in the territories, soon split the Democrats irrevocably into sectional halves: the Dred Scott decision of the Supreme Court (1857), the constitutional crisis in Kansas (1857), the Lincoln–Douglas debates in Illinois (1858), John Brown's raid in Virginia (1859), and Lincoln's election (1860). These incidents further polarized the negative images each culture held of the other and accelerated the nation down the road to civil war.

The Dred Scott Case

The events of 1857 reinforced the arguments of those who believed in a slave power conspiracy. Two days after James Buchanan's inauguration, the Supreme Court finally ruled in *Dred Scott* v. *Sanford*. The case had been before the Court for nearly three years. Back in 1846, Dred and Harriet Scott had filed suit in Missouri for their freedom. They argued that their master had taken them into territories where the Missouri Compromise prohibited slavery, and therefore they should be freed. By the time the case reached the Supreme Court, slavery in the territories was a hot political issue.

DOCUMENT

Opinion of the Supreme Court for *Dred Scott* v. *Sanford* (1857)

When the Court, with its southern majority, issued a 7–2 decision, it made three rulings. First, because blacks were, as Chief Justice Roger Taney put it, "beings of an inferior order [who] had no rights which white men were bound to respect," Dred Scott was not a citizen and had no right to sue in federal court. The second ruling stated that the Missouri Compromise was unconstitutional because Congress had no power to ban slavery in a territory. Third, the Court decided that the Scotts being taken in and out of free states did not affect their status.

The implications of these decisions went far beyond the Scotts' personal freedom. The arguments about black citizenship infuriated many northerners. Frederick Douglass called the ruling "a most scandalous and devilish perversion of the Constitution." Many citizens worried about the few rights free blacks still held.

IMAGE

Dred Scott

Even more troubling, the decision hinted that slavery might be legal in the free states of the North. People who suspected a conspiracy were not calmed when Buchanan endorsed the *Dred Scott* decision as a final settlement of the right of citizens to take their "property of any kind, including slaves, into the common Territories ... and to have it protected there under the Federal Constitution." Far from settling the issue of slavery in the territories, as Buchanan had hoped, *Dred Scott* threw it back into American politics. It opened new questions and increased sectional hostilities.

Constitutional Crisis in Kansas

The *Dred Scott* decision and Buchanan's endorsement fed northern suspicions of a slave power conspiracy to impose slavery everywhere. Events in Kansas, which still had two governments, heightened these fears. In the summer of 1857, Kansas had yet another election, with so many irregularities that only 2,000 out of a possible 24,000 voters participated. A proslavery slate of delegates was elected to a constitutional convention meeting at Lecompton as a preparation for statehood. The convention barred free blacks from the state, guaranteed the property rights of the few slaveholders in Kansas, and asked voters to decide in a referendum whether to permit more slaves.

The proslavery Lecompton constitution, clearly unrepresentative of the wishes of the majority of the people of Kansas, was sent to Congress for approval. Eager to retain southern Democratic support, Buchanan endorsed it. Stephen Douglas challenged the president's power and jeopardized his standing with southern Democrats by opposing it. Facing reelection to the Senate in 1858, Douglas needed to hold the support of the northern wing of his party. Congress sent the Lecompton constitution back to the people of Kansas for another referendum. This time they defeated it, which meant that Kansas remained a territory rather than becoming a slave state. While Kansas was left in an uncertain status, the larger political effect of the struggle was to split the Democratic party almost beyond repair.

No sooner had Douglas settled the Lecompton question than he faced reelection in Illinois. Douglas's opposition to the Lecompton constitution had restored his prestige in the North as an opponent of the slave power. This cut some ground out from under the Republican party's claim that only it could stop the spread of southern power. Party leaders from the West, however, had a candidate who understood the importance of distinguishing Republican moral and political views from those of the Democrats.

Lincoln and the Illinois Debates

Although relatively unknown nationally and out of elective office for several years, by 1858 Abraham Lincoln emerged in Illinois to challenge Seward for leadership of the Republican party. Lincoln's character was shaped on the midwestern frontier, where he had educated himself, developed mild abolitionist views, and dreamed of America's greatness.

Douglas was clearly the leading Democrat, so the 1858 Senate election in Illinois gave a preview of the presidential election of 1860. The other Douglass, Frederick, observed, "the slave power idea was the ideological glue of the Republican party." Lincoln's handling of this idea would be crucial in distinguishing him from Stephen Douglas. The Illinois campaign featured seven debates between Lincoln and Douglas, which took place in different cities. Addressing a national as well as a local audience, the debaters confronted the heated racial issues before the nation.

DOCUMENT

The Lincoln–Douglas Debates of 1858

Lincoln set a solemn tone when he accepted the Republican senatorial nomination. The American nation, he said, was in a "crisis" and building toward a worse one. "A House divided against itself cannot stand. I believe this government cannot endure, permanently half *slave* and half *free*." Lincoln said he did not expect the Union "to be dissolved" or "the house to fall," but rather that "it will become *all* one thing, or *all* the other." Then he rehearsed the history of the South's growing influence over national policy since the Kansas–Nebraska Act, which he blamed on Douglas. Lincoln stated his firm opposition to the *Dred Scott* decision, which he believed part of a conspiracy involving Pierce, Buchanan, Taney, and

Douglas. He and others like him opposing this conspiracy wished to place slavery on a "course of ultimate extinction."

Debating Douglas, Lincoln reiterated these controversial themes. Although far from a radical abolitionist, in these debates Lincoln also skillfully staked out a moral position on race and slavery not just in advance of Douglas but well ahead of his time.

Lincoln was also a part of his time. He believed in white superiority, opposed granting specific equal civil rights to free blacks, and said that differences between whites and blacks would "forever forbid the two races from living together on terms of social and political equality." "Separation" and colonization in Liberia or Central America was the best solution. But Lincoln differed from most contemporaries in his deep commitment to the equality and dignity of all human beings. Countering Douglas's racial slurs, Lincoln said that he believed not only that blacks were "entitled to all the natural rights ... in the Declaration of Independence," but also that they had many specific economic rights, like "the right to put into his mouth the bread that his own hands have earned." In these rights, blacks were "my equal and the equal of Judge Douglas, and the equal of every living man."

Unlike Douglas, Lincoln hated slavery. "I contemplate slavery as a moral, social, and political evil." The difference between a Republican and a Democrat was simply whether one thought slavery wrong or right. Douglas was more equivocal and dodged the issue in Freeport, pointing out that slavery would not exist if local legislation did not support it. But Douglas's moral indifference was clear: he did not care if a territorial legislature voted it "up or down." Republicans did care, Lincoln answered, and said that by stopping the expansion of slavery, the course toward "ultimate extinction" had begun. Although barred by the Constitution from interfering with slavery where it already existed, Lincoln said that Republicans believed slavery wrong, and "we propose a course of policy that shall deal with it as a wrong."

What Lincoln meant by "policy" was not yet clear, not even to himself. However, he did succeed in affirming that Republicans were the only moral and political force capable of stopping the slave power. It seems ironic now (though not then) that Douglas won the election. Elsewhere in 1858, however, Democrats did poorly, losing 18 congressional seats to the Republicans.

John Brown's Raid

IMAGE
John Brown
(ca. 1850)

Unlike Lincoln, John Brown was prepared to act decisively against slavery. On October 16, 1859, he and a band of 22 men attacked the federal arsenal at Harpers Ferry, Virginia (now West Virginia). He hoped to provoke a general uprising of slaves throughout the Upper South or at least provide arms for slaves to make their way to freedom. Federal troops soon overcame him. Nearly half his men died, including two sons. Brown was captured, tried, and hanged. So ended a lifetime of failures.

In death, however, Brown was not a failure. His daring if foolhardy raid and his dignified behavior during his trial and speedy execution unleashed powerful passions. The North–South gap widened. Although Brown's death was widely

John Brown as an Avenging Hero Describe the many images in this modern mural of John Brown. What do you see? What are the opposing forces? How violent is this depiction? Is the angry, stormy sky God's wrath? What do you think about John Brown? *(Kansas State Historical Society)*

DOCUMENT

John Brown's Address Before Sentencing (1859)

condemned, many northerners responded to it with an outpouring of sympathy. Thoreau compared him to Christ. Abolitionist William Lloyd Garrison, a pacifist, wished "success to every slave insurrection" in the South. Ministers called slave revolt a "divine weapon" and glorified Brown's treason as "holy." Brown's raid, Frederick Douglass said, showed that slavery was a "system of brute force" that would only be ended when "met with its own weapons."

Southerners were filled with "dread and terror" over the possibility of a wave of slave revolts led by hundreds of imaginary John Browns and Nat Turners, and concluded that northerners would stop at nothing to free the slaves. This suspicion further eroded freedom of thought and expression. A North Carolinian described a "spirit of terror, mobs, arrests, and violence" in his state. Twelve families in Berea, Kentucky, were evicted from the state for their mild abolitionist sentiments. A Texas minister who criticized the treatment of slaves in a sermon got 70 lashes.

With Brown's raid, southerners also became more convinced, as the governor of South Carolina put it, of a "black Republican" plot in the North "arrayed against the slaveholders," now a permanent minority. Southern Unionists lost their influence, and power passed to those favoring secession.

The Election of 1860

When the Democratic convention met in Charleston, South Carolina, a secessionist hotbed, it sat for a record 10 days and went through 59 ballots without being able to name a candidate. Reconvening in Baltimore, the Democrats acknowledged their irreparable division by choosing two candidates at two separate conventions: Douglas for northern Democrats, and John C. Breckinridge, Buchanan's vice president, for the proslavery South. The Constitutional Union party, made up

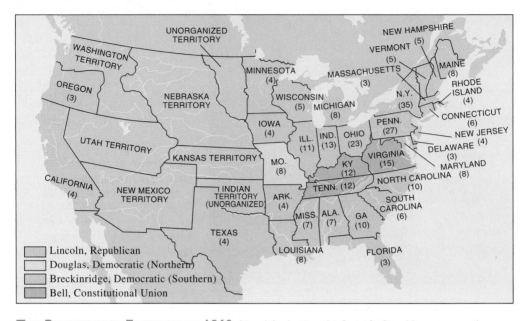

THE PRESIDENTIAL ELECTION OF 1860 Lincoln's election, the first of a Republican, was on the basis of a totally northern sectional victory; he received only 40 percent of the popular vote. How do you explain each candidate's success in each section of the country? Why didn't Douglas do better? Why did Lincoln win the election? Who would you have voted for in 1860?

of former southern Whigs and border-state nativists, claimed the middle ground and nominated John Bell, a slaveholder from Tennessee who favored compromise.

With Democrats split and a new party in contention, the Republican strategy aimed at keeping the states carried by Frémont in 1856 and adding Pennsylvania, Illinois, and Indiana. Seward, the leading candidate, had been tempering his antislavery views to appear more electable. So had Lincoln, who seemed more likely than Seward to carry those key states. After shrewd maneuvers emphasizing his "availability" as a moderate, Lincoln was nominated.

The Republican platform exuded moderation, opposing only slavery's extension. Mostly it spoke of tariff protection, subsidized internal improvements, free labor, and a homestead bill. Republicans, like southern Democrats, defended their view of what republican values meant for America's future, which did not include the equal rights envisioned by Frederick Douglass. An English traveler in 1860 observed that in America "we see, in effect, two nations—one white and another black—growing up together within the same political circle, but never mingling on a principle of equality."

The Republican moderate strategy worked as planned. Lincoln was elected by sweeping the entire Northeast and Midwest. Although he got less than 40 percent of the popular vote nationwide, his triumph in the North was decisive. Even a united Democratic party could not have defeated him. With victory assured, Lincoln finished his sandwich and coffee on election night in Springfield and prepared for his awesome responsibilities. They came even before his inauguration.

THE DIVIDED HOUSE FALLS

The Republicans overestimated Unionist sentiment in the South. A year earlier, some southern congressmen had walked out in protest when the House chose an antislavery speaker. A Republican leader, Carl Schurz, recalling this, said that the southerners had taken a drink and then come back. Now, Schurz predicted, they would walk out, take two drinks, and come back again. He was wrong.

Secession and Uncertainty

On December 20, 1860, South Carolina seceded, declaring the "experiment" of putting people with "different pursuits and institutions" under one government a failure. By February 1, the other six Deep South states (Mississippi, Florida, Alabama, Georgia, Louisiana, and Texas) also left. A week later, delegates meeting in Montgomery, Alabama, created the Confederate States of America and elected Jefferson Davis, a Mississippi senator and cotton planter, its provisional president. The divided house had fallen, as Lincoln had predicted. But it was not yet certain whether the house could be put back together, or whether there would be civil war.

The government in Washington had three options. First was compromise, but the emotions of the time ruled that out, as the compromises were mostly prosouthern. Second, as suggested by New York *Tribune* editor Horace Greeley, Washington might let the seven states "go in peace," taking care not to lose the border states. This was opposed by northern businessmen, who would lose profitable economic ties with the South, and by those who believed in an indissoluble Union. The third option was to compel secessionist states to return, which probably meant war.

Republican hopes that southern Unionism would assert itself and avoid all these options seemed possible in February 1861. No more states seceded. The nation waited, wondering what Virginia and the border states would do, what outgoing President Buchanan would do, and what Congress would do. Determined not to start a civil war in the last weeks of his already dismal administration, Buchanan did nothing. Congress made some feeble efforts to pass compromise legislation, waiting in vain for the support of the president-elect. And as Union supporters struggled with secessionists, Virginia and the border states, like the entire nation, waited for Lincoln.

Frederick Douglass waited, too, without much hope. He wanted the "complete and universal *abolition* of the whole slave system," as well as equal suffrage and other rights for free blacks. His momentary expectation during the presidential campaign, that Lincoln and the Republicans had the will to do this, had been thoroughly dashed. Douglass foresaw northern politicians and businessmen "granting the most demoralizing concessions to the Slave Power."

In his despair, Douglass began to explore possibilities for emigration and colonization in Haiti, an idea he had long opposed. To achieve full freedom and citizenship in the United States for all blacks, he said in January 1861, he would "welcome the hardships consequent upon a dissolution of the Union." In February, Douglass said, "Let the conflict come." He opposed all compromises, hoping that

The Causes of the Civil War

Starting with the seven items at the top of this chart, how would you explain the primary cause of the Civil War? Which four or five of the following "specific issues and events" would you use to support your argument? Can you make a distinction between underlying causes and immediate sparks?

Date	Issues and Events	Deeper, Underlying Causes of Civil War
1600s–1860s	Slavery in the South	Slavery as major, underlying, pervasive cause
1700s–1860s	Development of two distinct socio-economic systems and cultures	Further reinforced slavery as fundamental socioeconomic, cultural moral issue
1787–1860s	States' rights, nullification doctrine	Ongoing political issue, less fundamental as cause
1820	Missouri Compromise (36°30')	Background for conflict over slavery in territories
1828–1833	South Carolina tariff nullification crisis	Background for secession leadership in South Carolina
1831–1860s	Antislavery movements, southern justification	Thirty years of emotional preparation for conflict
1846–1848	War with Mexico (Wilmot Proviso, Calhoun, popular sovereignty)	Options for issue of slavery in territories

Date	Specific Issues and Events	Specific Impact on the Road to War
1850	Compromise of 1850	Temporary and unsatisfactory "settlement" of divisive issue
1851–1854	Fugitive slaves returned and rescued in North; personal liberty laws passed in North; Harriet Beecher Stowe's *Uncle Tom's Cabin*	Heightened northern emotional reactions against the South and slavery
1852–1856	Breakdown of Whig party and national Democratic party; creation of a new party system with sectional basis	Made national politics an arena where sectional and cultural differences over slavery were fought
1854	Ostend Manifesto and other expansionist efforts in Central America; formation of Republican party; Kansas–Nebraska Act	Reinforced image of Democratic party as favoring slavery; major party identified as opposing the extension of slavery; reopened "settled" issue of slavery in the territories
1856	"Bleeding Kansas"; Senator Sumner physically attacked in Senate	Foretaste of Civil War (200 killed, $2 million in property lost) inflamed emotions and polarized North and South
1857	*Dred Scott* decision; proslavery Lecompton constitution in Kansas	Made North fear a "slave power conspiracy," supported by President Buchanan and the Supreme Court
1858	Lincoln–Douglas debates in Illinois; Democrats lose 18 seats in Congress	Set stage for election of 1860
1859	John Brown's raid and reactions in North and South	Made South fear a "black Republican" plot against slavery; further polarization and irrationality
1860	Democratic party splits in half; Lincoln elected president; South Carolina secedes from Union	Final breakdown of national parties and election of "northern" president; no more compromises
1861	Six more southern states secede by February 1; Confederate Constitution adopted February 4; Lincoln inaugurated March 4; Fort Sumter attacked April 12	Civil War begins

with Lincoln's inauguration in March, it would "be decided, and decided forever, which of the two, Freedom or Slavery, shall give law to this Republic."

Lincoln and Fort Sumter

As Douglass penned these thoughts, Lincoln began a long, slow train ride from Springfield to Washington, writing and rewriting his inaugural address. Lincoln's quietness in the period between his election and his inauguration led many to judge him weak and indecisive. He was not. Lincoln firmly opposed secession and any compromise with the principle of stopping the extension of slavery. He would neither conciliate secessionist southern states nor force their return.

Lincoln believed in his constitutional responsibility to uphold the laws of the land. The focus of his attention was a federal fort in the harbor of Charleston. Major Robert Anderson, the commander of Fort Sumter, was running out of provisions and had requested new supplies from Washington. Lincoln would enforce the laws and protect federal property at Fort Sumter.

As the new president delivered his inaugural address on March 4, he faced a tense and divided nation. Lincoln asserted his unequivocal intention to enforce the laws of the land, arguing that the Union was "perpetual" and indissoluble. He reminded the nation that the "only substantial dispute" was that "one section of our country believes slavery is *right,* and ought to be extended, while the other believes it is *wrong,* and ought not to be extended." Still appealing to Unionist strength among southern moderates, Lincoln said that he would make no attempts to interfere with existing slavery and would respect the law to return fugitive slaves. Nearing the end, Lincoln put the burden of initiating civil war on the "dissatisfied fellow-countrymen" who had seceded. As if foreseeing the horrible events that would follow, he closed his speech eloquently:

> I am loath to close. We are not enemies, but friends. We must not be enemies. Though passion may have strained, it must not break our bonds of affection. The mystic chords of memory, stretching from every battlefield, and patriot grave, to every living heart and hearthstone, all over this broad land, will yet swell the chorus of the Union, when again touched, as surely they will be, by the better angels of our nature.

Frederick Douglass was not impressed with Lincoln's "honied phrases" and accused him of "weakness, timidity and conciliation." Also unmoved, Robert Allston wrote his son from Charleston, where he was watching the crisis over Fort Sumter, that the Confederacy's "advantage" was in having a "much better president than they have."

On April 6, Lincoln notified the governor of South Carolina that he was sending "provisions only" to Fort Sumter. No effort would be made "to throw in men, arms, or ammunition" unless the fort were attacked. On April 10, Jefferson Davis directed General P. G. T. Beauregard to demand the surrender of Fort Sumter. Davis told Beauregard to reduce the fort if Major Anderson refused.

On April 12, as Lincoln's relief expedition neared Charleston, Beauregard's batteries began shelling Fort Sumter, and the Civil War began. Frederick Douglass was about to leave for Haiti when he heard the news. He immediately changed

TIMELINE

1848	Arguments over slavery in the territories gained from Mexico		**1855–1856**	Bleeding Kansas
			1857	*Dred Scott* case
1850	Compromise of 1850, including Fugitive Slave Act		**1859**	John Brown's raid at Harpers Ferry
			1860	Abraham Lincoln elected president
1854	Kansas–Nebraska Act		**1861**	Confederate States of America founded
	Republican and Know-Nothing parties formed			Attack on Fort Sumter begins Civil War

his plans: "This is no time ... to leave the country." He announced his readiness to help end the war by aiding the Union to organize freed slaves "into a liberating army" to "make war upon ... the savage barbarism of slavery." The Allstons had changed places, and it was Benjamin who described the events in Charleston harbor to his father. On April 14, Benjamin reported the "glorious, and astonishing news that Sumter has fallen." With it fell America's divided house.

Conclusion

The "Irrepressible Conflict"

Lincoln had been right. The nation could no longer endure half-slave and half-free. The collision between North and South, William Seward said, was not an "accidental, unnecessary" event, but an "irrepressible conflict between opposing and enduring forces." Those forces had been at work for many decades, but developed with increasing intensity after 1848 over the question of the extension of slavery into the territories. Although economic, cultural, political, constitutional, and emotional forces all contributed to the developing opposition between North and South, slavery was the fundamental, enduring force that underlay all others, causing what Walt Whitman called the "red blood of civil war." Abraham Lincoln, Frederick Douglass, the Allston family, Michael Luark, and the American people all faced a radically altered national scene. All wondered whether the American democratic system would be able to withstand this challenge.

Questions for Review and Reflection

1. What options existed for dealing with slavery in the territories, and what compromises did Congress propose? How well did they work?

2. How did political party alignments change in the 1850s and how did that affect the path to civil war?

3. Examine how southerners and northerners viewed each other, especially in and after Kansas. How did cultural stereotypes and emotional attitudes contribute to the outbreak of civil war?

4. Can you explain four basic, underlying causes of the American Civil War? Which one cause do you think was most significant, and what specific events would you use to support your choice?

5. To what extent was the American democratic political system flexible enough to handle the issues of the 1850s? Could the Civil War have been avoided, or was it inevitable?

Discovering U.S. History Online

Compromise of 1850 www.loc.gov/exhibits/treasures/trm043.html
This exhibit shows digitized images of compromise documents by John C. Calhoun and Daniel Webster's notes for introductory remarks.

Bleeding Kansas www.kancoll.org/galbks.htm
A collection of contemporary and later accounts of America's rehearsal for the Civil War make up this University of Kansas site.

Africans in America 1831–1865 www.pbs.org/wgbh/aia/part4/index.html
A large collection of people and events, historical documents, and modern voices on antebellum slavery, abolitionism, slavery in the territories, John Brown's raid, and the Civil War is found in this site.

The Dred Scott Case www.library.wustl.edu/vlib/dredscott/
This site presents digital images and transcriptions of 85 original documents (HTML or Word format), as well as a timeline of events surrounding the case.

John Brown's Holy War www.pbs.org/wgbh/amex/brown
This companion Web site to the film contains primary source material (excerpts from letters, speeches, and an editorial), biographical information, a timeline, profiles of related people and events, information on the song "John Brown's Body," and a bibliography.

Lincoln's Election www.iath.virginia.edu/vshadow2/outlines/election.html
A thorough collection of sources on the 1860 election, including a breakdown of the votes and various contemporary newspaper articles.

Crisis at Fort Sumter www.tulane.edu/~latner/CrisisMain.html
This site presents "an interactive historical simulation and decision-making program. Using text, images, and sound, it reconstructs the dilemmas of policy formation and decision making in the period between Abraham Lincoln's election in November 1860 and the battle of Fort Sumter in April 1861."

Fiction and Film ————————————————————

The most important novel about slavery during the antebellum era was Harriet Beecher Stowe's *Uncle Tom's Cabin* (1852). Written in serial form, each episode stopped at a nail-biting moment and aroused the conscience of the North. Walt Whitman's collection of poems, *Leaves of Grass* (1855), celebrates not only the poet's own ego but also the common people and democratic American values in a decade that sorely tested those values. Russell Banks's *Cloudsplitter* (1998) is a long but riveting novel about John Brown and his activities during the 1850s, told through the eyes of one of his sons. *The Bondswoman's Daughter* by Hannah Crafts (2002), recently discovered by Henry Louis Gates, Jr., is a captivating story of a runaway slave woman in the 1850s. Toni Morrison's award-winning novel *Beloved* (1988), later made into a feature film, tells the story, based on a true event in 1856, of an escaped slave mother who killed her child as bounty hunters were about to seize her family and return them to slavery. Part I of Ken Burns's PBS film series, *The Civil War* (1989), sets the slavery and 1850s background for his haunting documentary portrayal of the Civil War. Another fine video is *John Brown's Holy War* (1999) from the PBS series *The American Experience*.

Recommended Reading ——————————————————

www.ablongman.com/nash

The Companion Website has a list of recommended readings about the 1850s and the causes of the Civil War.

The Union Severed

American Stories

A War that Touched Lives

In his remarks to Congress in 1862, Abraham Lincoln reminded congressmen that "We cannot escape history. We of this Congress and this administration will be remembered in spite of ourselves. No personal significance, or insignificance, can spare ... us. The fiery trial through which we pass, will light us down, in honor or dishonor, to the latest generation." Lincoln's conviction that Americans would long remember him and other major actors of the Civil War was correct. Jefferson Davis, Robert E. Lee, Ulysses S. Grant—these are the men whose characters, actions, and decisions have been the subject of continuing discussion and analysis, whose statues and memorials dot the American countryside and grace urban squares. Whether seen as heroes or villains, great men have dominated the story of the Civil War.

Yet from the earliest days, the war touched the lives of even the most uncelebrated Americans. From Indianapolis, 20-year-old Arthur Carpenter wrote to his parents in Massachusetts, begging for permission to volunteer: "I have always longed for the time to come when I could enter the army and be a military man, and when this war broke out, I thought the time had come, but you would not permit me to enter the service ... now I make one more appeal to you." The pleas worked, and Carpenter enlisted, spending most of the war fighting in Kentucky and Tennessee.

In that same year, in Tennessee, George and Ethie Eagleton faced anguishing decisions. Though not an abolitionist, George, a 30-year-old Presbyterian preacher, was unsympathetic to slavery and opposed to secession. But when his native state left the Union, George felt compelled to follow and enlisted in the 44th Tennessee Infantry. Ethie, his 26-year-old wife, despaired over the war, George's decision, and her own forlorn situation:

> Mr. Eagleton's school dismissed—and what for? O my God, must I write it? He has enlisted in the service of his country—to war—the most unrighteous war that ever was brought on any nation that ever lived. Pres. Lincoln has done what no other Pres. ever dared to do—he has divided these once peaceful and happy United States. And Oh! the dreadful dark cloud that is now hanging over our country—'tis enough to sicken the heart of any one. ... Mr. E. is gone. ... What will become of me, left here without a home and relatives, a babe just nine months old and no George.

Both Carpenter and the Eagletons survived the war, but it transformed their lives. Carpenter had difficulty settling down. Filled with bitter memories of the war years in Tennessee, the Eagletons moved to Arkansas. Ordinary people like Carpenter and the Eagletons are historically anonymous. Yet their actions on and off the battlefield helped to shape the course of events, as their leaders realized, even if today we tend to remember only the famous and influential.

For thousands of Americans, from Lincoln and Davis to Carpenter and the Eagletons, war was both a profoundly personal and a major national event. Its impact reached far beyond the four years of hostilities. The war that was fought to conserve two political, social, and economic visions ended by changing familiar ways of political, social, and economic life in both North and South. War was a transforming force, both destructive and creative in its effect on the structure and social dynamics of society and on the lives of ordinary people. This theme underlies this chapter's analysis of the war's three stages: the initial months of preparation, the years of military stalemate between 1861 and 1865, and, finally, resolution.

ORGANIZING FOR WAR

The Confederate bombardment of Fort Sumter on April 12, 1861, and the surrender of Union troops the next day ended uncertainties. The North's response to Fort Sumter was a virtual declaration of war as President Lincoln called for state militia volunteers to crush the "insurrection." His action pushed Virginia, North Carolina, Tennessee, and Arkansas into the secessionist camp. Three other slave states (Maryland, Kentucky, and Missouri) agonizingly debated which way to go. The "War Between the States" was a reality.

Many Americans were dismayed. Southerners like George Eagleton only reluctantly followed their states out of the Union. When he enlisted, Eagleton complained of the "disgraceful cowardice" of those who were "now refusing self and means for the prosecution of war." Robert E. Lee of Virginia was equally hesitant to resign his federal commission but finally decided that he could not "raise [a] hand against ... relatives ... children ... home." Whites in the southern uplands (where blacks were few and slaveholders were heartily disliked), yeomen farmers in the Deep South (who owned no slaves), and many border state residents opposed secession and war. Many would eventually join the Union forces.

In the North, large numbers supported neither the Republicans nor Lincoln. Irish immigrants fearing the competition of free black labor and southerners living in Illinois, Indiana, and Ohio opposed war. Northern Democrats at first blamed Lincoln and the Republicans almost as much as the secessionists for the crisis.

Nevertheless, the days following Fort Sumter and Lincoln's call for troops saw an outpouring of support on both sides, fueled in part by relief at decisive action, in part by patriotism and love of adventure, and in part by unemployment. The conviction that the conflict would rapidly come to a glorious conclusion also fueled the eagerness to enlist. Lincoln's call for 75,000 state militiamen for only 90 days of service, and a similar enlistment term for Confederate soldiers, supported the notion that the war would be short.

The war fever produced so many volunteers that officials could not handle the throng. Both sides sent thousands of white would-be soldiers home.

The Balance of Resources

The Civil War was one of several military conflicts during the nineteenth century that sought national independence. In Europe, Italian and German patriots struggled to create new nations out of individual states. Unlike their European counterparts, however, southern nationalists proclaimed their independence by withdrawing from an already unified state. Likening their struggle to that of the Revolutionary generation that had broken away from Great Britain's tyranny, southerners argued that they were "now enlisted in The Holy Cause of Liberty and Independence." While they legitimized secession by appealing to freedom, however, southerners were also preserving freedom's antithesis, slavery.

The outcome of the southern bid for autonomy was uncertain. Although statistics of population and industrial development suggested a northern victory, Great Britain with similar advantages in 1775 had lost that war. Many northern assets would become effective only with time.

The North's white population greatly exceeded the South's, giving the appearance of a military advantage. Yet early in the war, the armies were more evenly matched. Almost 187,000 Union troops bore arms in July 1861, while just over 112,000 men marched under Confederate colors. Southerners believed that their army would prove to be superior fighters. Many northerners feared so, too. And slaves could carry on vital work behind the lines, freeing most adult white males to serve the Confederacy.

The Union also enjoyed impressive economic advantages. In the North, 1 million workers in 110,000 manufacturing concerns produced goods valued at $1.5 billion annually, while 110,000 southern workers in 18,000 manufacturing concerns produced goods valued at only $155 million a year. But northern industrial resources had to be mobilized. That would take time, especially because the government did not intend to direct production. A depleted northern treasury made the government's first task the raising of funds to pay for military necessities.

The South depended on imported northern and European manufactured goods. If Lincoln cut off that trade, the South would have to create its industry almost from scratch. Its railroad system was organized to move cotton, not armies and supplies. Yet the agricultural South did have important resources of food, draft animals, and, of course, cotton, which southerners believed would secure British and French support. By waging a defensive war, the South could tap regional loyalty and enjoy protected lines. Because much of the South raised cotton and tobacco rather than food crops, Union armies could not live off the land, and extended supply lines were always vulnerable. The Union had to conquer and occupy; the South merely had to survive until its enemy gave up.

The Border States

Uncertainty and divided loyalties produced indecision in the border states. When the seven Deep South states seceded in 1860 and 1861, all the border states except

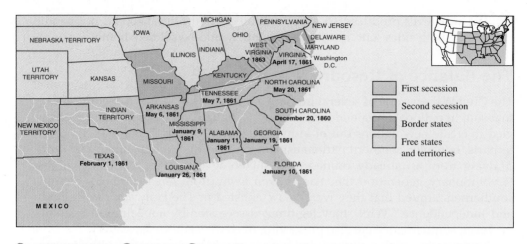

SECESSION OF THE SOUTHERN STATES The map provides a chronology of secession and shows the geographical importance of the border states. The map also highlights the vulnerable position of Washington and explains many of Lincoln's actions in the early days of the war.

Unionist Delaware adopted a wait-and-see attitude. Their decisions were critically important to both North and South.

The states of the Upper South could provide natural borders for the Confederacy along the Ohio River, access to its river traffic, and vital resources, wealth, and population. The major railroad link to the West ran through Maryland and western Virginia. Virginia boasted the South's largest ironworks, and Tennessee provided its principal source of grain. Missouri opened the road to the West and controlled Mississippi River traffic.

For the North, every border state remaining loyal was a psychological triumph. Nor was the North unaware of the economic and strategic advantages of keeping the border states with the Union. However, Lincoln's call for troops precipitated the secession of Virginia, Arkansas, Tennessee, and North Carolina between April 17 and May 20, 1861. Maryland, precariously balanced between the pro-Confederate southern and Eastern Shore counties and Unionist western and northern areas, and with pro-southern enthusiasts abounding in Baltimore, vividly demonstrated the significance of border state loyalty.

AUDIO

Battle Hymn of the Republic

On April 19, the 6th Massachusetts Regiment, heading for Washington, marched through Baltimore and was attacked by a mob of some 10,000 southern sympathizers, some carrying Confederate flags. The bloody confrontation and confusion allowed would-be secessionists to burn the railroad bridges to the north and south, cutting Washington temporarily off from the rest of the Union.

Lincoln took stern measures to secure Maryland. The president agreed temporarily to route troops around Baltimore. In return, the governor called the state legislature into session at Frederick in Unionist western Maryland. This action and Lincoln's swift violation of civil liberties dampened secessionist enthusiasm. Hundreds of southern sympathizers, including 19 state legislators and Baltimore's mayor, were imprisoned without trial. Although Chief Justice Roger B. Taney challenged the president's action and issued a writ of habeas corpus for the release of a southern supporter, Lincoln ignored him. A month later, Taney ruled in *Ex Parte Merryman* that if the public's safety was endangered, only Congress could suspend habeas corpus. By then, Lincoln had secured Maryland.

Although Lincoln's quick and harsh response ensured Maryland's loyalty, he was more cautious elsewhere. Above all, he had to deal with slavery prudently, for hasty action would push border states into the Confederacy. Thus, when General John C. Frémont issued an unauthorized declaration of emancipation in Missouri in August 1861, Lincoln revoked the order and recalled him. The president expected a chain reaction if certain key states seceded. After complex maneuvering, Kentucky and Missouri, like Maryland, remained in the Union.

Challenges of War

The tense weeks after Fort Sumter spilled over with unexpected challenges. Both North and South faced enormous organizational problems.

Southerners had to create a nation–state and devise everything from a constitution to a flag. An important question hovered behind the frantic organizational efforts: could the new political entity succeed in creating bonds of nationhood and inspire the feelings of patriotism that would be necessary if the conflict proved long and difficult?

In February 1861, the original seceding states began the work of creating a nation. The first task was to establish a provisional framework and choose a provisional president and vice president. The delegates swiftly wrote a constitution, much like the federal constitution but emphasizing the "sovereign and independent character" of the states and explicitly recognizing slavery. Provisional President Jefferson Davis tried to assemble a balanced and moderate cabinet. His appointees took on the daunting challenge of creating government departments from scratch. When an army captain came to the treasury with a warrant from Davis for blankets, he found only one clerk. After reading the warrant, the clerk offered the captain a few dollars of his own, explaining, "This, Captain, is all the money that I will certify as being in the Confederate Treasury at this moment."

Despite the challenges, the new Confederate government enjoyed enthusiastic civilian support and a growing sense of nationalism. Ordinary people spoke proudly of the South as "our nation" and referred to themselves as the "southern people." Georgia's governor insisted that "poor and rich, have a common interest, a common destiny." Southern Protestant ministers encouraged a sense of collective identity and reminded southerners that they were God's chosen people. The conflict was a sacred one.

While Lincoln inherited the federal government, he lacked administrative experience, and, like his Confederate counterpart, faced organizational problems. Military officers and government clerks defected daily to the South. The treasury was empty. Floods of Republican office seekers thronged into the White House.

Lincoln did not know many of the "prominent men of the day" and so appointed important Republicans to cabinet posts whether they agreed with him or not. Several scorned him as a backwoods bumbler. Treasury Secretary Salmon P. Chase hoped to replace Lincoln as president in four years' time. Secretary of State William Seward sent Lincoln a memo condescendingly offering to oversee the formulation of presidential policy.

Lincoln and Davis

A number of Lincoln's early actions illustrated that he was no fool. As his Illinois law partner, William Herndon, pointed out, Lincoln's "mind was tough—solid—knotty—gnarly, more or less like his body." The president firmly told Seward that he would run his own administration. After Sumter, he called up the state militias, expanded the navy, suspended habeas corpus, blockaded the South, and approved spending funds for military purposes—all without congressional sanction, because Congress was not in session. As Lincoln told legislators later, "The dogmas of the quiet past are inadequate to the stormy present. ... As our case is new, so must we think anew, and act anew." This willingness to "think anew" was a valuable personal asset, even though some criticized his expansion of presidential power as despotic.

By coincidence, Lincoln and his rival, Jefferson Davis, were born only 100 miles apart in Kentucky. However, the course of their lives diverged radically. Lincoln's father migrated north and eked out a simple existence as a farmer. Lincoln himself had only a rudimentary education. Davis's family moved to Mississippi to become cotton planters. Davis grew up in comfortable circumstances, went to West Point, fought in the Mexican-American War, was elected to the U.S. Senate, and served as secretary of war under Franklin Pierce.

Although Davis had not been eager to accept the presidency, he had loyally responded to the call of the provisional congress in 1861 and worked tirelessly as chief executive. As his wife observed, "the President hardly takes time to eat his meals and works late at night." Some, however, criticized this endless busyness as the result of Davis's inability to delegate details. Others found him sickly, reserved, humorless, and sensitive to criticism. He was hardly the kind of magnetic leader who might serve as a national symbol for the new nation. But Davis, like Lincoln, found it necessary to "think anew." He reassured southerners in his inaugural address that his aims were conservative, "to preserve the Government of our fathers in spirit." Yet under the pressure of events, he moved toward creating a new kind of South.

CLASHING ON THE BATTLEFIELD, 1861–1862

The Civil War
Part I:
1861–1862

The Civil War was the most brutal and destructive conflict in American history. Much of the bloodshed resulted from inadequate communications combined with changing military technology. The range of rifles had increased from 100 to 500 yards, in part owing to the new French minié bullet, which had tremendous velocity and accuracy. Because it was no longer possible to move artillery close enough to enemy lines to support an infantry charge, attacking infantry soldiers faced a 500-yard dash into deadly fire.

As it became clear that infantry charges produced horrible carnage, military leaders increasingly valued strong defensive positions. Although Confederate soldiers at first criticized General Lee as "King of Spades," the epithet evolved into one of affection as it became obvious that earthworks saved lives. Union commanders followed suit.

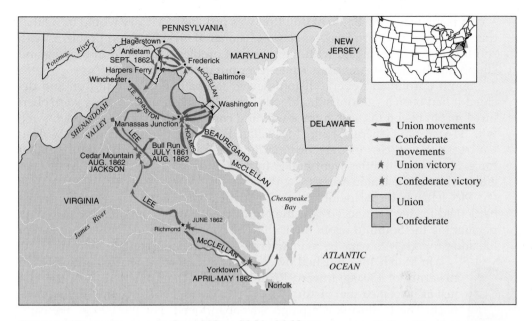

EASTERN THEATER OF THE CIVIL WAR, 1861–1862 The map reveals the military actions in the East during the early years of the war. Initially, military planners hoped to end the war quickly by capturing Richmond. They soon discovered that the Confederate army was too powerful to allow them an easy victory. Eventually, Lincoln decided to combine military pressure on Virginia with an effort in the West aimed at cutting the Confederacy in two.

War in the East

The war's brutal character only gradually revealed itself. The Union's commanding general, 70-year-old Winfield Scott, at first pressed for a cautious, long-term strategy, the Anaconda Plan. Scott proposed weakening the South gradually through blockades on land and sea until the northern army was strong enough for the kill. The public, however, hungered for quick victory. So did Lincoln: He knew that the longer the war lasted, the more embittered the South and the North would both become, making reunion ever more difficult. So 35,000 partially trained men led by General Irwin McDowell left Washington in sweltering July weather, heading for Richmond.

On July 21, 1861, only 25 miles from the capital at Manassas Creek (also called Bull Run), inexperienced northern troops confronted 25,000 raw Confederate soldiers commanded by Brigadier General P. G. T. Beauregard, a West Point classmate of McDowell's. Although sightseers, journalists, and politicians gaily accompanied the Union troops, Bull Run was no picnic. The battle was inconclusive until the arrival of 2,300 fresh Confederate troops, brought by trains, decided the day. Terrified and bewildered Union soldiers and sightseers fled toward Washington. Defeated though the Union forces were, inexperienced Confederate troops failed to turn the rout into a quick, decisive victory. As General Joseph E. Johnston pointed out, his men were disorganized, confused by victory, and insufficiently supplied with food to chase the Union army back toward Washington.

In many ways, the Battle of Bull Run was prophetic. Victory would be neither quick nor easy. Both armies were unprofessional. Both sides faced problems with short-term enlistments and with the logistical problems involved in moving and supplying the largest American armies ever put in the field.

South Carolinian Robert Allston viewed the battlefield at Bull Run and decided it had been a "glorious tho bloody" day. For the Union, the loss was sobering. Lincoln began his search for a winning commander by replacing McDowell with 34-year-old General George McClellan. Formerly an army engineer, McClellan began the process of transforming the Army of the Potomac into a fighting force. Short-term militias went home. In the fall of 1861, McClellan became general in chief of the Union armies.

McClellan had considerable organizational ability but no desire to be a daring battlefield leader. Convinced that the North must combine military victory with persuading the South to rejoin the Union, he sought to avoid embittering loss of life and property—to win "by maneuvering rather than fighting."

Robert E. Lee on Horseback

In March 1862, pushed by an impatient Lincoln, McClellan finally led his army of 130,000 toward Richmond, now the Confederate capital. But just as it seemed that victory was within grasp, Lee drove the Union forces back. The Peninsula campaign was abandoned. For the Union, the campaign was a frustrating failure. For Lee, the success in repelling the invasion was one step in the process that was making him and the Army of Northern Virginia into a symbol of the spirit of the new nation.

Other Union defeats followed in 1862 as commanders came and went. In September, the South took the offensive with a bold invasion of Maryland. But after a costly defeat at Antietam, in which more than 5,000 soldiers were slaughtered and another 17,000 wounded on the grisliest day of the war, Lee withdrew to Virginia. The war in the East was stalemated.

War in the West

The early struggle in the East focused on Richmond, the Confederacy's capital and one of the South's most important railroad, industrial, and munitions centers. But the East was only one of three theaters. Between the Appalachians and the Mississippi lay the western theater. The Mississippi River, with its vital river trade and its great port, New Orleans, was a major strategic objective. Here both George Eagleton and Arthur Carpenter served. Beyond lay the trans-Mississippi West—Louisiana, Arkansas, Missouri, Texas, and the Great Plains—where Native American tribes joined the conflict on both sides.

Union objectives in the West were twofold. The army sought to dominate Kentucky and eastern Tennessee, the avenues to the South and West, and to win control of the Mississippi in order to split the South in two.

Military Brass Bands

In the western theater, Ulysses S. Grant rose to prominence. His modest military credentials included education at West Point, service in the Mexican-American War, and an undistinguished stint in the peacetime army. After his resignation, he went bankrupt. Shortly after Fort Sumter, Grant enlisted as a colonel in an Illinois militia regiment. Within two months, he was a brigadier general. He proved to be a military genius, able to see beyond individual battles to larger goals. In 1862, he realized that the

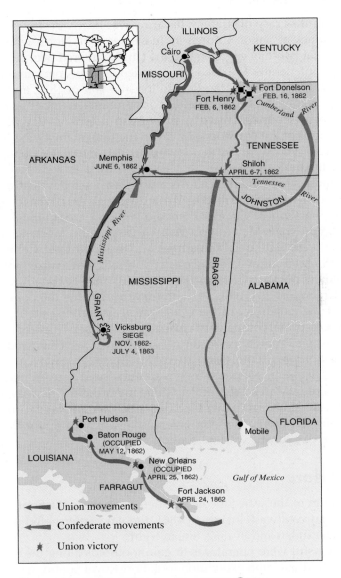

TRANS-MISSISSIPPI CAMPAIGN OF THE CIVIL WAR Union forces operating in the Mississippi Valley were attempting to separate Texas, Arkansas, and Louisiana from other southern states as part of an attempt to squeeze the Confederacy.

Tennessee and Cumberland rivers offered pathways for the successful invasion of Tennessee. A premature Confederate invasion of Kentucky allowed Grant to bring his forces into that state without arousing sharp local opposition. Assisted by gunboats, Grant was largely responsible for the capture of Fort Henry and Fort Donelson, key points on the rivers, in February 1862. His successes there raised fears among Confederate leaders that southern mountaineers, loyal to the Union, would rush to Grant's support.

Despite Grant's grasp of strategy, his army was nearly destroyed by a surprise Confederate attack at Shiloh Church in Tennessee. The North won, but at enormous cost. In that two-day engagement, the Union suffered over 13,000 casualties, while 10,000 Confederates lay dead or wounded. More American men fell in this single battle than in the American Revolution, the War of 1812, and the Mexican-American War combined. Because neither army offered sufficient care on the battlefield, untreated wounds caused many of the deaths. A day after the battle ended, nine-tenths of the wounded still lay in the rain, many dying of exposure or drowning. Those who survived the downpour had infected wounds by the time they received medical attention.

Though more successful than efforts in the East, such devastating Union campaigns failed to bring decisive results. Western plans were never coordinated with eastern military activities. Victories there did not force the South to its knees.

The war in the trans-Mississippi West was a sporadic, far-flung struggle. California was the prize that lured both armies into the Southwest. Confederate Texan troops held Albuquerque and Santa Fe briefly in 1862, but a mixed force, including volunteer soldiers from the Colorado mining fields and Mexican Americans, drove them out. A Union force recruited in California arrived after the Confederates were gone. It spent the remainder of the Civil War years fighting the Apache and the Navajo, and with brutal competence crushed both Native American nations.

Farther east was another prize, the Missouri River, which flowed into the Mississippi River, bordered Illinois, and affected military campaigns in Kentucky and Tennessee. Initially, Confederate troops were successful here, as they had been in New Mexico. But in March 1862, at Pea Ridge in northern Arkansas, Union forces whipped a Confederate army that included a brigade of Native Americans from the Five Civilized Nations. Missouri entered the Union camp for the first time in the war, but fierce guerrilla warfare continued.

Naval Warfare

At the beginning of the war, Lincoln decided to strangle the South with a naval blockade. But success was elusive. In 1861, the navy intercepted only about one blockade runner in ten and in 1862, one in eight.

More successful were operations to gain footholds along the southern coast. In November 1861, a Union expedition took Port Royal Sound, where it freed the first slaves, and the nearby South Carolina sea islands. By gaining these and other important coastal points, the navy increased the possibility of an effective blockade. The Union's major naval triumph in the early war years was the capture of the South's biggest port, New Orleans, in 1862. The success of this amphibious effort stimulated other joint attempts to cut the South in two.

The Confederates, recognizing that they could not match the Union fleet, concentrated on developing new weapons like torpedoes and ironclad vessels. The *Merrimac* was one key to southern naval strategy. Originally a U.S. warship that had sunk as the federal navy hurriedly abandoned the Norfolk Navy Yard early in the war, the Confederates raised the vessel and covered it with heavy iron armor. Rechristened the *Virginia,* the ship steamed out of Norfolk in March 1862, heading directly for the Union ships blocking the harbor. Using its 1,500-pound ram and guns, the *Virginia* drove one-third of the vessels aground and destroyed the squadron's largest ships. But the victory was short-lived. The next day, the *Virginia* confronted the *Monitor,* a newly completed Union iron vessel. They dueled inconclusively, and the *Virginia* withdrew. It was burned during the evacuation of Norfolk that May. Southern attempts to buy ironclad ships abroad faded and, with them, southern hopes of escaping the northern noose.

Still, Confederate attacks on northern commerce brought some success. Southern raiders, many of them built in Britain, wreaked havoc on northern shipping. In its two-year career, the *Alabama* destroyed 69 Union merchant vessels valued at more than $6 million. But such blows did not seriously damage the North's war effort.

Thus the first two years brought victories to both sides, but the war remained deadlocked. The South was far from defeated; the North was equally far from giving up. Costs in manpower and supplies far exceeded what either side had expected.

Cotton Diplomacy

Both sides realized that attitudes in Europe could be decisive. Diplomatic recognition would give the Confederacy international credibility, and European loans and assistance might bring the South victory—just as French and Dutch aid had helped the American colonies win independence. If the European powers refused to recognize the South, however, the fiction of the Union was kept alive. Such a refusal undermined both long-term Confederate survival and the critical process of knitting the Confederacy together as one nation. European powers, of course, consulted their own interests. Neither Britain nor France wished to back a loser. Nor did they wish to upset Europe's delicate balance of power by hasty intervention in American affairs. One by one, therefore, the European states declared neutrality.

Southerners were sure that cotton would be their trump card. British and French textile mills needed cotton, and southerners believed that their owners would eventually force their governments to recognize the Confederacy and to end the northern blockade. But a glut of cotton in 1860 and 1861 left foreign mill owners oversupplied. As stockpiles dwindled, European industrialists found cotton in India and Egypt. The faith that cotton was "king" was unfounded.

Union Secretary of State Seward's goal was to prevent diplomatic recognition of the Confederacy. The North had its own economic ties with Europe, so the Union was not as disadvantaged as southerners thought. Seward threatened Great Britain with war if it interfered. Some called his boldness reckless, but it succeeded. Although Britain allowed the construction of Confederate raiders in its ports, it did not intervene in American affairs in 1861 or 1862. Nor did the other powers. Unless the military situation changed dramatically, Europeans would sit on the sidelines.

Common Problems, Novel Solutions

As the conflict dragged on into 1863, unanticipated problems arose. In response, Union and Confederate leaders devised novel approaches to solve them.

The challenge of the long conflict was partly monetary. Both treasuries had been empty initially, and the war proved extraordinarily expensive. Neither side

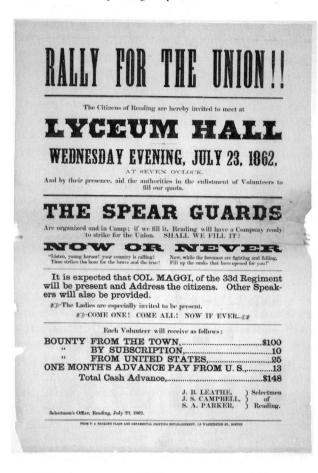

Recruiting the Troops This 1862 poster invites "one" and "all" to come to the rally in Reading, Massachusetts. While there would be speeches and perhaps even patriotic music, the point of the meeting was to fill the town's military quota with "volunteers." How does the poster encourage young men to enlist? Can you discover how much $148 would be worth today? *(Library of Congress, Rare Book Room)*

considered imposing direct taxes, which would have alienated support, but both introduced taxation on a small scale. Ultimately, taxes financed 21 percent of the North's war expenses, but only 1 percent of southern expenses. Both treasuries also tried borrowing. Northerners purchased over $2 billion worth of bonds, but southerners proved reluctant to buy their government's securities. As in the American Revolution, printing paper money provided the unwelcome solution. In August 1861, the Confederacy put into circulation $100 million in crudely engraved bills. Millions more followed the next year. Five months later, the Union issued $150 million in paper money, soon nicknamed "greenbacks." The result of this paper money policy was inflation. Inflation was particularly bad in the Confederacy, but even a "modest" 80 percent increase in food prices brought Union city families near starvation and contributed to wartime urban misery.

Both sides faced manpower problems as initial enthusiasm for the war evaporated. Soldiering, with its carnage and deadly diseases along with the boredom of life in camp, was nothing like militia parades familiar to most American males. Those in the service longed to go home. The swarm of volunteers disappeared. Rather than filling their military quotas from within, rich northern communities began offering bounties of $800 to $1,000 to outsiders who would join up.

Arthur Carpenter's letters give a good picture of life in the ranks and a young man's growing disillusionment with the war. As Carpenter's regiment moved into Kentucky and Tennessee in 1862, his spirits sank. "Soldiering in Kentucky and Tennessee is not so pretty as it was in Indianapolis. ... We have been half starved, half frozen, and half drowned. The mud in Kentucky is awful." Soldiering often meant marching with 50 or 60 pounds of equipment and insufficient food, water, or supplies. One blanket was insufficient in the winter. In the summer, stifling woolen uniforms attracted lice. Poor food, bugs, inadequate sanitation, and exposure invited disease. Carpenter marched through Tennessee suffering from diarrhea and fever. His regiment left him behind in a convalescent barracks in Louisville, which he fled as soon as he could. "[Ninety-nine] Surgeons out of a hundred," he wrote his parents, "would not know whether his patient had the horse distemper, lame toe, or any other disease."

Confederate soldiers, even less well supplied than their northern foes, complained similarly. In 1862, a Virginia captain described what General Lee called the best army "the world ever saw":

> During our forced marches and hard fights, the soldiers have been compelled to throw away their knapsacks and there is scarcely a private in the army who has a change of clothing of any kind. Hundreds of men are perfectly barefooted and there is no telling when they can be supplied with shoes.

AUDIO

When This Cruel
War Is Over

Such circumstances often led to desertion. An estimated one of every nine Confederate soldiers and one of every seven Union troopers deserted.

As manpower problems became critical, both governments resorted to the draft. Despite sacrosanct states' rights, the Confederate Congress passed the first conscription act in American history in March 1862. Four months later, the Union Congress also approved a draft measure. Both laws encouraged men already in the army to reenlist and sought volunteers rather than men forced to serve. Ultimately, over 30 percent of the Confederate army and 6 percent of the Union forces were draftees. The South relied more heavily on the draft because the North's manpower pool was larger and growing. During the war, 180,000 foreigners of military age poured into the northern states. Some came specifically to claim bounties and fight. Immigrants made up at least 20 percent of the Union army.

Although necessary, draft laws were very unpopular. The first Confederate conscription declared all able-bodied men between the ages of 18 and 35 eligible for military service but allowed numerous exemptions and the purchase of substitutes. The exemption from military service granted to every planter with more than 20 slaves fed class tension and encouraged disloyalty and desertion, particularly among mountaineers. The advice one woman shouted after her husband as he was dragged off to the army was hardly unique: "You desert again, quick as you kin. ... Desert, Jake!"

Northern legislation was neither more popular nor more fair. The 1863 draft allowed the hiring of substitutes, and $300 bought an exemption from military service. Workers, already suffering from inflation, resented the ease with which moneyed citizens could avoid army duty. In July 1863, the resentment boiled over in New York City in the largest civil disturbance of the nineteenth century, a three-day riot that erupted a month after a work stoppage on the New York waterfront. Events spun out of control as a mob (mainly Irish workmen) burned draft records and the armory, plundered the houses of the rich, and looted jewelry stores. Blacks, hated as economic competitors and the cause of the war, became special targets. Mobs beat and lynched blacks and burned the Colored Orphan Asylum. More than 100 people died. There was much truth in the accusation that the war on both sides was a rich man's war but a poor man's fight.

Political Dissension, 1862

As the war continued, rumbles of dissension grew louder. On February 24, 1862, the *Richmond Examiner* summarized many southerners' frustration. "The Confederacy has had everything that was required for success but one, and that one thing it was and is supposed to possess more than anything else, namely Talent." Criticism of Confederate leaders mounted. Vice President Alexander Stephens became one of the administration's most bitter accusers.

Because the South had no party system, dissatisfaction with Davis's handling of the war tended to be factional, petty, and personal. Detractors rarely offered alternative policies. Without a party leader's traditional weapons and rewards, Davis had no mechanism to generate political support.

Although Lincoln has since become a folk hero, at the time of the Civil War, many northerners derided his performance. Peace Democrats, called Copperheads, claimed that Lincoln betrayed the Constitution and that working-class Americans bore the brunt of his conscription policy. Immigrant workers in eastern cities and citizens in the southern Midwest had little sympathy for abolitionism or blacks, and they supported the antiwar Copperheads. Even pro-war Democrats found Lincoln arbitrary and tyrannical, and worried that extremist Republicans would push Lincoln into making the war an antislavery crusade. Some Republicans judged Lincoln indecisive and inept.

Republicans were themselves divided. Moderates favored a cautious approach toward winning the war, fearing the possible consequences of emancipating slaves, confiscating Confederate property, or arming blacks. The radicals, however, urged Lincoln to make emancipation a wartime objective. They sought a victory that would revolutionize southern social and racial arrangements. The reduction of the congressional Republican majority in the fall elections of 1862 made it imperative that Lincoln heed both factions as well as the Democratic opposition.

THE TIDE TURNS, 1863–1865

Harsh political realities and Lincoln's sense of the public's mood help explain why he delayed action on emancipation until 1863. Many northerners supported a war for the Union, not for emancipation. Most whites saw blacks as inferior and feared that emancipation would lure former slaves north to steal white jobs and political rights. Northern urban race riots dramatized white attitudes.

The Emancipation Proclamation, 1863

If the president moved too fast on emancipation, he risked losing the allegiance of northern racists, offending the border states, and increasing the Democrats' chances for political victory. Moreover, he at first hoped that pro-Union sentiment would emerge in the South and compel its leaders to abandon their rebellion. But

A French View of Emancipation This depiction of African Americans celebrating the Emancipation Proclamation appeared in the French publication *Le Monde Illustre.* How has the artist provided a triumphant and sympathetic picture of rejoicing freed people? What does this picture, published in France, suggest about the diplomatic importance to the Union cause of the Emancipation Proclamation?

if Lincoln did not move at all, he would alienate abolitionists and lose the support of radical Republicans, which he could ill afford.

So Lincoln proceeded cautiously. At first, he thought the border states might take the initiative. In the early spring of 1862, he urged Congress to pass a joint resolution offering federal compensation to states beginning a "gradual abolishment of slavery." Border state opposition killed the idea. Abolitionists and northern blacks, however, greeted Lincoln's proposal with a "thrill of joy."

That summer, Lincoln told his cabinet he intended to emancipate the slaves. Secretary of State Seward urged the president to delay any general proclamation until the North won a decisive military victory. Otherwise, Lincoln would appear to be urging racial insurrection behind the Confederate lines to compensate for northern military bungling. Lincoln took Seward's advice, using the summer and fall to prepare the North for the shift in the war's purpose. To counteract white fears of free blacks, he promoted schemes for establishing black colonies in Haiti and Panama. In August, Horace Greeley, the influential abolitionist editor of the New York *Tribune,* printed an open letter to Lincoln attacking him for failing to act on slavery. Replying, Lincoln linked emancipation to military necessity:

> If I could save the Union without freeing any slave, I would do it; and if I could save it by freeing all the slaves, I would do it; and if I could do it by freeing some and leaving others alone, I would also do that. What I do about Slavery and the colored race, I do because I believe it helps to save this Union.

If Lincoln attacked slavery, then, it would be only because emancipation would save white lives, preserve the democratic process, and restore the Union.

In September 1862, the Union victory at Antietam gave Lincoln the opportunity to issue a preliminary emancipation proclamation. It stated that unless rebellious states (or parts of states in rebellion) returned to the Union by January 1, 1863, the president would declare their slaves "forever free." Although supposedly aimed at bringing the southern states back into the Union, Lincoln never expected the South to lay down arms after two years of bloodshed. Rather, he was preparing northerners to accept the eventuality of emancipation on the grounds of necessity. Frederick Douglass greeted the president's action with jubilation. But not all northerners shared Douglass's joy. The September proclamation probably harmed Republicans in the fall elections.

Although the elections of 1862 weakened the Republicans' grasp on the national government, they did not destroy it. Still, cautious cabinet members begged Lincoln to forget about emancipation. His refusal demonstrated his vision and humanity. So did his efforts to reduce racial fears. "Is it dreaded that the freed people will swarm forth and cover the whole land?" he asked. "Are they not already in the land? Will liberation make them any more numerous? Equally distributed among the whites of the whole country, and there would be but one colored to seven whites. Could the one, in any way, greatly disturb the other?"

Finally, on New Year's Day, 1863, Lincoln issued the final Emancipation Proclamation as he had promised. It was an "act of justice, warranted by the Constitution upon military necessity." Thus, what began as a war to save the Union became a struggle that, if victorious, would free the slaves. Yet the proclamation had no immediate impact on slavery. It affected only slaves living in the unconquered portions of the Confederacy and said nothing about slaves in the border states and in parts of the South already in northern hands. These limitations led Elizabeth Cady Stanton and Susan B. Anthony to establish the woman's Loyal National League to lobby Congress to emancipate all southern slaves.

Yet the Emancipation Proclamation had a tremendous symbolic importance. On New Year's Day, blacks gathered outside the White House to cheer the president and tell him that if he would "come out of that palace, they would hug him to death." They realized that the proclamation had transformed the nature of the war. For the first time, the government had committed itself to freeing slaves. Jubilant blacks could only believe that the president's action heralded a new era for their race. More immediately, the proclamation sanctioned the policy of accepting blacks as soldiers. Blacks also hoped that the news would reach southern slaves, encouraging them either to flee to Union lines or subvert the southern war effort.

Diplomatic concerns also lay behind the Emancipation Proclamation. Lincoln and his advisers anticipated that the commitment to abolish slavery would favorably impress foreign powers. European statesmen did not abandon their cautious stance toward the Union. However, important segments of the British public who opposed slavery now came to regard any attempt to help the South as immoral. Foreigners could better understand and sympathize with a war to free the slaves than they could with a war to save the Union. In diplomacy, where image is so important, Lincoln had created a more attractive picture of the North. The Emancipation Proclamation became the North's symbolic call for human freedom.

Unanticipated Consequences of War

The Emancipation Proclamation was but one example of the war's surprising consequences. In the final two years of the war, both North and South experimented on the battlefields and behind the lines in desperate efforts to win.

One of the Union's experiments involved using black troops in combat. Blacks had offered themselves as soldiers in 1861 but had been turned away. They were serving as cooks, laborers, teamsters, and carpenters in the army, however, and composed as much as a quarter of the navy. As white casualties mounted, so did pressure for black service on the battlefield. The Union government allowed states to escape draft quotas if they enlisted enough volunteers, and they allowed them to count southern black enlistees on their state rosters. Northern governors grew increasingly interested in black military service.

Anticipating blacks' postwar interests, Frederick Douglass pressed for military service. "Once let the black man get upon his person the brass letter, U.S., let him get an eagle on his button, and a musket on his shoulder and bullets in his pocket," Douglass believed, "there is no power on earth that can deny that he has earned the right to citizenship." By the war's end, 186,000 blacks (10 percent of the army) had served the Union cause, 134,111 of them escapees from slave states.

But the black experience in the army highlighted some of the obstacles to racial acceptance. Black soldiers, usually led by white officers, were second-class soldiers for most of the war, receiving lower pay, poorer food, often more menial work, and fewer benefits than whites. Even whites working to equalize black and white pay often considered blacks inferior.

The army's racial experiment had mixed results. But the faithful and courageous service of black troops helped modify some of the most demeaning white racial stereotypes of blacks. The black soldiers who conquered the South, many of them former slaves, felt pride and dignity. Wrote one, "We march through these fine thoroughfares where once the slave was forbid being out after nine P.M. ... Negro soldiers!—with banners floating."

As the conflict continued, basic assumptions about how it should be waged weakened. One wartime casualty was the courtly idea that war involved only armies. Early in the war, many officers tried to protect civilians and their property. Such concern for rebel property soon vanished. Southern troops, on the few occasions when they came North, also lived off the land.

Changing Military Strategies, 1863–1865

In the early war years, southern strategy combined defense with selected maneuvers. Until the summer of 1863, the strategy seemed to be succeeding, at least in the East. But an occasional victory over the invading northern army, such as at Fredericksburg in December 1862, did not change the course of the war. Realizing this, Lee concluded, "There is nothing to be gained by this army remaining quietly on the defensive." Without victories in the North, he believed, it could not prevail.

In the summer of 1863, Lee led the Confederate army of northern Virginia into Maryland and southern Pennsylvania. His goal was a victory that would threaten Philadelphia and Washington; he even dreamed of capturing a northern city. Such

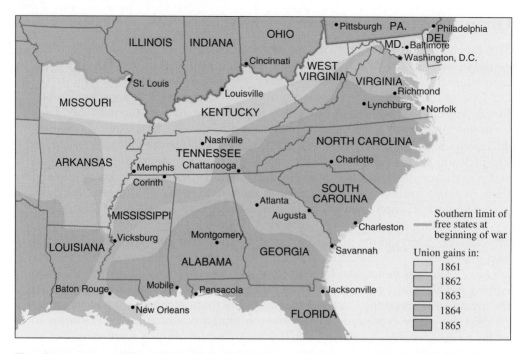

THE PROGRESS OF WAR, 1861–1865 In this map you can see the very slow progression of the North's effort to defeat the South. For much of the war, the South controlled large areas of contiguous territory. This control of the southern homeland helped southerners to feel that it was possible for them to win the war. At what point in time might the realities depicted in this map have made southerners decide their cause was lost?

feats would surely win diplomatic recognition and might force the North to sue for peace.

The Civil War Part II: 1863–1865

At Gettysburg on a hot and humid July 1, Lee confronted a Union army led by General George Meade. During three days of fighting, the fatal obsession with the infantry charge returned as Lee ordered costly assaults that probably lost him the battle. On July 3, Lee sent about 15,000 men against the Union center. The assault, known as Pickett's Charge, was gallant but futile. At 700 yards, the Union artillery opened fire. One southern officer described the scene: "Pickett's division just seemed to melt away in the blue musketry smoke which now covered the hill. Nothing but stragglers came back."

Despite his losses, Lee did procure the food and fodder he needed and captured thousands of prisoners. Gettysburg was a defeat, but neither Lee, nor his men, nor southern civilians regarded it as conclusive. Fighting would continue for another year and a half. In 1864, one high army officer revealed his continuing belief in the struggle's outcome. "Our hearts are full of hope," he wrote. "Oh! I do pray that we may be established as an independent people, ... [and] recognized as God's Peculiar People!" While many remained hopeful, Lee's Gettysburg losses were so heavy that he could never mount another southern offensive.

Despite the Gettysburg victory, Lincoln was dissatisfied with General Meade, who had failed to finish off Lee's retreating army. His disappointment faded with news of a great victory on July 4 at Vicksburg in the western theater. The capture of the city completed the Union campaign to gain control of the Mississippi River and to divide the South. Ulysses S. Grant, who was responsible for the victory, demonstrated the boldness and flexibility that Lincoln had been looking for in a commander.

DOCUMENT

Abraham Lincoln, *The Gettysburg Address* (1863)

By the summer of 1863, the military situation finally looked promising for the North. The Union controlled much of Arkansas, Louisiana, Mississippi, Missouri, Kentucky, and Tennessee. In March 1864, Lincoln appointed Grant general in chief of all Union armies. Grant planned for victory within a year. "The art of war is simple enough," he reasoned. "Find out where your enemy is. Get at him as soon as you can. Strike at him as hard as you can, and keep moving on."

As an outsider to the prewar military establishment, Grant had no difficulty rejecting conventional military wisdom: "If men make war in slavish observance of rules, they will fail." He sought not one decisive engagement but rather a grim campaign of annihilation, using the North's superior resources to grind down the South. Although Grant's plan entailed large casualties on both sides, he justified it by arguing that "now the carnage was to be limited to a single year."

A campaign of annihilation involved the destruction not only of enemy armies but also of enemy resources. Although the idea of cutting the enemy off from needed supplies was implicit in the naval blockade, economic or "total" warfare was a relatively new and shocking idea. Grant, however, "regarded it as humane to both sides to protect the persons of those found at their homes, but to consume everything that could be used to support or supply armies." Following this policy, he set out after Lee's army in Virginia. General William Tecumseh Sherman, striking from Tennessee toward Atlanta, refined this plan.

DOCUMENT

William T. Sherman, *The March Through Georgia* (1875)

War, Sherman believed, must also be waged on the minds of civilians, to make southerners "fear and dread" their foes. Therefore, his campaign to seize Atlanta and his march to Savannah spread destruction and terror. Ordered to forage "liberally" on the land, his army left desolation in its wake. This destruction, with its goal of total victory, showed once more how conflict produced the unexpected. The war that both North and South had hoped would be quick and relatively painless was ending after four long years with great cost to both sides. But the grimness of warfare during that final year threatened Lincoln's hopes for reconciliation.

IMAGE

Ruins of Atlanta (1864)

CHANGES WROUGHT BY WAR

As bold new tactics emerged both on and off the battlefield, both governments took steps that changed their societies in surprising ways. Of the two, the South, which had left the Union to preserve a traditional way of life, experienced the more radical transformation.

RECOVERING THE PAST

Photography

The invention of photography in 1839 expanded the visual and imaginative world of nineteenth-century Americans. For the first time, Americans could visually record events in their own lives and see the images of unfamiliar people and places. Photographs also expand the boundaries of the historian's world. As photographic techniques became simpler, more and more visual information about the nineteenth century was captured. Historians can use photographs to discover many aspects of daily life: what people wore, how they celebrated events like marriages and funerals, what their families, houses, and cities looked like. Pictures of election campaigns, parades, strikes, and wars show the texture of public life. But historians also study photographs, as they do paintings, to glean information about attitudes and values. The choice of subjects, the way in which people and objects are arranged, and the relationships between people in the photographs all provide clues to the social and cultural values of the past.

Some knowledge of the early history of photography helps place the visual evidence in the proper perspective. The earliest type of photograph, the daguerreotype, was not a print, but the negative itself on a sheet of silver-plated copper. The first daguerreotypes required between 15 and 30 minutes for the proper exposure. The long exposure time explains why nineteenth-century images often seem stiff and formal. Glass ambrotypes (negatives on glass) and tintypes (negatives on gray iron bases), developed after the daguerreotypes, were easier and cheaper to produce. But both techniques produced only one picture and required what to us would seem an interminable time for exposure.

A major breakthrough came in the 1850s with the development of the wet-plate process. In this process, the photographer coated a glass negative with a sensitive solution, exposed the negative (that is, took the picture), and then quickly developed it. The new procedure required a relatively short exposure time of about five seconds outside and one minute indoors. The resulting photographs looked more natural, but action shots were not yet possible. The entire process tied the photographer to the darkroom. Traveling photographers carried their darkrooms with them. The advantage of the wet-plate process was that it was possible to make many paper prints from one negative, opening new commercial vistas for professional photographers.

Mathew Brady, a fashionable Washington photographer, realizing that the camera was the "eye of history," asked Lincoln for permission to record the war with his camera. He and his team of photographers left about 8,000 glass negatives, currently stored in the Library of Congress and the National Archives, as their record of the Civil War. Shown are two photographs. In the photograph entitled Confederate Captives, study and describe the soldiers. How are they posed? What kinds of clothes are they wearing? What do you notice about their equipment? Their health? This one photograph just begins to suggest what can be discovered through the study of images. In family attics and cellars, there may well be photograph albums that, when examined carefully, will reveal many aspects of your own family's history.

The second picture was taken in April 1865, about a year after the battle at Cold Harbor. In the background, you can see 2 Union soldiers digging graves. In the foreground are the grisly remains of the battle. What do you think is the intent of the photograph? The choice of subject matter shows clearly that photography reveals attitudes as well as facts. Why is the burial taking place a full year after the battle? What does this tell us about the nature of civil warfare? Notice that the soldiers ordered to undertake this ghastly chore are black, as was customary. What might this scene suggest about the experience of black soldiers in the Union army?

Top, Mathew Brady, Confederate Captives, Gettysburg. (National Archives) Bottom, Mathew Brady, Burial Party at Cold Harbor. *(Alexander Gardner Chicago Historical Society [ICHi-07868])*

REFLECTING ON THE PAST   Using these photographs as evidence, what might you conclude about the southern soldiers' physical condition? What attitudes are conveyed through the men's facial expressions and poses? What kind of mood was the northern photographer trying to create? What attitude toward war and death is conveyed?

A New South

The expansion of the central government's power in the South, starting with the passage of the 1862 Conscription Act, continued in the last years of the war. States' rights had inspired secession, but winning demanded centralization. Many southerners denounced Davis as a despot because he recognized the need for the central government to take the lead. Despite the accusations, the Confederate Congress cooperated with him and established important precedents, including serious interference with property rights. For example, government impressment of slaves for war work in 1863 affected the very form of private property that had originally driven the South from the Union.

The Conscription Act of 1862 did not solve the Confederate army's manpower problems. By 1864, the southern armies were only one-third the size of the Union forces. Hence, in February 1864, an expanded conscription measure made all white males between the ages of 17 and 50 subject to the draft. By 1865, the necessities of war had led to the unthinkable: arming slaves as soldiers. Black companies were recruited, but the war was over before any blacks could fight for the Confederacy.

In a message sent to Congress in November 1864, Davis speculated on some of the issues involved in arming slaves. "Should a slave who had served his country" be kept in servitude, he wondered, "or should his emancipation be held out to him as a reward for faithful service, or should it be granted at once on the promise of such service ...?" The South had begun the war to preserve slavery but ended it contemplating emancipation.

Southern agriculture also changed under the pressure of war. Earlier, the South had imported food from the North, concentrating on producing cotton and tobacco for market. Now, more and more land was turned over to food crops. Some farmers voluntarily shifted crops, but others responded only to state laws reducing the acreage permitted for cotton and tobacco cultivation. These measures raised enough food to feed southerners adequately, but they helped dramatically cut the production of cotton.

The South had always depended on imported manufactured goods. Although some blockade runners evaded Union ships, the noose tightened after 1862. The Confederacy could not, in any case, rely on blockade runners to equip the army. Thus, war triggered the expansion of military-related industries in the South. Here, too, the government played a crucial role. The war and navy offices directed industrial development, awarding contracts to private manufacturing firms like Richmond's Tredegar Iron Works and operating other factories themselves. The number of southerners working in industry rose dramatically. At the end of the war, rebel soldiers were better supplied with arms and munitions than with food.

Although the war did not transform the southern class structure, relations between the classes began to change. The pressures of the struggle undermined white solidarity, based on racism, and the supposed political unanimity that masked class differences. Draft resistance and desertion reflected growing alienation from a war perceived as serving only the interests of plantation owners. More and more yeoman families suffered grinding poverty as the men went to war and officials requisitioned resources.

The Victorious North

Although changes in the South were more noticeable, the Union's government and economy also responded to the demands of war. Like Davis, Lincoln was accused of being a dictator. Although he rarely tried to control Congress, veto its legislation, or direct government departments, Lincoln freely exercised executive power. He violated the writ of habeas corpus by locking up more than 13,000 northerners without trials; he curbed press freedom by suppressing supposedly disloyal and inflammatory articles; he established conscription; he issued the Emancipation Proclamation; and he fired generals. Lincoln argued that this vast extension of presidential power was temporarily justified because, as president, he was responsible for defending and preserving the Constitution.

Many changes in government proved more permanent than Lincoln had imagined. Wartime financial necessities helped revolutionize the country's banking system. Ever since Jackson's destruction of the Bank of the United States, state banks had served American financial needs. Treasury Secretary Chase found this system inadequate and chaotic and proposed to replace it. In 1863 and 1864, Congress reestablished a federal banking system by passing legislation that established a national currency issued by federally chartered banks and backed by government bonds.

Northern agriculture expanded to feed soldiers and civilians, and so did investment in farm machinery. With so many men off soldiering, farmers were short of labor. Mechanical reapers performed the work of four to six men, and farmers began to buy them; McCormick sold 165,000 during the war. Northern farming, especially in the Midwest, was well on the way to becoming mechanized. Farmers even accumulated a surplus for export.

The war selectively stimulated manufacturing, although overall the war retarded economic growth by consuming rather than generating wealth. Between 1860 and 1870, the annual rate of increase in real manufacturing value added was only 2.3 percent, in contrast with 7.8 percent for the years between 1840 and 1860 and 6 percent for the period from 1870 to 1900. However, war industries, especially those with advantages of scale, expanded and made large profits. Each year, the Union army required 1.5 million uniforms and 3 million pairs of shoes; the woolen and leather industries grew accordingly. Meatpackers and producers of iron, steel, and pocket watches all profited from wartime opportunities.

On the Home Front, 1861–1865

Events on the battlefield were intimately connected to life behind the lines. As both northern and southern leaders realized, civilian morale was crucial to the war's outcome. If civilians lost faith, they would lack the will to continue the conflict.

The war stimulated religious efforts to generate enthusiasm and loyalty on the home front. On both sides, Protestant clergymen threw themselves behind the war effort. As northern preacher Henry Ward Beecher proclaimed, "God hates lukewarm patriotism as much as lukewarm religion, and we hate it too." Southern ministers gave similar messages and urged southerners to reform their lives,

The Impact of the War in the South The dislocations caused by the war were many. These southerners, forced to leave their home by invading troops, have packed what few belongings they could transport and stand ready to evacuate their homestead. How many children can you find in the picture? What does the fact that the woman in the foreground is smoking a pipe suggest about the social class of this group? *(Library of Congress)*

for victory could not come without moral change. In North and South, every defeat was a cause for soul searching. Fast days and revivals provided a spiritual dimension to the conflict and helped people deal with discouragement and death.

In numerous, less tangible ways, the war transformed northern and southern society. The very fact of conflict established a new perspective for most civilians. They read newspapers and national weekly magazines with a new eagerness, and used the mail often. As one North Carolina woman explained, "I never liked to write letters before, but it is a pleasure as well as a relief now." Distant events became almost as real and vivid as those at home. The war helped make Americans part of a larger world.

For some northerners like John D. Rockefeller and Andrew Carnegie, war brought unanticipated riches from army contracts. The New York *Herald* reported that New York City had never been "so gay, … so crowded, so prosperous," as in March 1864. Southern blockade runners made fortunes slipping in luxury goods.

For the majority of Americans, however, war meant deprivation. The war effort gobbled up a large part of each side's resources and, ultimately, ordinary people suffered. To be sure, the demand for workers ended unemployment and changed employment patterns. Many women and blacks entered the workforce, as they would in all future American wars. But whereas work was easy to get, real income declined. Inflation, especially destructive in the South, was largely to blame. By 1864, eggs sold in Richmond for $6 a dozen; butter brought $25 a pound. Strikes and union organizing pointed to working-class discontent.

Low wages compounded the problem of declining income and particularly harmed women workers. Often forced into the labor market because husbands could save little or nothing from small army stipends, army wives and other women took what pay they could get. As more women entered the workforce, employers cut costs by slashing wages.

In the South, which bore the brunt of the fighting, conflict and wartime dislocation drastically affected civilian life. Most white southerners suffered shortages in food, manufactured goods, and medicine. Farming families without slaves fared poorly, but food riots in Richmond and other cities suggest that urban conditions were the most dismal. Thousands of southerners fleeing from the advancing Union armies lost their homes at least temporarily. "The country for miles around is filled with refugees," noted an officer in 1862. "Every house is crowded and hundreds are living in churches, in barns and tents." Caught up in the effort of mere survival, worried about what had happened to homes and possessions left behind, these southerners must have wondered if the cause was worth the sacrifices. Life was probably just as agonizing for those who chose to stay put when Union troops arrived.

White flight also disrupted slave life. Even the arrival of Union forces could prove a mixed blessing. White soldiers were unknown quantities and might be hostile to blacks whom they were supposed to be liberating. One slave described the upsetting arrival of the Yankees at his plantation in Arkansas: "Them folks stood round there all day. Killed hogs ... killed cows ... Took all kinds of sugar and preserves ... Tore all the feathers out of the mattresses looking for money. Then they put Old Miss and her daughter in the kitchen to cooking." The next day found the Yanks gone and the Confederates back.

Throughout the South, insubordination, refusal to work, and refusal to accept punishment testified to the discontent of slaves, especially the fieldhands. Probably 20 percent of all slaves, many of them women, fled toward Union lines after the early months of the war. Their flight pointed to the changing nature of race relations and the harm slaves could do to the southern cause. Reflected one slave owner, "The 'faithful slave' is about played out."

Women and the War

The war made it impossible for many women to live according to conventional norms, which exalted their domestic role and minimized their economic importance. With so many men in the armies, women had to find jobs and sustain farms. During the war years, southern women who had no slaves to help with the farmwork and northern farm wives who labored without the assistance of husbands or sons carried new physical and emotional burdens.

DOCUMENT

Chesnut Diary
CW (1861)

Women also participated in numerous war-related activities. North and South, they entered government service in large numbers. In the North, hundreds of women became military nurses. Under the supervision of Drs. Emily and Elizabeth Blackwell; Dorothea Dix, superintendent of army nurses; and Clara Barton, northern women nursed the wounded and dying for low or even no pay. They also fought the red tape that worsened hospital conditions. In the South, men largely staffed southern military hospitals, but Confederate women played an important part in caring for the sick and wounded in their homes and in makeshift hospitals behind battle lines. Grim though the work was, many women felt that they were participating in the real world for the first time in their lives.

DOCUMENT

Susie King Taylor, Reminiscences of an Army Laundress (1902)

Women moved outside the domestic sphere in other forms of volunteer war work. Some women gained administrative experience in soldiers' aid societies and in the United States Sanitary Commission. Many others made bandages and clothes, put together packages for soldiers at the front, and helped army wives and disabled soldiers find jobs. Fund-raising activities realized substantial sums. By the end of the war, the Sanitary Commission had raised $50 million for medical supplies, nurses' salaries, and other wartime necessities.

Many of the changes women experienced during the war years ended when peace returned. Jobs disappeared when men reclaimed them. Women turned over the operation of farms to returning husbands. But for women whose men came home maimed or did not come home at all, the work had not ended. Nor had the discrimination. Trying to pick up the threads of their former lives, they found it impossible to forget what they had done in the war effort. Some of them were sure they had equaled their men in courage and commitment.

The Election of 1864

In the North, the election of 1864 brought some of the transformations of wartime into the political arena. The Democrats, capitalizing on war weariness, nominated General McClellan, branded the war a failure, and demanded an armistice. Democrats accused Lincoln of arbitrarily expanding executive power and denounced sweeping economic measures like the banking bills. Arguing that the president had transformed the war from one for Union into one for emancipation, they insinuated that a Republican victory would mean race mixing.

Although Lincoln controlled the party machinery and easily gained the Republican renomination, his party did not unite behind him. The outcome of the presidential election was much in doubt. Lincoln seemed to please no one. His veto of the radical reconstruction plan for the South, the Wade–Davis Bill, led to cries of "usurpation." The Emancipation Proclamation did not sit well with conservatives. In August 1864, a gloomy Lincoln, recognizing the many internal conflicts that divided northerners, told his cabinet that he expected to lose. As late as September, some Republicans hoped to reconvene the convention and select another candidate.

Sherman's capture of Atlanta in September 1864 and his march to Savannah helped swing voters to Lincoln. In the end, Republicans had no desire to see the Democrats oust their party. Lincoln won 55 percent of the popular vote and swept the Electoral College.

Why the North Won

In the months after Lincoln's reelection, the war drew to an agonizing conclusion. Sherman moved north from Georgia to North Carolina, while Grant pummeled Lee in Virginia. Grant's losses were staggering, but new recruits replaced the dead. On April 9, 1865, Grant accepted Lee's surrender at Appomattox. Southern soldiers and officers were allowed to go home with their personal equipment after promising to remain there peaceably. The war was over.

Grant's military strategy succeeded because the Union's manpower and economic resources could survive staggering losses of men and equipment while the Confederacy's could not. Naval strategy eventually paid off because the North could build enough ships to make its blockade work.

The South had taken tremendous steps toward satisfying war needs. But despite the impressive growth of manufacturing and food production, southern troops and southern people were poorly fed and clothed. New industries could not meet the extraordinary demands of wartime, and advancing Union forces destroyed many of them. Women working alone or with disgruntled slaves could not produce enough food. Worn-out farm equipment was not replaced. Impressments of slaves and animals and the flight to Union lines of half a million blacks cut production. A Confederate officer in northern Virginia described the consequences. "Many of our soldiers are thinly clothed and without shoes and in addition to this, very few of the infantry have tents. With this freezing weather, their sufferings are indescribable." Skimpy rations—only one-third of a pound of meat for each soldier a day by 1864—weakened the Confederate force, whose trail was "traceable by the deposit of dysenteric stool." By that time, the Union armies were so well supplied that soldiers often threw away extra blankets and coats.

The South's woefully inadequate transportation system also contributed to defeat. Primitive roads deteriorated and became all but impassable without repairs. The railroad system was inefficient. When tracks wore out or were destroyed, they were not replaced. Food intended for the army rotted awaiting shipment, while soldiers went hungry and cities rioted.

Ironically, measures that the Confederacy took to strengthen its ability to win the war, as one Texan later observed, "weakened and paralyzed it." Conscription, impressment, and taxes bred resentment and even open resistance. The proposal to use slaves as soldiers called into question the war's purpose. The many southern governors who refused to contribute men, money, and supplies on the scale Davis requested implicitly condoned disloyalty and undermined any sense of southern nationalism. The belief in states' rights and the sanctity of private property that gave birth to the Confederacy also helped kill it.

By the final months of the war, Davis had recognized how dangerous defeatism was to the Confederacy's cause. But such realization did not prompt any vigorous attempts to influence public opinion or to control internal dissent.

It is tempting to compare Lincoln and Davis as war leaders. There is no doubt that Lincoln's humanity, his awareness of the terrible costs of war, his determination to save the Union, and his eloquence set him apart as one of this country's most extraordinary presidents. Yet the men's personal characteristics were probably less important than the differences between the political and social systems of the two regions. Without the support of a party behind him, Davis failed to engender enthusiasm or loyalty. Even though the Republicans rarely united behind Lincoln, they uniformly wanted to keep the Democrats from office. Despite squabbles, Republicans tended to support Lincoln's policies in Congress and back in their home districts. Commanding considerable resources of patronage, Lincoln was able to line up federal, state, and local officials behind his party and administration.

Just as the northern political system provided Lincoln with more flexibility and support, its social system also proved more able to meet the war's extraordinary demands. Although both societies innovated to secure victory, northerners were more cooperative and disciplined. In the southern states, old attitudes impeded the war effort. Wedded to states' rights, southern governors undermined the Confederate government. When Sherman approached Atlanta, Georgia's governor would not turn over the 10,000 men in the state army to Confederate commanders. Slaveholders resisted the impressment of their slaves for war work.

In the end, the Confederacy collapsed, exhausted and bleeding. The belief that the southern cause might triumph disappeared. Hungry soldiers got letters revealing desperate situations at home. Some were perhaps horrified by the possibility that black troops might join the struggle. Soldiers in the Army of Virginia feared that Lee, who, rather than Davis, had symbolized their new nation, might take another post. Hungry, worried, and uncertain, the men slipped away. By December 1864, the Confederate desertion rate exceeded 50 percent. Replacements could not be found. Farmers hid livestock and produce from tax collectors. Many southerners resigned themselves to defeat, but some fought to the end. One Yankee described them as they surrendered at Appomattox:

> Before us in proud humiliation stood the embodiment of manhood: men whom neither toils and sufferings, nor the fact of death, nor disaster, nor hopelessness could bend from their resolve; standing before us now, thin, worn, and famished, but erect, and with eyes looking level into ours, waking memories that bound us together as no other bond.

The Costs of War

The war was over, but its memories would fester for years. About 3 million American men, one-third of all free males between the ages of 15 and 59, had served in the army. Each would remember his personal history of the war. For George Eagleton, who had worked in army field hospitals, the history was one of "Death and destruction! Blood! Blood! Agony! Death! Gaping flesh wounds, broken bones, amputations, bullet and bomb fragment extractions." Of all American wars, none has been more deadly. The death rate was more than five times that of World War II. About 360,000 Union soldiers and another 258,000 Confederate soldiers died, about one-third of these because their wounds were either improperly treated or not treated at all. Disease claimed more lives than combat.

Thousands upon thousands of men would be reminded of the human costs of war by the injuries they carried with them to the grave and by the missing limbs that marked them as Civil War veterans. About 275,000 on each side were maimed. Another 410,000 (195,000 northerners and 215,000 southerners) would recall their time in wretchedly overcrowded and unsanitary prison camps. The lucky ones would remember only the boredom. The worst memory was of those who rotted in prison camps, such as Andersonville in Georgia, where 31,000 Union soldiers were confined. At the war's end, over 12,000 graves were counted there.

Some Americans found it hard to readjust to peace. As Arthur Carpenter's letters suggest, he gradually grew accustomed to army life. War provided him with a sense of purpose, and afterward he felt aimless. A year after the war's end, he wrote, "Camp life agrees with me better than any other." Many others had difficulty returning to civilian routines. Even those who adjusted successfully discovered that they looked at life from a different perspective. The experience of fighting, of mixing with all sorts of people from many places, and of traveling far from home had lifted former soldiers out of their familiar local world and widened their vision. Fighting the war made the concept of national union real.

Unanswered Questions

What had the war accomplished? Certainly death and destruction. Physically, the war devastated the South. Historians have estimated a 43 percent decline in southern wealth during the war years, exclusive of the value of slaves. Great cities like Atlanta, Columbia, and Richmond lay in ruins. Fields were weed-choked and uncultivated. Tools were worn out. One-third or more of the South's mules, horses, and swine were gone. Two-thirds of the railroads had been destroyed. Thousands were hungry, homeless, and bitter about their four years of what now appeared useless sacrifice. More than 3 million slaves, a vast financial investment, were free.

On the other hand, the war had resolved the question of union and ended the debate over the relationship of the states to the federal government. Republicans had seized the opportunity to pass legislation that would foster national union and economic growth: the Pacific Railroad Act of 1862, which set aside huge tracts of public land to finance the transcontinental railroad; the Homestead Act of 1862, which was to provide yeoman farmers cheaper and easier access to the public domain; the Morrill Act of 1862, which established support for agricultural (land-grant) colleges; and the banking acts of 1863 and 1864.

The war had also resolved the issue of slavery that for so long had plagued American life. Yet uncertainties outnumbered certainties. What would happen to ex-slaves? When blacks had fled to Union lines, commanders had not known what to do with them. Now the problem became more pressing. Should blacks have the same civil and political rights as whites? In the Union army, they had been second-class soldiers. The behavior of Union forces toward liberated blacks in the South showed how deep the stain of racism went. Would blacks now get land and economic independence? What would be their relations with their former owners?

What, indeed, would be the status of the conquered South in the nation? Should it be punished for the rebellion? Some people thought so. Should southerners keep their property? Some people thought not. There were clues to Lincoln's intentions. As early as December 1863, the president had announced a generous plan of reconciliation. He was willing to recognize the government of former Confederate states established by a group of citizens equal to 10 percent of

TIMELINE

1861	Lincoln calls up state militia and suspends habeas corpus		**1863**	Lincoln issues Emancipation Proclamation
	First Battle of Bull Run			Congress adopts military draft
	Union blockades the South			Battles of Gettysburg and Vicksburg
1862	Battles at Shiloh, Bull Run, and Antietam		**1864**	Sherman's march through Georgia
	First black regiment authorized by Union			Lincoln reelected
	South institutes military draft		**1865**	Lee surrenders at Appomattox
				Lincoln assassinated

those voting in 1860, as long as the group swore to support the Constitution and to accept the abolition of slavery. He began to restore state governments in three former Confederate states on that basis. But some northerners disagreed with this leniency, and the debate continued.

In his 1865 inaugural address, Lincoln urged Americans to harbor "malice towards none ... and charity for all." "Let us strive," he urged, "to finish the work we are in; to bind up the nation's wounds ... to do all which may achieve a just and lasting peace." Privately, the president said the same thing. Generosity and goodwill would pave the way for reconciliation. On April 14, he pressed the point home to his cabinet. His wish was to avoid persecution and bloodshed. That same evening, only five days after the surrender at Appomattox, the president attended a play at Ford's Theatre. And there, said an eyewitness,

DOCUMENT

Abraham Lincoln, Second Inaugural Address (1865)

> a pistol was heard and a man ... dressed in a black suit of clothes leaped onto the stage apparently from the President's box. He held in his right hand a dagger whose blade appeared about 10 inches long. ... Every one leaped to his feet, and the cry of "the President is assassinated" was heard—Getting where I could see into the President's box, I saw Mrs. Lincoln ... in apparent anguish.

John Wilkes Booth had killed the president.

Conclusion

An Uncertain Future

As the war ended, many Americans grieved for the man whose decisions had so marked their lives for five years. "Strong men have wept tonight & the nation will mourn tomorrow," wrote one eyewitness to the assassination. Many more wept for friends and relations who had not survived the war, but whose actions had in one way or another contributed to its outcome. The lucky ones, like Arthur Carpenter and George and Ethie Eagleton, now faced the necessity of putting their lives back together and moving forward into an uncertain future. Perhaps not all Americans realized how drastically the war had altered their lives, their prospects, their nation. It was only as time passed that the war's impact became clear to them. And it was only with time that they recognized how many problems the war had left unsolved. It is to these years of Reconstruction that we turn next.

Questions for Review and Reflection

1. Assess the strengths and weaknesses of the North and South at the beginning of the war. What northern strengths actually led to northern victory and what Confederate weaknesses explain southern defeat?

2. What were the most important transformations in the Union and Confederacy during the war and why, in your opinion, were these changes so significant?

3. Compare and contrast Lincoln and Davis as war leaders and the two governments over which they presided.

4. What role did race play during the war?

5. Consider the Civil War as a struggle between differing beliefs and values and assess the importance of northern victory for this struggle. In what ways did the war's outcome realize or fail to realize the founding principles of this nation?

Discovering U.S. History Online

Index of Civil War Information on the Internet www.cwc.lsu.edu/
A good starting place for research, this index has as its mission to "locate, index, and make available all appropriate private and public data on the Internet regarding the Civil War" and to promote the study of the Civil War from the perspectives of all professions, occupations, and academic disciplines. It includes a guide on evaluating sources of information on the Internet.

Causes of the Civil War www.members.aol.com/jfepperson/causes.html
The site contains "primary documents from the period of the secession crisis ... with the goal of shedding light on the causes of secession, hence of the war." Document sections include "Party Platforms and Secession Documents," "Compromise Proposals," and "Abraham Lincoln's Speeches and Letters."

Crisis at Fort Sumter www.tulane.edu/~latner/CrisisMain.html
This well-crafted use of hypermedia with assignments and problems explains and explores the events and causes leading to the Civil War.

Charleston www.awod.com/gallery/probono/cwchas/cwlayout.html
William Hamilton, the author, attorney, and Civil War reenactor, presents the history of the Civil War in and around Charleston, South Carolina.

Abraham Lincoln www.ipl.org/ref/POTUS/alincoln.html
This site contains basic factual data about Lincoln, including his presidency, speeches, cabinet members, and election information.

Black American Contributions to Union Intelligence During the Civil War www.odci.gov/cia/
publications/dispatches/
This illustrated article, reprinted from the CIA journal *Studies in Intelligence* (Winter 1998–1999) offers
information about this little-known contribution to the Union war effort.

Fiction and Film

Stephen Crane's *The Red Badge of Courage* (1895) examines the soldier's experience during the war,
while MacKinlay Kantor's novel *Andersonville* (1955) depicts the Civil War's worst prison camp.
Enemy Women (2002) by Paulette Jiles follows the journey of a young Missouri woman who tries to rescue her father, who has been carried off by the Union militia to St. Louis. The feature film *Glory* (1989)
focuses on a black regiment, the 54th Massachusetts, that demonstrated its heroism in the midst of battle, while the classic *Gone with the Wind* (1939) offers a romanticized but powerful picture of southern
life before, during, and after the Civil War. Ken Burns's famous documentary series *The Civil War*
(1990) powerfully evokes the period.

Recommended Reading

www.ablongman.com/nash
The Companion Website has a list of recommended readings about the Civil War.

The Union Reconstructed

American Stories

Blacks and Whites Redefine Their Dreams and Relationships

In April 1864, a year before Lincoln's assassination, Robert Allston died, leaving his wife Adele and his daughter Elizabeth to manage their many rice plantations. With Union troops moving through coastal South Carolina in the winter of 1864–1865, Elizabeth's sorrow turned to "terror" as Union soldiers arrived and searched for liquor, firearms, and valuables. The women fled. Later, Yankee troops encouraged the Allston slaves to take furniture, food, and other goods from the Big House. Before they left, the Union soldiers gave the keys to the crop barns to the semifree blacks.

After the war, Adele Allston swore allegiance to the United States and secured a written order for the newly freed African Americans to relinquish those keys. She and Elizabeth returned in the summer of 1865 to reclaim the plantations and reassert white authority. She was assured that although the blacks had guns, "no outrage has been committed against the Whites except in the matter of property." But property was the issue. Possession of the keys to the barns, Elizabeth wrote, would be the "test case" of whether former masters or former slaves would control land, labor, and its fruits, as well as the subtle aspects of interpersonal relations.

Nervously, Adele and Elizabeth Allston confronted their ex-slaves at their old home. To their surprise, a pleasant reunion took place as the Allston women greeted the blacks by name and caught up on their lives. A trusted black foreman handed over the keys to the barns. This harmonious scene was repeated elsewhere.

But at one plantation, the Allston women met defiant and armed African Americans, who ominously lined both sides of the road as the carriage arrived. An old black driver, Uncle Jacob, was unsure whether to yield the keys to the barns full of rice and corn, put there by slave labor. Mrs. Allston insisted. As Uncle Jacob hesitated, an angry young man shouted: "If you give up the key, blood'll flow." Uncle Jacob slowly slipped the keys back into his pocket.

The African Americans sang freedom songs and brandished hoes, pitchforks, and guns to discourage anyone from going to town for help. Two blacks, however, slipped away to find some Union officers. The Allstons spent the night safely, if restlessly, in their house. Early the next morning, they were awakened by a knock at the unlocked front door. There stood Uncle Jacob. Silently, he gave back the keys.

The story of the keys reveals most of the essential human ingredients of the Reconstruction era. Defeated southern whites were determined to resume control of both land and labor. The law and federal enforcement generally supported property owners. The Allston women were friendly to the blacks in a maternal way and insisted on restoring prewar deference in black–white relations. Adele and Elizabeth, in short, both feared and cared about their former slaves.

The African American freedpeople likewise revealed mixed feelings toward their former owners: anger, loyalty, love, resentment, and pride. They paid respect to the Allstons but not to their property and crops. They wanted not revenge, but economic independence and freedom.

Northerners played a most revealing role. Union soldiers, literally and symbolically, gave the keys of freedom to the freed men and women but did not stay around long enough to guarantee that freedom. Despite initially encouraging blacks to plunder the master's house and seize the crops, in the crucial encounter after the war, northern officials had disappeared. Understanding the limits of northern help, Uncle Jacob ended up handing the keys to land and liberty back to his former owner. The blacks realized that if they wanted to ensure their freedom, they had to do it themselves.

This chapter describes what happened to the conflicting goals and dreams of three groups as they sought to redefine new social, economic, and political relationships during the postwar Reconstruction era. Amid vast devastation and bitter race and class divisions, Civil War survivors sought to put their lives back together. Victorious but variously motivated northern officials, defeated but defiant southern planters, and impoverished but hopeful African Americans could not all fulfill their conflicting goals, yet each had to try. Reconstruction would be divisive, leaving a mixed legacy of human gains and losses.

THE BITTERSWEET AFTERMATH OF WAR

"There are sad changes in store for both races," the daughter of a Georgia planter wrote in the summer of 1865. To understand the bittersweet nature of Reconstruction, we must look at the state of the nation after the assassination of President Lincoln.

The United States in April 1865

Constitutionally, the "Union" faced a crisis in April 1865. What was the status of the 11 former Confederate states? The North had denied the South's constitutional right to secede but needed four years of war and more than 600,000 deaths to win the point. Lincoln's official position had been that the southern states had never left the Union and were only "out of their proper relation" with the United

The United States in 1865: Crises at the End of the Civil War

Given the enormous casualties, costs, and crises of the immediate aftermath of the Civil War, what attitudes, goals, dreams, and behaviors would you predict for white southerners, white northerners, and black freedpeople?

Military Casualties

360,000 Union soldiers dead
260,000 Confederate soldiers dead
620,000 Total dead
375,000 Seriously wounded and maimed
995,000 Casualties nationwide in a total male population of 15 million (nearly 1 in 15)

Physical and Economic Crises

The South devastated; its railroads, industry, and some major cities in ruins; its fields and livestock wasted

Constitutional Crisis

Eleven former Confederate states not a part of the Union, their status unclear and future states uncertain

Political Crisis

Republican party (entirely of the North) dominant in Congress; a former Democratic slaveholder from Tennessee, Andrew Johnson, in the presidency

Social Crisis

Nearly 4 million freedpeople throughout the South facing challenges of survival and freedom, along with thousands of hungry demobilized white southern soldiers and displaced white families

Psychological Crisis

Incalculable stores of resentment, bitterness, anger, and despair throughout North and South

---

States. The president, therefore, as commander in chief, had the authority to decide how to set relations right again. Lincoln's congressional opponents retorted that the ex-Confederate states were now "conquered provinces" and that Congress should resolve the constitutional issues and direct Reconstruction.

Politically, differences between Congress and the White House over Reconstruction mirrored a wider struggle between the two branches of the national government. During war, as has usually been the case, the executive branch assumed broad powers. Many believed, however, that Lincoln had far exceeded his constitutional authority, and his successor, Andrew Johnson, was worse. Would Congress reassert its authority?

In April 1865, the Republican party ruled nearly unchecked. Republicans had made immense achievements in the eyes of the northern public: winning the war, preserving the Union, and freeing the slaves. They had enacted sweeping economic programs on behalf of free labor and free enterprise. But the party remained an uneasy grouping of former Whigs, Know-Nothings, Unionist Democrats, and antislavery idealists.

The Democrats were in shambles. Republicans depicted southern Democrats as rebels, murderers, and traitors, and they blasted northern Democrats as weak-willed, disloyal, and opposed to economic growth and progress. Nevertheless, in the election of 1864, needing to show that the war was a bipartisan effort, the Republicans nominated a Tennessee Unionist Democrat, Andrew Johnson, as Lincoln's vice president. Now the tactless Johnson headed the government.

Economically, the United States in the spring of 1865 presented stark contrasts. Northern cities and railroads hummed with productive activity; southern cities and railroads lay in ruins. Southern financial institutions were bankrupt; northern banks flourished. Mechanizing northern farms were more productive than ever; southern farms and plantations, especially those along Sherman's march, resembled a "howling waste." The widespread devastation in the South affected southern attitudes. As a later southern writer explained, "If this war had smashed the Southern world, it had left the essential Southern mind and will ... entirely unshaken." Many white southerners braced to resist Reconstruction and restore their former life and institutions; others, the minority who had remained quietly loyal to the Union, sought reconciliation.

Socially, nearly 4 million newly freedpeople faced the challenges of freedom. After initial joy and celebration in jubilee songs, freedmen and freedwomen quickly realized their continuing dependence on former owners. A Mississippi woman said:

Free at Last

> I used to think if I could be free I should be the happiest of anybody in the world. But when my master come to me, and says, Lizzie, you is free! it seems like I was in a kind of daze. And when I would wake up in the morning I would think to myself, Is I free? Hasn't I got to get up before day light and go into the field of work?

For Lizzie, and 4 million other blacks, everything—and nothing—had changed.

Hopes Among the Freedpeople

Throughout the South in the summer of 1865, optimism surged through the old slave quarters. The slavery chain, however, broke slowly, link by link. After Union troops swept through an area, "we'd begin celebratin'," one man said, but Confederate soldiers would follow, or master and overseer would return and "tell us to go back to work." The freedmen and women learned, therefore, not to rejoice too quickly or openly.

Gradually, though, African Americans began to test the reality of freedom. Typically, their first step was to leave the plantation, if only for a few hours or days. "If I stay here I'll never know I am free," said a South Carolina woman who went to work as a cook in a nearby town. Some freedpeople cut their ties entirely—returning to an earlier master, or, more often, going into towns and cities to find jobs, schools, churches, and association with other blacks, safe from whippings and retaliation.

Freedmen at Rest on a Levee

Many blacks left the plantation in search of a spouse, parent, or child sold away years before. Advertisements detailing these sorrowful searches filled African American newspapers. For those who found a spouse or who had been living together in slave marriages, freedom meant getting married legally, some-

Consequences of War This 1867 engraving shows two southern women and their children soon after the Civil War. In what ways are they similar and in what ways different? Is there a basis for sisterhood bonds? What separates them, if anything? From *Frank Leslie's Illustrated Newspaper*, February 23, 1867. *(The Granger Collection, New York)*

times in mass ceremonies common in the first months of emancipation. Legal marriage was important morally, but it also established the legitimacy of children and meant access to land titles and other economic opportunities. Marriage brought special burdens for black women, who assumed the double role of housekeeper and breadwinner. Their determination to create a traditional family life and care for their children resulted in the withdrawal of women from plantation field labor.

Freedpeople also demonstrated their new status by choosing surnames. Names connoting independence, such as Washington, were common. Revealing their mixed feelings toward their former masters, some would adopt their master's name while others would pick "any big name 'ceptin' their master's." Emancipation changed black manners around whites as well. Masks fell, and expressions of deference—tipping a hat, stepping aside, calling whites "master" or "ma'am"—diminished. For African Americans, these changes were necessary expressions of selfhood, proving that race relations had changed; whites, however, saw such behaviors as "insolence" and "insubordination."

The freedpeople made education a priority. A Mississippi farmer vowed to "give my children a chance to go to school, for I consider education next best ting to liberty." One traveler through the South counted "at least five hundred" schools "taught by colored people." Other than a persisting desire for education, the primary goal for most freedpeople was getting land. "All I want is to git to own fo' or five acres ob land, dat I can build me a little house on and call my home," a Mississippi black said. Through a combination of educational and economic independence, basic American means of controlling one's own life, labor, and land, freedpeople like Lizzie would make sure that emancipation was real.

During the war, some Union generals had put liberated slaves in charge of confiscated and abandoned lands. In the Sea Islands of South Carolina and Georgia, blacks had been working 40-acre plots of land and harvesting their own crops for several years. Farther inland, freedmen who received land were the former slaves of the Cherokee and the Creek. Some blacks held title to these lands. Northern philanthropists had organized others to grow cotton for the Treasury Department to prove the superiority of free labor. In Mississippi, thousands of ex-slaves worked 40-acre tracts on leased lands that ironically had formerly been owned by Jefferson Davis. In this highly successful experiment, they made profits sufficient to repay the government for initial costs, then lost the land to Davis's brother.

Many freedmen expected a new economic order as fair payment for their years of involuntary work. "Give us our own land," said one, "and we take care ourselves; but widout land, de ole massas can hire us or starve us, as dey please." Freedmen had every expectation that "forty acres and a mule" had been promised. Once they obtained land, family unity, and education, some looked forward to civil rights and the vote—along with protection from vengeful defeated Confederates.

The White South's Fearful Response

White southerners had equally strong dreams and expectations. Middle-class (yeoman) farmers and poor whites stood beside rich planters in bread lines, all hoping to regain land and livelihood. White southerners responded with feelings of outrage, loss, and injustice. Said one man, "My pa paid his own money for our niggers; and that's not all they've robbed us of. They have taken our horses and cattle and sheep and everything."

A dominant emotion was fear. The entire structure of southern society was shaken, and the semblance of racial peace and order that slavery had provided was shattered. Having lost control of all that was familiar, whites feared everything—from losing their cheap labor to having blacks sit next to them on trains. Ironically, given the rape of black women during slavery, southern whites' worst fears were of rape and revenge. African American "impudence," some thought, would lead to legal intermarriage and "Africanization," the destruction of the purity of the white race. African American Union soldiers seemed especially ominous. These fears were greatly exaggerated, as demobilization of black soldiers came quickly, and rape and violence by blacks against whites was extremely rare.

Believing their world turned upside down, the former planter aristocracy tried to set it right again. To reestablish white dominance, southern legislatures

passed "Black Codes" in the first year after the war. Many of the codes granted freedmen the right to marry, sue and be sued, testify in court, and hold property. But these rights were qualified. Complicated passages explained under exactly what circumstances blacks could testify against whites, own property (mostly they could not), or exercise other rights of free people. Forbidden rights were racial intermarriage, bearing arms, possessing alcoholic beverages, sitting on trains (except in baggage compart-

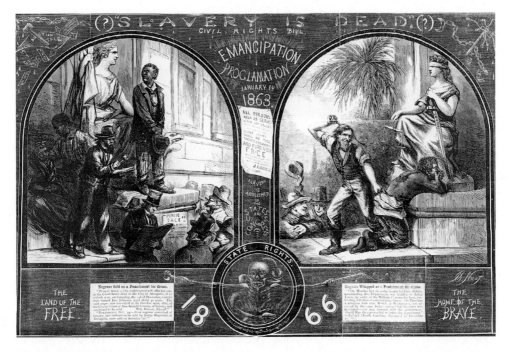

The End of Slavery? The Black Codes, widespread violence against freedpeople, and President John-son's veto of the civil rights bill gave rise to the sardonic title "Slavery Is Dead?" in this Thomas Nast car-toon. What do you see in the two scenes? Describe the two images of justice. What is Nast saying? *(Courtesy of the Newberry Library, Chicago)*

ments), being on city streets at night, or congregating in large groups. Many of the qualified rights guaranteed by the Black Codes were only passed to induce the federal government to withdraw its remaining troops from the South. This was a crucial issue, for in many places marauding whites were terrorizing virtually de-fenseless African Americans.

Key provisions of the Black Codes regulated freedpeople's economic status. "Vagrancy" laws provided that any blacks not "lawfully employed" (by a white employer) could be arrested, jailed, fined, or hired out to a man who would as-sume responsibility for their debts and behavior. The codes regulated black labor-ers' work contracts with white landowners, including severe penalties for leaving before the yearly contract was fulfilled. A Kentucky newspaper was blunt: "The tune ... will not be 'forty acres and a mule,' but ... 'work nigger or starve.'"

NATIONAL RECONSTRUCTION POLITICS

The Black Codes directly challenged the national government in 1865. Would it use its power in the South to uphold the codes, white property rights, and racial intimidation, or to defend the liberties of freedpeople? Although the primary drama of Reconstruction pitted white landowners against African American freedmen over land and labor in the South, in the background of these local struggles lurked the debate over Reconstruction policy among politicians in Washington. This dual drama would extend well into the twentieth century.

Presidential Reconstruction by Proclamation

After initially demanding that the defeated Confederates be punished for treason, President Johnson adopted a more lenient policy. On May 29, 1865, he issued two proclamations setting forth his Reconstruction program. Like Lincoln's, it rested on the claim that the southern states had never left the Union.

Johnson's first proclamation continued Lincoln's policies by offering "amnesty and pardon, with restoration of all rights of property" to most former Confederates who would swear allegiance to the Constitution and the Union. Johnson revealed his Jacksonian hostility to "aristocratic" planters by exempting ex–Confederate government leaders and rebels with taxable property valued over $20,000. They could, however, apply for individual pardons, which Johnson granted to nearly all applicants.

In his second proclamation, Johnson accepted the reconstructed government of North Carolina and prescribed the steps by which other southern states could reestablish state governments. First, the president would appoint a provisional governor, who would call a state convention representing those "who are loyal to the United States," including persons who took the oath of allegiance or were otherwise pardoned. The convention must ratify the Thirteenth Amendment, which abolished slavery; void secession; repudiate Confederate debts; and elect new state officials and members of Congress.

Under Johnson's plan, all southern states completed Reconstruction and sent representatives to Congress, which convened in December 1865. Defiant southern voters elected dozens of former officers and legislators of the Confederacy, including a few not yet pardoned. Some state conventions hedged on ratifying the Thirteenth Amendment, and some asserted former owners' right to compensation for lost slave property. No state convention provided for black suffrage, and most did nothing to guarantee civil rights, schooling, or economic protection for the freedmen. Eight months after Appomattox, the southern states were back in the Union, freedpeople were working for former masters, and the new president was firmly in charge. Reconstruction seemed to be over.

Congressional Reconstruction by Amendment

Late in 1865, northern leaders painfully saw that almost none of their moral or political postwar goals were being fulfilled and that the Republicans were likely to lose their political power. Would Democrats and the South gain by postwar elections what they had lost by civil war?

Congressional Republicans, led by Congressman Thaddeus Stevens of Pennsylvania and Senator Charles Sumner of Massachusetts, decided to set their own policies for Reconstruction. Although labeled "radicals," the vast majority of Republicans were moderates on the economic and political rights of freedmen.

Rejecting Johnson's position that the South had already been reconstructed, Congress exercised its constitutional authority to decide on its own membership.

Reconstruction Amendments

What three basic rights were guaranteed in these three amendments? What patterns do you see? How well were the dreams of the freedpeople fulfilled? Was that fulfillment immediate or deferred? For how long?

Substance	Outcome of Ratification Process	Final Implementation and Enforcement
Thirteenth Amendment—Passed by Congress January 1865		
Prohibited slavery in the United States	Ratified by 27 states, including 8 southern states, by December 1865	Immediate, although economic freedom came by degrees
Fourteenth Amendment—Passed by Congress June 1866		
(1) Defined equal national citizenship; (2) reduced state representation in Congress proportional to number of disfranchised voters; (3) denied former Confederates the right to hold office	Rejected by 12 southern and border states by February 1867; Congress made readmission depend on ratification; ratified in July 1868	Civil Rights Act of 1964
Fifteenth Amendment—Passed by Congress February 1869		
Prohibited denial of vote because of race, color, or previous servitude	Ratification by Virginia, Texas, Mississippi, and Georgia required for readmission; ratified in March 1870	Voting Rights Act of 1965

It refused to seat the new senators and representatives from the old Confederate states. It also established the Joint Committee on Reconstruction to investigate conditions in the South. Its report documented white resistance, disorder, and the appalling treatment and conditions of freedpeople.

Congress passed a civil rights bill in 1866 to protect the fragile rights of African Americans and extended for two more years the Freedmen's Bureau, an agency providing emergency assistance at the end of the war. Johnson vetoed both bills and called his congressional opponents "traitors." His actions drove moderates into the radical camp, and Congress passed both bills over his veto—both, however, watered down by weakening the power of enforcement. Southern courts regularly disallowed black testimony against whites, acquitted whites of violence, and sentenced blacks to compulsory labor.

In such a climate, southern racial violence erupted. In a typical outbreak, in May 1866, white mobs in Memphis, encouraged by local police, rampaged for over 40 hours of terror, killing, beating, robbing, and raping virtually helpless African American residents and burning houses, schools, and churches. Forty-eight people, all but two of them black, died. The local Union army commander took his time restoring order, arguing that his troops had "hated Negroes too." A congressional inquiry concluded that Memphis blacks had "no protection from the law whatever."

RECOVERING THE PAST

We usually read novels, short stories, and other forms of imaginary literature for pleasure, for the enjoyment of plot, style, symbolism, and character development. "Classic" novels such as *Moby Dick, Huckleberry Finn, The Great Gatsby, The Invisible Man,* and *Beloved,* for example, are not only written well, but also explore timeless questions of good and evil, of innocence and knowledge, of noble dreams fulfilled and shattered. We enjoy novels because we often find ourselves identifying with one of the major characters. Through that person's problems, joys, relationships, and search for identity, we gain insights about our own.

Even though they may be historically untrue, we can also read novels as historical sources, for they reveal much about the attitudes, dreams, fears, and ordinary everyday experiences of human beings in a particular period. In addition, they show how people responded to the major events of that era. The novelist, like the historian, is a product of time and place and has an interpretive point of view. Consider the two novels about Reconstruction quoted here. Neither is reputed for great literary merit, yet both reveal much about the various interpretations and impassioned attitudes of the post–Civil War era. *A Fool's Errand* was written by Albion Tourgée, a northerner; *The Clansman,* by Thomas Dixon, Jr., a southerner.

Tourgée was a young northern teacher and lawyer who fought with the Union army and moved to North Carolina after the war to begin a legal career. He became a judge and was an active Republican, supporting black suffrage and helping to shape the new state constitution. Because he boldly criticized the Ku Klux Klan, his life was threatened many times. When he left North Carolina in 1879, he published an autobiographical novel about his experiences as a judge challenging the Klan's campaign of violence and intimidation against the freedpeople.

The "fool's errand" in the novel is that of the northern veteran, Comfort Servosse, who, like Tourgée, seeks to fulfill humane goals on behalf of both blacks and whites in post–Civil War North Carolina. His efforts are thwarted, however, by threats, intimidation, a campaign of violent "outrages" against Republican leaders in the county, and a lack of support from Congress. Historians have verified the accuracy of many of the events in Tourgée's novel. While exposing the brutality of the Klan, Tourgée features loyal southern Unionists, respectable planters ashamed of Klan violence, and even guilt-ridden poor white Klansmen who try to protect or warn intended victims.

In the year of Tourgée's death, 1905, another North Carolinian published a novel with a very different analysis of Reconstruction and its fate. Thomas Dixon, Jr., was a lawyer, state legislator, Baptist minister, pro-Klan lecturer, and novelist. *The Clansman,* subtitled *A Historical Romance of the Ku Klux Klan,* reflects turn-of-the-century attitudes most white southerners still had about Republican rule during Reconstruction. According to Dixon, a power-crazed, vindictive, radical Congress, led by scheming Austin Stoneman (Thaddeus Stevens), sought to impose corrupt carpetbagger and brutal black rule on a helpless South. Only through the inspired leadership of the Ku Klux Klan was the South saved from the horrors of rape and revenge.

Dixon dedicated *The Clansman* to his uncle, a Grand Titan of the Klan in North Carolina during the time when two crucial counties were being transformed from Republican to Democratic through intimidation and terror. No such violence shows up in Dixon's novel. When the novel was made the basis of D. W. Griffith's film classic, *Birth of a Nation* in 1915, its attitudes were firmly implanted on the twentieth-century American mind.

Both novels convey Reconstruction attitudes toward the freedpeople. Both create clearly defined heroes and villains. Both include exciting chase scenes, narrow escapes, daring rescues, and tragic deaths. Both include romantic subplots. Yet the two novels are strikingly different.

A Fool's Errand,

Albion Tourgée (1879)

When the second Christmas came, Metta wrote again to her sister:

"The feeling is terribly bitter against Comfort on account of his course towards the colored people. There is quite a village of them on the lower end of the plantation. They have a church, a sabbath school, and are to have next year a school. You can not imagine how kind they have been to us, and how much they are attached to Comfort. ... I got Comfort to go with me to one of their prayer-meetings a few nights ago. I had heard a great deal about them, but had never attended one before. It was strangely weird. There were, perhaps, fifty present, mostly middle-aged men and women. They were singing in soft, low monotone, interspersed with prolonged exclamatory notes, a sort of rude hymn, which I was surprised to know was one of their old songs in slave times. How the chorus came to be endured in those days I can not imagine. It was—

'Free! free! free, my Lord, free!
An' we walks de hebben-ly way!

"A few looked around as we came in and seated ourselves; and Uncle Jerry, the saint of the settlement, came forward on his staves, and said, in his soft voice,

"'Ev'nin', Kunnel! Sarvant, Missuss! Will you walk up, an' hev seats in front?'

"We told him we had just looked in, and might go in a short time; so we would stay in the back part of the audience.

"Uncle Jerry can not read nor write; but he is a man of strange intelligence and power. Unable to do work of any account, he is the faithful friend, monitor, and director of others. He has a house and piece of land, all paid for, a good horse and cow, and, with the aid of his wife and two boys, made a fine crop this season. He is one of the most promising colored men in the settlement: so Comfort says, at least. Everybody seems to have great respect for his character. I don't know how many people I have heard speak of his religion. Mr. Savage used to say he had rather hear him pray than any other man on earth. He was much prized by his master, even after he was disabled, on account of his faithfulness and character."

The Clansman,

Thomas Dixon, Jr. (1905)

At noon Ben and Phil strolled to the polling-place to watch the progress of the first election under Negro rule. The Square was jammed with shouting, jostling, perspiring negroes, men, women, and children. The day was warm, and the African odour was supreme even in the open air. ...

The negroes, under the drill of the League and the Freedman's Bureau, protected by the bayonet, were voting to enfranchise themselves, disfranchise their former masters, ratify a new constitution, and elect a legislature to do their will. Old Aleck was a candidate for the House, chief poll-holder, and seemed to be in charge of the movements of the voters outside the booth as well as inside. He appeared to be omnipresent, and his self-importance was a sight Phil had never dreamed. He could not keep his eyes off him. ...

[Aleck] was a born African orator, undoubtedly descended from a long line of savage spellbinders, whose eloquence in the palaver houses of the jungle had made them native leaders. His thin spindle-shanks supported an oblong, protruding stomach, resembling an elderly monkey's, which seemed so heavy it swayed his back to carry it.

The animal vivacity of his small eyes and the flexibility of his eyebrows, which he worked up and down rapidly with every change of countenance, expressed his eager desires.

He was already mellow with liquor, and was dressed in an old army uniform and cap, with two horse-pistols buckled around his waist. On a strap hanging from his shoulder were strung a half-dozen tin canteens filled with whiskey.

REFLECTING ON THE PAST   Even in these brief excerpts, what differences of style and attitude do you see in the depictions of Uncle Jerry and Old Aleck? What emotional responses do you have to these passages? How do you think late nineteenth-century and early twentieth-century Americans might have responded?

A month later, Congress sent to the states for ratification the Fourteenth Amendment, the single most significant act of the Reconstruction era. The first section of the amendment promised permanent constitutional protection of the civil rights of blacks by defining them as citizens. States were prohibited from depriving "any person of life, liberty, or property, without due process of law," and citizens were guaranteed the "equal protection of the laws." Section 2 granted black male suffrage in the South, inserting the word "male" into the Constitution for the first time. Other sections of the amendment barred leaders of the Confederacy from national or state offices (except by act of Congress), repudiated the Confederate debt, and denied claims of compensation to former slave owners. Johnson urged the southern states to reject the Fourteenth Amendment, and 10 immediately did so.

The Fourteenth Amendment was the central issue of the 1866 midterm election. Johnson barnstormed the country asking voters to throw out the radical Republicans and trading insults with hecklers. Democrats north and south appealed openly to racial prejudice in attacking the Fourteenth Amendment. Republicans responded by attacking Johnson personally and freely "waved the bloody shirt," reminding voters of the Democrats' treason. Self-interest and local issues moved voters more than fiery speeches, and the Republicans won an overwhelming victory. The mandate was clear: presidential Reconstruction had not worked, and Congress could present its own.

Early in 1867, Congress passed three Reconstruction acts. The southern states were divided into five military districts, whose commanders had broad powers to maintain order and protect civil and property rights. Congress also defined a new process for readmitting a state. Qualified voters—including blacks but excluding unreconstructed rebels—would elect delegates to state constitutional conventions that would write new constitutions guaranteeing black suffrage. After the new voters of the states had ratified these constitutions, elections would be held to choose governors and state legislatures. When a state ratified the Fourteenth Amendment, its representatives to Congress would be accepted, completing its readmission to the Union.

DOCUMENT

Thirteenth, Fourteenth, and Fifteenth Amendments (1864)

The President Impeached

Congress also restricted presidential powers and established legislative dominance over the executive branch. The Tenure of Office Act, designed to prevent Johnson from firing the outspoken Secretary of War Edwin Stanton, limited the president's appointment powers. Other measures trimmed his power as commander in chief.

Johnson responded exactly as congressional Republicans had anticipated. He vetoed the Reconstruction acts, hindered the work of Freedmen's Bureau agents, limited the activities of military commanders in the South, and removed cabinet officers and other officials sympathetic to Congress. The House Judiciary Committee charged the president with "usurpations of power" and of acting in the "interests of the great criminals" who had led the rebellion. But moderate House Republicans defeated the impeachment resolutions.

In August 1867, Johnson dismissed Stanton and asked for Senate consent. When the Senate refused, the president ordered Stanton to surrender his office, which he refused, barricading himself inside. The House quickly approved impeachment resolutions, charging the president with "high crimes and misdemeanors." The three-month trial in the Senate in 1868 featured impassioned oratory, similar to the trial of President Bill Clinton 130 years later. And, as with Clinton, evidence was skimpy that Johnson had committed any constitutional crime justifying his removal. With seven moderate Republicans joining Democrats against conviction, the effort to find the president guilty fell one vote short of the required two-thirds majority. Not until the late twentieth century (Nixon and Clinton) would an American president face removal from office through impeachment.

Moderate Republicans were fearful that by removing Johnson, they might get Ohio Senator Benjamin Wade, a leading radical Republican, as president. Wade had endorsed woman suffrage, rights for labor unions, and civil rights for African Americans in both southern and northern states. As moderate Republicans gained strength in 1868 through their support of the eventual presidential election winner, Ulysses S. Grant, radicalism lost much of its power within Republican ranks.

What Congressional Moderation Meant for Rebels, Blacks, and Women

Congress's political battle against President Johnson was not matched by an idealistic resolve on behalf of the freedpeople. State and local elections of 1867 showed that voters preferred moderate Reconstruction policies. It is important to look not only at what Congress did during Reconstruction, but also at what it did not do.

With the exception of Jefferson Davis, Congress did not imprison Confederate leaders, and only one person, the commander of the infamous Andersonville prison camp, was executed. Congress did not insist on a long probation before southern states could be readmitted. It did not reorganize southern local governments. It did not mandate a national program of education for the freedpeople. It did not confiscate and redistribute land to the freedmen. It did not prevent Johnson from taking land away from those who had gained titles during the war. It did not, except indirectly and with great reluctance, provide economic help to the new black citizens.

Congress did, however, halfheartedly grant citizenship and suffrage to freedmen, but not to freedwomen. Northerners were no more prepared than southerners to make African Americans equal citizens. Proposals to give black men the vote gained support in the North only after the presidential election of 1868, when General Grant, the supposedly invincible military hero, barely won the popular vote in several states. To ensure grateful black votes, Congressional Republicans, who had twice rejected a suffrage amendment, took another look at the idea. After a bitter fight, the Fifteenth Amendment, forbidding all states to deny the vote to anyone "on account of race, color, or previous condition of servitude," became part of the Constitution in 1870.

One casualty of the Fourteenth and Fifteenth Amendments was the goodwill of women who had worked for suffrage for two decades. They had hoped that male legislators would recognize their wartime service in support of the Union and were shocked that black males got the vote but not loyal white (or black) women. Elizabeth Cady Stanton and Susan B. Anthony, veteran suffragists and opponents of slavery, campaigned against the Fourteenth Amendment, breaking with abolitionist allies such as Frederick Douglass, who had long supported woman suffrage yet declared that this was "the Negro's hour."

When the Fifteenth Amendment was proposed, many suffragists wondered why gender was still a barrier to the right to vote. Disappointment over the suffrage issue helped split the women's movement in 1869. Anthony and Stanton continued their fight for a national amendment for woman suffrage and a long list of other rights, while other women concentrated on securing the vote state-by-state. Abandoned by radical and moderate men alike, women had few champions in Congress, and their efforts did not bear fruit for half a century.

Congress compromised the rights of African Americans as well as women. It gave blacks the vote but not land, the opposite of what they wanted first. Thaddeus Stevens argued that "forty acres ... and a hut would be more valuable ... than the ... right to vote." But Congress never seriously considered his plan to confiscate the land of the "chief rebels" and give a small portion of it, divided into 40-acre plots, to freedpeople, which would have violated deeply held beliefs of the Republican party and the American people on the sacredness of private property. Moreover, northern business interests looking to develop southern industry and invest in southern land liked the prospect of a large pool of propertyless African American workers.

Congress did pass the Southern Homestead Act of 1866, making public lands available to blacks and loyal whites in five southern states. But the land was poor and inaccessible, and most black laborers were bound by contracts that prevented them from making claims before the deadline. Only about 4,000 African American families even applied for the Homestead Act lands, and fewer than 20 percent of them saw their claims completed. White claimants did little better.

THE LIVES OF FREEDPEOPLE

Union army major George Reynolds boasted late in 1865 that in the area of Mississippi under his command, he had "kept the negroes at work, and in a good state of discipline." Clinton Fisk, a well-meaning white who helped found a black college in Tennessee, told freedmen in 1866 that they could be "as free and as happy" working again for their "old master ... as any where else in the world." Such pronouncements reminded blacks of white preachers' exhortations during slavery to work hard and obey masters. Ironically, Fisk and Reynolds were agents of the Freedmen's Bureau, the agency intended to aid the black transition from slaves to freedpeople.

The Freedmen's Bureau

Never in American history has one small agency—underfinanced, understaffed, and undersupported—been given a harder task than was the Bureau of Freedmen, Refugees, and Abandoned Lands. Controlling less than 1 percent of southern lands, the Bureau's name is telling; its fate epitomizes Reconstruction.

The Freedmen's Bureau performed many essential services. It issued emergency food rations, clothed and sheltered homeless victims of the war, and established medical and hospital facilities. It provided funds to relocate thousands of freedpeople. It helped blacks search for relatives and get legally married. It represented African Americans in local civil courts to ensure that they got fair trials and learned to respect the law. Working with northern missionary aid societies and southern black churches, the Bureau became responsible for an extensive program of education, and by 1870 there were almost 250,000 pupils in 4,329 agency schools.

The Bureau's largest task was to promote African Americans' economic well-being. This included settling them on abandoned lands and getting them started with tools, seed, and draft animals, as well as arranging work contracts with white landowners. But in this area the Freedmen's Bureau, determined not to instill a new dependency, more often than not supported the needs of white landowners to find cheap labor than of blacks to become independent farmers.

Although a few agents were idealistic New Englanders eager to help freedpeople adjust to freedom, most were Union army officers more concerned with social order than social transformation. Working in a postwar climate of resentment and violence, Freedmen's Bureau agents were overworked, underpaid, spread too thin (at its peak only 900 agents were scattered across the South), and constantly harassed by local whites. Even the best-intentioned agents would have agreed with Bureau commissioner General O. O. Howard's belief in the nineteenth-century American values of self-help, minimal government interference in the marketplace, the sanctity of private property, contractual obligations, and white superiority.

On a typical day, overburdened agents would visit local courts and schools, file reports, supervise the signing of work contracts, and handle numerous complaints, most involving contract violations between whites and blacks or property and domestic disputes among blacks. A Georgia agent wrote that he was *"tired out* and *broke down.* … Every day for 6 months, day after day, I have had from 5 to 20 complaints, *generally trivial* and of no moment, yet requiring consideration & attention coming from both Black & White." To find work for freedmen, agents implored freedwomen to hold their husbands accountable as providers and often sided with white landowners by telling blacks to obey orders, trust employers, and accept disadvantageous contracts. One agent sent a man who had complained of a severe beating back to work: "Don't be sassy [and] don't be lazy when you've got work to do."

Despite numerous constraints, the agents accomplished much. In little more than two years, the Freedmen's Bureau issued 20 million rations (nearly one-third to poor whites), reunited families and resettled some 30,000 displaced war refugees, treated some 450,000 people for illness and injury, built 40 hospitals and 4,000 schools, provided books, tools, and furnishings—and even some land—to the freedmen, and occasionally protected their economic and civil rights. The great African American historian and leading black intellectual of the twentieth century, W. E. B. Du Bois, wrote that, "In a time of perfect calm, amid willing neighbors and streaming wealth," it "would have been a herculean task" for the bureau to fulfill its many purposes. But in the midst of hunger, sorrow, spite, suspicion, hate, and cruelty, "the work of any instrument of social regeneration was … foredoomed to failure." But Du Bois, reflecting the varied views of freedpeople themselves, recognized that in

DOCUMENT

Southern Skepticism of the Freedmen's Bureau (1866)

laying the foundation for black labor, future land ownership, a public school system, and recognition before courts of law, the Freedmen's Bureau was "on the whole successful beyond the dreams of thoughtful men."

Economic Freedom by Degrees

Despite the best efforts of the Freedmen's Bureau, the failure of Congress to provide the promised 40 acres and a mule forced freedmen and women into a new dependency on former masters. Blacks made some progress, however, in degrees of economic autonomy and were partly responsible, along with international economic developments, for forcing the white planter class into making major changes in southern agriculture.

First, a land-intensive system replaced the labor intensity of slavery. Land ownership was concentrated into fewer and even larger holdings than before the war. From South Carolina to Louisiana, the wealthiest tenth of the population owned about 60 percent of the real estate in the 1870s. Second, these large planters increasingly specialized in one crop, usually cotton, and were tied into the international market. This resulted in a steady drop in postwar food production (both grain and livestock). Third, one-crop farming created a new credit system whereby most farmers, black and white, were forced into dependence on local merchants for renting land, housing, seed, and farm implements and animals. These changes affected race relations and class tensions.

This new system took a few years to develop after emancipation. At first, most African Americans signed contracts with white landowners and worked in gangs as during slavery. All members of the family had to work to receive their rations. The freedpeople resented this new semiservitude, refused to sign the contracts, and sought a measure of independence working the land themselves. Freedwomen especially wanted to send their children to school rather than to apprenticeships, and insisted on "no more outdoor work," preferring small plots of land to grow vegetables rather than plantation labor.

Many blacks therefore broke contracts, ran away, engaged in work slowdowns or strikes, burned barns, and sought other means of negotiation. In the Sea Islands and rice-growing regions of coastal South Carolina and Georgia, where slaves had long held a degree of autonomy, resistance was especially strong. On the Heyward plantations, near those of the Allstons, the freedmen "refuse work at any price," a Freedman's Bureau agent reported, and the women "wish to stay in the house or the garden all the time."

Blacks' insistence on autonomy and land of their own was the major impetus for the change from the contract system to tenancy and sharecropping. Families would hitch mules to their old slave cabin and drag it to their plot, as far from the

DOCUMENT

A Sharecrop
Contract (1882)

Big House as possible. Sharecroppers received seed, fertilizer, implements, food, and clothing. In return, the landlord (or a local merchant) told them what and how much to grow, and he took a share—usually half—of the harvest. The cropper's half usually went to pay for goods bought on credit (at high interest rates) from the landlord. Thus sharecroppers remained tied to the landlord.

Tenant farmers had only slightly more independence. Before a harvest, they promised to sell their crop to a local merchant in return for renting land, tools,

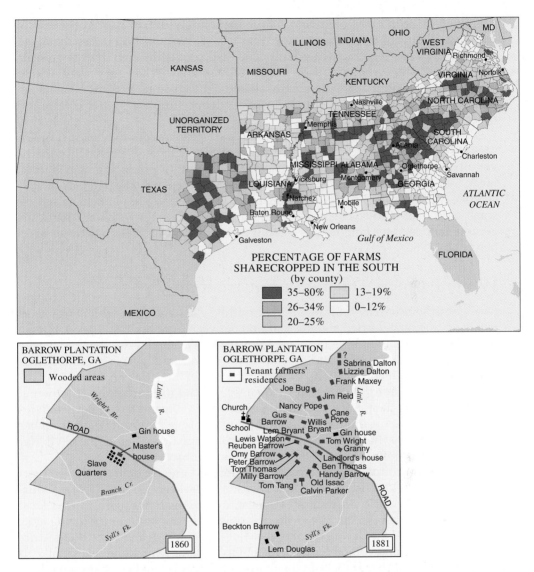

PERCENTAGE OF FARMS
SHARECROPPED IN THE SOUTH
(by county)

35–80%   13–19%
26–34%   0–12%
20–25%

BARROW PLANTATION
OGLETHORPE, GA

Wooded areas

Wright's Br.
Little R.
ROAD
Gin house
Master's house
Slave Quarters
Branch Cr.
Syll's Fk.

1860

BARROW PLANTATION
OGLETHORPE, GA

Tenant farmers' residences

?
Sabrina Dalton
Lizzie Dalton
Frank Maxey
Joe Bug
Jim Reid
Church
Nancy Pope
Gus Barrow
Cane Pope
Willis Bryant
School
Lem Bryant
Bryant
Gin house
Lewis Watson
Tom Wright
Reuben Barrow
Omy Barrow
Granny
Peter Barrow
Landlord's house
Tom Thomas
Ben Thomas
Milly Barrow
Handy Barrow
Tom Tang
Old Issac
Calvin Parker
Beckton Barrow
Syll's Fk.
Lem Douglas
ROAD
Little R.

1881

THE RISE OF TENANCY IN THE SOUTH, 1880 Although no longer slaves and after resisting labor contracts and the gang system of field labor, the freedmen (as well as many poor whites) became tenant farmers, working on shares, in the New South. The former slaves on the Barrow plantation in Georgia, for example, moved their households to individual 25- to 30-acre tenant farms, which they rented from the Barrow family in annual contracts requiring payment in cotton and other cash crops. Where was the highest percentage of tenant farms, and how do you explain it? How would you explain the low-percentage areas? What do you notice about how circumstances have changed—and not changed—on the Barrow plantation?

and other necessities. From the merchant's store they also had to buy goods on credit (at higher prices than whites paid) against the harvest. At "settling up" time, income from sale of the crop was compared to accumulated debts. It was possible, especially after an unusually bountiful season, to come out ahead and eventually to own one's own land. But tenants rarely did; in debt at the end of each year, they had to pledge the next year's crop. World cotton prices remained low, and whereas big landowners still generated profits through their large scale of operation, sharecroppers rarely made much money. When they were able to pay their debts, landowners frequently altered loan agreements. Thus peonage replaced slavery, ensuring a continuing cheap labor supply to grow cotton and other staples in the South.

Despite this bleak picture, painstaking, industrious work by African Americans helped many gradually accumulate a measure of income, personal property, and autonomy, especially in the household economy of producing eggs, butter, meat, food crops, and other staples. Debt did not necessarily mean a lack of subsistence. In Virginia, the declining tobacco crop forced white planters to sell off small parcels of land to blacks. Throughout the South, a few African Americans became independent landowners—about 3 to 4 percent by 1880, but closer to 25 percent by 1900.

White Farmers During Reconstruction

Changes in southern agriculture affected middle-class and poor white farmers as well, and planters worried about a coalition between poor black and pro-Unionist white farmers. As a Georgia farmer said in 1865, "We should tuk the land, as we did the niggers, and split it, and giv part to the niggers and part to me and t'other Union fellers." But confiscation and redistribution of land was no more likely for white farmers than for the freedmen. Whites, too, had to concentrate on growing staples, pledging their crops against high-interest credit, and facing perpetual indebtedness. In the upcountry piedmont area of Georgia, for example, the number of whites working their own land dropped from nine in ten before the Civil War to seven in ten by 1880, while cotton production doubled.

Reliance on cotton meant fewer food crops and greater dependence on merchants for provisions. In 1884, Jephta Dickson of Jackson County, Georgia, purchased over $50 worth of flour, meal, meat, syrup, peas, and corn from a local store; 25 years earlier, he had been almost completely self-sufficient. Fencing laws seriously curtailed the livelihood of poor whites raising pigs and hogs, and restrictions on hunting and fishing reduced the ability of poor whites and blacks alike to supplement incomes and diets. In the worn-out flatlands and barren mountainous regions of the South, the poverty, health, and isolation of poor whites worsened after the war. They lived a marginal existence, hunting, fishing, and growing crops that, as a North Carolinian put it, were "puny." Some became farmhands at $6 a month (with board). Others fled to low-paying jobs in cotton mills.

The cultural life of poor southern whites reflected their lowly position and their pride. Their emotional religion centered on camp meeting revivals in backwoods clearings. There, ballads and folklore told of debt, chain gangs, herbal remedies for poor health, and deeds of drinking prowess. Their quilt making and house construction reflected a marginal culture in which everything was saved and reused.

In part because their lives were so hard, poor whites clung to their belief in white superiority. Many joined the Ku Klux Klan and other southern white terror groups that emerged between 1866 and 1868. A federal officer reported, "The poorer classes of white people ... have a most intense hatred of the Negro," which expressed itself in midnight raids on teachers in black schools, Republican voters, and any black whose "impudence" caused him not to "bow and scrape to a white man, as was done formerly."

Black Self-Help Institutions

But however hard life was for poor whites, things were even worse for blacks, whose hopes slowly soured. Recalled an African American Texan, "We soon found out that freedom could make folks proud but it didn't make 'em rich." Many African American leaders realized that because white institutions could not fulfill the promises of emancipation, freedpeople would have to do it themselves.

Black community self-help survived in the churches and schools of the antebellum free Negro communities and in the "invisible" cultural institutions of the slave quarters. Emancipation brought a rapid increase in the growth of membership in African American churches. The Negro Baptist Church grew from 150,000 members in 1850 to 500,000 in 1870, while the membership of the African Methodist Episcopal Church increased fourfold in the postwar decade, from 100,000 to over 400,000 members. African American ministers continued to exert community leadership. Many led efforts to oppose discrimination, some by entering politics; over one-fifth of the black officeholders in South Carolina were ministers. Most preachers, however, focused on sin, salvation, and revivalist enthusiasm. An English visitor to the South in 1867 and 1868 noted the intensity of black "devoutness." As one woman explained: "We make noise 'bout ebery ting else ... I want to go to Heaben in de good ole way."

The freedpeople's desire for education was as strong as for religion. A school official in Virginia said that the freedmen were "down right crazy to learn." In addition to black teachers from the churches, "Yankee schoolmarms taught black children and adults." Sent by aid societies such as the American Missionary Association, these high-minded young women sought to convert blacks to Congregationalism and their version of moral behavior. In October 1865, Esther Douglass found "120 dirty, half naked perfectly wild black children" in her schoolroom near Savannah, Georgia. Eight months later, she reported that they could read, sing hymns, and repeat Bible verses and had learned "about right conduct which they tried to practice."

Such glowing reports waned as white teachers grew frustrated with crowded facilities, limited resources, local opposition, and absenteeism caused by fieldwork. In Georgia, for example, only 5 percent of black children went to school for part of any one year between 1865 and 1870, as opposed to 20 percent of white children. As white teachers left, they were increasingly replaced by blacks, who boarded with families and were more persistent and positive. Charlotte Forten, for example, noted that even after a half day's "hard toil" in the fields, her older pupils were "as bright and as anxious to learn as ever," showing "a desire for knowledge, and a capability for attaining it." Under teachers like Forten, by 1870 there was a 20 percent gain in adult literacy, a figure that, against difficult odds, continued to grow for all ages to the end of the century, when more than 1.5 million black children attended school. To train African American teachers and

Black Schoolchildren with Their Books and Teacher Along with equal civil rights and land of
their own, what the freedpeople wanted most was education. Despite white opposition, one of the most
positive outcomes of the Reconstruction era was education in Freedmen's Bureau schools. What do you
see in this photograph? Is it sad or uplifting? Why? *(Cook Collection, Valentine Richmond History Center)*

preachers, northern philanthropists founded Howard, Atlanta, Fisk, Morehouse,
and other black universities in the South after 1865.

African American schools, like churches, became community centers. They
published newspapers, provided training in trades and farming, and promoted
political participation and land ownership. These efforts made black schools objects of local white hostility. As a Virginia freedman told a congressional committee, in his county, anyone starting a school would be killed and blacks were
"afraid to be caught with a book." In 1869, in Tennessee alone, 37 black schools
were burned to the ground.

White opposition to black education and land ownership stimulated African
American nationalism and separatism. In the late 1860s, Benjamin "Pap" Singleton, a former Tennessee slave, urged freedpeople to abandon politics and migrate
westward. He organized a land company in 1869, purchased public property in
Kansas, and in the early 1870s took several groups from Tennessee and Kentucky
to establish separate black towns in the prairie state. In following years, thousands of "exodusters" from the Lower South bought some 10,000 infertile acres in
Kansas. But natural and human obstacles to self-sufficiency often proved insur-

mountable. By the 1880s, despairing of ever finding economic independence in the United States, Singleton and other nationalists advocated emigration to Canada and Liberia. Other black leaders like Frederick Douglass continued to press for full citizenship rights within the United States.

RECONSTRUCTION IN THE SOUTHERN STATES

Douglass's confidence in the power of the ballot seemed warranted in the enthusiastic early months under the Reconstruction Acts of 1867. With President Johnson neutralized, Republican congressional leaders finally could prevail. Local Republicans, taking advantage of the inability or refusal of many southern whites to vote, overwhelmingly elected their delegates to state constitutional conventions in the fall of 1867. Guardedly optimistic and sensing the "sacred importance" of their work, black and white Republicans began creating new state governments.

MAP

Reconstruction

Republican Rule

Contrary to early pro-southern historians, southern state governments under Republican rule were not dominated by illiterate black majorities intent on "Africanizing" the South. Nor were these governments unusually corrupt or extravagant, nor did they use massive numbers of federal troops to enforce their will. By 1869, only 1,100 federal soldiers remained in Virginia, and most federal troops in Texas were guarding the frontier against Mexico and hostile Indians. Lacking strong

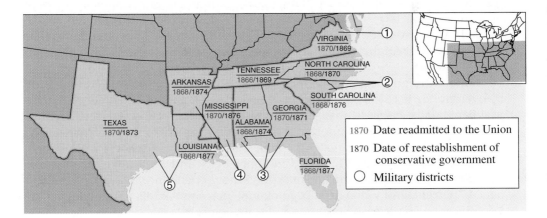

THE RETURN OF CONSERVATIVE DEMOCRATIC CONTROL IN SOUTHERN STATES DURING RECONSTRUCTION Note that the duration of Republican governments in power to implement even moderate Reconstruction programs varied from state to state. In North Carolina and Georgia, for example, Republican rule was very brief, while in Virginia it never took place at all. "Redemption," the return of conservative control, took longest in three Deep South states. How would you explain these variations among the southern states?

military backing, the new state governments faced economic distress and increasingly violent harassment.

Diverse coalitions made up the new governments elected under congressional Reconstruction. These "black and tan" governments (as opponents called them) were actually predominantly white, except for the lower house of the South Carolina legislature. Many of the new leaders were local bankers, industrialists, and others interested more in economic growth and sectional reconciliation than in radical social reforms. A second group consisted of northern Republican capitalists who headed south to invest in land, railroads, and new industries. Others included Union veterans, and missionaries and teachers inspired to work in Freedmen's Bureau schools. Such people were unfairly labeled "carpetbaggers."

Moderate African Americans made up a third group in the Republican state governments. A large percentage of black officeholders were mulattos, many of them well-educated preachers, teachers, and soldiers from the North. Others were self-educated tradesmen or representatives of the small landed class of southern blacks. In South Carolina, for example, of some 255 African American state and federal officials elected between 1868 and 1876, two-thirds were literate and one-third owned real estate; only 15 percent owned no property at all. This class composition meant that black leaders often supported policies that largely ignored the economic needs of the African American masses. Their goals fit squarely into the American republican tradition. Black leaders reminded whites that they were also southerners, seeking only, as an 1865 petition put it, "that the same laws which govern white men shall govern black men [and that] we be dealt with as others are—in equity and justice."

The primary accomplishment of Republican rule in the South was to eliminate undemocratic features from prewar state constitutions. All states provided universal male suffrage and loosened requirements for holding office. Underrepresented counties got more legislative seats. Automatic imprisonment for debt was ended, and laws were enacted to relieve poverty and care for the handicapped. Many southern states passed their first divorce laws and provisions granting property rights to married women. Lists of crimes punishable by death were shortened.

Republican governments financially and physically reconstructed the South by overhauling tax systems and approving generous railroad and other capital investment bonds. Harbors, roads, and bridges were rebuilt; hospitals and asylums were established. Most important, the Republican governments created the South's first public school systems. As in the North, these schools were largely segregated, but for the first time rich and poor, black and white alike had access to education. By the 1880s, African American school attendance increased from 5 to over 40 percent, and white from 20 to over 60 percent. All this cost money, so the Republicans also increased tax rates and state debts.

These considerable accomplishments came in the face of opposition like that expressed at a convention of Louisiana planters, which labeled the Republican leaders the "lowest and most corrupt body of men ever assembled in the South." There was some corruption, mostly in land sales, railway bonds, and construction contracts. Such graft had become a way of life in postwar American politics,

South and North. Given their lack of experience with politics, the black role was remarkable. As Du Bois put it, "There was one thing that the White South feared more than negro dishonesty, ignorance, and incompetence, and that was negro honesty, knowledge, and efficiency."

The Republican coalition did not survive. It lasted for different periods in different states, surviving longest in the Deep South, where the black population was equal to or greater than the white. In Virginia, Republicans ruled hardly at all, joining with Democrats to encourage northern investors to rebuild shattered cities and develop industry. In South Carolina, African American leaders' unwillingness to use their power to help black laborers contributed to their loss of political control to the Democrats, and class divisions among blacks in Louisiana helped weaken the Republican regime there. But the primary reason for the return of Democrats to power was the use of violence.

Violence and "Redemption"

A southern editor said, "We must render this either a white man's government, or convert the land into a Negro man's cemetery." The Ku Klux Klan was only one of several secret organizations that forcibly drove black and white Republicans from office. Although violence was pervasive throughout the South, North Carolina and Mississippi typified the pattern.

After losing a close election in North Carolina in 1868, conservatives waged a concentrated terror campaign in several piedmont counties, areas of strong Unionist support. If the Democrats could win these counties in 1870, they would most likely win statewide. In the year before the election, several prominent Republicans were killed, including a white state senator and a leading black Union League organizer, who was hanged in the courthouse square with a sign pinned to him: "Bewar, ye guilty, both white and black." Scores of citizens were flogged, fired from their jobs, or driven in the middle of the night from burning homes and barns. The courts consistently refused to prosecute anyone for these crimes, which local papers blamed on "disgusting negroes and white Radicals." The conservative campaign worked. In the election of 1870, some 12,000 fewer Republicans voted in the two crucial counties than had voted two years earlier, and the Democrats swept back into power.

In Mississippi's state election in 1875, Democrats used similar tactics in what became known as the "Mississippi Plan." Local Democratic clubs formed armed militias, marching defiantly through black areas, breaking up Republican meetings, and provoking riots to justify killing hundreds. Armed men posted during voter registration intimidated Republicans. At the election itself, voters were either "helped" by gun-toting whites to cast a Democratic ballot or chased away. Counties that had given Republicans majorities in the thousands managed a total of less than a dozen votes in 1875!

Democrats called their victory "redemption." As conservative Democrats resumed control of each state government, Reconstruction ended. Redemption succeeded with a combination of persistent white southern resistance, including violence and coercion, and a failure of northern will.

"The negroes of the South are free—ree as air," says the parliamentary Watterson. This is what the *State*, a well-nown Democratic organ of Tennessee, says, in huge capitals, on the subject: 'Let it be known before the election that the farmers have agreed to spot every leading Radical negro in the county, and treat him as an enemy for all time to come. The rotten ring must and shall be broken at any and all costs. The Democrats have determined to withdraw all employment from their enemies. Let this fact be known."

Ensuring Votes for the Democratic Ticket Although the Fourteenth and Fifteenth Amendments gave African American males the right to vote, almost immediately white southerners opposed to black suffrage found many illegal ways of influencing and eventually depriving them of that vote, thus returning white Democrats to office. In this cartoon, titled "Of course he wants to vote the Democratic Ticket," one of the two pistol-wielding men is saying: "You're as free as air, ain't you? Say you are, or I'll blow your black head off!" Note that another freedman is being led down the street to the polling place. Do you think he will also vote Democratic or for the party of Lincoln? *(Corbis)*

Congress and President Grant did not totally ignore southern violence. Three Force Acts, passed in 1870 and 1871, gave the president strong powers to use federal supervisors to ensure that citizens were not prevented from voting by force or fraud. The third act, also known as the Ku Klux Klan Act, declared illegal secret organizations that used disguise and coercion to deprive others of equal protection of the laws. Congress created a joint committee to investigate Klan violence, and in 1872 its report filled 13 huge volumes with horrifying testimony. Grant sent messages to Congress proclaiming the importance of the right to vote and condemning lawlessness, and dispatched additional troops to South Carolina, where violence against blacks was the worst. However, reform Republicans lost interest in defending African Americans, and regular Republicans decided that they could keep political power without black votes. In 1875, Grant's advisers told him that Republicans might lose important Ohio elections if he continued protecting African Americans, so he rejected appeals by Mississippi blacks for troops to guarantee free elections. He and the nation, Grant said, "had tired of these annual autumnal outbreaks."

The success of the Democrats' Mississippi Plan in 1875, repeated a year later in South Carolina and Louisiana, indicated that congressional reports, presidential proclamations, and the Force Acts did little to stop the reign of terror against black and white Republicans throughout the South. Despite hundreds of arrests, all-white juries refused to find whites guilty of crimes against blacks. The U.S. Supreme Court backed them in two 1874 decisions throwing out cases against whites convicted of preventing blacks from voting and declaring key parts of the Force Acts unconstitutional. Officially, the Klan's power ended, but the attitudes (and tactics) of Klansmen would continue long into the next century.

Shifting National Priorities

The American people, like their leaders, were tired of battles over the freedpeople. The easiest course was to give citizenship and the vote to African Americans, and leave them to fend for themselves. Americans of increasing ethnic diversity were primarily interested in starting families, finding work, and making money. Slovakian immigrants fired furnaces in Pittsburgh; Chinese men pounded in railroad ties for the Central Pacific over the Sierra Nevada mountains and across the Nevada desert; Yankee women taught in one-room schoolhouses in Vermont for $23 a month; Mexican *vaqueros* drove Texan cattle herds to Kansas; and Scandinavian families battled heat, locusts, and high railroad rates on farmsteads in the Dakotas.

American priorities had shifted, at both the individual and national levels. Failing to effect a smooth transition from slavery to freedom for freedpeople, northern leaders focused their efforts on accelerating and solidifying programs of economic growth and industrial and territorial expansion.

As North Carolina Klansmen convened in dark forests in 1869, the Central Pacific and Union Pacific railroads met in Utah, linking the Atlantic and the Pacific. As southern cotton production revived, northern iron and steel manufacturing and western settlement of the mining, cattle, and agricultural frontiers also surged. As black farmers haggled over work contracts with landowners in Georgia, white workers were organizing the National Labor Union in Baltimore. As Elizabeth and Adele Allston demanded the keys to their barns in the summer of 1865, the Boston Labor Reform Association was demanding that "our ... education, morals, dwellings, and the whole Social System" needed to be "reconstructed." If the South would not be reconstructed, labor relations might be.

The years between 1865 and 1875 featured not only the rise (and fall) of Republican governments in the South, but also a spectacular surge of working-class organization. Stimulated by the Civil War to improve working conditions in northern factories, trade unions, labor reform associations, and labor parties flourished, culminating in the founding of the National Labor Union in 1866. Before the depression of 1873, an estimated 300,000 to 500,000 American workers enrolled in some 1,500 trade unions, the largest such increase in the nineteenth century. This growth inevitably stirred class tensions. In 1876, hundreds of freedmen in the rice region along the Combahee River in South Carolina went on strike to protest a 40-cent-per-day wage cut, clashing with local sheriffs and white Democratic rifle clubs. A year later, also fighting wage cuts, thousands of northern railroad workers went out in a nationwide wave of strikes, clashing with police and the National Guard.

As economic relations changed, so did the Republican party. Heralded by the moderate tone of the state elections of 1867 and Grant's election in 1868, the Republicans changed from a party of moral reform to one of material interest. In the continuing struggle in American politics between "virtue and commerce," self-interest was again winning. Abandoning the Freedmen's Bureau as an inappropriate federal intervention, Republican politicians had no difficulty handing out huge grants of money and land to the railroads. As freedpeople were told to fend for themselves, the Union Pacific was getting subsidies of between $16,000 and $48,000 for each mile of track it laid. As Susan B. Anthony and other women tramped through the snows of upstate New York with petitions for women's rights, Boss Tweed and other politicians defrauded New York taxpayers of millions of dollars. As Native Americans in the Great Plains struggled to preserve the sacred Black Hills from gold prospectors protected by U.S. soldiers, corrupt government officials in the East "mined" public treasuries.

DOCUMENT

Trial of Susan B. Anthony, on the charge of Illegal Voting, at the Presidential Election in November 1872

By 1869, the year financier Jay Gould almost cornered the gold market, the nation was increasingly defined by its sordid, materialistic "go-getters." President Grant's cabinet was filled with his old army cronies and rich friends to whom he owed favors. Henry Adams, descended from two former presidents, charged that Grant's administration "outraged every rule of decency." Honest himself, Grant showed poor judgment of others. The scandals of his administration touched his relatives, his cabinet, and two vice presidents. Outright graft, loose prosecution, and generally negligent administration flourished in a half dozen departments. The Whiskey Ring affair, for example, cost the public millions of dollars in tax revenues siphoned off to government officials. Gould's gold scam was aided by Grant's Treasury Department and by the president's brother-in-law.

Nor was Congress pure. Crédit Mobilier, a dummy corporation supposedly building the transcontinental railroads, received generous bonds and contracts in exchange for giving congressmen money, stock, and railroad lands. An Ohio congressman described the House of Representatives in 1873 as an "auction room where more valuable considerations were disposed of under the speaker's hammer than any place on earth."

The election of 1872 showed the public uninterested in moral issues. "Liberal" Republicans, disgusted with Grant, formed a third party calling for lower tariffs and fewer grants to railroads, civil service reform, and the removal of federal troops from the South. Their candidate, Horace Greeley, editor of the New York *Tribune,* was also nominated by the Democrats, whom he had spent much of his career condemning. But despite his wretched record, Grant easily won a second term.

The End of Reconstruction

Soon after Grant's second inauguration, a financial panic, caused by railroad mismanagement and the collapse of some eastern banks, started a terrible depression that lasted throughout the mid-1870s. In these hard times, economic issues dominated politics, further diverting attention from freedpeople. As Democrats took control of the House of Representatives in 1874 and looked toward winning the White House in 1876, politicians talked about new Grant scandals, unemployment and public works, the currency, and tariffs. No one said much about freed-

The End of Reconstruction This 1868 Thomas Nast cartoon ran under a caption quoting a Democratic party newspaper, "This is a white man's government." Describe each of the four (stereotyped) figures in this cartoon. Note the details in what each person carries in his raised (or outstretched) arm. You will see symbols of Irish workers in the "5 Points" neighborhood of New York City, the "lost cause" of the CSA, Confederate general Nathan Bedford Forrest, capitalist wealth, a Union soldier's uniform, and the ballot box. Note also the images in the background. In short, what do you see, and what does it mean? No single image better captures the story of the end of Reconstruction. (Harper's Weekly, September 5, 1868)

people. In 1875, a guilt-ridden Congress did pass Senator Charles Sumner's civil rights bill to put teeth into the Fourteenth Amendment. But the act was not enforced, and eight years later the Supreme Court declared it unconstitutional. Congressional Reconstruction, long dormant, was over. The election of 1876, closest in American history until 2000, sealed the end.

As their presidential candidate in 1876, the Republicans chose a former governor of Ohio, Rutherford B. Hayes, partly because of his reputation for honesty, partly because he had been a Union officer (a necessity for post–Civil War candidates), and partly because, as Henry Adams put it, he was "obnoxious to no one." The Democrats nominated Governor Samuel J. Tilden of New York, a well-known civil service reformer who had broken the corrupt Tweed ring.

Tilden won a popular-vote majority and appeared to have enough electoral votes for victory—except for 20 disputed electoral votes, all but one in Louisiana, South Carolina, and Florida, where some federal troops remained and where Republicans still controlled the voting apparatus despite Democratic intimidation. To settle the dispute, Congress created a commission of eight Republicans and seven Democrats who voted along party lines to give Hayes all 20 votes and a narrow electoral college victory, 185 to 184.

Outraged Democrats protested the outcome and threatened to stop the Senate from officially counting the electoral votes, preventing Hayes's inauguration. There was talk of a new civil war. But unlike the 1850s, a North–South compromise

TIMELINE

1865	Civil War ends	**1868–1870**	Ten former Confederate states readmitted to the Union
	Thirteenth Amendment ratified		
	Freedmen's Bureau established	**1870**	Fifteenth Amendment ratified
1865–1866	Black Codes	**1876–1877**	Three remaining former Confederate States of America readmitted to the Union
	Repossession of land by whites		
	Ku Klux Klan formed		
1867	Reconstruction acts passed over Johnson's veto	**1880s**	Tenancy and sharecropping prevail in the South
1868	Fourteenth Amendment ratified		Disfranchisement and segregation of southern blacks begins

emerged. Northern investors wanted the government to subsidize a New Orleans-to-California railroad. Southerners wanted northern dollars but not northern political influence—no social agencies, no federal enforcement of the Fourteenth and Fifteenth amendments, and no military occupation, not even the symbolic presence left in 1876.

As the March 4 inauguration date approached, the forces of mutual self-interest concluded the "compromise of 1877." On March 2, Hayes was declared president-elect. After his inauguration, he ordered the last federal troops out of the South, sending them west to fight Plains Indians, appointed a former Confederate general to his cabinet, supported federal aid for economic and railroad development in the South, and promised to let southerners handle race relations themselves. On a goodwill trip to the South, he told blacks that "your rights and interests would be safer if this great mass of intelligent white men were let alone by the general government." The message was clear: Hayes would not enforce the Fourteenth and Fifteenth Amendments, initiating a pattern of executive inaction that lasted to the 1960s. But the immediate crisis was averted, officially ending Reconstruction.

Conclusion

A Mixed Legacy

In the 12 years between Appomattox and Hayes's inauguration, victorious northern Republicans, defeated white southerners, and hopeful black freedpeople each wanted more than the others would give. Each got something. The compromise of

1877 cemented the reunion of North and South, providing new opportunities for economic development in both regions. The Republican party achieved its economic goals and generally held the White House, though not always Congress, until 1932. The ex-Confederate states came back into the Union, and southerners retained their grip on southern lands and black labor, though not without struggle and some changes. The Allstons' freedpeople refused to sign work contracts, even when offered livestock and other favors, and in 1869, Adele Allston had to sell much of her lands, albeit to whites.

In 1880, Frederick Douglass wrote: "Our Reconstruction measures were radically defective. ... To the freedmen was given the machinery of liberty, but there was denied to them the steam to put it in motion. ... The old master class ... retained the power to starve them to death, and wherever this power is held there is the power of slavery." The wonder, Douglass said, was "not that freedmen have made so little progress, but, rather, that they have made so much; not that they have been standing still, but that they have been able to stand at all."

Freedpeople had made strong gains in education and in economic and family survival. Despite sharecropping and tenancy, black laborers organized themselves to achieve a measure of autonomy and opportunity in their lives. The three great Reconstruction amendments, despite flagrant violation over the next 100 years, held out the promise that equal citizenship and political participation would yet be realized.

Questions for Review and Reflection

1. At the end of the Civil War, what were the goals and dreams of defeated southern whites, victorious northerners, and emancipated freedpeople? Can you name three for each group?

2. How did each group pursue its goals and dreams, what resources did each have, and how did they conflict with each other between 1865 and 1877?

3. What differences existed *within* each of the three major groups?

4. What were the major differences between northern presidential and congressional plans for reconstruction? In your judgment, which was more important—reconstruction politics in the North or daily life, race relations, and politics in the South?

5. What is your assessment of how well American democratic politics and values served the dreams of diverse American peoples in the postwar era?

Discovering U.S. History Online

A Documentary History of Emancipation, 1861–1867 www.inform.umd.edu/ARHU/Depts/History/Freedman/home.html

A rich collection of primary sources from the Freedom and Southern Society Project of the University of Maryland, containing superb links to nine projected volumes of collected documents.

Freedmen's Bureau Online http://freedmen'sbureau.com/

An excellent collection of Freedmen's Bureau sites, including marriage records and accounts of "murders and other outrages," as well as links to other African American and Freedmen's Bureau sites.

The Impeachment of Andrew Johnson www.andrewjohnson.com
Over 200 excerpts from contemporary issues of *Harper's Weekly* (1865–1869) provide in-depth information about Andrew Johnson and the impeachment process.

Images of African Americans from the Nineteenth Century www.digital.nypl.org/schomburg/images_aa19/
A vast collection of visual images by artists, engravers, and photographers capturing elements of African American life in the nineteenth century.

Reports on Black America, 1857–1874 www.blackhistory.harpweek.com
Fascinating text and imagery found in the pages of *Harper's Weekly* magazine.

African American Perspectives, 1818–1907 www.memory.loc.gov/ammem/aap/aaphome.html
This searchable collection is filled with links to Reconstruction topics and political speeches and manuscripts from the Federal Writers' Project interviews with ex-slaves in the 1930s.

Fiction and Film

W. E. B. Du Bois's *The Quest of the Silver Fleece* (1911) is a little-known novel by the sociologist-historian about the lives of sharecroppers during Reconstruction. Howard Fast's *Freedom Road* (1944) is a novel about the heroic but ultimately failed efforts of poor whites and blacks to unite for mutual benefit during the era. Ernest Gaines's *The Autobiography of Miss Jane Pittman* (1971), framed as an autobiography, is a gripping fictional account of a proud centenarian black woman who lived from the time of the Civil War to the era of civil rights. In *A Fool's Errand* (1879), as described in this chapter's "Recovering the Past" section, Albion Tourgée takes the viewpoint of a sympathetic white judge who helps the freedpeople in North Carolina during Reconstruction.

Margaret Walker's *Jubilee* (1966) is a black female novelist's epic version of the African American experience in the Civil War era, and Alice Randall's *The Wind Done Gone* (2001) is a parody of Margaret Mitchell's *Gone with the Wind* (1936); both follow black and white families from slavery to Reconstruction. Toni Morrison's *Beloved* (1988), an extraordinary novel set near Cincinnati in 1873 that includes flashbacks, is about the lasting traumas of slavery as black women especially seek to put their lives together and pursue their dreams of freedom. The film of the same name (1998), though slow moving, follows the time disconnections of the novel well with many moving scenes. *Birth of a Nation,* the classic 1913 film by D. W. Griffith that portrays the rise of the Ku Klux Klan as the defender of white supremacy and womanhood, is based on Thomas Dixon's *The Clansman* (1905) (also described in the "Recovering the Past" section). A quite different film portrayal is seen in Oscar Micheaux's *Within Our Gates* (1919), the first feature film by an African American, available from the Library of Congress's early American film collection.

Recommended Reading

www.ablongman.com/nash
The Companion Website has a list of recommended readings about the post–Civil War period.

THE DECLARATION OF INDEPENDENCE IN CONGRESS, JULY 4, 1776

The Unanimous Declaration of the Thirteen United States of America

When, in the course of human events, it becomes necessary for one people to dissolve the political bonds which have connected them with another, and to assume, among the powers of the earth, the separate and equal station to which the laws of nature and of nature's God entitle them, a decent respect to the opinions of mankind requires that they should declare the causes which impel them to the separation.

We hold these truths to be self-evident: That all men are created equal; that they are endowed by their Creator with certain unalienable rights; that among these are life, liberty, and the pursuit of happiness; that, to secure these rights, governments are instituted among men, deriving their just powers from the consent of the governed; that whenever any form of government becomes destructive of these ends, it is the right of the people to alter or to abolish it, and to institute new government, laying its foundation on such principles, and organizing its powers in such form, as to them shall seem most likely to effect their safety and happiness. Prudence, indeed, will dictate that governments long established should not be changed for light and transient causes; and accordingly all experience hath shown that mankind are more disposed to suffer, while evils are sufferable, than to right themselves by abolishing the forms to which they are accustomed. But when a long train of abuses and usurpations, pursuing invariably the same object, evinces a design to reduce them under absolute despotism, it is their right, it is their duty, to throw off such government, and to provide new guards for their future security. Such has been the patient sufferance of these colonies; and such is now the necessity which constrains them to alter their former systems of government. The history of the present King of Great Britain is a history of repeated injuries and usurpations, all having in direct object the establishment of an absolute tyranny over these states. To prove this, let facts be submitted to a candid world.

He has refused his assent to laws, the most wholesome and necessary for the public good.

He has forbidden his governors to pass laws of immediate and pressing importance, unless suspended in their operation till his assent should be obtained; and, when so suspended, he has utterly neglected to attend to them.

He has refused to pass other laws for the accommodation of large districts of people, unless those people would relinquish the right of representation in the legislature, a right inestimable to them, and formidable to tyrants only.

He has called together legislative bodies at places unusual, uncomfortable, and distant from the depository of their public records, for the sole purpose of fatiguing them into compliance with his measures.

He has dissolved representative houses repeatedly, for opposing, with manly firmness, his invasions on the rights of the people.

He has refused for a long time, after such dissolutions, to cause others to be elected; whereby the legislative powers, incapable of annihilation, have returned to the people at large for their exercise; the state remaining, in the mean time, exposed to all the dangers of invasions from without and convulsions within.

He has endeavored to prevent the population of these states; for that purpose obstructing the laws for naturalization of foreigners; refusing to pass others to encourage their migration hither, and raising the conditions of new appropriations of lands.

He has obstructed the administration of justice, by refusing his assent to laws for establishing judiciary powers.

He has made judges dependent on his will alone, for the tenure of their offices, and the amount and payment of their salaries.

He has erected a multitude of new offices, and sent hither swarms of officers to harass our people and eat out their substance.

He has kept among us, in times of peace, standing armies, without the consent of our legislatures.

He has affected to render the military independent of, and superior to, the civil power.

He has combined with others to subject us to a jurisdiction foreign to our constitution, and unacknowledged by our laws, giving his assent to their acts of pretended legislation:

For quartering large bodies of armed troops among us;

For protecting them, by a mock trial, from punishment for any murder which they should commit on the inhabitants of these states;

For cutting off our trade with all parts of the world;

For imposing taxes on us without our consent;

For depriving us, in many cases, of the benefits of trial by jury;

For transporting us beyond seas, to be tried for pretended offenses;

For abolishing the free system of English laws in a neighboring province, establishing therein an arbitrary government, and enlarging its boundaries, so as to render it at once an example and fit instrument for introducing the same absolute rule into these colonies;

For taking away our charters, abolishing our most valuable laws, and altering fundamentally the forms of our governments;

For suspending our own legislatures, and declaring themselves invested with power to legislate for us in all cases whatsoever.

He has abdicated government here, by declaring us out of his protection and waging war against us.

He has plundered our seas, ravaged our coasts, burned our towns, and destroyed the lives of our people.

He is at this time transporting large armies of foreign mercenaries to complete the works of death, desolation, and tyranny already begun with circumstances of cruelty and perfidy scarcely paralleled in the most barbarous ages, and totally unworthy the head of a civilized nation.

He has constrained our fellow-citizens, taken captive on the high seas, to bear arms against their country, to become the executioners of their friends and brethren, or to fall themselves by their hands.

He has excited domestic insurrection among us, and has endeavored to bring on the inhabitants of our frontiers the merciless Indian savages, whose known rule of warfare is an undistinguished destruction of all ages, sexes, and conditions.

In every stage of these oppressions we have petitioned for redress in the most humble terms; our repeated petitions have been answered only by repeated injury. A prince, whose character is thus marked by every act which may define a tyrant, is unfit to be the ruler of a free people.

Nor have we been wanting in our attentions to our British brethren. We have warned them, from time to time, of attempts by their legislature to extend an unwarrantable jurisdiction over us. We have reminded them of the circumstances of our emigration and settlement here. We have appealed to their native justice and magnanimity; and we have conjured them, by the ties of our common kindred, to disavow these usurpations, which would inevitably interrupt our connections and correspondence. They, too, have been deaf to the voice of justice and of consanguinity. We must, therefore, acquiesce in the necessity which denounces our separation, and hold them, as we hold the rest of mankind, enemies in war, in peace friends.

We, therefore, the representatives of the United States of America, in General Congress assembled, appealing to the Supreme Judge of the world for the rectitude of our intentions, do, in the name and by the authority of the good people of these colonies, solemnly publish and declare, that these United Colonies are, and of right, ought to be, FREE AND INDEPENDENT STATES; that they are absolved from all allegiance to the British crown, and that all political connection between them and the state of Great Britain is, and ought to be, totally dissolved; and that, as free and independent states, they have full power to levy war, conclude peace, contract alliances, establish commerce, and do all other acts and things which independent states may of right do. And for the support of this declaration, with a firm reliance on the protection of Devine Providence, we mutually pledge to each other our lives, our fortunes, and our sacred honor.

JOHN HANCOCK

BUTTON GWENNETT	THS. NELSON, JR.	RICHD. STOCKTON
LYMAN HALL	FRANCIS LIGHTFOOT LEE	JNO. WITHERSPOON
GEO. WALTON	CARTER BRAXTON	FRAS. HOPKINSON
WM. HOOPER	ROBT. MORRIS	JOHN HART
JOSEPH HEWES	BENJAMIN RUSH	ABRA. CLARK
JOHN PENN	BENJA. FRANKLIN	JOSIAH BARTLETT
EDWARD RUTLEDGE	JOHN MORTON	WM. WHIPPLE
THOS. HEYWARD, JUNR.	GEO. CLYMER	SAML. ADAMS
THOMAS LYNCH, JUNR.	JAS. SMITH	JOHN ADAMS
ARTHUR MIDDLETON	GEO. TAYLOR	ROBT. TREAT PAINE
SAMUEL CHASE	JAMES WILSON	ELBRIDGE GERRY
WM. PACA	GEO. ROSS	STEP. HOPKINS
THOS. STONE	CAESAR RODNEY	WILLIAM ELLERY
CHARLES CARROLL	GEO. READ	ROGER SHERMAN
OF CARROLLTON	THO. MÍKEAN	SAMÍEL. HUNTINGTON
GEORGE WYTHE	WM. FLOYD	WM. WILLIAMS
RICHARD HENRY LEE	PHIL. LIVINGSTON	OLIVER WOLCOTT
TH. JEFFERSON	FRANS. LEWIS	MATHEW THORNTON
BENJA. HARRISON	LEWIS MORRIS	

THE CONSTITUTION OF THE UNITED STATES OF AMERICA

PREAMBLE

We the People of the United States, in Order to form a more perfect Union, establish Justice, insure domestic Tranquility, provide for the common defence, promote the general Welfare, and secure the Blessings of Liberty to ourselves and our Posterity, do ordain and establish this Constitution for the United States of America.

ARTICLE I.

Section 1   All legislative Powers herein granted shall be vested in a Congress of the United States, which shall consist of a Senate and House of Representatives.

Section 2   The House of Representatives shall be composed of Members chosen every second Year by the People of the several States, and the Electors in each State shall have the Qualifications requisite for Electors of the most numerous Branch of the State Legislature.

No Person shall be a Representative who shall not have attained to the Age of twenty five Years, and been seven Years a Citizen of the United States, and who shall not, when elected, be an Inhabitant of that State in which he shall be chosen.

Representatives and direct Taxes shall be apportioned among the several States which may be included within this Union, according to their respective Numbers, *which shall be determined by adding to the whole Number of free Persons, including those bound to Service for a Term of Years, and excluding Indians not taxed, three fifths of all other Persons.* The actual Enumeration shall be made within three Years after the first Meeting of the Congress of the United States, and within every subsequent Term of ten Years, in such Manner as they shall by Law direct. The Number of Representatives shall not exceed one for every thirty Thousand, but each State shall have at Least one Representative; *and until such enumeration shall be made, the State of New Hampshire shall be entitled to chuse three, Massachusetts eight, Rhode-Island and Providence Plantations one, Connecticut five, New-York six, New Jersey four, Pennsylvania eight, Delaware one, Maryland six, Virginia ten, North Carolina five, South Carolina five, and Georgia three.*

When vacancies happen in the Representation from any State, the Executive Authority thereof shall issue Writs of Election to fill such Vacancies.

The House of Representatives shall chuse their Speaker and other Officers; and shall have the sole Power of Impeachment.

Section 3   The Senate of the United States shall be composed of two Senators from each State, chosen by the Legislature thereof, for six Years; and each Senator shall have one Vote.

Immediately after they shall be assembled in Consequence of the first Election, they shall be divided as equally as may be into three Classes. The Seats of the Senators of the first Class shall be vacated at the Expiration of the second Year, of the second Class at the Expiration of the fourth Year, and of the third Class at the Expiration of the sixth Year, so that one third may be chosen every second Year; and if Vacancies happen by Resignation, or otherwise, during the Recess of the Legislature of any State, the Executive thereof may make temporary Appointments until the next Meeting of the Legislature, which shall then fill such Vacancies.

No Person shall be a Senator who shall not have attained to the Age of thirty Years, and been nine Years a Citizen of the United States, and who shall not, when elected, be an Inhabitant of that State for which he shall be chosen.

The Vice President of the United States shall be President of the Senate, but shall have no Vote, unless they be equally divided.

The Senate shall choose their other Officers, and also a President *pro tempore*, in the Absence of the Vice President, or when he shall exercise the Office of President of the United States.

The Senate shall have the sole Power to try all Impeachments. When sitting for that Purpose, they shall be on Oath or Affirmation. When the President of the United States is tried the Chief Justice shall preside: And no Person shall be convicted without the Concurrence of two thirds of the Members present.

Judgment in Cases of Impeachment shall not extend further than to removal from Office, and disqualification to hold and enjoy any Office of honor, Trust or Profit under the United States: but the Party convicted shall nevertheless be liable and subject to Indictment, Trial, Judgment and Punishment, according to Law.

Section 4   The Times, Places and Manner of holding Elections for Senators and Representatives, shall be prescribed in each State by the Legislature thereof; but the Congress may at any time by Law make or alter such Regulations, except as to the Places of chusing Senators.

The Congress shall assemble at least once in every Year, and such Meeting *shall be on the first Monday in December, unless they shall by Law appoint a different Day.*

Section 5   Each House shall be the Judge of the Elections, Returns and Qualifications of its own Members, and a Majority of each shall constitute a Quorum to do Business; but a smaller Number may adjourn from day to day, and may be authorized to compel the Attendance of absent Members, in such Manner, and under such Penalties as each House may provide.

Each House may determine the Rules of its Proceedings, punish its Members for disorderly Behaviour, and, with the Concurrence of two thirds, expel a Member.

Each House shall keep a Journal of its Proceedings, and from time to time publish the same, excepting such Parts as may in their Judgment require Secrecy; and the Yeas and Nays of the Members of either House on any question shall, at the Desire of one fifth of those Present, be entered on the Journal.

Neither House, during the Session of Congress, shall, without the Consent of the other, adjourn for more than three days, nor to any other Place than that in which the two Houses shall be sitting.

Section 6   The Senators and Representatives shall receive a Compensation for their Services, to be ascertained by Law, and paid out of the Treasury of the United States. They shall in all Cases, except Treason, Felony and Breach of the Peace, be privileged from Arrest during their Attendance at the Session of their respective Houses, and in going to and returning from the same; and for any Speech or Debate in either House, they shall not be questioned in any other Place.

No Senator or Representative shall, during the Time for which he was elected, be appointed to any civil Office under the Authority of the United States, which shall have been created, or the Emoluments whereof shall have been encreased during such time; and no Person holding any Office under the United States, shall be a Member of either House during his Continuance in Office.

Section 7   All Bills for raising Revenue shall originate in the House of Representatives; but the Senate may propose or concur with Amendments as on other Bills.

Every Bill which shall have passed the House of Representatives and the Senate, shall, before it become a Law, be presented to the President of the United States; If he approve he shall sign it, but if not he shall return it, with his Objections to that House in which it shall have originated, who shall enter the Objections at large on their Journal, and proceed to reconsider it. If after such Reconsideration two thirds of that House shall agree to pass the Bill, it shall be sent, together with the Objections, to the other House, by which it shall likewise be reconsidered, and if approved by two thirds of that House, it shall become a Law. But in all such Cases the Votes of both Houses shall be determined by yeas and Nays, and the Names of the Persons voting for and against the Bill shall be entered on the Journal of each House respectively. If any Bill shall not be returned by the President within ten Days (Sundays excepted) after it shall have been presented to him, the Same shall be a Law, in like Manner as if he had signed it, unless the Congress by their Adjournment prevent its Return, in which Case it shall not be a Law.

Every Order, Resolution, or Vote to which the Concurrence of the Senate and House of Representatives may be necessary (except on a question of Adjournment) shall be presented to the President of the United States; and before the Same shall take Effect, shall be approved by him, or being disapproved by him, shall be repassed by two thirds of the Senate and House of Representatives, according to the Rules and Limitations prescribed in the Case of a Bill.

Section 8   The Congress shall have Power:

To lay and collect Taxes, Duties, Imposts and Excises, to pay the Debts and provide for the common Defence and general Welfare of the United States; but all Duties, Imposts and Excises shall be uniform throughout the United States;

To borrow Money on the credit of the United States;

To regulate Commerce with foreign Nations, and among the several States, and with the Indian Tribes;

To establish an uniform Rule of Naturalization, and uniform Laws on the subject of Bankruptcies throughout the United States;

To coin Money, regulate the Value thereof, and of foreign Coin, and fix the Standard of Weights and Measures;

To provide for the Punishment of counterfeiting the Securities and current Coin of the United States;

To establish Post Offices and post Roads;

To promote the Progress of Science and useful Arts, by securing for limited Times to Authors and Inventors the exclusive Right to their respective Writings and Discoveries;

To constitute Tribunals inferior to the supreme Court;

To define and punish Piracies and Felonies committed on the high Seas, and Offences against the Law of Nations;

To declare War, grant Letters of Marque and Reprisal, and make Rules concerning Captures on Land and Water;

To raise and support Armies, but no Appropriation of Money to that Use shall be for a longer Term than two Years;

To provide and maintain a Navy;

To make Rules for the Government and Regulation of the land and naval Forces;

To provide for calling forth the Militia to execute the Laws of the Union, suppress Insurrections and repel Invasions;

To provide for organizing, arming, and disciplining, the Militia, and for governing such Part of them as may be employed in the Service of the United States, reserving to the States respectively, the Appointment of the Officers, and the Authority of training the Militia according to the discipline prescribed by Congress;

To exercise exclusive Legislation in all Cases whatsoever, over such District (not exceeding ten Miles square) as may, by Cession of particular States, and the Acceptance of Congress, become the Seat of the Government of the United States, and to exercise like Authority over all Places purchased by the Consent of the Legislature of the State in which the Same shall be, for the Erection of Forts, Magazines, Arsenals, dock-Yards, and other needful Buildings;

To make all Laws which shall be necessary and proper for carrying into Execution the foregoing Powers, and all other Powers vested by this Constitution in the Government of the United States, or in any Department or Officer thereof.

Section 9 *The Migration or Importation of such Persons as any of the States now existing shall think proper to admit, shall not be prohibited by the Congress prior to the Year one thousand eight hundred and eight, but a Tax or duty may be imposed on such Importation, not exceeding ten dollars for each Person.*

The Privilege of the Writ of Habeas Corpus shall not be suspended, unless when in Cases of Rebellion or Invasion the public Safety may require it.

No Bill of Attainder or ex post facto Law shall be passed.

No Capitation, or other direct, Tax shall be laid, unless in Proportion to the Census or Enumeration herein before directed to be taken.

No Tax or Duty shall be laid on Articles exported from any State.

No Preference shall be given by any Regulation of Commerce or Revenue to the Ports of one State over those of another: nor shall Vessels bound to, or from, one State, be obliged to enter, clear, or pay Duties in another.

No Money shall be drawn from the Treasury, but in Consequence of Appropriations made by Law; and a regular Statement and Account of the Receipts and Expenditures of all public Money shall be published from time to time.

No Title of Nobility shall be granted by the United States: And no Person holding any Office of Profit or Trust under them, shall, without the Consent of the Congress, accept of any present, Emolument, Office, or Title, of any kind whatever, from any King, Prince, or foreign State.

Section 10 No State shall enter into any Treaty, Alliance, or Confederation; grant Letters of Marque and Reprisal; coin Money; emit Bills of Credit; make any Thing but gold and silver Coin a Tender in Payment of Debts; pass any Bill of Attainder, ex post facto Law, or Law impairing the Obligation of Contracts, or grant any Title of Nobility.

No State shall, without the Consent of the Congress, lay any Imposts or Duties on Imports or Exports, except what may be absolutely necessary for executing it's inspection Laws: and the net Produce of all Duties and Imposts, laid by any State on Imports or Exports, shall be for the Use of the Treasury of the United States; and all such Laws shall be subject to the Revision and Controul of the Congress.

No State shall, without the Consent of Congress, lay any Duty of Tonnage, keep Troops, or Ships of War in time of Peace, enter into any Agreement or Compact with another State, or with a foreign Power, or engage in War, unless actually invaded, or in such imminent Danger as will not admit of delay.

ARTICLE II.

Section 1 The executive Power shall be vested in a President of the United States of America. He shall hold his Office during the Term of four Years, and, together with the Vice President, chosen for the same Term, be elected, as follows

Each State shall appoint, in such Manner as the Legislature thereof may direct, a Number of Electors, equal to the whole Number of Senators and Representatives to which the State may be entitled in the Congress: but no Senator or Representative, or Person holding an Office of Trust or Profit under the United States, shall be appointed an Elector.

The Electors shall meet in their respective States, and vote by Ballot for two Persons, of whom one at least shall not be an Inhabitant of the same State with themselves. And they shall make a List of all the Persons voted for, and of the Number of Votes for each; which List they shall sign and certify, and transmit sealed to the Seat of Government of the United States, directed to the President of the Senate. The President of the Senate shall, in the Presence of the Senate and House of Representatives, open all the Certificates, and the Votes shall then be counted. The Person having the greatest Number of Votes shall be the President, if such Number be a Majority of the whole Number of Electors appointed; and if there be more than one who have such Majority, and have an equal Number of Votes, then the House of Representatives shall immediately chuse by Ballot one of them for President; and if no Person have a Majority, then from the five highest on the List the said House shall in like Manner chuse the President. But in chusing the President, the Votes shall be taken by States, the Representation from each State having one Vote; A quorum for this Purpose shall consist of a Member or Members from two thirds of the States, and a Majority of all the States shall be necessary to a Choice. In every Case, after the Choice of the President, the Person having the greatest Number of Votes of the Electors shall be the Vice President. But if there should remain two or more who have equal Votes, the Senate shall chuse from them by Ballot the Vice President.

The Congress may determine the Time of chusing the Electors, and the Day on which they shall give their Votes; which Day shall be the same throughout the United States.

No Person except a natural born Citizen, *or a Citizen of the United States, at the time of the Adoption of this Constitution,* shall be eligible to the Office of President; neither shall any Person be eligible to that Office who shall not have attained to the Age of thirty five Years, and been fourteen Years a Resident within the United States.

In Case of the Removal of the President from Office, or of his Death, Resignation, or Inability to discharge the Powers and Duties of the said Office, the Same shall devolve on the Vice President, and the Congress may by Law provide for the Case of Removal, Death, Resignation or Inability, both of the President and Vice President declaring what Officer shall then act as President, and such Officer shall act accordingly, until the Disability be removed, or a President shall be elected.

The President shall, at stated Times, receive for his Services, a Compensation, which shall neither be increased nor diminished during the Period for which he shall have been elected, and he shall not receive within that Period any other Emolument from the United States, or any of them.

Before he enter on the Execution of his Office, he shall take the following Oath or Affirmation: "I do solemnly swear (or affirm) that I will faithfully execute the Office of President of the United States, and will to the best of my Ability, preserve, protect and defend the Constitution of the United States."

Section 2   The President shall be Commander in Chief of the Army and Navy of the United States, and of the Militia of the several States, when called into the actual Service of the United States; he may require the Opinion, in writing, of the principal Officer in each of the executive Departments, upon any Subject relating to the Duties of their respective Offices, and he shall have Power to grant Reprieves and Pardons for Offences against the United States, except in Cases of Impeachment.

He shall have Power, by and with the Advice and Consent of the Senate, to make Treaties, provided two thirds of the Senators present concur; and he shall nominate, and by and with the Advice and Consent of the Senate, shall appoint Ambassadors, other public Ministers and Consuls, Judges of the supreme Court, and all other Officers of the United States, whose Appointments are not herein otherwise provided for, and which shall be established by Law: but the Congress may by Law vest the Appointment of such inferior Officers, as they think proper, in the President alone, in the Courts of Law, or in the Heads of Departments.

The President shall have Power to fill up all Vacancies that may happen during the Recess of the Senate, by granting Commissions which shall expire at the End of their next Session.

Section 3   He shall from time to time give to the Congress Information of the State of the Union, and recommend to their Consideration such Measures as he shall judge necessary and expedient; he may, on extraordinary Occasions, convene both Houses, or either of them, and in Case of Disagreement between them, with Respect to the Time of Adjournment, he may adjourn them to such Time as he shall think proper; he shall receive Ambassadors and other public Ministers; he shall take Care that the Laws be faithfully executed, and shall Commission all the Officers of the United States.

Section 4   The President, Vice President and all civil Officers of the United States, shall be removed from Office on Impeachment for, and Conviction of, Treason, Bribery, or other high Crimes and Misdemeanors.

ARTICLE III.

Section 1   The judicial Power of the United States, shall be vested in one supreme Court, and in such inferior Courts as the Congress may from time to time ordain and establish. The Judges, both of the supreme and inferior Courts, shall hold their Offices during good Behaviour, and shall, at stated Times, receive for their Services, a Compensation which shall not be diminished during their Continuance in Office.

Section 2   The judicial Power shall extend to all Cases, in Law and Equity, arising under this Constitution, the Laws of the United States, and Treaties made, or which shall be made, under their Authority;—to all Cases affecting Ambassadors, other public Ministers and Consuls;—to all Cases of admiralty and maritime Jurisdiction;—to Controversies to which the United States shall be a Party;—to Controversies between two or more States;—*between a State and Citizens of another State;*—between Citizens of different States;—between Citizens of the same State claiming Lands under Grants of different States, and between a State, or the Citizens thereof, and foreign States, Citizens or Subjects.

In all Cases affecting Ambassadors, other public Ministers and Consuls, and those in which a State shall be Party, the supreme Court shall have original Jurisdiction. In all the other Cases before mentioned, the supreme Court shall have appellate Jurisdiction, both as to Law and Fact, with such Exceptions, and under such Regulations as the Congress shall make.

The Trial of all Crimes, except in Cases of Impeachment, shall be by Jury; and such Trial shall be held in the State where the said Crimes shall have been committed; but when not committed within any State, the Trial shall be at such Place or Places as the Congress may by Law have directed.

Section 3   Treason against the United States, shall consist only in levying War against them, or in adhering to their Enemies, giving them Aid and Comfort. No Person shall be convicted of Treason unless on the Testimony of two Witnesses to the same overt Act, or on Confession in open Court.

The Congress shall have Power to declare the Punishment of Treason, but no Attainder of Treason shall work Corruption of Blood, or Forfeiture except during the Life of the Person attainted.

ARTICLE IV.

Section 1   Full Faith and Credit shall be given in each State to the public Acts, Records, and judicial Proceedings of every other State. And the Congress may by general Laws prescribe the Manner in which such Acts, Records and Proceedings shall be proved, and the Effect thereof.

Section 2   The Citizens of each State shall be entitled to all Privileges and Immunities of Citizens in the several States.

A Person charged in any State with Treason, Felony, or other Crime, who shall flee from Justice, and be found in another State, shall on Demand of the executive Authority of the State from which he fled, be delivered up, to be removed to the State having Jurisdiction of the Crime.

No Person held to Service or Labour in one State, under the Laws thereof, escaping into another, shall, in Consequence of any Law or Regulation therein, be discharged from such Service or Labour, but shall be delivered up on Claim of the Party to whom such Service or Labour may be due.

Section 3   New States may be admitted by the Congress into this Union; but no new State shall be formed or erected within the Jurisdiction of any other State; nor any State be formed by the Junction of two or more States, or Parts of States, without the Consent of the Legislatures of the States concerned as well as of the Congress.

The Congress shall have Power to dispose of and make all needful Rules and Regulations respecting the Territory or other Property belonging to the United States; and nothing in this Constitution shall be so construed as to Prejudice any Claims of the United States, or of any particular State.

Section 4   The United States shall guarantee to every State in this Union a Republican Form of Government, and shall protect each of them against Invasion; and on Application of the Legislature, or of the Executive (when the Legislature cannot be convened) against domestic Violence.

ARTICLE V.

The Congress, whenever two thirds of both Houses shall deem it necessary, shall propose Amendments to this Constitution, or, on the Application of the Legislatures of two thirds of the several States, shall call a Convention for proposing Amendments, which, in either Case, shall be valid to all Intents and Purposes, as Part of this Constitution, when ratified by the Legislatures of three fourths of the several States, or by Conventions in three fourths thereof, as the one or the other Mode of Ratification may be proposed by the Congress; Provided that *no Amendment which may be made prior to the Year One thousand eight hundred and eight shall in any Manner affect the first and fourth Clauses in the Ninth Section of the first Article; and* that no State, without its Consent, shall be deprived of its equal Suffrage in the Senate.

ARTICLE VI.

All Debts contracted and Engagements entered into, before the Adoption of this Constitution, shall be as valid against the United States under this Constitution, as under the Confederation.

This Constitution, and the Laws of the United States which shall be made in Pursuance thereof; and all Treaties made or which shall be made, under the Authority of the United States, shall be the supreme Law of the Land; and the Judges in every State shall be bound thereby, any Thing in the Constitution or Laws of any State to the Contrary notwithstanding.

The Senators and Representatives before mentioned, and the Members of the several State Legislatures, and all executive and judicial Officers, both of the United States and of the several States, shall be bound by Oath or Affirmation, to support this Constitution; but no religious Test shall ever be required as a Qualification to any Office or public Trust under the United States.

ARTICLE VII.

The Ratification of the Conventions of nine States, shall be sufficient for the Establishment of this Constitution between the States so ratifying the Same.

Done in Convention by the Unanimous Consent of the States present the Seventeenth Day of September in the Year of our Lord one thousand seven hundred and Eighty seven and of the Independence of the United States of America the Twelfth. IN WITNESS whereof We have hereunto subscribed our Names,

GEORGE WASHINGTON,
President and Deputy from Virginia

North Carolina
WILLIAM BLOUNT
RICHARD DOBBS
  SPRAIGHT
HU WILLIAMSON

Pennsylvania
BENJAMIN FRANKLIN
THOMAS MIFFLIN
ROBERT MORRIS
GEORGE CLYMER
THOMAS FITZSIMONS
JARED INGERSOLL
JAMES WILSON
GOUVERNEUR MORRIS

Delaware
GEORGE READ
GUNNING BEDFORD, JR.
JOHN DICKINSON
RICHARD BASSETT
JACOB BROOM

South Carolina
J. RUTLEDGE
CHARLES C. PINCKNEY
PIERCE BUTLER

Virginia
JOHN BLAIR
JAMES MADISON, JR.

New Jersey
WILLIAM LIVINGSTON
DAVID BREARLEY
WILLIAM PATERSON
JONATHAN DAYTON

Maryland
JAMES MCHENRY
DANIEL OF ST. THOMAS
  JENIFER
DANIEL CARROLL

Massachusetts
NATHANIEL GORHAM
RUFUS KING

Connecticut
WILLIAM S. JOHNSON
ROGER SHERMAN

New York
ALEXANDER HAMILTON

New Hampshire
JOHN LANGDON
NICHOLAS GILMAN

Georgia
WILLIAM FEW
ABRAHAM BALDWIN

AMENDMENTS TO THE CONSTITUTION*

*The first ten amendments (the Bill of Rights) were adopted in 1791.

AMENDMENT I

Congress shall make no law respecting an establishment of religion, or prohibiting the free exercise thereof; or abridging the freedom of speech, or of the press; or the right of the people peaceably to assemble, and to petition the Government for a redress of grievances.

AMENDMENT II

A well regulated Militia, being necessary to the security of a free State, the right of the people to keep and bear Arms, shall not be infringed.

AMENDMENT III

No Soldier shall, in time of peace be quartered in any house, without the consent of the Owner, nor in time of war, but in a manner to be prescribed by law.

AMENDMENT IV

The right of the people to be secure in their persons, houses, papers, and effects, against unreasonable searches and seizures, shall not be violated, and no Warrants shall issue, but upon probable cause, supported by Oath or affirmation, and particularly describing the place to be searched, and the persons or things to be seized.

AMENDMENT V

No person shall be held to answer for a capital, or otherwise infamous crime, unless on a presentment or indictment of a Grand Jury, except in cases arising in the land or naval forces, or in the Militia, when in actual service in time of War or public danger; nor shall any person be subject for the same offence to be twice put in jeopardy of life or limb; nor shall be compelled in any criminal case to be a witness against himself, nor be deprived of life, liberty, or property, without due process of law; nor shall private property be taken for public use, without just compensation.

AMENDMENT VI

In all criminal prosecutions, the accused shall enjoy the right to a speedy and public trial, by an impartial jury of the State and district wherein the crime shall have been committed, which district shall have been previously ascertained by law, and to be informed of the nature and cause of the accusation; to be confronted with the witnesses against him; to have compulsory process for obtaining witnesses in his favor, and to have the Assistance of Counsel for his defence.

AMENDMENT VII

In Suits at common law, where the value in controversy shall exceed twenty dollars, the right of trial by jury shall be preserved, and no fact tried by a jury, shall be otherwise re-examined in any Court of the United States, than according to the rules of the common law.

AMENDMENT VIII

Excessive bail shall not be required, nor excessive fines imposed, nor cruel and unusual punishments inflicted.

AMENDMENT IX

The enumeration in the Constitution, of certain rights, shall not be construed to deny or disparage others retained by the people.

AMENDMENT X

The powers not delegated to the United States by the Constitution, nor prohibited by it to the States, are reserved to the States respectively, or to the people.

AMENDMENT XI [ADOPTED 1798]

The Judicial power of the United States shall not be construed to extend to any suit in law or equity, commenced or prosecuted against one of the United States by Citizens of another State, or by Citizens or Subjects of any Foreign State.

AMENDMENT XII [ADOPTED 1804]

The Electors shall meet in their respective states, and vote by ballot for President and Vice-President, one of whom, at least, shall not be an inhabitant of the same state with themselves; they shall name in their ballots the person voted for as President, and in distinct ballots the person voted for as Vice-President, and they shall make distinct lists of all persons voted for as President, and of all persons voted for as Vice-President, and of the number of votes for each, which list they shall sign and certify, and transmit sealed to the seat of the government of the United States, directed to the President of the Senate;—The President of the Senate shall, in the presence of the Senate and House of Representatives, open all the certificates and the votes shall then be counted;—The person having the greatest number of votes for President, shall be the President, if such number be a majority of the whole number of Electors appointed; and if no person have such majority, then from the persons having the highest numbers not exceeding three on the list of those voted for as President, the House of Representatives shall choose immediately, by ballot, the President. But in choosing the President, the votes shall be taken by states, the representation from each state having one vote; a quorum for this purpose shall consist of a member or members from two thirds of the states, and a majority of all the states shall be necessary to a choice. And if the House of Representatives shall not choose a President whenever the right of choice shall devolve upon them, before the *fourth day of March* next following, then the Vice-President shall act as President, as in the case of the death or other constitutional disability of the President.

The person having the greatest number of votes as Vice-President, shall be the Vice-President, if such number be a majority of the whole number of Electors appointed, and if no person have a majority, then from the two highest numbers on the list, the Senate shall choose the Vice-President; a quorum for the purpose shall consist of two thirds of the whole number of Senators, and a majority of the whole number shall be necessary to a choice. But no person constitutionally ineligible to the office of President shall be eligible to that of Vice-President of the United States.

AMENDMENT XIII [ADOPTED 1865]

Section 1 Neither slavery nor involuntary servitude, except as a punishment for crime whereof the party shall have been duly convicted, shall exist within the United States, or any place subject to their jurisdiction.

Section 2 Congress shall have power to enforce this article by appropriate legislation.

AMENDMENT XIV [ADOPTED 1868]

Section 1 All persons born or naturalized in the United States, and subject to the jurisdiction thereof, are citizens of the United States and of the State wherein they reside. No State shall make or enforce any law which shall abridge the privileges or immunities of citizens of the United States; nor shall any State deprive any person of life, liberty, or property, without due process of law; nor deny to any person within its jurisdiction the equal protection of the laws.

Section 2 Representatives shall be apportioned among the several States according to their respective numbers, counting the whole number of persons in each State, excluding Indians not taxed. But when the right to vote at any election for the choice of electors for President and Vice-President of the United States, Representatives in Congress, the Executive and Judicial officers of a State, or the members of the Legislature thereof, is denied to any of the male inhabitants of such State, being twenty-one years of age, and citizens of the United States, or in any way abridged, except for participation in rebellion, or other crime, the basis of representation therein shall be reduced in the proportion which the number of such male citizens shall bear to the whole number of male citizens twenty-one years of age in such State.

Section 3 No person shall be a Senator or Representative in Congress, or elector of President and Vice-President, or hold any office, civil or military, under the United States, or under any State, who, having previously taken an oath, as a member of Congress, or as an officer of the United States, or as a member of any State legislature, or as an executive or judicial officer of any State, to support the Constitution of the United States, shall have engaged in insurrection or rebellion against the same, or given aid or comfort to the enemies thereof. But Congress may by a vote of two thirds of each House, remove such disability.

Section 4 The validity of the public debt of the United States, authorized by law, including debts incurred for payment of pensions and bounties for services in suppressing insurrection or rebellion, shall not be questioned. But neither the United States nor any State shall assume or pay any debt or obligation incurred in aid of insurrection or rebellion against the United States, or any claim for the loss or emancipation of any slave; but all such debts, obligations and claims shall be held illegal and void.

Section 5 The Congress shall have power to enforce, by appropriate legislation, the provisions of this article.

AMENDMENT XV [ADOPTED 1870]

Section 1 The right of citizens of the United States to vote shall not be denied or abridged by the United States or by any State on account of race, color, or previous condition of servitude.

Section 2 The Congress shall have power to enforce this article by appropriate legislation.

AMENDMENT XVI [ADOPTED 1913]

The Congress shall have power to lay and collect taxes on incomes, from whatever source derived, without apportionment among the several States, and without regard to any census or enumeration.

AMENDMENT XVII [ADOPTED 1913]

The Senate of the United States shall be composed of two Senators from each State, elected by the people thereof, for six years; and each Senator shall have one vote. The electors in each State shall have the qualifications requisite for electors of the most numerous branch of the State legislatures.

When vacancies happen in the representation of any State in the Senate, the executive authority of such State shall issue writs of election to fill such vacancies: *Provided,* That the legislature of any State may empower the executive thereof to make temporary appointments until the people fill the vacancies by election as the legislature may direct.

This amendment shall not be so construed as to affect the election or term of any Senator chosen before it becomes valid as part of the Constitution.

AMENDMENT XVIII [ADOPTED 1919; REPEALED 1933]

Section 1 After one year from the ratification of this article the manufacture, sale, or transportation of intoxicating liquors within, the importation thereof into, or the exportation thereof from the United States and all territory subject to the jurisdiction thereof for beverage purposes is hereby prohibited.

Section 2 The Congress and the several States shall have concurrent power to enforce this article by appropriate legislation.

Section 3 This article shall be inoperative unless it shall have been ratified as an amendment to the Constitution by the legislatures of the several States, as provided in the Constitution, within seven years from the date of the submission hereof to the States by the Congress.

AMENDMENT XIX [ADOPTED 1920]

Section 1 The right of citizens of the United States to vote shall not be denied or abridged by the United States or by any State on account of sex.

Section 2 Congress shall have power to enforce this article by appropriate legislation.

AMENDMENT XX [ADOPTED 1933]

Section 1 The terms of the President and Vice-President shall end at noon on the 20th day of January, and the terms of Senators and Representatives at noon on the third day of January, of the years in which such terms would have ended if this article had not been ratified; and the terms of their successors shall then begin.

Section 2 The Congress shall assemble at least once in every year, and such meeting shall begin at noon on the third day of January, unless they shall by law appoint a different day.

Section 3 If, at the time fixed for the beginning of the term of the President, the President elect shall have died, the Vice-President elect shall become President. If a President shall not have been chosen before the time fixed for the beginning of his term, or if the President elect shall have failed to qualify, then the Vice-President elect shall act as President until a President shall have qualified; and the Congress may by law provide for the case wherein neither a President elect nor a Vice-President elect shall have qualified, declaring who shall then act as President, or the manner in which one who is to act shall be selected, and such person shall act accordingly until a President or Vice-President shall have qualified.

Section 4 The Congress may by law provide for the case of the death of any of the persons from whom the House of Representatives may choose a President whenever the right of choice shall have devolved upon them, and for the case of the death of any of the persons from whom the Senate may choose a Vice-President whenever the right of choice shall have devolved upon them.

Section 5   Sections 1 and 2 shall take effect on the 15th day of October following the ratification of this article.

Section 6   This article shall be inoperative unless it shall have been ratified as an amendment to the Constitution by the legislatures of three fourths of the several States within seven years from the date of its submission.

AMENDMENT XXI [ADOPTED 1933]

Section 1   The eighteenth article of amendment to the Constitution of the United States is hereby repealed.

Section 2   The transportation or importation into any State, Territory, or possession of the United States for delivery or use therein of intoxicating liquors, in violation of the laws thereof, is hereby prohibited.

Section 3   This article shall be inoperative unless it shall have been ratified as an amendment to the Constitution by conventions in the several States, as provided in the Constitution, within seven years from the date of the submission hereof to the States by the Congress.

AMENDMENT XXII [ADOPTED 1951]

Section 1   No person shall be elected to the office of the President more than twice, and no person who has held the office of President, or acted as President, for more than two years of a term to which some other person was elected President shall be elected to the office of the President more than once. But this Article shall not apply to any person holding the office of President when this Article was proposed by the Congress, and shall not prevent any person who may be holding the office of President, or acting as President, during the term within which this Article becomes operative from holding the office of President or acting as President during the remainder of such term.

Section 2   This article shall be inoperative unless it shall have been ratified as an amendment to the Constitution by the legislatures of three fourths of the several States within seven years from the date of its submission to the States by the Congress.

AMENDMENT XXIII [ADOPTED 1961]

Section 1   The District constituting the seat of Government of the United States shall appoint in such manner as the Congress may direct:

A number of electors of President and Vice-President equal to the whole number of Senators and Representatives in Congress to which the District would be entitled if it were a State, but in no event more than the least populous State; they shall be in addition to those appointed by the States, but they shall be considered, for the purposes of the election of President and Vice-President, to be electors appointed by a State; and they shall meet in the District and perform such duties as provided by the twelfth article of amendment.

Section 2   The Congress shall have power to enforce this article by appropriate legislation.

AMENDMENT XXIV [ADOPTED 1964]

Section 1   The right of citizens of the United States to vote in any primary or other election for President or Vice-President, for electors for President or Vice-President, or for Senator or Representative in Congress, shall not be denied or abridged by the United States or any State by reason of failure to pay any poll tax or other tax.

Section 2   The Congress shall have power to enforce this article by appropriate legislation.

AMENDMENT XXV [ADOPTED 1967]

Section 1   In case of the removal of the President from office or his death or resignation, the Vice-President shall become President.

Section 2   Whenever there is a vacancy in the office of the Vice-President, the President shall nominate a Vice-President who shall take the office upon confirmation by a majority vote of both houses of Congress.

Section 3   Whenever the President transmits to the President pro tempore of the Senate and the Speaker of the House of Representatives his written declaration that he is unable to discharge the powers and duties of his office, and until he transmits to them a written declaration to the contrary, such powers and duties shall be discharged by the Vice-President as Acting President.

Section 4   Whenever the Vice-President and a majority of either the principal officers of the executive departments, or of such other body as Congress may by law provide, transmit to the President pro tempore of the Senate and the Speaker of the House of Representatives their written declaration that the President is unable to discharge the powers and duties of his office, the Vice-President shall immediately assume the powers and duties of the office as Acting President.

Thereafter, when the President transmits to the President pro tempore of the Senate and the Speaker of the House of Representatives his written declaration that no inability exists, he shall resume the powers and duties of his office unless the Vice-President and a majority of either the principal officers of the executive department, or of such other body as Congress may by law provide, transmit within four days to the President pro tempore of the Senate and the Speaker of the House of Representatives their written declaration that the President is unable to discharge the powers and duties of his office. Thereupon Congress shall decide the issue, assembling within 48 hours for that purpose if not in session. If the Congress, within 21 days after receipt of the latter written declaration, or, if Congress is not in session, within 21 days after Congress is required to assemble, determines by two-thirds vote of both houses that the President is unable to discharge the powers and duties of his office, the Vice-President shall continue to discharge the same as Acting President; otherwise, the President shall resume the powers and duties of his office.

AMENDMENT XXVI [ADOPTED 1971]

Section 1   The right of citizens of the United States, who are eighteen years of age or older, to vote shall not be denied or abridged by the United States or any state on account of age.

Section 2   The Congress shall have power to enforce this article by appropriate legislation.

AMENDMENT XXVII [ADOPTED 1992]

No law, varying the compensation for the services of Senators and Representatives, shall take effect until an election of Representatives have intervened.

Presidential Elections

Year	Candidates	Parties	Popular Vote	Electoral Vote	Voter Participation
1789	GEORGE WASHINGTON		*	69	
	John Adams			34	
	Others			35	
1792	GEORGE WASHINGTON		*	132	
	John Adams			77	
	George Clinton			50	
	Others			5	
1796	JOHN ADAMS	Federalist	*	71	
	Thomas Jefferson	Democratic-Republican		68	
	Thomas Pinckney	Federalist		59	
	Aaron Burr	Dem.-Rep.		30	
	Others			48	
1800	THOMAS JEFFERSON	Dem.-Rep.	*	73	
	Aaron Burr	Dem.-Rep.		73	
	C. C. Pinckney	Federalist		64	
	John Jay	Federalist		1	
1804	THOMAS JEFFERSON	Dem.-Rep.	*	122	
	C. C. Pinckney	Federalist		14	
1808	JAMES MADISON	Dem.-Rep.	*	122	
	C. C. Pinckney	Federalist		47	
	George Clinton	Dem.-Rep.		6	
1812	JAMES MADISON	Dem.-Rep.	*	128	
	De Witt Clinton	Federalist		89	
1816	JAMES MONROE	Dem.-Rep.	*	183	
	Rufus King	Federalist		34	
1820	JAMES MONROE	Dem.-Rep.	*	231	
	John Quincy Adams	Dem.-Rep.		1	
1824	JOHN Q. ADAMS	Dem.-Rep.	108,740 (10.5%)	84	26.9%
	Andrew Jackson	Dem.-Rep.	153,544 (43.1%)	99	
	William H. Crawford	Dem.-Rep.	46,618 (13.1%)	41	
	Henry Clay	Dem.-Rep.	47,136 (13.2%)	37	
1828	ANDREW JACKSON	Democratic	647,286 (56.0%)	178	57.6%
	John Quincy Adams	National Republican	508,064 (44.0%)	83	
1832	ANDREW JACKSON	Democratic	687,502 (55.0%)	219	55.4%
	Henry Clay	National Republican	530,189 (42.4%)	49	
	John Floyd	Independent		11	
	William Wirt	Anti-Mason	33,108 (2.6%)	7	
1836	MARTIN VAN BUREN	Democratic	765,483 (50.9%)	170	57.8%
	W. H. Harrison	Whig		73	
	Hugh L. White	Whig	739,795 (49.1%)	26	
	Daniel Webster	Whig		14	
	W. P. Magnum	Independent		11	

*Electors elected by state legislators.

Presidential Elections

Year	Candidates	Parties	Popular Vote	Electoral Vote	Voter Participation
1840	WILLIAM H. HARRISON	Whig	1,274,624 (53.1%)	234	80.2%
	Martin Van Buren	Democratic	1,127,781 (46.9%)	60	
	J. G. Birney	Liberty	7,069	—	
1844	JAMES K. POLK	Democratic	1,338,464 (49.6%)	170	78.9%
	Henry Clay	Whig	1,300,097 (48.1%)	105	
	J. G. Birney	Liberty	62,300 (2.3%)	—	
1848	ZACHARY TAYLOR	Whig	1,360,967 (47.4%)	163	72.7%
	Lewis Cass	Democratic	1,222,342 (42.5%)	127	
	Martin Van Buren	Free-Soil	291,263 (10.1%)	—	
1852	FRANKLIN PIERCE	Democratic	1,601,117 (50.9%)	254	69.6%
	Winfield Scott	Whig	1,385,453 (44.1%)	42	
	John P. Hale	Free-Soil	155,825 (5.0%)	—	
1856	JAMES BUCHANAN	Democratic	1,832,955 (45.3%)	174	78.9%
	John C. Fremont	Republican	1,339,932 (33.1%)	114	
	Millard Fillmore	American	871,731 (21.6%)	8	
1860	ABRAHAM LINCOLN	Republican	1,865,593 (39.8%)	180	81.2%
	Stephen A. Douglas	Democratic	1,382,713 (29.5%)	12	
	John C. Breckinridge	Democratic	848,356 (18.1%)	72	
	John Bell	Union	592,906 (12.6%)	39	
1864	ABRAHAM LINCOLN	Republican	2,213,655 (55.0%)	212	73.8%
	George B. McClellan	Democratic	1,805,237 (45.0%)	21	
1868	ULYSSES S. GRANT	Republican	3,012,833 (52.7%)	214	78.1%
	Horatio Seymour	Democratic	2,703,249 (47.3%)	80	
1872	ULYSSES S. GRANT	Republican	3,597,132 (55.6%)	286	71.3%
	Horace Greeley	Democratic; Liberal Republican	2,834,125 (43.9%)	66	
1876	RUTHERFORD B. HAYES	Republican	4,036,298 (48.0%)	185	81.8%
	Samuel J. Tilden	Democratic	4,300,590 (51.0%)	184	
1880	JAMES A. GARFIELD	Republican	4,454,416 (48.5%)	214	79.4%
	Winfield S. Hancock	Democratic	4,444,952 (48.1%)	155	
1884	GROVER CLEVELAND	Democratic	4,874,986 (48.5%)	219	77.5%
	James G. Blaine	Republican	4,851,981 (48.2%)	182	
1888	BENJAMIN HARRISON	Republican	5,439,853 (47.9%)	233	79.3%
	Grover Cleveland	Democratic	5,540,309 (48.6%)	168	
1892	GROVER CLEVELAND	Democratic	5,556,918 (46.1%)	277	74.7%
	Benjamin Harrison	Republican	5,176,108 (43.0%)	145	
	James B. Weaver	People's	1,041,028 (8.5%)	22	
1896	WILLIAM McKINLEY	Republican	7,104,779 (51.1%)	271	79.3%
	William J. Bryan	Democratic People's	6,502,925 (47.7%)	176	
1900	WILLIAM McKINLEY	Republican	7,207,923 (51.7%)	292	73.2%
	William J. Bryan	Dem.-Populist	6,358,133 (45.5%)	155	
1904	THEODORE ROOSEVELT	Republican	7,623,486 (57.9%)	336	65.2%
	Alton B. Parker	Democratic	5,077,911 (37.6%)	140	
	Eugene V. Debs	Socialist	402,283 (3.0%)	—	

Presidential Elections

Year	Candidates	Parties	Popular Vote	Electoral Vote	Voter Participation
1908	WILLIAM H. TAFT	Republican	7,678,908 (51.6%)	321	65.4%
	William J. Bryan	Democratic	6,409,104 (43.1%)	162	
	Eugene V. Debs	Socialist	420,793 (2.8%)	—	
1912	WOODROW WILSON	Democratic	6,293,454 (41.9%)	435	58.8%
	Theodore Roosevelt	Progressive	4,119,538 (27.4%)	88	
	William H. Taft	Republican	3,484,980 (23.2%)	8	
	Eugene V. Debs	Socialist	900,672 (6.0%)	—	
1916	WOODROW WILSON	Democratic	9,129,606 (49.4%)	277	61.6%
	Charles E. Hughes	Republican	8,538,221 (46.2%)	254	
	A. L. Benson	Socialist	585,113 (3.2%)	—	
1920	WARREN G. HARDING	Republican	16,152,200 (60.4%)	404	49.2%
	James M. Cox	Democratic	9,147,353 (34.2%)	127	
	Eugene V. Debs	Socialist	919,799 (3.4%)	—	
1924	CALVIN COOLIDGE	Republican	15,725,016 (54.0%)	382	48.9%
	John W. Davis	Democratic	8,386,503 (28.8%)	136	
	Robert M. La Follette	Progressive	4,822,856 (16.6%)	13	
1928	HERBERT HOOVER	Republican	21,391,381 (58.2%)	444	56.9%
	Alfred E. Smith	Democratic	15,016,443 (40.9%)	87	
	Norman Thomas	Socialist	267,835 (0.7%)	—	
1932	FRANKLIN D. ROOSEVELT	Democratic	22,821,857 (57.4%)	472	56.9%
	Herbert Hoover	Republican	15,761,841 (39.7%)	59	
	Norman Thomas	Socialist	881,951 (2.2%)	—	
1936	FRANKLIN D. ROOSEVELT	Democratic	27,751,597 (60.8%)	523	61.0%
	Alfred M. Landon	Republican	16,679,583 (36.5%)	8	
	William Lemke	Union	882,479 (1.9%)	—	
1940	FRANKLIN D. ROOSEVELT	Democratic	27,244,160 (54.8%)	449	62.5%
	Wendell L. Willkie	Republican	22,305,198 (44.8%)	82	
1944	FRANKLIN D. ROOSEVELT	Democrat	25,602,504 (53.5%)	432	55.9%
	Thomas E. Dewey	Republican	22,006,285 (46.0%)	99	
1948	HARRY S TRUMAN	Democratic	24,105,695 (49.5%)	304	53.0%
	Thomas E. Dewey	Republican	21,969,170 (45.1%)	189	
	J. Strom Thurmond	State-Rights Democratic	1,169,021 (2.4%)	38	
	Henry A. Wallace	Progressive	1,156,103 (2.4%)	—	
1952	DWIGHT D. EISENHOWER	Republican	33,936,252 (55.1%)	442	63.3%
	Adlai E. Stevenson	Democratic	27,314,992 (44.4%)	89	
1956	DWIGHT D. EISENHOWER	Republican	35,575,420 (57.6%)	457	60.5%
	Adlai E. Stevenson	Democratic	26,033,066 (42.1%)	73	
	Other	—	—	1	
1960	JOHN F. KENNEDY	Democratic	34,227,096 (49.9%)	303	62.8%
	Richard M. Nixon	Republican	34,108,546 (49.6%)	219	
	Other	—	—	15	

Presidential Elections

Year	Candidates	Parties	Popular Vote	Electoral Vote	Voter Participation
1964	LYNDON B. JOHNSON	Democratic	43,126,506 (61.1%)	486	61.7%
	Barry M. Goldwater	Republican	27,176,799 (38.5%)	52	
1968	RICHARD M. NIXON	Republican	31,770,237 (43.4%)	301	60.6%
	Hubert H. Humphrey	Democratic	31,270,633 (42.7%)	191	
	George Wallace	American Indep.	9,906,141 (13.5%)	46	
1972	RICHARD M. NIXON	Republican	47,169,911 (60.7%)	520	55.2%
	George S. McGovern	Democratic	29,170,383 (37.5%)	17	
	Other	—	—	1	
1976	JIMMY CARTER	Democratic	40,828,587 (50.0%)	297	53.5%
	Gerald R. Ford	Republican	39,147,613 (47.9%)	241	
	Other	—	1,575,459 (2.1%)	—	
1980	RONALD REAGAN	Republican	43,901,812 (50.7%)	489	52.6%
	Jimmy Carter	Democratic	35,483,820 (41.0%)	49	
	John B. Anderson	Independent	5,719,722 (6.6%)	—	
	Ed Clark	Libertarian	921,188 (1.1%)	—	
1984	RONALD REAGAN	Republican	54,455,075 (59.0%)	525	53.3%
	Walter Mondale	Democratic	37,577,185 (41.0%)	13	
1988	GEORGE H.W. BUSH	Republican	48,886,000 (45.6%)	426	57.4%
	Michael S. Dukakis	Democratic	41,809,000 (45.6%)	111	
1992	WILLIAM J. CLINTON	Democratic	43,728,375 (43%)	370	55.0%
	George H.W. Bush	Republican	38,167,416 (38%)	168	
	Ross Perot	—	19,237,247 (19%)	—	
1996	WILLIAM J. CLINTON	Democratic	45,590,703 (50%)	379	48.8%
	Robert Dole	Republican	37,816,307 (41%)	159	
	Ross Perot	Independent	7,866,284 (9%)		
2000	GEORGE W. BUSH	Republican	50,456,062 (47%)	271	51.0%
	Albert Gore	Democratic	50,996,582 (49%)	267	
	Ralph Nader	Independent	2,858,843 (3%)	—	
2004	GEORGE W. BUSH	Republican	60,934,251 (51%)	286	
	John F. Kerry	Democrat	57,765,291 (48%)	252	
	Ralph Nader	Independent	405,933 (0%)	—	

Index

The World

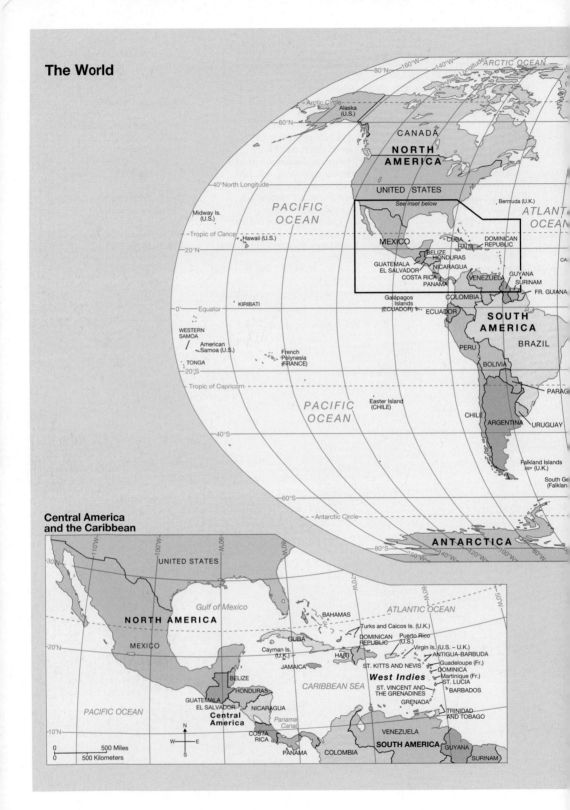

Central America and the Caribbean

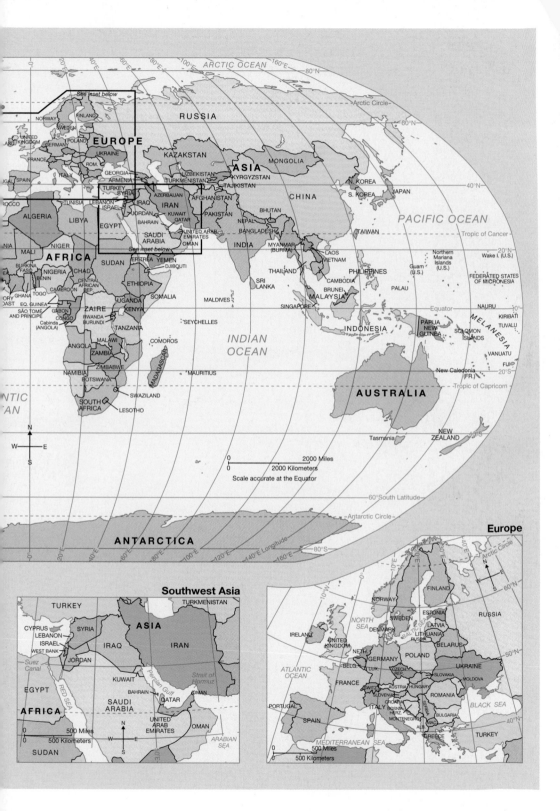